English Language

WORD BUILDER

Second Edition

Bob Jackman

Order this book online at www.trafford.com
or email orders@trafford.com

Most Trafford titles are also available at major online book retailers.

Printed in the United States of America.

ISBN: 978-1-4669-5254-6 (sc)
ISBN: 978-1-4669-5253-9 (e)

Trafford rev. 08/14/2012

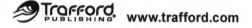 www.trafford.com

North America & international
toll-free: 1 888 232 4444 (USA & Canada)
phone: 250 383 6864 ✦ fax: 812 355 4082

CONTENTS

CONTENTS

1.1 INTRODUCTION

The **English Language Word Builder** is a useful reference for people wishing to improve their English vocabulary. It contains the basic form of every word up to eight letters in length acceptable in international SCRABBLE® competition, along with selected nine-letter words. It is designed to assist people to learn, or even master the English language, especially through playing the board game SCRABBLE®.

The book is organised in chapters by word length, from two to nine letters. All words up to and including eight letters in length are listed with formatting and symbols to indicate the valid forms of each main word. The formatting indicates the part of speech enabling standard extensions to be inferred for nouns and verbs, while the symbols indicate valid extensions which cannot be inferred from formatting. Other single letter extensions of each capitalised main word to make a different word are shown by a lower case letter at the end of the capitalised main word. Throughout the book, italicising indicates words which have been recently added to the international SCRABBLE® word list, with the most recent new words being shaded as well.

Within each chapter, words are further grouped according to their familiarity. Familiar words are broadly defined as those that are judged to be in relatively common use in countries where English is the first language. These are the words that readers whose first language is not English may wish to study in order to communicate better in English. All familiar words are further grouped according to their part of speech. Definitions of most of these words can be found in any standard English dictionary.

Less familiar words are those that are judged to be in less common use in English-speaking countries and are therefore not necessarily defined in a standard English dictionary. The sections containing less familiar words are arranged primarily to suit SCRABBLE® enthusiasts. They are divided into words formed by hooking one letter onto words listed in the previous chapter (hook words) and words which do not contain a word from the previous chapter (non-hook words). New words in italics recently introduced are deemed less familiar and will always be found in these sections. Definitions of all less familiar words can be found in the 2012 edition of the Collins SCRABBLE® Dictionary ISBN 978-0-00-743606-4.

Each capitalised main word is listed only in one section, the exception being when a less familiar word is both a front hook and an end hook of other words. Standard verb, plural and adjectival forms of words will not appear as main words in other sections, unless the word is used in a different part of speech in which case it will appear as a familiar word.

The **English Language Word Builder** has been manually compiled and interpretations have been applied to categorise words as either familiar or less familiar. For this reason some readers in English-speaking countries may find words which they consider to be familiar listed in the sections of less familiar words, while others may find words unfamiliar to them listed as familiar words. Although thoroughly researched, there may be accidental omissions of words and single-letter extensions to words.

1.2 BASIS FOR WORD PLACEMENT

FAMILIAR WORDS
Words which are in relatively common use in countries where English is the first language

> **VERBS IN COMMON USE**
> Commonly used words for which a main use is as a verb (e.g JUMP)

> **VERBS MORE OFTEN USED IN OTHER PARTS OF SPEECH**
> Verbs (and words acting as verbs) which are more familiar as commonly used nouns (e.g. REFUGE, ANNEXE) or adjectives (e.g. HAPPY) or which are plural or adjectival extensions of words from an earlier chapter (e.g. SUDS, HIGHER)

> **NOUNS IN COMMON USE**
> Commonly used words which are not verbs and for which a main use of the word is as a noun (e.g. ANIMAL)

> **NOUNS MORE OFTEN USED IN OTHER PARTS OF SPEECH**
> Nouns (and words acting as nouns) which are more familiar in adjectival and other forms in which the plural is not expected to occur (e.g. GIVEN, MALTED, FOURS, BESIDE)

> **NOUNS WHICH ARE VERB FORMS ENDING IN 'ING'**
> Words ending in ING which are derived from verbs and which can be pluralised by adding an S (e.g. SAYING)

> **NON-PLURALS IN COMMON USE**
> Commonly used words which are not verbs or nouns and which therefore cannot be pluralised (e.g. AGAIN)

LESS FAMILIAR WORDS
Words which are in less common use in countries where English is the first language

> **LESS FAMILIAR WORDS WHICH ARE HOOK WORDS**
> Less familiar words formed by placing one letter in front or at the end of a word from the previous chapter (e.g. GLEDGE, POTHERB). Standard verb, plural, and adjectival forms are excluded

> **LESS FAMILIAR NON-HOOK WORDS**
> Less familiar but more probable (in terms of SCRABBLE® tile distribution) words which are not formed by hooking one letter onto a shorter word, presented in various ways depending on the word length (e.g. PICUL)

> **LESS FAMILIAR BUT LESS PROBABLE NON-HOOK WORDS**
> Less familiar words which are not formed by hooking one letter onto a shorter word and which contain a pair of B, C, F, H, M, P, S. V, W or Y (e.g. DEICTIC)

> **VERY IMPROBABLE LESS FAMILIAR WORDS**
> All less familiar words containing three or more of B, C, F, H, M, P, V, W and Y or two or more of J, K, X, Q or Z (e.g. ZYZZYVA)

1.3 FORMATTING, SYMBOLS AND TERMS

Guide to Formatting

Underlining
Underlining indicates the word is a verb (or a word acting as a verb).
The standard extensions which can be inferred from an underlined word are S, ED and ING
Example: JUMP => JUMPS, JUMPED, JUMPING

The main exceptions are as follows:
If the word ends in E but not IE, the extensions are formed by adding S and D direct, and adding ING after dropping E
Example: MERGE => MERGES, MERGED, MERGING
If the word ends in a consonant followed by Y, extensions are formed by adding IES and IED after dropping Y
Example: REPLY => REPLIES, REPLIED, REPLYING
If the word ends in CH, SH, X, S or Z, the plural extension is ES
Example: BLITZ => BLITZES, BLITZED, BLITZING
Exceptions for words ending in CH are shown with an end hook of s
Example: PECHs => PECHS, PECHED, PECHING
If the word ends in IE, extensions are formed by adding S and D directly, and adding YING after dropping IE
Example: VIE => VIES, VIED, VYING
Variations to the above standards are covered by symbols (see Guide to Symbols Used)

Bold Type
Bold type indicates the word is a non-plural in that it cannot be pluralised, either by adding S or ES, or by adding IES after dropping a Y ending. Symbols following bold print indicate adjectival forms of the word.

Plain Type
Plain type (neither underlined or bold) indicates the word is either a noun or a word acting as a noun. The standard extension which can be inferred for words with plain type is S. Variations to this are covered by symbols (see Guide to Symbols Used).

Italics
Underlined, bold or plain formatted words which are also in italics are words which were introduced into the International SCRABBLE® lexicon in 2007 and 2012.

Shading
Shaded words are those that were introduced into the International SCRABBLE® lexicon in 2012

Guide to Symbols

*   indicates adjectival extensions of R and ST for words ending in E or IE
Examples: **SUAVE*** => SUAVER, SUAVEST; **BLUDIE*** => BLUDIER, BLUDIEST
indicates adjectival extensions of IER and IEST for words ending in Y, after dropping the Y
Example: **RAINY*** => RAINIER, RAINIEST
indicates adjectival extensions of IER and IEST for words ending in EY, after dropping the EY
Example: **DICEY*** => DICIER, DICIEST
indicates adjectival extensions of ER, EST for words not ending in E or Y
Example **HUMID*** => HUMIDER, HUMIDEST

^   indicates adjectival extensions of ER, EST, repeating the last letter if not Y
Examples: **LOYAL^** => LOYALLER, LOYALLEST; **SPRY^** => SPRYER, SPRYEST

+   for verbs, indicates a plural extension of ES
Example: <u>FORGO</u>+ => FORGOES
for nouns ending in O or I, indicates a plural extension of ES
Examples: DINGO+ => DINGOES; CURLI+ => CURLIES
for nouns ending in Y, indicates a plural extension of IES after dropping Y
Example: FORTY+ => FORTIES
for nouns ending in CH, SH, S, J, X, Z, indicates a plural extension of ES
Example: FINCH+ => FINCHES
for nouns ending in CH, SH, S, J, X and Z, + is inferred if there is an end hook
Example: TENNISt => TENNISES; KLUTZy => KLUTZES

>   for verbs, the last letter is repeated for both ED and ING extensions
Example: <u>EXCEL</u>> => EXCELLED, EXCELLING
for nouns, the last letter is repeated for the plural extension
Example: AVGAS> => AVGASSES

đ   for verbs, indicates (E)D extension is not available (i.e. verb is irregular)
Example: <u>DRIVE</u>đ => DRIVING, but not DRIVED
for verbs, both a đ and a > symbol indicate doubling of last letter only for the ING extension
Example: <u>REBID</u>đ <u>REBID</u>> => REBIDDING only

@   for verbs ending in I, indicates a YING extension after dropping I
Example: <u>TAXI</u>@ => TAXYING

=   for verbs ending in E or I, indicates an extension by directly adding ING
Examples: <u>WINGE</u>= => WINGEING; <u>BIRDIE</u>=> BIRDIEING; <u>ALIBI</u> = => ALIBIING
for adjectives ending in EY, indicates extensions of IER and IEST after dropping the Y
Example: **TOEY=** => TOEIER, TOEIEST

    &   for verbs ending in C, indicates KED and KING extensions
                 Example: <u>MIMIC</u>& => MIMICKED, MIMICKING

    #   for verbs ending in E or Y, indicates an extension by directly adding ED
                 Example: <u>GLACE</u># => GLACEED

Important note: The sequence of the symbols within sets of words provide an indication of the various forms available.

Examples: <u>EQUIP</u>>, <u>EQUIP</u>e => EQUIPPED, EQUIPE , but not EQUIPED
              <u>GOSSIP</u>y, <u>GOSSIP</u>> => GOSSIPED, GOSSIPY, GOSSIPPED

Definitions of Key Terms

Hook Word
A word formed by hooking one letter on the front or end of another word and which therefore contains a different word that is shorter by one letter.

Non-Hook Word
A word which has not been formed by hooking and which therefore does not contain a different word which is shorter by one letter.

Non-Plural
A word which cannot be pluralised by extending with S or ES, or with IES after dropping a Y ending.

Adjective
For the purposes of this book, a word which can be extended with (I)ER and (I)EST.

Verb
For the purposes of this book , a word which can be extended with (E)S, (E)D and ING.

Noun
For the purposes of this book, a word which can be extended with S or ES, or by IES. after dropping a Y ending.

2. TWO-LETTER WORDS

2.1 FAMILIAR TWO-LETTER WORDS

ADd ADo ADz

AMa **AM**e **AM**i **AM**p **AM**u

ANa ANd ANe ANi ANn ANt ANy

ASh **AS**k **AS**p **AS**s

ATe ATt

BE~~e~~ <u>BE</u>d <u>BE</u>e <u>BE</u>g <u>BE</u>l <u>BE</u>n <u>BE</u>t <u>BE</u>y <u>BE</u>z

BYe **BY**s

<u>DO</u>~~e~~ <u>DO</u>b <u>DO</u>c <u>DO</u>d <u>DO</u>e <u>DO</u>f <u>DO</u>g <u>DO</u>h <u>DO</u>l <u>DO</u>m <u>DO</u>n <u>DO</u>o <u>DO</u>p <u>DO</u>r <u>DO</u>t <u>DO</u>w
<u>DO</u>y <u>DO</u>+

<u>GO</u>~~e~~ <u>GO</u>a <u>GO</u>b <u>GO</u>d <u>GO</u>e <u>GO</u>n <u>GO</u>o <u>GO</u>r <u>GO</u>t <u>GO</u>v <u>GO</u>x <u>GO</u>y <u>GO</u>+

HAd HAe HAg HAh HAj HAm HAn HAo HAp HAt HAw HAy

HEh HEm HEn HEp HEr HEt HEw HEx HEy

HIc HId HIe HIm HIn HIp HIt

IFf

<u>IN</u>> INg <u>IN</u>k <u>IN</u>n

ISh **IS**m **IS**o

ITa

MAa MAc MAd MAe MAg MAk MAl MAm MAn MAp MAr MAt MAw MAx MAy

MEd MEe MEg MEh MEl MEm MEn MEt MEu MEw

MYc

NOb NOd NOg NOh NOm NOn NOo NOr NOt NOw NOx NOy NO+

OFf **OF**t

<u>ON</u>> ONe ONo ONy

ORa ORb ORc ORd ORe ORf ORt

OX+ OXo OXy

PAc PAd PAh PAl PAm PAn PAp PAr PAt PAv PAw PAx Pay

SOb SOc SOd SOg SOh SOl SOm SOn SOp SOt SOu SOv SOw SOx SOy SOz

TOc **TO**d **TO**e **TO**g **TO**m **TO**n **TO**o **TO**p **TO**r **TO**t **TO**w **TO**y

<u>UP</u>> UPo

USe

WEb **WE**d **WE**e **WE**m **WE**n **WE**t **WE**x **WE**y

YEa YEh YEn YEp YEt YEw YEx

2.2 LESS FAMILIAR TWO-LETTER WORDS

AAh AAl
ABa ABb ABo ABy
AE
AGa AGe AGo
<u>AHa</u> <u>AHi</u>
AIa AId AIl AIm AIn AIr AIt
ALa ALb ALe Alf ALl ALp Alt ALu
ARb ARc ARd ARe ARf ARk ARm ARt ARy
AWa **AW**e **AW**k **AW**l **AW**n
<u>AXe</u>
AYe AYu
BAa BAc BAd BAg BAh BAl BAm BAn BAp BAr BAt BAy
BIb BId BIg BIn BIo BIt BIz
BOa BOb BOd BOg BOh BOi BOk BOn BOo BOp BOr BOt BOw BOx BOy
CHa **CH**e **CH**i
DAb DAd DAe DAg DAh DAk DAl DAm DAn DAp DAw DAy
DEb **DE**e **DE**f **DE**g **DE**i **DE**l **DE**n **DE**v **DE**w **DE**x **DE**y
DIb DId DIe DIf DIg DIm DIn DIp DIt DIv
EAn EAr EAt EAu
EDh
EEk **EE**l **EE**n
<u>EF></u> <u>EFf</u> <u>EFt</u>
<u>EH</u>
ELd ELf ELk ELl ELm ELt
EMe EMo EMu
ENe ENd ENg
ERa ERe ERf ERg ERk ERm ERn ERr
ES+ ESs ESt
ETa **ET**h
<u>EXo</u>
FAa FAb FAd FAe FAg FAh FAn FAp FAr FAt FAw FAx FAy
FEd FEe FEg FEh FEm FEn FEr FEt FEu FEw FEy FEz
FY
GIb GId GIe GIf GIg GIn GIo GIp GIt
GUb GUe GUl GUm GUn GUp GUr GUt GUv GUy
HMm
<u>HOa</u> <u>HOb</u> <u>HOc</u> <u>HOd</u> <u>HOe</u> <u>HOg</u> <u>HOh</u> <u>HOi</u> <u>HOm</u> <u>HOn</u> <u>HOo</u> <u>HOp</u> <u>HOt</u> <u>HOw</u> <u>HOx</u> <u>HOy</u>
IDe
IOn
JAb ***JA***g ***JA***i ***JA***k ***JA***m ***JA***p ***JA***r ***JA***w ***JA***y
JO+ JOb JOe JOg JOl JOr JOt JOw JOy
<u>KAb</u> <u>KAe</u> <u>KAf</u> <u>KAi</u> <u>KAk</u> <u>KAm</u> <u>KAt</u> <u>KAw</u> <u>KAy</u>
KId KIf KIn KIp KIr KIt
KOa KOb KOi KOn KOp KOr KOw
KYe **KY**u
LAb LAc LAd LAg LAh LAm LAp LAr LAt LAv LAw LAx LAy
LIb LId LIe LIg LIn LIp Lit
LOb LOd LOg LOo LOp LOr LOt LOu LOw LOx LOy
MIb MIc MId MIg MIl MIm MIr MIx MIz

8

MM

MOa MOb MOc MOd MOe MOg MOi MOl MOm MOn MOo MOp MOr MOt MOu MOw
    MOy MOz

MUd MUg MUm MUn MUt MUx

NAb NAe NAg NAh NAm NAn NAp NAt NAw NAy

NEb **NE**d **NE**e **NE**f NEg **NE**k **NE**p **NE**t NEw

NUb NUn NUr NUt

NY+ NYe NYs

OBa OBe OBi OBo

ODa ODd ODe

OE

OHm OHo

OIk OIl

OM

OOf OOh OOm OOn OOp OOr OOt

OPe OPt

OS+ OSe

OUd OUk OUp OUr OUt

OWe **OW**l **OW**n **OW**t

OYe

PEa PEc PEd PEe PEg PEh PEl PEn PEp PEr PEt Pew

PIa PIc PIe PIg PIn PIp PIr PIt PIu PIx

POa POd POh POi POl POm POo POp POt POw POx POz

QIn

REb REc REd REe REf REg REh REi REm REn REo REp REt REv REw REx
    REz

SHa **SH**e **SH**h **SH**y

SIb SIc SIf SIk SIm SIn SIp SIr SIt SIx

STy

TAb TAd TAe TAg TAi TAj TAk TAm TAn TAo TAp TAr TAt TAu TAv TAw
    TAx TAy

TEa TEc TEd TEe TEf TEg TEl TEn TEt TEw TEx

TIc TId TIe TIg TIk TIl TIn TIp TIt TIx

UG> UGh

UH

UM> UMm UMp UMu

UNi

URb **UR**d **UR**e **UR**n **UR**p

UTa UTe UTu

WOe WOf WOg WOk WOn WOo WOp WOw WOx

XI

XU

YAd **YA**e **YA**g **YA**h **YA**k **YA**m **YA**p **YA**r **YA**w **YA**y

YOb **YO**d **YO**k YOm **YO**n **YO**u YOw

YUg YUk YUm YUp

ZAg ZAp ZAx

ZOa ZOl ZOo

3. THREE-LETTER WORDS

3.1 FAMILIAR THREES

3.1.1 VERBS IN COMMON USE

ACTa
ADDy
AGEe AGEn AGEr AGE=
AIDa AIDe
AIL
AIM
AIR* AIRn AIRt AIRy
ARMy
ASK
AXEl
BAAl
BAG> BAGh
BAN> BANc BANd BANe BANg BANi
     BANk BANt
BAR> BARb BARd BARe BARf BARk
     BARm BARn BARp
BAT> BATe BATh BATt
BEG> BEGo
BET> BETa BETe BETh
BIDd BID> BIDe BIDi
BOB> BOBa
BOG> BOGy
BOOb BOOh BOOk BOOl BOOm BOOn
     BOOr BOOt
BOP>
BOWl BOWr
BOXy
BUG>
BUYd
CAN> CANe CANg CANn CANt CANy
CAP> CAPa CAPe CAPh CAPi CAPo
CAWk
CON> CONd CONe CONf CONi CONk
     CONn CONy
COOf COOk COOl COOm COOn COOP
     COOt
COP> COPe COPy
CRY
CUTd CUT> CUTe
DAB>
DAM> DAMe DAMn DAMp
DIEb DIEl DIEt DIE=
DIG>
DIM> DIM^ DIMe DIMp
DIP> DIPt
DOT> DOTe DOTh DOTy

DRY* DRY^ DRYs
DUB>
DYE= DYEr
EATd EATh
EBB
EKE
END
ERR
EYEn EYEr EYE=
FAN> FANd FANe FANg FANk FANo
FAX
FIB>
FIT> FIT^ FITt
FIXt
FLY* FLY^
FOB>
FRY
GAD> GADe GADi
GAG> GAGa GAGe
GAS> GASh GASp GASt GAS+
GETd GET> GETa
HEWn
HITd HIT>
HOEr HOE=
HOG> HOGg HOGh
HOP> HOPe
HUG> HUGe HUGy
HUM> HUMa HUMf HUMp
ICEr
IRK
JAB>
JAG> JAGa JAGg
JAM> JAMb
JAR> JARk JARl JARp
JIG>
JOG>
JOT> JOTa
JUT> JUTe
KEY
LAG>
LAY
LET>
LIEf LIEn LIEr LIEu
LOB> LOBe LOBi LOBo
LOG> LOGe LOGo LOGy
LOP> LOPe

11

3. Three-Letter Words

<table>
<tr><td>

LUG> LUGe
MAP>
MAR> MARa MARc MARd MARe MARg
    MARk MARl MARm MARt MARy
MIXt MIXy
MOB> MOBe MOBy
MOOd MOOi MOOk MOOl MOOn MOOp
    MOOr MOOt
MOP> MOPe MOPy
MOWa MOWn
MUG> MUGg
NAB> NABe NABk
NAG> NAGa
NAP> NAPa NAPe
NET> NETe NETt
NIP> NIPa
NOD> NODe NODi
OILy
OPT
OWEr
OWN
PAD> PADi
PAN> PANd PANe PANg PANt
PAT> PATe PATh PATu PATy
PAY
PEEk PEEl PEEn PEEp PEEr
PEG> PEGh
PET>
PIN> PINa PINe PINg PINk PINt
    PINy
PIP> PIPa PIPe PIPi PIPy
PIT> PITa PITh PITy
PLY
POP> POPe
POT> POTe POTt
PRYs
PUT> PUTt PUTz
RAM> RAMi RAMp
RAP> RAPe RAPt
RID> RIDe
RIG> RIGg
RIP> RIPe RIPp RIPt
ROB> ROBe
ROT> ROTa ROTe ROTi ROTl ROTo
ROWt
RUB> RUBe RUBy
RUEr RUE=
~~RUNe~~ RUN> RUNd RUNe RUNg RUNt
SAG> SAGa SAGe SAGo SAGy
SAWn
SAY

</td><td>

SEEk SEEl SEEm SEEn SEEp SEEr
~~SETd~~ SET> SETa SETt
SEWn
SIN> SINd SINe SINg SINh SINk
SIP> SIPe
~~SITd~~ SIT> SITe SITh SITz
SKI= SKId SKIm SKIn SKIo SKIp
    SKIt
SOB> SOBa
SOWf SOWl SOWm SOWn SOWp
SPY
SUEr SUEt
SUM> SUMo SUMp SUMy
TAG>
TAN^ TAN> TANa TANe TANg TANh
    TANk
TAP> TAPa TAPe TAPu
TAR> TARa TARe TARn TARo TARp
    TARt
TAXa TAXi
TIEr TIE=
TIP> TIPi TIPt
TOT> TOTe
TOWn TOWt TOWy
TRYe TRYp
TUG>
USEr
VEXt
VIEr VIEw
VOW
WAG> WAGe
WAXy
WED>
WEE* WEEd WEEk WEEl WEEm WEEn
     WEEp WEEt
WET> WET^ WETa
WIN> WINd WINe WINg WINk WINn
    WINo WINy
WOOd WOOf WOOl WOOn WOOt
YAP> YAPp
YIP> YIPe
ZAP>
ZIP>

</td></tr>
</table>

3.1.2 VERBS MORE OFTEN USED IN OTHER PARTS OF SPEECH

ACEr
AMP
ANTa ANTe ANTi
APEr APEx
APT*
ARCh ARCo ARC&
ARK
ASHy
AWEe AWE=
BAYe BAYt
BED> BEDe BEDu
BIB> BIBb
BIG^ BIG> BIGa BIGg
BIN> BINd BINe BINg BINk BINt
BIT> BITe BITo BITt
BOYf BOYg BOYo
BUD> BUDa BUDi BUDo
BUM^ BUM> BUMf BUMp
BUSh BUSk BUSs BUSt BUSy BUS>
BUT> BUTe BUTt
CAB> CABa
CAT> CATe
COB> COBb
COD> CODa CODe
COG>
COT> COTe COTh COTt
COWk COWl COWp COWy
COXa COXy
COY*
CUB> CUBe
CUE CUE=
CUP>
DAD> DADa DADo
DAG> DAGo
DEN> DENe DENi DENt DENy
DEWy
DIN> DINe DINg DINk DINo DINt
DIS> DISa DISc DISh DISk DISs
DOG> DOGe DOGy
DUEl DUEt
EARd EARl EARn
EGGy
ELF
EREv
FAG>
FAR> FARd FARe FARl FARm FARo
     FARt
FAT^ FAT> FATe

FEEb FEEl FEEn FEEr FEEt
FIG> FIGo
FIN> FINd FINe FINi FINk FINo
FOG> FOGy
FOP>
FOXy
FUN> FUN^ FUNd FUNg FUNk
FUR> FURl FURr FURy
GAP> GAPe GAPo GAPy
GEEk GEEp GEEz
GEL> GELd GELt
GEM>
GIG> GIGa
GIN> GINg GINk GINn
GOB> GOBi GOBo GOBy
GOD>
GUM> GUMp
GUN> GUNg GUNk
GUT>
GUY
HADd HAD> HADe HADj
HAG> HAGg
HAM> HAMe
HAT> HATe HATh
HAY
HEM> HEMe HEMp
HEN> HENd HENt
HEX
HEY
HIP> HIP^ HIPt
HOT> HOT^ HOTe
HUT>
IMPi
INKy
INN
IRE
JAW
JET> JETe
JIB> JIBb JIBe
JOB> JOBe
JOY
JUG> JUGa
KEG
KID>
KIP> KIPe KIPp
KIT> KITe KITh
LAP>
LAW* LAWk LAWn

3. Three-Letter Words

LEEk LEEp LEEr LEEt
LEG>
LID> LIDo
LIP> LIPa LIPe LIPo
LOOf LOOk LOOm LOOn LOOp LOOr
     LOOt
LOT> LOTa LOTe LOTh LOTi LOTo
LOW* LOWe LOWn LOWp LOWt
MAN> MANa MANd MANe MANg MANi
     MANo MANy
MAD^ MAD> MADe
MAT> MATe MATh MATt MATy
MAYa MAYo
MUD>
MUM> MUMm MUMp MUMu
NEW* NEWt
NIB>
NIL> NILl
NIXe NIXy
NUB>
NUT>
OARy
OFFy
ORBy
OUT
OWLy
PAL> PALe PALl PALm PALp PALy
PAR> PARa PARd PARe PARk PARp
     PARr PARt
PAWa PAWk PAWl PAWn
PEN> PENd PENe PENi PENk PENt
PEP> PEPo
PIE= PIEr PIEt
PIG>
POD>
POXy
PUB> PUBe
PUG> PUGh
PUN> PUNa PUNg PUNk PUNt PUNy
PUP> PUPa PUPu
RAG> RAGa RAGe RAGg RAGi RAGu
RAT> RATa RATe RATh RATo RATu
RAYa
RED^ RED> REDd REDe REDo
REF> REFt
REV>
RIB> RIBa
RIM> RIMa RIMe RIMu RIMy
ROD> RODe

RUG> RUGa
RUT> RUTh
SAD^ SAD> SADe SADi SADo
SAP>
SEXt SEXy
SHY* SHY^
SIR> SIRe SIRi
SKYr SKYf SKY#
SOD> SODa
SPAe SPAg SPAm SPAn SPAr SPAt
     SPAw SPAy SPAz
STYe STY#
SUB> SUBa
SUN> SUNi SUNg SUNk SUNn
TAB> TABi TABu
TEAd TEAk TEAl TEAm TEAr TEAt
TEEk TEEl TEEm TEEn TEEr
TIC> TICe TICh TICk
TIN> TINa TINd TINe TINg TINk
     TINy
TIT> TITe TITi
TOEa TOEy TOE=
TOG> TOGa TOGe
TOM> TOMb TOMe TOMo
TOP> TOPe TOPh TOPi TOPo
TOYo
TUB> TUBa TUBe
TUT> TUTu
URN
VAN> VANe VANg VANt
VAT> VATu
VET> VETo
WAD> WADd WADe WADi WADt WADy
WAN> WAN^ WANd WANe WANg WANk
     WANt WANy
WAR> WARb WARd WARe WARk WARm
     WARn WARp WARt WARy
WAY
WEB>
WIG>
WIT> WITe WITh
WON> WONk WONt
WOWf
WRY* WRY^
YAK>
YEN>
YES> YESk YESt YES+
ZAG>
ZIG>

3.1.3 NOUNS IN COMMON USE

```
ADO                                  IVY+
ALEc ALEe ALEf ALEw                  JAY
ARTi ARTy                            KINa KINd KINe KINg KINk KINo
ASP                                  LAB
ASS+                                 LADe LADy
AYE                                  LEAd LEAf LEAk LEAl LEAm LEAn
BEEf BEEn BEEp BEEr BEEt                  LEAp LEAr LEAt
BOAb BOAk BOAr BOAt                  LEIr
BRAd BRAe BRAg BRAk BRAn BRAt        NITe
     BRAw BRAy                       NOB
BUNa BUNd BUNg BUNk BUNn BUNt        NUN
BYE                                  OAF
CADe CADi                            OAKy
CARb CARd CARe CARk CARl CARn        OATh OATy
     CARp CARr CARt                  ODEa
CUD                                  ONEr
CURb CURd CURe CURf CURl CURn        ORE
     CURr CURt                       PEAg PEAk PEAl PEAn PEAr PEAt
DAY                                  PEW
DOEk DOEn DOEr                       RUM^ RUMe RUMp
DUDe                                 RYE
DUO                                  SACk
EELy                                 SEAl SEAm SEAn SEAr SEAt
EGO                                  SIX+
ELK                                  SONe SONg
ELMy                                 SOYa
EMU                                  TAD
EON                                  TENd TENe TENt
ERA                                  TONe TONg TONk TONy
EVEn EVEr                            TWO
EWE*                                 UTE
FADe FADo FADy                       VIM
FENd FENi FENt                       WOE
FEZ+ FEZ>                            WOG
FIRe FIRk FIRm FIRn                  YAM
FOEn                                 ZOOm ZOOn ZOOt
GALa GALe GALl
GNU
GOOd GOOf GOOg GOOk GOOl GOOn
     GOOp GOOr
GYMp
HUB
HUEd HUEr
ILKa
ION
```

3.1.4 NOUNS MORE OFTEN USED IN OTHER PARTS OF SPEECH

ALLy

AND

AREa AREd AREg AREt AREw

ATE

BAD^ BADe

BES+ BESt

DUG

ERS+

FED

FEW*

FROe FROg FROm FROw

GAY*

HERb HERd HERe HERl HERm HERn
    HERo HERy

HIM

HOWe HOWf HOWk HOWl

ILL* ILLy

KOS+ KOS> KOSs

LAX*

LIS> LISk LISp LISt

LITe LITh LITu

METa METe METh

MIDi

NOWl NOWn NOWt NOWy

ODD*

OLD* OLDe OLDy

OURn

RAW* RAWn

RES+ RESh RESt

ROEd

SHEa SHEd SHEt SHEw

VIAe VIAl

WHYs

YEP

YOUk YOUr

3.1.5 NON-PLURALS IN COMMON USE

AFT

AGOg **AGO**n

ANY

DIDo **DID**y

FORa **FOR**b **FOR**d **FOR**e **FOR**k **FOR**m
    FORt

GOTh

HIDe

ICY*

LED

MENd **MEN**e **MEN**g **MEN**o **MEN**t **MEN**u

NORi **NOR**k **NOR**m

NOTa **NOT**e **NOT**t

PERe **PER**i **PER**k **PER**m **PER**n **PER**p
    PERt **PER**v

RANa **RAN**d **RAN**g **RAN**i **RAN**k **RAN**t

SATe **SAT**i

SLY* **SLY^**

THEe **THE**m **THE**n **THE**w **THE**y

THY

TOOk **TOO**l **TOO**m **TOO**n **TOO**t

WASe **WAS**h **WAS**p **WAS**t

WHOa **WHO**m **WHO**p **WHO**t **WHO**w

YETi **YET**t

3.2 LESS FAMILIAR THREES WHICH ARE HOOK WORDS

3.2.1 FRONT HOOKS OF TWOS TO MAKE THREES

AA	*CAA*				*WAId*	*WAIf* *WAIl* *WAIn* *WAIr*
	FAAd̶ *FAA*n				*WAIt*	
	MAAr			AL	AAL	
AB	FAB^				BALd BALe BALk BALl BALm
	GAB> GABy				BALu	
	KAB				DALe DALi DALt
	SAB> SABe				MALa MALe MALi MALl MALm
	WAB				MALt	
AD	RAD> RAD^ RADe				SALe SALl SALp SALt
	YAD			**AM**	BAM>
AE	DAEd̶ DAE=				CAM> CAMa CAMe CAMo CAMp
	FAE				GAM> GAMa GAMb GAMe GAMp
	GAE= GAEn				GAMy	
	HAE= HAEm HAEn HAEt				**KAM**a **KAM**e **KAM**i
	KAE=				LAM> LAMa LAMb LAMe
	MAE				LAMp	
	NAE				MAMa	
	SAE				NAMe NAMu
	TAE= TAEl				PAM	
	VAE				SAM> SAMa SAMe SAMp
	WAE				TAMe TAMp
	YAE			AN	DANg DANk DANt
AG	*CAGe* *CAGy*				EAN	
	MAG> MAGe MAGg MAGi				GAN> GANe GANg GANt
	VAG> *VAGi*				**HAN**d **HAN**g **HAN**k **HAN**t
	YAGi				NANa NANe
AH	AAH				SANd SANe SANg SANk
	BAHt **BAH**u				SANt	
	DAHl			AR	GAR> GARb GARe GARi
	FAH				GARt	
	HAHa				LARd LARe LARi LARk
	LAH				LARn	
	NAH				SARd SARi SARk
	PAH				VARa VARe VARy
	RAH				**YAR**d **YAR**e **YAR**k **YAR**n **YAR**r
YAH				**AS**	RASe RASh RASp RASt
AI	**JAI**l				VASa VASe **VAS**t
	KAId KAIe KAIf KAIk KAIl			AT	GATe GATh
	KAIm KAIn				KATa KATi
	RAIa RAId RAIk RAIl RAIn				LATe LATh LATi LATu
	RAIt				NAT	
	SAIc SAId SAIl SAIm SAIn				QAT	
	SAIr				TAT> TATe TATh TATt
	TAIg TAIl TAIn TAIt				TATu	

3. Three-Letter Words

WAT^ WATe WATt
AW DAWd DAWk DAWn DAWt
FAWn
GAWd GAWk
HAWk HAWm
KAWa
MAWk MAWn MAWr
NAW
TAWa TAWt
VAW
WAWa WAWe WAWl
YAWl YAWn YAWp YAWy
AX MAXi
PAX+
RAX
SAX+ SAXe
ZAX+
AY CAY
FAY*
KAYo
NAY
TAY
YAY
BA ABAc
OBA
BE OBEy
BI OBIa OBIt
BO ABO
OBOe OBOl
BY ABYd ABYe
CH **ACHe** **ACHy**
ECHe ECHo ECHt
ICHs
OCHe
DA ODAh ODAl
DE IDEa IDEe IDEm
DO UDOn
EA KEA
YEAd YEAh YEAn YEAr
ZEAl
ED GED
KED
MED
NED
PED
SED
TED> TEDy
ZED
EE CEE

DEEk DEEm DEEn DEEp DEEr
DEEt DEEv
JEEl JEEp JEEr JEEz
MEEd MEEk MEEr MEEt
NEE **NEE**d **NEE**m **NEE**p
REEd REEf REEk REEl REEn
VEEp VEEr
ZEE
EF **DEF^ DEFi DEFo DEFt DEFy**
KEF
NEF
TEFf
EH FEHm
HEH
MEH
PEH
REH
YEH
EL BELl BELt
CELl CELt
DELe DELf DELi DELl DELo
DELt
MELa MELd MELl MELt
PELa PELl PELt
SELd SELe SELf SELl
TELa TELd TELe TELl TELt
ZEL
EM FEMe
MEMe MEMo
REM
WEMb
EN BENd BENe BENi BENj BENt
EEN
GEN> GENa GENe GENt GENu
KEN> KENo KENt
REN> RENd RENk RENt RENy
SENa SENd SENe SENt
WENa WENd WENt
ER **FERe FERm FERn**
GERe GERm GERt
SERa SERe SERf SERk SERr
ES+ LES+ LESs LESt
ET **FET> FETa FETe FETt**
HETe HETh
KETa KETe KETo
RET> RETe
TETe TETh
EX DEX+ DEXy
KEX+

	LEX+						YIN			
	REX+						ZINc	ZINe	ZINg	
	TEX+	*TEXt*				IO	BIOg			
	WEXe						GIO			
	YEX					**IS**	**CIS**t			
	ZEX+						NIS>	NISh	NISi	
GO	**YGO**e						VIS+	VISa	VISe	
HA	**AHA**						WIS+	WIS>	WISe	WISh	WISp
	CHAd	CHAi	CHAl	CHAm	CHAo		WISs	WISt		
	CHAp	CHAr	CHAt	CHAv	CHAw	IT	AITu			
	CHAy						CITe	CITo	CITy	
	SHAd	**SHA**g	**SHA**h	**SHA**m	**SHA**n		DIT>	DITa	DITe	DITt	DITz
	SHAt	**SHA**w	**SHA**y				GIT>	GITe		
	WHAe	**WHA**m	**WHA**p	**WHA**t			RIT>	RITe	RITt	RITz
HE	**CHE**f	**CHE**r	**CHE**w	**CHE**z			ZITe	ZITi		
HI	*AHI*					KA	*AKA*			
	CHIa	CHIb	CHIc	CHId	CHIk		OKAy			
	CHIn	CHIp	CHIt	CHIv	CHIz		SKAg	SKAt	SKAw	
	GHI					LA	ALAe	ALAn	ALAp	ALAr	ALAy
	KHI					MA	AMAh			
	PHIz						**SMA**			
HM	OHM					ME	*AME*n	EMEu		
HO	MHO					MI	AMIa	AMId	AMIe	AMIn	AMIr
	OHO					**MM**	**HMM**			
	PHOh	PHOn	PHOt				UMMa			
	RHO					MO	*EMO*			
	THOn	**THO**u				MU	AMU			
	ZHO						*UMU*			
ID	CIDe					NA	ANAl	ANAn		
	FIDo						MNA			
	GID					**NE**	ANEw			
	NIDe	NIDi					ENEw			
	TIDe	TIDy				NO	*ONO*			
	VIDe					NY	**ONY**x			
	YID						SNY+	SNYe		
IF	*DIF*f					OB	DOB>	DOBy		
	GIFt						HOB>	HOBo		
	KIFf						KOBo			
	RIF>	RIFe	RIFf	RIFt			YOB			
	SIFt					OD	BODe	BODy		
IN	AINe						DOD>	DODo		
	HINd	HINg	HINt				HOD>			
	JINk	JINn	JINx				LODe			
	QIN						MOD>	MODe	MODi	
	LIN>	LINd	LINe	LINg	LINk		TOD>	TODy		
	LINn	LINo	LINt	LINy			YODe	YODh		
	RIN~~d~~	RIN>	RINd	RINe	RINg	OE	GOEl	GOEr	GOEy	
	RINk						JOEy			
	VINa	VINe	VINo	VINt	VINy		MOEr			

19

3. Three-Letter Words

VOE
OF *DOF*f
OOFy
WOF
OH BOHo
DOH
FOHn
HOHa
NOH
OOH
POH
SOHo
OI *BOI*l
HOIk
KOI
MOIl **MOI**t
POI
OM DOMe DOMy
*HOM*a *HOM*e *HOM*o *HOM*y
MOMe MOMi
NOMa NOMe
OOM
POMe POMo POMp
ROMa ROMp
*SOM*a *SOM*e *SOM*y
YOMp
ON **BON**a **BON**d **BON**e **BON**g **BON**k
BONy
DON> DONa DONe DONg
FON> FONd FONe FONt
GONe GONg GONk
HONd HONe HONg HONk
KONe KON> KONd KONk
MONa MONg MONk MONo MONy
NONa **NON**e **NON**g **NON**i
OONt
YONd **YON**i **YON**t
OO DOOb DOOk DOOl DOOm DOOn
DOOr
HOOd **HOO**f **HOO**k **HOO**n **HOO**p
HOOr **HOO**t
NOOk **NOO**n **NOO**p
POOd POOf POOh POOk POOl
POOn POOp POOr POOt
ROOd ROOf ROOk ROOm ROOn
ROOp ROOt
OP DOP> DOPa DOPe DOPy
KOPh
OOP

SOP> SOPh
WOP
OR BORa BORd BORe BORk BORm
BORn BORt
CORd CORe CORf CORk CORm
CORn CORy
DOR> DORb DORe DORk DORm
DORp DORr DORt DORy
GORA **GOR**e **GOR**i **GOR**m **GOR**p
GORy
JOR
KORa KORe KORo KORu
LORd **LOR**e **LOR**n **LOR**y
MORa MORe MORn MORt
OOR
TORa TORc TORe TORi TORn
TORo TORr TORt TORy
VOR>
OS+ COS+ COSe COSh COSs COSt
COSy
OU FOU* FOUd FOUl FOUr
*LOU*d *LOU*n *LOU*p *lOU*r *LOU*t
MOUe MOUp
SOUk SOUl SOUm SOUp SOUr
SOUt
OW DOWd DOWf DOWl DOWn DOWp
DOWt
JOWl
KOW
POWn
YOWe YOWl
OX+ GOX+
HOX
LOX
NOX+
SOX
VOX
WOX
OY *DOY*
FOY
GOY
HOYa
LOY
MOYa MOYl
NOY
PE OPEn
PO *APO*d
UPOn
RE **PRE**e **PRE**m **PRE**p **PRE**x **PRE**y

	PREz					HUP>		
	UREa					OUPa OUPh		
SH	ISH+					SUP> SUPe		
SI	PSI					TUP>		
SO	DSO					YUP		
	ISO			**UR**	BUR> BURa BURb BURd BURg			
					BURk BURl BURn BURp BURr			
ST	EST				BURy			
	PST				GURl GURn GURu			
TA	ETAt				LURe LURk			
	ITA				NURd NURl NURr			
	UTA				PUR> PURe PURi PURl PURr			
UG	FUG> FUGu				**SURa SURd SURe SURf**			
	SUG> SUGh SUGo			**US**	JUSt			
	VUGg VUGh				PUS+ PUSh PUSs			
	YUGa				SUS+ SUSs SUSu			
UH	*DUH*				WUS+ WUSs			
	HUHu			UT	MUTe MUTi MUTt			
	PUHa			**YA**	PYAt			
UM	CUM				RYAl			
	FUMe FUMy			YE	HYEn HYE=			
	LUMa LUMp				KYE			
	TUMp				LYE			
	VUM>				NYE			
	YUMp				OYEr OYEz			
UN	DUN^ DUN> DUNe DUNg DUNk				PYE= PYEt			
	DUNt				SYEn			
	HUNg HUNh HUNk HUNt				TYEe TYEr TYE=			
	JUNk				WYE			
	MUNg MUNi MUNt			YU	AYU			
	TUN> TUNa TUNd TUNe TUNg				KYU			
	TUNy			ZO	**AZO**n			
UP	DUP> DUPe				DZO			
	GUP							

3.2.2 END HOOKS OF TWOS TO MAKE THREES

AA	AAH				AITu	
	AAL		AL	ALAe ALAn ALAp ALAr ALAy		
AB	ABAc			ALBa ALBe		
	ABBa ABBe			*ALFa*		
	ABO			ALP		
	ABYd ABYe			ALTo		
AD	ADZe			*ALUm*		
AG	AGAr		AM	AMAh		
AH	**AHA**			*AMEn*		
	AHI			AMIa AMId AMIe AMIn AMIr		
AI	AIA			AMU		
	AINe		AN	ANAl ANAn		

21

3. Three-Letter Words

ANEw

ANIl

ANNa ANNo

AR   ARBa

ARD

ARF

ARYl

AT   **ATT**

AW   **AWA**y

AWK

AWL

AWNy

AY   AYU

BA   BACh BACk

BAHt **BAH**u

BALd BALe BALk BALl BALm

BALu

BAM>

BAPu

BE   BELl BELt

BEN BENd BENe BENi BENj

BENt

BEY

BEZ+

BI   BIOg

BIZe BIZ>

BO   BODe BODy

BOHo

*BOI*l

BOKe BOKo

BONa **BON**d **BON**e **BON**g **BON**k

BONy

BORa BORd BORe BORk BORm

BORn BORt

BOT> BOTa BOTe BOTh BOTt

CH   CHAd CHAi CHAl CHAm CHAo

CHAp CHAr CHAt CHAv CHAw

CHAy

CHEf **CHE**r **CHE**w **CHE**z

CHIa CHIb CHIc CHId CHIk

CHIn CHIp CHIt CHIv CHIz

DA   DAE= DAEd

DAHl

DAK

DALe DALi DALt

DANg DANk DANt

DAP>

DAWd DAWk DAWn DAWt

DE   DEBe DEBt

DEEd DEEk DEEm DEEn DEEp

DEEr DEEt DEEv

DEF^ **DEF**i **DEF**o **DEF**t **DEF**y

DEG> *DEG*u

DEIf **DEI**d **DEI**l

DELe DELf DELi DELl DELo

DELt

DEVa

DEX+ DEXy

DEY

DI   DIB>

*DIF*f

DIT> DITa DITe DITt DITz

DIVa DIVe DIVi DIVo

DO   DOB> DOBy

DOCk DOCo

DOD> DODo

***DOF*f**

DOH

DOLe DOLl DOLt

DOMe DOMy

DON> DONa DONe DONg

DOOb DOOk DOOl DOOm DOOn

DOOr

DOP> DOPa DOPe DOPy

DOR> DORb DORe DORk DORm

DORp DORr DORt DORy

DOWd DOWf DOWl DOWn DOWp

DOWt

DOY

EA   EAN

EAUx

ED   EDH

EE   **EEK**

EEN

EF   EFF

EFT

EL   ELD*

ELL

ELT

EM   EMEu *EMO*

EN   ENEw

ENG

ER   **ERF**

ERGo

ERK

ERM

ERNe

ES+   ESSe

	EST					HETe	HETh		
ET	ETAt				HI	HICk			
	ETHe					HIE	HIE=		
EX	EXOn					HINd	HINg	HINt	
FA	FAAd FAAn				HM	HMM			
	FAB^				HO	HOAr	HOAx		
	FAE					HOB>	HOBo		
	FAH					HOCk			
	FAP					HOD>			
	FAWn					HOHa			
	FAY*					HOIk			
FE	FEG					HOMa	HOMe	HOMo	HOMy
	FEHm					HONd	HONe	HONg	HONk
	FEM					HOOd	HOOf	HOOk HOOn HOOp	
	FERe FERm FERn					HOOr HOOt			
	FET> FETa FETe FETt					HOX			
	FEUd					HOYa			
	FEY*				ID	IDEa	IDEe	IDEm	
GI	GIB> GIBe				IF	IFFy			
	GID				IN	INGo			
	GIE= GIEn				IS	ISH+			
	GIFt					ISM			
	GIO					ISO			
	GIP>				IT	ITA			
	GITe				JA	JAIl			
GO	GOAd GOAf GOAl GOAt					JAKe			
	GOEl GOEr GOEy					JAP> JAPe			
	GONe GONg GONk				JO	JOEy			
	GORa GORe GORi GORm GORp					JOL> JOLe JOLl JOLt			
	GORy					JOR			
	GOV					JOWl			
	GOX+				KA	KAB			
	GOY					KAE=			
GU	GUB>					KAF			
	GUE					KAId KAIe KAIf KAIk KAIl			
	GULa GULe GULf GULl GULp					KAIm KAIn			
	GULy					KAKa KAKi			
	GUP					KAMa KAMe KAMi			
	GUR GURl GURn GURu					KATa KATi			
	GUV					KAWa			
HA	HAE= HAEm HAEn HAEt					KAYo			
	HAHa				KI	KIFf			
	HAJ+ HAJi HAJj					KIRn			
	HANd HANg HANh HANt				KO	KOAn KOAp			
	HAO					KOBo			
	HAP> HAPu					KOI			
	HAWk HAWm					KONd KON> KONd KONk			
HE	HEH					KOPh			
	HEP^ HEPt					KORa KORe KORo KORu			

3. Three-Letter Words

KOW
KY KYE
KYU
LA LACe LACk LACy
LAH
LAM> LAMa LAMb LAMe LAMp
LARd LARe LARi LARk LARn
LATe LATh LATi LATu
LAVa LAVe
LI LIB>
LIG>
LIN> LINd LINe LINg LINk
LINn LINo LINt LINy
LO LODe
LORd **LOR**e **LOR**n **LOR**y
LOUd LOUn LOUp LOUr LOUt
LOX
LOY
MA MAAr
MACe MACh MACk
MAE
MAG> MAGe MAGg MAGi
MAKe MAKi MAKo
MALa MALe MALi MALl MALm
MALt
MAMa
MAWk MAWn MAWr
MAXi
ME MED
MEEd MEEk MEEr MEEt
MEGa
MEH
MELa MELd MELl MELt
MEMe MEMo
MEU
MEWl
MI MIB
MICa MICe MICh MICk MICo
MIGg
MILd MILe MILf MILk MILl
MILo MILt
MIM^ MIMe
MIRe MIRi MIRk MIRo MIRv
MIRy
MIZ> MIZz
MO MOAi MOAn MOAt
MOCh MOCk
MOD> MODe MODi
MOEr

MOG>
MOIl **MOI**t
MOLa MOLd MOLe MOLl MOLt
MOLy
MOMe MOMi
MONa MONg MONk MONo MONy
MORa MORe MORn MORt
MOTe MOTh MOTi MOTt MOTu
MOUe MOUp
MOYa MOYl
MOZe MOZo MOZz
MU MUNg MUNi MUNt
MUTe MUTi MUTt
MUX
MY MYC
NA **NAE**
NAH
NAMe NAMu
NANa NANe NANg
NAT
NAW
NAY
NE NEB>
NED
NEEd **NEE**m **NEE**p
NEF
NEG
NEK
NEP
NO NOG> NOGg
NOH
NOMa NOMe
NONa **NON**e **NON**g **NON**i
NOOb **NOO**k **NOO**n **NOO**p
NOX+
NOY
NU NURd NURl NURr
NY NYE
OB OBA
OBEy
OBIa OBIt
OBOe OBOl
OD ODAh ODAl
OF OFT*
OH OHM
OHO
OI OIK
ON ONO

	ONYx	RE	REB
OO	OOFy		RECk
	OOH		REEd REEf REEk REEl REEn
	OOM		REGo
	OONt		REH
	OOP		REIf REIk REIn
	OOR		REM
	OOT		REN> RENd RENk RENt RENy
OP	OPEn		*REO*
OR	**ORA**d **ORA**l		REP> REPo REPp
	ORCa		RET>
	ORDo		REW
	ORFe		REX+
	ORT		REZ>
OS+	OSE	SH	**SHA**d **SHA**g **SHA**h **SHA**m **SHA**n
OU	OUD		**SHA**t **SHA**w **SHA**y
	OUK		**SHH**
	OUPa OUPh	SI	SIBb
OW	OWT		SIC> SICe SICh SICk
OX+	**OXO**		***SIF*t**
	OXY+		***SIK*a *SIK*e**
OY	OYEr OYEz		SIMa SIMi SIMp
PA	PACa PACe PACk PACo PACt	SO	SOCa SOCk
	PACy		SOG>
	PAH		SOHo
	PAM		SOLa SOLd SOLe SOLi SOLo
	PAP> PAPa PAPe		*SOMa SOMe SOMy*
	PAVe		SOP> SOPh SOUk SOUl SOUm
	PAX+		SOT> SOTh
PE	PECh PECk		SOUp SOUr
	PED		SOUt
	PEH		SOV
	PELa PELl PELt		**SOX**
PI	PIAl PIAn		***SOZ***
	PICa PICe PICk	TA	TAE= TAEl
	PIRl PIRn		TAIl TAIn TAIt
	PIUm		TAJ+
	PIX+ PIXy		TAKa TAKe TAKi TAKy
PO	POA		TAMe TAMp
	POH		TAO
	POI		TAT> TATe TATh TATt TATu
	POLe POLk POLl POLo POLt		TAUt
	POLy		TAVa
	POMe POMo POMp		TAWa TAWt
	POOd POOf POOh POOk POOl		TAY
	POOn POOp POOr POOt	TE	*TECh*
	POWn		TED> TEDy
	POZz		TEFf
QI	*QIN*		TEGg TEGu

		WO	WOF
	TELa TELd TELe TELl TELt		WOKe
	TETe TETh		WOP>
	TEW		WOT>
	TEX+ *TEX*t		**WOX**
TI	TIDe TIDy		YAD
	TIG> TIGe	**YA**	**YAE**
	*TIK*a *TIK*e *TIK*i		YAGi
	TILe TILl TILt		YAH
	TIX		**YAR**d **YAR**e **YAR**k **YAR**n **YAR**r
TO	TOCk TOCo		YAWl YAWn YAWp YAWy
	TOD> TODy		YAY
	TORa TORc TORe TORi TORn	YE	YEAd YEAh YEAn YEAr
	TORo TORr TORt TORy		**YEH**
UG	UGH		YEW
UM	**UMM**a		YEX
	UMPh UMPy	YO	YOB
	UMU		YODe YODh
UN	UNIt		YOK> YOKe
UP	**UPO**n		**YOM**p
UR	URB		**YON**d **YON**i **YON**t
	URDe URDy		YOWe YOWl
	UREa	YU	YUGa
	URP		YUK> YUKe YUKo YUKy
UT	UTA		**YUM**p
	UTU		YUP
WE	WEMb	ZO	**ZOA**
	WENa WENd WENt		*ZOL*
	WEXe		
	WEY		

3.3 LESS FAMILIAR NON-HOOK THREES

3.3.1 VERBS

AKEe

CLY

EIK

EUK

EWK

FIZ> FIZz

FUB>

GYP>

HYP> HYPe HYPo

IGG

JEW

KEB>

KEP> KEPi KEPt

LEK> LEKe LEKu

LEP> LEPt

NIE

NIM> NIMb

PYX

RUD> RUDe RUDd

TSK

VAC&

VEG+ VEG> VEGa VEGo

WAP>

WUD> WUDu

ZIZ> ZIZz

3.3.2 NOUNS

APP

AUA

AUF

AUK

AVAl

AVEl AVEr

AVO

BROd BROg BROo BROw

BRUt BRUx

BUBa BUBo BUBu

CEPe

CIG

COLa COLd COLe COLl COLt COLy

COZe COZy

CRUd CRUe CRUx

CUZ>

CWM

DUX+

ECOd

ECU

EVOe

EWT

FILa FILe FILm FILo

FLUb FLUe FLUx

FRAb FRAe FRAg FRAp FRAt FRAu

FRAy

FUD

GAK

GAUd GAUm GAUn GAUp GAUr

GEO

GJU

HUIa HUIc

IWI

JIZ> JIZz

JUDo JUDy

KUEh

LEY

LEZ+ LEZ> LEZz

LUDe LUDo

LUV

LUX+ LUXe

LUZ>

LYMe

OCA

OKEh

OLEa OLEo

OLM

PLUe PLUg PLUm

PROa PROb PROd PROf PROg PROm

PROo PROp PROw

PUDu

PULa PULe PULi PULk PULl PULp

PULu PULy

PUY

RAJ+ RAJa

RAVe

RHY+

RIAd RIAl

ROCk

ROKe ROKy

RUCk

SAVe

SAZ+ SAZ>

SECh SECo SECt

SEGo

SEIf SEIk SEIl SEIr

SEY

SRI

SUDd

SUKh

SUQ

SWY+

TUI

TUX+

TWAe TWAl TWAt TWAy

TYG

UEY

UFO

UKE

ULEx

ULU

UVAe

VAUt

VAV

VIGa

VLY+

VOLa VOLe VOLk VOLt

WIZ+ WIZ>

WYNd WYNn

ZEP

ZEK

ZZZ

3.3.3 NON-PLURALS

AFFy
AUE
BRRr
CAZ
DUIt
FIE* FIEf
GEY*
ICKy
JEUx
LEUd
LEVa LEVe LEVo LEVy
LEWd
NTH
OVAl
PHT
PST
QUAd QUAg QUAi QUAt QUAy
RIZa
SAUl SAUt
SEZ
SUId SUIt
SYNc SYNd SYNe
TWP
UDS
ZUZ

4. FOUR-LETTER WORDS

4.1 FAMILIAR FOURS

4.1.1 VERBS IN COMMON USE

ACHE ARCH* AVOW

BACK   BAITh BAKEn BAKEr BALKy BANDa BANDh BANDy BANG   BANK   BARE* BARKy
BASE* BASEn BASHo BASK   BATHe BAWL   BEAMy BEARd BEARe BEAT~~d~~ BEATh BEATy
BEEP   BELT   BENDy BIDEr BIDEt BIFFo BIFFy BILLy BIND~~d~~ BINDi BITE~~d~~ BITEr
BLOT> BLOWn BLOWy BLUR> BLURb BLURt BOIL   BOLT   BOMBe BOMBo BOND   BOOKy
BOOMy BOOTh BOOTy BOREe BOREl BOREr BOSS* BOSSy BOWL   BRAG^ BRAG> BREW
BUCKo BUCKu BUFF* BUFFa BUFFe BUFFi BUFFo BUFFy BUMPh BUMPy BURNt BURP
BURY   BUSTi BUSTy BUTTe BUTTy BUZZy

CAGEr CAGEy CALLa CALM* CALMy CAMP* CAMPi CAMPo CAMPy CANEh CANEr CANT*
CANTo CANTy CAREr CAREt CAREx CARTa CARTe CASE   CASH   CASTe CAVEl CAVEr
CHAR> CHARa CHARd CHARe CHARk CHARm CHARr CHARt CHARy CHAT> CHEWy CHIP>
CHOP> CITEr CLAP> CLAPt CLAW   CLIP> CLIPe CLIPt CLOG> CLOT> CLOTe CLOTh
CLUB> COATe COATi COAX   CODEc CODEn CODEr CODEx COIL   COIN   COMBe COMBi
COMBo COMBy COME~~d~~ COMEr COMEt COOKy COOL* COOLy COOPt COPEn COPEr COPY
COSTa COSTe CRAM> CRAMe CRAMp CROWd CROWn CULLy CURB   CUREr CUREt CURLi
CURLy

DAMN   DAREr DARN   DART   DASHi DASHy DATEr DAUBe DAUBy DAZEr DEAL~~d~~ DEALt
DEEM   DEFY   DENT   DENY   DIAL   DIAL> DICEr DICEy DIET   DINEr DINT   DIVEr
DOCK   DOPEr DOPEy DOTEr DOWNa DOWNy DOZEn DOZEr DRAG> DRAW~~d~~ DRAWl DRAWn
DRIP> DRIPt DROP> DROPt DRUB> DRUG> DUCKy DUEL   DUEL> DUMPy DUNK   DUSTy

EARN   EASEl EASEr ECHO   ECHO+ EDGEr EDIT   EMIT> ENVY   ETCH   EVEN* EVENt
EXIT

FACEr FACEt FADEr FAIL   FAKEr FAKEy FALL~~d~~ FAREr FARM   FAST* FASTi FEARe
FEARt FEED~~d~~ FEEL~~d~~ FENDy FILEr FILEt FILLe FILLo FILLy FILMi FILMy FIND~~d~~
FINE* FIRer FIRM* FISHy FIZZy FLAG> FLAP> FLEE~~d~~ FLEEr FLEEt FLEXo FLIP^
FLIP> FLIT> FLITe FLITt FLOG> FLOP> FLOWn FOAMy FOIL   FOLD   FOOL   FORDo
FORKy FORMe FOUL* FOULe FRAY   FREE* FREEt FRET> FUMEr FUMEt FUNDi FUNDy
FUSEe FUSEl FUSSy

GAIN* GAPEr GASH* GASPy GAWKy GAWP   GAZEr GIRD   GIVEn GIVEr GLOW   GLUEr
GLUEy GLUE= GNAWn GOAD   GOAL   GOOFy GORE   GRAB> GRIN> GRINd GRIP> GRIPe
GRIPt GRIPy GRIT^ GRIT> GRITh GROW~~d~~ GROWl GROWn GULPh GULPy GUSHy GUSTo
GUSTy

HACK   HAILy HALT   HANDy HANGi HARM   HATEr HAULd HAULm HAULt HAVE~~d~~ HAVEn
HAVEr HEADy HEAL~~d~~ HEAPy HEAR~~d~~ HEARd HEARe HEARt HEATh HEEDy HELP   HERD
HIDEr HIKEr HIREe HIRER HISSy HOCK   HOLD~~d~~ HOLEy HONEr HONEy HONKy HOOKa

HOOKy HOOTy HOPEr HOSEl HOSEn HOSEr HOSEy HOSTa HOWL HUFFy HUNT HURLy
HURTe

IRONe IRONy ITCHy

JACKy JAIL JEER JERKy JEST JILT JIVEr JIVEy JOINt JOKEr JOKEy JOLTy
JUMPy

KEEPe KICKy KILL KISSy KNEEl KNIT> KNOWe KNOWe KNOWn

LACEr LACEt LACEy LACK LANDe LASH LAST LAUD LAZE LEADy LEAKy LEAN*
LEANt LEANy LEAPt LEERy LENDe LICK LIFT LIKE* LIKEn LILT LIMP* LIMPa
LINEn LINEr LINEy LINKy LISP LIST LIVE* LIVEn LOAD LOAF LOCK LOFTy
LOLLy LONG* LONGa LONGe LOOK LOOM LOOPy LOOT LOPEr LOSEl LOSEn LOSEr
LOVEr LOVEy LUREr LUREx LURK

MAILe MAILl MAIM MAKEe MAKEr MARKa MASHy MASK MATEr MATEy MAUL MEAN*
MEANe MEANt MEANy MEET* MEETe MELD MELTy MEND MESSy MILKo MILKy MIND
MINEr MISSa MISSy MOAN MOCK MOORy MOPEr MOPEy MOVEr MUCKy MULLa

NAIL NAMEr NEAR* NEEDy NEST NICKy NOSEr NOSEy NOTEr

OBEY OGLEr OMIT> OOZE OPEN* OUST

PACEr PACEy PACK PAGEr PAIR* PAIRe PANTo PANTy PAREo PAREr PAREu PAREv
PARKa PARKi PARKy PARTi PARTy PASSe PAVEn PAVEr PAWN PEAL PECKe PECKy
PEEK PEEL PEEPe PEERy PELTa PENDu PERKy PERM PICKy PILEa PILEi PILEr
PINEy PIPEr PIPEt PITY PLAN> PLANe PLANk PLANt PLAYa PLOD> PLOP> PLOT>
PLOTz PLUG> POKEr POKEy POLLy PONGa PONGo PONGy POOP POSEr POSEy POST
POUR POUTy PRAY PREY PROD> PROP> PUFFy PUKEr PUKEy PULLi PUMP PUNTo
PUNTy PURR PUSHy PUTTi PUTTo PUTTy

QUIT> QUITe

RACEr RACK RAGEe RAGEr RAID RAINe RAINy RAKEe RAKEr RANK* RANKe RANT
RAPEr RASPy RATEl RATEr RAVEl RAVEn RAVEr RAZEe RAZEr READe READd READy
REAP REARm REDOe REDOn REDOx REDO+ REEKy REEL RELY RENTe RESTo RESTy
RIDEe RIDEr RILEy RING RIOT RISEe RISEn RISEr RISKy ROAM ROARy ROCKy
ROLL ROMP ROOTy ROPEr ROPEy ROUTe ROUTh ROVEn ROVEr RUINg RULEr RUSHy
RUSTy

SACK SAIL SAVEr SAVEy SCAN> SCANd SCANt SCAR> SCARe SCARf SCARp SCARt
SCARy SEAL SEAR* SEARe SEAT SEEDy SEEKe SEEM SEEPy SELLe SELLa SELLe
SEND SHED> SHIP> SHOOk SHOOl SHOOn SHOOt SHOP> SHOPe SHOWd SHOWn SHOWy
SHUN> SHUNt SHUTe SHUT> SHUTe SIDE SIDEr SIFT SIGHt SIGNa SINGe SINKe
SINKy SIZEl SIZEr SKID> SKIM> SKIMo SKIMp SKIN> SKINk SKINt SKIP> SLAM>
SLAP> SLAY SLIM^ SLIM> SLIMe SLIMy SLIP> SLIPe SLIPt SLIT> SLOG> SLOP>
SLOPe SLOPy SLOW* SLUR> SLURb SLURp SNAG> SNAP> SNIP> SNIPe SNIPy SNOWk
SNOWy SNUB> SOAK SOARe SORTa SPAN> SPANe SPANg SPANk SPAR> SPARd SPARe
SPARk SPARt SPEWy SPINe SPIN> SPINa SPINe SPINk SPINy SPIT> SPITe SPITz

```
SPOT> STAB> STAR> STARe STARk STARn STARr STARt STAY  STEM> STEMe STEP>
STEPt STEWy STIR> STIRe STIRk STIRp STOP> STOPe STOPt STOWn STOWp STUB>
STUN> STUNg STUNk STUNt SUCKy SUITe SULKy SURFy SWAP> SWAPt SWAT> SWATh
SWOT> SWAYl SWIG> SWIM~~e~~ SWIM>
```

```
TACKy TAIL  TAKE~~d~~ TAKEn TAKEr TALKy TAME* TAPEn TAPEr TAPEt TEARy TEEM
TELL~~d~~ TELLy TENDu TESTa TESTe TESTy THAWy THIN^ THIN> THINe THINg THINk
TICKy TIDY* TILEr TILLy TILTh TIMEr TINTy TIRE  TOILe TOLLy TONEr TONEy
TOOTh TOSSy TOUR  TOUT  TRAP> TRAPe TRAPt TREK> TRIM^ TRIM> TRIP> TRIPe
TRIPy TROT> TROTh TUCK  TUNEr TURN  TYPEy
```

```
UNDO~~d~~ URGEr
```

```
VARY  VEERy VEND  VENT  VIEWy VOTEr
```

```
WADEr WAFT  WAGEr WAIL  WAITe WAKEn WAKEr WALK  WANEy WANKy WANTy WARD
WARM* WARN  WARP  WASHy WAVEr WAVEy WEAN  WEARy WEEDy WEEP~~d~~ WEEPy WELD
WEND  WHIP> WHIPt WHIZ> WHIZz WILT  WINDy WINGe WINGy WINK  WIPEr WIREr
WISHa WISHt WOOFy WORDy WORK  WRAP> WRAPt
```

```
YACKa YANK  YAWNy YELL  YELP
```

```
ZOOM
```

4.1.2 VERBS MORE OFTEN USED IN OTHER PARTS OF SPEECH

```
ABLE* ABLEt ADZE  ALLYl AMENd AMENe AMENt ANTE= ARSEy AUTO
```

```
BABY* BAIL  BALD* BALDy BALEr BALLy BANE  BARBe BARBy BARDe BARDo BARDy
BARNy BASS* BASSe BASSi BASSo BASSy BEADy BEANo BEANy BEEFy BEET  BELLe
BELLy BESTi BIAS  BIAS> BIKEr BILE  BIRD  BLOB> BLUE* BLUEt BLUEy BLUE=
BOAT  BODY  BONEr BONEy BONGo BOOBy BRAN> BRANd BRANe BRANk BRANt BRIM>
BULB  BULKy BULLa BULLy BUNGy BUNKo BUOY  BURRo BURRy BUSHy BUSY*
```

```
CAKEy CAPEr CAPEx CARDi CARDy CARPi CASKy CELLa CELLi CELLo CHAP> CHAPe
CHAPt CHEF  CHEF> CHIN> CHINa CHINe CHINk CHINo CHIT> CHOWk CHUM> CHUMp
CLAD> CLADe CLAG> CLAM> CLAMe CLAMp CLAY  CLOD> CLUE  CLUE= COALa COALy
COKE  COLT  COMPo COMPt CONEy CORD  COREr COREy CORKy CORNi CORNo CORNu
CORNy COSY* COUPe COVEn COVEr COVEt COVEy COWL  CRAB> CRAP> CRAPe CRAPy
CREWe CRIB> CROP> CUBEb CUBEr CUFFo CURDy
```

```
DAMP* DAMPy DARK* DARKy DAWN  DEAD* DEAN  DEAR* DEARe DEARn DEARy DECKo
DEED* DEEDy DEMOb DEMOn DICKy DIKEr DIKEy DILLi DILLy DINGe DINGo DINGy
DIRTy DISHy DISCi DISCo DISK  DOLE  DOLLy DOME  DONGa DOOMy DOSEh DOSEr
DOVEn DOVEr DRAB^ DRAB> DRAM> DRAMa DRAT> DRAY  DRUM> DUAL> DUCT  DUDE
DUET  DUET> DUETt DUFF* DUKE  DULL* DULLy DUMB* DUMBo DUNGy DUSK* DUSKy
DYKEy
```

```
EAST  EASY* EDDY
```

4. Four-Letter Words

```
FAIR*  FAIRy  FAME   FANGa  FANGo  FATE   FAWNy  FEAT*  FELL*  FELLa  FELLy  FELTy
FETE   FEUD   FIFEr  FINK   FISTy  FLAT^  FLAT>  FLAWn  FLAWy  FLUX   FOAL   FOND*
FONDa  FONDu  FOOTy  FORTe  FORTh  FORTy  FOWL   FROG>  FUEL   FUEL>  FULL*  FULLy
FUZZy

GAITa  GAITt  GALLy  GAME*  GAMEr  GAMEy  GANG   GAOL   GARBe  GARBo  GATER  GEARe
GERMy  GIFT   GILLy  GIRTh  GLAD^  GLAD>  GLADe  GLADy  GLEEk  GLEEt  GLIB^  GLIB>
GLUT>  GLUTe  GOLF   GONG   GOWN   GRAY*  GREW   GREY*  GROG>  GRUB>  GULFy  GULLy
GUTSy

HAIRy  HALE*  HALOn  HALO+  HAREm  HARK   HARPy  HASHy  HAWK   HAZEl  HAZEr  HEEL
HEIR   HELLo  HELM   HIGH*  HIGHt  HILLo  HILLy  HILT   HINT   HIVEr  HOAX   HOBO
HOBO+  HOMEr  HOMEy  HOODy  HOOF   HOON   HOOP   HORNy  HOVEa  HOVEl  HOVEn  HOVEr
HULKy  HULLo  HULLy  HUMPh  HUMPy  HUSHy  HUSKy  HYMN   HYPEr

IDLE*  INCH   IRIS   ISLEt  ITEM

JADE   JAMBe  JAMBo  JAMBu  JAZZy  JEEP   JIBEr  JINX   JOWLy  JUNKy  JURY   JUST*

KEEL   KEEN*  KEENo  KELPy  KERB   KILN   KILTy  KIND*  KINDa  KINDy  KING   KINKy
KITEr  KNOB>  KNOT>  KOOK

LAID   LAIRd  LAIRy  LAKEr  LAMBy  LAME*  LAMP   LANK*  LANKy  LARDy  LARKy  LAZY*
LEAFy  LENSe  LEST   LEVY   LIMBa  LIMBi  LIMBo  LIMBy  LIMEn  LIMEy  LINTy  LOAMy
LOAN   LOBE   LOCO   LOCO+  LORDy  LOUT   LUBE   LUCKy  LUGEr  LULL   LUMPy  LUSH*
LUSHy  LUSTy  LUTEr

MACEr  MAID   MAIN*  MALL   MALTy  MARLe  MARLy  MART   MASSa  MASSe  MASSy  MASTy
MATTe  MAZEr  MAZEy  MEALy  MERE*  MEREl  MESHy  MEWS   MIKE   MILD*  MILLe  MINTy
MIREx  MISTy  MOAT   MOONg  MOONy  MOOT*  MORNe  MOSSo  MOSSy  MUFF   MULEy  MUSEr
MUSEt  MUSHa  MUSHy  MUSKy  MUSTh  MUSTy  MUTE*

NAPE   NECK   NEWSy  NIGH*  NIGHt  NOON   NULLa  NUMB*

OKAY   OMEN   OUCHt  OVEN   OVERt

PAINt  PALE*  PALEa  PALEt  PALMy  PANEl  PANGa  PATH   PEAKy  PERVe  PERVy  PIKEr
PIKEy  PILL   PIMP   PINGo  PINK*  PINKo  PINKy  PITHy  PLEAd  PLEAt  PLOY   PLUSh
PLUS>  POLEr  POLEy  POND   PONY   POOL   PORer  PORKy  PORTa  PORTy  POSH*  POSHo
PRIM^  PRIM>  PRIMa  PRIMe  PRIMi  PRIMo  PRIMp  PRIMy  PUCKa  PULPy  PURE*  PUREe

QUAD>  QUIP>  QUIPo  QUIPu  QUIZ>

RAFT   RAILe  RAMP   RANDy  RARE*  RAREe  RASH*  REAMe  REAMy  REEDe  REEDy  REEFy
REINk  RICEr  RICEy  RICH*  RICHt  RICK   RIFTe  RIFTy  RILLe  RINDy  RINK   RIPE*
RIPEn  ROBE   RODEo  ROOFy  ROOKy  ROOMy  ROSEt  ROSY*  ROTE   RUBY*  RUCK   RUMPo
RUMPy
```

```
SAFE*  SALT*  SALTo  SALTy  SANDy  SANE*  SASH   SCAB>  SCAM>  SCAMp  SCAT>  SCUM>
SEAMe  SEAMy  SELF   SENTe  SENTi  SHAG>  SHAM>  SHAMa  SHAMe  SHIN>  SHINe  SHINy
SHIT>  SHITe  SHOE=  SHOEr  SHOT>  SHOTe  SHOTt  SICK*  SICKo  SILKy  SILO   SILTy
SIREe  SIREn  SITE   SKEW*  SLAB>  SLAG>  SLAT>  SLATe  SLATy  SLED>  SLEW   SLOT>
SLOTh  SLUG>  SLUM>  SLUMp  SMUG^  SMUG>  SMUT>  SNOT>  SNUG^  SNUG>  SOAPy  SOCKo
SOFT*  SOFTa  SOFTy  SOILy  SOLEi  SOLEr  SOLOn  SOOK   SOOTe  SOOTh  SOOTy  SORE*
SOREe  SOREl  SOREx  SOUPy  SOUR*  SPAT>  SPATe  SPEC>  SPECk  SPUD>  SPUR>  SPURn
SPURt  STAG>  STAGe  STAGy  STUD>  STUDe  STUDy  STYE   SUDSy  SURE*  SWAG>  SWAGe
SWAN>  SWANg  SWANk

TALCy  TALC&  TANGa  TANGi  TANGo  TANGy  TANKa  TANKy  TARE   TART*  TARTy  TASK
TAUT*  TAXI+  TAXI=  TAXI@  TEAM   TEENd  TEENe  TEENy  TEMPi  TEMPo  TEMPt  TENTh
TENTy  TERM   TERNe  TEXT   THEEk  THOU   THUD>  TIDE   TIER   TIFF   TINEa  TOMB
TONGa  TOOL   TOTEm  TOTEr  TRAM>  TRAMp  TREEn  TRUE*  TRUE=  TUBEr  TUFTy  TURFy
TUSKy  TUTS   TWIG>  TWIN>  TWINe  TWINk  TWINy  TWIT>  TWITe  TYRE

UGLY*

VEALe  VEALy  VEILy  VEINy  VESTa  VETO+  VIAL   VIAL>  VICE   VINEr  VINEw  VISA
VIVAt  VOID   VOLTa  VOLTe

WAIFt  WALLa  WALLy  WAREz  WEIRd  WELLy  WELT   WEST   WHIM>  WICKy  WIFEy  WILD*
WILE   WILL*  WILLy  WIMPy  WINEy  WISE*  WISPy  WITHe  WITHy  WOLF   WOMBy  WONT
WOODy  WORMy

YARD   YARN   YOKEl  YOKEr  YUCKo  YUCKy

ZANY*  ZERO   ZERO+  ZESTy  ZINCo  ZINCy  ZINC&  ZINGy  ZONEr
```

4.1.3 NOUNS IN COMMON USE

```
ACID*  ACIDy  ACNEd  ACREd  AIDEr  ANUS+  APEX+  AREAd  AREAe  AREAl  AREAr  ARIA
ARMY+  ATOMy  AUNTy  AURAe  AURAl  AURAr  AXIS+
BEAKy  BEAUt  BEAUx  BEERy  BEVY+  BOARd  BOARt  BOONg  BRAT   BRIG   BROWn  BYTE
CAFÉ   CALF   CENTo  CENTu  CITY+  CLANg  CLANk  COLD*  COMAe  COMAl  CRAG   CRUX+
CULTi  CULTy  CUSPy  CYST
DAGO   DAGO+  DAISy  DALEd  DAME   DEBT   DELLy  DESK   DIMEr  DODO   DODO+  DOLT
DOORn  DUNE   DUTY+
EARLy  EPIC   EVIL*  EVIL^  EXAM
FACT   FERNy  FIVEr  FLAB   FLAKe  FLAKy  FLEAm  FONT   FOODy  FOREl  FOREx  FOUR
FURY+
GALAh  GALAx  GALEa  GEEKy  GENEt  GENTy  GIRLy  GLENt  GNAT   GOATy  GOLD*  GOLDy
GOONy  GOUTy  GRAMa  GRAMe  GRAMp  GRIDe
HALFa  HALLo  HEMPy  HERBy  HEROe  HEROn  HERO+  HICK   HOURi  HUNKy
ICON   IDEAl  IDOLa  INFO   IOTA
JUBE   JUDO   JUTE
KILO   KIWI
LADY+  LANE   LASS+  LASSi  LASSo  LASSu  LAVA   LAWNy  LEEK   LIARd  LIARt  LIFEr
LILY+  LINO   LION   LOGOi  LOGOn  LOIN   LOREl  LOSS+  LOSSy  LUDO   LUNGe  LUNGi
LYRE
MANEd  MANEh  MANEt  MARE   MEAD   MEATh  MEATy  MEMO   MENU   MICA   MILEr  MINKe
MITEr  MODEl  MODEm  MODEr  MOLE   MONK   MOODy  MOTHy  MUTT   MYTHi  MYTHy
NAVY+  NEON   NERDy  NINE   NODE   NONG   NOOKy  NORMa  NOUNy
```

33

```
OATH  OBOE  OGRE  ONUS+  OPAL  ORGY+
PACTa PAIL  PEARe PEARl  PEARt PEATy PESTo PESTy PIERt PINTa PINTo PLEBe
PLUM^ PLUMb PLUMe PLUMp  PLUMy POEM  POET  POLO  POMP  PORNo PORNy PRAM
PROMo PUMA  PUNK* PUNKa  PUNKy
QUAYd QUID  QUINa QUINe  QUINo QUINt
RITE  ROAD  ROLE  RUNG   RUNTy RUSE
SAGA  SAGE* SAGO  SAKEr  SALEp SALEt SARIn SECT  SERF  SILLy SKITe SLOB
SLUT  SMOG  SNOB  SODA   SOFAr SONG  SOUL  SUMPh
TACO  TACT  TALEa TALEr  TEAK  TEAL  TEAT  THUG  TOFFy TOGAe TOME  TOWNy
TRAY  TRIOl TRIOr TUBAe  TUBAl TUBAr TUNA  TYPO
UNITe UNITy USER
VANEd VASE  VERB  VIBEx  VIBEy VOLTi
WAND  WARTy WASPy WATT*  WEEKe WOOLd WOOLy WREN  WRITe
YEARd YEARn YOGA  YOLKy
```

4.1.4 NOUNS MORE OFTEN USED IN OTHER PARTS OF SPEECH

```
AFARa AMIDe AMIDo AMIS+  AMISs AMOK  ANTIc ARTY* AWAY
BAAS+ BENTo BENTy BOLD*  BRAS+ BRASh BRASs BRASt BREDe
CAMEl CAMEo CHIC* CHICa  CHICh CHICk CHICo CUTE* CUTEy
DANK*
EWER
FLEW  FOXY*
GILT  GLUM^ GLUMe GOODy
HAHA  HARD* HARDy HECK   HERE  HIND  HOLY*
LEFTe LEFTy LESS+ LIFEr
MAAS+ MANY+ MOREl MOSTe  MUCHo
NEAT* NEATh NETTy NEXT   NONEt NOSY* NUDE*
ONCEr ONCEt ORAL  OVAL   OYES+ OYES>
PASTa PASTe PASTy PENT   PERT* POKY*
REAL* REALm REALo REIS+  REISt ROAN  RUDE*
SAID  SAMEk SAMEl SAMEn  SAMEy SANGa SANGh SANGo SOLDe SOLDi SOLDo SUNK
TALL* TALLy THANa THANe  THANg THANk THEN  TINY* THUS+ TORE  TRODe
UTAS+
VAST* VASTy
WAVY* WENT  WHATa WHEN   WIDE* WIDEn
YOURn YOURt
```

4.1.5 NON-PLURALS IN COMMON USE

```
AGOGe AIRY* AJAR  AKINg  ALSO  ANEW  ARID* AVID* BADE  BEEN  BLED  BLEW
BONY* BORNa BORNe BOTHy  CAGY* CURT* DAFT* DATAl DEAF* DEFT* DEWY* DIRE*
DONEe DONEr DOPY* DOUR*  DOURa DOZY* DREW  DULY  EACH  EDGY* ELSE  EVERt
EVERy FEET  FROM  GAVEl  GONEf GONEr GOSHt GRIM^ GRIMe GRIMy HAZY* HELD
HEWN  HUGE* IDLY  INTO   KEPT  KNEW  LAIN  LATE* LATEd LATEn LATEx LENTi
LENTo LEWD* LICE  LONEr  LOST  LOUD* MADE  MEEK* MICE  MOWN  NICE* OILY*
ONLY  ONTO  OXEN  PAID   POOR* POORi POORt PUNY* RANGa RANGe RANGi RANGy
RIFE* SANKo SAWN  SEEN   SEWN  SEXY* SLIDe SOME  SOON* SOWNd SOWNe SPED
SPUNk SUCH  SUNG  SWAMi  SWAMp SWAMy SWUM  THAT  THEMa THEMe THEY  THIS
TOLD  TOOK  TORN  UNTO   UPON  VAIN* VERY* VILE* WARY* WEAK* WEPT  WERE
WHOMp WILY* WIRY* WOKEn  WORE  WORN  WOVEn
```

4.2 LESS FAMILIAR FOURS WHICH ARE HOOK WORDS

4.2.1 FRONT HOOKS OF THREES TO MAKE FOURS

AAL	BAAL	*DAAL*	**KAAL**	*PAAL*
	TAAL			
AAS	**KAAS**			
ABA	BABA	CABAl	*YABA*	
ABY	GABY+			
ACE	DACE	TACEt		
ACH	BACHa	BACHs	MACHe	MACHi
	MACHo	NACH+	NACHe	NACHo
	RACH+	RACHe	TACHe	TACHo
ADD	WADDy			
ADO	DADO	DADO+	FADO	*SADO*
ADS	*NADS*			
AFF	BAFFy	CAFF	DAFFy	FAFF
	GAFFe	HAFF	NAFF*	RAFF
	WAFF	YAFF		
AFT	BAFT	HAFT	*SAFT**	
AGA	**GAGA**	*JAGA*	NAGA	RAGA
AGE	GAGEr	MAGE		
AGO	KAGO			
AHA	*MAHA*	TAHA		
AIA	RAIA			
AID	CAID	GAID	KAID	QAID
	WAIDe			
AIL	KAIL	VAIL		
AIM	KAIM	SAIM		
AIN	CAIN	FAIN*	FAINe	FAINt
	HAINt	KAINg	**NAIN**	SAINe
	SAINt	TAINt	WAIN	
AIR*	GAIR	MAIRe	SAIR*	VAIRe
	VAIRy	WAIR		
AIS	**PAIS**a	**PAIS**e		
AIT	RAITa	TAIT		
AKA	HAKAm	KAKA	TAKA	WAKA
AKE	HAKEa	JAKEy		
ALA	*MALA*m	*MALA*r	*MALA*x	NALA
	TALAk	TALAq	TALAr	
ALE	EALE	KALE	RALE	VALEt
	WALEr	YALE		
ALL	LALL	PALLa	PALLy	**SALL**e
	SALLy			
ALP	CALPa	PALPi	SALPa	
ALT	DALT			
ALU	BALUn			

AMA	*CAMA*n	GAMAy	KAMA	LAMA
	MAMA	SAMAn		
AME	HAME	KAME	WAMEd	
AMI	KAMIk	RAMIe	RAMIn	
AMP	GAMP	SAMPi	TAMP	VAMPy
AMU	*NAMU*			
ANA	KANAe	LANAi	MANAt	NANA
	RANA	TANA		
AND	FAND	**MAND**i	PANDa	PANDy
ANE	FANE	**GANE**f	**GANE**v	JANE
	KANEh	**NANE**	**TANE**	
ANI	**BANI**a	MANIa	MANIc	RANId
ANN	CANNa	CANNy	JANNy	
ANS	KANS+			
ANT	BANTu	BANTy	DANT	GANT
	HANT	KANT	LANT	SANTo
	VANT			
APE	JAPEr	PAPEr		
APP	YAPPy			
APO	CAPOn	CAPOt	GAPO	
APT*	**RAPT**			
ARB	CARBo	CARBy	DARB	*WARBy*
ARC	MARCh	NARCo		
ARD	EARD	FARD	**MARD**y	NARD
	PARDi	PARDy	SARD	
ARE	**GARE**	LAREe	NARE	VAREc
	YARE*			
ARF	BARF	ZARF		
ARK	CARK	JARK	KARK	NARKy
	RARK	SARKy	WARK	*YARK*
ARM	BARMy	MARM		
ART	FART	**GARTh**	HART	KART
ARY	MARY+	**NARY**	**OARY***	
ASH	FASH	PASHa	PASHm	TASH
ASK	HASK			
ASP	HASP	JASPe		
ASS+	JASS+	SASSe	SASSy	TASS+
	TASSe			
ATE	BATE	CATEr	PATEd	PATEn
	PATEr	SATEm	TATEr	**WATE**r
	YATE			
ATT	BATTa	BATTu	BATTy	TATTy
AUA	PAUA			
AUF	**CAUF**	*HAUF*	LAUF	
AUK	BAUK	CAUK	JAUK	WAUK

4. Four-Letter Words

AVA	*CAVA* FAVA JAVA KAVAl TAVAh				**EAS**	CEAS+ CEASe			
AVE	EAVEd FAVE* FAVEl LAVEr NAVEl NAVEw				EAT	GEAT JEAT LEAT			
AWA	*KAWA*u PAWAw TAWAi *WAWA*				ECH	EECH **HECH**t LECH PECHs *SECH* TECHy YECHy			
AWE	WAWE				ECO	DECOr DECOy **SECO**			
AWK	CAWK DAWK LAWK MAWKy PAWKy				**EEK**	**DEEK** KEEK ***TEEK***			
AWL	PAWL WAWL YAWL				EEL	JEELy SEELd SEELy TEEL WEEL			
AWN	BAWN **MAWN** RAWN				**EEN**	DEEN *FEEN* PEEN REEN WEENy			
AXE	*SAXE*				EFF	JEFF *MEFF* TEFF			
AYE	BAYE				EFT	HEFTe HEFTy **REFT** WEFTe			
AZO	LAZO LAZO+				EGG	TEGG YEGG			
BAC	ABACa ABACi ABACk				EGO	BEGOd BEGO+ BEGOt REGO SEGOl *VEGO*			
BAR	KBAR				EIK	REIKi **SEIK***			
BED	**ABED**				EKE	DEKE DEKE= **LEKE** PEKE REKEy			
BET	ABET> **YBET**				ELD	GELD **SELD** **TELD** VELDt **YELD**			
BID	**ABID**e				ELF	DELFt PELF			
BIS	IBIS+				ELK	WELKe WELKt YELK			
BIT	OBIT				ELL	JELLo JELLy KELLy MELL PELL VELL			
BON	EBONy				ELM	YELM			
BUT	ABUT>				**ELS**	*WELS*h			
BYE	ABYEd ABYE=				ELT	CELT DELTa GELT KELTy **TELT** YELT			
CAD	ECAD SCAD				EME	DEME FEME HEME LEMEl MEME SEMEe SEMEn TEMEd			
CAG	SCAG>				**EMS**	TEMSe			
CAW	SCAW				END	HEND REND			
CHE	ECHE OCHEr				ENE	BENEt DENEt MENE NENE PENE SENE TENEt			
COD	**ECOD**				ENG	LENG* MENGe			
COG	SCOG>				**ENS**	CENS+ CENSe			
COP	SCOPa SCOPe				EON	AEON **JEON** PEONy			
COT	SCOT				ERA	**SERA**c **SERA**i **SERA**l **VERA**			
COW	SCOWl SCOWp				ERE	BEREt CERE DERE FERE* GERE LERE PEREa SERE*			
CRU	ECRU				**ERF**	KERF TERFe			
CRY	SCRY				ERG	BERG			
CUD	SCUD> SCUDi SCUDo				ERK	BERKo MERK NERKa SERK YERK ZERK			
CUP	SCUP				***ERM***	BERMe DERMa FERMi HERMa			
CUR	SCUR> SCURf				ERN	DERN HERN KERNe PERN			
CUT	SCUTa SCUTe				ERR	SERRa SERRe SERRy			
DAH	*ODAH*				ERS+	VERS+ VERSe VERSo VERSt			
DAL	ODAL UDAL				ESS+	CESSe FESSe JESSe NESS+ SESS+ SESSa			
DAW	ADAW								
DEE	IDEE								
DIT	ADIT								
DON	*UDON*								
DOR	ODOR								
DRY*	**ADRY**								
DSO	**ODSO**								
EAN	GEAN JEAN PEAN REAN SEAN YEAN								
EAR	LEARe LEARn LEARy								

Root	Words
EST	FESTa FESTy GESTe HEST
	KESTd YESTy
ETA	BETA FETAl GETA KETA
	METAl **SETA**e **SETA**l WETA
	ZETA
ETH	BETH HETH METHo TETH
EUK	NEUK YEUKy
EVE	LEVEe LEVEl LEVEr MEVE
	NEVEl NEVEr YEVEd YEVEn
EVO	**LEVO**
EWT	NEWT
FAY*	OFAY
FRO	AFRO
GAD	EGAD **IGAD**
GAL	**EGAL**
GAM	OGAM
GAR	AGAR
GEE	**AGEE** OGEEd
GEN	**AGEN**e **AGEN**t
GER	AGER EGER
GIN	**AGIN**g
GIO	AGIO
GIS	EGIS+
GOE	**YGOE**
GON	AGONe AGONy
GUE	AGUEd
HAD	CHADo SHADe SHADy
HAE	**THAE** ***WHAE***
HAH	SHAH
HAM	CHAMp WHAM> WHAMo
HAN	KHAN SHANd SHANk
HAO	CHAO
HAP	WHAP>
HAT	***BHAT*** GHAT KHAT **PHAT^**
	SHAT
HAW	CHAWk SHAWl SHAWm SHAWn
HAY	CHAYa SHAYa
HEM	**AHEM**
HER	**CHER**e **CHER**t
HET	KHETh SHETd SHET> WHET>
HEW	**PHEW** SHEWn THEWy WHEW
HID	CHIDe WHID>
HIM	SHIM>
HIN	WHINe WHINy
HIT	WHITe WHITy
HOA	**WHOA**
HOC	CHOCk CHOCo
HOD	**SHOD**
HOG	*CHOG* SHOG> SHOGi
HOH	**PHOH**
HON	**CHON** PHONe PHONo PHONy
	THONg
HOP	WHOP>
HOT	PHOTo **WHOT**
HOW	DHOW **WHOW**
HOY	**AHOY**
HUB	CHUB
HUG	CHUG>
HUP	*WHUP>*
HUT	BHUT **CHUT**e PHUT>
ICE	BICEp FICE **PICE** SICE
	TICE **WICE**
ICH	**DICH**t LICH+ LICHi LICHt
	*MICH*e *MICH*t **SICH**t TICH+
	TICHy WICH+
ICK	MICKy
ICY*	**RICY***
IDE	CIDEr **EIDE**r NIDE **VIDE**o
IFF	*DIFF* JIFFy ***KIFF*** MIFFy
	NIFFy RIFF ZIFF
IGG	BIGGy MIGG RIGG
ILK	BILK
ILL*	CILL JILL LILL NILL
	VILLa VILLi YILL ZILLa
IMP	*DIMP* GIMPy **JIMP*** JIMPy
	SIMP
ING	BINGe BINGo BINGy GINGe
	HINGe LINGa LINGo LINGy
	MINGe MINGy TINGe
INK	BINK **DINK*** DINKy GINK
	JINK OINK TINK
INN	**GINN**y JINNe JINNi LINNy
	WINNa
ION	CION PIONy
IRE	CIRE **LIRE** VIREo
IRK	BIRK DIRKe FIRK KIRK
	LIRK MIRKy YIRK
ISH+	BISH+ ***EISH*** HISH KISH+
	NISH+ PISH
ISM	GISMo JISM
ISO	MISO PISO
ITA	DITAl PITA VITAe VITAl
IVY+	***JIVY*** **TIVY**
JEE	**AJEE**
JIN	DJINn
JOE	***SJOE***
KAT	IKAT SKATe SKATt
KAW	SKAW
KEG	SKEGg
KEN	*SKEN>* *SKENe*

KEP	SKEP>		
KET	*SKET>*		
KON	IKON		
LAB	BLAB>		
LAD	BLAD>	BLADe	BLADy
LAG	BLAG>		
LAH	BLAH		
LAM	BLAMe	FLAM>	FLAMe FLAMm
	FLAMy	GLAM>	
LAP	ALAPa	*KLAP>*	PLAP>
LAR	**ALARm**	**ALARy**	
LAT	BLAT>	BLATe	BLATt CLAT>
	PLAT>	PLATe	PLATy
LAX*	FLAXy		
LAW	BLAWn	SLAW	
LAY	ALAY	BLAY	FLAY
LEA	**ILEAc**	**ILEAl**	**OLEA**
LED	GLEDe	**PLED**	
LEE	**ALEE**	BLEEd	BLEEp **SLEE***
	SLEEk	**SLEEp**	**SLEEt**
LEG	CLEG	FLEG	**GLEG^**
LEI	GLEI	VLEI	
LET	BLET>		
LEW	ALEW	CLEW	PLEW
LEX+	ILEX+	*PLEX+*	ULEX+
LEY	BLEY	FLEY	GLEY SLEY
LID	**GLID^**	**GLIDe**	**OLID**
LIE	PLIEr		
LIN	BLIN>	BLINd	BLINg BLINi
	BLINk	BLINy	
LIP	BLIP>		
LIT	**ALIT**	*BLIT>*	*BLITe* *BLITz*
	CLIT	GLITz	
LOB	*FLOB>*	GLOBe	GLOBi GLOBy
LOD	ALOD		
LOG	*BLOG>*	*VLOG*	
LOO	*ALOOf*		
LOP	CLOP>	GLOP>	
LOR	FLORa	FLORy	
LOU	CLOUd	CLOUr	CLOUt
LOW	**ALOWe**	CLOWn	PLOW
LOX	***FLOX***		
LOY	CLOYe		
LUG	GLUG>		
LUM	ALUM		
MAM	IMAM		
MEE	SMEEk		
MEU	EMEU		
MEW	SMEW		
MIC	**EMIC**		

MID	IMIDe	IMIDo	
MIR	AMIR	EMIR	SMIR> SMIRk
	SMIRr		
NAB	SNAB		
NAG	KNAG		
NAN	**ANANa**		
NAP	KNAP>		
NAW	SNAW		
NEB	SNEB>		
NED	SNED>		
NEE	SNEEr		
NEW*	ENEW		
NIB	SNIB>		
NIE	*ONIE*		
NIL	ANILe		
NIT	SNIT		
NOD	SNOD>	SNOD^	
NOG	SNOG>		
NON	**ANON**		
NOW	**ANOW**	ENOW	*GNOW*
NUB	KNUB		
NUR	KNURl	KNURr	
NUT	KNUT		
NYE	SNYE		
OAF	GOAF		
OAK	BOAK		
OAR	HOARd	HOARy	VOAR
OAT	DOAT		
OBA	BOBAc	BOBAk	*SOBA*
OBE	JOBE	*MOBE*	
OBI	**LOBI**		
OBO	GOBO	GOBO+	KOBO LOBO
	ZOBO		
OCA	COCA	**LOCAl**	SOCA
OCH	COCH+	LOCH	MOCHa MOCHy
	ROCH+		
ODA	CODA		
ODE	BODE	LODEn	**YODEl**
OFF	BOFFo	COFF	DOFF GOFF
	KOFF		
OFT	**COFT**	TOFT	
OHO	*BOHO*	COHOe	COHOg **SOHO**
	TOHO		
OIK	HOIK		
OIL	MOIL	NOILy	ROILy
OKA	*HOKA*		
OKE	BOKE	HOKEy	LOKE MOKE
	ROKEr	SOKEn	TOKEn TOKEr
OLD*	MOLDy	WOLD	**YOLD**

OLE	BOLE	COLEd	COLEy	GOLEm		OWN	LOWNd	LOWNe	**NOWN**	POWNd
	JOLE	NOLE	TOLE	VOLEt			POWNy			
OLM	HOLM					OWT	DOWT	LOWT	NOWTy	ROWTh
OMS	**COMS**						TOWT			
ONE	**FONE**	PONEy	RONEo	SONE		OXY+	**BOXY***	**COXY***	DOXY+	**POXY***
ONO	MONO					PAH	OPAH			
ONS	**PONS**					PAM	SPAM>			
ONY	CONY+	MONY+	TONY*			PAS	UPAS+			
OOF	COOF	LOOFa	POOFy	YOOF		PAW	SPAWl	SPAWn		
OOH	BOOH	POOH				PAY	APAYd	APAYd	SPAYd	
OOM	COOMb	COOMy	SOOM	TOOM*		PEE	EPEE			
OON	COON	**DOON**a	LOONy	POON		**PER**	APERt	APERy		
	ROON	TOON	WOON	ZOON		PET	SPET>			
OOP	GOOPy	MOOP	NOOP	ROOPy		PIC	SPICa	SPICe	SPICk	SPICy
	SOOP	YOOP				PIE	SPIEl	SPIEr		
OOR	BOORd	GOORy	HOORd	**LOOR**d		POD	APODe	SPODe		
OOT	POOT	**WOOT**z	ZOOTy			POS	EPOS+			
OPE	**NOPE**	POPE	TOPEe	TOPEk		PRY	**SPRY***	**SPRY^**		
	TOPEr					PUG	SPUG			
ORA	BORAk	BORAl	BORAx	**FORA**m		PUS+	OPUS+			
	FORAy	GORAl	HORAh	HORAl		**QUA**	AQUAe			
	KORAi	KORAt	MORAe	MORAl		RAD^	BRAD>	**DRAD**	GRADe	**ORAD**
	MORAt	MORAy	SORAl	TORAh			PRAD	TRADe		
	TORAn					RAG	FRAG>			
ORB	DORBa	FORBy	SORBo			**RAN**	CRANe	CRANk	GRANa	GRANd
ORC	TORCh						GRANt			
ORD	BORDe	SORDa	SORDo			RAP	DRAP>	DRAPe	FRAP>	FRAPe
ORE	DOREe	**HORE**	KORE	RORE		RAT	FRATe	FRATi	**GRATe**	PRAT>
	YORE						PRATe	PRATt	PRATy	TRATt
ORF	**CORF**					RAV	GRAVe	GRAVy		
ORS	HORS+	HORSe	HORSt	HORSy		RAW*	BRAW*	BRAWl	BRAWn	CRAWl
ORT	BORTy	BORTz	DORTy	MORT		RAY	BRAY	CRAY	XRAY	
	TORTa	TORTe	WORTh			RED	**ARED**d	**ARED**e	CREDo	
OSE	COSEc	COSEt	COSEy	MOSEy		REE	BREEd	BREEm	BREEr	CREEd
	OOSE	TOSE					CREEk	CREEl	CREEp	DREE
OUD	FOUD						GREEk	GREEn	GREEt	PREEn
OUK	BOUK	DOUK	GOUK	JOUK		REF	**TREF**a			
	POUKd	POUKe	SOUK	TOUK		REG	**AREG**	DREG		
	YOUK	ZOUK				REI	BREId	BREI=	BREId	
OUP	DOUP	LOUPe	MOUP	NOUP		REM	CREMe	PREMy		
	ROUPy					REN	BRENt	GREN>	GRENz	
OUR	COURb	COURd	COURe	COURt		REP	PREP>			
	JOUR	LOURe	LOURy			RES+	**TRES**s	**TRES**t		
OUS	NOUS+					RET	ARET>	ARETe	ARETt	TRET
OUT	DOUT	HOUT	**NOUT**	SOUTh		REV	EREV			
OVA	NOVAe					REW	**AREW**	TREW		
OWE	HOWE	LOWEr	YOWE			REX+	GREX+	PREX+	PREXy	
OWL	DOWLe	DOWLy	GOWL	NOWL		**REZ**	PREZ+	TREZ+		
	SOWLe	YOWL				RIA	CRIA			
						RIB	DRIB>	FRIB		

RID	IRID
RIG	FRIG> GRIG> PRIG> TRIG^
	TRIG> TRIGo
RIM	CRIMe CRIMp
RIN	BRINe BRINg BRINk BRINy
	TRINe
RIT	BRITh BRITt CRITh FRIT>
	FRITh FRITt FRITz
RIZ	FRIZe FRIZz
ROB	PROBe
ROC	CROCi CROCk
ROD	BROD>
ROE	FROE
ROK	*GROK* *GROK>*
ROO	BROOd BROOk BROOl BROOm
	PROOf
ROT	GROT ***VROT***
ROW	**AROW** DROWn FROWn FROWy
	PROW* PROWl TROW VROW
RUD	CRUD> CRUDe CRUDy
RUE	CRUEl CRUEt GRUEl GRUE=
RUG	FRUG> TRUGo
RUM^	ARUM **GRUM^** **GRUM**e **GRUM**p
RUT	BRUTe
RYE	**TRYE**r
SAR	**ASAR** KSAR **OSAR** TSAR
SEA	**ASEA**
SHY*	**ASHY***
SIT	***ISIT***
SKY	ESKY+
SPY	ESPY
TAP	ATAP STAP> STAPh
TAT	ETAT STATe
TAW	STAW
TED	STED> STEDd STEDe
TEN	ETEN STEN> STENd STENo
	STENt
TET	STET>
THE	**ETHE**r
TIC	**ETIC** **OTIC**
TIE	STIE
TIS	UTIS+
TOC	ATOC
TOP	**ATOP**y
TOT	STOT> STOTt
TUI	ETUI ***PTUI***
TUM	STUM> STUMm STUMp
UDO	BUDO KUDO

UEY	QUEYn
UFO	BUFO
UGH	EUGH **PUGH** SUGH VUGHy
UKE	BUKE CUKE JUKE **LUKE**
	NUKE YUKE
ULE	DULE GULE HULE PULEr
	TULE YULE
ULU	LULU PULU SULU ZULU
UMM	**MUMM**
UMP	GUMP MUMP TUMPy YUMP
UMU	MUMU
UNI	MUNI *SUNI*
URB	*BURB*
URD	BURD NURDy SURD TURD
URE	DURE **IURE** **JURE**l MUREx
URN	CURNy DURN GURN **OURN**
URP	RURP
UTA	*KUTA*
UTE	BUTEo JUTE
UTU	*KUTU* TUTU
VAE	**UVAE**
VAS+	KVAS+ KVASs
VET	EVET
VOE	**EVOE**
VUM	**OVUM**
WAD	SWAD
WAE	TWAE
WAN^	**HWAN**
WAT^	TWAT
WAY	TWAY
WEE	**AWEE**l SWEEl SWEEp SWEEr
	SWEEt **TWEE*** **TWEE**d **TWEE**l
	TWEEn TWEEt
WEY	SWEY
WIS	**YWIS**
WIZ+	SWIZ> SWIZz
WOP	SWOP> SWOPt
WRY*	**AWRY**
YAD	DYAD
YAH	AYAH
YAK	KYAK
YAM	LYAM
YAR	KYAR
YEN	**EYEN** HYENa SYEN
YET	PYET
YIN	AYIN PYIN ***TYIN***g
ZEE	MZEE
ZHO	DZHO

4.2.2 END HOOKS OF THREES TO MAKE FOURS

ABA	ABACa	ABACi	ABACk		BAA	BAAL		
ABB	ABBA	ABBEd	ABBEy		BAC	BACH	BACHs	BACHa
ABY	ABYEd	ABYE=			BAG	*BAGH*		
ACE	ACERb				**BAH**	BAHT	*BAHUt*	
ACH	**ACHY***				BAL	BALMy	BALUn	
ACT	**ACTA**				BAN	BANCo	**BANI**a	BANTu BANTy
ADD	*ADDY*+				BAP	BAPU		
AFF	AFFY				BAR	BARF	BARMy	BARP
AGA	AGAR				**BAS**	BASTa	BASTe	BASTi BASTo
AGE	**AGEE**	**AGEN**e	**AGEN**t AGER		BAT	BATE	BATTa	BATTu BATTy
AGO	AGONe	AGONy			BAY	BAYE	BAYT	
AID	*AIDA*				BED	BEDEl	BEDEw	**BEDU**
AIN	**AINE**e				BEG	BEGOd	BEGO+	BEGOt
AIR*	AIRN	AIRTh			BEN	BENEt	BENI	BENJ+
AIT	AITU				BET	BETA	BETEl	BETH
AKE	AKEE				BID	*BIDI*		
ALA	**ALAE**	ALANd	ALANe ALANg		BIG^	**BIGA**e	BIGGy	
	ALANt	ALAPa	**ALAR**m **ALAR**y		BIN	BINEr	BINGe	BINGo BINGy
	ALAY					BINK	BINT	
ALB	ALBA	**ALBE**e			BIO	BIOG		
ALE	ALECk	**ALEE**	ALEFt ALEW		**BIS**	BISE	BISH+	BISK **BIST**
ALF	ALFA				BIT	BITOu	BITTe	BITTy
ALT	ALTO				BIZ>	BIZE		
ALU	ALUM				BOA	*BOAB*	BOAK	
AMA	AMAH				BOB	BOBAc	BOBAk	
AMI	AMIA	AMIE	AMINe AMINo		BOD	BODE		
	AMIR				BOG	BOGY+		
ANA	**ANAL**	**ANAN**a			BOH	*BOHO*		
ANI	ANILe				BOK	BOKE	BOKO	
ANN	ANNAl	ANNAt	**ANNO**y		**BON**	**BONA**	BONK	
ANS	ANSAe				BOO	BOOH	BOOL	BOORd
ANT	ANTAe	ANTAr			BOR	BORAk	BORAl	BORAx BORDe
APE	APERt	APERy				*BORK*	*BORM*	BORTy BORTz
APO	APODe				**BOS**	BOSH+	BOSKy	
ARB	ARBA				BOT	BOTA	*BOTE*l	BOTTe BOTTy
ARC	ARCO				BOW	BOWR		
ARE	**ARED**d	**ARED**e	**AREG** ARET>		BOX	**BOXY***		
	ARETe	ARETt	**AREW**		BOY	*BOYF*	BOYG	BOYO
ARS	**ARSY***				BRA	BRAD>	BRAE	*BRAKe BRAKy*
ART	*ARTIc*					BRAW*	BRAWl	BRAWn BRAY
ARY	ARYL				BRO	BROD>	BROG>	BROGh BROOd
ASH	**ASHY***					BROOk	BROOl	BROOm
AVA	AVALe				**BRR**	**BRRR**		
AVE	*AVEL*	AVER>	AVERt		*BRU*	BRUTe	*BRUX*	
AWE	**AWEE**l				BUB	BUBAl	BUBO+	*BUBU*
AWN	**AWNY***				BUD	*BUDA*	*BUDI*	BUDO
AXE	AXEL				BUM^	BUMF		
AZO	AZON							

4. Four-Letter Words

BUN	BUNA	BUNDe	BUNDh	BUNDt
	BUNDu	BUNDy	BUNNy	BUNTy
BUR	BURAn	*BURB*	BURD	BURGh
	BURKa	BURKe	BURLy	
BUS	BUSKy	BUSSu		
BUT	BUTEo			
CAB	CABAl			
CAD	CADEe	CADEt	CADIe	
CAM	*CAMAn*	*CAMO*		
CAN	CANG	CANNa	CANNy	**CANY***
CAP	CAPA	CAPH	**CAPI**z	CAPOn
	CAPOt			
CAR	CARBo	CARBy	CARK	CARLe
	CARNy	CARRy		
CAT	CATEr			
CAW	CAWK			
CEL	CELT			
CEP	CEPE			
CHA	CHADo	CHAIn	CHAIr	CHALk
	CHAMp	CHAO	*CHAVe*	CHAWk
	CHAYa			
CHE	**CHERe**	**CHERt**	**CHEZ**	
CHI	CHIAo	*CHIB>*	**CHIDe**	CHIK
	CHIV>	CHIVe	CHIVy	CHIZ>
	CHIZz			
CID	CIDEr			
CIS	CIST			
CIT	**CITO**			
COB	COBBy			
COD	CODA			
COL	COLA	COLEd	COLEy	COLLy
	COLY+			
CON	**COND**o	CONF	**CONI**a	**CONI**c
	CONIn	CONKy	CONNe	CONY+
COO	COOF	COOMb	COOMy	COON
COR	**CORF**	CORM	CORY+	
COS+	COSEc	COSEt	COSEy	COSH
	COSS+			
COT	COTE	COTH	COTTa	
COW	*COWK*	COWP	**COWY***	
COX	**COXA**e	**COXA**l	**COXY***	
COZ+	COZEn	COZEy	COZY*	
CRU	CRUD>	CRUDe	CRUDy	CRUEl
	CRUEt			
CUR	CURF	CURNy	CURRy	
DAD	DADAh	DADO	DADO+	
DAH	DAHL			
DAL	DALI	DALT		
DAN	DANG	DANT		
DAW	DAWD	DAWK	DAWT	

DEB	*DEBE*l			
DEE	**DEEK**	DEEN	DEET	DEEVe
DEF^	DEFI	***DEFO*g**		
DEG	*DEGU*m			
DEI	DEID*	***DEIF***	***DEIF*y**	DEIL
DEL	DELE=	DELFt	DELI	*DELO*
	DELTa			
DEN	DENEt	*DENI*m		
DEV	DEVA			
DEX+	DEXY+			
DID	DIDO	DIDO+	DIDY+	
DIE	DIEB	**DIEL**		
DIF	*DIFF*			
DIM^	*DIMP*			
DIN	DINK*	DINKy	DINO	
DIP	**DIPT**			
DIS	DISA	DISS		
DIT	DITAl	DITE	DITTo	DITTy
	DITZ+	DITZy		
DIV	DIVAn	DIVI@	*DIVO*	
DOB	DOBY+			
DOC	*DOCO*			
DOE	DOEK	**DOEN**	DOER	
DOF	DOFF			
DOG	DOGEy	DOGY+		
DOM	**DOMY***			
DON	DONAh			
DOO	DOOB	DOOK	DOOLe	DOOLy
	DOONa			
DOP	DOPA			
DOR	*DORB*a	DOREe	DORKy	DORMy
	DORP	DORR	DORTy	DORY+
DOS	DOSH+	DOSS	**DOST**	
DOT	**DOTH**	**DOTY***		
DOW	DOWDy	**DOWF**	DOWLe	DOWLy
	DOWP	DOWT		
DUI	DUIT			
DUN^	DUNT			
DUP	DUPEr			
DYE	DYER			
EAR	EARD			
EAT	**EATH**e			
EAU	**EAUX**			
ECH	ECHE	**ECHT**		
ECO	**ECOD**			
EEL	**EELY***			
EGG	**EGGY***			
ELM	**ELMY***			
EME	EMEU			
ENE	ENEW			

ERE	*EREV*			
ERG	ERGOn	ERGOt		
ERN	ERNE			
ERS+	**ERST**			
ESS+	ESSE			
ETA	ETAT			
ETH	**ETHE**r			
EVE	EVET			
EVO	**EVOE**			
EXO	EXON			
EYE	**EYEN**	EYER		
FAD	FADO	**FADY***		
FAA	***FAAN***			
FAN	FAND	FANE	FANK	FANOn
FAR	FARD	FARLe	FARO	FART
FAS	FASH			
FEE	*FEEB*	*FEEN*	FEER	
FEH	**FEHM**e			
FEM	FEME			
FEN	FENI	FENT		
FER	FERE*	FERMi		
FES	FESSe	FESTa	FESTy	
FET	FETAl	FETTa		
FID	FIDO			
FIE*	FIEF	FIERe	FIERy	
FIG	FIGO			
FIL	**FILA**r	FILO		
FIN	FINI	FINO		
FIR	FIRK	FIRN		
FIT^	FITTe			
FIX	**FIXT**			
FLU	FLUB>	FLUEd	FLUEy	
FOE	**FOEN**			
FOG	FOGY+			
FOH	FOHN			
FON	**FONE**			
FOR	**FORA**m	**FORA**y	FORBy	
FOU*	FOUD			
FRA	FRAB	**FRAE**	FRAG>	FRAP>
	FRAPe	FRATe	FRATi	FRAUd
FRO	FROE	FROWn	FROWy	
FUG	FUGUe			
FUM	**FUMY***			
FUN^	FUNGi	FUNGo	FUNKy	
FUR	FURL	FURRy		
GAB	GABY+			
GAD	GADE	GADId		
GAE	**GAEN**			
GAG	**GAGA**	GAGEr		

GAM	GAMAy	GAMBa	GAMBe	GAMBo
	GAMP	**GAMY***		
GAN	**GANE**f	**GANE**v	GANT	
GAP	GAPO	**GAPY***		
GAR	**GARE**	*GARI*	**GART**h	
GAS	GAST			
GAT	GATH			
GAU	GAUDy	GAUMy	**GAUN**t	GAUP
	GAUR			
GAW	GAWD			
GEE	GEEP	**GEEZ**		
GEL	GELD	GELT		
GEN	GENAl	GENUa		
GER	***GERT***			
GET	GETA			
GIB	GIBEl	GIBEr		
GIE	**GIEN**			
GIG	GIGA			
GIN	GINGe	GINK	**GINN**y	
GIS	GISMo	GIST		
GIT	GITE			
GOA	GOAF			
GOB	GOBO	GOBO+	GOBY+	
GOE	GOEL	GOER	**GOEY***	
GON	GONK			
GOO	*GOOG*	GOOKy	GOOLd	GOOLy
	GOOPy	GOORy		
GOR	GORAl	*GORI*	GORMy	GORP
	GORY*			
GOS	*GOSS*e			
GOT	*GOTH*			
GUL	GULAg	GULAr	GULEt	**GULY**
GUM	GUMP			
GUN	***GUNG*e**	***GUNG*y**	GUNKy	
GUR	GURLy	GURN		
GYM	GYMP			
HAD	HADE	HADJ+	HADJi	
HAE	HAEM	**HAEN**	HAET	
HAG	HAGG			
HAJ+	HAJI	HAJJi		
HAM	HAME			
HAN	HANKy	HANT		
HAP	*HAPU*			
HAS	HASK	HASP	*HASS*+	**HAST**a
	HASTe	**HAST**y		
HAT	**HATH**a			
HAW	HAWM			
HEM	HEME			
HEN	HEND	HENT		
HEP^	**HEPT**			

43

4. Four-Letter Words

HER	HERL	HERMa	HERN	HERYe
HES	HESP	HEST		
HET	HETEd	HETH		
HIN	HINGe			
HIP^	**HIPT**			
HIS	HISH	**HISN**	HIST	
HOA	HOARd	HOARy		
HOE	HOER			
HOG	HOGG	HOGH		
HOH	**HOHA**			
HOI	HOIK			
HOM	HOMA	HOMO	HOMY*	
HON	HONDa	HONGe	HONGi	
HOO	HOORd			
HOS	HOSS+			
HOT^	**HOTE**l	**HOTE**n		
HOW	HOWE	HOWFf	HOWK	
HOY	HOYA			
HUE	**HUED**	HUER		
HUG	**HUGY**			
HUH	HUHU			
HUI	HUIA	**HUIC**		
HUM	HUMAn	HUMF		
HUN	**HUNH**			
HYE	HYENa			
HYP	HYPO			
ICE	ICER			
ICK	ICKY*			
IDE	IDEE	**IDEM**		
IFF	IFFY*			
ILK	**ILKA**			
ILL*	**ILLY**			
IMP	IMPI	IMPI+		
ING	INGO+	INGOt		
INK	**INKY***			
JAG	JAGA	JAGGy		
JAK	JAKEy			
JAP	JAPEr			
JAR	JARK	JARL	JARP	
JEE	JEELy	**JEEZ**		
JET	JETE			
JEU	**JEUX**			
JIB	JIBBa			
JIN	JINK	JINNe	JINNi	
JIZ>	JIZZ+			
JOB	JOBE			
JOE	JOEY			
JOL	JOLE	JOLLy		
JOT	JOTA			
JUD	JUDY+			

JUG	JUGAl			
JUT	JUTE			
KAI	KAID	KAIE	KAIF	KAIKa
	KAIL	KAIM	KAINg	
KAK	KAKA	KAKI		
KAM	KAMA	KAME	KAMIk	
KAT	KATAl	KATI		
KAW	KAWAu			
KAY	KAYO	KAYO+		
KEN	KENO	KENTe		
KEP	KEPI			
KET	KETA	KETE	**KETO**l	
KIF	**KIFF**			
KIN	KINA	KINE	KINO	
KIP	KIPE	KIPPa		
KIR	KIRK	KIRN		
KIS	KISH+	KIST		
KIT	KITHe			
KOA	KOAN	KOAP		
KOB	KOBO			
KON	**KOND**o	KONK		
KOP	KOPH			
KOR	KORAi	KORAt	KORE	KORO
	KORUn			
KOS+	KOSS+			
KUE	**KUEH**			
LAC	**LACY***			
LAD	LADEn	LADEr		
LAM	LAMA			
LAR	LAREe	LARI	LARN	
LAS	LASEr			
LAT	LATHe	LATHe	LATHi	LATHy
	LATI	*LATU*		
LAV	LAVEr			
LAW*	LAWK			
LEA	**LEAL***	LEAM	LEARe	LEARn
	LEARy	LEAT		
LEE	LEEP	LEET		
LEI	LEIR			
LEK	**LEKE**	**LEKU**		
LEP	**LEPT**a			
LEU	LEUD			
LEV	**LEVA**	LEVEe	LEVEl	LEVEr
	LEVO			
LEZ+	LEZZa	LEZZy		
LID	LIDO			
LIE	LIEF*	LIEN	LIER	LIEU
LIN	LINDy	LINGa	LINGo	LINGy
	LINNy	**LINY***		
LIP	*LIPA*	**LIPE**	*LIPO*	

LIS	LISK				
LIT	LITEr	LITHe	LITHo	**LITU**	
LOB	**LOBI**	LOBO			
LOD	LODEn				
LOG	LOGE	LOGY*			
LOO	LOOFa	LOONy	**LOORd**		
LOR	**LORN**	LORY+			
LOS	**LOSH**				
LOT	LOTAh	LOTE	**LOTH***	LOTIc	
	LOTO				
LOU	LOUNd	LOUPe	LOURe	LOURy	
LOW*	LOWEr	LOWNd	LOWNe	*LOWP*	
	LOWT				
LUD	LUDE	LUDO			
LUM	*LUMA*				
LUX+	LUXE				
LYM	LYME				
MAA	MAARe				
MAC	MACHe	MACHi	MACHo	MACK	
MAG	MAGE	MAGG	**MAGI**c		
MAK	*MAKI*	MAKO			
MAL	*MALA*m	*MALA*r	*MALA*x	MALIc	
	MALIk	MALMy			
MAM	MAMA				
MAN	MANAt	**MAND**i	MANGa	MANGe	
	MANGo	MANGy	MANIa	MANIc	
	MANOr				
MAR	MARAe	MARAh	MARCh	**MARD**y	
	MARGe	MARM	MARY+		
MAS	MASA	MASEr	MASU		
MAT	MATH	MATY*			
MAW	MAWKy	**MAWN**	MAWR		
MAX	MAXIm				
MAY	MAYAn	MAYOr			
MEE	MEED	MEER			
MEG	**MEGA**				
MEL	MELA	MELL			
MEM	MEME				
MEN	MENE	MENGe	**MENO**	**MENT**a	
	MENTo				
MES	MESAl	MESEl			
MET	**META**l	METEr	METHo		
MEW	MEWL				
MIC	*MICH*e	*MICH*t	MICKy	MICO	
MID	MIDI				
MIG	MIGG				
MIL	*MILF*	MILOr	MILTy	MILTz	
MIR	**MIRI**n	MIRKy	*MIRO*	MIRV	
	MIRY*				
MIS	MISEr	MISO			

MIX	**MIXT**e	**MIXY***		
MIZ>	MIZZy			
MOA	***MOAI***			
MOB	*MOBE*y	*MOBY*+		
MOC	MOCHa	MOCHy		
MOD	**MODI**i			
MOE	*MOER*			
MOI	MOIL	MOIT		
MOL	MOLAl	MOLAr	MOLDy	MOLLa
	MOLLy	MOLTo	MOLY+	
MOM	MOME	**MOMI**		
MON	MONAd	MONAl	MONGo	MONO
	MONY+			
MOO	**MOOI**	MOOK	MOOLa	MOOLi
	MOOLy	MOOP		
MOP	**MOPY***			
MOR	MORAe	MORAl	MORAt	MORAy
	MORT			
MOS	MOSEy	*MOSH*	MOSK	
MOT	MOTEd	MOTEl	MOTEn	MOTEt
	MOTEy	*MOTI*f	MOTTe	MOTTo
	MOTTy	MOTU		
MOU	MOUE	MOUP		
MOW	MOWA			
MOY	MOYA	MOYLe		
MOZ+	MOZE	MOZO	MOZZ+	
MUG	MUGGa	MUGGy		
MUM	MUMMy	MUMP	MUMU	
MUN	*MUNG*a	*MUNG*e	*MUNG*o	
	MUNI	MUNTu		
MUS	MUSO	MUSSe	MUSSy	
MUT	MUTI			
NAB	NABE	NABK		
NAG	NAGA			
NAM	*NAMU*			
NAN	NANA	***NANE***	***NANG***	
NAP	NAPA			
NEE	NEEMb	NEEP		
NET	NETE			
NID	NIDE	**NIDI**		
NIE	NIEF			
NIL	NILL			
NIM	NIMBi			
NIP	NIPA			
NIS	*NISH*+	**NISI**		
NIT	NITEr			
NIX	NIXEr	NIXY+		
NOD	**NODI**			
NOG	NOGG			
NOM	NOMAd	NOMEn		

4. Four-Letter Words

NON	NONA	NONG	NONI	
NOO	*NOOB*	NOOP		
NOR	NORIa	NORK		
NOS	NOSH			
NOT	**NOTAl**	**NOTT**		
NOW	NOWL	**NOWN**	NOWTy	**NOWY**
NUR	NURDy	NURL	NURR	
OAK	OAKY*			
OAR	**OARY***			
OAT	*OATY***			
OBI	OBIA	OBIT		
OBO	OBOLe	OBOLi		
OCH	OCHEr			
ODA	*ODAH*	ODAL		
ODE	**ODEA**			
ODS	**ODSO**			
OFF	*OFFY+*			
OKE	OKEH			
OLD*	*OLDEn*	*OLDEr*	OLDY+	
OLE	**OLEA**	OLEO		
ONE	ONERy			
ONS	**ONST**			
ONY	ONYX+			
OOF	*OOFY***			
OON	OONT			
OOS	OOSE	**OOSY***		
ORA	**ORAD**			
ORB	**ORBY***			
ORC	ORCA			
ORD	ORDO			
ORF	ORFE			
OUP	*OUPA*	OUPHe		
OUR	**OURN**			
OWE	**OWER**			
OWL	**OWLY***			
OYE	OYER	OYEZ+		
PAC	PACA	PACO	**PACY***	
PAD	PADI			
PAL	PALLa	PALLy	PALPi	**PALY***
PAN	PANDa	PANDy		
PAP	PAPAl	PAPAw	PAPEr	
PAR	PARAe	PARDi	PARDy	PARP
	PARRa	PARRy		
PAS	PASEo	PASHa	PASHm	
PAT	PATEd	PATEn	PATEr	*PATU*
	PATY			
PAW	PAWAw	PAWKy	PAWL	
PEA	PEAGe	PEAN		
PEC	PECHs			
PEE	PEEN			
PEG	PEGH			
PEL	PELA	PELE	PELF	
PEN	PENE	PENIe	PENK	
PEP	PEPO			
PER	PEREa	PERIl	PERN	*PERP*
PES	PESO			
PHI	PHIZ+	PHIZ>		
PHO	**PHOH**	PHONe	PHONo	PHONy
	PHOTo			
PIA	**PIAL**	PIANi	PIANo	
PIC	PICAl	**PICE**		
PIE	PIETa	PIETy		
PIN	PINA	PINY*		
PIP	PIPAl	PIPIt	**PIPY***	
PIR	PIRL	PIRN		
PIS	PISE	PISH	PISO	PISS
PIT	PITA			
PIU	PIUM			
PIX+	PIXY+			
PLU	*PLUE*			
POL	POLKa	POLT	POLY+	POLYp
	POLYs			
POM	POME	*POMO*		
POO	POOD	POOFy	POOH	POOKe
	POOKa	POON	POOT	
POP	POPE			
POS	POSSe	POSY*		
POT	POTE	POTTo	POTTy	
POW	POWNd	POWNy		
POX	**POXY***			
POZ	**POZZy**			
PRE	PREEn	*PREMy*	PREP>	PREX+
	PREXy	PREZ+		
PRO	PROA	PROBe	PROF	PROG>
	PROOf	PROW*	PROWl	
PRY	PRYSe			
PUB	*PUBE*			
PUD	PUDU			
PUG	**PUGH**			
PUH	*PUHA*			
PUL	PULAo	PULEr	PULIk	PULKa
	PULU	**PULY***		
PUN	PUNA	PUNGa		
PUP	PUPAe	PUPAl	*PUPU*	
PUR	PURIm	PURIn	PURL	
PUS+	PUSS+	PUSSy		
PUT	PUTZ			
PYA	PYAT			
PYE	PYET			
QUA	QUAG	QUAIl	QUAIr	QUATe

46

RAD*	**RADE**			
RAG	RAGA	RAGGa	RAGGy	RAGI
	RAGU			
RAI	RAIA	RAIK	RAITa	
RAJ+	RAJAh			
RAM	RAMIe	RAMIn		
RAN	RANA	RANId		
RAP>	**RAPT**			
RAS+	RASEr	**RASTa**		
RAT	RATAl	RATAn	RATHa	RATHe
	RATOo	RATU		
RAW*	RAWN			
RAY	RAYAh			
REC	RECK			
RED	REDDy	REDE		
REE	REEN			
REF	**REFT**			
REG	REGO			
REI	REIFy	REIKi		
REN	REND	*RENK**	RENY	
REP	REPOt	REPP		
RES+	RESH+			
RET	**RETEm**			
RIA	*RIAD*	RIAL		
RIB	*RIBA*			
RIF	RIFF			
RIG	RIGG			
RIM	**RIMAe**	RIMEr	RIMU	**RIMY***
RIN	RINE			
RIP	RIPP	**RIPT**		
RIT	RITT	RITZ+	RITZy	
RIZ	RIZA			
ROC	ROCH+			
ROE	**ROED**			
ROK	ROKEr	**ROKY***		
ROM	**ROMAl**	**ROMAn**		
ROO	ROOD	ROON	ROOPy	
ROT	ROTAl	ROTAn	ROTI	ROTL
	ROTOn	ROTOr		
ROW	ROWTh			
RUB	RUBEl			
RUD	RUDDy			
RUE	RUER			
RUG	**RUGAe**	**RUGAl**		
RUM^	RUMEn			
RUN	RUND	RUNEd		
RUT	RUTH			
RYA	RYAL			
SAB	SABE=	SABEr		
SAD^	SADE	SADI	*SADO*	

SAG	**SAGY***			
SAI	SAICe	SAICk	SAIM	SAINe
	SAINt	SAIR*		
SAL	**SALLe**	**SALLy**	SALPa	
SAM	SAMAn	SAMPi		
SAN	SANTo			
SAR	SARD	SARKy		
SAT	SATEm	SATIn		
SAU	SAULt	SAUTe		
SAX+	*SAXE*			
SEA	SEAN			
SEC	*SECH*	**SECO**		
SEE	SEELd	SEELy	SEER	
SEG	SEGOl			
SEI	SEIF	**SEIK***	SEIL	SEIR
SEL	**SELD**	SELE		
SEN	SENA	SENE		
SER	**SERAc**	**SERAi**	**SERAl**	SERE*
	SERK	SERRa	SERRe	SERRy
SET	**SETAe**	**SETAl**	SETT	
SEX	SEXTo			
SHA	SHADe	SHADy	SHAH	SHANd
	SHANk	**SHAT**	SHAWl	SHAWm
	SHAWn	SHAYa		
SHE	SHEAf	SHEAl	SHEAr	SHETe
	SHET>	SHEWn		
SIB	SIBB			
SIC	SICE	**SICHt**		
SIK	SIKA	SIKEr		
SIM	SIMAr	SIMI	SIMP	
SIN	SIND	SINEw	SINH	
SIP	SIPE			
SIR	SIRIh			
SIS+	SISS+	SIST		
SIT	**SITHe**	*SITZ*		
SKA	SKAG	SKATe	SKATt	SKAW
SKI	SKIO			
SKY	*SKYF*	SKYRe		
SNY+	SNYE			
SOB	SOBA			
SOC	SOCA			
SOH	**SOHO**			
SOL	SOLAh	SOLAn	SOLAr	**SOLId**
SOM	SOMAn	*SOMY*		
SON	SONE			
SOP	SOPHy			
SOS	SOSS			
SOT	SOTH			
SOU	SOUK	SOUM	SOUTh	
SOW	SOWFf	SOWLe	SOWM	SOWP

SOY   SOYA
SPA   SPAE= SPAG> SPAM> SPAWl
     SPAWn SPAYd SPAZ> SPAZa
     SPAZz
SUB   SUBAh
SUD   SUDD
SUE   SUER SUETy
SUG   SUGH SUGO
SUI   SUID
SUK   SUKH
SUM   SUMO SUMY
SUN   SUNI SUNNa SUNNy
SUP   SUPEr
SUR   SURAh SURAl SURAt SURD
SUS   SUSS SUSU
SYE   SYEN
SYN   SYNCh SYND SYNE
TAB   TABId TABUn
TAE   TAEL
TAI   TAIGa TAINt TAIT
TAK   TAKA TAKIn TAKY*
TAM   TAMP
TAN^   TANA TANE TANH
TAP   TAPA TAPU
TAR   TARA TARN TAROc TAROk
     TAROt TARP
TAS   TASH TASS+ TASSe
TAT   TATEr TATH TATTy TATU
TAV   TAVAh
TAW   TAWAi TAWT
TAX   TAXA
TEA   TEADe
TEC   TECHy
TED   TEDY*
TEE   TEEK TEEL TEER
TEF   TEFF
TEG   TEGG TEGUa
TEL   TELAe TELD TELEx TELT
TEN   TENEt
TET   TETE TETH
THE   THEWy
THO   THONg
TIC   TICE TICH+ TICHy
TIG   TIGEr
TIK   TIKA TIKE
TIN   TINA TIND TINGe TINK
TIP   TIPI TIPT
TIT   TITEr TITI
TOC   TOCKy TOCO
TOD   TODY+

TOE   TOEA TOEY*
TOG   TOGEd
TOM   TOMO
TON   TONKa TONY*
TOO   TOOM* TOON
TOP   TOPEe TOPEk TOPEr TOPHe
     TOPHi TOPIc TOPOi
TOR   TORAh TORAn TORCh TORIc
     TORIi TOROt TORR TORTa
     TORTe TORY+
TOW   TOWT TOWY*
TOY   TOYOn
TRY   TRYEr TRYP
TUM   TUMPy
TUN   TUND TUNG TUNY*
TUT   TUTU
TWA   TWAE TWAL TWAT TWAY
TYE   TYEE TYER
UDO   UDON
ULE   ULEX+
UMM   UMMAh
UMP   UMPH UMPY+
UPS   UPSY+
URD   URDEe URDY
URE   UREAl
UVA   UVAE
VAG   VAGI
VAN   VANG VANT
VAR   VARAn VAREc
VAS   VASAl
VAT   VATU
VAU   VAUTe
VEE   VEEP
VEG+   VEGAn VEGO
VEX   VEXT
VIA   VIAE
VID   VIDEo
VIE   VIER
VIG   VIGA
VIN   VINAl VINO VINT VINY*
     VINYl
VIS   VISE VISE# VISE=
VOL   VOLAe VOLAr VOLEt VOLK
VUG   VUGGy VUGHy
WAD   WADDy WADI WADT WADY+
WAI   WAIDe WAIN WAIR
WAN^   WANG WANY*
WAR   WARBy WARK
WAS   WASE WASTe
WAT*   WATEr

WAW	*WAWA*	WAWE	WAWL		YAP	YAPPy		
WAX	**WAXY***				**YAR**	**YARE***	*YARK*	YARR
WEE*	WEEL	WEEM	WEENy	WEET*	YAW	YAWL	YAWP	**YAWY**
	WEETe				YEA	YEADe	YEAH	YEAN
WEM	WEMB				YES	YESK	YESTy	
WEN	***WENA***				**YET**	YETI	YETT	
WET^	WETA				**YGO**	**YGOE**		
WEX	WEXE				YIP	YIPE		
WHA	***WHAE***	WHAMo	WHAMo	WHAP>	YOD	**YODE**l	YODH	
WHO	**WHOA**	WHOP>	**WHOT**	**WHOW**	**YOM**	YOMP		
WIN	WINNa	WINO	WINO+	**WINY***	WON	**YOND**	YONIc	**YONT**
WIS	WISS	WIST			**YOU**	YOUK		
WIT	WITE				YOW	YOWE	YOWL	
WON	WONKy				YUG	YUGA		
WOO	WOON	**WOOT**z			YUK	YUKE	YUKO	**YUKY***
WOS	**WOST**				**YUM**	YUMP		
WOW	**WOWF***				ZIN	ZINEb		
WUD	*WUDU*				ZIT	**ZITE**	ZITI	
WUS+	WUSS+	WUSSy			ZIZ	ZIZZ		
WYN	WYND	WYNN			ZOO	ZOON	***ZOOT***y	
YAG	YAGI							

4.3 LESS FAMILIAR NON-HOOK FOURS

4.3.1 ADJECTIVES ENDING IN 'Y'

AERY* **CAKY*** **COKY*** **EERY*** **FIKY*** **FOZY*** **GAZY*** **JOKY*** **LAKY*** **LIMY*** LUNY* **MAZY***
MINY* **MITY*** **OOZY*** **PORY*** *PUKY** **RACY*** **ROPY*** **RORY*** **RULY*** **SIZY*** **TYPY*** WALY*

4.3.2 OTHERS CONTAINING HEAVY LETTERS

VERBS

FAZE FLIX FUTZ FUZEe HIZZ JAUP JOOK JOSH *MUZZ*y PIZE QUOD> QUOP>
RAZZ TOZE VIZY ZONK

NOUNS

AXILe AXONe AZAN AZYMe BAJU BOZO CALX+ CZAR DIXY+ DOJO EXEC EXPO
EXULt *FIQH* FUJI GAJO GIZZ+ *GOJI* IBEX+ IXIA IZARd *JAAP* *JAFA* JASY+
JATO *JAXY*+ JAZY+ *JEDI* JEFE JEHU JIAO JIRD JOCKo JOHN JOMOn *JONG*
JOSS+ JUBA *JUCO* JUJU *JUKU* JUPE JUVE JYNX+ KAZI *KOJI* KUZU LUTZ+
LYNX+ MEZE MEZZ+ MINX+ MOJO MOJO+ MOXA *MYXO* NAZE NAZIr ORYX+ ORZO
OUZO OXER OXIDe OXIMe PUJAh QADI QOPH QUIM ROJI SIJO SOJA TIZZ+
TIZZy TUZZ+ TZAR WAQF XYSTi YUNX+ YUTZ+ *YUZU* ZACK *ZARI* ZATI ZEBUb
ZEIN ZEZE ZILA ZIMBi ZOBU ZOEAe ZOEAl ZORIl ZUPAn ZURF ZYME

NON-PLURALS

AXAL　DIXIe　DIXIt　DOUX　**FAIX**　**FALX**　**FAUX**　JOCO　JURAl　JURAt　**LANX**　**QUEP**
RONZ　ROUX　ZOIC　ZONAe　ZONAl　ZYGAl

4.3.3 OTHER VERBS

ARLE
BECKe　BIRLe　BIRR　BLUB>　BOCK　BOLL　BOUNd　*BREY*　*BYDE*　BYKE　BYRL
CALK　CAUM　CEDEr　CEILi　CIEL　CLEM>　COIF　*CROG*>　CULM　CUSSo
DACK　DAUD　DAUR　DAUT　DICTa　DICTy　DIRL　DUSH　DWAM>
*EMPT*y
FAIK　*FAUT*　FEAL　FECK　FIAT　FIKE　FISK　FLOC>　FLOCk　FOIN　FUCK　FUFFy
FUSTy
FYKE
GEAL　GECKo　GILD　GIRN　GLOM>　GNAR>　GNARl　GNARr　GOWF　GYBE　GYRE　GYVE
HARL　HAUDe̶　HEIL　HELE　HOLK　HOUFf
KECK　KEMBo　KEMPt　KEMPy　KNAR>　KNARl　KRIS　KYNDe
LAER　LAIKa　LIMN　LOID　LOME　LUFFa　LUNT　LUSK　LYSE　LYTE
MEINt　MEINy　MEOU　MEOW　*MIHI*=　MURLy
NEAL　NEAP　NEMN　NIRLy　NOCK
OINT
PAIK　PEIN　PLIM>　POCKy　POGO　PONK　POUFf　PUER　PYNE
REAK　RISP　RIVEl　RIVEn　RIVEr　RIVEt　ROIN　ROLF　RORTy　ROSTi　RUFFe　RYKE
SCUG>　SHIV>　SHIVa　SHIVe　SILEn　SILER　SILEx　SKEEf　SKEEn　SKEEr　SKEEt　SKER>
SKOL>　SKRY　SKUG>　SLUB>　SLUBb　SLUE　SLUE=　SMIT>　SMITe　SMITh　SMUR>　SNAR>
SNARe　SNARf　SNARk　SNARl　SNARy　SNIG>　*SOOL*e　SORN　SPUEr　SPUE=　STOR>　SWOB>
SYPE
THIGe̶　THIG>　THIGh　TIFT　TIKI　TIRL　TIRR　TOIT　TOSHy　TRIEr　TROG>　TUSHy
TYNE
UPGOe̶　UPGO+
VADE　VERTu　VULN
WAULk　WAUR　WHIG>　WHIR>　WHIRl　WHIRr　WIVEr　WULL　WYLE　WYTE
YAUP　YEDEe̶　YEEDe̶　YERD　YIKE　YIRD　YIRR　YMPEe̶　YOCK　YORK　*YORP*

4.3.4 OTHER NOUNS

ABRIm　ABRIn　*ACAI*　*ACCA*　ACME　ACYL　AERO　AGHA　*AGLU*　AGMA　*AIGA*　*ALCO*
ALGAe　ALGAl　ALIF　*ALKO*　ALKY+　ALKYd　ALKYl　ALMAh　ALMEh　ALOEd　AMBO　AMLA
AMMOn　AMYL　ANGA　ANKH　ANOA　APSE　*APSO*　ARAK　ARAR　ARIL　ARIS+　ARISe
ARISh　ARNA　*ARPA*　ARVO　ATMAn　ATOKe　*ATUA*　AULA　AUNE　AWDL　AWOL　AYRE

BABEl　BABUl　BAEL　BAUD　BAUR　BAWDy　BAWR　BEMAd　*BHAI*　BHEL　BIER　BIMAh
BIRO　BLAE*　BLEB　BLOCk　*BOEP*　*BOET*　BOLAr　BOLO　BOMA　BRERe　BRIEf　BRIEr
*BRIK*i　BRIO　BRIS+　BRISs　BUAT　BUHL　BUHR　BUIK　BYRE

CACAo　*CACK*y　CALO　CASA　CAULd　CAULk　CAUP　CAVY+　CEDI　CERO　CERTy　CETE
CINE　CIRL　CIVEt　CLEFt　CLONe　CLONk　COCOa　COED　COIR　COIT　*COMM*a　*COMM*o

COMMy CRIS+ CRISe CRISp CUIF CUIT CUNT CUSH+ CUSHy CUSK CYANo CYMAe
CYMAr CYME CYTE

DARGa DARIc DATO DAVY+ DEAWy DEMY+ *DERO* DERV DHAK DHAL DHOLe DHOL1
DIKA DIOL *DIYA* DOAB DOIT DOUCe DOUMa DREK DREY DUAD DUAN DUAR
DUCE *DUKA* DUMA DURA1 DUROc DUROy DURRa DURRy DYNE1

EDDO+ EEVN EGER EGMA EILD EKKA ELANd EMMA *EMMYs* EMYDe ENOL EORL
EPHAh *ERHU* ERICa ERICk EROS+ EROSe *ERUV* ESNE ETNA EURO EYAS+ EYASs
EYOT EYRA EYRE EYRY+

FAUNa FEOD FIAR FICO FICO+ FISC FLANk FLICk *FLIMp* *FLIRt* FLOE FOID
FOSSa FOSSe FRIS+ FRISe FRISt FYCE FYLE FYRD

GEIT GEUM GHEE GILA GIROn GIRR GLIA1 GLIMe GOGO GOLPe GOWD* GOWK
GRIS+ GRISe GRISt GRISy *GRRL* GUANa GUANo GUARd GUCKy GUDE GUFF GUGA
GUIDe GYAL GYNY+ GYROn GYTE

HAAF HAAR HABU HAIKa HAIKu *HAKU* HALMa HARN HARO HEBEn HEID HELOt
HIOI HOKI HOLT *HORI* HUCK HULA HUSO HUSS+ HUSSy HWYL HYKE HYLA
HYLEg

IAMBi IDYL1 IGLU *IKAN* IMMY+ INTI1 ISBA

KADE KADI KAGU KALIf KANGa KAON KAPA KAPH KARAt KARN *KAROo* KEEF
KEET KEIR *KERO* KESH+ KHAF KHOR KHUD KIBEi KIEF KIER *KIEVe* KIKE
KILP KIVA *KLIK* KNOP KOEL *KOHA* KOHL KOLA KOLO KOTOw KRAB KUDU
KUFI *KUIA* KUKU *KULAk* *KULAn* KURI KURU *KUTI* KYAT *KYBO* KYLE *KYPE*
KYTE

LAICh LAKH LEHR LENO LERP *LIAS+* LILO LIMAn LIMAx LIMO LIRA LOIR
LOMA LUAU LUCE LUNAr LUNEt LUNK LWEI *LYCH+* LYNE

MABE MAIKo MAUD MAUT *MECK* MERCh MERCy MERI1 MERIt MERLe MIEN *MIHA*
MINAe MINAr MINIm MINOr MITT *MOFO* MOHR MOKI MOKO MUID MUIL MUIR
MUON MURA1 MURK* MURKy MURRa MURRe MURRi MURRy MYNAh

NAAM NAAN NADA NAIF* NAIK NAOS+ NEIF NEMA NEUMe NIFE *NOAH* NOEL
NOIR NOLL NOLO *NONI* NOULd NOULe NUFF NYAS+

OAST *OCCY+* OCTAd OCTA1 OCTAn ODYLe OHIA OKRA OKTA OLIO OLLAv OLPE
OMBU OMER *OMOV* OPPO ORLE OTTO OULK *OUMA* *OVEL* OWRE

PAAN PAUL PEBA PIKAu PIKI PILI PIMA PIOYe *POEP* POGY+ PONTy PRAO
PRAU PUCE* *PUKA* PUKU PUMY+ PYOT PYREx PYRO

RABIc RABId RAKIa RAKU RAUN RHEA RHUS+ RIEL RIEM RIVA1 RONTe ROUEn
ROULe ROUM RUKH RURU RUSA RUSK RYND RYOT

SAAG	SAKIa	SCULk	SCULl	SCULp	SCYE	SEKT	SEMIe	SEPTa	*SESH+*	SHIRe	SHIRk
SHIRr	SHIRt	SHMO+	SHRI	SHULe	SHULn	SHWA	SIAL	SIDA	SIENt	SILD	SKEO
SKUA	SLAE	*SLEB*	SLOE	SPEK	SPIKe	SPIKy	*SPIFf*	*SPIM*	SPIV	*STIMe*	*STIMy*
STOAe	STOAi	STOAt	SYBO+	SYBOe	SYBOw	SYCEe	SYKEr	SYLI	SYPH		

TAHR	TEHR	TEIL	*TEINd*	TEPAl	THARm	*TIAN*	TIARa	TIRO	TIRO+	TOBY+	TOFU
TOKO	TOLAn	TOLAr	TOLT	TOLU	TOSA	TOUN	TREY	TRONa	TRONc	TRONe	TRONk
TROY	TUAN	TUFA	TUFFe	TURK	TURMe	TYKE	TYMP	TYPP	TYRO	TYRO+	

ULAN	ULNAd	ULNAe	ULNAr	ULVA	UMBO	*UMRAh*	UNAI	UNAU	UNCE	UNCOy	UNCO+
UNCO*	UNDY+	UPDO	URAO	URUS+	URVA	UVEAl					

VALId	VELE	VIOLa	VIOLd	VIRL	VIVEr	*VOIP*	VRIL	*VROUw*

WAAC	WACK*	WACKe	WACKo	WACKy	WAKF	WALDo	WALI	WEALd	WEID	WEIL	WEKA
WERO	*WHIO*	WIELd	*WIKI*	WILI	WOAD	WOCK	WYCH+				

YAAR	YANG	YAUD	YITE	YLEM	YLKE	YOGH	YOGIc	YOGIn	YUAN	YUCA	YUFT
YURTa											

4.3.5 OTHER NON-PLURALS

ABLY	AESC	AGLY	ALMS	ANCE	*ARGH*	ASCI	AULD*	***AWFY***			
BEINg	BIEN										
CECAl	CHOUt	CHOUx	*CHURl*	*CHURn*	*CHURr*	CIAO					
DESI	DEUS	*DOUN*	*DRACk*	*DRACo*	DUCI						
ECCE	ECCO	*EINA*	EINE	ELHI	EMYS	*ENUF*	EOAN	EUGE	EUOI	EYNE	
*FAUR**	*FAURd*	FEISt	FOCI	FUCI	FUSC						
GYRI											
HAUTe	HILAr	HILD	HILI	HIYA	HOLP	HOLS	HYTE				
ILIAc	ILIAd	ILIAl	INBYe	INIA	INLY	INRO	*ISNAe*				
KEKS	*KEWL**	KILD	*KUNA*	*KUNE*	KYNE						
LANG*	LIRI	LOCI	LUES	LUIT	*LYRA*						
MAUNd	*MIPS*	*MWAH*	MYALl								
NAOI	NESH*	NEVI	*NGAIo*								
ODIC	ORRA	OSSA	OULD*	OWSEn							
PFFT	PFUI	PILAf	PILAo	PILAr	PILAu	PILAw	PILY	POCO	PRUH	PSST	PUIR*
PYIC											
RACA	RIVO	RONG	RYFE	RYPEr							
SEPS	SESEy	*SIDHa*	*SIDHe*	*SIES*	SORI	STEY*					
TALI	THIOl	THIRd	THIRl	THROb	THROe	THROw	THRUm	TOST	TROPe	TYDE	TYNDe
TYTE											
UNBEd	UNCIa	UNDEe	UNDEr	UPBYe	*UPTAk*	URIC	URSAe				
VEHMe	VELAr	VENAe	VENAl	*VERD*	VIBS	VILDe	VITEx	VIVO			
WERT	WHEEl	WHEEn	WHEEp								
YALD	*YEBO*	YMPT	YUCH								

5. FIVE-LETTER WORDS

5.1 FAMILIAR FIVES

5.1.1 VERBS IN COMMON USE

ABATEr	ABHOR>	ABIDEr	ABORT	ABUSEr	ADAPT	ADDLE	ADMIT>	ADOPT	ADOREr
ADORN	AFFIX	AGREE	ALARM	ALERT*	ALIGN	ALLAY	ALLOT>	ALLOW	ALTERn
AMASS	AMAZE	AMBLEr	AMENDe	AMUSEr	ANGLEr	ANNEXe	ANNOY	ANNUL>	ANNULi
APPAL>	APPALl	APPLY	ARGUEr	ARISEd	ARISEn	ASSAY	ATONEr	AUDIT	AVAILe
AVERT	AVOID	AWAIT	AWARD					

BASTEr	BATHEr	BAULKy	BEFIT>	BEGETd	BEGET>	BEGINd	BEGIN>	BELCH	BELIEf
BELIEr	BESETd	BESET>	BESOT>	BEVEL	BEVEL>	BLAMEr	BLARE	BLASTy	BLAZEr
BLEAT	BLEED	BLENDe	BLESS	BLINK	BLITZ	BLOAT	BLOCKy	BLOOMy	BLUFF*
BLURT	BLUSH	BOARD	BOAST	BOOST	BOTCHy	BRACEr	BRAKE	BRANDy	BRAWLy
BREAKd	BREEDd	BRIBEe	BRIBEr	BRINGd	BROIL	BROODy	BRUSHy	BUDGEr	BUDGEt
BUILD	BULGEr							

CADGEr	CALVEr	CARRY	CARVEl	CARVEn	CARVEr	CATCHt	CATCHy	CATER	CAUSEn
CAUSEr	CAUSEy	CEASE	CHAFEr	CHAINe	CHANTy	CHARM	CHARTa	CHASEr	CHEAT
CHECKy	CHEEP	CHEERo	CHEERy	CHIDEr	CHILL*	CHILLi	CHILLy	CHIMEr	CHIRPy
CHOCKo	CHOKEr	CHOKEy	CHOMP	CHUCKy	CHURN	CLAIM	CLAMP	CLANG	CLANKy
CLASH	CLASPt	CLASSy	CLEAN*	CLEAR*	CLICK	CLIMB	CLINGy	CLINK	CLONEr
CLOSE*	CLOSEt	CLOUT	CLUCKy	CLUNKy	COLORy	COUGH	COUNTy	COVERt	COVET
COWER	CRACKa	CRACKy	CRANE	CRANK*	CRANKy	CRASH	CRAVEn	CRAVEr	CRAWLy
CREAKy	CREEPy	CROAKy	CROON	CROSS*	CROSSe	CROWN	CRUSH	CURSEr	CYCLEr

DALLY	DANCEr	DANCEy	DAUNT	DEBUG>	DECAY	DECRY	DEFER>	DEIGN	DELAY
DELVEr	DESEX	DETER>	DIVVY*	DODGEm	DODGEr	DOUBT	DOUSEr	DRAFTy	DRAIN
DRAPEr	DRAPEt	DRAPEy	DRAWLy	DREAD	DREAMt	DREAMy	DRESSy	DRIFTy	DRILL
DRINKd	DRIVEd	DRIVEl	DRIVEn	DRIVEr	DROOLy	DROOPy	DROWNd	DWELL	

EDIFY	EJECTa	ELECT	ELOPEr	ELUDEr	EMBED>	EMPTY*	ENACT	ENDOW	ENJOY
ENROL>	ENROLl	ENSUE	ENTERa	EQUALi	EQUAL>	EQUIP>	EQUIPe	ERASEr	ERECT
ERODE	ERUPT	EVADEr	EVICT	EVOKEr	EXALT	EXCEL>	EXERT	EXILEr	EXIST
EXPEL>	EXTOL>	EXTOLd	EXTOLl	EXUDE	EXULT			

FAINT*	FAINTy	FANCY*	FAULTy	FEIGN	FENCEr	FETCH	FIGHTd	FLAIL	FLARE
FLASH*	FLASHy	FLICK	FLINGd	FLIRTy	FLOATy	FLOUT	FLUKEy	FLUNKy	FLUSH*
FLUSHy	FOCUS	FOCUS>	FOIST	FORCEr	FORGEr	FORGEt	FORGOd	FORGO+	FORGOt
FRAMEr	FRISKa	FRISKy	FROWN	FUDGE				

GAUGEr	GLARE	GLAZEn	GLAZEr	GLEAMy	GLEAN	GLIDEr	GLINTy	GLOAT	GNARLy
GNASH	GORGEr	GORGEt	GOUGEr	GRADEr	GRANT	GRAPH	GRASP	GRATEr	GRAZEr
GREETe	GRILLe	GRIND	GRIPEr	GRIPEy	GROAN	GROOM	GROPEr	GROWLy	GRUNT
GUARD	GUESS	GUIDEr						

5. Five-Letter Words

HALVEr HATCH HAUNT   HEAVEn HEAVEr HITCHy HOARD HOIST HONOR HOVER
HURRY

IMPEL> IMPLY INCUR> INFER> INFERe INTER> INTERn ISSUEr

JOUST JUDGEr

KNEAD KNEEL KNIFEr KNOCK

LABEL LABEL> LABOR LAPSEr LAUGHy LEACHy LEARNt LEASEr LEAVEn LEAVEr
LIGHT* LIKEN LIMIT LIVEN LOBBY LODGEr LOWERy LUNGEe LUNGEr LUNGE=
LURCH LYNCH

MARCH MARRY MATCH MERGEe MERGEr MIMIC& MINCEr MODEL MODEL> MOOCH
MOTORy MOULDy MOULT MOUNT MOURN MUNCH

NEIGH NUDGEr NURSEr

OCCUR> OFFER ORATE ORBITa ORBITy ORDER OUTDOd OUTDO+

PAINTy PANIC& PANICk PARCH PASTEl PASTEr PATCHy PAUSEr PEDALo PEDAL>
PEEVEr PERCH PETER PHONEr PHONEy PINCH PIQUEt PITCHy PIVOT PLACEr
PLACEt PLAIT PLANEr PLANEt PLANTa PLEAD PLUCKy POACHy POINTe POINTy
POUND POWER PREEN PRESS PRICKy PRINT PROBEr PROVEn PROVEr PROWL
PRUNEr PUNCHy PURGEr

QUACKy QUAFF QUAKEr QUASH QUELL QUEUEr QUEUE= QUOTEr

RAISEr RALLYe REACH REACT REARM REBEL> REBIDd REBID> REBUT> RECAP>
RECUR> RECUREe REFER> REFIT> REIGN REJIG> REKEY RELAX RELAY REMIT>
RENEW REOIL REPAYd REPEL> REPLY REPOT> RERUNd RERUN> RESET> RESITd
RESIT> RESITe RETIE RETIE= RETRY REUSE REVEL REVEL> RHYMEr RINSEr
RIPEN ROAST RONEO ROOST ROUSEr ROUST

SAVORy SCALEr SCAREr SCAREy SCOFF SCOLD SCOOP SCOOT SCOREr SCORN
SCOUR SCOUTh SCOWL SCREWy SCRUB> SCUFF SEIZEr SENSEi SERVEr SEVEREe
SEVERy SHADEr SHAKEn SHAKEr SHAMEr SHAPEn SHAPEr SHAREr SHAVEn SHAVEr
SHEAR SHELLy SHIFTy SHINEr SHIRK SHOCK SHOOTd SHOUTy SHOVEl SHOVEr
SHRED> SHRUG> SHUNT SIDLEr SIGHT SINGEr SINGE= SKATEr SKIMPy SKITE
SKULK SLAKEr SLANTy SLASH SLEEPy SLICEr SLIDEr SLINGd SLINKy SLOPEr
SLOSHy SLUMPy SLURPy SMACK SMASH SMEARy SMELLy SMILEr SMILEt SMILEy
SMIRKy SMOKEr SMOKEy SNAREr SNARLy SNEAKy SNEERy SNIFFy SNIPEr SNOOPy
SNOREr SNORTy SOLVEr SOUND* SPANK SPARE* SPARKe SPARKy SPAWNy SPEAKd
SPEARy SPEEDo SPEEDy SPELL SPENDd SPENDy SPILL SPLIT> SPOILt SPRAY
SPURNe SPURT SQUAT^ SQUAT> STACK STAGEr STAGEy STAIN STAKE STALKo
STALKy STALL STAMP STANDd STAREr START STASH STATEr STAVE STEALe
STEALt STEAMy STEERy STICKy STIMY STINGo STINGy STINKd STINKo STINKy
STOCKy STOKEr STOMP STONEn STONEr STONEy STOOPe STOREr STOREy STORMy
STRAP> STRAY STREWn STRIP> STRIPe STRIPt STRIPy STRUM> STRUMa STRUT>
STUDY STUFFy STYLEe STYLEr STYLEt SULLY SURGEr SWARM SWEARd SWEARd

SWEARy SWEATy SWEEPe̶d̶ SWEEPy SWELL* SWILL   SWINGe SWINGy SWIPEr SWIPEy
SWIRLy SWOONy SWOOPy

TAINT TALLY TAPER TASTEr TAUNT TEACHe̶d̶ TEASEl TEASEr TEMPT THANK
THINKe̶d̶ THROB> THROWe̶d̶ THROWe THROWn THUMP TOASTy TOTAL TOTAL> TOUCHe
TOUCHy TRACEr TRACK TRADEr TRAIL TRAIN TRAMPy TRAWL TREAD TREATy
TRICKy TROLLy TRUMP TRUSTy TWEAKy TWEET TWIRLy TWISTy

UNIFY UNITEr UNTIE UNZIP> UPEND UPSETe̶d̶ UPSET> USHER USURP UTTER*

VALUEr VAUNTy VISITe VOMITo VOUCH

WAGER WAIVEr WAKEN WALTZ WASTEl WASTEr WATCH WATERy WAVERy WEAVEr
WEDGE WEIGHt WHACKo WHACKy WHEELy WHINEr WHINEy WHIRLy WHIRRy WHISKy
WHIZZy WIDEN WIELDy WINCEr WINCEy WORRY WOUNDy WRACK WREAK WRECK
WREST WRING WRITEe̶d̶ WRITEr

YEARN YIELD YODEL YODEL>

5.1.2 VERBS MORE OFTEN USED IN OTHER PARTS OF SPEECH

ABODE AGENT AISLE ALIBI= ALIBI+ ALIEN ALLOY ANGEL ANGER ANKLEt
ANTIC& ANTICk ANVIL ANVIL> APRON ARMORy ARRAY ARROWy AWAKEn

BADGEr BANDY* BARGEe BATCH BATIK BATON BEACHy BEARDy BEAST BELLE
BELLY BENCHy BERRY BERTHa BERTHe BIGHT BILGE BINGEr BINGE= BIRCH
BIRTH BITCHy BLACK* BLADEr BLAND* BLANK* BLANKy BLEEP BLIND* BLISS
BLOODy BLUNT* BLURB BOGEY BOGIE= BOOZEr BOOZEy BOSOMy BOUND BOWEL
BOWEL> BRAID* BRAIDe BRAINy BRASH* BRASHy BRASSy BRAVE* BRAVO BRAVO+
BREADy BREAM BRICKy BRIDE BRIEF* BRINEr BRISK* BRISKy BROKEn BROKEr
BROOK BROOMy BROWN* BROWNy BRUNT BRUTEr BUDDY* BUGLEr BUGLEt BULLY*
BUNCHy BURST

CABIN CABLEr CABLEt CACHEt CADDY CAMEO CANAL CANAL> CANDY CANOE=
CANOEr CAPER CARGO CARGO+ CAROLi CAROL> CASTEr CHAFFy CHAIR CHALKy
CHAMPy CHEAP* CHEAPo CHEAPy CHEEKy CHESTy CHILDe CHINKy CHIVE CHOIR
CHOOK CHORDa CHOREa CHOREe CHUMP CHUNKy CHUTE CINCH CLEAT CLEFT
CLERK CLOAK CLOCK CLOTHe CLOUDy CLOWN CLUMPy COAST COLLY CONCHa
CONCHe CONCHo CONCHs CONCHy CONGA COOEE COPSE COUCHe COUPEe COUPEr
COURT CRAFTy CRAMPy CRATEr CRAZE CREAMy CREPEy CRESTa CRICKy CRIMEn
CRISP* CRISPy CROCK CROOK* CROUPe CROUPy CROWDy CRUMBy CRUSTa CRUSTy
CURRY CURVEt CURVEy

DEBIT DEBUT DECOY DEMUR> DEMUR* DEMURe DEUCE DEVIL DEVIL> DINGO+
DINGY* DIRTY* DISCO DITCH DITTO DITTY DIZZY* DOLLY DONUT> DOWEL
DOWEL> DOZEN DROLL* DROLLy DRONEr DROVEr DUMMY* DWARF*

EAGLEt EARTHy ELBOW EMAIL EMERY EPOXY ESSAY EVENT EXACT* EXACTa

FABLEr FACETe FACET> FAITH FALSE* FANNY FARCEr FAVOR FEAST FEINT*
FERRY FEVER FIELD FLAKEr FLAKEy FLAMEn FLAMEr FLANK FLECKy FLEER
FLEET* FLESHy FLINTy FLOCKy FLOOD FLOOR FLOSSy FLOURy FLUFFy FLUME
FLUTEr FLUTEy FOLIO FOLLY FORAY FORTE FOUND FRANK* FREAKy FRESH*
FRILLy FRIZZy FROCK FRONT FROSTy FROTHy FRUITy FRUMPy

GABLEt GAUNT* GAVEL GAVEL> GIDDY* GHOSTy GIPSY GIRTH GLASSy GLITZy
GLOBE GLOOMy GLORY GLOSSa GLOSSy GLOVEr GOLLY GOOSEy GRACE GRAFT
GRAINe GRAINy GRAPEy GRASSy GRAVE* GRAVEl GRAVEn GREEN* GREENy GRIME
GROIN GROSS* GROUPy GROUTy GRUFF* GRUFFy GRUMPh GRUMPy GUEST GUILEr
GUISEr GULCH GULLY GYPSY

HABIT HAPPY* HARSH* HASTEn HAVEN HAVOC& HEARTh HEARTy HEDGEr HEIST
HELLO HELLO+ HENNA HINGEr HOMER HONEY HORDE HORSEy HOUND HOUSEl
HOUSEr HOUSEy HOVEL HOVEL> HOWDY HULLOa HULLOo HULLO+ HUMOR HUNCH
HUTCH

IMAGEr INDEX INGOT INLAYd INLETd INLET> INPUT> INSET>

JAUNTy JELLY JEMMY* JETTY* JEWEL JEWEL> JOINT JOIST JOLLY* JOULE
JUICEr

KAYAK KEBAB> KNACKy KNELL KNOLLy

LADEN LADLEr LAGER LANCEr LANCEt LASSO LASSO+ LATCH LATHEe LATHEn
LATHEr LAYER LEASH LEECH LEMONy LEVEL^ LEVEL> LEVER LIBEL LIBEL>
LITHE* LIVERy LOOSE* LOOSEn LOUSEr LUNCH

MADAMe MAGIC& MAJOR MASON MEDAL MEDAL> MERIT METAL METAL> METER
METRE MINOR MITER MITRE MODEM MOIST* MOODY* MORAL> MORALe MORALl
MOUND MOUSEr MOUSEy MOUTHy MUDDY* MULCH MULES MUMMY MUSIC& MUSICk

NANNY NAVVY NERVEr NICHEr NOISE NOOSEr NORTH NOTCHy

OCHREa OCHREy OLDEN ONIONy ONSETd ONSET> OTTER OUGHT OVATE

PALLY* PALSY* PANEL PANEL> PAPERy PARTY PEACE PEACHy PEARLy PERIL
PERIL> PHASE PHIAL> PHONY* PHOTOg PHOTOn PIECEn PIECEr PILOT PLAID
PLAIN* PLAINt PLANK PLATEn PLATEr PLEAT PLONKo PLONKy PLUMB PLUME
PLUMP* PLUMPy POESY POISEr POLKA POOCH POSSEr POSSEt POUCHy PRANG
PRANKy PRAWN PRICEr PRICEy PRIDE PRIMEr PRIZEr PRONG PROOF PROSEr
PSALM PULSEr PUPPY PUREE PURSEr PURSEw PUTTY

QUAIL QUEENy QUEER* QUERY QUEST QUIET* QUILL QUILT QUIRE QUIRKy
QUITE QUOIT

RADIO RANCHo RANGEr RAVEN RAZOR READY* REGALe REHAB> RESINy RIDGEl
RIDGEr RIFLEr RIGHT* RIGHTo RIGHTy RIVAL RIVAL> RIVET RIVET> ROACH

RODEO	ROGER	ROGUEd	ROGUE=	ROSINg	ROSINy	ROUGE	ROUGH*	ROUGHt	ROUGHy
ROUND*	ROUTEr	ROUTE=	RUDDY*	RULER	RUMOR				

SABER	SABLE	SABRE	SAINT	SALSA	SAMBAl	SAMBAr	SATINg	SATINy	SAUCEr
SAUNA	SAVVY*	SCALP	SCAMPi	SCANT*	SCANTy	SCARF	SCENE	SCENT	SCOPE
SCRAG>	SCRAM>	SCRAMb	SCRAP>	SCRAPe	SCRUM>	SCRUMp	SCUBA	SEGUE=	SEWER
SHACKo	SHAFT	SHALEy	SHANK	SHARK	SHARP*	SHARPy	SHAWL	SHEAFy	SHEENy
SHEER*	SHEETy	SHELFy	SHIRE	SHIRTy	SHOAL*	SHOALy	SHOREr	SHORT*	SHORTy
SHREWd	SHRUB>	SHUSH	SHUTE	SIEGEr	SIEVE	SINEWy	SKEIN	SKIFF	SKILLy
SKINK	SKIRT	SKULL	SKUNKy	SLACK*	SLANGy	SLATEr	SLATEy	SLAVEr	SLAVEy
SLEEK*	SLEEKy	SLEETy	SLICK*	SLIME	SLOTH	SLUSHy	SMALL*	SMART*	SMARTy
SMELT	SMOCK	SNACK	SNAILy	SNAKEy	SNIDE*	SNIDEy	SNOUTy	SNUFFy	SOBER*
SOUTH	SPACEr	SPACEy	SPADEr	SPASM	SPECKy	SPICEr	SPICEy	SPIEL	SPIKEr
SPIKEy	SPIREa	SPIREm	SPITE	SPLAT>	SPOKEn	SPOOFy	SPOOKy	SPOOL	SPOONy
SPORE	SPORTy	SPOUTy	SPREE	SPRIG>	SPUME	SPUNKy	SQUAD>	SQUIB>	SQUID>
STAFF	STALE*	STANK	STARK*	STEEDy	STEELd	STEELy	STEEP*	STEEPy	STEIN
STENT	STERN*	STERNa	STIFF*	STIFFy	STILEt	STILL*	STILLy	STILTy	STINTy
STONY*	STOOK	STOOL	STORY	STOVEr	STRAWn	STRAWy	STROP>	STUMPy	STUNT
SUEDE	SUGARy	SUITEr	SUPERb	SWAMPy	SWEET*	SWEETy	SWIFT*	SWIFTy	SWISH*
SWISHy	SWORD	SYRUPy							

TABBY	TABLEt	TABOO	TANGO	TARDY*	TELEX	TENSE*	THEME	THICK*	THICKo
THICKy	THIRD	THORNy	THROE=	THUMBy	TINGE	TINGE=	TITLEr	TOKEN	TOOTHy
TOOTSy	TORCHy	TOUGH*	TOUGHy	TOWEL	TOWEL>	TOWERy	TRACT	TRASHy	TRENDy
TRESSy	TRIAL	TRIAL>	TRICEp	TROOP	TRUCE	TRUCK	TRUNK	TRUSS	TUTOR
TWANGy	TWEER	TWINEr							

ULCER	UNCLEw	UNFIT^	UNFIT>	URINE

VAGUE*	VALETa	VALETe	VALVE	VAPORy	VAULTy	VENOM	VERGEr	VERSEr	VERSEt
VIDEO	VISOR	VISTAl	VIZOR	VOGUEr	VOGUEy	VOGUE=	VOICEr	VOWEL>	

WAFERy	WAGON	WAIST	WEARY*	WEIRD*	WEIRDo	WEIRDy	WENCH	WHALEr	WHARF
WHIFFy	WHILE	WHIST	WHITE*	WHITEn	WHITEy	WHORE	WIDOW	WINCH	WITCHy
WOLVEr	WOMAN	WOOPS	WORSEn	WORSEr	WORSEt	WORST	WORTHy	WRATHy	WRONG*

YABBY	YACHT	YEASTy

5.1.3 NOUNS IN COMMON USE

ABBEY	ABYSS+	ACORN	ACTOR	ADAGE	ADDER	ADULT	AGATE	AGGRO	AGONY+
AIMER	AIRER	ALBUM	ALIAS+	ALLEY	ALPHA	ALTAR	AMBERy	AMBIT	AMIGO
ANGSTy	AORTAe	AORTAl	APPLEt	APPLEy	ARDOR	ARENA	AROMA	ARSON	ASSET
ATLAS+	ATOLL	ATTIC	AUDIO	AUGER	AUNTY+	AXIOM	AZURE		

BACON	BAGEL	BAKERy	BALSAm	BANJO	BANJO+	BARONg	BARONy	BASIL	BASINg
BAYOU	BEAUTy	BEECH+	BEECHy	BEIGEl	BERET	BIBLE	BIDET	BIGOT	BIKER
BIKIE	BILLY+	BILLYo	BIMBO	BIMBO+	BINGO	BINGO+	BISON	BLIMP	BLOKEy

BOBBY+ BONUS+ BOOTH BOOTY+ BORER BORON BOUGHt BOXER BRAWNy BRIARd
BRIARy BRINK BROTHy BUGGY* BUNNY+ BUYER BYLAW

CABER CADET CAMEL CANON CARER CARATe CAROB CAVERn CEDARn CEDARy
CELLO CHAOS+ CHASMy CHESS+ CHICK CHIEF* CHIMP CHINAr CIDERy CIGAR
CLIFFy CLOVEn CLOVEr COBRA COCOA CODER COLIC COLONe COLONi COMER
COMETh COMICe COMMA CONDOm CONDOr CONDO+ COPRAh CORAL CORGI CORSO
COVENt CREED CREEKy CRIER CRONY+ CRYPTo CUPID CURIO CYNIC

DADDY+ DAIRY+ DAISY+ DEATHy DÉCOR DEITY+ DELTA DEMON DENIM DEPOT
DEPTH DERBY+ DIARY+ DICER DIGIT DILDOe DINERo DIRGE DIVAN DIVERt
DIVOT DOGMAn DONOR DOONA DOUGHt DOUGHy DOYEN DOZER DRAKE DRAMA
DROSSy DUNCE DUNNY* DUVET

EASEL EATERy EBONY+ EDGER EDICT EIGHTh EIGHTy EMBER ENEMY+ ENTRY+
ENVOY EPOCHa ERROR ETHER ETHIC ETHOS+

FAIRY+ FAUNAe FAUNAl FELONy FIBER FIBREd FIBRO FIEND FIFTH FIFTY+
FILLY+ FILTHy FINALe FINCH+ FIVER FIXER FLAIR FLASK FLIER FLORAe
FLORAl FLUID FLYER FORTY+ FORUM FOUNT FOYER FRANCo FRAUD FRIARy
FROND FUTON

GALAH GAMMAt GAMUT GAUZE GECKO GECKO+ GENIE GENRE GENUS+ GETUP
GHOUL GIANT GIVER GLADE GLAND GNOME GONER GRAILe GRAVY+ GREEDy
GRIEF GROVEd GROVEl GROVEt GUAVA GUILD GUILTy GUSTO GUSTO+

HAREM HAZEL HEATHy HERON HIKER HIPPO HIPPY* HIRER HOBBY+ HOLLY+
HOTEL HUBBY+ HUMANe HUSSY+ HYENA

IDIOM IDIOT IGLOO IRONY* IVORY+

JIFFY+ JIVER JOKER JUMBO JUNTA JUROR

KARMA KHAKI KIOSK KITTY+ KLUTZy KNAVE KOALA

LAPEL LARCH+ LARVAe LARVAl LASER LATEX+ LAYUP LEDGEd LEDGEr LEMUR
LEPER LETUP LIFER LILAC LIMBO LINENy LINER LINGO+ LINGOt LITRE
LLAMA LOCALe LOGIC LOLLY+ LONER LORRY+ LOSER LOTTO LOTUS+ LOVER
LUPINe LYMPH LYRIC

MAIZE MAKER MANGEl MANGEr MANGEy MANGO MANGO+ MANIAc MANOR MANSE
MAPLE MARSH+ MARSHy MATER MAUVE* MAXIMa MAYOR MECCA MEDICk MEDICo
MELEE MELON MERCY+ METRO MIDST MIGHTy MILER MINER MINUS+ MIRTH
MISERe MISERy MIXER MIXUP MOLAR MONEY MONTH MORON MOTEL MOTIF
MOTTO MOTTO+ MOVER MOVIE MOWER MUFTI MULGA MURAL

NANNA NAPPY* NAVEL NEGRO+ NIECE NIGHTy NINTH NOMADe NOMADy NOVEL
NYLON NYMPHa NYMPHo

OCEAN OCKER OCTETt ODOUR OFFAL OLIVEr OLIVEt OPERA OPIUM ORGANa
OTHER OUNCE OVARY+ OWNER OXIDE OZONE

PACER PADDY+ PAGAN PAGER PANDAr PANSY+ PARERa PASTA PATIO PATTY+
PAVER PAYEE   PECAN PENIS+ PENNY+ PEONY+ PETAL   PIANO PIETY+ PIGGY*
PIKER PINUP   PIPER PIXEL PIZZAz PLAZA   POKER   POLIO POLYPe POLYPi
POPPY+ PORCH+ POSER PRISMy PROXY+ PRUDE   PUPIL   PUSSY* PYGMY+ PYLON

QUALMy QUARTe QUARTo QUARTz QUOTA

RABBIn RABBIt RABBI+ RACER RADAR RAGER   RAJAH   RATIOn RAVER RAYON
REALM RELICt RIDER   RIGOR RISER RIVERy ROBINg ROBOT ROOKY* ROTOR
ROVER ROWER RUGBY+ RUMMY* RUPEE RUPIAh

SALADe SALON SATAY SAVER SCONE SEDAN SEMEN SEPIA   SERUM SETUP
SEVEN SHEIKh SINUS+ SIREN SISSY* SITUP SIXTH SIXTY+ SKIER SLOOP
SONAR SPATE SPERM SPINEd SPINEl SPINEt SQUAWk STAIR   STEAK STORK
SUNUP SWEDE

TAKER TALON TAROT TEDDY+ TEMPO TENET TENOR TENTH   THEFT THIGH
THINGy THONG THREEp THYMEy TIARA TIGERy TILERy TIMER   TONER TONIC
TONNEr TOPAZ+ TOPIC TORSO TOTEM TOXINe TRAIT TRIBE   TRIER TRIPEy
TROUTy TRUTHy TULIP TUMMY+ TUMOR TUNER TUNICa TWEEDy TWERPy

UDDER UNION UNITY+ USAGEr

VALOR VELDT VENUE VERVEl VERVEn VERVEt VICARy VIGIL   VIGORo VILLAe
VILLAn VILLAr VINYL VIOLA VIPER VIRUS+ VIXEN VODKA   VOTER

WADER WHEATy WIDTH WIPER WORLD WRISTy

YAHOO YOBBO YOBBO+ YOUTHy YUPPY+

ZEBRA

5.1.4 NOUNS MORE OFTEN USED IN OTHER PARTS OF SPEECH

ABOUT ABOVE ACUTE* ADEPT AFTER AGAPE AGING AGONE ALOHA AMISS+
AMUCK ANGRY* ASIDE
BAGGY* BASIC BATTY* BAWDY* BEING BELOW BLEAK* BLEAKy BLOND* BLONDe
BLOWY* BOLAS+ BONNY* BOSSY* BRINY* BROAD* BUSHY* BUTCH*
CAMAS+ CAMASh CAMASs CATTY* CHEWY* CHOSEn CIVIC CIVIL COCKY* COKES+
COUTH* COUTHy CRAZY* CRUDE* CRUEL* CRUEL^ CUBBY* CUBICa CURLY* CUSHY*
DAFFY* DAILY+ DANDY* DATUM DEMOS+ DICKY* DOING DOWDY* DRIER DRUNK
DRYER DUCKY* DUMPY* DYING
EAGER* EARLY* ELDER ELFINg ELITE EXTRA
FATTY* FERAL FINERy FINIS+ FINISh FIRST FLAKY* FOURS+ FRAIL* FREER
FUNNY* FURRY*

```
GAMER  GAUDY* GAWKY* GIVEN  GLEED  GOING  GRAND* GRANDe GREAT* GUMMY*
HALERu HARDY* HEARD  HEAVY* HUMPY* HUNKS+ HUSKY*
ICING  IDEAL  IDLER  INANE* INERT* INNER  IONIC
JAKES+ JAMMY* JERKY* JUNKY*
KAMIS+ KECKSy KNOWN  KOOKY* KUDOS+
LAMEDh LARGE* LARGEn LEAST  LEGAL  LEGGY* LIKER  LOONY* LOTOS+ LUCKY*
LUNARy LYING
MACHO  MANIC  MAYBE  MEDIAd MEDIAe MEDIAl MEDIAn MERRY* MONAS+ MOPED
MOSSY* MOUSY*
NAÏVE* NASAL  NASTY* NEWSY* NIFTY* NOBLE*
OPTIC  OUTER  OVINE
PASTY* PENCEl PETTY* PLIER  PLUSH* PLUSHy POLAR  PORKY* POTTY* PRIORy
PRIVY* PRONE*
QUICK* QUICKy
RANDY* RAPID* RIGID* RIPER  ROOMY* ROOTY* ROWDY* ROYAL^ RUING  RURAL
SALTY* SASSY* SAYED  SEMIS+ SHIER  SHINY* SHOOK  SHYER  SILKY* SILLY*
SMOKY* SOAPY* SOLAR  SOLID* SOLIDi SONIC  SPELTz STOIC  STOLEd STOLEn
STOUT* STOUTh STUCK  SUING  SULKY* SUNNY* SWINE
TACKY* TAMER  TANGY* TATTY* TAWNY* THEIR  THERE  THESE  TIGHT* TINNY*
TODAY  TOFFY* TOXIC  TRITE*
UPPER  USUAL
VITAL  VOCAL  VYING
WEENY* WEEPY* WHERE  WHOLE  WINDS+ WOODY* WOOLY* WOULD  WOVEN  WUSSY*
YOUNG  YUMMY*
```

5.1.5 NON-PLURALS

```
ABACK  ABUZZ  ACRID* AFOOT  AGAIN  AGILE* AHEAD  ALGAE  ALIKE  ALIVE
ALOFT  ALONE  ALONG  ALOOF  ALOUD  AMONG  AMPLE* APACE  APART  AROSE
ASKEW  AWARE* AWASH  AWFUL^ AWOKEn
BADLY  BARMY* BASIS  BEADY* BEGAN  BEGOT  BEGUNk BLASÉ  BLOWN  BOGGY*
BOGUS  BOOZY* BORNE  BUILT  BULKY* BUMPY* BURLY* BURNT  BUSTY* BUXOM*
CANNY* CLUNG  COMFY* CORNY* CORPSe COULD  COYLY  CRASS* CREPT  CURVY*
DAGGY* DEALT  DENSE* DIMLY  DODGY* DOTTY* DOWNY* DRANK  DRAWN  DUSTY*
DWELT
EATEN  EERIE* ELVES  EVERY
FATAL  FERNY* FIERY* FISHY* FIZZY* FLOWN  FLUKY* FLUNG  FOAMY* FOCAL
FOGGY* FORTHy FROZEn FULLY  FUNKY* FUSSY* FUZZY*
GAMMY* GAYLY  GEESE  GLANS  GLARY* GODLY* GOOEY* GOOFY* GRIMY* GROWN
GUSTY* GUTSY*
HAIRY* HANDY* HASTY* HEADY* HEFTY* HENCE  HILLY* HORNY* HOTLY  HUFFY*
HUMID*
INEPT* IRATE* ITCHY*
JAZZY* JUICY* JUMPY*
KINKY* KNELT
LAIRY* LANKY* LEAFY* LEAKY* LEANT  LEAPT  LIVID* LOATH* LOATHe LOATHy
LOFTY* LOOPY* LOUSY* LOWLY* LOYAL* LOYAL^ LUCID* LUMPY* LURID* LUSTY*
MADLY  MANLY* MANGY* MEANT  MEATY* MESSY* MILKY* MINGY* MISTY* MOOSE
MUGGY* MURKY* MUSTY*
```

NAKED* NATTY* NAVAL NEEDY* NERVY* NEVER NEWLY NIPPY* NOBLY NOISY*
NUTTY*
OASES OASIS OBESE* ODDLY OFTEN* OVERT
PAPAL PENAL PERKY* PESKY* PICKY* PIOUS PITHY* PONGY* POOFY* PRICY*
PROUD* PUFFY* PUSHY*
QUOTHa
RABID* RADII RAINY* RATTY* REDID REEDY* RENAL RERAN RESAT RISEN
RISKY* RITZY* ROCKY* RUNNY* RUSTY*
SADLY SAGGY* SANDY* SAUCY* SCALY* SCARY* SEAMY* SEEDY* SHADY* SHAKY*
SHALLi SHALT SHALY* SHEEPo SHEEPy SHONE SHORN SHOWN SHOWY* SHYLY
SILTY* SINCE SLAIN SLEPT SLIMY* SLOPY* SLUNG SLUNK SLYLY SNAKY*
SNOWY* SOGGY* SOOTY* SOPPY* SORRY* SPENT SPICY* SPIKY* SPILTh STAID*
STOOD STUNG STUNK SUAVE* SURLY* SWEPT SWORE SWORN SWUNG
TACIT TAKEN TASTY* TEARY* TEETHe TEPID* TERSE* TESTY* THIEF THOSE
THREW TIDAL TIMID* TIPSY* TIRED* TRULY TUBBY* TWICEr
UNCUTe UNDERn UNDID UNDUE UNFED UNLET UNLIT UNMET UNTILe UNWED
URBAN* URBANe
VALID* VIRAL VIVID*
WACKY* WEEDY* WHICH WHOSE WINDY* WITTY* WOKEN WOMEN WONKY* WORDY*
WROTE WRUNG WRYLY
YUCKY*

5.2 LESS FAMILIAR FIVES WHICH ARE HOOK WORDS

5.2.1 FRONT HOOKS OF FOURS TO MAKE FIVES

UNIQUE FRONT HOOKS WITH VOWELS

AARGH ABAFT ABAND ABASEr ABASH ABASK ABEAM ABEAR~~d~~ ABLET ABLOW
ABOIL ABOMA ABOON ABORD ABRAY ABRIM ABRIN ABUNA *ACHAR* ACOCK
ACOLD ACRED ADAYS ADEEM ADOWN ADOZE ADUST AEGIS+ AFEARd AFIRE
AFORE AFOUL AFRIT AGAMA AGAST AGAVE AGAZEd AGENE AGILA AGISM
AGIST AGLEE AGLEY AGLOW AGOOD AGORAe AGRIN AHIND AHINT AHOLD
AHULL AJUGA ALOWE ALURE AMAIN AMATE *AMAUT* AMENEd AMENTa AMICE
AMITY+ AMOLE AMORT ANEAR ANIGHt ANODE ANOLE APAGE APAID APEEK
APERT APHIS APIAN APISH APOOP APSIS AREDD ARETE ASHET ASPICk
ASTIR ASTUN> ASWAY ASWIM AURIC AVALE AVANTi AVAST AVISE AWARN
AWAVE AWORK AYELP AYONT AZINE AZOIC AZYME
EBOOK ECLAT EDUCE EDUCT EGESTa EIKON ELOGE *EMACS* EMULE EMURE
ENEMA ENORM EPACT ESILE ESTOP> ETAPE ETWEE EVITE EWEST EWHOW
IBRIK IDANT *IDENT* IGAPO ILEAL
OBANG OBOLE OCHERy OFLAG *OGEED* OGIVE OMASAl OMEGA OOBIT ORACY+
UPLED USUREr UVEAL

UNIQUE FRONT HOOKS WITH 'S'

SALTO SCAFF SCALLy SCAPA SCAPE SCAPI SCARPa SCARPh SCARTh SCAUP
SCHAV SCION SCOUP SCOWP SCRAB> SCRAN SCRAWl SCRAWm SCRAWp SCRAYe
SCREEd SCREEn SCREEt SCRIMp SCROG SCROWl SCULLe SCURFy SEINEr SENVY+
SEPIC SEYEN SHALM SHANDy SHARNy SHASH SHAUL SHAWM SHEND~~e~~ SHERD
SHEWN SHOER SHOPE SHOTE SHULE SILEX+ SIZAR SKAIL SKARTh *SKEEF*
SKEEN SKEET SKELLy SKELP SKOFF SKYTE SLILY SLOAN SLOID SLUIT
SMAIK SMALMy SMALTi SMALTo SMARMy SMEEK SMERK SMITE~~d~~ SMITEr SMOKO
SMOOR SMOOTh SMORE *SMUSH* SNARKy SNEAP SNECK SNICK SNOOK SOLDEr
SPACY* SPAIL SPAINg SPALE SPALLe SPANE SPANG SPARD SPAULd SPAWL
SPEAL SPEAN SPEAT SPEEL SPEER SPIAL SPICAe SPICK* SPIER SPILE
SPINAe SPINAl SPINAr SPINK SPINY* SPOOR SPOOT *SPORK* SPOSHy SPRAD
SPRAT SPROD SPROG *SPUER* SPULE SPUMY* SPYRE SQUIT SQUIZ> STAIG
STANE STANG STARN STEADy STEARd STEARe STEEK STEEM STEEN STEIL
STELAe STELAi STELAr STELE STELLa STEME STEND STICHs STIME STIRE
STIVY* STOIT STONG STONK STOPEr STOSS+ STOUN~~e~~ STOUNd STOURe STOURy
STOWNd STRAD STRIG> STRIGa *STRIM>* STROWn STROY STYRE STYTE SWACK
SWAGEr SWAIL SWALY* SWARTh SWARTy SWEAL SWEIRt SWEIR* SWISS+ SWITHe
SWIVEl SWIVEt

UNIQUE FRONT HOOKS WITH OTHER CONSONANTS

BALOO BEAUX BEGAD *BHAJIa* BLAUD BLEST *BLINY* BLORE *BOBOL>* BOCHE
BOINK BROCHe BROCHo BROCHs BRUIN BRULE BRUSK* BUNDEd BURSAe BURSAl
BURSAr *CAPEX+* CARET CEORL *CHAWK* CHILI CHILI+ *CHOWK* CHUFF* CHUFFy
CLEVEr COBIA CONTO COPEN CREEL CTENE CULEX+ DECADe DJINNi DJINNy
DORADo DWILE FAERY+ FAGIN FASCIa FASCIo FAYRE *FLAVA* FLEMEd FLOTA

FLYTE	FOSSAe	FRITZ+	**FRORY**	***FUGLY*** *	GAZON	GHAST	GHAUT	GIRON	GLAIK
GLAZY *	*GLOBIn*	**GLODE**	GLOST	GODSOn	GOLPE	**GOATY** *	GOOSY*	GREGO	GREIN
GRUND	GRYPE	GYELD	HALFA	HAZAN	JALAP	JIMMY	KARSY+	KLUGE	KNISH+
KNURLy	KNURR	KOKRA	KOMBU	*KVELL*	KYACK	KYANG	LAURAe	LEGER	**LEISH** *
LETHEe	**LOTIC**	**LYARD**	MANTA	**MANUS**	MARID	MESNE	METIC	*MOBEY*	MOPUS+
MURVA	NACREd	NOVUM	NOYES+	NYAFF	**PACTA**	PAEONy	PALAY	PARVO	**PAVID**
PHYLAe	**PHYLAr**	PILEA	PINTO	PORGY+	PRIMAl	*PROTOn*	PROUL	PSHAW	PSORA
RAGEE	RAKEE	RAYAH	RECCE=	RECCE#	**REGMA**	REVET>	**TANTI**	TASAR	TEPEE
TERAS	THEBE	THERM	*THESP*	THETE	THOWL	TOKAY	**TRAGIc**	TRAIK	TRIAD
TROMPe	TSADE	TSADI	TSUBA	TWEENy	TWILT	**TWINY** *	TWITE	VARNA	VEALEr
VIBEX	**VIRID**	VULVAe	VULVAl	VULVAr	**WAIDE**	WATAPe	WHELM	**WHIPT**	WHISS
WHOOP	WROOT	XYLEM	YCLAD	YCOND	YFERE	YOGEE	**YSAME**	**YTOST**	ZANTE
ZHOMO	**ZOPPO**								

FRONT HOOK SETS

ABBA — *DABBA* *GABBA* YABBA
ACCA — BACCAe YACCA
ACER — FACER LACER MACER
ACHE — MACHE NACHE RACHEt TACHE
ADDY+ — BADDY+ **FADDY** * WADDY
AFFY — BAFFY+ TAFFY+
AGER — CAGER GAGER JAGER YAGER
AGMA — MAGMA **TAGMA**
AIGA — SAIGA TAIGA
AINE — DAINE FAINE* RAINE SAINEd
AIRN — BAIRN CAIRNy
AKIN — LAKINg TAKINg
ALAR — MALAR TALAR
ALAS — BALAS+ PALAS+
ALKY+ — **BALKY** * TALKY*
ALIF — CALIF KALIF
ALLY — BALLY+ GALLY SALLY WALLY*
ALMA — HALMA TALMA
AMBO — GAMBO+ GAMBOl **JAMBOk** MAMBO MAMBO+ SAMBO ZAMBO
AMEN — RAMEN **SAMEN** YAMEN
AMIA — LAMIAe ZAMIA
AMIE — MAMIE RAMIE
AMIN — GAMINe GAMINg RAMIN TAMINe TAMINg
AMIS+ — CAMIS+ CAMISa CAMISe TAMIS+ TAMISe
AMUS — CAMUS+ **RAMUS** WAMUS+

ANAL — **BANAL** * FANAL
ANCE — HANCE NANCE PANCE RANCEl
ANGA — FANGA KANGA MANGAl PANGA *RANGA* SANGAr TANGA
ANNA — CANNAe MANNAn TANNAh **WANNA**
ANSA — HANSA SANSAr
APER — GAPER JAPERy RAPER
ARCO — NARCO *YARCO*
ARIA — **MARIA** VARIA
ARIS+ — **NARIS** PARIS+ PARISh
ARLE — CARLE FARLE MARLE PARLEy
ARSE — CARSEy FARSE MARSE PARSEc PARSEr
ARTI — *AARTI* PARTIm
ARTY* — **TARTY** * **WARTY** *
ARUM — GARUM LARUM
ASHY* — **DASHY** * **HASHY** * MASHY* WASHY*
AULD* — CAULD* FAULD HAULD **TAULD** **YAULD**
AUNT — NAUNT SAUNT
AVEL — CAVEL **FAVELa** **FAVELl** JAVEL RAVEL RAVEL>
AVER — HAVER LAVER TAVERn TAVERt
AWNY* — **FAWNY** * **LAWNY** * **YAWNY** *
AXON — CAXON TAXON
AYIN — *LAYINg* ZAYIN
BORE — **ABORE** YBORE

DRAD	**ADRAD**	YDRAD	
EASE	FEASE	MEASE	PEASEn
	SEASE		
EAST	HEASTe	REASTy	
EATH	BEATH	MEATHe	**NEATH**
EAVE	DEAVE	REAVEr	
ECCO	RECCO	SECCO	
ECHT	FECHTe	HECHTe	WECHT
EDDY	NEDDY*	**REDDY***	
EDGE	KEDGEr	SEDGEd	
EDGY*	**HEDGY***	**KEDGY***	**LEDGY***
	SEDGY*	WEDGY*	
EECH	KEECH+	REECHo	REECHy
EELY*	*DEELY*	JEELY	**SEELY***
EERY*	**BEERY***	**LEERY***	PEERY*
	VEERY+		
EMIC	**DEMIC**	HEMIC	
EMMA	**GEMMA**e	**GEMMA**n	LEMMA
EMMY	*FEMMY**	**GEMMY***	
EMPT	**DEMPT**	**KEMPT**	**NEMPT**
ERIC	**CERIC**	**SERIC**	**XERIC**
ERNE	CERNE	GERNE	KERNEl
	TERNE		
ERST	**PERST**	VERSTe	
ESSE	CESSEr	DESSE	FESSE
	GESSE	JESSE	
ETCH	LETCH	RETCH	VETCHy
EUGH	HEUGH	**LEUGH**	TEUGH*
EVEN	EEVEN	**YEVEN**	
HACK	CHACK	THACK	
HANG	BHANG	CHANGa	CHANGe
	PHANG	*THANG*	WHANG
HARD	CHARD	SHARD	
HARM	*PHARM*a	THARM	
HARE	CHAREt	PHARE	WHARE
HEAL	SHEAL	WHEAL	
HELP	*CHELP*	WHELP	
HENT	**AHENT**	**SHENT**	
HERE	**CHERE**	**SHERE**	
HETH	CHETH	KHETH	
HILL	SHILL	THILL	
HISH	*SHISH*a	WHISHt	
HOLE	DHOLE	THOLE	
HONE	**OHONE**	RHONE	
HOOF	CHOOF	WHOOF	
HOON	*CHOON*	**SHOON**	
HOOT	BHOOT	WHOOT	
HURL	CHURL	THURL	
HYLE	CHYLE	**PHYLE**	

ICKY*	MICKY+	TICKY+	WICKY+
IFFY*	BIFFY+	**MIFFY***	**NIFFY***
ILIA	**CILIA**	**MILIA**	
ILLY	DILLY*	GILLY	TILLY*
	WILLY		
INGO+	JINGO+	PINGO	PINGO+
INKY*	DINKY*	*HINKY**	LINKY*
	PINKY*	**SINKY***	**ZINKY***
IOTA	BIOTA	DIOTA	
ITCH	AITCH+	FITCHe	FITCHy
	MITCH	TITCHy	
LACK	**ALACK**	CLACK	FLACK
	PLACK		
LADE	CLADE	SLADE	
LADY+	*BLADY**	**GLADY***	
LAIN	BLAIN	ELAIN	
LAND	ALAND	ELAND	
LANE	**ALANE**	SLANE	
LANG*	ALANG	KLANG	
LASH	BLASHy	PLASHy	
LAST	CLAST	**PLAST**e	
LATE	ALATEd	**BLATE***	ELATEr
LAWN	**BLAWN**	FLAWN	
LEEK	CLEEK	GLEEK	
LENT	**BLENT**	GLENT	**OLENT**
LIFT	CLIFTy	GLIFT	
LIKE	GLIKE	**YLIKE**	
LIME	CLIME	GLIME	
LINE	ALINEr	CLINE	
LING	*BLING**	*BLING*y	PLING
LISK	FLISKy	GLISK	
LINT	CLINT	ELINT	
LIPE	CLIPE	SLIPE	
LIST	**ALIST**	**BLIST**	
LITE	BLITE	FLITE	
LIVE	**BLIVE**	SLIVEn	SLIVEr
LOAM	CLOAM	GLOAM	
LOGY+	ELOGY+	OLOGY+	
LOIN	ALOIN	ELOIN	
LONG	FLONG	KLONG	PLONGd
	PLONGe		
LOOK	*BLOOK*	PLOOKy	
LOOP	BLOOP	CLOOP	GLOOPy
LOOT	CLOOT	SLOOT	
LOTE	CLOTE	FLOTEl	**ZLOTE**
LUFF	PLUFFy	SLUFF	
LUNK	BLUNK	PLUNKy	
MEER	AMEER	EMEER	
MINE	AMINE	IMINE	
MINO	**AMINO**	**IMINO**	

MOLT	SMOLT	**YMOLT**	
MOTE	EMOTEr	**SMOTE**	
MOVE	AMOVE	EMOVE	
NANA	ANANA	JNANA	
NARY	SNARY*	**UNARY**	
OARY*	GOARY	HOARY*	ROARY*
OAST	HOAST	**LOAST**	
ODAL	MODAL	**NODAL**	PODAL
ODIC	IODIC	SODIC	
OGLE	BOGLE	FOGLE	
OILY*	DOILY+	**NOILY***	ROILY*
	SOILY*		
OLDY+	GOLDY*	MOLDY*	
OLLA	HOLLA	MOLLAh	
OMER	*GOMER*	VOMER	
ONCE	BONCE	NONCE	PONCEy
	SONCE		
ONER	BONER	*DONER*	HONER
	MONERa	ZONER	
ONIE	BONIE*	MONIEd	
ONLY	FONLY	SONLY	
ONUS+	CONUS	TONUS+	
OOFY*	*BOOFY***	**POOFY***	ROOFY*
	WOOFY*		
OOSE	BOOSE	ROOSEr	*WOOSEl*
OOZY*	DOOZY+	WOOZY*	
OPAL	COPALm	NOPAL	
ORAL	BORAL	GORAL	**HORAL**
	LORAL	PORAL	RORAL
	SORAL		
ORBY*	CORBY+	FORBYe	
ORDO	FORDOe	FORDO+	SORDOr
ORRA	MORRA	SORRA	
OUMA	DOUMA	*LOUMA*	
OURN	BOURNe	YOURN	
OVEN	DOVEN	**HOVEN**	ROVEN
OWER	BOWERy	DOWERy	SOWER
	VOWER		
OWLY*	*DOWLY***	JOWLY*	
OWRE	HOWRE	POWRE	
OWSE	BOWSEr	BOWSEy	DOWSEr
	DOWSEt	LOWSE*	SOWSE
	TOWSEr		
OXEN	BOXEN	WOXEN	
PLAY	SPLAY	UPLAYd	
RACH+	BRACHs	BRACH+	ORACH+
	ORACHe		
RACK	BRACK	*DRACK*	FRACK
RAFF	DRAFFy	GRAFF	
RAIL	BRAIL	DRAIL	

RANA	**GRANA**	PRANA	
RANG	KRANG	ORANGe	ORANGy
	WRANG		
RANK	BRANKy	TRANK	
RANT	BRANT	DRANT	ORANT
	TRANT		
RAPE	CRAPE	*FRAPE*	TRAPE
RAPT	**TRAPT**	**WRAPT**	**YRAPT**
RARE	CRARE	URARE	
RASE	PRASE	URASE	
RAST	BRASTe	WRAST	
RATE	FRATEr	PRATEr	URATE
	WRATE		
RAVE	**DRAVE**	TRAVEl	
READ	AREADe	OREAD	
REAL	**AREAL**	**UREAL**	
REAR	**AREAR**	DREAR*	DREARe
	DREARy		
RECK	DRECKy	TRECK	
REDE	AREDEe	BREDE	
REDO	CREDO	UREDO	
REIF	PREIFe	**TREIFa**	
RENT	BRENT*	**DRENT**	PRENT
	URENT	**YRENT**	
REST	**DREST**	PRESTo	TREST
RIAL	PRIAL	URIAL	
RICE	DRICE	GRICEr	
RICK	ERICK	WRICK	
RIDE	GRIDE	**TRIDE**	
RIEL	ARIEL	ORIEL	
RIFF	GRIFFe	**TRIFF***	
RILL	BRILL*	BRILLo	KRILL
	PRILL	TRILLo	
RINE	CRINE	TRINE	
RIOT	**ARIOT**	GRIOT	
RIPT	**DRIPT**	**GRIPT**	
RISE	BRISE	CRISE	FRISEe
	GRISE	PRISEr	
RITT	BRITT	FRITT	
ROCK	BROCK	TROCK	
ROKE	PROKEr	TROKE	**WROKEn**
ROLE	DROLE*	PROLEg	PROLEr
RONE	CRONEt	GRONE	IRONEr
	KRONEn	KRONEr	TRONE
RORE	CRORE	**FROREn**	PRORE
ROSE	BROSE	EROSE	
ROST	**CROST**	**PROST**	
ROSY*	BROSY*	PROSY*	
RUME	BRUME	GRUME	
RUSE	CRUSEt	DRUSEn	

RUST	BRUSTe	FRUSTa		UNDY	BUNDY	CUNDY+	FUNDY+
RYKE	GRYKE	TRYKE			GUNDY+	OUNDY	
SCAR	ESCARp	OSCAR		UNTO	JUNTO	PUNTO	
SCOT	ASCOT	ESCOT	ESCOT>	UPON	JUPON	YUPON	
SKER	ASKER	ESKER		URDY	CURDY*	NURDY*	
ULAN	KULAN	YULAN		USER	LUSER	MUSER	
UMBO	BUMBO	DUMBO	GUMBO	WAIN	SWAIN	TWAIN	
	RUMBO			WALE	DWALE	SWALE	
UMMA	GUMMA	SUMMAe	SUMMAr	WANG	DWANG	SWANG	
	SUMMAt			WANK	SWANK*	SWANKy	TWANKy
UMPH	BUMPH	HUMPH	SUMPH	WEEL	AWEEL	SWEEL	TWEELy
UMPY+	RUMPY+	TUMPY*		WINE	DWINE	GWINE	
UNCE	BUNCE	PUNCE		WINK	SWINK	TWINK	
UNCO	BUNCO	JUNCO	JUNCO+	WIRE	SWIRE	TWIRE	

OTHER FRONT HOOKS

AHEAP AHIGH ALANT ALEFT APEAK APORT ATILT ATOKE ATONY+ ATRIP
AURES KAVAL AVINE BANNS BEVER BLEAR* BLEARy BLIMY BLUDE BOWES
BRAZEn BRAZEr BRUNG CHAFT CHANK CHARKa CHAVE CHOUT CLAME CLAVEr
CLEEP CLEPT CLOKE CLOUR COOZE CRAKE CREPS CRIPE CROUTe CRUCK
CRUMP* CRUMPy CUTIS+ DEARN DEMIT> DOVER DROIL DROOK ELOPS+ ELUTE
EMEND EMONG EQUID EVERT EWEST FANON FIDES FLEAM FLIMP FLORY*
FLOSH+ FLUMP FRUSH GHEST GLACE# GLACE= GLAIRe GLAIRy GLEETy GLOUT
GLUTEi GLUTEn GOUCH GRAMPa GREEK GRIFT GROMA GROOF GURGE HABLE
HEWER IRADE JONES KAVAL KEECH+ KEVIL KLOOF KNOUT KRAFT KRAIT
KROONi LENES LINCH+ LISLE LITAS MOUCH MOUST NATES NIMPS NOINT
NOMEN NOULDe NOWED OAKED OAVES OPINE OVOID PEGGY+ PLINKy POTTO
PRIMY PRINK PROInE PROLL PRUNT RHEME RICER SCUTE SHAPS SHEEL
SHIST SHIVE SHUCK SLAID SLANK SLOOMy SLOVEn SMAZE SPARTh SWARDy
SWARE SWASHy SWEERt SWELT SWITS+ TABID TALUS+ TERES THALEr THUNK
TIMPS TOYER TREEN TROADe TRODE TROPE TROVEr TWILLy ULAMA URITE
UTILE VAIRY* VAKAS+ VROOM WHEARe WHEFT WHUMP YEARD

5.2.2 END HOOKS OF FOURS TO MAKE FIVES

END HOOKS WITH 'A'

ABACA AFARA ALAPA ANANA BACHA BANDAr BANIAn BASTA BATTA BORNA
BUFFA BULLAe BURKA BURSAe BURSAl BURSAr CALLAn CALPAc CANNAe CARTA
CELLAe CELLAr CHARA CHAYA CHICA COALA CONIA COSTAe COSTAl COSTAr
COTTAe COTTAr DARGAh DERMAl DICTA DONGA DORBA DORSAd DORSAl DOUMA
DOURAh DOWNA DURRA ERICA FANGA FELLAh FESTAl FETTA FONDA FOSSAe
GAITA GALEAe GAMBA GENUA GRAMA GRANA GUANAy HAIKAi HAKEA HALFA
HALMA HASTA HATHA HERMAe HERMAi HONDA HOOKAh HOSTA HOVEA IDOLA
JIBBAh KANGA KINDA KIPPA LAIKA LEPTA LIMBA LIMPA LINGAm LONGAn
LOOFAh LUFFA LUTEAl MANGAl MARKA MASSA MENTAl MISSAe MISSAl MISSAw
MISSAy MOCHA MOLLAh MOOLAh MUGGAr MULLAh MUNGA MURRAm MURRAy MUSHA
NERKA NORIA NORMAl NORMAn NULLAh PACTA PAISAn PALEAe PALEAl PALLAe
PALLAh PANGA PARKA PARRAl PASHA PELTAe PEREA PIETA PILEA PINTA
PLAYA PONGA POOKA PORTAl PRIMAl PUCKA PULKA PUNGA PUNKAh QUINA

```
RAGGA   RAITA   RAKIA   RANGA   RASTA   RATHA   ROOSA   RUEDA   SAKIA   SALPAe
SANGAr  SANSAr  SCOPAe  SCUTAl  SELLAe  SENSA   SEPTAl  SERRAe  SERRAn  SESSA
SHAMAn  SHAYA   SHIVAh  SIDHA   SIGNAl  SOFTA   SORDA   SORTAl  SPAZA   SPICAe
SPINAe  SPINAl  SPINAr  SUNNAh  TAIGA   TALEAe  TANGA   TANKA   TEGUA   TESTAe
THANAh  THEMA   TINEAl  TONGA   TONKA   TORTA   TREFAh  TRONA   UNCIAe  UNCIAl
VESTAl  VOLTA   WALLAh  WHATA   WINNA   WISHA   YACKA   YURTA   ZILLAh
```

END HOOKS WITH 'E'

```
ABASEr  AGENE   AGOGE   AINEE   ALANE   ALBEE   ALOWE   AMENEd  AMIDE   AMINE
ANILE   ANISE   ANSAE   ANTAE   APODE   AQUAE   AREAE   AREDEd  ARETE   ATOKE
AURAE   AVALE   AXILE   AXONE   AZYME   BARBEl  BARBEr  BARBEt  BARDE   BASSE*
BASSEt  BEAREr  BECKEt  BERME   BIGAE   BIRLEr  BITTEd  BITTEn  BITTEr  BLATE*
BLITE   BOMBEr  BOOSE   BORDEl  BORDEr  BOREEn  BOTTE   BOWSEr  BOWSEy  BRANE
BREDE   BRERE   BRISE   BROSE   BUFFEd  BUFFEl  BUFFEr  BUFFEt  BUNDEd  BURKEr
BURSE   BUTTEr  CADEE   CADIE   CARLE   CARSEy  CARTEl  CARTEr  CENSEr  CESSEr
CHAPEl  CHAREt  CHAVE   CHERE   CHINE   CLADE   CLAME   CLIPE   CLOTE   CLOYE
COATEe  COATEr  COHOE   COMAE   COMBEr  CONNEr  CORSEt  CORSEy  COSTEr  COURE
COXAE   CRAME   CRAPE   CRÈME   CREWEl  CRISE   CRUSEt  CYMAE   DAUBEr  DEARE*
DEERE   DEEVE   DHOLE   DINGEr  DINGEy  DIRKE   DIXIE   DONEE   DOOLEe  DOREE
DORSEl  DORSEr  DOUCE*  DOUCEt  DOWLE   DOWSEr  DOWSEt  EATHE   EMYDE   EROSE
FAINE*  FARLE   FARSE   FEAREr  FEESE   FEHME   FESSE   FIERE   FILLEr  FILLEt
FITTE*  FLITE   FORMEe  FORMEr  FOSSE   FOULE*  FRAPE   FRATEr  FRISEe  FRIZEr
FUGUE   FUSEE   FUZEE   GAFFEr  GAMBEt  GARBE   GEARE   GESTE   GINGEr  GLEDE
GLIME   GLUME   GLUTEi  GLUTEn  GOLPE   GOSSE   GRAME   GRIDE   GRISE   GRUME
GUNGE   GUYSE   HAUTE   HAWSEr  HEAREr  HEFTEd  HEFTEr  HERSEd  HERYE   HIREE
IMIDE   INBYE   IRONEr  ISNAE   JAMBEe  JAMBEr  JASPEr  JESSE   JINNEe  KANAE
KENTE   KERNEl  KIEVE   KITHE   KNOWEr  KYNDE   LANDEr  LAREE   LEARE   LEESEd
LEFTE*  LENSE   LEVEE   LONGE=  LOUPEn  LOURE   LOWNE   LOWSE*  MAARE   MACHEr
MAILEr  MAIRE   MARAE   MARGE   MARLE   MARSE   MASSE   MATTEr  MEANE*  MENGE
MERLE   MEUSE   MICHEr  MILLEr  MILLEt  MINAE   MINGEr  MINKE   MIXTE   MORAE
MORNE   MORSEl  MOSTE   MOTTE   MOYLE   MUNGE   MURREe  MURREn  MURREy  MUSSEl
NACHE   NEUME   NOULE   NOVAE   OBOLE   ODYLE   OUPHE   OXIME   PAIRE*  PAISE
PARAE   PARSEc  PARSEr  PASSEe  PASSEl  PASSEr  PEAGE   PEARE   PEASEn  PECKEr
PEEPEr  PENIE   PERVE   PIOYE   PLEBE   POUKEd  PRATEr  PRYSE   PUPAE   QUATE
QUINE   RACHEt  RAGEE   RAILEr  RAINE   RAKEE   RAMIE   RANKE*  RAREE   RATHE*
RAZEE   REAMEr  REEDEn  REEDEr  RENTEr  RIFTEd  RILLEt  RIMAE   RONTE   ROOSEr
ROULE   RUFFE   RUGAE   SAICE   SAINEd  SALLEe  SALLEt  SALSE   SASSE   SAUTE
SAUTE=  SAUTE#  SAUTE+  SCUTE   SEAMEn  SEAMEr  SEARE*  SEAREd  SEASE   SEISEr
SELLEr  SEMEEd  SEMIE   SENTEd  SERRE   SETAE   SHITE   SHIVEr  SHOPE   SHOTE
SHULE   SIDHE   SIREE   SITHEe  SITHEn  SKENE   SKYRE   SLIPE   SMITEd  SMITEr
SOARE   SOLDEr  SONSE   SOOLE   SOOTE   SOREE   SOUSE   SOWLE   SOWNE   SOWSE
SPANE   SPODE   STEDE   STEME   STIME   STIRE   STOAE   STOPEr  STUDE   SWAGEr
SYBOE   SYCEE   TACHE   TASSEl  TASSEt  TAWSE   TEADE   TEENEr  TELAE   TEMSE
TERFE   TERNE   TESTEe  TESTEr  THANE   THINE   TOGAEd  TOILEr  TOILEt  TOPEE
TOPHE   TORSEl  TORTEn  TOWSEr  TRAPE   TRINE   TRODE   TRONE   TROPE   TUBAE
TUFFEt  TURME   TWITE   TYNDE   ULNAE   UNDEE   UPBYE   URDEE   URSAE   VAIRE
VAUTE   VEALEr  VEHME   VENAE   VILDE   VITAE   VOLAE   VOLTE   WACKE*  WAIDE
WAITEr  WEEKE   WEETE*  WEETEd  WEETEn  WEFTE   WELKE   WINGEr  WINGE=  WITHEr
WOOSEl  YOUSE   ZOEAE   ZONAE
```

5. Five-Letter Words

END HOOKS WITH 'I'

ABACI　BASSI　*BASTI*　*BESTI*r　BINDI　BLINI　*BRIKI*　**BUFFI**　*BUSTI*c　**CAMPI**
CARDIa　CARDIe　CARDIo　**CARPI**　CEILI　**CELLI**　COATI　COMBI　**CORNI**　**CROCI**
CULTIc　*CURLI*+　**CURSI**　DASHI　DILLI　**DISCI**　**FASTI**e　FERMI　*FILMI*c　**FRATI**
FUNDIc　FUNDIe　**FUNGI**c　*GLOBI*n　HADJI　*HANGI*　HONGI=　HONGI+　HOURI　**IAMBI**c
JINNI　KIBEI　**KORAI**　LANAI　LASSIe　LATHI　**LENTI**c　**LENTI**l　LICHI　**LIMBI**c
LOGOI　LUNGIe　*MACHI*　*MANDI*r　**MODII**　MOOLI　*MURRI*n　**MYTHI**c　NIMBI　OBOLI
PALPI　PARDIe　PARKIe　PARKIn　PARTIm　*PIANI*　**PILEI**　POORI　**PRIMI**　*PULLI*
PUTTIe　*RANGI*　REIKI　*ROSTI*　SAMPI　**SCUDI**　*SENSI*　**SENTI**　SERAIl　SHOGI
SOLDI　SOLEIn　**STOAI**　SWAMI　TANGIe　**TARSI**a　*TAWAI*　**TEMPI**　**TOPHI**　**TOPOI**
TORII　**TORSI**　**VILLI**　**VOLTI**　**XYSTI**　ZIMBI

END HOOKS WITH 'O'

AMIDOl　**AMINO**　BANCO　BARDO　**BASHO**　BASSO　BASTO　BEANO　*BENTO*　**BERKO**
BIFFO　BOFFO　BOMBO　BONGO　BONGO+　BUCKO　BUCKO+　BUFFO　BUNKO　BURROw
BUTEO　CACAO　CAMPO　CANSO　CANTOn　CANTOr　CARBOn　CARBOy　CENTO　*CHADO*r
CHIAO　CHICOn　CHINO　CHOCO　COMBO　COMMOn　COMMOt　COMPOt　**CORNO**　CREDO
CUFFO　CUSSO　**CYANO**　DECKO　DIPSO　*DRACO*　DUMBO　FANGO　FATSO　FATSO+
FILLO　*FLEXO*r　FORDOd　FORDO+　FUNGO+　**GADSO**　GAMBO+　GAMBOl　GARBO　GISMO
GODSOn　GUANO　HALLOa　HALLOo　HALLOt　HALLOw　HALLO+　HILLOa　HILLO+　**HOWSO**
IMIDO　**JAMBO**k　JELLO　JOCKO　KAROO　*KEENO*　KEMBO　*KONDO*　LENTOr　LITHO
MAIKO　MENTOr　*METHO*d　MILKO　MIMEO　**MOLTO**　MONGOe　MONGOl　**MOSSO**　*MUCHO*
MUNGO　MUNGO+　NACHO　NARCO　NGAIO　*NUTSO*　PANTOn　PAREO　PASEO　PESTO
PHONOn　*PILAO*　PINGO　PINGO+　PINKO　PINKO+　PINTO　PINTO+　PONGO　PONGO+
PORNO　*POSHO*　POTTO　PRIMO　PROMO　PROSO　*PULAO*　PUNTO　**PUTTO**　*QUINO*a
*QUINO*l　QUIPO　RATOOn　REALO　*RESTO*　*RUMPO*　SALTO　*SANGO*　SANKO　SANTOl
SANTOn　**SCUDO**　SEXTOn　SICKO　SKIMO　SOCKO　**SOLDO**　*SORBO*　SORDOr　STENO
TACHO　TRIGOn　*TRUGO*　VERSO　VIREO　WACKO　*WALDO*　*WALDO*+　**WHAMO**　*YUCKO*
ZINCO

END HOOKS WITH 'U'

BANTU　**BATTU**　*BITOU*　BUCKU　BUNDU　BUSSU　*CENTU*m　CORNUa　FONDUe　HAIKU
JAMBUl　*KAWAU*　LASSU　MUNTU　PAREU　**PENDU**　*PIKAU*　PILAU　QUIPU　*TENDU*
VERTUe

END HOOKS WITH 'D'

ABBED　**ACNED**　**ACRED**　**AGUED**　ALAND　ALKYD　**ALOED**　**APAYD**　AREADd　**AREDD**
AXLED　BEMAD>　BOORDe　*BREID*　CAULD*　CHARD　**COLED**　**COURD**　*DALED*h　**EAVED**
ELAND　**FAURD**　**FLUED**　GADID　GOOLD　HAULD　HEALD　HOORD　ILIAD　IZARD
LAIRD　**LATED**　LIARD　LOORD　LOUND　LOWND　**MANED**　MAUNDy　MONAD　**MOTED**
NOULDe　OCTAD　*OGEED*　**PATED**　**PAYSD**　POWND　**QUAYD**　RANID　READD　**RUNED**
SCAND　**SEELD**　SHANDy　*SHOWD*　SOWND　**SPARD**　SPAYD　STEDDe　STEDDy　STEND
TABID　TEEND　TEIND　**TEMED**　TOGED　ULNAD　UNBED>　**VANED**　**VIOLD**　**WAMED**
WEALD　WOOLD　YEARD

END HOOKS WITH 'L'

ALGAL　ALKYL　ALLYL　ANNAL　**AREAL**　**AURAL**　**AWEEL**　BABEL　BABUL　BEDELl
BETEL　BORAL　**BOREL**　BOTEL　BROOL　BUBALe　CABAL>　CABALa　CAVEL　**CECAL**
COMAL　**COXAL**　CREEL　DATAL　DEBEL>　DHOLL　DITAL　DURAL　DYNEL　FAVELa
FAVELl　**FETAL**　FOREL　FUSEL　**GENAL**　GIBEL　**GLIAL**　GORAL　GRUEL　GRUEL>

HORAL	HOSEL	IDYLL	**ILEAL**	**ILIAL**	**INTIL**	JUGAL	**JURAL**	JUREL	*KATAL*
KAVAL	KETOL	KNARLy	KNURLy	LEMEL	LOREL	LOSEL	MAILL	MERELl	MERELy
MERIL	**MESAL**	MESEL	**MOLAL**	MONAL	MOREL	MYALL	NEVEL>	**NOTAL**	OCTAL
PICAL	PIPAL	**PUPAL**	RATAL	RATEL	RAVEL	RAVEL>	RIVEL>	ROMAL	**ROTAL**
RUBEL	**RUGAL**	SAMELy	SCULLe	SEGOL	**SERAL**	**SETAL**	SHEAL	SHOOLe	SIZEL
SORAL	SORELl	SORELy	SPAWL	**SURAL**	SWAYL	SWEEL	TEPAL	THIOL	THIRL
TRIOL	**TUBAL**	TWEELy	**UREAL**	**UVEAL**	**VASAL**	**VENAL**	VINAL	YOKEL	**ZOEAL**
ZONAL	ZORIL	**ZYGAL**							

END HOOKS WITH 'N'

ABRIN	AMMONo	ATMAN	**BAKEN**	*BASEN*	*BALUN*	**BLAWN**	BURAN	CAMAN	CAPON
CODEN	CONINe	CONINg	COPEN	COZEN	DEARN	DJINNi	DJINNy	DOORN	DOVEN
ERGON	FANON	FLAWN	GIRON	**GNAWN**	GYRON	HALON	HEBEN	**HOSEN**	**HOTEN**
HOVEN	*JOMON*	KORUNa	KORUNy	KULAN	LATENt	LIMAN	LIMEN	LODEN	LOGON
LOSEN	**MAYAN**	MIRINg	**MOTEN**	**NOMEN**	OCTANe	OCTANt	**OWSEN**	PATENt	PAVEN
PURINe	PURINg	QUEYN	RAMIN	RATANy	REDON>	REDONe	**RIVEN**	ROMANo	*ROTAN*
ROTON	ROUEN	**ROVEN**	RUMEN	SAMAN	**SAMEN**	SARINg	**SHAWN**	**SHEWN**	**SHOON**
SHULN	SILENe	SILENi	SILENt	SKEEN	SOKEN	SOLANd	SOLANo	SOLON	SOMAN
STARN	**STOWN**	TABUN	TAKINg	**TAPEN**	TOLANe	TORANa	TOYON	TREEN	TWEENy
VARAN	VEGAN	WHEEN	**YEVEN**	YOGINi	**YOURN**	ZUPAN			

END HOOKS WITH 'R' OF VERBS

AIDER	BALER	BIDER	BITER	BONER	CAGER	CANER	CEDER	CITER	CORER
CUBER	CURER	DARER	DATER	DAZER	DIKER	DOPER	DOSER	DOTER	DUPERy
EASER	FACER	FADER	FAKERy	FARER	FIFER	FILER	FIRER	FUMER	GAGER
GAPER	*GATER*	GAZER	GIBER	GLUER	HATER	HAZER	HIDER	HIVER	HONER
HOPER	*HOSER*	HYPER	JAPERy	JIBER	KITER	LACER	LADER	LAKER	LAVER
LITER	LOPER	LUGER	LURER	LUTER	MACER	MASER	MAZER	MIMER	MOPERy
MUSER	NAMER	*NIXER*	NOSER	NOTER	OGLER	PILER	PLIER	POLER	PORER
PUKER	PULER	RAKERy	RAPER	RASER	RATER	RAZER	RICER	RIMER	ROKER
ROPERy	SHOER	SIDER	SILER	SIZER	SOLERa	SPAER	*SPUER*	TOKER	TOPER
TOTER	TUBER	URGER	VINERy	WAKER	WALER	WIRER	WIVERn	ZONER	

OTHER END HOOKS WITH 'R'

ANTARa	**AREAR**	**AURAR**	*BINER*	**BOLAR**	BREER	BRIERy	CHARRo	CHARRy	CHURRo
CLOUR	COPER	CYMAR	DIMER	*DONER*	DOVER	EIDER	**FILAR**	GNARR	**GULAR**
HAVER	**HILAR**	KNURR	MILORd	MINAR	MODERn	NAZIR	NITERy	OCHERy	ONCER
PATERa	**PILAR**	QUAIR	**RYPER**	SAKER	SHIRRa	**SIKER**	SIMAR	SKEERy	SMIRRy
SOFAR	SPIER	STARRy	SWEERt	**SYKER**	TALAR	TALER	TATER	TITER	*TOLAR*
TRIOR	TRYER	**TUBAR**	ULNARe	VELAR	VIVER	**VOLARy**	*YOKER*		

END HOOKS WITH 'T'

ABLET	**AGAST**	**ALANT**	**ALEFT**	AMENTa	ANNAT	**APERT**	ARETT	**AVAST**	BAHUT
BENET>	BLATT	BLUET	BOART	BRANT	BRASTe	BRENT*	BRITT	BRUSTe	BUNDT
CANST	CAPOT>	CAPOTe	CARET	**CHAPT**	CHERTy	CHOUT	CIVET	**CLAPT**	**CLIPT**
COMPT	COOPT	**COOST**	COSET	CRUET	CURET	**CURST**	DELFT	DENET>	**DICHT**
DIXIT	**DOEST**	**DRIPT**	**DROPT**	DUETTi	DUETTo	**EARST**	ERGOT	**EVERT**	**EWEST**
FEART	FEISTy	FILET	**FLITT**	FREETy	FRIST	FRITT	FUMET	GAITT	GEEST
GENET	GLEETy	GLENT	*GOEST*	GOSHT	**GRIPT**	GRIST	*GULET*	**HADST**	*HAINT*

5. Five-Letter Words

HAULT	HECHTd	HELOT	HIGHT	HOAST	HORSTe	ISLET	JURAT	KARATe	**KEMPT**
KORAT	LACET	**LIART**	LICHT*	LUNET	*MANATi*	*MANATu*	**MANET**	**MAYST**	**MEINT**
MICHT	MORAT	MOTETt	MOUST	MUSET	NONET	**ONCET**	OUCHT	PALET	**PEART***
PIERT	PIPET	PIPIT	POORT	**PRATT**	**PROST**	QUINTa	QUINTe	REESTy	REIST
RICHT*	ROSETy	**SAIST**	SALET	SAULT	**SAYST**	SCARTh	SCATTy	SHOTTe	*SICHT*
SIENT	SKATT	SKEET	**SKINT***	**SLIPT**	SPARTh	**STEPT**	STOAT	**STOPT**	*STOTT*
SURAT	**SWAPT**	**SWOPT**	**TACET**	TAPETa	TAPETi	**TOROTh**	**TRAPT**	TRATT	TREST
VERSTe	VIVAT	VOLET	WAIFT	**WARST**	**WELKT**	WHIPT	*WISHT*	**WRAPT**	YOURT

END HOOKS WITH 'Y' TO MAKE ADJECTIVES

ACIDY*	ANTSY*	*ARSEY*	ARTSY*	BALDY*	**BALKY***	**BALMY***	BARDY*	**BARKY***	**BARNY***
BASSY*	**BEAKY***	**BEAMY***	*BEATY*	**BEEFY***	**BEERY***	BENDYs	BENDY*	**BENTY***	**BITSY***
BITTY*	*BLADY*	BLUEY*	**BONEY***	**BONEY^**	BOOKY*	**BOOMY***	**BORTY***	**BOSKY***	*BOYSY*
BRAKY*	BROSY*	**BUFFY***	**BUNTY***	**BURRY***	**BUSTY***	CAGEY*	CAKEY*	CALMY*	CAMPY*
CANTY*	CARNY*	CARNYx	CASKY*	**CHARY***	COALY*	**COBBY***	COMBY*	**CONKY***	**COOMY***
COPSY*	**CORKY***	COZEY*	**CRAPY***	*CULTY*	**CURDY***	**CURNY***	*CUSPY*	DAMPY*	DASHY*
DAUBY*	**DEEDY***	**DICEY***	**DICTY***	**DIKEY***	DILLY*	DINKY*	**DISHY***	**DITSY***	**DITZY***
DONSY*	**DOOMY***	**DOPEY***	**DORKY***	**DORTY***	*DOWLY*	**DULLY***	**DUNGY***	**DUSKY***	**DYKEY***
FAKEY*	FAWNY*	**FELTY***	**FENDY***	**FERNY***	*FESTY*	FILMY*	**FISTY***	**FLAMY***	**FLAWY***
FLAXY*	FLORY*	**FLUEY***	FOLKY*	FOOTY*	**FORKY***	**FROWY***	**FUBSY***	**FUSTY***	**GAMEY***
GASPY*	**GAUMY***	**GEEKY***	**GENTY***	**GERMY***	**GIMPY***	**GINNY***	GIRLY*	**GLADY***	**GLUEY***
GOATY*	**GOLDY***	GOODY*	GOONY*	**GOOPY***	GOOSY*	**GORMY***	**GOUTY***	**GRIPY***	**GUCKY***
GULFY*	**GULPY***	**GUNGY***	**GUNKY***	**GURLY***	**GUSHY***	**HAILY***	**HASHY***	**HEAPY***	HEMPY*
HERBY*	HISSY*	**HOARY***	**HOKEY***	**HOLEY***	**HOLEY^**	HOMEY*	HOODY*	HOOKY*	**HOOTY***
HORSY*	**HULKY***	**HULLY***	HUNKY*	**HUSHY***	JAGGY*	**JIMPY***	**JIVEY***	**JOKEY***	**JOLTY***
JOWLY*	*KEMPY*	KISSY*	LACEY*	LAMBY*	**LARDY***	**LARKY***	**LATHY***	**LAWNY***	**LEADY***
LEAKY*	**LEARY***	**LEERY***	**LIMBY***	LINEY*	LINGY*	**LINKY***	LINTY*	**LOAMY***	**LOSSY***
LOURY*	**LUSHY***	**MALMY***	**MALTY***	MARDY*	**MARLY***	MASHY*	**MASSY***	**MASTY***	**MAWKY***
MAZEY	MEALY*	**MELTY***	**MESHY***	**MIFFY***	**MILTY***	**MINTY***	**MIRKY***	MISSY*	**MOCHY***
MOLDY*	**MOONY***	**MOORY***	**MOPEY***	**MOTEY***	**MOTHY***	MOTTY*	**MUCKY***	**MUMSY***	**MURLY***
MUSHY*	MUSKY*	**MUSSY***	**MYTHY***	**NARKY***	**NERDY***	NETTY*	**NIFFY***	**NIRLY***	**NOILY***
NOOKY*	NOSEY*	**NOUNY***	*NOWTY*	*NURDY*	NUTSY*	ONERY*	PACEY*	PALMY*	PARKY*
PAWKY*	**PEAKY***	**PEATY***	**PECKY***	PEERY*	*PERVY*	**PESTY***	**PINEY***	PINKY*	PLATY*
PLATYs	**PLUMY***	POCKY*	**POOFY***	**PORNY***	**PORTY***	**POSEY***	**POUTY***	**PROSY***	**PUDSY***
PUFFY*	*PUKEY*	**PULPY***	PUNKY*	**PURSY***	RAGGY*	**RANGY***	**RASPY***	**REAMY***	**REDDY***
REEFY*	**REEKY***	**RESTY***	RICEY*	**RIFTY***	**RILEY***	**RINDY***	**RITZY***	ROARY*	**ROILY***
ROOFY*	ROOKY*	**ROOPY***	**ROPEY***	**RORTY***	**ROUPY***	RUNTY*	**RUSHY***	**SAMEY***	**SARKY***
SEAMY*	**SEELY***	**SEEPY***	SINKY*	**SLATY***	**SNARY***	**SNIPY***	**SOILY***	**SONSY***	**SOUPY***
SPEWY*	**STAGY***	**STEWY***	*SUCKY*	**SUDSY***	**SUETY***	SURFY*	**TALCY***	TALKY*	**TARTY***
TEARY*	**TECHY***	**TEENY***	**TENTY***	**THAWY***	**THEWY***	**TICHY***	**TILLY***	**TINTY***	*TOCKY*
TONEY*	**TOSHY***	**TOSSY***	TOWNY*	**TOWSY***	**TRIPY***	**TUFTY***	**TUMPY***	**TURFY***	**TUSKY***
TWINY*	**TYPEY***	VAIRY*	*VAMPY*	**VASTY***	**VEALY***	**VEILY***	**VEINY***	*VIBEY*	VIEWY*
VUGGY*	*VUGHY*	**WACKY***	WALLY*	WANEY*	**WANKY***	**WARBY***	**WARTY***	**WASHY***	WASPY*
WAVEY*	**WHINY***	WHITY*	**WIMPY***	**WINEY***	**WINGY***	**WISPY***	WITHY*	**WOMBY***	**WOOFY***
WORMY*	YAPPY*	**YAWNY***	YECHY*	YEUKY*	YOLKY*	**ZESTY***	ZINCY*	**ZINGY***	ZOOTY*

OTHER END HOOKS WITH 'Y'

ALARY	APERY+	ATOMY+	ATOPY+	BAFFY+	BALLY+	BANTY+	*BARBY+*	*BEANY+*	BIFFY+
BIGGY+	BINGY+	*BLINY*	BOOBY+	BOTHY+	BOTTY+	*BUNDY*	BUNGY+	**BUSKY**	BUTTY+
CARBY+	CARDY+	*CERTY*	CHIVY	COLEY	COMMY+	CONEY	COOKY+	COOLY+	COREY

COSEY* COVEY **CRUDY** CRUSY+ CULLY CUTEY DARKY+ DEARY+ **DEAWY** DEIFY
DELLY+ DOGEY DOOLY+ **DORMY** DUROY *DURRY+* FELLY+ FOODY+ **FORBY**e FUNDY+
GALLY GAMAY GILLY **GLOBY** **GOOKY** GOOLY+ *GOORY+* **GRISY** HANKY+ HARPY+
HEEDY HONKY+ *HOSEY* HURLY+ JACKY+ *JAKEY* JANNY+ JEELY KELLY+ KELPY+
KELTY+ KILTY+ KINDY+ **LEANY** LEFTY+ LIMEY LINDY+ LINNY+ **LORDY** LOVEY
MATEY* MEANY+ MEINY+ *MOBEY* MOLLY+ MOOLY+ MOPSY+ MORAY MOSEY MULEY
MURRY+ PANDY PANTY+ **PARDY** PARRY PATSY+ *PIKEY* PIONY+ POKEY* POLEYn
POLLY+ PONEY PONTY+ POPSY+ POTSY+ POWNY+ PRATY+ PREMY+ PREXY+ **PRIMY**
PUNTY+ REIFY RUMPY+ SALLY SAVEY SERRY **SESEY** SOFTY+ SOPHY+ SWAMY+
TANKY+ TANSY+ TELLY+ TELLYs TICKY+ TOADY *TOLLY+* TUSHY+ **UNCOY** VEERY+
WADDY WANTY+ WELLY+ WICKY+ *WIFEY* WILLY **YESTY**

OTHER END HOOKS

ABASH **ABASK** **ABRIM** ABYSM **ACERB*** AIRTH ALANG *ALECK* ALMAH ALMEH
ARISH+ ARTIC **BAITH** *BANDH* BEATH **BEAUX** BEDEW *BICEP* BIMAH *BLING**
BOBAC BOBAK BOONGa BORAK BORAX+ BORTZ+ BRANK **BREEM** *BRISS+* *BRITH*
BROGH **BRUSK*** BUMPH *BUNDH* BURGH CANEH *CAPEX+* CAPIZ+ **CAREX** CAULK
CHAWK CHICH+ CHICHa CHICHi **CHOUX** *CHOWK* CLONK CODEC **CODEX** COHOG
CONIC COOMBe COSECh COURB CRIMPy CRITH CUBEB *DADAH* DARIC DEFOG>
DEGUM> DEMOB> DONAH DOSEH **DRACK** DUNSH DUROC EPHAH ERICK *EYASS+*
FLAMM FLIMP FORAM *FOREX+* FRASS+ FRITH FRITZ+ FROSH+ GALAXy GANEF
GANEV GARTH GAUSS+ GLEEK GOLEM GONEF **GREEK** GRITH GULAG GULPH
GURSH+ HAKAM HAULMy HORAH HOUFF HOWFF HUMPH HYLEG **ILEAC** **ILIAC**
JAMES+ KALIF KAMIK KANEH KHETH KOTOW KVASS+ LAICH **LEISH*** **LIMAX**
LOTAH **LOTIC** *LUREX+* *MALAM* MALAX **MALIC**e MALIK MANEH MARAH MEATHe
MERCH+ MILTZ+ MINIMa *MIREX+* **MOONG** MUREX+ MUSTH MYNAH NAVEW **NEATH**
NEEMB OLLAV PAPAW **PAREV**e PASHM PAWAW PILAFf PILAW PLOTZ POUFFe
POUFFy PRIMP PROSS+ PUJAH **PULIK** *PYREX+* **RABIC** RAYAH REDOX+ REINK
RETEM ROUTH ROWTH SAICK SALEP SAMEKh SANGH **SATEM** SCARPa SCARPh
SCATHe SCOWP SCULK SCULPt SCURFy SEISM SERAC SHAWM SILEX+ SIRIH
SKEEF SKEGG SLUBBy SLURB SMEEK SMITHy *SNARF* SNARKy SNOWK SOLAH
SOOTH* SOOTHe SOREX+ SOWFF SPANG SPICK* *SPIFF*y SPINK SPITZ+ STAPH
STIRK STIRP STOWP **STUMM** SUBAH SUMPH SURAH **SWANG** SWATHe SWATHy
SYBOW SYNCH TAISH+ TALAK TALAQ TAROC TAROK TAVAH *THANG* THEEK
THRUM> TILTH TOPEK TORAH TORIC TORSK TRONC *TRONK* TROTH TUISM
TWINK *UMMAH* *UMRAH* UPTAKe VARECh **VIBEX** VINEW VITEX+ VROUW ***WAREZ***
WAULK WELSH WHEEP WHOMP WOOSH WOOTZ+ **YOGIC** **YONIC** ZEBUB ZINEB

5.3 LESS FAMILIAR NON-HOOK FIVES

5.3.1 VERBS COMPRISED OF A COMMON PREFIX PLUS A VERB

BEBOP> BECAP> BEDIM> BEDYE= BEFOG> BEGEM> BELAY BELEE BEMIXt BEMUD>
BEPAT> BERAY BEROB> BESEEd BESEEm BESEEn BESITd BEWET> BEWIG>

DEAIR DEASH DEBAG> DEBAR> DEBARk *DEBUD> DEBUR> DEBURr* DEBUS DEBUS>
DEFAT> DEGAS> DEGAS+ DEICEr DEMAN> DEMANd DERAT> DERATe DERAY DERIG>
DEWAX

EMBAR> EMBARk EMBAY EMBOG> EMBOX EMBOW EMBUSy EMBUS> EMMEW

ENARM ENDEW ENDUE ENFIX ENMEW ENSEW ENSKY ENSKY# *ENURN*

IMBAR> IMBARk IMBED> IMMEW IMMIX

INARM INDEW INDOW INDUE INFIX INORB INURN

REBUYd RECON> RECUTd REDIP> REDIPt REDRY REDUB> REDYE= REFIX REFLYd
REFRY REHEM> RELETd RELET> RELIEf RELIEr REMAN> REMANd REMAP> REMIXt
REPEG> REPIN> REPINe RERIG> RESAWn RESAYd RESEEk RESEEn RESEWn RESOD>
RESOWn RETAG> RETAX REVIEw REWAX REWED> REWET> REWINd REWIN> REWINd

UNARM UNBAG> UNBAN> UNBAR> UNBARe UNBARk UNBOX UNCAP> UNCAPe UNDAM>
UNFIXt UNGAG> UNGETd UNGOD> UNGUM> *UNJAM>* UNHAT> UNLAW UNLAYd UNLID>
UNMAN> UNMEW UNMIXt UNPAYd UNPEG> UNPEN> UNPENt UNPIN> UNRIG> UNRIP>
UNRIPe UNSAYd UNSETd UNSET> UNSEWn UNSEXy UNTAX UNTIN> UNWIT>

UPDRY UPJET> UPRUNd UPRUN> UPTIE

5.3.2 OTHER VERBS

CONTAINING HEAVY LETTERS

ADMIXt AVIZE AVYZE BAIZE BOLIX CEAZE COZIE* DETOX DIZEN EXEEM
EXEME FEAZE *FEDEX* FEEZE GLOZE HEEZE JAPAN> JODEL> JUMARt JUMAR>
JUTTY NEEZE NUDZH+ OXTER PEAZE PEIZE QUANTa QUEME QUICHe QUIRT
QUOIF QUOIN QUONK QUYTE ROZET ROZIT SEAZE SQUAB> SQUEG> TEAZEl
TOAZE TOUZE TOWZE WANZE WEIZE WIZEN ZINKE

OTHERS

ACCOY ADVEW ALEYE ANELE APPAYd APPAYd APPUI@ APPUY AREFY ARGLE
ASSOT> ASSOTt AUGURy

BARRE# BARRE= BARREl BARREn BARREt BESOM BEVVY BIELDy BIVVY *BLART*
BLUME BODGEr BOING BOODY BOOGY BOUGEt BOULT BOUSE BOWNE *BRAAI=*
BRUIT BUIST BUTLEr

CABOB> CAROM CAVIL CAVIL> CHACE CHEVY CHIRK* CHIRL CHIRM CHIRRe
CHIRT CHUSEd CLARTy CLAUT CLECKy CLEPE CLOMP CLYPEi COACT COAPT
COIGNe CONGE= CONGEe CONGEr COOEY COSIE* CRAAL CROFT CROMB CROME
CROOL CUPEL CUPEL> *CWTCH*

DAKER DARRE DAVEN *DAYCH* DECAL DECAL> DENAY DEVEL DEVEL> DIGHT
DONNEe *DOOCE* DROUK DUNCH DUPLY DWALM DWAUM

ELIDE EMCEE ENNUI@ ENURE ERUCT ETTLE

FADGE FAGOT FAYNE *FELCH* FERLY* FIDGEt FILCH FLURRy FLYPE FOYLE
FOYNE FRACTi FUGLE

GALOP GALOP> GAMMEr GANCH GARREt GAVOT> GIUSTo GLAUM GRYDE GUIMPe
GUSSY GUYLEr

HALAL> HALALa HALSEr HANCH HARRY HAUSEn HELVE HERRY *HIKOI=* HILCH
HINNY HOCUS HOCUS> HOICK HOISE HOLLOa HOLLOo HOLLOw HOLLO+ HOOSH
HOOVEn HOOVEr HOTCH HOUGH HURRAh HURRAy

IMBUE IMMIT> INCUSe INKLE INURE

KABAB> KABOB> KEBOB> KERVE KIDDY KIMBO KNIVE *KOTCH* KRAAL KYTHE

LANCH LAUCHd LAUCHs LEGGEr LIGGEr LOAVE LOTTEr

MEAREd MEDLEy MENSE MENSH MIAOU MIAOW MIAUL MIEVE MISDOd MISDO+
MISGOd MISGO+ MOBLE *MODGE* MOOVE MORPHo MUDGEr MUIST MULCT MULSH
MUTCH

NAPOO NAPPEr NEESE

OBEAH OUTGOd OUTGO+

PANNEr PARGEt PAROLe PATTEe PATTEn PATTEr PEISE PENNEr PERCEn PERSEd
PEYSE PHESE PICOTe PIGHT PLOAT POIND PORGE POSIT POTCHe POUPE
POYNT POYSE PREDY PREVE PRISSy PRONK PROYNe PSYCHe PSYCHo PUSLEy

RABAT> RABATo RALPH *RAPPEe* *RAPPEl* *RAPPEn* *RAPPEr* RATCH RAVINe RAVINg
RAYLEt RECAL> RECALl RECCY REEVE REFEL> REFELl REFELt REIVEr RENAY
RENEY RENIG> RENNEt RIEVEd RIEVEr ROATE ROIST ROSIT ROTTEn ROTTEr
ROWEL ROWEL> ROWND ROYNE ROYST RUCHE RUMBA RYMME

SALUE SALVEr SALVOr SALVO+ SCAIL SCALD SCAUD SCAURy SCEND SCLIM>
SCOOG SCOUG SCRAT> SCUSE SDAYN SDEIN SEPAD> SERGEr SHIELd SHLEP>
SHLEPp SHROWd SHTUP> SIRUPy SKEARy SKIRL SKIRR SKIVEr SKLIM> SKOAL
SLART *SLORM* SMAAK *SMEIK* *SMEKE* SMOUT SNAFU SNASH SNELL* SNELLy
SNIFTy SNOKE SNOOD SNOOL SNOOTy SNUSH SOUCE SOUGHt SOWCE SOWTH
SPALT SPEIL SPEIR SPELD SPIRT SPOOM SPRAG> *STAUNd* STEANe STIVEr
STONNe STUPE STURT STYME STYMY SWARF SWERF SWOUNd SWOUNe

TABERd	TABOR	TAMMY	TARGEt	TARRE	TARRY*	TASER	TENON	THRAWn	THRID>
TINCT	TITHEr	TITUPy	TITUP>	TODDE	TOMMY	TOUSEr	TROAK	TROAT	TRYSTe
TYPTO	TYRANt	TYRAN>	TYTHE						

UMBERy

VALSE	VAUCH	VAWTE	VENGEr	VISIE=	VISIEr	VOLVE

WAUFF	WAUGHt	WEDELn	WEISE	WELCH	WIGHT	WONGI=	WRAWL

YEALM	YODLEr	YOICK

5.3.3 ADJECTIVES ENDING IN 'Y'

BARRY*	BEIGY*	BILGY*	BIRSY*	BLUDY*	BOUSY*	BULGY*	CACKY*	CADGY*	CHOKY*
CISSY*	CREPY*	CUPPY*	CUTTY*	DANCY*	DEBBY*	DIDDY*	DIPPY*	DODDY*	DOGGY*
DRONY*	DRUSY*	DRUXY*	DUDDY*	DURGY*	FABBY*	FAGGY*	FENNY*	FINNY*	FIRRY*
FITLY*	FLARY*	FLUTY*	FUBBY*	FUGGY*	FURZY*	GABBY*	GAPPY*	GASSY*	GAUCY*
GAUZY*	GAWCY*	GAWSY*	GLEBY*	GOBBY*	GORSY*	GRAPY*	GRODY*	GUTTY*	HAMMY*
HAYEY*	HENNY*	HOOLY*	HOPPY*	HUGGY*	JANTY*	JIGGY*	JOTTY*	LEAVY*	LIPPY*
LOGGY*	LOOBY*	LOPPY*	LUMMY*	MANKY*	MARVY*	MIDGY*	MIMSY*	MINCY*	MIRLY*
MOPPY*	NAGGY*	NITTY*	NOBBY*	NODDY*	NUBBY*	PODDY*	PODGY*	PONCY*	POOVY*
PUDGY*	PUGGY*	PUNNY*	PURTY*	QUAKY*	RAMMY*	RATTY*	RIBBY*	RIDGY*	RUGGY*
RUTTY*	SAPPY*	SCODY*	SKIEY^	SKIVY*	SKYEY*	SODDY*	SPIRY*	SURGY*	TAGGY*
THYMY*	TIDDY*	TIPPY*	TOPPY*	TOTTY*	TOUSY*	TOUZY*	TOWZY*	VUTTY*	WALTY*
WEBBY*	WENNY*	WIFTY*	WIGGY*	ZAPPY*	ZIPPY*	ZOOEY*			

5.3.4 OTHERS CONTAINING HEAVY LETTERS

NOUNS CONTAINING 'J'

AJIVA	AJWAN	BAJAN	BAJRA	BAJRI	BIJOUx	BUNJEe	BUNJY+	EEJIT	FJELD
FJORD	GADJE	GANJAh	GAUJE	HEJAB	HEJRA	HIJAB	HIJRAh	HODJA	JABOT
JACAL	JAFFA	JAGIR	JAGRA	JALOPy	JARTA	JARUL	JASEY	JAWAN	JAXIE
JEBEL	JEHADi	JELAB	JEMBE	JENNY+	JERID	JERRY+	JETON	JEWIE	JHALA
JIGOT	JIHADi	JIRGA	JONTY+	JORAM	JORUM	JOTUNn	JOUAL	JOWARi	JUDAS+
JUGUM	JULEP	JUMBY+	JUVIE	KANJI	KHOJA	KOPJE	LAPJE	MUJIK	NINJA
OBJET	OJIME	OUIJA	POLJE	POOJAh	PUNJI	RIOJA	ROJAK	SAJOU	SHOJI
SLOJD	SUJEE	THUJA	WILJA	YOJANa	ZANJA				

NOUNS CONTAINING 'Q'

BURQA	FAQIR	FIQUE	GUQIN	MAQUI	NIQAB	QANAT	QIBLA	QORMA	QUARK
QUASS+	QUBIT	QUEAN	QUENA	QUERN	QUIFF	QUIST	QUOLL	QURSH+	ROQUEt
TOQUEt	TRANQ	TUQUE	UMIAQ	USQUE					

NOUNS CONTAINING 'X'

ADDAX+	AUXIN	ATAXY+	AXION	AXITE	AXOID	*BOXTY*+	BRAXY+	CALYX+	*COXIB*
DEXIE	DOXIE	EXEAT	EXINE	EXODE	EXPAT	EXURB	*FOXIE**	HAPAX+	HELIX+
HEXADe	HEXER	HEXYL	HYRAX+	*INBOX*+	IXORA	IXTLE	*JAXIE*	LEXIS+	*LINUX*+
MIXEN	MOXIE	NEXUS+	NIXIE	*ORIXA*	OXBOW	OXEYE	OXLIP	PANAX+	PHLOX+
PIXIE	PODEX+	PYXIE	RADIX+	SEXER	SIXER	SIXMO	SIXTE	TAXER	TAXOL
TAXOR	TEXAS+	VEXER	VEXIL	VOXEL	WAXER	*WUXIA*	XEBEC	XENIAl	XENON
XERUS+	XYLAN	XYLOL	XYLYL						

NOUNS CONTAINING 'Z'

AIZLE	AZIDE	AZLON	AZOLE	AZOTEd	AZOTH	*AZUKI*	AZYGY+	BAIZA	BAZAR
BAZOO	BEZEL	BEZIL	BONZEr	BRAZA	BRIZE	BUAZE	BWAZI	*CEZVE*	CLOZE
COBZA	COLZA	CROZEr	DARZI	DIAZO	DIAZO+	*DURZI*	ENZYMe	FURZE	FUZIL
GAZAL	GAZAR	GAZOOn	GHAZI	GHAZI+	*GINZO*+	GIZMO	GRIZE	*GYOZA*	HAFIZ+
HAMZAh	HERTZ+	HIZEN	KANZU	KARZY+	KAZOO	*KHAZI*	KRANZ+	KUDZU	LAZAR
LEAZE	LOZEN	MATZAh	MATZOh	MATZOt	MAZUT	MIRZA	MIZEN	MOTZA	NIZAM
OUZEL	OZEKI	*PONZU*	PUZEL	RAZOO	SADZA	SOYUZ+	SOZINe	TOZIE	ULZIE
VEZIR	VIZIR	VOZHD	WAZIR	*WAZOO*	WINZE	ZABRA	ZAIRE	ZAKAT	ZAMANg
ZANJA	ZEBECk	ZERDA	ZIBETh	ZIGAN	ZILCH+	ZIPPO	ZIRAM	ZLOTY+	ZLOTYs
*ZOAEA*e	ZOCCO	ZOISM	ZOIST	ZOMBIe	ZONDA	ZOOEAe	ZOOEAl	ZOOID	ZORRO

NON-PLURALS

AFLAJ	*ASSEZ*	**AXIAL**	**AXMAN**	**AXMEN**	**AZIDO**	**AZURN**	**AZURY**	***BASIJ***	**BONZA**
CAJON	**CAJUN**	**CALIX**	**CIMEX**	**COMIX**	**CYLIX**	**DEOXY**	**EXIES**	**FALAJ**	**FIXITy**
FORZA	***FORZE***	***GADJO***	**GONZO**	**GROSZe**	**GROSZy**	***JAMON***	**JESUS**	**JEUNE**	***JIRRE***
JOKOL	**JOUGS**	**KYLIX**	**LAXLY**	***LEEZE***	**NERTZ**	**NOXAL**	**PIEZO**	**PYXIS**	**QUALE**
QUARE*	**QUASI**	**QUOAD**	**QUOTHa**	**REDUX**	**REJON**	**REMEX**	**SALIX**	**SENZA**	**TAXUS**
TROOZ	**TWIXT**	**VARIX**	**WAXEN**	**XENIC**	**XOANA**	**XYLIC**	**ZOOKS**	**ZOPPA**	**ZOWIE**
ZYGON	**ZYMIC**								

5.3.5 OTHER NOUNS

AALII	ABAKA	ABAMP	ABAYA	ABBOT	ABCEE	ABELE	ABMHO	ABOHM	ABSEY
ABSIT	ACKEE	*ACKER*	ACTINg	ACTON	*ADHAN*	ADIEUx	ADMIN	ADOBE	ADOBO
ADUKI	AERIE*	AERIEd	AGAMIc	AGAMId	AGGER	AGGIE	*AGITA*	AGLET	*AGLOO*
AGRIA	AGUTI	*AHURU*	AIERY+	*AINGA*	AIOLI	AIVER	AKELA	AKENE	*AKITA*
ALAAP	ALAMO	ALCID	ALDEA	ALDERn	ALDOL	ALEPH	ALGIN	ALGOR	ALGUM
ALIYAh	ALKIE	ALLEE	ALLELe	ALLIS+	ALLOD	ALMUDe	ALMUG	ALULAe	ALULAr
ALWAY	AMBAN	AMBRY+	AMEBAe	AMEBAn	AMIGA	AMMAN	AMNIOn	AMOUR	*AMOWT*
AMPULe	AMRITa	*ANATA*	ANCHOr	ANCLE	*ANDRO*	ANGLO	ANIMAl	ANIME	ANIMI
ANION	ANKER	ANKUS+	ANKUSh	ANLAS+	ANOMY+	ANTRE	*ANYON*e	APHID	APIOL
APISM	APNEAl	APPEL	*APPRO*	ARABA	ARAME	ARBOR	ARCUS+	ARDEB	ARDRI
ARECA	*ARENE*	*AREPA*	ARGALa	ARGALi	ARGANd	ARGIL	ARGOL	ARGON	ARGOT
ARGUS+	ARHAT	*ARIKI*	ARMER	ARMET	ARMIL	ARNUT	AROBA	*AROHA*	AROID
ARPENt	ARRAS+	ARRET	ARRIS+	ARRISh	ARTEL	*ARUHE*	ASANA	ASDIC	ASPEN
ASPER	ASPISh	*ASPRO*	ASSAIl	*ASSAM*	ASTERn	ASTERt	*ATIGI*	ATIMY+	ATTAP
ATTAR	AUDAD	AUGHT	AUMIL	AURUM	AVENS+	AVGAS+	AVGAS>	AVIAN	AVION
AVISO	*AWATO*	AWETO	AWMRY+	AWNER	AYRIE				

5. Five-Letter Words

```
BABKA  BABOOl BABOOn BACCO  BACCO+ BACCY+ BAGIE  BAKRA  BALTIc BAMBI
BANAK  BANYAn BARCA  BARRAt BARYE  BASANt BASON  BAVIN  BAWTY+ BAYLE
BEEDI+ BEEDIe BEGAR  BEGUM  BEKAH  BELAH  BELAR  BELGA  BELONg BENGA
BENNEt BENNI  BENNY+ BERYL  BETONy BETTA  BETTY+ BEVOR  BEVUE  BHUNA
BIACH+ BIALI  BIALY+ BIALYs BICCY+ BIDDY+ BIDON  BIGHA  BIGOS+ BILBOa
BILBO+ BILBY+ BINIT  BIOME  BIONT  BIPED  BIPOD  BIRSE  BISOM  BLAFF
BLERT  BLUIDy BLYPE  BOCCA  BOCCE  BOCCIa BOCCIe BODLE  BOGAN  BOHEA
BOITE  BOLUS+ BONNEt BOOAI  BOOAY  BORGO  BOSIE  BOSON  BOSUN  BOULE
BOURD  BOURG  BOVID  BOWAT  BOWET  BOYARd BOYLA  BRACT  BRAME  BRAVA
BREVEt BROME  BROMO  BRONCo BROND  BRUGH  BUCHU  BUFTY+ BULSE  BUNIA
BUNYA  BUPPY+ BURET  BURIN  BUROO  BUSBY+ BUTUT  BUTYL  BWANA  BYWAY

CABBY+ CABOC  CADRE  CAGOT  CAHOW  CAIRD  CANID  CAPLEt CAPUL  CARAP
CARON  CARVY+ CASCO  CAVIEr CEBID  CEIBA  CELEB  CELOM  CERCI  CERGE
CERIA  CESTA  CETYL  CHACO  CHACO+ CHANA  CHEKA  CHELAe CHEMO  CHIELd
CHILE  CHIMB  CHIRO  CHIRU  CHOKO  CHOLA  CHOLIc CHOLO  CHOOM  CHOTT
CHUFA  CHYME  CIBOL  CIGGY+ CIMAR  CISCO  CISCO+ CITAL  CIVIE  CIVVY+
CLACHs CLARO  CLARO+ CLARY+ CLAVIe CLEIK  CLOFF  COARB  COBLE  CODON
COGIE  COGON  COGUE  COHAB  COHEN  COLBY+ COLBYs COLIN  COLOG  COMTE
COMUS+ CONGOu CONGO+ CONTE  CONVOy COOCH+ COOER  COPAY  COPPY+ CORBEl
COTAN  COUTA  COVINg COWAL  COWAN  COWRY+ COYPU  CRAIC  CRAIG  CRENA
CRESSy CRIOS+ CRUNK  CRUOR  CRUVE  CRWTH  CUBITi CUDDY+ CUISH+ CULCH+
CULET  CUMEC  CUMIN  CUPPA  CURATe CURCH+ CURIAe CURIAl CURIEt CUSEC
CUSUM  CUTCHa CUTIE  CUTIN  CUTTO+ CUTTOe CUTUP  CUVEE  CYCAD  CYCAS+
CYCLO  CYDER  CYMOL  CYTON

DACHA  DAGGA  DAIKOn DALLE  DAMAN  DAMAR  DANIO  DANNY+ DARAF  DARCYs
DARCY+ DATTO  DAULT  DAVIT  DAWAH  DAYAN  DEBYE  DECAFf DEISM  DEIST
DELPH  DENARi DENARy DERRO  DERRY+ DERTH  DEVON  DEVOTe DEWANi DEWAR
DHOBI  DHOTI  DHUTI  DICOT  DIDIE  DIENE  DINAR  DINIC  DIODE  DIRAM
DISME  DIWAN  DOBBY+ DOBIE  DOBLA  DOBRA  DOBRO  DOGIE  DOHYO  DOLCE
DOLMAn DOLOR  DONKO  DONNAt DONNY+ DOODY+ DORISe DOUAR  DOULA  DOWAR
DOWRY+ DOYLY+ DRERE  DROID  DROIT  DROME  DROOB  DROOG  DRUID  DRUPEl
DRYAD  DSOBO  DSOMO  DUBBO  DUCAT  DUCHY+ DUFUS+ DULIA  DULSE  DUNAM
DUOMO  DUPPY+ DURUM  DUTCH+ DWAAL  DWEEBy DYKON

EAGRE  EASLE  EBBET  EDEMA  EDILE  EGGAR  EGGERy EGRET  EISELl ELCHI
ELDINg ELEGY+ ELEMI  ELIAD  ELPEE  ELSIN  ELVAN  ELVER  EMMER  EMMET
ENATE  ENDER  ENIAC  ENNOG  ENOKI  ENVOI  EOSINe EPHOD  EPHORi EPODE
EPOPT  ERBIA  ERUGO  ERVIL  ESKAR  ESTER  ESTOC  ESTRO  ETAGE  ETHAL
ETHYL  ETTIN  ETUDE  EUPAD  EUSOL  EYRIE

FACIAe FACIAl FAENA  FAKIE* FAKIR  FANUM  FARAD  FARCY+ FATWAh FAUVE
FAVUS+ FELID  FEMALe FEMME  FEMUR  FERIAe FERIAl FETOR  FETUS+ FETWA
FEUAR  FICHE  FICHU  FICIN  FICUS+ FIENT  FINCA  FIORD  FIRIE  FIRTH
FITNA  FLUOR  FLUYT  FLYBYs FOEHN  FOGEY  FOGIE  FOGOU  FOLEY  FOLIE
FOUAT  FOUET  FOUTH  FOVEAe FOVEAl FOWTH  FRAIM  FREITy FREMD  FRERE
FRIER  FRYER  FUCUS+ FUDDY+ FUERO  FUGIE  FUGIO  FURAL  FURANe FUROLe
FURORe FUSILe FYTTE

GADDI  GADGEt GALUTh GALVO  GANOF  GATOR  GAULT  GAYAL  GEBUR  GEIST
GELEE  GELLY+ GEMEL  GEMOTe GENIP  GENNY+ GENOA  GENOMe GENRO  GEODE
GEOID  GERAH  GERBE  GERLE  GESSO+ GHYLL  GIBLI  GIBUS+ GIGOT  GIGUE
```

GILET	GILPY+	GIMEL	GIMMEr	GIPON	GIPPO	GIPPO+	GIPPY+	GIRSH+	GLAURy
GLEBE	GLIFF	GLOGG	GLUON	GLYPH	GOBANg	GODET	GOETY+	GOFER	GOGGA
GOMBO	GOMPA	GONAD	GONIFf	GONOF	GONYS+	GOOBY+	GOPAK	GOPIK	GORSE
GOURA	GOURDe	GOURDy	GOWANy	GOYLE	GRAAL	GRAIP	GREBE	GREBO	GRECE
GRESE	GREVE	GRIKE	GROAT	GROUF	GRRRL	GRUFE	GRYCE	GUACO	GUIRO
GUNNY+	GUPPY+	GURRY+	GUSLAr	GUSLE	GUSLI	GUTTAe	GUYOT	GYNAE	GYNIE
GYNNY+	GYPPO	GYPPY+	GYRUS+						

HACEK	HAICK	HAKIM	HALIDe	HALVAh	HAMAL	HANAP	HANSEl	HAOLE	HAOMA
HARAM	HARIM	HAUGHt	HAYER	HAYLE	HEDERa	HELIO	HEMINa	HENGE	HENRY+
HENRYs	HEPAR	HEUCHs	HEVEA	HIMBO	HINAU	HITHEr	HOAGY+	HODAD	HOGAN
HOGEN	HOKUM	HOLON	HOMIE*	HOMME	HONAN	HOOCH+	HOOEY	HORME	HOTTY+
HOYLE	HUDNA	HUDUD	HUMUSy	HURST	HUTIA	HYDRAe	HYDRO	HYMEN	HYNDE
HYOID	HYPHY+	HYSON	HYTHE						

ICHOR	ICKER	ICTUS+	IFTAR	IHRAM	ILEUS+	ILLTH	IMAGO	IMAGO+	IMARI
IMAUM	IMPOT	INCLE	INCOG	INDIA	INDIE	INDOLe	INDRI	INGAN	INGLE
INION	INKER	INRUN	INTEL	INTROn	INULA	INVAR	INWITh	IODIDe	IODINe
IPPON	IROKO	ISSEI	ISTLE						

KAAMA	KABAR	KAFIR	KAHAL	KALAM	KALPAc	KALPAk	KANDY+	KAPPA	KARRI
KARST	KASHA	KATTI	KAUGH	KAURI	KAURU	KAURY+	KAYLE	KEBAR	KEEMA
KEEVE	KEFIR	KEHUA	KELEP	KELIM	KENAF	KENCH+	KENDO	KEREL	KERMA
KERRY+	KESAR	KEVEL	KHADI	KHAPH	KHAYAl	KHEDAh	KHOUM	KIAAT	KIANG
KIBBEh	KIBBI	KIBLAh	KIDDO	KIDDO+	KIDEL	KIGHT	KILEY	KILIM	KININ
KIORE	KIRRI	KISAN	KITUL	KLETT	KNAUR	KNAWEl	KNOSP	KOBANg	KOFTA
KOGAL	KOINE	KONBU	KOORI	KOORI+	KOPPA	KORMA	KOURA	KRANS+	KRAUT
KREEP	KRENG	KREWE	KRUBI	KUGEL	KULFI	KUMYS+	KURRE	KURTA	KUSSO
KUTCH+	KUTCHa	KWELA	KYLIE	KYLIN	KYLOE	KYRIE			

LAARI	LABDA	LABIS+	LAGAN	LAHAR	LAIGH*	LAITY+	LAKSA	LALDY+	LAMMY+
LAPIN	LAPIS+	LARGO	LATAH	LATKE	LATTEn	LATTEr	LAUAN	LAUND	LAVRA
LAVVY+	LAWINe	LAWINg	LEBEN	LECCY+	LEDUM	LEEAR	LEGIT	LEHUA	LEMAN
LEONE	LEPRA	LESBO	LEVIN	LEWIS+	LIANA	LIANE	LIANG	LIBERo	LIBRAe
LIDAR	LIEGEr	LIEVE*	LIGANd	LIGER	LIGNE	LIKINg	LIMMA	LINAC	LININg
LINUM	LIPIDe	LIPIN	LIVOR	LIVRE	LLANO	LOACH+	LOCUM	LOESS+	LOGAN
LOGIE*	LOGIN	LOHAN	LOLOG	LOOEY	LOOIE	LORAN	LORICa	LORIS+	LOUGH
LOUIE	LOVAT	LOWAN	LOWRY+	LUBRA	LUCRE	LUMEN	LUPUS+	LURGI	LURGY+
LURRY+	LURVE	LUSUS+	LUVVY+	LYASE	LYCEE	LYCRA	LYSINe	LYSINg	LYSOL
LYSSA	LYTHE	LYTTAe							

MACAW	MACLEd	MACON	MACROn	MADGE	MADRE	MAERL	MAFIA	MAFIC	MAGOT
MAHOE	MAHUA	MAHWA	MAISE	MAIST	MAKAR	MALVA	MALWA	MAMBA	MAMEE
MAMEY	MANTO	MANTO+	MANTY+	MANUL	MAPAU	MARON	MAROR	MARRI	MATAI
MATINg	MATLOw	MAUBY+	MAURI	MAVEN	MAVIE	MAVIN	MAVIS+	MBIRA	MEBOS+
MEITH	MELICk	MELIK	MENAD	MENSAe	MENSAl	MERDE	MERSE	MESON	METIF
METOL	MHORR	MIASMa	MICROn	MIDDY+	MIDGEt	MILPA	MINNY+	MITIS+	MNEME
MOBBY+	MOBIE	MOGGY+	MOGUL	MOHEL	MOHUA	MOHUR	MOIRE	MOMUS+	MONDE
MONDO	MONTEm	MONTY+	MORIA	MORROw	MOWRA	MPRET	MUCIN	MUCOR	MUCRO
MUCUS+	MUDIR	MUDRA	MUHLY+	MULSE	MURID	MURTI	MUSAR	MUSIT	MUTHA
MUTON	MVULE	MYLAR	MYOMA	MYOPE	MYOPS+	MYOPY+	MYRRH	MYSID	

5. Five-Letter Words

```
NABLA  NABOB  NADIR  NAEVE  NAGOR  NAHAL  NAIAD  NAIRA  NAIRU  NAKER
NAKFA  NALED  NALLAh NANCY+ NANDU  NANUA  NAPPA  NARAS+ NASHI  NATCH+
NAUCH+ NAVAR  NAWAB  NEAFE  NEBEK  NEBEL  NEELD  NEELE  NEGUS+ NEIVE
NELLY+ NEPER  NEPIT  NERAL  NEROLi NETOP  NEWELl NEWIE  NGANA  NGATI
NGOMA  NICAD  NICHT  NICOL  NIDOR  NIDUS+ NIEVE  NIGER  NIHIL  NIKAB
NIKAH  NIKAU  NINNY+ NINON  NISEI  NISSE  NITON  NITRE  NITROx NKOSI
NONNY+ NONYL  NOWAY  NOYAU  NUBIA  NUDDY+ NUDIE  NYALA  NYSSA


OAKER  OAKUM  OATER  OCCAMy OCTYL  ODEON  ODEUM  ODISM  ODIUM  ODIST
OFFIE  OGGIN  OGHAM  OILERy OKAPI  OLDIE  OLEINe OLEUM  OLLER  OLLIE
OMBER  OMBRE  OMLAH  OMRAH  ONIUM  ONLAY  OOMPH  OOTID  OPEPE  OPSIN
OPTER  ORCINe ORGIAc ORGUE  ORIBI  ORLON  ORLOP  ORMER  ORNIS+ ORPINe
ORRIS+ ORTHO  ORVAL  OSHAC  OSIERy OSMIC  OSMOLe OTARY+ OTTAR  OUBIT
OUSEL  OUTROw OVIST  OVOLO  OVULE  OWCHE  OWLERy OWLET


PACHAk PADLE  PADMA  PADRE  PAEAN  PAEDO  PAGLE  PAGODa PAGRI  PALKI
PAMPA  PANIM  PANKO  PARGO  PARLY+ PASPY+ PATINa PATINe PATKA  PAVANe
PAVINg PAVISe PAWER  PAYER  PAYOR  PEAVY+ PEDRO  PEECE  PEEOY  PEKAN
PEKIN  PEKOE  PELMA  PENGO  PENNIa PERAI  PERDUe PERRY+ PETARd PETARy
PETREl PEWEE  PEWIT  PHAGE  PHEERe PHENE  PHEON  PHOCAe PIBAL  PICCY+
PICRA  PICUL  PIEND  PIGMY+ PIKUL  PILCH+ PILOW  PINOT  PINNAe PINNAl
PINNY+ PINON  PIPUL  PIRAI  PISCO  PISKY+ PISTE  PITON  PITTA  PLAAS+
PLAGE  PLASMa PLEON  PLESH+ PLOUKy PLYER  POAKA  POAKE  POBOY  PODGE
POGEY  POGGE  POILU  POKAL  POKIE* POLISh POMBE  POMMY+ POOVE  PORAE
POTAE  POTINg POTOO  POULE  POULPe POULT  POWAN  POWIN  POYOU  PRAAM
PRAHU  PREON  PREOP  PRESEt PRIEFe PRIER  PRION  PROEM  PRYER  PSEUDo
PSION  PSOAS+ PSYOP  PUBCO  PUBIS+ PUCAN  PUDDY+ PUDGE  PUDOR  PUGIL
PUMIE  PURDAh PURPY+ PUTON  PYGAL  PYRAN


RACON  RADGE* RADON  RAHUI  RAIRD  RAMEE  RAMET  RANEE  RAPHE  RASSE
RAUPO  RAWINg RAYNE  REATA  REATE  REBAR  REBBE  REBECk REBOP  REBUS+
RECITe RECTOr REDAN  REDIAe REDIAl REFFO  REGARd REGGO  REGIE  REGUR
REIRD  REMENd RENGA  RENIN  REPRO  RESIDe RETROd REVUE  REWTH  RHEUMy
RHIME  RHINE  RHINO  RHODY+ RHOMBi RHUMBa RHYNE  RIATA  RICINg RIGOLl
RISHI  RISUS+ RIYAL  ROBLE  ROLAG  ROMEO  RONDE  RONDO  RONIN  ROSHI
ROTCHe ROWAN  ROWEN  ROWME  RUANA  RUBBY+ RUBINe RUBLE  RUDAS+ RUDIE
RUMAL  RUNCH+ RUSMA  RUTIN  RYBAT


SABAL  SABHA  SABINe SABIR  SABOT  SABRA  SADDO  SADDO+ SADHE  SADHU
SAHEB  SAHIBa SAITHe SAKAI  SALAL  SALMI  SALOL  SALOP  SAMFU  SAMMY+
SAOLA  SAPAN  SAPOR  SARAN  SAREE  SARGE  SARGO  SARODe SAROS+ SARUS+
SASER  SASINe SATAI  SATYRa SAUBA  SAUCHs SAUGHy SAURY+ SAVINe SAVINg
SAVOY  SAWAH  SAWER  SAYER  SAYID  SAYON  SCENA  SCHMOe SCHULn SCHWA
SCRAE  SCRIPt SCROD  SCUFT  SEBUM  SEDER  SEDUM  SEGAR  SEGNO  SEHRI
SEITY+ SEKOS+ SELAH  SELVA  SENNA  SENORa SEPAL  SEPOY  SERIF  SERINe
SERINg SERON  SEROW  SERVO  SETON  SEWAN  SEWAR  SEWEL  SEWEN  SEWINg
SHAKO  SHAKO+ SHCHI  SHEOL  SHEVA  SHIAI  SHISO  SHLUB  SHMEK  SHOAT
SHOLA  SHORL  SHOYU  SHTIK  SHURA  SIBYL  SIETH  SIEUR  SIGIL  SIGLA
SIGMA  SILVAe SILVAn SIMBA  SIMUL  SIROC  SIRRAh SISAL  SITAR  SITUS+
SIVER  SKALD  SKEANe SKELF  SKELM  SKOOL  SKORT  SKOSH+ SKRAN  SKYER
SLISH+ SLOYD  SLUSE  SLYPE  SMOWT  SNATHe SNEAD  SNIRT  SNOEK  SOAVE
SOCLE  SODOMy SOGER  SOHUR  SOKAH  SOKOL  SOLUM  SONDEr SONNEt SONNY+
SOPOR  SORGO  SOTOL  SOWAR  SOYLE  SPADO  SPADO+ SPAHI  SPAIT  SPALD
```

78

SPELK SPEOS+ *SPEUG* SPIDEr *SPLOG* SPREDd SPREW SPRITe SPRITz SPRUE
SPRUG SPYAL STADE STERE STILB STIPA STIPEd STIPEl STOEP STOGY+
STOMAl STOND STOOR STOUP STRAE STRAG STREP STULL STULM STUPA
STYLO SUBBY+ SUBER *SUBHA* SUCRE SUDOR *SUGAN* *SUHUR* SUINT SULFA
SULPHa SUMACh SURRA SUSHI SUTOR SUTRA SUTTA SYBBE SYBIL SYLPHy
SYLVAe SYLVAn SYMAR SYNOD SYNTH SYRAH SYREN SYSOP SYTHE SYVER

TAATA TABLA TACAN TAFIA TAIRA TAKHI *TAIKO* TALPAe TALUKa TAMALe
TAPIR TAPIS+ TAPISt TAPPA TATAR TATIE TATOU TAUBE *TAUON* TAUPE
TAWERy TAYRA TEIID *TELCO* TENCH+ *TENGE* TENIAe TENNEr TENNO TENNY+
TENUE TEPOY TERAI TERCEl TERCEt TEREK TERRAe TERRY+ TESLA TETRAd
TETRI TEWEL TEWIT THAGI *THALI* THEGN THEIC THEINe THEOW THETA
THOFT THORPe THRIP THUYA TIBIAe TIBIAl TICAL TIGON TILAK TILDE
TIMBO TIMON TITAN TITRE TITTY+ *TIYIN* TODDY+ TOGUE *TOING* TOISE
TOLYL TOMAN TONDO TOWIE* TRASS+ TREMA TRIACt TRIKE TRULL TUART
TUATH TUGRA TUINA *TUKTU* TULLE *TULPA* TUNNY+ TUPEK TUPIK *TUPLE*
TURBOt TUTEE TUTTI TUTTY+ TUYERe TWIER TWIRPy TWOER TWYERe *TYIYN*
TYLER

UGALI UHLAN UHURU UKASE ULEMA ULMIN ULTRA ULYIE *UMAMI* UMBEL
UMBLE UMBRAe UMBRAl UMBREl UMIACk UMIAK *UMPIE* UPBOW UPSEE UPSEY
URALI URARI URBIA URENA URMAN *URSID* URSON URUBU USNEA USURY+
UVULAe UVULAr

VAKIL VANDAl VARDY+ VARUS+ VARVEd VARVEl VEENA VEGIE VENEY VENINe
VENUS+ VESPA VIAND VICHY+ VIFDA VIGIA VINCA VIRGA VIRGEr VIRTUe
VISNE VISON VISTO VIVDA VOCAB *VODDY+* *VODOUn* VODUN *VOEMA* VOILE
VOLVAe VOUGE VRAIC

WAGGA *WAGYU* WAHOO WEAMB WEBER *WENGE* WHAUP WHAUR WHELKy WHIFT
WHORL WHORT WICCAn WIDDY+ WIFIE WIGAN *WIGGA* WILGA WITAN WOALD
WODGE WOLLY+ WONGA WOOER WURST WUSHU

YAIRD YAKOW *YAMPY+* YAMUN YAPOK YAPON YARFA YARTA YARTO YECCHs
YENTA YENTE YERBA YIPPY+ YIRTH *YITIE* YOWIE YUCCA

5.3.6 OTHER NON-PLURALS

ABRAM ABUNE ACARId ACETAl ACHOO ACINIc ACMIC ACRID* ADDIO ADIOS
ADMAN ADMEN ADRED ADSUM ADUNC ADYTA AECIAl AEDES AESIR AFALD
AGGRI AGGRY *AGUNAh* AIDOI AIDOS *AIGHT* ALGID ALTHO AMICI AMNIA
AMNIC AMPLY ANCONe ANENT ANTRAl *APGAR* APRES APTLY AREIC ARERE
ARRAH ARSIS ARTAL ARVAL ASCUS ASHEN ASKOI ASKOS ASYLA ATRIAl
AULIC AULOI AULOS AUREI AURIS AYGRE

BARIC *BARROw* BASALt BEDAD BEGAT BESAT BESAW BETIDe BIFID BIGLY
BINAL BIVIA *BODHI* *BOEUF* BORIC *BOWIE* BOYAUx BRAVI BREME BYSSI

CABRE CACTI CAECAl CAESE CALID CAPUT CASUS *CAUDAd* *CAUDAe* *CAUDAl*
CAUSAe CAUSAl CECUM CESTI CHIMO CHODE CHOTA CHYND CINCT CIPPI
CIRCAr CIRCS CIRRI CLAES CLOMB CNIDAe CORAM CORIA COUDE CRONK*
CRURAl CULPAe *CUNEI* *CYBER*

```
DAINTy DAMMEd DAMMEr DAWEN  DAYNT  DEDAL  DEFFO  DESHI  DIACT  DIANE
DIBBS  DIDST  DINNAe DIVNA  DOCHT  DOETH  DOGGO  DOILT* DOLCI  DOLIA
DOLOS  DOMAL  DOMIC  DORIC  DOTAL  DOVIE* DOWIE* DRILY  DRYLY  DUCAL
DUMKA  DUMKY  DUNNO  DUOMI  DUPLEt DUPLEx DURST
```

```
EIDOS  EIGNE  ELMEN  ENLIT  ENTIA  EPRISe ERVEN  ETYMA  EVHOE  EVOHE
EYRIR
```

```
FARCIe FARCIn FATLY  FAUGH  FECAL  FECES  FECIT  FENKS  FETID* FEYLY
FILII  FILUM  FOLIAr FOLIC  FOMES  FRENA  FRONS  FRORNe FUBAR  FUGAL
FURCAe FURCAl FURTH*
```

```
GAILY  GAMIC  GANDY  GARDAi GARNI  GELID* GENIC  GENII  GEYAN  GIGHE
GLEBAe GOBAR  GOBBI  GOBBO  GOETH  GONIA  GONNA  GOTTA  GOYIM  GREGE
GRYPT  GYRAL
```

```
HADAL  HAITH  HAMBA  HAPLY  HEAME  HEIGHt HEMAL  HEWGH  HIANT  HIEMS
HILUM  HILUS  HIPLY  HOWBE  HUMIC  HURDS  HYLIC  HYPHAe HYPHAl
```

```
ICILY  ICKLE* ICTAL  ICTIC  ILEUM  ILIUM  IMSHI  IMSHY  INAPT  INCUT
INERM  INFRA  INNIT  INTRA  INUST  ITHER
```

```
KACHA  KAMME  KAPUTt KASME  KIDGE  KIRBY  KLIEG  KOHEN  KRONA  KYDST
```

```
LABIAl LABRAl LAEVO  LAITH  LEGES  LENIS  LEPID  LEUCH  LEUCO  LEVIS
LIBRI  LICIT  LIROTh LITAI  LOBAR  LOBUS  LOCUSt LOGIA  LOIPEn LOUIS
LUACH  LUDIC  LUMME  LYART  LYCEA  LYSIS  LYTIC
```

```
MADID  MAGUS  MEDII  MELBA  MESIC  MESTOm METIS  MEYNT  MICRA  MIFTY
MIKRA  MILCH  MISCH  MODUS  MOIRAi MOOBS  MOULS  MUCIC  MUCID  MUSCAe
MUSCAt MYOID
```

```
NABIS  NAEVI  NAMMA  NARIC  NARRE  NATAL  NATIS  NEIST  NELIS  NERTS
NEVUS  NGWEE  NIDAL  NISUS  NITID  NITRYl NIVAL  NODUS  NOHOW  NOMIC
NOMOI  NOMOS  NOOIT  NOTUM  NUCHAe NUCHAl NUGAE  NUMEN  NUNNY
```

```
OAKEN  OASES  OATEN  OBELIa OBIIT  OCHRY  OCREAe OCULI  OGMIC  OHMIC
OIDIA  OLEIC  OLPAE  ONCUS  ONELY  ONKUS  ONTIC  OORIE* ORGIC  OSSIA
OSTIAl OTAKU  OUENS  OURIE* OUTBYe OUTREd OVOLI  OWRIE*
```

```
PADRI  PAOLI  PAOLO  PARVE  PATLY  PEDES  PELON  PENNAe PENNAl PEPLA
PERDY  PETITe PETRI  PETTI  PETTO  PHPHT  PILUM  PILUS  PIROGi PLENA
PLICAe PLICAl PODIAl POUPT  PRESA  PRUTAh PSOAE  PSOAI  PUDIC  PULMO
PUTID  PYOID  PYRAL  PYRIC
```

```
RAGDE  RAMAL  RAWLY  REBITe RECTAl RECTI  REDLY  REFED  REGESt REGNAl
RELIT  REMET  REPLAn REPLAy RETIAl REWAN  REWON  RHYTA  RIANT  RIBES
ROGUY  RONNEl RORIC  RORID  RORIE* RUBAI  RUBUS  RUMLY  RUNIC  RUSSEl
RUSSEt
```

SACRAl	SAGUM	SALIC	SAPID	SAYNE	SCALAe	SCALAr	SCEATt	SEDES	*SEFER*
SEGNI	SENGI	SHAKT	SHILY	*SHIUR*	SHTUMm	SIELD	*SIPPY*	*SITKA*	*SNOEP*
SNUCK	SOLUS	SOOEY	SOPRA	SORUS	SOUCT	SPAKE	SPUTA	STOLN	*STRAKe*
STRIAe	STURE	STYLIe	SUCCI	*SUENT*	SULCI	SULFO	SUPRA	SWOLN	

TABES	TANTO	TARDO	*TARGA*	TAWIE*	TECTAl	TELIAl	TELIC	TELOI	TELOS
TERGAl	TERTS	TEUCH*	THAIM	THECAe	THECAl	THELF	THILK	THOLI	THORON
THRAE	THYMIc	TICCA	TOMIAl	TONAL	TONDI	TORUS	*TRABS*	TRANSe	TRILD
TRISTe	TROIS	TRYMA	TUMID	TURPS	TYPAL	TYPIC			

ULPAN	UMPTY	UNAPT	UNBID	UNCUS	UNDUG	UNETH	UNGOT	UNHIP^	UNKED
UNKET	UNKID	UNLED	UNREDy	UNRID	UNSOD	UNWET	UNWONt	UPLIT	*UPTER*
URAEI	UREIC	URNAL	UTERI						

VACUA	VAGAL	VAGUS	VAPID*	VATIC	VELUM	*VERRA*	VERRY	VIMEN	VINIC
VITTAe	VOCES	VOGIE*	VOILA	VOULU	VULGO				

WANLE	WANLY	WARREd	WARREn	WARREy	WERSH*	WETLY	WHILK	WHOSO	WILCO
WIRRAh	WOFUL^	*WOMYN*	WOWEE	WROTH					

YAWEY	YCLED	YDRED	YEWEN	YINCE	YOKUL	YOMIM	YONKS	YRIVD	YUCCH
YUMMO									

5.4 VERY IMPROBABLE LESS FAMILIAR FIVES

AKKAS	*BIZZO*	*BIZZY+*	*BUBBA*	BUBBY+	**BUZZY***	CHIZZ	COCCIc	COCCId	COCCO
DEKKO	*DUKKAh*	FEOFF	*FEZZY*	FLAFF	**FUFFY***	HAJJI	**HOKKU**	HUZZAh	HUZZY+
IZZAT	KAIAK	*KAIKAi*	KAPOK	**KERKY***	**KICKY***	KIKOI	*KLICK*	KOKER	KOKUM
KOPEK	*KRUNK*	KUKRI	KULAKi	**LAZZI**	**LAZZO**	*LEZZA*	LEZZY+	MAMMAe	MAMMAl
MAMMY+	*MEKKA*	MEZZE	MEZZO	*MIZZY*	MOMMA	MOMMY+	**MUZZY***	*OZZIE*	**PAKKA**
PAPPI	PAPPY*	**PEPPY***	PIPPY*	POPPA	POZZY+	**PUKKA**	PZAZZ+	SCUZZy	SKANKy
SKRIKe	SPAZZ	*SUKUK*	SWIZZ	TAZZA	**TAZZE**	TIKKA	TIZZY+	*WOKKA*	XEROX
YAKKA	YUKKY*	ZANZA	ZANZE	ZAZEN	ZIZEL	ZIZITh	**ZUZIM**		

81

6. SIX-LETTER WORDS

6.1 FAMILIAR SIXES

6.1.1 VERBS IN COMMON USE

ABDUCT	ABOUND	ABRADEr	ABSEIL	ABSORB	ACCEDEr	ACCEPT	ACCESS	ACCOST
ACCRUE	ACCUSEr	ACQUIT>	ACQUITe	ADHEREr	ADJOINt	ADJUST	ADMIREr	ADVISEe
ADVISEr	AERATE	AFFECT	AFFIRM	AFFORD	ALIGHT	ALLEGEr	ALLUDE	ALLUREr
AMBUSH	ANCHOR	ANOINT	ANSWER	APPEAL	APPEAR	APPEND	AROUSEr	ARREST
ARRIVEr	ASCEND	ASPIREr	ASSAIL	ASSERT	ASSESS	ASSIGN	ASSIST	ASSUMEr
ASSUREr	ATTACHe	ATTACK	ATTAINt	ATTEND	ATTEST	ATTIRE	ATTUNE	AVENGEr
AVIATE	AWAKEN							

BAFFLEr	BANISH	BANTER	BARTER	BATTERo	BATTERy	BATTLEr	BECALM	BECKON
BECOMEd	BEFALLd	BEHAVEr	BEHEAD	BEHOLDd	BEHOVE	BELLOW	BELONG	BEMOAN
BERATE	BESTOW	BETRAY	BICKER	BILLET	BILLOWy	BISECT	BLANCH	BLEACH
BLUDGEr	BOGGLEr	BOOGIE	BOOGIE=	BORROW	BOTHER	BOTTLEr	BOUNCEr	BRAISE
BRANCHy	BREACH	BROACH	BROWSEr	BRUISEr	BUBBLEr	BUCKLEr	BUDGET	BUMBLEr
BUNDLEr	BUNGLEr	BURDEN	BURGLE	BURROW	BUSTLEr	BUTTERy	BUTTONy	BYPASS

CACKLEr	CAJOLEr	CANCEL	CANCEL>	CANTER	CARESS	CAVORT	CEMENTa	CENSOR
CHANGEr	CHARGEr	CHOOSEd	CHOOSEr	CHOOSEy	CIRCLEr	CIRCLEt	CLAMOR	CLEAVEr
CLENCH	CLINCH	CLOTHE	CLUTCHy	COBBLEr	CODDLEr	CODIFY	COERCEr	COHOST
COLOURy	COMMIT>	COMPEL>	COMPLY	CONCUR>	CONFER>	CONVEY	CORNER	COSIGN
COSSET	COSTAR>	COSTARd	COUPLEr	COUPLEt	CRADLEr	CREASEr	CREATE	CREDIT
CRINGEr	CROUCH	CRUISEr	CRUNCHy	CUDDLEr	CURDLEr			

DABBLEr	DAMAGEr	DAMPEN	DANGLEr	DARKEN	DAWDLEr	DAZZLEr	DEADEN	DEAFEN
DEBASEr	DEBATEr	DECANT	DECIDEr	DECODEr	DECREEr	DECREEt	DEDUCE	DEDUCT
DEEPEN	DEFACEr	DEFAMEr	DEFEAT	DEFECT	DEFEND	DEFILEr	DEFINEr	DEFRAY
DEFUSEr	DELETE	DELIST	DELUDEr	DEMAND	DEMEANe	DEMIST	DEMOTE	DENOTE
DENUDEr	DEPART	DEPEND	DEPICT	DEPLOY	DEPORT	DEPOSEr	DERAIL	DERIDEr
DERIVEr	DESERT	DESIGN	DESIREr	DESIST	DETACH	DETAIL	DETAIN	DETECT
DETEST	DETOUR	DEVISEe	DEVISEr	DEVOTEe	DEVOUR	DIDDLEr	DIDDLEy	DIFFER
DIGEST	DILATEr	DILUTEe	DILUTEr	DIRECT*	DISARM	DISMAYd	DISMAYl	DISOWN
DISPEL>	DISTIL>	DISTILl	DITHERy	DIVERT	DIVEST	DIVIDEr	DODDERy	DONATE
DOODLEr	DOUBLEr	DOUBLEt	DREDGEr	DRENCH				

ELAPSE	ELICIT	EMBALM	EMBARK	EMBODY	EMBOSS	EMERGE	EMPLOYe	ENABLEr
ENCAGE	ENCODEr	ENDEAR	ENDUREr	ENGAGEe	ENGAGEr	ENGULF	ENLIST	ENRICH
ENSUREr	ENTAIL	ENTICEr	ENTOMB	ENTRAP>	EQUATE	ESCAPEe	ESCAPEr	ESCORT
EVOLVEr	EXCEED	EXCITEr	EXCUSEr	EXEMPT	EXHALE	EXHUMEr	EXPAND	EXPECT
EXPEND	EXPIREr	EXPORT	EXPOSEr	EXTEND	EXTORT			

FALTER	FASTEN	FATHER	FATTEN	FAVOUR	FESTER	FIDDLEr	FIDDLEy	FIDGETy
FIGUREr	FILLET	FILTER	FINISH	FIZZLE	FLAUNTy	FLAVORy	FLEECEr	FLINCH

FLOWERy FOLLOW FONDLEr FORAGEr FORBIDe FORBID> FOREGOe FORGETe FORGET>
FOSTER FREEZEe FREEZEr FROLIC& FULFILl FULFIL> FUMBLEr

GABBLEr GALLOP GAMBLEr GAMBOL GAMBOL> GARBLEr GARDEN GARGLEr GATHER
GIGGLEr GLANCEr GOBBLEr GOSSIPy GOSSIP> GOVERN GREASEr GRIEVEr GROVEL
GROVEL> GURGLEt GUZZLEr GYRATE

HAGGLEr HAMMER HAMPER HANDLEr HANKER HAPPEN HARASS HARDEN HASSLE
HASTEN HECKLEr HIJACK HINDER HOBBLEr HOGTIE= HONOUR HUDDLEr HURDLEr
HURTLE HUSTLEr

IGNITEr IGNOREr IMBIBEr IMPACT IMPALEr IMPAIR IMPART IMPEDEr IMPORT
IMPOSEr IMPOSEx INCANT INCITEr INDENT INDICT INDUCEr INDUCT INFECT
INFEST INFORM INHALEr INJECT INJUREr INSERT INSIST INSTAL> INSTALl
INSTIL> INSTILl INSULT INSUREr INTEND INVADEr INVENT INVERT INVEST
INVITEe INVITEr INVOKEr IONISEr IONIZEr

JABBER JANGLEr JIGGLE JOSTLEr JUGGLEr JUMBLEr

KIDNAP KIDNAP> KINDLEr KOWTOW

LABOUR LAMENT LATHERy LESSEN LIAISE LIMBER* LINGER LISTEN LITTERy
LOCATEr LOITER LOOSEN LOATHE*

MADDEN MALIGN MANAGEr MANGLEr MARKET MAROON MASTERy MATTERy MATURE*
MEDDLEr MELLOW* MELLOWy MENACEr MINGLEr MISLAYe MISUSEr MODIFY MOLEST
MOTHERy MUDDLEr MUFFLEr MUMBLEr MURDER MURMUR MUSTER MUTATE MUTTER

NARROW* NATTERy NEATEN NEEDLEr NEGATEr NESTLEr NIBBLEr NIGGLEr NOBBLEr
NOTATE NOTICEr NOTIFY NUMBER NUZZLEr

OBJECT OBLIGEe OBLIGEr OBSESS OBTAIN OCCUPY OFFEND OFFSETe OPPOSEr
ORDAIN ORIENT OUTBIDe OUTBID> OUTBOX OUTEATe OUTLAYe OUTRUNe OUTRUNg
OUTRUN> OUTWIT> OUTWITh OVERDOe OVERDOg

PACIFY PADDLEr PAMPERo PANDER PARDON PATROL> PEDDLEr PERISH PERMIT>
PERUSEr PESTER PICKET PICKLEr PIDDLEr PIERCEr PILFERy PLAGUEr PLAGUEy
PLEASEr PLEDGEe PLEDGEr PLEDGEt PLOUGH PLUNGEr POCKET POISON POLICEr
POLISH PONDER POTTERy POUNCEr POUNCEt POWDERy PRAISEr PRANCEr PREACHy
PREFER> PREPAYe PROFIT PROMPT* PROPEL> PUCKERy PUMMELo PUMMEL> PUNISH
PURIFY PURSUEr PUZZLEr

QUAVERy QUENCH QUIVERy

RAFFLEr RAMBLEr RANKLE RATIFY RATION RATTLEr RAVAGEr RAVISH REBINDe
REBOOT REBUFF REBUKEr RECALL RECANT RECEDE RECITEr RECKON RECOIL
RECOOK RECORD RECOUPe REDDEN REDEALe REDEALt REDEEM REDIAL REDIAL>
REDRAWe REDRAWn REDUCEr REFILL REFILM REFINEr REFORM REFUEL REFUEL>

REFUND REFUSEr REFUTEr REGAIN REGALEr REGARD REGRET> REHANG REHASH
REHEAR~~d~~ REHEAR~~d~~ REHEAT REHEEL REJECT REJOIN RELATEr RELENT RELINE
RELISH RELIST RELIVEr RELOAD REMAIN REMARK REMIND REMOVEr RENAME
RENDER REOPEN REPACK REPAIR REPEAL REPEAT REPENT REPLANt REPLAY
REPORT REREAD~~d~~ RESCUEr RESEAL RESELL~~d~~ RESEND~~d~~ RESENT RESIDEr RESIGN
RESIST RESIZE RESORT RESULT RESUMEr RETAIL RETAIN RETELL~~d~~ RETEST
RETIREe RETIREr RETURN RETYPE REVAMP REVEAL REVEREr REVERT REVIEW
REVILEr REVISEr REVIVEr REVOKEr REVOLT REWARD REWIND REWORD REWORK
REWRAP> REWRAPt REZONE ROTATE RUFFLEr RUMBLEr RUSTLEr

SADDEN SADDLEr SALUTEr SAMPLEr SAVOURy SCATHE SCORCH SCOTCH SCRAPEr
SCRAWLy SCREAMo SCREEN SCROLL SCULPT SCURRY SEARCH SECEDEr SECURE*
SEDATE* SEDUCEr SEETHEr SELECTa SETTLEr SHELVEr SHIELD SHIVERy SHOWERy
SHRIEKy SHRINK~~d~~ SICKEN SIGNAL SIGNAL> SIMMER SIMPER SIZZLEr SKETCHy
SMOOCHy SMOOTH* SMOOTHy SMOOTH+ SMUDGEr SNATCHy SNEEZEr SNIVEL SNIVEL>
SNOOZEr SOFTEN SOLDER SOOTHE* SOZZLE SPLASHy SPLICEr SPONGEr SPRAINt
SPRAWLy SPREAD~~d~~ SPRINGe SPRINGy SPRINT SPROUT SPRUIK SQUARE* SQUASHy
SQUAWKy SQUEAKy SQUEAL SQUINT* SQUINTy SQUIRMy SQUIRT STAPLEr STARVEr
STEADY* STIFLEr STITCH STRAFEr STRAINt STRAND STREAMy STRESS STRIDE~~d~~
STRIDEr STRIKE~~d~~ STRIKEr STRINGy STRIPEr STRIPEy STRIVEn STRIVEr STROKEn
STROKEr STROLL STYMIE STYMIE= SUBDUEr SUBLET~~d~~ SUBMIT> SUCKLEr SUFFER
SUMMON SUPPLY SURVEY SWATHEr SWERVEr SWITCHy SWIVEL SWIVEL>

TACKLEr TAMPER TANGLEr TARGET TATTOO TEETER TEETHEr TETHER THATCHt
THATCHy THIEVE THRASH THREADy THRESH THRILLy THRIVEn THRIVEr THRUST
THWART TICKLEr TINGLEr TINKER TINKLEr TIPPLEr TITTER TODDLEr TOGGLEr
TOOTLEr TOPPLE TOTTERy TOUSLE TRAVEL TRAVEL> TRIPLEt TRIPLEx TRUDGEn
TRUDGEr TUMBLEr TWITCHy TYPIFY

UNBOLT UNCORK UNFOLD UNHANDy UNHOOK UNLACE UNLOAD UNLOCK UNPACK
UNPLUG> UNROLL UNSEAT UNVEIL UNWIND~~d~~ UNWRAP> UPDATEr UPHOLD~~d~~ UPLOAD
UPROOT

VACATE VANISH VERIFY VILIFY

WADDLEr WAFFLEr WAGGLEr WALLOP WALLOW WANDER WANGLEr WARBLEr WAYLAY~~d~~
WEAKEN WHEEZEr WHINGEr WHINGE= WHINNY* WHITEN WIGGLEr WINNOW WITHER
WOBBLEr WONDER WORSEN WRENCH WRITHEn WRITHEr

6.1.2 VERBS MORE OFTEN USED IN OTHER PARTS OF SPEECH

ABJECT ABSENT ACCENT ACCORD ACTION ADDICT AMOUNT ANNEXE ANTHEM
ARCADE ARMOURy ASPECT ASSENT AUTHOR

BABBLEr BADGER BALLADe BALLET BALLOT BALSAMy BANNER BARBER BARNEY
BARREL BARREL> BASSETt BASSET> BATTEN BEACON BEAGLEr BEAUTY BEAVERy
BEETLEr BEGGARy BETTER BEWARE BINGLE BIOPSY BIRDIE= BISHOP BITTER*

BITTERn	BLIGHTy	BLOODY*	BLOTCHy	BLOUSE	BONNET	BORDER	BOTTOM	BRANDY
BRAZEN	BREAST	BREATHe	BREATHy	BREECH	BREEZE	BRIDGE	BRIDLEr	BROKERy
BRONZEn	BRONZEr	BROOCH	BRUNCH	BUCKET	BUFFER	BUFFET	BUGGERy	BULLET
BUMPER	BUNKER	BURLEY*	BUSHEL	BUSHEL>	BUTLERy	BYLINEr		

CALLUS	CAMBER	CAMPUS	CANARY	CANDLEr	CANNON	CANOPY	CANVASs	CAREER
CARNAL>	CARPET	CARTON	CASKET	CASTLE	CATNAP>	CAUCUS	CAVEAT	CAVERN
CELLAR	CENSUS	CENTER	CENTRE	CENTRE=	CHANCEl	CHANCEr	CHANCEy	CHEESE
CHERRY*	CHISEL	CHISEL>	CHORUS	CHORUS>	CHROMEl	CHURCHy	CINDERy	CLARET
CLIMAX	CLIQUEy	CLOSET	COCKLEr	COCOON	COFFER	COFFINg	COLLARd	COLLIEr
COMBAT	COMBAT>	COMMON	CONVEX	CONVOY	COPPERy	COQUET>	CORDON	CORPSE
CORRAL>	CORSET	COTTONy	COURSEr	COWARD	COWBOY	CRANNY	CRATER	CRAVAT>
CRAYON	CRUTCH	CUCKOO	CUDGEL	CUDGEL>	CURATE	CUTTLE		

DAGGER	DANGER	DAPPLE	DEACON	DELUGE	DEMISE	DEMURE*	DIALOG	DIAPER
DIESEL	DIMPLE	DINNER	DISUSE	DIVINE*	DOCKET	DOCTOR	DOGEAR	DOGLEG>
DOLLOP	DOUCHE	DRIVEL	DRIVEL>	DUPLEX				

EARWIG>	EFFECT	EGRESS	EMBLEMa	ENAMEL	ENAMEL>	ENCORE	ENGINEr	ENSIGN
ESTATE	ESTEEM	EUCHRE	EXCEPT	EXCESS	EXCISE	EXPERT	EYELET	EYELET>

FABRIC&	FACTORy	FAGGOTy	FALLOW*	FAMOUS	FATHOM	FEEBLE*	FELLOW	FERRETy
FETTLEr	FICKLE*	FILLIP	FINGER	FLANGEr	FLIGHTy	FLURRY	FODDER	FONDUE
FONDUE=	FOOTER	FOREST	FORMATe	FORMAT>	FRENCH	FRENZY	FRIDGE	FRIEND
FRIEZE	FRIGHT	FRINGE	FULLERy	FUNNEL	FUNNEL>	FURROWy		

GAGGLE	GAMBIT	GANDER	GARAGEy	GARISH	GARLIC&	GARTER	GASBAG>	GENDER
GENTLE*	GETTER	GHETTO	GHETTO+	GIBBER	GINGERy	GIRDLEr	GLAMOR	GOGGLEr
GOLDEN*	GOPHER	GOSPEL>	GRANNY	GRAVELy	GRAVEL>	GROOVEr	GROUCHy	GROUND
GROUSE*	GRUDGEr	GUFFAW	GUTTERy					

HACKLEr	HACKLEt	HALTERe	HANGAR	HARBOR	HARROW	HATTER	HAUNCH	HAZARD
HEARSE	HEEHAW	HELMET	HERALD	HICCUPy	HICCUP>	HIGHER	HITHER	HOICKS
HOLLOW*	HOMAGEr	HONCHO	HOODOO	HOORAY	HOOVER	HOSTEL	HOSTEL>	HOTDOG>
HOTTER	HUMBLE*	HUMBUG>	HUMOUR	HUNGER	HYPHEN			

IMPOST	INFIRM*	INTERNe	ISLAND

JACKAL>	JACKET	JARGONy	JIGGER	JIGSAWn	JINGLEr	JINGLEt	JOCKEY	JUNKET
JUNKET>							

KENNEL	KENNEL>	KERNEL	KERNEL>	KIPPER	KITTENy	KNIGHT	KOSHER	KYBOSH

LACKEY	LADDERy	LARIAT	LAUREL	LAUREL>	LAVISH*	LAWYER	LEADEN	LEAGUEr
LECHERy	LEDGER	LESION	LESSON	LETTERn	LICHEN	LIQUOR	LOCUSTa	LOGJAM>
LOPPER	LOUNGEr	LOUNGEy	LUMBER	LUSTER	LUSTRE			

```
MADAME  MALICE  MANTLEt  MANUREr  MARBLEr  MARGIN  MARROWy  MARTYRy  MARVEL
MARVEL> MENAGE  MENTOR   MIDDLEr  MILDEWy  MINUTE* MIRROR   MISFIT>  MISHAP>
MISHAPt MISHITd MISHIT>  MISTERm  MISTERy  MOCKERy MONKEY   MORSEL   MORSEL>
MORTARy MOTION  MOTIVE   MOUSSE   MUSCLE   MUTINY  MUZZLEr

NAPALM  NATURE  NETTLEr  NEUTER   NICKEL   NICKEL> NIGGERy  NIPPER   NIPPLE
NOODLE  NUANCE  NUGGETy  NUGGET>  NUTMEG>

OCCULT  OPAQUE* OPIATE   OPTION   ORACLE   ORGASM  ORPHAN   OUTCRY   OUTFIT>
OUTLAW  OUTPUTd OUTPUT>  OYSTER

PACKET  PALATE  PALLET   PARADEr  PARCEL   PARCEL> PARENT   PARODY   PAROLEe
PARROTy PASTOR  PATENT   PATTERn  PAUNCHy  PAUPER  PEBBLE   PELLET   PENCIL
PENCIL> PEOPLEr PEPPERy  PERIOD   PESTLE   PETROL> PHONEY   PHRASEr  PICNIC&
PIFFLEr PIGEON  PILLAR   PILLOWy  PINCER   PINION  PIRATE   PISTOLe  PISTOL>
PLIGHT  POLLENt PORTER   POSSUM   POSTERn  POTASH  POWWOW   PRECIS*  PRECISe
PRECUTd PREFIX  PRESETd  PRETTY   PRIEST   PRINCE  PRISON   PSYCHE   PUDDLEr
PUMICEr PURPLE* PUTTER

QUARRY  QUICHE

RABBITo RABBITy RABBLEr  RACKETt  RACKETy  RAFTER  RANSOM   RAVINE   REALLY
REASON  REBATEr RECESS   REFLEX   REFLUX   REFUGEe REMAKEd  REMAKEr  REMAND
REMEDY  RENOWN  REPAST   REPOSEr  REPUTE   RETAKEd RETAKEn  RETAKEr  RETARD
RETORT  RHUMBA  RIBBONy  RIDDLEr  RIPPLEr  RIPPLEt RIPSAWn  ROCKET   ROSTER
ROTUND* ROTUNDa RUBBERy  RUBBLE   RUMOUR   RUSSETy

SAFARI  SAFETY  SALARY   SALLOW*  SALLOWy  SANDAL  SANDAL>  SAVAGE*  SCHEMEr
SCHOOLe SCREED  SCRIBEr  SCRIPT   SCUNGE   SCYTHEr SEASON   SECONDe  SECONDi
SECONDo SECRET* SECRETa  SECRETe  SECTOR   SEESAW  SEQUIN   SERENE*  SERMON
SETTER  SHADOWy SHAMMY   SHEATHe  SHEATHy  SHOVEL  SHOVEL>  SHRIKE   SHRILL*
SHRILLy SHRIMPy SHRINE   SHROUDy  SHROVE   SICKLE  SICKLY*  SIGNET   SILAGE
SILAGE= SILKEN  SILVERn  SILVERy  SIMPLE*  SIMPLEx SINGLEt  SINNER   SIPHON
SISTER  SKEWER  SKIVVY   SLALOM   SLAVERy  SLEDGEr SLEEVEr  SLEIGHt  SLEUTH
SLIGHT* SLIVER  SLOUCHy  SLUDGE   SLUICE   SLURRY  SMITHY   SOCKET   SODDEN
SOLACEr SOMBER* SOMBRE*  SONNET   SORROW   SORTIE= SOURCE   SPEECH   SPHERE
SPIRAL  SPIRAL> SPIRITy  SPLINE   SPLINT   SPOUSE  SPRUCE*  SQUALLy  SQUIRE
STABLE* STARCHy STENCHy  STEREO   STICKY   STOOGE  STOUSH   STRAIT*  STREAKy
STREETy STROBE  STUCCO   STUCCO+  SUBWAY   SUCKER  SUFFIX   SUITOR   SUMMERy
SUMMIT  SUNTAN> SUPPER   SUPPLE*  SURETY   SUTURE  SYMBOLe  SYPHON

TABLET  TABLET> TAILOR   TAMPON   TARIFF   TARMAC& TASSEL1  TASSEL>  TATTERy
TELLER  TEMPERa TENANT   TENDER*  TENURE   THIRSTy THREAT   THROATy  THRONE
THRONG  TICKET  TILLER   TIMBERy  TINSEL   TINSEL> TIPTOE=  TISSUEy  TOILET
TOMCAT> TONGUE  TORQUEr  TRANCEy  TRAPES   TREBLE  TREMOR   TRENCH   TRIAGE
TRIFLEr TRIPLY  TROPHY   TROUGH   TROUPEr  TROWEL  TROWEL>  TRUANT   TUCKER
TUMULT  TUNNEL  TUNNEL>  TURNIPy  TURTLEr  TUSSLE  TWINGE   TWINGE=  TYRANT
```

UMPIRE UNFAIR* UNREST UNTIDY* UPLIFT UPROAR UPTAKEd UPTAKEn UPTURN
UPWINDd

VACUUM VAPOURy VECTOR VELVETy VENEER VERBAL> VIRGIN VISION VITTLE
VOLLEY VOLUME VOODOO VOYAGEr

WAGGON WAITER WANTON* WARDEN WARDER WASHERy WASTERy WATTLE WEAPON
WEASELy WEASEL> WEEWEE WEIGHTy WELTER WHOOSH WIDDLE WILDER WILLOWy
WINDOWy WINTERy WOODEN* WORTHY WREATHe WREATHy

YABBIE YELLOW* YELLOWy YOICKS

ZIGZAG> ZIPPER

6.1.3 NOUNS IN COMMON USE

ABACUS+ ACACIA ACUMEN ADVENT ADVERB ADVICE AFFAIRe AGENCY+ AGENDA
AIRWAY ALBINO ALCOVEd ALKALIc ALKALIn ALKALI+ ALMONDy AMOEBAe AMOEBAn
AMPERE AMULET ANGINAl ANGLER ANGORA ANIMAL ANORAK ANTLER APATHY+
APIARY+ APLOMB ARCHERy ARDOUR ARMADA ARMFUL ARMORY+ ARMPIT ARTERY+
ARTISTe ASCENT ASTHMA ASYLUM ATRIUM AUNTIE AURORAe AURORAl AUTISM
AUTUMNy AVENUE AVIARY+ AWNING AZALEA

BABOON BACKER BACKUP BAILER BAKERY+ BAMBOO BANANA BANDITo BANGER
BANGLEd BANKER BANTAM BARIUM BARLEY BARROW BASALT BASKET BATHER
BAUBLE BAZAAR BEAKER BEANIE BEARER BEATER BEDBUG BEDLAMp BEDPAN
BEDSIT BEEPER BEIGEL BELFRY+ BELIEF BENDER BESIDE BIDDER BIGAMY+
BIGWIG BIKINI BINDERy BISTRO BLAZER BLONDE* BLOWER BLOWUP BOATER
BOBCAT BODICE BOFFINg BOILERy BOLTER BOMBER BONBON BOOBOOk BOOKIEr
BOOTEE BOOTIE BOOZER BOPPER BOTANY+ BOUNTY+ BOWLER BOWSER BREWERy
BRIBERy BROLGA BRUMBY+ BUDGIE BUGLER BUMBAG BUMMER BUNKUM BUNYIP
BUREAUx BURGER BURIAL BURNER BUSKER BUSTER BUTANE BUZZER BYROAD

CABBIE CACTUS+ CADGER CALICO CALICO+ CALLER CALORY+ CAMERAe CAMERAl
CAMPERy CANAPE CANCAN CANCER CANDOR CANNERy CANYON CAPTOR CARAFE
CARBON CARROTy CARTEL CARTER CARVERy CASHEW CASINO CASTORy CATGUT
CAVIARe CAVITY+ CELERY+ CEREAL CERVIX+ CHALET CHAPEL CHASER CHEQUEr
CHERUB CHILLI CHOICE* CICADAe CINEMA CIRCUSy CITRUSy CLAUSE CLERGY+
CLERIC CLICHEd CLIENT CLINIC CLOVERy COBALT COBBER COBWEB COFFEE
COGNAC COHORT COLONY+ COLUMN COMEDY+ CONDOM CONDOR CONSOLe CONSULt
COOKERy COOKIE COPIER CORNEAe CORNEAl CORNETt CORONAe CORONAl COUGAR
COUNTY+ COUPON COUSIN COYOTE CRECHE CRETIN CRITIC CROTCH+ CUPFUL
CURFEW CURLER CURLEW CURSORy CUSTOM CUTLET CUTOFF CUTTER CYGNET
CYMBALo

DAMSEL DANCER DASHER DEALER DEARTH DEBTOR DECADE DECEIT DEGREEd
DENIAL DEPUTY+ DESPOT DEVICE DIGGER DIMWIT DINGHY+ DISCUSs DOBBER
DOCKER DODDLE DODGERy DOLLAR DOMAINe DOMINO DOMINO+ DONKEY DOSAGE
DOTAGE DOWNER DRAGON DRAWER DRIVER DRONGO DRONGO+ DROPSY+ DROVER
DUFFER DUGONG DUGOUT DURESSe DURIAN DUSTER DYNAMO

EARFUL EARNER EATERY+ ÉCLAIR EDITOR EFFIGY+ EFFORT EGGCUP EIGHTH
EIGHTY+ ELEVEN ELIXIR EMBRYOn EMPIRE ENDIVE ENERGY+ ENIGMA ENTITY+
ENTRÉE ENZYME EQUITY+ ERASER ERMINEd ERRAND EULOGY+ EUNUCH EXODUS+
EXPIRY+ EXTENT EYEFUL EYELID

FAÇADE FALCON FAMILY+ FAMINE FARMERy FAUCET FEEDER FEELER FELONY+
FEMALE FENCER FENDER FERVOR FETISH+ FIANCEe FIASCO FIASCO+ FIBBERy
FIESTA FILLER FINALE FINDER FINERY+ FISHERy FITTER FIZZER FLAGON
FLORIN FOETUS+ FOIBLE FOLDER FORGERy FOSSIL FOURTH FRAMER FRYPAN
FUNGUS+ FUSION FUTURE

GADGETy GAIETY+ GAITER GALAXY+ GALLEY GALLON GANGER GANNET GARNET
GASKET GAZEBO GAZEBO+ GEISHA GENIUS+ GENTRY+ GERUND GEYSER GIBBON
GIGOLO GIRDER GLIDER GLITCHy GOALIE GOANNA GOATEEd GOBLET GOBLIN
GODSON GOITREd GOLFER GRADER GRANGEr GRATER GRINGO GROCERy GROPER
GROTTO GROTTO+ GROWER GROWTHy GUINEA GUITAR GULLET GUMNUT GUNNERa
GUNNERy GUSHER GUTFUL GYPSUM

HACKERy HAILER HAIRDO HAMLET HANGER HANGUP HARLOT HATPIN HATRED
HAWKER HEADER HEALER HEALTHy HEARTH HEATER HEAVEN HEELER HEIGHTh
HELIUM HELPER HERESY+ HERMIT HERNIAe HERNIAl HEROINe HEYDAY HIATUS+
HIPPIE* HITTER HOBBIT HOCKEY HOLDER HOLDUP HOMBRE HOOKER HOOKEY
HOOKUP HOOPLA HOOTER HOPPER HORNER HORNET HORROR HOTBED HOTPOT
HOTROD HOWLER HUBCAP HUNTER HYBRID

ICEBOX+ ICECAP ICICLEd IDIOCY+ IGUANA IMPALA INCEST INCOMEr INDIGO
INDIGO+ INDOOR INFANTa INFANTe INFLUX+ INJURY+ INMATE INROAD INSECT
INSIDEr INSTEP INTAKE INTENT* INWARD IODINE ITALIC

JAGUAR JAILER JALOPY+ JAMJAR JERSEY JESTER JETSAM JOGGER JOINERy
JOTTER JUGFUL JUICER JUMPER JUNGLEd JUNIOR

KARATE KEEPER KETTLE KEYPAD KICKER KIDNEY KILLER KIMONO KISSER

LAGOON LANCER LAPTOP LARDER LARYNX+ LAYOFF LEADER LEAVER LEEWAY
LEGACY+ LEGEND LEGION LEGUME LENDER LENGTHy LENTIL LESSEE LESSOR
LEVITY+ LIBIDO LIFTER LINEUP LIQUID LITANY+ LITMUS+ LIZARD LOADER
LOAFER LOCALE LOCKER LOCKET LOCKUP LODGER LOGGER LOOKER LOOTER
LOQUAT LOTION LOUVREd LOWBOY LUNACY+ LURKER LUXURY+ LYCHEE

MAGGOTy MAGNETo MAGNUM MAGPIE MAIDEN MAILER MAKEUP MALADY+ MALLET
MAMMAL MANGER MANIAC MANNER MANTRAm MANTRAp MANUAL MAPPERy MARINA

```
MARKER  MARLINe MARLINg MASCOT  MATRIX+ MATRON  MAYDAY  MAYHEM  MEADOWy
MEDIANt MEDICO  MEDIUM  MEDLEY  MELODY+ MEMBER  MEMOIR  MEMORY+ MERGER
MERINO  MERLOT  METEOR  METHOD  METTLEd MIDGET  MILKER  MILLER  MILLET
MINCER  MINDER  MINNOW  MINUET  MIRAGE  MISERY+ MITTEN  MOANER  MODULE
MOHAIR  MOMENTa MOMENTo MONGOL  MOPOKE  MORALE  MORASSy MORGUE  MORNAY
MOSAIC  MOSQUE  MUESLI  MUFFINg MUGGER  MULLET  MUSEUM  MUSKET  MUSSEL
MUTTONy MYOPIA  MYRIAD  MYRTLE

NAPKIN  NATION  NATIVE  NAUSEA  NECTARy NEPHEW  NESTER  NEURONe NICETY+
NINETY+ NITWIT  NODULEd NOGGINg NOTION  NOUGAT  NOUGHT  NOVICE  NOZZLE
NUDISM  NUDIST  NUDITY+ NUTTERy

OBOIST  OCTANE  OCTAVE  ODDITY+ OFFCUT  OFFICEr OILCAN  ONWARD  OPENER
ORANGE* ORANGEy ORATORy ORCHID  ORDEAL  ORIGIN  OUTAGE  OUTLET  OUTSET
OXYGEN

PACKER  PAGODA  PALACEd PALLOR  PANTRY+ PAPAYAn PARISH+ PARITY+ PARLOR
PARSON  PASTEL  PASTIEr PASTRY+ PATHOS+ PATRON  PAWPAW  PAYDAY  PAYOFF
PAYOLA  PAYOUT  PEANUT  PECKER  PEDLARy PEELER  PEEPER  PEEWIT  PELVIS+
PERSONa PEWTER  PHOBIA  PICKERy PICKUP  PIGLET  PIGPEN  PIGSTY+ PILEUP
PIMPLEd PIRACY+ PISTON  PLANET  PLAQUE  PLASMA  PLATEN  PLAYER  PLOVERy
PLURAL  PODIUM  POETRY+ POLICY+ POMPOM  PONCHO  POODLE  POPGUN  POPLAR
PORTAL  POTATO+ POTION  POURER  PRAYER  PRIMERo PRIVET  PROTEAn PROTON
PRUNER  PUFFERy PUFFINg PULLET  PULLEY  PULPIT  PUNDIT  PUNNET  PUNTER
PUPPET  PURIST  PURITY+ PURSER  PUSHER  PUSHUP  PUTOFF  PYRITE  PYTHON

QUARTO  QUARTZy QUINCE  QUORUM

RACISM  RACIST  RADISH+ RADIUM  RADIUS+ RAIDER  RAISINg RAISINy RANCOR
RANGER  RAPIER  RAPIST  RARITY+ RASCAL  RATBAG  READER  REALTY+ REAPER
RECIPE  RECTORy RECTUM  REEFER  REGGAE  REGIMEn REGION  RELIEF  RENTAL
RENTER  RESALE  RETINAe RETINAl RHYTHMi RIGGER  RIGOUR  RINGER  RINSER
RIOTER  RIPOFF  RIPPER  RITUAL  ROADIE  ROBBERy ROCKERy RODENT  ROLLER
ROMPER  ROOFER  ROSARY+ ROTGUT  ROTTER  RUCKUS+ RUDDER  RUNNER  RUNOFF
RUNOUT  RUNWAY  RUPIAH  RUTILE

SACHET  SADISM  SADIST  SAILOR  SALAMI  SALIVAl SALMONy SALOON  SANDER
SANITY+ SAPPER  SARONG  SATIRE  SAUCER  SAVIOR  SCHISMa SCORER  SCRUFFy
SCURVY* SEALERy SÉANCE  SEEKER  SELLER  SENATE  SENDER  SENDUP  SENIOR
SENSORy SENTRY+ SEQUELa SERIAL  SERVERy SESAME  SETTEE  SEWAGE  SEXISM
SEXIST  SEXPOT  SHAKER  SHANDY+ SHANTY+ SHARER  SHAVER  SHEIKH  SHEILA
SHERPA  SHERRY+ SHINER  SHRIFT  SIESTA  SILICA  SIMILE  SINGER  SINKER
SITTER  SKATER  SKYWAY  SLAYER  SLICER  SLIPUP  SLOGAN  SMILER  SMOKER
SNIPER  SNORER  SOCCER  SODIUM  SODOMY+ SOIREE  SONATA  SORTER  SPIDERy
SPLEENy SPRITE  STAGERy STANCE  STANZA  STATUEd STATUSy STAYER  STIGMAl
STOKER  STORER  STOREY  STRIFE  STUDIO  STUPOR  STYLUS+ SUBSET  SUBURB
SULTANa SUNDAE  SUNDRY+ SUNHAT  SUNSET  SURFER  SURFIE* SYNTAX+ SYSTEM
```

TACTIC TAIPAN TALCUM TALENT TALKER TANDEM TANKER TANNERy TAPPET
TARTANa TARTANe TASTER TAVERNa TEACUP TEAPOT TEASER TEDIUM   TEEPEE
TEMPLEd TEMPLEt TENDON TENNER TENNISt TENPIN TERROR TESTERn THEORY+
THIRTY+ THORAX+ THRIFTy THRUSH+ TICKER TIDBIT TIEPIN TINDERy TIPOFF
TIPPER TIRADE TITBIT TOERAG TOFFEE TOILER TOMATO+ TOMBOY   TONSIL
TORPOR TOSSER TOSSUP TOUCAN TOUPEEd TOURER TOWARD TOWBAR   TRACERy
TRADER TRAUMA TREATY+ TRIPODy TROPIC TRUISM TUFFET TUMOUR   TUNDRA
TUNEUP TURBANd TURBANt TURKEY TURNERy TURNUP TURRET TUXEDO   TUXEDO+
TWELVE TWENTY+ TYCOON TYPHUS+ TYPIST

UNISON UPKEEP UPSHOT UPSIDE URCHIN URINAL UTERUS+ UTOPIAn

VAGINAe VAGINAl VALLEY VALOUR VALUER VANDAL VANITY+ VENDOR VERGER
VERMINy VERTEX+ VESSEL VESTRY+ VICARY+ VICTIM VICTORy VIEWER VIGOUR
VIOLET VIOLIN VIRTUE VORTEX+ VOYEUR

WALKER WALLET WALNUT WALRUS+ WANKER WARMTH WARMUP WARREN WEALTHy
WEAVER WEEDERy WEEVILy WEIRDO WEIRDO+ WELDER WETHER WHALERy WHISKY+
WICKER WICKET WIGWAM WINDER WINDUP WINERY+ WINGER WINNER WISDOM
WIZARD WOMBAT WORKER WOWSER WRETCH+ WRITER

YELLER YODLER YOGURT

ZAPPER ZEALOT ZENITH ZEPHYR ZINNIA ZIRCON ZITHERn ZODIAC ZOMBIE

6.1.4 NOUNS MORE OFTEN USED IN OTHER PARTS OF SPEECH

ABROAD ABRUPT* ABSURD* ACTIVE ACTUAL AERIAL AIRING ALPINE ANANAS+
ANNUAL ANYONE ANYWAY ARABLE ARCTIC ASTRAL ATOMIC AUBURN AUGUST*
AUGUSTe
BARREN* BEHIND BEYOND BICEPS+ BINARY+ BIONIC BIOTIC BOLSHY* BOUGHT
BOVINE BRASSY* BRAVERy BRIDAL BRIGHT* BUBBLY* BYGONE
CALLOW* CANDID* CANDIDa CANINE CASUAL CERCIS+ CHARAS+ CHATTY* CHILLY*
CHUMMY* CLOSER COOLER CORNUS+ COSIER COVERT COZIER CRAPPY* CREEPY*
CRUMMY* CRUSTY* CUTOUT
DAINTY* DAMPER DAPPER* DEADER DENTAL DIMMER DINGES+ DINKUM DISMAL*
DISMAL^ DODGEM DREARY* DRUGGY* DULCET
EDIBLE ENDING ENOUGH ENTIRE EQUINE EROTICa ERRANT ERRATA ETHNIC
EVENER EXOTICa
FACIAL FALSER FASTER FELINE FELLER FILING FINITE FIRMER FISCAL
FLEECY* FLIMSY* FLOPPY* FLORAL FLUENT FORMAL FORMER FRACAS+ FRILLY*
FRIZZY* FUNGAL
GAINER GALORE GLASSY* GLOSSY* GRAVER GREASY*
HEARTY* HECTIC HERBAL HEROIC HERPES+ HIDING HOURLY+
IMMUNE INBRED INDRIS+ INNING INLAND
JUSTER
KEENER KINDER KITSCHy

```
LANGER   LATENT   LATEST   LEANER   LETHAL   LIKING   LIMPER   LITTLE*  LIVING
LONGER   LOVELY*  LUMBAR   LUSHER
MADCAP   MADDER   MAKING   MALTED   MARINEr  MEAGRE*  MEANER   MEDIAL   MEETER
MENIAL   METRIC   MIDAIR   MIDDAY   MIDWAY   MOBILE   MODERN*  MODERNe  MOOTER
MORTAL   MOTLEY*  MOTLEY^  MUTANT   MUTUAL   MYOPIC   MYSTIC
NOBODY+  NORMAL
OBLONG   ONSIDE   OUTING
PAMPAS+  PARING   PAVING   PEARLY*  PELVIC   PEPTIC   PETITE   PINKER   PLENTY+
POETIC   PORTAS+  POSTAL   POTENT   PRISSY*  PROPER*  PUBLIC   PUNKER
RADIALe  RAGMAN   RANDOM   RANKER   RASHER   RATING   REDDER   REGENT   REMADE
REMOTE*  RIBALD   RISQUE   ROSIERe  ROTARY+  ROTTEN*  RULING   RUMMER   RUMPUS+
RUSTIC
SALINE   SALTERn  SARGOS+  SAVING   SAVORY*  SAYING   SCALARe  SCANTY*  SCENIC
SENILE   SEPTIC   SHODDY*  SIDING   SILENT*  SKINNY*  SLUSHY*  SMELLY*  SNOTTY*
SOCIAL   SOONER   SPARER   SPINAL   SPORTY*  SPOTTY*  SPRANG   SPUNKY*  STATICe
STEAMY*  STEELY*  STINGY*  STRATAl  STUBBY*  STUMPY*  STUPID*  STURDY*  SUDDEN
SULLEN*
TAKING   TAWDRY*  TERRAS+  THRIPS+  TIDDLY*  TIDIER   TIDING   TIMING   TINPOT
TIPTOP   TORPID   TRAGIC   TRENDY*  TRIBAL   TRUSTY*
UNIQUE*  UNISEX+  UNLIKEd  UNSEEN   UPBEAT   UPHILL   UPTOWN   UPWARD   USEFUL
UTMOST
VISUAL   VULGAR*
WARMER   WEEKLY+  WETTER   WHENCE   WHIRLY*  WICKED*  WILLER   WIRING   WITHINg
WOBBLY*  WOOLEN   WOOLLY*
YEARLY+  YONDER
```

6.1.5 OTHER NOUNS WHICH ARE VERB FORMS ENDING IN 'ING'

```
ABLING   ACHING   ACTING   ADDING   AGEING   ANTING   ARCING   ARMING   ASKING
BAAING   BAKING   BIDING   BIKING   BITING   BLUING   BODING   BONING   BORING
BOWING   BOXING   BUSING   BUYING   CAKING   CANING   CARING   CASING   CAVING
CAWING   CODING   COMING   COOING   COPING   COVING   CRYING   CUEING   DARING
DATING   DICING   DIVING   DOPING   DOTING   DOZING   DRYING   DYEING   EARING
EASING   EATING   EDGING   EFFING   ERRING   FACING   FADING   FINING   FIRING
FIXING   FLYING   FOXING   FRYING   GAMING   GAPING   GATING   GAZING   GIVING
GORING   HAVING   HAYING   HAZING   HEWING   HEXING   HIRING   HOLING   HOMING
HYPING   IMPINGe  JAPING   JAWING   KEYING   KITING   LACING   LADING   LAKING
LASING   LAWING   LAYING   LIMING   LOBING   LOSING   LOVING   LOWING   LUGING
LURING   LUTING   MATING   MAYING   MERING   MINING   MOWING   MUSING   NAMING
NIDING   NOSING   OFFING   OGLING   PAGING   PALING   PAYING   PIKING   PILING
PIPING   POLING   POSING   PRYING   PULING   RACING   RAGING   RAKING   RAVING
RIDING   RISING   ROBING   RODING   ROPING   ROVING   ROWING   RUEING   SAWING
SEEING   SEWING   SEXING   SIRING   SIZING   SKIING   SORING   SOWING   SPAING
SPYING   TAMING   TARING   TAWING   TAXING   TILING   TIRING   TOLING   TONING
TOWING   TOYING   TRYING   TUBING   TUNING   TYPING   UPPING   URGING   URNING
VEXING   VOTING   WADING   WAKING   WANING   WAVING   WAXING   WIPING   WOOING
YOKING   ZONING
```

6.1.6 NON-PLURALS IN COMMON USE

ABLAZE ABOARD ACIDIC ACROSS ADRIFT ADROIT* AFLOAT AFRAID AFRESH
AGHAST AIRMAN AIRMEN ALBEIT ALMOST AMIDST ANYHOW APIECE ARDENT
ARISEN AROUND ARTFUL ASHORE ASLEEP ASTERN ASTRAY ASTUTE* AVERSE
AVIDLY AWOKEN

BARELY BARMAN BARMEN BATMAN BATMEN BEATEN BECAME BEFELL BEFORE
BEHALF BEHELD BENIGN* BEREFT BITCHY* BITTEN BLEARY* BLIMEY BLITHE*
BLOTTO BLURRY* BODILY BOLDLY BOUNCY* BOYISH BRAINY* BRAWNY* BREEZY*
BROKEN BROODY* BRUTAL BUSILY

CALMLY CANNOT CATCHY* CATTLE CAUGHT CHALKY* CHANCY* CHASTE* CHASTEn
CHEEKY* CHEESY* CHIRPY* CHOOSY* CHOPPY* CHOSEN CHUBBY* CHUNKY* CLAMMY*
CLASSY* CLEVER* CLINGY* CLOUDY* CLUCKY* CLUMSY* CLUNKY* COARSE* COARSEn
COGENT COLDLY COMELY* COOLLY COSMIC COSTLY* CRABBY* CRAFTY* CRAGGY*
CRANKY* CREAMY* CRIKEY CRISIS CROAKY* CRUDDY* CUDDLY* CURSED* CYCLIC

DAMNED* DEADLY* DEARLY DEBRIS DECENT* DEEPLY DEFTLY DEVOID DEVOUT*
DIMPLY* DOABLE DOCILE* DOGGED* DOUBLY DOUGHY* DOURLY DRAFTY* DREAMT
DREAMY* DRESSY* DRIVEN DROOPY* DROWSY*

EARTHY* EASILY EITHER EVENLY

FAIRLY FALLEN FAULTY* FEEBLY FEISTY* FERVID* FEUDAL FIDDLY* FIERCE*
FILTHY* FINELY FIRMLY FITFUL FLABBY* FLATLY FLESHY* FLORID* FLOURY*
FLUFFY* FOETAL FOETID* FONDLY FORGOT FOUGHTy FREAKY* FREELY FRIGID*
FRISKY* FROSTY* FROTHY* FROZEN FRUGAL FRUITY* FRUMPY* FUTILE*

GAMELY GANGLY* GENIAL GENTLY GLADLY* GLITZY* GLOBAL GLOOMY* GOODLY*
GRAINY* GRASSY* GRATIS GRAVEN GREEDY* GRIMLY GRITTY* GROGGY* GROOVY*
GROTTY* GRUBBY* GRUMPY* GUILTY* GUNMAN GUNMEN

HAGGED* HARDLY HEREBY HEREIN HIDDEN HIGHLY HOARSE* HOARSEn HOMELY*
HOMELYn HONEST* HONESTy HORRID* HUGELY HUMANE* HUMBLY HUNGRY*

ICONIC IMPISH IMPURE* INDEED INNATE INSANE* INTACT IRONIC ITSELF

JAGGED* JOVIAL JOYFUL^ JOYOUS JUSTLY

KEENLY KINDLY* KINGLY* KNOTTY*

LACTIC LASTLY LATELY LATTER LAWFUL LAWMAN LAWMEN LAYMAN LAYMEN
LAZILY LEARNT LESSER LIABLE LIKELY* LIMPLY LINEAR LIVELY* LONELY*
LORDLY* LOUDLY*

6. Six-Letter Words

MADMAN	MADMEN	MAINLY	MANFUL	MARBLY*	MARSHY*	MEANLY	MEASLY*	MEEKLY
MENTAL	MERELY	MIGHTY*	MILDLY	MISFED	MISLED	MODEST*	MODESTy	MOLTEN
MORBID*	MOROSE*	MOSTLY	MOULDY*	MUSCLY*	MYSELF			

NAMELY	NEARBY	NEARLY*	NEATLY	NETHER	NICELY	NIGGLY*	NIMBLE*	NITRIC

OBTUSE*	ODIOUS	OFFISH	OODLES	OPENLY	ORALLY	ORNATE*	ORNERY*	OUTATE
OUTDID	OUTRANg	OUTRANk	OVERLY					

PALLID*	PALTRY*	PARTLY	PATCHY*	PEBBLY*	PIEMAN	PIEMEN	PIMPLY*	PLACID*
PLIANT	PLUCKY*	POINTY*	POLITE*	POORLY*	POROUS	PORTLY*	PRETAX	PRONTO
PROVENd	PURELY	PUTRID*						

QUAINT*	QUEASY*	QUIRKY*

RABIES	RACIAL	RAGGED*	RAGGEDy	RAGMENt	RANCID*	RARELY	RASHLY	RATHER
REBORN	RECENT*	REDONE	REDREW	REHUNG	REMISS	REPAID	RESOLD	RETOLD
RICHLY	RIDDEN	ROBUST*	ROBUSTa	RUDELY	RUEFUL	RUGGED*		

SACRED	SAFELY	SCABBY*	SCARCE*	SCARED*	SCATTY*	SCREWY*	SCUMMY*	SCUNGY*
SEAMAN	SEAMEN	SEEMLY*	SELDOM	SEVERE*	SEXILY	SEXUAL	SHABBY*	SHAGGY*
SHAKEN	SHAVEN	SHELLY*	SHIFTY*	SHIRTY*	SHITTY*	SHONKY*	SHOULD*	SHRANK
SHREWD*	SHRUNK	SIMPLY	SINFUL	SINGLY	SLEAZY*	SLEEPY*	SLOPPY*	SLOWLY
SLUDGY*	SLUMMY*	SMOGGY*	SMUGLY	SMUTTY*	SNAPPY*	SNARLY*	SNAZZY*	SNEAKY*
SNOBBY*	SNOOTY*	SNUGLY	SOFTLY	SOLELY	SOLEMN*	SORDID*	SORELY	SOUGHT
SOURLY	SPARSE*	SPEEDY*	SPOILT	SPOKEN	SPONGY*	SPOOKY*	SPRUNG	STARRY*
STINKY*	STOCKY*	STODGY*	STOLEN	STOLID*	STORMY*	STREWN	STRICT*	STRIPY*
STRODE	STRONG*	STROVE	STRUCK	STRUNG	STUFFY*	SUBTLE*	SUBTLY	SUGARY*
SULTRY*	SUNKEN	SUNLIT	SUPERB*	SURELY	SWEATY*	SWIRLY*		

TAMELY	TAUGHT	TAXMAN	TAXMEN	THESIS	THINLY	THORNY*	THOUGHt	THRICE
THROWN	TIMELY*	TINGLY*	TOOTHY*	TORRID*	TOUCHY*	TRASHY*	TRICKY*	TRIVIAl
TROPPO	TURBID	TURGID*	TWISTY*					

UNABLE	UNBORNe	UNDIES	UNDONE	UNDULY	UNEASY*	UNEVEN*	UNHOLY*	UNHURT
UNJUST*	UNKIND*	UNLESS	UNMADE	UNMOWN	UNOPEN	UNPAID	UNREADy	UNREAL
UNRIPE*	UNRULY*	UNSAFE*	UNSAID	UNSENT	UNSOLD	UNSUNG	UNSURE*	UNSUREd
UNTOLD	UNTRUE*	UNUSED	UNWARY*	UNWELL	UNWISE*	UNWORN	UPHELD	URBANE*
URGENT	USABLE							

VACANT	VAINLY	VASTLY	VERSUS	VIABLE	VIRILE

WARILY	WARMLY	WATERY*	WEAKLY*	WHEEZY*	WHILST	WHOLLY	WIDELY	WIDISH
WIFELY*	WIGGLY*	WILDLY	WILFUL	WINTRY*	WISELY*	WOEFUL^		

6.2 LESS FAMILIAR SIXES WHICH ARE HOOK WORDS

6.2.1 FRONT HOOKS OF FIVES TO MAKE SIXES

UNIQUE FRONT HOOKS WITH VOWELS

ABASER	**ABATTU**	ABIDER	**ABLINS**	**ABLOOM**	**ABLUSH**	**ABORAL**	**ABORNE**	ABRAID
ABURST	ACATER	**ACATES**	ACETYL	**ADOORS**	ADREAD	AEMULE	AERUGO	**AFIELD**
AFLAME	AFREET	**AFRONT**	**AGAZED**	AGEIST	**AGLARE**	**AGLEAM**	**AGOING**	AGOUTY+
AGREGE	AGRISE	AGRIZE	AGUISE	**AHORSE**	**AIDANT**	**AKIMBO**	ALARUM	ALEGGE
ALEVIN	ALINER	ALOGIA	AMOOVE	**AMORAL**	AMUSER	*AMUSIC*	APHONY+	**APODAL**
ARABICa	ARABISe	**ARILED**	ASEITY+	**ASHAKE**	ASHAME	ASHINE	ASLAKE	**ASLANT**
ASLOPE	*ASLOSH*	**ASMEAR**	ASPICK	ASPINE	ASPORT	ASPOUT	**ASQUAT**	ASTARE
ASTART	ASTONE	ASTONY	**ASTOOP**	**ASTRUT**	**ASWARM**	ASWING	ASWIRL	ASWOON
ATAATA	**ATHROB**	**ATONAL**	ATONIC	**ATOPIC**	**ATRIAL**	**ATWAIN**	ATWEEL	ATWEEN
ATWIXT	AVAUNT	**AVITAL**	AVOUCH	AVOWER	**AWEIGH**	AWHEEL	**AWHIRL**	**AWRACK**
AWRONG	**AXENIC**	AZONAL						
ECARTE	ECHARD	ECLOSE	ECURIE	**EGALLY**	**EIDOLA**	ELEGIT	*EMERSE*	EMETIC
EMUNGE	ENERVE	EPARCHs	EPARCHy	**EPERDU**e	EPULIS+	EQUANT	ESCARP	ESCROW
ESCUDO	ESPIAL	*ESPIER*	ESPRIT	ESTRUM	ETALON	ETAMINe	**ETERNE**	ETHANE
ETOILE	ETRIER							
IBICES	*INKOSI*	INYALA	IODISM	ISATINe				
OBENTO	**OBITER**	OBLASTi	**OBOLUS**	**OCELLI**	OEDEMA	*OLINGO*	OOLOGY+	**OPALED**
OPULUS+	ORACHE	**ORANGY***	**OSTEAL**	OSTENT	OTITIS+	OURALI		
UNITER	UPHANGed	**UPLAID**	UPLEADed	UPLINK	UPLOOK	UPRATE	UPREST	UPROLL
UPROSE	**UREDIA**l	USAGER	USURER	USWARD				

UNIQUE FRONT HOOKS WITH CONSONANTS

*BEIGNE*t	*BLADER*	*BLAZAR*	**BLEAKY**	**BLOUSY***	BLOWSEd	BRAIRD	**BRATTY***	**BREADY***
BREGMA	*BREIST*	BROMAL	**BROOMY***	BROOSE	**BRUMAL**	**BRUSHY***	BUNION	
CAMASS+	**CAUDAD**	CHAPPY*	CHEAPY+	CHAUNT	CHAZAN	CHEDER	CHEMIC	CHIDER
CHINKY*	CHINTS+	CHOKEY	CHOLLA	CHORALe	**CHUFFY***	**CLANKY***	CLAWER	CLEVIS+
CLOGGY*	CLONER	*COLDIE*	COPTER	COTTAR	COVARY	**CREEKY***	**CRIANT**	CROTALa
CROUTE	CRUMEN	**CRURAL**	CURARE	CURITE				
DELOPE	DELVER	DHOOLY+	DHURRA	DJEBEL	*DJEMBE*	**DJINNI**	**DOLENT**e	DRAGEE
DRAPERy	**DRIFTY***	DROGER	DROUTHy	DROWND				
FAERIE	**FILIAL**	FINGAN	FLASER	**FLEDGY***	FLENSEr	FLETCH	FLUTER	FOUTRE
FRAPPEe	FREMIT							
GABOON	GHAZEL	**GLAIRY***	*GLOBUS*	**GLOOPY***	*GNAMMA*	**GNATTY***	GORGIA	GRAILE
GRAINEr	GRAYLE	GREAVE	GRILLEr	GRIPER	GROSET			
HACKEE	HALLEL	HARTAL	HEXACT	HOUSEL	HOUSEL>	HOWLET		

JARRAH JASPIS+ JUNCUS+

KABAYA KABELE *KAINGA* KALONG KENTIA KHODJA KVETCHy

LALANG **LAROID** **LARVAL** LATRIA **LAURAE** LEVITE LEXEME LINGOT LINTEL
LOCULI LUNARY+

MAGISM MAIMER **MALIST** **MANENT** MANGEL MANTIS+ MATOKE **MEAGER** MEASLE
MEATHE METAGE METHYL MIMBAR MISTLE *MOFFIE* MORGAN MORRIS MUNIFY
MUNTINg MURENA

NAPRON NUNCLE

PALAPA PAPISH+ PAPISM PARPENd PARPENt PAVISEr **PEARST** PELITE PHAROS+
PHONER **PHOOEY** **PHYLIC** **PILEUM** **PILEUS** PLACER PLACET *PLODGE* PLONGE
PONTIC *POPERA* **PRAXES** PREACT PREARM *PREBIDe* *PREBID>* *PREBUYe* *PREDRY*
PREEVE **PREMAN** **PREMEN** PREMIXt PRESTO PREVUE **PRICEY*** PRIMUS+ PRISERe
PROSIT **PTOSES**

RAPHIS **RAPTLY** RAREFY RAZURE REBOOK REGEST *RELAND* **RELIDE** REMAIL
REMEND RENVOI RESILE RETAPE *REXINE* **RHEXES** **RICTAL** RICTUS+ RUNLET
RUNRIG

SAGENE SARGUS+ SCAMEL SCARER **SCARRY*** SCATCH+ SCERNE SCHOUT SCLAVE
SCLIFF *SCOOCH* SCORSEr SCOUTH SCREAKy SCRIMPy SCRINE *SCROME* SCRUMPy
SCULCH+ SCUTCH SDAINE SDEIGNe *SHAMAL* SHAMBA SHARPY+ SHAUGH SHEUCH
SHIPPOn SHOVER *SHUGGY+* SIDLER SKELLY* SKERRY+ **SKIDDY*** SLEAZE *SLIEVE*
SLIVEN **SMALMY** SMATCH SMEATH SMEUSE SMIDDY SMIDGEn SMIGHTe **SMIRKY***
SMITER SMOUCH SMOUSEr SMOYLE **SMURRY*** SMUTCHy **SNARKY*** **SNELLY** **SNIFFY***
SNIFTY* **SNIPPY*** SNUDGE **SOAKEN** SOAKER SOBOLE **SOLEIN** SOLIVE SPACER
SPACEY* SPARGE **SPARRY*** SPAVIN **SPECKY*** SPEISE SPENCEr **SPERSE** **SPERST**
SPHENE SPIKERy **SPIKEY*** SPINNY+ SPINTO *SPODDY*** **SPOOFY*** **SPORAL** **SPOUTY***
SPRENT **SPRONG** **SPUDDY*** *SPUGGY+* SPURGE SQUAIL *SQUARK* **SQUIFF**y SQUILLa
STAGGY* **STALKY*** STATER STEDDY **STELAE** **STILLY*** **STINTY*** **STOLED** *STOMIA*
STONEY* STONNE STOPER *STOTTY*** STOWER *STRACK* STRAIK STRAMP STRASS+
STRICK STROUT STYLER SUNBED SWADDY+ SWAGER **SWARTY** **SWASHY*** **SWEEPY***
SWIFTY+ **SWINGY*** SWIPER **SWITHE**r SWOOSH SWOUND

TALLISh TALMUD TANNOY **TAVERT** TAXITE TCHICK TERBIA THEIST TOCHER
TRAYNE TROULE TRUFFE TSAMBA **TSORES** TWAITE **TWEEDY*** **TWIGGY*** TWIGHT
TWILLY+

VAGILE VAWARD VENDUE VERVEN **VORANT**

WARRAY **WASHEN** **WHEARE** WOUBIT **WOUNDY** WRASSE

YBLENT **YBRENT** **YCLEPT** **YPLAST** YSHENDe **YSHENT** YUMPIE **YWROKE**

OTHER FRONT HOOKS

FRONT HOOK SETS

ABLER	*CABLER*	FABLER	
ABLET	CABLET	GABLET	
ACKER	DACKER	JACKER	LACKER
	RACKER	SACKER	TACKER
	WACKER	YACKER	
ADDER	GADDER	PADDER	WADDER
ADDLE	DADDLE	FADDLE	RADDLE
AFTER	HAFTER	WAFTER	
AGGER	BAGGER	GAGGERy	JAGGERy
	LAGGER	NAGGER	SAGGER
	TAGGER	WAGGERy	YAGGER
AGGIE	BAGGIE*	*MAGGIE*	
AGLET	EAGLET	HAGLET	
AIVER	TAIVERt	WAIVER	
ALANT	**GALANT**y	TALANT	
ALINE	MALINE	VALINE	
ALLEE	*CALLEE*	MALLEE	SALLEE
ALLOT	**HALLOT**h	TALLOT	
ALLOW	BALLOW	GALLOW	HALLOW
	MALLOW	TALLOWy	
AMATE	HAMATE	**RAMATE**	
AMBER	JAMBER	LAMBERt	TAMBER
AMBLE	HAMBLE	WAMBLE	
AMINE	GAMINE	TAMINE	
AMPLY	**CAMPLY**	**DAMPLY**	
ANANA	MANANA	ZANANA	
ANCHO	RANCHO	SANCHO	
ANGLE	CANGLE	FANGLE	
ANION	FANION	WANION	
ANKER	CANKERy	JANKER	YANKER
ANKLE	*CANKLE*	FANKLE	**WANKLE**
ANTAR	CANTAR	KANTAR	
ANTIC	**CANTIC**o	**MANTIC**	
ANTRA	TANTRA	YANTRA	
APERY+	JAPERY+	NAPERY+	**PAPERY**
APPEL	LAPPEL	RAPPEL	RAPPEL>
ARISH+	**BARISH**	**HARISH**	MARISH+
ARRAS+	NARRAS+	TARRAS+	
ARRET	BARRET	GARRET	
ARROW	FARROW	TARROW	YARROW
ARSEY*	CARSEY	KARSEY	
ASKER	MASKER	TASKER	
ASPER	GASPER	JASPERy	RASPER

ASTER	BASTER	CASTER	EASTERn
	GASTER	LASTER	PASTERn
	RASTER		
AUGER	**MAUGER**	SAUGER	
AUGHT	**HAUGHT**y	NAUGHTy	**RAUGHT**
	WAUGHT		
AUNTY+	JAUNTY*	**VAUNTY***	
AURIC	*LAURIC*	**TAURIC**	
AWNER	DAWNER	FAWNER	PAWNER
	YAWNER		
BLATE*	ABLATE	OBLATE	
EDGED	*LEDGED*	**SEDGED**	
EDGER	HEDGER	KEDGER	
EDILE	AEDILE	**SEDILE**	
EERIE*	FEERIE	PEERIE	
EGGER	*KEGGER*	LEGGER	
ELATE	BELATE	DELATE	GELATE
	VELATEd		
ELDER	GELDER	MELDER	
ELVES	**PELVES**	**SELVES**	
EMMER	HEMMER	*YEMMER*	
ENDER	MENDER	VENDER	
ENTER	TENTER	VENTER	
ENVOY	LENVOY	RENVOY	
ESTER	*MESTER*	RESTER	WESTERn
	YESTERn	ZESTER	
ETHER	AETHER	**HETHER**	PETHER
EVERY	REVERY+	SEVERY+	
GAMIC	**AGAMIC**	**OGAMIC**	
HAMMY*	CHAMMY	WHAMMY+	
HARRY	**CHARRY***	GHARRY+	
HEAVE	SHEAVE	THEAVE	
HENCE	**THENCE**	**WHENCE**	
HEUGH	SHEUGH	WHEUGH	
HEWER	CHEWER	SHEWER	
HIPPY*	CHIPPY*	**WHIPPY***	
HOUGH	CHOUGH	SHOUGH	
HOUSE	CHOUSEr	*SHOUSE*	
ICKER	DICKER	LICKER	NICKER
	RICKER	YICKER	
ICKLE*	MICKLE*	NICKLE	RICKLE
IDENT	BIDENT	**EIDENT**	**RIDENT**
ILIUM	**CILIUM**	**MILIUM**	

ILLER BILLER GILLER HILLER
SILLER
INDIE *KINDIE* *YINDIE*
INGLE DINGLE GINGLE KINGLEt
LINGLE PINGLEr
INKER JINKER LINKER WINKER
INNER FINNER GINNERy PINNER
TINNER
INTER HINTER LINTER MINTER
SINTERy TINTER
ITCHY* **FITCHY** **HITCHY*** **PITCHY***
TITCHY* **WITCHY***
ITHER CITHERn MITHER *NITHER*
TITHER
IZARD RIZARD VIZARD
LAKER FLAKER SLAKER
LAMER BLAMER FLAMER
LANCH FLANCH PLANCHe
LATCH CLATCH KLATCH+ SLATCH+
LATER ELATER PLATER SLATER
LEAVE GLEAVE SLEAVE
LEDGE FLEDGE GLEDGE
LEECH FLEECH SLEECHy
LEUCH CLEUCH PLEUCH
LEUGH CLEUGH PLEUGH
LINKY *PLINKY** SLINKY***
LINTY* FLINTY* *GLINTY**
LIPPY* FLIPPY* SLIPPY*
LOBBY GLOBBY* SLOBBY*
LOOEY **BLOOEY** FLOOEY
LOOIE **BLOOIE** FLOOIE
LOPER ELOPER SLOPER
LOUGH CLOUGH SLOUGHi SLOUGHy
LUMPY* **CLUMPY*** **GLUMPY*** **PLUMPY***
SLUMPY*
LUNCH CLUNCH+ GLUNCH
LUSHY* FLUSHY* PLUSHY*
MENTA AMENTAl OMENTAl
MESES EMESES TMESES
NAGGY* KNAGGY* SNAGGY*
NEATH **ANEATH** SNEATH **UNEATH**
NUBBY* KNUBBY* SNUBBY*
NODAL ANODAL ENODAL
NOMIC ANOMIC GNOMIC
NOSES ENOSES GNOSES
OATER COATER DOATER
OBANG GOBANG KOBANG
OCKER COCKER HOCKER

ODDER CODDER *MODDER* NODDER
ODIST CODIST MODISTe
OFFER DOFFER GOFFER
OILER COILER MOILER
OLDEN BOLDEN **HOLDEN**
OLDER MOLDER POLDER
OLLER GOLLER HOLLER LOLLER
POLLER SOLLER TOLLER
OLLIE MOLLIE *TOLLIE*
ONION **GONION** RONION
ONIUM CONIUM **GONIUM** IONIUM
OORIE* *COORIE=* *GOORIE* TOORIE
ORATE BORATE **LORATE**
ORMER DORMER WORMERy
OTARY+ NOTARY+ VOTARY+
OTHER FOTHER **NOTHER** POTHERb
POTHERy ROTHER **TOTHER**
OTTER COTTER DOTTER *LOTTERy*
OUGHT **DOUGHTy** **MOUGHT** **ROUGHT**
OUNCE JOUNCE ROUNCE
OURIE* *COURIE=COURIEr* *LOURIE**
POURIE TOURIE
OUTER COUTER DOUTER **FOUTER**
MOUTER POUTER ROUTER
SOUTER TOUTER
OVATE BOVATE *NOVATE*
OWLER FOWLER JOWLER YOWLER
OWRIE* COWRIE *LOWRIE*
PICAL APICAL **EPICAL**
PIGHT SPIGHT **YPIGHT**
PRISE **EPRISE** UPRISEd UPRISEn
UPRISEr
RAGGY* **BRAGGY*** **DRAGGY***
RAISE ARAISE FRAISE
RATCH CRATCH+ FRATCHy
RATER FRATERy KRATER PRATER
RAWLY BRAWLY* CRAWLY* DRAWLY*
RAZER BRAZER GRAZER
REACH AREACH CREACHs
RENNE BRENNEd FRENNE
REVET BREVETe BREVET> TREVET
RICER GRICER PRICER
RICHT* *BRICHT** FRICHT
RIGHT **ARIGHT** WRIGHT
RIVET GRIVET TRIVET
ROGUE BROGUE DROGUEt
ROUGH BROUGH GROUGH
ROUPY* **CROUPY*** GROUPY+

ROUSE	CROUSE	TROUSEr		UNITE	DUNITE	GUNITE	MUNITE
ROVER	PROVER	TROVER		URARI	CURARI	OURARI	
ROYNE	GROYNE	PROYNE		URGER	PURGER	SURGER	
RUMLY	DRUMLY*	GRUMLY		URINE	MURINE	PURINE	
TELIC	ATELIC	STELIC		USHER	BUSHER	HUSHER	MUSHER
TONER	ATONER	STONERn				RUSHER	
TYPIC	ATYPIC	ETYPIC		WANKY*	SWANKY*	TWANKY+	
UDDER	BUDDER	DUDDERy	JUDDERy	WATCH	AWATCH	SWATCH+	
	MUDDER	PUDDER	SUDDER	WEARY*	AWEARY	SWEARY*	
UMPTY	HUMPTY+	NUMPTY+		WEENY*	SWEENY+	TWEENY+	
UNDER	DUNDER	FUNDER	SUNDER				

OTHERS

ACRAWL	ALATED	ANIGHT	AURATEd	BADMAN	BADMEN	BLINGY*	BLUNGEr	BRACEROn
BREEKS	BREEST	BRISKY*	BROWED	CAMPLE	CENTRY+	CLAVER	COMBER	CORDER
CRANCH	CRANTS+	CRASES	CRAVEN	CRAVER	CROTON	CROWER	CRUMPY*	CUMBER
CUPPER	CURIAL	CYESES	DARGLE	DEJECTa	DOILED	DRUMMY+	DURNED*	ELANCE
ESTRAY	FLANES	FLAYER	FLOSSY*	FLOUSE	FRITES	GAMMON	GEMOTE	GLAMMY*
GLOPPY*	GLOVER	GLOWER	GLUMPS	GOOPED	GROVED	HARMER	HOGGINg	HOSIERy
ICONES	IRIDES	JEANED	JIMPLY	KEIGHT	KNOBBY*	LACHES+	LAWNED	LEASER
LOFTER	MALATE	MANTES	MARTEL>	MINION	MOILER	NACRED	NIMBED	OLIVER
PALTER	PETTLE	PHEEZE	PIONIC	PLEACH	PLOWER	PLUMMY*	PLURRY	PRIEVE
PROKER	RAWING	REALESt	REARLY	RURBAN	RUTTER	SANGER	SAPPLE	SAVINE
SEATER	SEGGAR	SHINNY	SHOPPY*	SPINED	STAPES	SUNKET	SUTILE	SWINGEr
SWINGE=	TASSET	TEAGLE	TEASEL	TEASEL>	TECHED	THALER	THEWED	TRIMER
TROWTH	ULOSES	UNOWED	URESES	UROSES	VATMAN	WHERRY	WHILLY	WINKLEr
YBOUND								

6.2.2 END HOOKS OF FIVES TO MAKE SIXES

END HOOKS WITH 'A'

AMENTAl	AMRITA	ANTARA	ARGALA	BERTHA	BHAJIA	BILBOA	BOCCIA	BOONGA
CABALA	CAMISA	CARDIAc	CARDIAe	CHANGA	CHARKA	CHARTA	CHICHA	CHORDAe
CHORDAl	CHOREAl	CONCHAe	CONCHAl	CORNUAl	CRACKA	CRESTAl	CRUSTAe	CRUSTAl
CUBICAl	CUTCHA	EGESTA	EJECTA	ENTERAl	EPOCHAl	EXACTA	FASCIAe	FASCIAl
FAVELA	FRISKA	FRUSTA	GLOSSAe	GLOSSAl	GRAMPA	HALALAh	HALLOA	HEDERAl
HEMINA	HILLOA	HOLLOA	HULLOA	KAINGA	KORUNA	KUTCHA	LORICAe	MAXIMAl
MIASMAl	MINIMAl	MINIMAx	MONERAn	NYMPHAe	NYMPHAl	OBELIA	OCHREAe	ORBITAl
ORGANA	PARERA	PATERAe	PATINAe	PENNIA	PETARA	PHARMA	PLANTAe	PLANTAr
QUANTAl	QUINOA	QUINTAl	QUINTAn	QUINTAr	QUOTHA	SAHIBAh	SATYRAl	SCARPA
SENORA	SHIRRA	SHISHA	SOLERA	SPIREA	STELLAr	STERNAl	STRIGAe	STRUMAe
SULPHA	TALUKA	TAPETAl	TARSIA	TORANA	TREIFA	TUNICAe	VALETA	YOJANA

END HOOKS WITH '(A)E'

AGORAE	ALULAE	AMEBAE	AORTAE	BACCAE	BULLAE	BURSAE	CANNAE	CAUDAE
CAUSAE	CELLAE	CHELAE	CNIDAE	COSTAE	COTTAE	CULPAE	CURIAE	DINNAE
FACIAE	FAUNAE	FERIAE	FLORAE	FOSSAE	FOVEAE	FURCAE	GALEAE	GEMMAE
GLEBAE	GUTTAE	HERMAE	HYDRAE	HYPHAE	LAMIAE	LARVAE	LAURAE	LIBRAE
LYTTAE	MEDIAE	MENSAE	MISSAE	MUSCAE	NUCHAE	OCREAE	PALEAE	PALLAE

PELTAE	PENNAE	PHOCAE	PHYLAE	PINNAE	PLICAE	REDIAE	SALPAE	SCALAE
SCOPAE	SELLAE	SERRAE	SILVAE	SPICAE	SPINAE	STELAE	STRIAE	SUMMAE
SYLVAE	TALEAE	TALPAE	TENIAE	TERRAE	TESTAE	THECAE	TIBIAE	UMBRAE
UNCIAE	UVULAE	VILLAE	VITTAE	*VOLVAE*	VULVAE	*ZOAEAE*	ZOOEAE	

OTHER END HOOKS WITH 'E'

ALLELE	ALMUDE	AMENDEr	AMPULE	ANCONE	AVAILE	BARGEE	BATTUE	*BEEDIE*
BERTHE	BETIDE	BLENDEr	BLOWSEd	BOCCIE	BOORDE	BOURNE	**BRAIDE***	**BRAIDE**d
BREESE	BRIBEE	BROCHE	BROOSE	BUBALE	BUNJEE	CAMESE	CAMISE	CAPOTE
CARATE	*CARDIE*	CHAINE	CHAISE	CHILDEr	CHIRREn	CHOREE	CHOWSE	CLAVIEr
COATEE	COIGNE	COLONEl	COMICE	CONCHE	CONGEE	CONINE	COOMBE	COUCHEe
COUCHEr	COUPEE	CREESE	CROSSE*	CROUPEr	CROUTE	CUTTOE	DERATE	DILDOE
DONNEE	DOOLEE	DORISE	DREARE*	DROWSE	EOSINE	**EPRISE**	EQUIPE	**FACETE**d
FARCIEd	*FASTIE*	**FILOSE**	FITCHEe	FITCHEt	FITCHEw	**FORBYE**	**FORMEE**	FRISEE
FRORNE	FUNDIE	FURANE	FUROLE	FURORE	**FUSILE**	GAMINE	GEMOTE	GENOME
GLAIRE	GOURDE	GRAILE	GRAINEr	**GRANDE***	**GRANDE**e	GREESE	GREETEr	GRIFFE
GRILLEr	**GROSZE**	GUIMPE	**GYROSE**	HALIDE	HEASTE	HEXADE	HORSTE	INCUSE
INDOLE	**INFERE**	IODIDE	JAMBEE	**JINNEE**	KINASE	LASSIE	LATHEE	LAWINE
LETHEE	LIPIDE	**LOBOSE**	LUNGEE	LUNGIE	LUPINE	LYSINE	MEATHE	*MERGEE*
MISERE	MONGOE	*MURREE*	NOMADE	**NOULDE**	OLEINE	ORACHE	ORCINE	ORPINE
OSMOLE	**OUTBYE**	**PARDIE**	**PAREVE**	PARKIE*	**PASSEE**	PATINE	**PATTEE**	PAVANE
PAVISEr	PERDUE	PHEERE	**PICOTE**d	**PICOTE**e	**PLASTE**r	PLONGE	POINTEl	POINTEr
POLYPEd	POTCHEr	POUFFE	POULPE	PREIFE	PRIEFE	**PROINE**	PROYNE	PURINE
PUTTIEr	QUARTEt	QUINTEt	RALLYE	RAPPEE	REBITEd	RECURE	REPINEr	RESITE
ROTCHE	RUBINE	SABINE	SAITHE	SALADE	SALLEE	SARODE	SASINE	SAVINE
SCHMOE	SCRAYE	SCULLEr	SERINE	SHOOLE	SHOTTEn	SILENE	SKEANE	STEARE
SNATHE	SOURSE	SOZINE	SPALLEr	SPARKEr	SPURNEr	STEALEr	STEANE	STEARE
STEDDE	STONNE	STOOPEr	STOURE	STRAKEd	*STYLEE*	**STYLIE***	SWINGEr	SWINGE=
SWITHEr	SWOUNE	TAMALE	TAMINE	TAMISE	TANGIE*	TESTEE	THEINE	THERMEl
THORPE	THROWEr	TOLANE	**TOROSE**	TOUCHEr	TOXINE	TRANSE	TRIOSE	**TRISTE**
TROADE	TROMPE	TRYSTEr	TUYERE	TWYERE	**ULNARE**	UNCAPE	**UNCUTE**	UNTILE
UREASE	VALETE	VALISE	VENINE	VERSTE	VERTUE	VISITEe	VISITEr	WALISE
WATAPE	**WHEARE**							

END HOOKS WITH 'I'

ANNULI	ARGALI	**AVANTI**	CAROLI	CHICHI	**CLYPEI**	COLONIc	*CUBITI*	*DENARI*i
DEWANI	**DJINNI**	**DUETTI**	**EPHORI**	*EQUALI*	FRACTI	GARDAI	GLUTEI	HAIKAI
HERMAI	*JEHADI*	*JIHADI*	JOWARI	**KROONI**	MANATI	**MOIRAI**	NEROLI	PIROGI+
POLYPI	**RHOMBI**c	SCAMPI	SCAMPI+	*SENSEI*	SHALLI	**SILENI**	**SMALTI**	**SOLIDI**
STELAI	TAPETI	YOGINI						

END HOOKS WITH 'O'

AMMONO	*BILLYO*h	*BRILLO*	**BROCHO**	BRONCO	*CARDIO*	CHARRO	CHEAPO	CHEERO
CHOCKO	*CHURRO*	*CONCHO*	CRYPTOn	DINERO	DORADO	DUETTO	ERINGO	ERINGO+
FASCIO	**FRANCO**	**GIUSTO**	HALLOO	HOLLOO	*HULLOO*	LIBERO	*LIVEDO*	MORPHO
NYMPHO	PEDALO	PEDALO+	*PLONKO*	PRESTO	PSEUDO	PSYCHO	RABATO	RABATO+
RANCHO	REECHO+	**RIGHTO**	ROMANO	SHACKO	SHACKO+	SHEEPO	SMALTO	SOLANO

SPEEDO STALKO+ STINGO **STINKO** THICKO THICKO+ TOLEDO TRILLO+ VIGORO
VOMITO WHACKO WHACKO+ **WHATSO**

END HOOKS WITH 'D'

ACARID **AERIED** **AFEARD** AGAMID **AGAZED** **ALATED** **APPAYD** ARGAND **AZOTED**
BOYARD BRIARD **CAUDAD** CHIELD **DORSAD** DROWND **EXTOLD** **FIBRED** **FOSSED**
GROVED **HERSED** *LEDGED* LIGAND **MACLED** **MEDIAD** MILORD **MONIED** **NACRED**
OUTRED> PETARD **PLONGD** REMEND RESEED **RETROD** SEDGED **SEMEED** **SHROWD**
SOLAND SPAULD **SPINED** SPREDDd SPREDDe **STEARD** **STEELD** **STIPED** **STOLED**
STOUND STOWND SWEARD SWOUND TABERD TETRAD **TOGAED** **VARVED**

END HOOKS WITH 'L'

ACETAL **AECIAL** AMIDOL **ANTRAL** **AORTAL** **APNEAL** APPALL **ATRIAL** BABOOL
BARBELl BEDELL BORDEL **BUFFEL** **BURSAL** **CAECAL** CARVEL **CAUDAL** CAUSAL
CORBEL CORBEL> COSTAL CREWEL> **CRURAL** **CURIAL** **DERMAL** DORSAL DORSEL
DRUPEL EISELL ENROLL EXTOLL **FAUNAL** FAVELLa **FERIAL** FESTAL FLOTEL
FOVEAL **FURCAL** HANSEL HANSEL> HOUSEL HOUSEL> **HYPHAL** JAMBUL *KHAYAL*
KNAWEL LABIAL **LABRAL** **LARVAL** **LUTEAL** MANGAL MANGEL **MENSAL** MERELL
MISSAL MORALLy NEWELL NITRYL NUCHAL **OMASAL** **OSTIAL** **PALEAL** PARRAL
PASSEL PENCEL PENNAL PETREL **PINNAL** **PLICAL** **PODIAL** **PRIMAL** QUINOL
RANCEL RAPPEL RAPPEL> **RECTAL** REFELL **REGNAL** **RETIAL** RIDGEL RIGOLL
RONDEL RONNEL RUSSEL SACRAL SAMBAL SANTOL SCROWLe **SCUTAL** **SEPTAL**
SERAIL SORELL *SORTAL* SPINEL STIPEL **STOMAL** TEASEL TEASEL> TEAZEL
TEAZEL> **TECTAL** **TELIAL** TERCEL **TERGAL** **THECAL** **TIBIAL** **TINEAL** **TOMIAL**
TORSEL **UMBRAL** UMBREL UNCIAL VARVEL VERVEL VESTAL **VISTAL** **VULVAL**
WASTEL WOOSELl **XENIAL** **ZOOEAL**

END HOOKS WITH 'N'

ALDERN **ALTERNe** **AMEBAN** AMNION BANIAN BANYAN **BESEEN** BOREEN CALLANt
CANTON **CARVEN** **CAUSEN** **CEDARN** CHICON **CLOVEN** CRAVEN **CRIMEN** DAIKON
DOGMAN DOLMAN **DRUSEN** FARCINg FLAMEN **FROREN** GAZOON **GEMMAN** **GLAZEN**
GLOBINg GLUTEN HAUSEN **HOOVEN** INTRON JOTUNN **KRONEN** LARGEN **LATHEN**
LATTEN LEAVEN **LOIPEN** LONGAN **LOUPEN** MACRON MANNAN MICRON MURREN
MURRINe NORMAN PAISANa PAISANo PANTON PARKINg PATTEN **PEASEN** **PERCENt**
PHONON PHOTON PIECEN POLEYN RABBIN **RAPPEN** RATOON **REEDEN** **RESAWN**
RESEEN **RESEWN** **RESOWN** SANTON **SCHULN** SERRANo SEXTON SHAMAN **SHAPEN**
SILVAN SITHEN **SLIVEN** SLOVEN **SOLEIN** **STONEN** **STRAWN** **STROWN** SYLVAN
THORON **THRAWN** **TORTEN** TRIGON UNDERN **UNSEWN** VERVEN VILLANy VODOUN
WEDELN **WEETEN** WICCAN WIVERN **WROKEN**

END HOOKS WITH 'R' OF VERBS

ABASER ABATER ABIDER ABUSER ADORER ALINER AMBLER AMUSER ARGUER
ATONER BASTER BELIER BINGER BIRLER *BLADER* BLAMER BODGER BRACERo
BRAZER BRINER BRUTER BUDGERo BULGER BURKER *CABLER* *CANOER* CASTER
CAUSER CENSER CESSER CHAFER CHIDER CHIMERa CHIMERe CHOKER CLONER
COATER COMBER CONGER CONNER COSTER COUPER CRAVER CURSER CYCLERy
DAMMER DAUBERy DEICER DELVER DINGER DOUSER DOWSER DRAPERy DRONER
ELATER ELOPER ELUDER EMOTER EVADER EVOKER *EXILER* FABLER FARCER

```
FEARER  FLAKER  FLAMER  FLUTER  FORCER  FRIZER  GAFFER  GAMMER  GAUGER
GLAZER  GLOVER  GORGER  GOUGERe GRAZER  GRIPER  GUIDER  GUILER  GUISER
GUYLER  HALSER  HALVER  HAWSER  HEARER  HEAVER  HEDGER  HEFTER  HINGER
HOUSER  IMAGERy IRONER  ISSUER  JAMBER  JUDGER  KEDGER  KNIFER  KNOWER
LADLER  LANDER  LAPSER  LEASER  LEGGER  LIGGER  LOTTERy LOUSER  LUNGER
MICHER  MINGER  MOUSERy MUDGER  NAPPER  NERVER  NOOSER  NUDGER  NURSERy
PANNER  PARSER  PASSER  PASTERn PAUSER  PEEVER  PENNER  PHONER  PIECER
PLACER  PLANER  PLATER  POISER  POSSER  PRATER  PRICER  PRISERe PRIZER
PROBER  PROKER  PROLER  PROSER  PROVER  PULSER  PURGER  QUAKER  QUEUER
QUOTER  RAILER  RAISER  RAPPER  REAMER  REAVER  REEDER  REIVER  RELIER
RHYMER  RIDGER  RIEVER  RIFLERy ROGUERy ROOSER  ROUSER  ROUTER  SALVER
SCALER  SCARER  SEAMER  SEINER  SEISER  SEIZER  SERGER  SHADER  SHAMER
SHAPER  SHORER  SHOVER  SIDLER  SIEGER  SLAKER  SLATER  SLIDER  SLOPER
SMITER  SNARER  SOARER  SOLVER  SPADER  SPICERy SPIKERy STARER  STATER
STIVER  STOKER  STONERn STOPER  STOVER  STYLER  SUITER  SWAGER  SWIPER
TEENER  TITHER  TITLER  TOUSER  TOWSER  TWINER  UNITER  USURER  VENGER
VERSER  VISIER  VOGUER  VOICER  WAIVER  WHINER  WINCER  WOLVER
```

OTHER END HOOKS WITH 'R'

```
ALULAR  BANDARi BESTIR> BONZER  BURSARy CALVER  CANTOR  CAVIER  CHADOR
CHINAR  CIRCAR  CLAVER  COTTAR  CROZER  DEBURR  DORSER  FLEXOR  FOLIAR
FRATERy GIMMER  GRICER  GUSLAR  JASPERy KRONER  LENTOR  LIEGER  MACHER
MANDIRa MUGGAR  NICHER  OLIVER  PANDAR  PHYLAR  SALVOR  SAMBAR  SANGAR
SANSAR  SKIVER  SONDER  SORDOR  SPINAR  STELAR  SUMMARy THALER  TONNER
TROVER  TWICER  USAGER  UVULAR  VEALER  VILLAR  VIRGER  VULVAR  WACKER
WORSER
```

END HOOKS WITH 'T'

```
ADMIXT  ANIGHT  ANKLET  APPLET  ARPENT  ASSOTT  ASTERT  AURIST  BARBET
BARRAT  BARRET  BASANT  BECKET  BEMIXT  BENNET  BOUGET  BREEST  BREIST
BREVETe BREVET> BROWST  BUGLET  CABLET  CACHET  CAPLET  CATCHT  CHARET
CLASPT  COMMOTe COMPOTe COVENT  CRONET  CRUSET  CURIET  CURVET  CURVET>
DEGUST  DIKAST  DONNAT  DOUCET  DOUGHTy DOWSET  DRAPET  DUPLET  EAGLET
FROWSTy GABLET  GAINST  GAMBET  GAMMAT  GARRET  GORGET  GROVET  HAIRST
HALLOTh HAUGHTy HAULST  JUMART  KAPUTT  LANCET  LINGOT  MALIST  MATZOTh
MONGST  MOTETT  MUSCAT  OCTANT  OCTETTe OLIVET  PARGET  PARGET> PEARST
PIERST  PIQUET  PLACET  PLAINT  POSSET  RACHET  RAYLET  REDIPT  REFELT
REGEST  RELICT  REMIXT  RENNET  REPOST  RILLET  ROQUET  ROUGHT  SAIDST
SALLET  SCEATT  SCREET  SMILET  SPINET  STEALTh STILET  STRIPT  STYLET
SUMMATe SWEERT  SWEIRT  SWIVET  TAPIST  TASSET  TAVERT  TERCET  TOQUET
TRIACT  TURBOT  UNFIXT  UNMIXT  UNPENT  UNWONT  VERSET  VERVET  WAUGHT
WAURST  WHISHT  WORSET
```

END HOOKS WITH '(ER)Y' TO NOUNS

```
AMBERY+ BOWERY+ DOWERY+ DUPERY+ EGGERY+ FAKERY+ JAPERY+ LIVERY+ MOPERY+
NITERY+ OILERY+ OSIERY+ OWLERY+ RAKERY+ ROPERY+ RUDERY+ SEVERY+ STEERY+
TAWERY+ TILERY+ VINERY+
```

END HOOKS WITH 'Y' TO ADJECTIVES

ANGSTY* BALLSY* BAULKY* BEACHY* BEARDY* BEECHY* BENCHY* BIELDY* BLASHY*
BLASTY* BLINGY* BLOCKY* BLOKEY* BLOOMY* BLOWSY* BLUESY* BLUIDY* BOOKSY*
BOOZEY* BOSOMY* BOTCHY* BRANKY* BRASHY* BRAWLY* BREADY* BRICKY* BRIERY*
BRISKY* BROOMY* BROTHY* BROWNY* BROWSY* BRUSHY* BUNCHY* CAIRNY* CHAFFY*
CHAMPY* CHARRY* CHASMY* CHECKY* CHEERY* CHERTY* CHESTY* CHINKY* CHOKEY*
CHUFFY* CLANKY* CLARTY* CLECKY* CLIFFY* CLIFTY* CLUMPY* COACHY* COCKSY*
COUTHY* CRAMPY* CRAWLY* CREAKY* CREEKY* CREPEY* CRESSY* CRIMPY* CRISPY*
CROUPY* CRUMBY* CRUMPY* CURVEY* CUTESY* DANCEY* DEATHY* DINGEY* DRAFFY*
DRAWLY* DRECKY* DRIFTY* DROOLY* DROSSY* DWEEBY* FAINTY* FLAKEY* FLASHY*
FLECKY* FLINTY* FLIRTY* FLISKY* FLOATY* FLOCKY* FLOSSY* FLUKEY* FLUSHY*
FLUTEY* FOLKSY* FREETY* FREITY* FROWSY* GAMESY* GHOSTY* GLAIRY* GLAURY*
GLEAMY* GLEETY* GLINTY* GLOOPY* GNARLY* GOOSEY* GOURDY* GRAPEY* GREENY*
GRIPEY* GROUTY* GROWLY* GRUFFY* HAULMY* HEARSY* HEATHY* HITCHY* HORSEY*
HOUSEY* JAUNTY* KLUTZY* KNARLY* KNOLLY* KNURLY* LAUGHY* LEACHY* LEMONY*
LIMPSY* LOWERY* MANGEY* MOUSEY* MOUTHY* NOTCHY* ONIONY* PAINTY* PAPERY*
PEACHY* PLASHY* PLINKY* PLONKY* PLOOKY* PLOUKY* PLUFFY* PLUMPY* PLUNKY*
PLUSHY* POACHY* PONCEY* POUCHY* POUFFY* PRANKY* PRICEY* PRICKY* PUNCHY*
QUACKY* QUALMY* QUEENY* REASTY* REECHY* REESTY* RHEUMY* ROOTSY* SCAREY*
SCURFY* SHALEY* SHARNY* SHEAFY* SHEENY* SHEEPY* SHEETY* SHELFY* SHOALY*
SHOUTY* SINEWY* SIRUPY* SKEARY* SKEERY* SKELLY* SKILLY* SKILLY+ SKIMPY*
SLANGY* SLANTY* SLATEY* SLEEKY* SLEETY* SLIMSY* SLINKY* SLOOMY* SLOSHY*
SLUBBY* SLURPY* SMARMY* SMEARY* SMILEY* SMIRKY* SMIRRY* SMOKEY* SNAILY*
SNAKEY* SNARKY* SNIDEY* SNIFFY* SNIFTY* SNOOPY* SNORTY* SNOUTY* SNUFFY*
SPACEY* SPARKY* SPAWNY* SPEARY* SPECKY* SPENDY* SPICEY* SPIFFY* SPOOFY*
SPOONY* SPOUTY* STAGEY* STALKY* STEEPY* STILLY* STILTY* STINTY* STONEY*
STOURY* STRAWY* SWAMPY* SWANKY* SWARDY* SWASHY* SWATHY* SWEARY* SWEEPY*
SWINGY* SWIPEY* SWISHY* SWOONY* SWOOPY* SYLPHY* SYRUPY* TEENSY* THINGY*
THUMBY* THYMEY* TITCHY* TOASTY* TORCHY* TOWERY* TRAMPY* TRESSY* TRIPEY*
TROUTY* TRUTHY* TWANGY* TWEAKY* TWEEDY* TWERPY* TWIRLY* TWIRPY* VAULTY*
VAUNTY* VETCHY* VOGUEY* WAVERY* WEENSY* WHACKY* WHEATY* WHEELY* WHELKY*
WHIFFY* WHINEY* WHITEY* WIELDY* WITCHY* WOODSY* WRATHY* WRISTY* YEASTY*
YOUTHY*

OTHER END HOOKS WITH 'Y'

APPLEY   ARROWY   AUGURY+ BARONY+ BETONY+ BLEAKY BOWSEY BRIARY   BRISKY
CARBOY   CARSEY   CAUSEY   CEDARY   CHANTY+ CHEAPY+ CHUCKY+ CIDERY   COLORY
CONCHY+ CORSEY   CRACKY   CRICKY   CROWDY+ DENARY+ DIMPSY+ DJINNY   DRAPEY*
DROLLY   EMBUSY   FITCHY   FIXITY+ FLUNKY+ FOOTSY+ FORTHY FRIARY+ GOWANY
GROSZY   GROUPY+ GUANAY   HUMUSY   HURRAY   JACKSY+ KORUNY LINENY   LOATHY
LUNARY+ MAUNDY+ MISSAYd MONOSY+ MOTORY   MURRAY MURREY NIGHTY+ NOMADY+
OCCAMY+ OCHERY   OCHREY   ORBITY+ PAEONY+ PARLEY PETARY+ PRIORY+ PRISMY
PUSLEY   QUICKY+ QUINSY+ RATANY+ RESINY   RIGHTY+ RIVERY ROSETY   ROSINY
ROUGHY+ SAMELY   SATINY   SAUGHY   SCALLY+ SCAURY+ SHARPY+ SHORTY+ SLAVEY
SMALMY   SMARTY+ SNELLY   STEDDY   STEEDY   STIFFY+ SWARTY SWEETY+ SWIFTY+
THICKY   TIGERY   TITUPY   TOOTSY+ TOUGHY+ TROLLY TWANKY+ TWEELY   TWEENY+
TWILLY+ UMBERY   UNREDY   UNSEXY   VAPORY   VOLARY+ WAFERY WARREY   WEIRDY+
WHIMSY* WHIRRY   WINCEY   WOUNDY

103

OTHER END HOOKS

ABBESS+	**ACINIC**	**ADIEUX**	**AGAMIC**	*AGUNAH*	ALIYAH	ANKUSH+	ANTICKe	ARRISH+
ASPICK	**ASPISH**	*BALTIC*	BARONG	BEGUNK	BESEEM	**BIJOUX**	**BOYAUX**	BUSTIC
CALPACk	CAMASH+	CAMASS+	*CARNYX*+	CAVASS+	CENTUM	CHIASMa	CHIASMi	**CHOLIC**
CITESS+	COHOSH+	**COMETH**	CONGOU	COPALM	COPRAH	COSECH	CREESHy	**CULTIC**
DALEDH	*DARGAH*	DEBARK	DECAFF	*DELISH*	DOURAH	ELDING	ESCARP	FATWAH
FELLAH	**FILMIC**	**FUNDIC**	**FUNGIC**	GALUTH	GAMASH+	GANJAH	GONIFF	GRUMPHy
HALERU	HALLOW	HALVAH	HAMZAH	HIGHTH	HIJRAH	HOOKAH	HURRAH	IAMBIC
IMBARK	**INWITH**	JAMBOK>	JIBBAH	*KALPAC*	KAVASS+	KHEDAH	KIBBEH	KIBLAH
LAMEDH	*LAVASH*+	**LENTIC**	**LIMBIC**	LINGAM	**LIROTH**	LOOFAH	MALISM	*MANATU*
MATLOW	MATZAH	MATZOH	MEDICK	MERISM	*MESTOM*e	**MISSAW**	MINISH
MOLLAH	MONTEM	MOOLAH	MORROW	MULLAH	MURRAM	*MUSICK*	MUTISM	**MYTHIC**
NALLAH	*NITROX*+	NULLAH	OGRESS+	**ORGIAC**	OUTROW	PACHAK	PALLAH	PANICKy
PARSEC	**PARTIM**	PHOTOG	PILAFF	POOJAH	PROLEG	**PRUTAH**	PUNKAH	PURDAH
PURISM	PURSEW	**RAKISH**	RAWING	REBECK	RESEEKed	SAMEKH	SCARPH	SCARTH
SCRAMB	SCRAWM	*SCRAWP*	SCRIMPy	SCRUMPy	SHEIKHa	SHIVAH	SHLEPP	**SHTUMM**
SIRRAH	SKARTH	SNEESH+	SPARTHe	SPELTZ+	SPILTH	SPIREMe	SPRITZ	STOUTH
SUMACH	SUNNAH	SWARTHy	TANNAH	TELESM	THANAH	THREEP	**THYMIC**	**TOROTH**
TREFAH	*TRICEP*	UMIACK	UNBARK	UNCLEW	VARECH	*WAIRSH**	WALLAH	*WIRRAH*
YOGISM	ZAMANG	ZEBECK	ZIBETH	ZILLAH				

6.3 LESS FAMILIAR NON-HOOK SIXES

6.3.1 VERBS COMPRISED OF A COMMON PREFIX PLUS A VERB

BECALL	BECLOG>	BECURL	BEDAMN	BEDASH	BEDAUB	BEDAZE	BEDECK	BEDROP>
BEDROPt	BEDRUG>	BEDUCK	BEDUMB	BEDUNG	BEDUST	BEFLAG>	BEFOAM	BEFOOL
BEFOUL	BEFRET>	BEGALL	BEGAZE	BEGIFT	BEGILD	BEGIRD	BEGLAD>	BEGNAW
BEGULF	BEHOWL	BEJADE	BEKISS	BEKNOT>	BELACE	BELAUD	BELEAPt	BELOVE
BEMAUL	BEMEANt	BEMETE	BEMIRE	BEMIST	BEMOCK	BEMOIL	BEMUSE	BENAME
BENUMB	BEPELT	BEPITY	BEPUFF	BERAKE	BERIME	BESIGH	BESINGed	BESMUT>
BESNOW	BESORT	BESPITed	BESPIT>	BESPOT>	BESTAR>	BESTUD>	BETAKEd	BETAKEn
BETEEMe	BETIME	BETOIL	BETOSS	BETRIM>	BEWAIL	BEWEEPed	BEWORM	BEWRAP>
BEWRAPt								

COEDIT	COHEAD	COJOIN	COLEADed	COMAKEed	COMAKEr	COPLOT>

DEBONEr	DEBOSS	DEBUNK	DECAMP	DECLAW	DECOKE	DECREW	DEFANG	DEFLEX
DEFOAM	DEFORM	DEFOUL	DEFRAG>	*DEFUEL*	*DEFUEL*>	DEFUND	DEFUZE	DEGERM
DEHORN	DELEAD	DELIME	DEMARK	DEMAST	DEPERM	DESALT	DESAND	DESCRY
DESEED	DESINE	DESORB	DESYNE	DETICK	DETUNE	DEVEIN	DEVEST	DEWORM
DEZINC	DEZINC&							

EMBAIL	EMBALE	EMBALL	EMBANK	EMBASE	EMBOIL	EMMESH	EMMOVE	EMPALEr
EMPARE	EMPART							

ENARCH	ENCALM	ENCAMP	ENCASE	ENCASH	ENCAVE	ENDART	ENDITE	ENDOSS
ENFACE	ENFIRE	ENFOLD	ENFORM	ENFREE	ENGAOL	ENGILD	ENGIRD	ENGLUT>
ENGORE	ENHALO	ENHALO+	ENISLE	ENJAMB	ENJOIN	ENLACE	ENLARD	ENLINK
ENLOCK	ENMESH	ENMOVE	ENRACE	ENRAGE	ENRANK	ENRING	ENROBEr	ENROOT
ENSEAL	ENSEAM	ENSEAR	ENSILE	ENTAME	ENTOIL	ENWALL	ENWINDd	ENWOMB
ENWRAP>	ENZONE							

IMBALM	IMBASE	IMBODY	IMBOSS	IMMASK	IMMESH	IMMURE	IMPARK	IMPAVE
IMPAWN	IMPEND							

INARCH	INCAGE	INCASE	INCAVE	INCEDE	INCLIP>	INDART	INDITEr	INFAME
INFILL	INFOLD	INFUSEr	INGULF	INHOOP	INISLE	INLACE	INLOCK	INMESH
INPOUR	INSEAM	INSEEM	INSHIP>	INSPAN>	INSTAR>	INTOMB	INTONEr	INWALL
INWICK	INWINDd	INWORK	INWRAP>					

MISACT	MISADD	MISAIM	MISCUE	MISCUE=	MISCUTd	MISCUT>	MISEATd	MISKEN>
MISKENt	MISKEY	MISLIEd	MISPEN>	MISSEEd	MISSEEm	MISSEEn	MISSETd	MISSET>

OUTACT	OUTADD	OUTASK	OUTBAR>	OUTBARk	OUTBEG>	OUTBUYd	OUTFLYd	OUTFOX
OUTGAS>	OUTGAS+	OUTGUN>	OUTHITd	OUTHIT>	OUTJUT>	OUTLIEr	OUTMAN>	*OUTRIG>*
OUTSAYd	OUTSEEd	OUTSEEn	OUTSIN>	OUTSINg	OUTSITd	OUTSIT>	OUTSUM>	OUTTOP>
OUTVIE	OUTWAR>	OUTWARd	OUTWINd	OUTWIN>	OUTWINd	OUTWINg		

REAVOW	REBACK	REBAIT	REBILL	REBODY	REBOIL	REBORE	REBURY	RECANE
RECASTd	RECHEW	*RECHIP>*	RECLAD>	RECOAL	*RECOAT*	RECOCK	RECODE	RECOIN
RECOMB	RECOPY	RECORK	REDATE	REDEFY	REDENY	REDOCK	REEARN	REEDIT
REEMIT>	REFACE	REFALLd	REFEEDd	REFEELd	REFILE	REFINDd	REFIRE	REFLAG>
REFLOWn	REFOLD	REFOOT	REGEAR	*REGIFT*	REGILD	REGIVEd	REGIVEn	REGLOW
REGLUE	REGROWd	REGROWn	REHIRE	*REHOME*	REKNIT>	*REKNOT>*	RELACE	RELENDd
RELINK	RELOAN	RELOCK	RELOOK	REMATE	REMEETd	REMELT	REMINT	REMOLD
RENAIL	RENEST	REPARK	REPASS	REPAVE	REPERK	REPLOT>	*REPLOW*	REPOLL
REPOUR	REPULP	REPUMP	REPURE	REQUITe	REQUIT>	RERACK	RERAIL	*RERENT*
RERISEd	RERISEn	REROLL	REROOF	RESAIL	RESEAT	RESHIP>	RESHOE=	RESHOWn
RESIFT	RESKEW	RESOAK	RESOLE	RESORB	RESPOT>	RESTEM>	RETACK	RETEAM
RETEARd	RETILE	RETIME	RETINT	RETOOL	RETOUR	RETRIM>	RETUND	RETUNE
RETURF	REURGE	REVEST	REVOTE	REWAKEn	REWARM	REWASH	*REWEARd*	REWELD
REWIRE	*REZERO*	*REZERO+*						

UNBALE	UNBARE	UNBEAR	UNBELT	UNBEND	UNBIAS	UNBIAS>	UNBINDd	UNBITT
UNBONE	UNBOOT	UNBURY	UNCAGE	UNCAKE	UNCART	UNCASE	UNCLIP>	UNCLIPt
UNCLOG>	UNCOCK	UNCOIL	UNCOLT	UNCOPE	UNCORD	UNCOWL	UNCUFF	UNCURB
UNCURL	UNDECK	UNDOCK	UNDRAWd	UNDRAWn	UNEDGE	UNFOOL	UNFORM	UNFREE
UNFURL	UNGEAR	UNGILD	UNGIRD	UNGLUE	UNGOWN	UNGYVE	UNHAIR	UNHANG
UNHASP	UNHEAD	UNHEAL	UNHELE	UNHELM	UNHIVE	UNHOOD	UNHOOP	UNHUSK
UNKING	UNKISS	UNKNIT>	UNKNOT>	UNLADEn	UNLASH	UNLEAD	UNLIME	UNLINE
UNLINK	UNLIVE	UNLORD	UNLOVE	UNMAKEd	UNMAKEr	UNMASK	UNMESH	UNMOLD
UNMOOR	UNNAIL	UNNEST	UNPICK	UNPILE	UNPRAY	UNPROP>	UNRAKE	UNREEL
UNREIN	UNROBE	UNROOF	UNROOT	UNROPE	UNSEAL	UNSEAM	UNSEEL	UNSELF

```
UNSELLd UNSHIP> UNSHOE= UNSHUTd UNSHUT> UNSNAG> UNSNAP> UNSPAR> UNSTEP>
UNSTOP> UNSTOW  UNSUIT  UNTACK  UNTAME  UNTEAM  UNTENTy UNTHAW  UNTOMB
UNTRIM> UNTUCK  UNTUNE  UNTURF  UNTURN  UNVAILe UNWILL  UNWIRE  UNWISH
UNWIVE  UNWORK  UNYOKE


UPBEARd UPBINDd UPBLOWd UPBLOWn UPBOIL  UPBRAY  UPCASTd UPCOIL  UPCURL
UPDART  UPDIVE  UPDRAG> UPDRAWd UPDRAWn UPFILL  UPFLOW  UPFOLD  UPFURL
UPGAZE  UPGIRD  UPGROWd UPGROWn UPGUSH  UPHAUDd UPHEAP  UPHURL  UPKNIT>
UPLEANt UPLEAPt UPLOCK  UPPILE  UPREAR  UPRUSH  UPSELLd UPSENDd UPSIZE
UPSOAR  UPSTAY  UPSTEP> UPSTIR> UPSWAY  UPTALK  UPTEARd UPTILT  UPTOSS
UPWAFT  UPWELL
```

6.3.2 OTHER VERBS

CONTAINING HEAVY LETTERS

```
ABJUREr ADJUREr AGNIZE  AGRYZE  AGUIZE  ASSIZEr BANJAX  BLAZON  BOLLIX
BOLLOX  CALQUE  CONFIX  CONJEE  DEEJAY  DORIZE  EXCAMB  EXCIDE  EXHORT
EXPUGN  EXSECT  EXSERT  EXTIRP  FIXATE  FIZGIG> FOOZLEr GAZUMP  IODIZEr
JAUNCE  JAUNSE  JEELIE  JEELIE= JERQUEr JIRBLE  JITTERy JOGGLEr JUSTLE
KIBITZ  KLAXON  LUXATE  NAZIFY  OBJURE  PICKAXe POLEAXe QUAERE= QUATCH
QUELCH  QUETCH  QUETHEd QUIGHT  QUITCH  SCRUZE  SQUINY  SQUIRR  SQUISHy
SQUUSH  STOOZEr SURTAX  TEAZLE  TOUZLE  TWEEZEr WEAZEN  WRAXLE
```

OTHER

```
ABDUCE  ACKNOWd ACKNOWn ADDEEM  ADDOOM  ADDUCEr ADDUCT  ADSORB  ADVECT
ADVENE  ADVERT  ADWARD  AERIFY  AGNISE  AMERCEr ANNEAL  ARAYSE  ARGUFY
AROINT  AROYNT  ARRIDE  ASHLAR  ASHLER  ASKANT  ASSART  ASSOIL  ASSORT
ATTASKt ATTONE  ATTORN  ATTRAP> ATTRITe ATTRIT> AUMAIL  AURIFY  AVULSE
AWHAPE


BALLAT  BARHOP> BARKEN  BASIFY  BATOON  BATTEL  BATTEL> BEFLEA  BEFLUM>
BEGRIMe BEGRIM> BEHOTEd BELADY  BENDAY  BERLEY  BEWRAY  BIRSLE  BITMAP>
BLANCO  BLENCH  BOGART  BOODIE  BOODLEr BOOGEY  BOOHOO  BRIGUE  BUDDLE
BULLER  BUTTLE


CADDIE  CAGMAG> CALEFY  CANDIE  CANTLEt CAREEN  CARHOP> CARNEY  CARNIE*
CARROM  CASEFY  CAUDLE  CHASSE= CHASSE# CHAUFEr CHERUP  CHIAUS  CIPHER
CITIFY  CITYFY  COEMPT  COGGLE  COHERER COLLET  CONFAB> COOPERy COOSEN
COOSIN  CORVET  CORVET> COSHERy COTISE  CRENEL  CRENEL> CUITER  CUPOLAr
CURRIEr CURTSY  CYPHER


DAGGLE  DAIDLE  DAIKER  DAMASK  DANDER  DANDLEr DANTON  DARKLE  DARTLE
DAUNER  DEBEAK  DEBOSH  DECARB  DECERN  DEFLEA  DEHORT  DEMENTi DEPONE
DEPUTE  DETORT  DEVALL  DEWITT  DEWOOL  DIADEM  DIDDER  DINDLE  DINNLE
DIPNET> DISBAR> DISBARk DISBUD> DISMAN> DISPLE  DOGNAP  DOGNAP> DONDER
DRAUNT  DRUDGEr DUMPLE  DUSKEN
```

```
ELOIGN  EMBACEd EMBOSK  EMBRUE  EMPARL  EMULGE  ENAMOR  ENCYST  ENSERF
ENSOUL  ESCHEW  ESLOIN  EVINCE  EVULSE

FAMISH  FEAGUE  FELTER  FERLIE*  FERREL  FERREL>  FERULE  FETTER  FEUTRE
FEWTER  FINEER  FISSLE  FLAMBE#  FLAMBE=  FLAMBEe  FLENCH  FLITCH  FLOUSH
FOMENT  FOOTLEr FOREDOd FORHOO  FORHOW  FORRAY  FORSAYd FRESCO  FRESCO+
FRIVOL  FRIVOL> FUDDLEr

GALLETa GALOSHe GARNER  GAROTE  GARROTe GARROT>  GASIFY  GAUNCH  GHERAO
GHERAO+ GHESSE  GIGGIT  GILLIE  GIMBAL  GIMBAL>  GIMLET  GODDAM>  GODDAMn
GOLIAS  GOLLAR  GOLLER  GOLLOP  GOLOSHe GOOGLE  GOSTER  GRAITH  GRUTCH
GUDDLE  GUGGLE  GULLEY  GUSSET  GUSSIE  GUTTLEr

HALLAL> HALLALi HARKEN  HARTEN  HECTOR  HEDDLE  HIGGLEr HIRPLE  HIRSEL
HIRSEL> HIRSLE  HOBDAY  HOCKLE  HODDLE  HOIDEN  HONDLE  HOWDIE  HOYDEN
HUCKLE  HUMECT  HUMEFY  HUMIFY  HUNKER

IDEATE  IGNIFY  ILLUDE  ILLUME  IMBOSK  IMBRUE  IMPARL  IMPONE  IMPUGN
IMPUTEr INCENT  INCEPT  INCISE  INGESTa INHERE  INHUMEr INSOUL  INTORT
INTUIT  IODATE  IODISEr IRRUPT

KASHER  KIBOSH  KIDDIEr KITTLE*  KLUDGEy KORERO  KREESE  KURVEY

LAAGER  LADIFY  LADYFY  LAIPSE  LARRUP  LAUNCE  LAVEER  LAVOLTa LEASOWe
LEGATEe LENIFY  LENITE  LEVANT  LIBATE  LIGATE  LINISH  LOADEN  LOLLOPy
LOUDEN  LUMINE

MACKLE  MACULE  MADEFY  MAKUTU  MALGRE  MANEGE  MARAUD  MARCEL>  MARVER
MAUGRE  MEEKEN  MICATE  MICKEY  MILDEN  MINIFY  MOIDER  MONGERy  MONISH
MOTTLEr MOUSLE  MUCKER  MUDCAP> MULLER  MUTINE

NIDATE  NIDIFY  NIELLO  NOCHEL  NOCHEL>  NODDLE  NOODGE  NORSEL>  NOUSLE
NURDLE  NURSLE  NUTATE

OBDURE  OBSIGN  OBTEND  OBTEST  OBTUND  OBVERT  OLFACT  OMNIFY  ONLOAD
OOMPAH  OSMOSE  OSSIFY  OUGHLY  OUGLIE=  OVERGOd OVERGOt

PANFRY  PARLAY  PASEAR  PEARCE  PEENGE  PEENGE=  PEINCT  PELTER  PERSUE
PHEESE  PHREAK  PINKEN  PITTER  PODDLE  POGROM  POMADE  POONCE  POOTLE
POSTIL  POSTIL> POWTER  POYSON  PRANCKe PREACE  PREASE  PROIGN  PROLOG
PRUSIK  PUGGLE  PULVER  PULVIL>  PUNGLE  PURFLEr PURVEY

RAGGLE  RAGOUT  RAMIFY  RAMROD>  RARIFY  RASSLE  RATTEN  RAUNCHy RAUNGE
RECULE  RECUSE  REDACT  REDDLE  REFECT  RELUCT  RELUME  REMBLE  REMEAD
REMEDE  REMEID  REMISE  RENEGEr REPONE  REPUGN  RESECT  RESKUE  REVERB
RICHEN  RIMPLE  RIPOSTe ROOTLEt RUBEFY  RUBIFY  RUCKLE  RUDDLE  RUMPLE
RUNKLE
```

SAGGARd	SALAAM	SALIFY	SANIFY	SASHAY	SAWDER	SCAITH	SCARRE	SCHLEP>
SCHLEPp	SCHUSS	*SCOOSH*	SCRIKE	SCRIVE	SCROOP	SEARCE	SECERN	SEMBLE
SHAMOY	SHIKAR>	SHIKARi	SHINNEy	SHINTY	SHLUMPy	SHREEK	SHREIK	SHRIVE1
SHRIVEn	SHRIVEr	*SHROOM*	SIWASH	SKAITH	SKIDOO	*SKITCH*	SKLATE	SKLENT
SKOOSH	SKRIMP	SKRUMP	SKURRY	SLAIRG	SLOKEN	SLOOSH	SMEECH	SMIRCH
SMOILE	*SMOOGE*	*SMOOSH*	SNITCHy	SODGER	SOLATE	SOOGEE	SOOGIE=	SOPITE
SOUPLE	SOWSSE	SPARREr	SPERRE	*SPLISH*	SPLOSH	SPRUSH	SPULYE=	STANCH*
STAYNE	STEEVE*	STERVE	STIMIE	STIRREr	STITHY	STODGEr	STREEK	STREEL
STROAM	STRUNT	SUBACT	SUBDEW	SUBFEU	SUBORN	SUDATE	SULFURy	SURBED>
SUTTLE	SWARVE	SYPHER						

TABEFY	TABOUR	TAIGLE	TATTLEr	TATTOW	TAUTEN	TEDDER	TELFER	TELLAR
TELNET	TELNET>	TEPEFY	TETTER	THRALL	THRANG	THREAP	THRISTy	THWACK
TIDDLEr	TIDDLEy	TITTLE	TITTUPy	TITTUP>	TITULE	*TOGGERy*	TOLTER	TOMPON
TRAMEL1	TRAMEL>	TRAPAN>	TREPAN>	TREPANg	TUMEFY			

UGLIFY	ULLAGE	UMLAUT	UNDEAF	UNSOUL

VAMOSE	VAROOM	VASSAL>	VAUNCE	VELURE	VENTRE	VERMIL>	VERMILy	VINIFY
VOUDOUn								

WADDIE	WADSET>	WADSETt	WARRANd	WARRANt	WARSLEr	WAUCHT	*WEBIFY*	WEDDER
WILLEY	WILLIE	WIMBLE	WIMPLE	WINDLE	WINTLE	WITTER	WORRIT	WRETHE
WUTHER								

YATTER

6.3.3 NOUNS BY COMMON ENDINGS

AGE

ACHAGE	ALNAGEr	AMBAGE	ANLAGEn	BOCAGE	BORAGE	*CEPAGE*	COWAGE	CUBAGE
EATAGE	ENNAGE	FUMAGE	GALAGE	GAVAGE	HIDAGE	HIRAGE	*INNAGE*	LAVAGE
LINAGE	LOVAGE	LYNAGE	MILAGE	MURAGE	NONAGEd	OARAGE	OHMAGE	PARAGE
PAVAGE	PELAGE	POTAGEr	RIVAGE	ROMAGE	SOCAGEr	SORAGE	*TIRAGE*	TOWAGE
TUBAGE	VISAGEd							

AL

ATABAL	AVOWAL	BEDRAL	BENZAL	BHARAL	BUNTAL	*CANTALa*	CARPALe	CENTAL
CHITAL	CITRAL	COEVAL	COTWAL	CURTAL	FALLAL	FAUCAL	FECIAL	FETIAL
FINIAL	*FUTSAL*	GARIAL	GAVIAL	GHAZAL	GINGAL1	GOORAL	GYMBAL	HYMNAL
JINGAL1	JUMBAL	*KEYPAL*	KOTWAL	MESCAL	MEZCAL	MISKAL	*MISTAL*	MONIAL
MUGHAL	NARWAL	OORIAL	PARDALe	PARIAL	PASCAL	*PAUCAL*	PINEAL	PUTEAL
QUEZAL	SALLAL	SANTAL	SENDAL	SERVAL	SPITAL	TARSAL	TIMBALe	TINCAL
TINDAL	TYMBAL	UNWEAL	VERSAL	WADMAL	WORRAL			

ANE

ALKANEt	BORANE	*BYLANE*	CETANE	*CUBANE*	DECANE	DOUANE	HEXANE	MOPANE
NONANE	SILANE	TISANE						

ANT

ACTANT BEJANT BEZANT BYZANT DOPANT DOTANT DURANT ELUANT ENFANT
GELANT JURANT OPTANT PEDANT PESANTe PEZANT SAVANTe SECANT SONANT
ZELANT

AR

ALEGAR ANTIAR ARREAR AVATAR BEZOAR BISMAR BORDAR BOXCAR CAESAR
CHADAR CHENAR CHIMAR CHUKAR DAFTAR *DARBAR* DEODARa DURBAR ESCHAR
EVEJAR EYEBAR FULMAR *GAYDAR* HANJAR HERBARy ISOBARe KEASAR *KHIMAR*
LANGAR LASCAR LEKVAR *LOUVAR* MEDLAR MINBAR NICKAR NONWAR NUGGAR
OCULAR PSYWAR PULSAR PULWAR QINDAR QINTAR QUASAR REDEAR *SALWAR*
SARDAR SECPAR SHMEAR SHOFAR SIRCAR SIRDAR SIRKAR SITTAR SOLLAR
SOUCAR SOUTAR SOWCAR SPHEARe SUNGAR TARTARe THENAR TRICAR TROCAR
TULWAR TUSKAR

ARY+

AMBARY+ ANGARY+ DATARY+ DONARY+ FEGARY+ PANARY+ SENARY+ SUDARY+ VAGARY+

ATE

AGNATE ALGATE CERATEd COMATE DOGATE ELUATE ERGATE FLUATE FOLATE
HUMATE HYPATE INGATE LUNATEd LYSATE METATE MUCATE OLEATE OSMATE
OXGATE SAVATE SCLATE SEBATE

EE

APOGEE *ASYLEE* BAILEE BAJREE BENDEE BHAGEE BHAJEE BUNGEE BURGEE
BURPEE BUSTEE CORVEE COULEE DEBTEE DRAWEE *DUMPEE* ELCHEE GIDGEE
GIDJEE *GIFTEE* HADJEE *HEALEE* HUMVEE IMPHEE *JAYCEE* JAYGEE JAYVEE
JESTEE LICHEE LISTEE *LOANEE* MENTEE MESTEE MUGGEE MUSTEE PALKEE
PARKEE PAWNEE PEEWEE PENSEE POLLEE PONGEE PUGREE PUNTEE PUTTEE
RAGGEE RETREE RUSHEE SICKEE SIGNEE SIRREE SPAHEE SUTTEE TAGGEE
TOUPEE TOWHEE TOWNEE VEEPEE VENDEE VESTEE VOIDEE WAMPEE *YANKEE*

EN

ALPEEN BALEEN *BERGEN* BIOGENy BUNSEN CHEVEN CUDDEN DOCKEN DOLMEN
DUDEEN DZEREN EXAMEN EXOGEN FARDEN FARREN GERMEN GIPSEN GODDEN
GORHEN GOWPEN GRABEN GULDEN HAGDEN HAPTENe HERDEN HODDEN HUMPEN
HURDEN KAIZEN KANTEN *KEIREN* KHAZEN KUCHEN KYOGEN LAGGEN LATEEN
LEDDEN LEGLEN LIBKEN LINDEN LUMPEN LURDEN MARTEN MIDDEN MOREEN
MORGEN *MUDHEN* MULLEN MYOGEN OROGENy PANGENe PEAHEN PECTEN POTEEN
PUDDEN *RATEEN* SATEEN SAZHEN SEITEN SEPHEN SKREEN STAMEN STEVEN
SUCKEN SWEVEN TELLEN TICKEN TUREEN VOTEEN WICKEN

ER *extensions of verbs*

BAITER BALKER BALLER BANDER BARKER BASHER BAWLER *BEADER* BEAMER
BEDDER BELTER BILKER BIRDER *BOGGER* BONDER BOOKER BOOMER BRAYER
BUCKER BULKER *BUNGER* BUNTER BURIER BURLER BURRER CALKER CARDER
CARPER CEILER CHAWER COALER COAXER COGGER COINER COLTER COMPERe
CONKER CORKER CULLER CURBER DAMNER DARNER DARTER DEANERy DECKER

DEFIER   DENIER   DIALER   DIETER   DOGGERy DORTER   DUCKER   DUELER   DUMPER
DUNGER DUNKER   ECHOER   ENVIER   ETCHER   FALLER   FANNER   FILMER   FOAMER
FOGGER   FORKER   FUCKER   FUELER   FUNKER   FURLER   GAOLER   GAUPER   GAWKER
GAWPER   GILDER   GIRNER   GNAWER   GOWFER   GULLERy GULPER   GUTSER   HANDER
HARPER   HAULER   *HEAPER* HEEDER   HELLERi HELLERy *HELMER* HENNERy HERDER
HOAXER   HOGGERy HONKER   HOOFER   HOOPER   HOWKER   HUGGER   HULLER   HUMPER
HURLER   HURTER   HUSKER   *INCHER* JEERER   JERKER   JILTER   *JOLLER* JOLTER
JOSHER   JUNKER   KEELER   KELPER   KEMPER   KENNER   KIDDER   KILTER   LAIKER
*LAMPER*n LARKER   LASHER   LAUDER   LEAKER   LEAPER   LEVIER   LIMNER   LISPER
LISTER   LOANER   LOOPER   LUGGER   *LULLER* LUMPER   MARRER   MASHER   MAULER
MEALER   MEETER   MELTER   MEWLER   MILTER   MINTER   MOLTER   MOONER   *MOSHER*
NAILERy NECKER   NEEDER   NETTER   NOONER   NOSHERy OBEYER   OUSTER   PALMER
PANTER   PARKER   PARTER   PETTER   PINGER   PIONER   *PISHER* PITIER   *POGOER*
POOLER POOTER   PORKER   PREYER   PULLER   PUNNER   PURLER   RAMPER   RANTER
RATTERy REARER   REEKER   REELER   RIDDER   RISKER   RITTER   ROAMER   ROARER
ROLFER   ROOMER   ROOTER   RORTER   RUGGER   RUINER   SAILER   SCRYER   SEEDER
SEEMER   SIFTER   SIGHER   SIGNER   SKRYER   SOAPER   SORNER   SOUPER   SPEWER
STEWER   SULKER   SWAYER   TAILER   TEAMER   TEARER   TEEMER   TERMER   *TEXTER*
THAWER   TILTER   TONGER   TONKER   TOOLER   TOOTER   TOSHER   TUFTER   TUGGER
TUSKER   UNDOER   VAMPER   VANNER   VARIER   VATTER   VEILER   VEINER   VETOER
VETTER VIZIER   VOIDER   WAILER   WALLER   WANTER   WARNER   WARPER   WAUKER
WEANER   WEARER   WEEPER   *WIGGERy* WISHER   WOLFER   WONNER   WOOFER   *YARDER*
YARNER   YAUPER   YAWPER   YELPER   YORKER   YUCKER   ZINGER

ER *other*

ALMNER   AMBEER   ANTHER   AUNTER   AVOYER   BATLER   BAXTER   BEEZER   *BIFTER*
BISTER   *BITSER* BOOGER   *BOONER* BOWYER   CAHIER   CAUKER   CAUTERy CAWKER
CHOLERa CIMIER   CODGER   CONDER   COOSER   COOTER   CRAYER   CULTER   CULVERt
CUNNER   CUTLERy DEXTER   DOOFER   DOOZER   DORPER   DUIKER   DUYKER   *EBAYER*
EGGLER   EPIMERe FAKEER   FUHRER   GAUFER   GEEZER   GOITER   GOOBER   GROSERt
GUIZER   GUNTER   GUTZER   HEIFER   HIDDER   HOSIERy INLIER   ISOMERe JAEGER
KAISER   KARTER   KEGLER   KELTER   LANNER   LEIGER   LIDGER   LIVIER   LIVYER
LOUVER   LUNKER   MENEER   MERCERy METIER   MOISER   MOTSER   *MUNTER* NIPTER
ONAGER   ONEYER   OSTLER   OUTLER   *PANEER* PANIER   PANZER   PATZER   PEDDER
PEDLERy PINDER   POTZER   POUDER   PYONER   REITER   RIBIER   ROEMER   *RONZER*
SAETER   SAWYER   SCOTER   SHODER   *SOWDER* SOWTER   SPHAERe SQUIER   STUMER
SUTLERy *SWILER* TATLER   TITFER   *TODGER* TWOFER   ULSTER   URETER   VESPER
VIOLER   WEEVER   WEINER   WIDDER   WIENER   WIZIER   WOOLER   WUNNER   XYSTER
YONKER   ZANDER   ZOSTER

ERY+

ALMERY+ ASHERY+ DUKERY+ EMPERY+ FIKERY+ JADERY+ ORRERY+ PINERY+ ROSERY+
VENERY+ VOLERY+

ET *excluding 'LET'*

AIGRET   AMORET   AVOCET   AVOSET   BACKET   BAGUET   BANKET   BANNET   *BARNET*
BASNET   BERRET   BOSKET   *BOTNET* BOWGET   BRUNET   *BUNNET* BURNET   BUSKET
CARNET   CERMET   CHENET   CHEVET   CHEWET   DECTET   DENNET   DOOKET   ELANET

FANJET	FEWMET	FLORET	FORPET	FUSTET	GARGETy	GENNET	GROMET	GURNET
HOGGET	IMARET	JENNET	*JULIET*	KENNETt	KEYSET	KISMET	*KITSET*	LABRET
LASKET	LIMPET	LINNET	LIONET	NACKET	NIDGET	NOCKET	OUTJET	PELMET
PINNET	POSNET	PROJET	RAMJET	*RICKET*y	ROCHET	RUNNET	SENNET	SEPTET
SEXTETt	SINNET	SORBET	SOVIET	SUBNET	SUCKET	SYNDET	TABRET	TACKETy
TERRET	THIBET	TORRET	TOUPET	TRIJET	TUCKET	VARLET	VERDET	WIDGET
WISKET								

EY

ASHKEY	BAILEY	BAWLEY	BUNGEY	COOKEY	DARKEY	DICKEY*	DINKEY*	GANSEY
GARVEY	GILPEY	GOOLEY	GOONEY	GURNEY	HAWKEY	*HENLEY*	HICKEY	HONKEY
HOOLEY*	HORKEY	*HUNKEY**	HURLEY	JARVEY	JITNEY	JOLLEY*	KERSEY	*LARNEY**
LINNEY	LINSEY	LOONEY*	MAGUEY	MEINEY	MILSEY	MOOLEY	MULLEY	OSPREY
PEAVEY	PINKEY*	PINKEYe	PIONEY	PODLEY	POWNEY	PUNKEY*	RICKEY	RIDLEY
SARNEY	SAWNEY	SOOJEY	STOGEY	SURREY	TAWNEY*	TICKEY	TINSEY	*TOLLEY*
TOLSEY	TOLZEY	WINSEY	WITNEY	WURLEY				

FUL

BAGFUL	BOXFUL	CANFUL	CAPFUL	CARFUL	HATFUL	JARFUL	LAPFUL	MUGFUL
NETFUL	PANFUL	PENFUL	POTFUL	TINFUL	TUBFUL	URNFUL	VATFUL	

IA

ABASIA	ABELIAn	ABULIA	ACEDIA	ALALIA	ALEXIA	AMELIA	AMUSIA	ANEMIA
ANOPIA	ANOXIA	ANURIA	APORIA	ARALIA	ATAXIA	ATOCIA	*ATONIA*	BUNNIA
CLIVIA	CLUSIA	CODEIA	*CUMBIA*	DAHLIA	FATSIA	FUNKIA	GAMBIA	GLORIA
HOLMIA	*HOODIA*	KALMIA	KERRIA	*KETMIA*	*KOCHIA*	LITHIA	LOGGIA	*MANAIA*
NUTRIA	PYEMIA	PYURIA	RAPHIA	SALVIA	SCOTIA	SHARIAh	SHARIAt	SHERIAt
STADIAl	SYLVIA	TAENIAe	TANKIA	TERTIAl	TERTIAn	THORIA	THULIA	URANIAn
UREMIA	YAUTIA	YTTRIA	ZOYSIA					

IC

AGARIC	AGOGIC	ATAXIC	BEYLIC	BIOPIC	*BORSIC*	DYADIC	EMBLIC	FUSTIC
GOTHIC	HAPTIC	HERDIC	HYPNIC	IRENIC	LUETIC	MASTICh	MATRICe	MIOTIC
MUNDIC	MYOTIC	NAUTIC	*NERDIC*	OVONIC	PATHIC	PHOBIC	PHONIC	PHOTIC
PHYSIC	PYKNIC	RUBRIC	SPIRIC	SYNDIC	VITRIC			

ID

ARAMID	BROMIDe	CAPRID	CAPSID	CERVID	CLERID	CORVID	*COSMID*	COTTID
CUSPID	CYANIDe	CYBRID	CYPRID	CYSTID	DESMID	DIACID	DIOXIDe	ELAPID
FURKID	GOBIID	HYDRIDe	IXODID	JERRID	KIDVID	LABRID	MAELID	MANTID
MASJID	MUSCID	MUSJID	NAVAID	NEREID	NITRIDe	*OZALID*	PIERID	PONGID
PSOCID	SAIYID	SALPID	SIALID	SPARID	SULFIDe	TINEID	TOLUIDe	VERBID
VESPID								

IE

ANOMIE	AWMRIE	*BACKIE*	BADDIE	BAILIE	*BALDIE**	*BARDIE**	*BARRIE**	BAWTIE
BICKIE	BIGGIE	BILLIE	BIRKIE*	BITTIE*	BLOWIE*	BOATIE	BODGIE*	BONNIE*
BONXIE	BOTHIE	BOUGIE	*BOWSIE*	*BOYKIE*	*BREDIE*	BRIDIE	BUCKIE	*BUFTIE*

BUNGIE BUNJIE BURDIE BURNIE *BUSHIE** BYRNIE CABRIE CATTIE* CHEWIE*
CIGGIE COGGIE CONDIE *CONNIE* COOLIE COOTIE CORBIE CORRIE COWPIE
CRUSIE *CRUZIE* CUDDIE *CUSHIE** DAFTIE DARKIE DAUTIE DAWTIE DEARIE
DEEPIE DICKIE* DINKIE* DOGGIE* *DOOBIE* DOOLIE DOOZIE DUCKIE* DURRIE
FALSIE FOLKIE* FOODIE FOOTIE* *FOULIE* GADGIE GARVIE *GEGGIE* GILGIE
GIRLIE* GOODIE* GOOLIE GOONIE* *GYMPIE* HACKIE HADDIE HANKIE HAWKIE
HEEZIE HEINIE HEMPIE* *HETTIE* *HICKIE* HOAGIE HONKIE HOODIE* HOOLIE*
HOSTIE HOTTIE HUMLIE *HUNKIE** JARVIE JILGIE JUMBIE JUNKIE* KEAVIE
KEELIE KELPIE KELTIE *KEWPIE* KIERIE KILLIE KILTIE LADDIE LALDIE
LAMBIE* LEFTIE *LEGGIE** LINTIE* *LOERIE* LOONIE* *LOOSIE* LUCKIE* LUGGIE
LUNYIE MASHIE* MATTIE MEALIE* MEANIE MEINIE MENYIE *MIDDIE* *MIDGIE**
MIELIE MILLIEr MINNIE MOGGIE MOUSIE* *MOWDIE* MUSKIE* NANNIE NELLIE
NETTIE* NEWBIE NEWSIE* *NOOGIE* NOOKIE* PALMIE* PALMIEt PANTIE PATTIE
PERMIE PIGGIE* *PILLIE* PINKIE* PINNIE PIRNIE *PODDIE** PONTIE PORGIE
POSTIE *POTJIE* POTSIE POWNIE PRATIE PREMIEr PUGGIE* PUNKIE* QUINIE
RANDIE* *RASHIE* *RELLIE* RHODIE *RONNIE* *ROOFIE** ROOKIE* ROOMIE* *SADDIE*
SALTIE* SANNIE *SARMIE* SARNIE SAULIE SELKIE SHAVIE SICKIE SILKIE*
*SMOKIE** SOAPIE* SOFTIE *SOUTIE* SPAVIEt SPECIE STOGIE SUNKIE TADDIE
TALKIE* *TANNIE* TATTIE* TAUPIE TAWPIE TECHIE* TEDDIE TINNIE* TITTIE
TOEBIE *TOOLIE* *TOONIE* TOTTIE* TOWNIE* TREMIE TUSHIE *TWONIE* TYSTIE
VEGGIE WALLIE* WASPIE* WEDGIE* WEENIE* WEEPIE* WELLIE *WESTIE* *WETTIE*
WIDDIE WIDGIE WIENIE WOODIE* WOOLIE* WOOPIE *WURLIE* YANKIE *YETTIE*
YONNIE YORKIE

INE

ALKINE ARSINE *BOLINE* COSINE DOLINE DOMINEe EXTINE INGINE INTINE
MOLINEt NERINE ONDINE OSCINE PRUINE RAPINE RATINE RETINE SUPINE
TAGINE TAJINE UNDINE VAHINE WAHINE

ION

BASION CAMION CATION DUPION DURION ETHION GABION KATION LOGION
MORION NASION SOLION TALION TURION ULTION USTION VIRION

IS+

ABATIS+ ADONISe BREVIS+ BREWIS+ CADDISh CERRIS+ CULLIS+ DEIXIS+ DERMIS+
DERRIS+ EXOMIS+ FACTIS+ GLACIS+ HAGGISh HUBRIS+ HYBRIS+ IBERIS+ IRITIS+
KALPIS+ KERMIS+ KOUMISs MAJLIS+ MEJLIS+ NEBRIS+ ORCHIS+ OREXIS+ OXALIS+
PARVISe *PIERIS*+ PRAXIS+ PTYXIS+ RACHIS+ RHEXIS+ TRAVIS+ TREVISs TURKIS+
ULITIS+ VENDISs *WERRIS*+

ISM

AGEISM BONISM CHRISMa CIVISM CUBISM DUDISM EGOISM EONISM FAVISM
HOLISM HYLISM LAXISM LYRISM NANISM OBEISM OBIISM OGRISM PORISM
THEISM VERISMo

IST

AORIST	*AUTIST*	BONIST	CUBIST	CUEIST	EGOIST	HOLIST	HYLIST	JURIST
LAXIST	LEGIST	LUTIST	LYRIST	MONIST	OECIST	OIKIST	QUOIST	SCHIST
TANIST	TIMIST	TUBIST	UPRIST	VERIST	VIBIST			

IT

BAGGIT	*BANKIT*	CABRIT	COMFIT	CONFIT	DACOITy	DAKOITi	DAKOITy	FORPIT
GODWIT	HENBIT	JESUIT	KAINITe	KARAIT	MUSKIT	PANDIT	PLACITa	PROBITy
REDUIT	SAWPIT	SCHUIT	SENNIT	SPRUIT	SUMPIT	TALLITh	TERRIT	TEWHIT
TIRRIT	TOMTIT	TURBITh	VERDITe	WESKIT				

ITE

ACMITE	ALBITE	APLITE	ARKITE	AUGITE	BARITE	CERITE	DACITE	*DUGITE*
FOMITE	HALITE	HUMITE	ILLITE	IOLITE	KARITE	*KUMITE*	*LUCITE*	*LUTITE*
NANITE	NERITE	NORITE	OOLITE	OPHITE	PINITE	PODITE	RATITE	SAMITE
SOMITE	TONITE	VENITE	VERITE	ZYMITE				

ITY+

ACUITY+	COMITY+	DIMITY+	EGOITY+	ENMITY+	FERITY+	LAXITY+	LENITY+	MOYITY+
NOVITY+	POLITY+	VERITY+						

IUM

ALLIUM	CERIUM	CESIUM	CORIUM	CURIUM	*ECHIUM*	ERBIUM	FOLIUM	INDIUM
KALIUM	LOLIUM	SEPIUM						

LET

AIGLET	ARMLET	AUKLET	BATLET	CALLET	CAMLET	CULLET	EYALET	GIBLET
GIGLET	GILLET	GOGLET	GOSLET	GUGLET	GURLET	HASLET	JILLET	JUGLET
KIDLET	LEGLET	NUTLET	OILLET	OMELET	PIOLET	REFLET	REGLET	RIBLET
SAMLET	TALLET	TASLET	TONLET	VELLET	WIGLET	WILLET		

MAN

ATAMAN	CAIMAN	CAYMAN	DESMAN	DODMAN	FIRMAN	GERMANe	HARMAN	HETMAN
PITMAN								

OID

CEBOID	CONOID	CUBOID	FUCOID	GADOID	GANOID	HALOID	KELOID	LIPOID
MELOID	MUCOID	OPIOID	PELOID	TOROID	TOXOID	VIROID		

OR

ABATOR	BAILOR	BETTOR	BITTOR	CHIKOR	CHUKOR	CREMOR	ELUTOR	FAITOR
FAUTOR	FICTOR	FOETOR	FRAGOR	FULGOR	HAVIOR	HUZOOR	JAILOR	LECTOR
LICTOR	MAHZOR	MAINOR	NESTOR	OCTUOR	OVATOR	PAVIOR	PAWNOR	*PHASOR*
PLEXOR	PRETOR	RAPTOR	RHETOR	SAMLOR	SARTOR	SEIZOR	SENHORa	SIGNORa
SIGNORe	SIGNORi	SIGNORy	SPINOR	STATOR	TENSOR	TERMOR	TONSOR	TURGOR
VIATOR	WELDOR							

6. Six-Letter Words

OSE
ALDOSE ARKOSE FUCOSE HEXOSE KETOSE POROSE RIBOSE VIROSE XYLOSE
ZYGOSE

OUR
ARBOUR DOLOUR DYVOURy GIAOUR SAPOUR TENOUR VELOUR

OUT
BUGOUT BUYOUT *COPOUT* DEGOUT DIMOUT LAYOUT LOGOUT MAHOUT MAZOUT
PIGOUT PUTOUT REDOUT *RIGOUT* RUBOUT SETOUT TRYOUT

UM *excluding 'IUM'*
ANTRUM ASARUM CRINUM CUNDUM CUPRUM DICTUM DIRDUM DURDUM *EXACUM*
FACTUM FERRUM FRENUM HYPNUM KHANUM LABRUM LIGNUM LYCEUM NICKUM
NINCUM PABLUM *PELLUM* PENSUM PLENUM QUOTUM SACRUM SEPTUM SKELUM
SUBGUM TECTUM VALLUM VELLUM VISCUM ZYTHUM

UP
BALLUP CATSUP DUSTUP EYECUP *FOLDUP* FUCKUP GILCUP LINKUP LOOKUP
MARKUP *MASHUP* MOCKUP OILCUP SANNUP STROUP TAKEUP WALKUP WASHUP
WIKIUP WORKUP

US+
AIRBUS+ AIRBUS> ANIMUS+ CEREUS+ CLONUS+ COITUS+ COLEUS+ CORMUS+ CORPUS+
CORVUS+ COTTUS+ CULTUS+ CYPRUS+ DINGUS+ DOOFUS+ ERINUS+ FLATUS+ GALLUS+
GAUPUS+ GAWPUS+ GRADUS+ HOUMUS+ IAMBUS+ LACMUS+ LIMBUS+ LITUUS+ MANCUS+
MAWPUS+ MEATUS+ MEDIUS+ MIURUS+ MORBUS+ NIMBUS+ PANNUS+ PLEXUS+ PRUNUS+
TELLUS+ THYMUS+ URAEUS+ VALGUS+ VULGUS+ WAMPUS+

6.3.4 ADJECTIVES ENDING IN 'Y'

AUNTLY* BLOTTY* BLOWZY* BLUGGY* BRANNY* BRONZY* CHEQUY* CHITTY* *CHROMY*
CLAGGY* CLAYEY* CLIQUY* CLODDY* CLOTTY* COGGLY* CREASY* CURNEY* DANGLY*
DARKLY* DICKTY* DREGGY* ECHOEY* FEATLY* FLAGGY* FOUSTY* FRANZY* FRETTY*
FRINGY* FROGGY* FROUZY* FROWZY* GAINLY* GIGGLY* GOGGLY* GOUSTY* GRISLY*
GROOLY* GRUNGY* HACKLY* JANGLY* JIGGLY* JINGLY* JOUNCY* JUMBLY* JUNGLY*
KITTLY* *KLUDGY* KNARRY* MAUNGY* MUDDLY* NEEDLY* NETTLY* PHRASY* PIDDLY*
PLAGUY* PLOTTY* *PREGGY* PUDDLY* PUDSEY* QUAGGY* QUEAZY* RATTLY* RUMBLY*
RUMPLY* SCHIZY* SHELVY* SKEELY* SLAGGY* SLEEZY* *SLITTY* SLUICY* SLUTTY*
SMUDGY* SNEEZY* SNOOZY* SPHERY* SPRUCY* SPURRY* STUDLY* STUGGY* SUETTY*
SWANNY* *SWATTY* *SWOTTY* TACKEY* TALCKY* TANGLY* TEENTY* TETCHY* TICKLY*
TINKLY* TOWNLY* WADDLY* WAGGLY* WAMBLY* WHEYEY* *WHINGY* ZINCKY*

6.3.5 NON-PLURALS BY COMMON ENDINGS

AL

AGONAL	ANURAL	ATOKAL	AUDIAL	AXONAL	BIAXAL	BOREAL	BYSSAL	*CHEVAL*
CHIRAL	CLINAL	CLONAL	COAXAL	COITAL	CREDAL	CRINAL	CUNEAL	CURSAL
CUSPAL	DAEDAL	DISCAL	DISTAL	DUCTAL	ESTRAL	FAECAL	FEODAL	FONTAL
HAEMAL	HIATAL	HIEMAL	HYETAL	IRIDAL	IRREAL	LAICAL	LIENAL	LINEAL
LOREAL	MEATAL	MESIAL	MITRAL	MORSAL	NARIAL	NASIAL	NERVAL	NEURAL
NOUNAL	OBITAL	OGIVAL	OOIDAL	PAUSAL	PENIAL	PHONAL	PLAGAL	PLEXAL
PONTAL	RAMEAL	RETRAL	RHINAL	ROSEAL	SIMIAL	STATAL	SULCAL	TARNAL
TERNAL	THENAL	TOMBAL	*TRAGAL*	TRINAL	TUSSAL	UNGUAL	UNITAL	UNLEAL
VARSAL	VEINAL	VENIAL	VERMAL	VERNAL	VIDUAL	VINEAL	VORPAL	WITHAL
ZOONAL								

ANT

ARRANT	CREANT	EXTANT	GYRANT	LIBANT	NAIANT	NATANT	NUTANT	SEJANT
TONANT	VOLANTe							

AR

ACINAR	*FOOBAR*	*GHUBAR*	MAGYAR	NONPAR	OVULARy	PALMARy	*PHWOAR*	PLANAR
PREWARm	PREWARn	PROWAR	STYLAR	SUBPARt	UNDEAR	VALLARy		

ATE

ACUATE	ADNATE	ANSATEd	BINATE	ENSATE	JUBATE	JUGATE	LANATEd	LOBATEd
LYRATEd	MISATE	PEDATE	RUGATE	TOGATEd	TUBATE	UNCATE	UNDATEd	ZONATEd

ED

AXISED	BEAKED	BESPED	CARIED	CISTED	CITIED	CUSPED	DARNED*	DEBTED
DOITED	DUTIED	FLEWED	*GEEKED*	HERBED	HONIED	IDEAED	*IMPLED*	INTOED
LILIED	*MAFTED*	MALFED	MEATED	*MONGED*	MOTHED	NEONED	NORMED	ODORED
OUTLED	PARDED	PAVEED	PIOTED	REBRED	REPLED	RUNTED	SLEDED	SOULED
TEATED	*TUTUED*	UNAGED	UNAWED	*UNAXED*	UNBRED	UNDYED	UNEYED	UNFEED
UNSHED	UNSPED	WARTED	WEBFED	WOADED	WOOLED	YOLKED		

EN

BIDDEN	BIRKEN	BOLLEN	CULMEN	DAIMEN	*DOGMEN*	EOTHEN	EUGHEN	EWGHEN
FLAXEN	FORREN	GILDEN	GOTTEN	GUNNEN	GYLDEN	HADDEN	HALFEN	HEMPEN
HOLPEN	HUDDEN	LENTEN	LITTEN	LOOTEN	LUCKEN	LUITEN	LUTTEN	MILKEN
PITMEN	PITTEN	PUTTEN	RUSHEN	SITTEN	TEGMEN	TOSSEN	TURFEN	UNBEEN
VATMEN	WHATEN	*YITTEN*						

ENT

BEWENT	CADENT	INBENT	JACENT	LUCENT	PONENT	PUDENT	SCIENT	SEDENT
UNBENT	UNKENT	UNRENT	UPSENT	UPWENT	VIRENT			

ES

AESCES	APICES	AWAYES	BEEVES	*BUPKES*	CARIES	CAULES	CAUVES	CERTES
CORVES	DEIXES	DIESES	EWFTES	FACIES	FAECES	FAIKES	FALCES	FASCES
FAUCES	FOLLES	FRIGES	GENTES	HAERES	ILICES	KERMESs	LEUDES	LOOVES

6. Six-Letter Words

MATJES	MATRES	MEAWES	*MERCES*	MIOSES	MYASES	MYOSES	NELIES	NOESES
PARIES	PEONES	PHYSES	PONTES	*PRECES*s	PTYXES	PYOSES	SANIES	*SORDES*
SORTES	SYRTES	THEWES	TURVES	*ULICES*	UNGUES	VEGGES	VERMES	

FUL

AIDFUL	AIMFUL	BARFUL	DINFUL	DUEFUL	IREFUL	SAPFUL	SOBFUL	TOPFUL1
WAEFUL								

IA

ALODIA1	ANTLIAe	CAMBIA1	CHORIA1	CRANIA1	ELUVIA1	EXUVIAe	EXUVIA1	HYDRIAe
ISCHIA1	LOCHIA1	ORARIAn	PALLIA1	PEREIA	PREMIA	PTERIA	QUALIA	REALIA
SCOLIA	SCORIAc	SCORIAe	SEMEIA	SKOLIA	ZOARIA1	ZOECIA		

IC

ABULIC	ADIPIC	AEONIC	AGONIC	ALEXIC	AMEBIC	AMIDIC	AMINIC	AMYLIC
ANEMIC	ANETIC	ANISIC	ANODIC	ANOXIC	ANURIC	AORTIC	APNEIC	ATAVIC
AXONIC	AZONIC	AZOTIC	BARDIC	BROMIC	DEIFIC	DELTIC	DERMIC	*DOMOIC*
DROMIC	EDENIC	ENATIC	ENOLIC	EPODIC	EREMIC	ETYMIC	EXILIC	EXODIC
EXONIC	FEHMIC	FELSIC	FERRIC	FISTIC	FORMICa	GALLICa	GEODIC	GESTIC
GOETIC	GYMNIC	HAEMIC	HOLMIC	*HORMIC*	HYDRIC	HYENIC	HYMNIC	IATRIC
IMIDIC	IRIDIC	IRITIC	*KAONIC*	KARMIC	LESBIC	LIMNIC	*LIPOIC*	LITHIC
LUBRIC	MALEIC	MUONIC	NASTIC	NEANIC	NEUMIC	NIOBIC	NOETIC	NORDIC
ONIRIC	ORPHIC	OTITIC	OXALIC	OXIDIC	OZONIC	PHAEIC	PHASIC	PHATIC
PHENIC	PIANIC	PSORIC	PTOTIC	PYEMIC	QUINIC	RHIZIC	RHODIC	RHOTIC
SIALIC	SODAIC	SORBIC	STERIC	TANNIC	TERBIC	THETIC	THORIC	*TIGLIC*
TOLUIC	TOMBIC	UNIFIC	URANIC	URATIC	UREMIC	URETIC	VEHMIC	VIATICa
YTTRIC	ZOETIC	ZOONIC						

ID

BEDRID	CALLID	FORDID	FULGID	FULVID	GRAVIDa	HISPID	INLAID	LIMPID
MISDID	RAUCID	RELAID	RESAID	ROSCID	SEXFID	SPRAID	TREPID	TRIFID
UNLAID	VISCID							

IE

BARMIE*	BLUDIE*	CANNIE*	*CERTIE*	DEAWIE	DONSIE*	DORMIE	DUDDIE*	FEIRIE*
FROWIE*	GAUCIE*	GAWSIE*	GIRNIE*	GRYSIE	GUSTIE*	HEARIE	HISTIE	KIDGIE*
LAESIE	LOGGIE*	MOCHIE*	NIRLIE*	PERDIE	RECHIE	REEKIE*	ROARIE*	*SEELIE*
SKIVIE*	SONSIE*	*STOBIE*	TAWTIE*	TENTIE*	TOUTIE*			

ILY *derived from adjectives*

AERILY	AIRILY	ARTILY	*BOXILY*	CAGILY	COSILY	COZILY	DEWILY	*DOPILY*
DOZILY	EDGILY	EERILY	FOXILY	GAMILY	GLUILY	*GOOILY*	GORILY	HAZILY
HOKILY	HOLILY	ICKILY	JOKILY	LACILY	LOGILY	MATILY	MAZILY	*MOPILY*
NOSILY	OILILY	OOZILY	POKILY	PUNILY	RACILY	ROPILY	ROSILY	TIDILY
TINILY	UGLILY	VERILY	WAVILY	WAXILY	WILILY	WIRILY	ZANILY	

INE
AEDINE	ALVINE	FERINE	LARINE	NARINE	ONLINEr	PICINE	RANINE	RUSINE
THYINE	UNFINE	URSINE					

IS
BUPKIS	CAPRIS	CAULIS	*CLOVIS*	*CNEMIS*	COULIS	CRASIS	CUSPIS	CYESIS
CYPRIS	DIESIS	EMESIS	FOLLIS	FORTIS	GNOSIS	*GRAVIS*	MIOSIS	MYASIS
MYOSIS	NEREIS	PALAIS	PATOIS	PHASIS	PHYSIS	POLEIS	PTOSIS	PUTOIS
PYOSIS	SYRTIS	TENUIS	TESTIS	TMESIS	TSORIS	TZURIS	ULOSIS	UNGUIS
URESIS	UROSIS	VERMIS					

ISH
AGUISH	BLUISH	COWISH	COYISH	DAWISH	DOTISH	DOVISH	DRYISH	DUDISH
ELFISH	ELVISH	FIKISH	*FLUISH*	GLUISH	GOYISH	JADISH	LAKISH	LAMISH
LATISH	LOWISH	MODISH	MOPISH	MORISH	MULISH	NEWISH	NICISH	OAFISH
ODDISH	OGRISH	OLDISH	OWLISH	PALISH	RAWISH	RUDISH	SKYISH	SLYISH
TONISH	TOYISH	TYKISH	WINISH				

IT
DAYLIT	DITTIT	DOITIT	FLEMIT	FORRIT	GASLIT	GEDDIT	HAWKIT	LOUPIT
LOWSIT	MISLIT	NIRLIT	PINXIT	PIRNIT	POOKIT	POUKIT	ROOPIT	ROUPIT
SKYLIT	SOBEIT	TAUTIT	TWILIT				

LY *derived from adjectives, excluding ILY*
ACIDLY	ARCHLY	ARIDLY	BALDLY	BASELY	BASSLY	BLUELY	BRAGLY	CURTLY
CUTELY	DAFTLY	DANKLY	DEAFLY	DINKLY	DIRELY	DRABLY	DUMBLY	DUSKLY
EVILLY	FAINLY	FASTLY	FICKLY	FOULLY	GASHLY	GLEGLY	GLIBLY	GLUMLY
LAMELY	LANKLY	LEANLY	LEWDLY	LIEFLY	LONGLY	LUSHLY	MEETLY	MURKLY
MUTELY	*NAIFLY*	NIGHLY	NIMBLY	NUDELY	NUMBLY	PALELY	PERTLY	PINKLY
POSHLY	PRIMLY	RANKLY	RIFELY	RIPELY	SAGELY	SALTLY	SANELY	SLIMLY
STABLY	TARTLY	TAUTLY	TRIGLY	TRIMLY	VILELY		

LY *other*
AGEDLY	ANALLY	ANERLY	CLODLY	DERNLY	DUALLY	EATHLY	FECKLY	HOSTLY
LAIDLY	LANELY	LEALLY	LIONLY	MUCHLY	OVALLY	NEBULY	NEXTLY	PACKLY
PARKLY	PURFLY	RAGULY	RICKLY	SUABLY	SUTTLY	THUSLY	TITELY	TREBLY
USABLY	VIABLY	VIEWLY	VILDLY	WHALLY	WISTLY		

MAN->MEN
AIDMAN	APEMAN	ASHMAN	AXEMAN	BAGMAN	BAYMAN	BINMAN	*BOGMAN*	BOWMAN
BUSMAN	CABMAN	CARMAN	COWMAN	CUPMAN	FENMAN	FLYMAN	FOEMAN	FOGMAN
GAGMAN	GASMAN	GIGMAN	*HITMAN*	HODMAN	ICEMAN	LEGMAN	NONMAN	OILMAN
PENMAN	POTMAN	RODMAN	SKYMAN	SOCMAN	SUBMAN	SUBMENu	TINMAN	TITMAN
TOPMAN	TOYMAN	TUTMAN	VANMAN	WARMAN	YEOMAN		

OID
ALGOID	CYMOID	CYTOID	HEMOID	HYPOID	*LUPOID*	MYXOID	NEVOID	XYLOID
ZONOID	ZYGOID	ZYMOID					

OSE

ARIOSE	COMOSE	CYMOSE	DUMOSE	FAVOSE	HAMOSE	JOCOSE	LANOSE	MUCOSE
NODOSE	OTIOSE	PILOSE	RAMOSE	REROSE	RIMOSE	RUGOSE	SETOSE	VADOSE
VENOSE								

OUS

ALMOUS	AUROUS	AWMOUS	CEROUS	COMOUS	CYMOUS	DUMOUS	FAVOUS	FUCOUS
FUMOUS	GYROUS	HAMOUS	HUMOUS	IODOUS	LIMOUS	LUPOUS	MUCOUS	NODOUS
NOYOUS	OSMOUS	PAROUS	PILOUS	RAMOUS	RIMOUS	RUFOUS	RUGOUS	SEROUS
SETOUS	TIMOUS	TOROUS	UVEOUS	VENOUS	VINOUS	VIROUS		

UM

ACETUM	ADYTUM	AECIUM	BIVIUM	*DADGUM*	DOLIUM	DORSUM	GRANUM	IDOLUM
INGRUM	ITERUM	LABIUM	LUTEUM	OIDIUM	OSTIUM	PACTUM	PHYLUM	REGNUM
REPLUMb	*SCHTUM*	SCUTUM	SENSUM	*SIGLUM*	SPUTUM	TELIUM	TERGUM	*VALIUM*
XENIUM								

US

ACARUS	ACINUS	AENEUS	AMICUS	AUREUS	*BUPKUS*	CANTUS	CARPUS	CIRRUS
CLAVUS	*CUNEUS*	CURSUS	*FILIUS*	FUNDUS	GLOMUS	*MAGNUS*	MODIUS	MYTHUS
NAEVUS	OBELUS	OCULUS	PIGNUS	*PULLUS*	RECTUS	REGIUS	SCAPUS	SULCUS
TARSUS	THOLUS	TOPHUS	TRAGUS	*VELLUS*	VILLUS	VISCUS	XYSTUS	

6.3.6 OTHERS CONTAINING HEAVY LETTERS

NOUNS CONTAINING 'J'

ACAJOU	*ADJIGO*	AJOWAN	BAJADA	BHAJAN	*BOOJUM*	CROJIK	DONJON	FAJITA
FEIJOA	*FIGJAM*	FINJAN	GARJAN	*GOUJON*	GURJUN	*GYTTJA*	HEJIRA	INJERA
JABIRU	JACANA	*JACARE*	JAGHIRe	*JAMAAT*	JAMPANi	JAMPOT	JANSKYs	JARINA
JAROOL	JASMINe	JATAKA	JAWARI	JAWBOX+	JERBIL	JERBOA	JEREED	JERKINg
JETLAG	JETSOM	JETSON	JETTON	*JETWAY*	JEZAIL	*JHATKA*	JICAMA	JINGKO+
JOANNA	JOHNNY+	*JOLLOP*	JORDAN	JOSEPH	JOSKIN	JOURNO	*JOYPAD*	JUBILEe
JUDOGI	JUDOKA	JUNGLI	JUPATI	*MOJITO*	MOUJIK	MUZJIK	*NUTJOB*	PAJAMA
PAJOCKe	*PRAJNA*	*PUJARI*	PYJAMA	*RAKIJA*	RHANJA	*ROMAJI*	SANJAK	*SHINJU*
SVARAJ+	SWARAJ+	TINAJA	UJAMAA	VEEJAY	WILTJA			

NOUNS CONTAINING 'Q'

BARQUE	BASQUEd	BISQUE	BOSQUEt	BUQSHA	CAIQUE	CASQUEd	CINQUE	CIRQUE
CLAQUEr	CLOQUE	DIQUAT	EXEQUY+	FAQUIR	HAIQUE	LASQUE	MARQUEe	MASQUEr
PULQUE	*QABALAh*	QASIDA	QIGONG	QIVIUT	QUAGGA	QUAHOG	QUAICH+	QUAIGH
QUANGO	QUATRE	*QUBYTE*	QUEACHy	*QUEBEC*	QUEEST	QUELEA	QUETHE	QUIDAM
QUININa	QUININe	QUINZE	QUOHOG	QURUSH+	QWERTYs	QWERTY+	REQUIN	SACQUE
SAIQUE	SHEQEL	SQUAME	YANQUI	YAQONA				

NOUNS CONTAINING 'X'

ALEXINe	AXILLAe	AXILLAr	AXSEED	CARFAX+	CARFOX+	CAUDEX+	CHENIX+	CLAXON
CORTEX+	COWPOX+	DENTEX+	DIAXON	DIOXANe	DIOXIN	DOGFOX+	EARWAX+	ETHOXYl
EUTAXY+	EXARCHs	EXARCHy	EXEQUY+	*EXERGY+*	EXONYM	EXOPOD	EXTASY+	EXTERNe

FIXURE	*GUANXI*	*HANDAX*+	HATBOX+	HAYBOX+	HEXENE	HEXONE	HOTBOX+	IMPLEX+
ISOLEX+	MAGNOX+	MASTIX+	NONTAX+	*OREXIN*	ORIFEX+	OXCART	OXFORD	OXGANG
OXHEAD	*OXHIDE*	OXLAND	OXSLIP	OXTAIL	OXYMEL	PEGBOX+	PHENIX+	SAXAUL
SAXONY+	SEXTANt	SILVEX+	SIXAINe	SKYBOX+	SMILAX+	SPADIX+	SPHINX+	*SPHYNX*+
STORAX+	STYRAX+	SUBFIX+	*SUPLEX*+	SYRINX+	TAXEME	TEABOX+	TETTIX+	*TRIMIX*+
TUTRIX+	URTEXT	VERNIX+	*WAXEYE*	XEROMA	XYLENE	XYLOMA		

NOUNS CONTAINING 'Z'

ABRAZO	ADZUKI	ALTEZA	AMAZON	APOZEM	AZIONE	AZOLLA	AZYGOS+	BANZAI
BARAZA	BENZIL	BENZINe	BENZOLe	BENZYL	BIZONE	BLINTZe	BLOWZEd	BORZOI
BRAIZE	BRAZIL	BROUZE	BUZUKIa	CHINTZy	COROZO	CORYZAl	*COUZIN*	CZAPKA
DIAZINe	DIZAIN	DONZEL	DRAZEL	ECZEMA	ENZIAN	ERSATZ+	EVZONE	FLOOZY+
FRAZIL	GAZABO	GAZABO+	*GEEZAH*	*HAZMAT*	HUTZPAh	*IMBIZO*	JEZAIL	KAMEEZ+
KOLHOZy	KRANTZ+	KWANZA	LAZULI	LOZELL	LUZERN	MAZARD	MAZHBI	MEAZEL
MEZAIL	*MIZUNA*	MUZHIK	MUZJIK	MZUNGU	NYANZA	OZAENA	PHIZOG	PODZOL
POZOLE	QUINZE	RANZEL	REBOZO	SCAZON	SCHIZO	SCHNOZ+	SCHNOZz	SEIZINg
SHITZU	STANZE	STANZO	STANZO+	TARZAN	TENZON	TIZWAS+	*TZADDI*q	TZETSE
UMFAZI	VIZSLA	WEZAND	WURZEL	ZABETA	ZADDIK	ZAIKAI	ZAMBUK	ZARAPE
ZAREBA	ZARIBA	ZARNEC	ZEATIN	ZECHIN	ZENANA	ZENDIK	ZEREBA	ZERIBA
ZEUGMA	ZINGEL	*ZOCALO*	ZONULAe	ZONULAr	ZONULEt	ZONURE	ZORINO	ZOUAVE
ZYDECO	ZYGOMA	ZYGOTE	ZYMASE					

NON-PLURALS

*ACQUIS*t	ADNEXAl	ALKOXY	AUSPEX	AXLIKE	*AZERTY*	*BASEEJ*	BIFLEX	BLAIZE
CIZERS	DELUXE	DESOXY	DEXTRO	DIPLEX	ENTREZ	EPIZOAn	EXEDRAe	EXEUNT
EXODOI	EXODOS	FIXIVE	FORNIX	FRIJOLe	FRUTEX	GAIJIN	HALLUX	HALUTZ
HOWZAT	*HOWZIT*	IMBREX	INKJET	JABERS	JANTEE	JIMINY	*JIMSON*	JOCUND
JUGULAr	JYMOLD	KUVASZ	LARNAX	LEXICAl	MANQUE	MENINX	*MUSKOX*	MUZAKY
OXLIKE	*PEROXO*	PEROXY	POLLEX	PROLIX	QUEINT	QUOOKE	SCOLEX	*SHAZAM*
SLEAZO	SQUAMAe	SUIVEZ	UBIQUE	UNVEXT	XOANON	XYSTOI	XYSTOS	YAKUZA
ZAFTIG	ZAPATA	ZELOSO	ZEROTH	ZOFTIG	ZONARY	ZOUNDS	ZUFOLI	ZUFOLO

6.3.7 OTHER NOUNS

ABITUR	ABLAUT	ABOLLAe	ABREGE	ABVOLT	ABWATT	ACANTHa	ACANTHi	ACETIN
ACHENE	ACHKAN	ACNODE	ACTURE	ADAGIO	ADDENDa	ADENYL	ADLAND	ADNOUN
ADSUKI	*ADWARE*	AEROBE	AFGHANi	AFTOSA	*AGGADA*h	AGNAIL	AGNAMEd	AGOUTA
AGOUTI	AGRAFE	AHIMSA	AIKIDO	*AIRBAG*	*AIRCON*	AIRGAP	*AIRGUN*	*AKATEA*
AKEDAH	*AKHARA*	ALANINe	ALANYL	ALASKA	ALBATA	ALBEDO	ALBEDO+	ALBERT
ALBUGO	ALCADE	*ALCOOL*	ALDRIN	ALERCE	ALFAKI	ALIDADe	ALIPED	ALISMA
ALISON	ALKENE	ALKYNE	ALLICE	ALMAIN	ALMUCE	ALNICO	ALPACA	ALPHYL
ALSIKE	ALTHEA	ALUDEL	ALUMINa	ALUMINe	AMADOU	AMATOL	*AMBACH*+	AMBARI
AMIDINe	AMORCE	AMTRACk	ANABAS+	ANADEM	ANALOGa	ANALOGy	ANANKE	ANARCHy
ANATTA	ANATTO	ANBURY+	ANCOME	ANERGY+	ANGICO	ANICUT	ANILINe	ANLACE
ANNONA	ANONYMa	ANURAN	AOUDAD	APACHE	APEDOM	APERCU	APNOEAl	APOLLO
APOLOGy	APTOTE	*ARAARA*	ARABIN	ARBUTE	ARCANA	ARCHIL	ARCHON	*ARCMIN*

AREOLAe AREOLAr AREOLE ARGENT ARGHAN ARGOSY+ ARGYLE ARGYLL ARIOSO
ARISTAe ARISTO ARMURE ARNICA AROLLA ARRACK ARROBA ARROYO ARSHINe
ASCIAN ASHCAN ASHRAMa *ASIAGO* ASKARI ASRAMA ASTELY+ ATABEG ATABEK
ATHAME ATLATL ATTENT AUBADE AUCEPS+ AUCUBA AUDILE AUDING AUGEND
AUMBRY+ AUSUBO AUTEUR AVENIR AVIDIN AVOURE AVOWRY+ *AVRUGA* *AWHATO*
AWHETO AYWORD

BACKRA BAETYL BAGNIO BAGUIO BAGWIG BAHADA BAILLIe BAININ BALATA
BALISE BALLANt BALLON BAMPOT BANDOG BAREGE BARFLY+ BARKAN BARLOW
BAROCK *BAROLO* BARRIO BARTON BARYON BARYTA BARYTE BASHAW BASTLE
BASUCO BATATA BATHOS+ BATTIK BAUERA BAWDRY+ BAYAMO BAYARD BEADLE
BEDUIN BEEGAH BEENAH *BEENTO* BEFANA BEGUINe BEHEST BEHOOF BELAMY+
BELDAMe BELUGA BERLINe BESOIN BETHEL BETISE BEURRE BEYLIK BHAKTA
BHAKTI *BHAVAN* *BHAWAN* BHINDI BHISTIe *BHOONA* *BIATCH+* *BICHIR* BICORNe
BICRON BIFACE *BIFTAH* BIGEYE BIGGINg *BIGGON* BILIAN BILLON *BINDHI*
BINDLE BINGHI *BINIOU* *BIODOT* BIOGAS+ BIOTIN BIPACK BIREME BISTREd
BITTUR BLAGUEr BLENNY+ BOATEL BODACH BODDLE BODEGA BODKIN BODRAG
BOGOAK BOGONG BOHUNK BOLERO BOLETE BOLIDE BOLSON BONACI BONDUC
BONHAM BONITA BONITO BONITO+ BONSAI *BOOCOO* *BOOHAI* BOOKOO BOORKA
BOREAS+ BORIDE *BORNYL* BORSCHt BORSHT BOSCHE BOSTON BOTFLY+ BOTHAN
BOUCHEe BOUCLEe *BOUDIN* BOULLE BOURSE BOUTON BOWFIN BOWLEG BOWPOT
BRAATA BRAHMAn BRANLE *BRASCO* BRASIL BREARE BREHON BRETON *BRINNY+*
BRIONY+ BROGAN BROLLY+ BROMINe BRUCINe BRULOT BRYONY+ BUCKRAm BUDDHA
BUGEYE BUGGANe BUGGINg BUGONG BUGSHA *BUHUND* BUKSHI BULGUR BULIMY+
BUMKIN BURGOO BURHEL BURITI *BURKHA* BURLAP BURRELl BURTON *BUSERA*
BUSHWAh BUSKINg BUTENE BYELAW BYNAME BYPATH BYRLAW BYROOM BYTALK
BYWORD BYWORK

CABANA *CABRIO* *CADAGA* *CADAGI* CAEOMA CAFARD CAFILA CAFTAN CAGOULe
CAHOOT CAILLE *CALALU* CALASH+ CALESA CALIGO CALIGO+ CALIMA CALIPH
CALKINg *CALLOP* CALTHA CAMAIL CAMOTE CANADA CANARD CANGUE CANNEL
CANOLA CANULAe CANULAr CAPIAS+ CAPLIN CAPTAN *CARDON* CAREME CARIBE
CARINAe CARINAl CARLINe CARLINg CARLOT CARPEL CARRAT CARRELl CASABA
CASAVA CASBAH CASEIN CASERNe CASHAW CASHOO CASITA CATALOg CATALO+
CATENAe CATKIN CATLINg CATNEP CATNIP CAUTEL CAYUSE CEDULA CEMBRA
CENOTE CERIPH CERISE CEROON CERUSE CESTUI CESURAe CESURAl CESURE
CHABUK CHAGAN CHAKRA CHALAN CHALLAh CHALLAn CHALLY+ CHAPKA CHATON
CHATTA CHATTI CHEGOE CHESIL CHEVIN CHEVREt CHIBOL *CHIGGA* CHIGOE
CHIGRE CHIMLA CHITIN CHITON CHOKRA CHOKRI CHOPINe CHOWRI CHOWRY+
CHROMA CHROMO CHUDDY+ CHYPRE CIERGE CINEOLe CITOLA CITOLE CITRINe
CITRON CLEEVE CLEOME COAITA *COBAEA* COBURG COBNUT CODEINa CODEINe
CODLINg COELOMe COGITO COGWAY COHEIR COHORN COHUNE COLLOP *COLTAN*
COLUGO COLURE COMARB COMART COMBLE COMEDO CONIMA CONTRAt CONURE
COOLTH COONTY+ COPITA COPULAe COPULAr CORBAN CORKIR CORMEL CORNEL
CORODY+ *CORREA* CORTINa CORYMB COSMEA *COSMINe* COTYLE COTYPE *COUGAN*
COUTIL COVYNE COWPAT COWPEA COYDOG COYPOU CRAMBE CRAMBO CRAMBO+
CRAPLE CRATON CRATUR CREAGH CREOLE CREPON CRESOL CRESYL *CROGGY+*
CROOVE *CROWEA* CRUIVE *CUATRO* CUDDIN CUESTA CULLAY CUPULE CURAGH

CURARA CURPEL CURRANt CUSHAT CUSHAW CUTLASs CYANINe CYBORG CYMENE
CYMLINg CYPRESs CYTASE CYTODE

DACRON DACTYLi DAEMON DAGABA DAGOBA DAHOON DAIMIO DAIMON DAIMYO
DALASI DALETH DALLOP DALTON DAMSON DANISH+ DAPHNE DARNEL DARTRE
DATCHA DATIVE DATURA DAUBRY+ DAWBRY+ DAYBED DAYFLY+ DEASIL DECARE
DECILE DECIME DECKEL DECKLEd DECURY+ DEEWAN DEGAME DEGAMI DEKARE
DELICE DELICT DEMAINe DENGUE DENTEL DENTIL DENTINe DENTINg DERHAM
DETENTe DETENUe DEUTON DEVOIR DEVORE DEWLAPt DHARMA DHARNA DHOORA
DHOOTIe DHURNA DIABLE DIAMINe DIAPIR DIATOM DICAST DIDACT DIDDLY+
DIEDRE DIGAMY+ DIGLOT DIKTAT DIMBLE DIOBOL DIOECY+ DIPLOE DIPLONt
DIPODY+ DIPOLE DIRDAM DIRHAM DIRHEM DIRIGE DIRNDL DISEUR *DISOMY+*
DITONE DITTAY DIURON DOBLON DOBSON DOCENT DODKIN DOGDOM DOLINA
DOMETT DONGLE DONING DONNOT DOOCOT DOODAD DOODAH *DOODOO* *DOOLAN*
DOOSRA *DOOWOP* DORBUG DORMIN DOTARD *DOTCOM* DOTTEL DOTTLE* DOTTLEd
DOWLAS+ DOWLNEy DRACHMa DREIDL DROICHy DROMONd DROOME DROSKY+ DRYLOT
DUALIN DUELLO DUENDE DUENNA DUNLIN DUOLOG *DURGAH* DURGAN DYNASTy
DYNEIN DYNODE DYSURY+

EADISH+ *EARBUD* EARCON EARLAP EATCHE ECBOLE *ECOMAP* ECONUT ECTOPY+
ECTYPE EDDISH+ EGENCE EGENCY+ EGGNOG EIRACK ELENCHi ELEVON *ELICHE*
ELLOPS+ ELODEA ELSHIN ELTCHI ELUENT EMBOLY+ *EMDASH+* EMEROD EMETINe
EMEUTE ÉMIGRÉ EMODIN EMPUSA EMPUSE ENCINAl *ENDASH+* ENDRIN ENDURO
ENGOBE ENGRAM ENNEAD *ENVIROn* EOLITH EPAULEt EPEIRA EPHEBE EPIGONe
EPIGONi EPILOG EPONYMy ERIACH *ERLANG* ERYNGO ERYNGO+ ESCROLl ESNECY+
ESPADA ESTRIN ETHENE ETHNOS+ ETHYNE ETYMON EUCAINe *EUMONG* *EUMUNG*
EUOUAE EUPHONy EUPNEA EUREKA EUROKY+ EVOLUE EYLIAD

FADEIN FADEUR FAIBLE FAILLE *FAINNE* *FANBOY* FANDOM FANEGA FANNELl
FANSUB FLANNY+ FANTAD FANTOD FANTOM FARDEL FARINA FEALTY+ FECULAe
FEDORA FEERINg FELLOE FENNEC FENNEL FERBAM FERULAe FESCUE FETICHe
FIACRE FIAUNT FIBRIL FIBRIN FIBULAe FIBULAr FIMBLE FINNACk FINNAN
FIORIN FIRKINg FIRLOT FISGIG FLACON *FLANNY+* FLATTY+ FLAUNE *FLAUTA*
FLAVINe *FLEADH* FLECHE FLOOSY+ FLUGEL FLYSCH+ FOGASH+ FOGBOW FOGDOG
FOGRAM FOISON FOOTRA FORCAT FORINT FORMOL FORMYL FOUTRA FRATRY+
FRIANDe FRIGOT FRIPON *FROING* FROISE FRUICT FUGATO FULHAM FULLAM
FULLAN FUMADO FUMADO+ FUREUR FURPHY+ FUSAIN FUSTOC FYNBOS+

GADFLY+ GAGAKU GALAGO GALENA GALERE GALIOT GALOOT GALYAC GALYAK
GAMBIR GAMETE *GAMONE* GANGUE GANOINe GANTRY+ GARCON GARRAN GARRON
GARRYA GARUDA GASCON GASKINg GATEAUx GAUCHO GAUFRE GAYETY+ *GEDACT*
GEEBAG GEEGAW GELADA GELATIn GELATO *GELCAP* GELOSY+ GEMINY+ GENEVA
GENNEL GENTOO GERBIL GERENT GERMINa GERMINg GHARRI GHIBLI GIBSON
GIGLOT GILGAI GINGKO GINGKO+ GINKGO GINKGO+ GINNEL GIRKIN GIRNEL
GITANA GITANO GLAIVEd GLIOMA GLOIRE GLUCAN *GLURGE* GLYCAN GLYCINe
GLYCOL GNOMON GODOWN GOLLANd GOMBRO GOMOKU GOMUTI GOMUTO *GONGYO*
GONOPH GOODBYe GOODBYs GOOGLY+ GOOGOL GOONDA GOOROO GOPURAm GORAMY+
GORGIO GORGON *GOTCHA* GOUTTE GOWLANd GRADINe GRADINg GRADINi GRADINo

```
GRAHAM  GRAKLE  GRAPLE  GRATINe GRATINg GREEBO+ GREECE  GREIGE  GRIECEd
GRIGRI  GRILSE  GRINCH+ GRINGA  GRISON  GRUGRU  GRUNGEr GRUNGEy GRYFON
GUAIAC  GUANGO  GUANINe GUENON  GUIDON  GUNDOG  GUNNEL  GUNSEL  GUNYAH
GURAMI  GURRAH  GUTROT  GWEDUCk GYRASE  GYRENE

HADRON  HAEMIN  HAGBUT  HAGDON  HAIDUK  HAIRIF  HAKARI  HAKEEM  HALLAN
HAMADA  HAMAUL  HANSOM  HANTLE  HAPUKA  HAPUKU  HAREEM  HARELD  HARIRA
HARMEL  HARMINe HARMINg HARPINg HATPEG  HAUYNE  HAWALA  HAYMOW  HAYSEL
HEAUME  HEBONA  HEGARI  HEGIRA  HENNINg HEPCAT  HEPTAD  HERIOT  HEROON
HETERO  HODDINg HOGNUT  HOISINg HOLARD  HOMILY+ HOMINY+ HOOPOE  HOOPOO
HOPDOG  HORSON  HOSTRY+ HOUDAN  HRYVNA  HUIPIL  HUNGAN  HUMINT  HUPIRO
HYAENA  HYALINe

IGNARO  IGNARO+ IGNOMY+ ILLIAD  ILLIPE  ILLUPI  IMPROVe INANGA  INDABA
INDENE  INDULT  INDUNA  INFALL  INFAMY+ INFARE  INFLOW  INGENUe INHAUL
INKPAD  INKPOT  INRUSH+ INSOLE  INTIMAe INTIMAl INTURN  INTUSE  INULIN
IONONE  ISABEL  ISOGONe ISOGONy ISOHEL  ISOLOG  ISOPOD  ISTANA

KABALA  KAFILA  KAFTAN  KAGOOL  KAGOULe KAHUNA  KALIAN  KALIPH  KAMAHI
KAMALA  KAMEES+ KAMELA  KAMILA  KAMSIN  KANBAN  KANGHA  KANTHA  KAOLINe
KARAMU  KARORO  KARROO  KARYON  KASBAH  KATANA  KATIPO  KEBELE  KEBLAH
KEDDAH  KEIRIN  KELSON  KELVIN  KEMBLA  KEMPLE  KEPHIR  KERERU  KETENE
KETONE  KGOTLA  KHALAT  KHALIFa KHANDA  KHANGA  KHARIF  KHILAT  KHILIM
KHURTA  KIAUGH  KIDDLE  KIDULT  KILERG  KILLAS+ KILLUT  KIMCHI  KINARA
KINCOB  KINEMA  KINONE  KINRED  KIRANA  KIRBEH  KIRPAN  KIRSCH+ KIRTAN
KIRTLEd KISMAT  KITBAG  KITTEL  KITTUL  KLEPHT  KLEPTO  KLOOCH+ KNITCH+
KOBOLD  KONFYT  KONINI  KOODOO  KOOLAH  KORARI  KORORA  KOTARE  KOULAN
KOUMYSs KOWHAI  KRUBUT  KULTUR  KUMARA  KUMARI  KUMERA  KURGAN  KWACHA
KWAITO

LABRYS+ LACTAM  LACUNAe LACUNAl LACUNAr LACUNE  LADINO  LADRONe LAGENA
LAGEND  LAGGINg LAGUNA  LAGUNE  LALLANd LAMBDA  LAMINAe LAMINAl LAMINAr
LAMPAD  LAMPAS+ LANDAU  LANGUEd LANGUEt LANGUR  LANUGO  LAOGAI  LAPDOG
LARDON  LATIGO  LATIGO+ LATINA  LATINO  LATRON  LATTIN  LAURYL  LAVABO
LAVABO+ LEALTY+ LECHWE  LECTIN  LEGATOr LEGGINg LEGLAN  LEGLIN  LEGONG
LEGUAN  LEHAIM  LEIPOA  LEPTIN  LEPTON  LETTRE  LEUCINe LEUKON  LIERNE
LIGASE  LIGNAN  LIGNIN  LIGULAe LIGULAr LIGULE  LIGURE  LIMAIL  LIMBECk
LINGEL  LINGUAe LINGUAl LINHAY  LINTOL  LIONEL  LIPASE  LIPOMA  LISTEL
LITCHI  LOBALA  LOBOLO  LOBULE  LOCHAN  LOCULEd LOGGAT  LOGLOG  LOGWAY
LOLIGO  LOMEIN  LOMENTa LORCHA  LORING  LORIOT  LOSLYF  LUCERNe LUCUMA
LUCUMO  LUNGAN  LUNGYI  LUNULE  LURDANe LUTEIN

MABELA  MACHAN  MACOYA  MACULAe MACULAr MADAFU  MADRASa MADURO  MAENAD
MAFTIR  MAGIAN  MAGILP  MAGLEV  MAGNES+ MAGNON  MAHEWU  MAHSIR  MAIDAN
MAIGRE  MALKIN  MALTHA  MALTOL  MANAWA  MANCHEt MANILA  MANIOCa MANITOu
MANITU  MANOAO  MANRED  MANTEL  MANTUA  MANUKA  MARABI  MARACA  MARARI
MARERO  MARGAY  MARRON  MARTINg MARTINi MASALA  MASCLEd MASCON  MASHUA
MASKEG  MASLIN  MASULA  MATATA  MATICO  MATIPO  MATSAH  MATTINg MATATU
```

MAULVI	MAUVINe	MAWKIN	MAYFLY+	MAYVIN	MEDAKA	MEDFLY+	MEDINA	MEDUSAe
MEDUSAl	MEDUSAn	MEGILPh	*MEHNDI*	MEISHI	MELANO	*MELENA*	MELLAY	MELTON
MENHIR	MENSCHy	*MENUDO*	MERCAT	MERKIN	MERLINg	MERLON	MESAIL	MESETA
METEPA	METOPE	*MEVROU*	MGANGA	*MIBUNA*	MICELLa	MICELLe	MIDGUT	MIDLEG
MIDRIB	MIGGLE	MIGNON	MIHRAB	MIKADO	MIKRON	MIKVAH	MIKVEH	MILADI
MILADY+	MILIEUx	MILNEB	MINYAN	MIRITI	MOBCAP	*MOBLOG*	MODENA	MOGGAN
MOGHUL	MOHAWK	MOIETY+	*MOKIHI*	*MOKORO*	*MOKSHA*	MOLOCH	MONAUL	MONETH
MONOAO	MONODY+	MONTRE	*MOOLOO*	*MOOLVIe*	MOORVA	MOPANI	*MORCHA*	MORGAY
MORKIN	MORULAe	MORULAr	MOTILE	MOTUCA	MOULIN	MOUTAN	MOUTON	MUCHELl
MUCKLE	MUCOSAe	MUCOSAl	*MUDBUG*	MUDCAT	*MUDEYE*	MUFLON	MUGGUR	MULETA
MUNSHI	MUREIN	MURLAN	MURLINg	MURPHY+	MURRHA	MUSANG	MUSKEG	MUSKLE
MUSLIN	MUSROL	MUTASE	MUTUCA	MUTUEL	MUTULE	MYCELE	MYELINe	MYELON
MYGALE	MYOSIN	MYRICA						
NAGANA	NAGARI	NANDINa	NANDINe	NANDOO	NANKIN	*NANOBE*	*NANOOK*	NARDOO
NASARD	NASUTE	NATRON	NAUTCH+	NEBECK	NEBISH+	NEBULAe	NEBULAr	NEBULE
NEKTON	*NEINEI*	NELSON	*NEOCON*	NEPETA	NEWTON	NHANDU	NIACIN	*NIGIRI*
NILGAI	NILGAU	NIMROD	NINCOM	*NISGUL*	NITRILe	NOCAKE	NOCENT	NOCTUA
NONART	NONCOM	NONEGO	NONFAN	NONGAY	NONUSEr	NOSEAN	NOSODE	NOSTOC
NOVENAe	NOYADE	*NUBUCK*	NUCULE	NUDNIK	NUMBAT	NUMDAH	NUMNAH	NUNCIO
NURHAG								
OBECHE	OCELOT	OCTAVO	OCTROI	OEUVRE	OGDOAD	*OILGAS+*	OILNUT	OILWAY
OLEFINe	OLLAMH	OMERTA	*ONBEAT*	ONCOME	ONCOST	ONDING	ONEYRE	ONFALL
ONFLOW	ONRUSH+	ONYCHA	OOCYST	OOCYTE	OOGAMY+	OOGENY+	OOLITH	OOLONG
OOMIACk	OOMIAK	OORALI	OPCODE	OPERON	OPTIME	ORCEIN	ORCHAT	ORCHEL
ORCHIL	ORDURE	OREIDE	ORFRAY	ORGEAT	ORGONE	ORIGANe	*ORIHOU*	ORIOLE
ORISHA	ORISON	ORMOLU	OROIDE	ORRICE	OSCULE	*OSETRA*	OSMUNDa	OSTOMY+
OTALGY+	OTTAVA	*OUBAAS+*	OULONG	OURANG	OUREBI	OVIBOS+	OVISAC	OWELTY+
PADANG	PADAUK	PADNAG	PADOUK	PADSAW	PAELLA	PAESANi	PAESANo	PAIDLE
PAIGLE	PAINCH+	PAINIM	PAIOCKe	*PAKAHI*	PAKEHA	*PAKIHI*	PAKORA	PALAGI
PALOLO	PANADA	PANAMA	*PANINI*	PANISC	PANISK	PANTUN	PARAMO	PARANG
PARDAH	PARIAH	PARIAN	PARORE	PARREL	PARTAN	PARTON	PARURA	PARURE
PASELA	PASHIM	*PASHKA*	PASTILy	PATACA	*PATAKA*	*PATIKI*	PATTLE	PAULIN
PAUNCE	PAVONE	PAWNCE	PAYNIM	PEACOD	PECHAN	PECTIN	PELHAM	PELORY+
PELOTA	PELTRY+	PENANG	PENNON	PENSEL	PENSILe	PENTAD	PENTYL	PENULT
PENURY+	PEREON	*PERFINg*	PERKINg	*PERNOD*	*PEROGI+*	PERONE	PERRON	PERUKEd
PESADE	PESETA	PESEWA	PESHWA	PETSAI	PEYOTE	PEYOTL	PHENOL	PHENOM
PHENYL	PHLEGMy	PHLOEM	PHOEBE	PHYLLO	PHYSED	PHYSIO	*PHYTIN*	PHYTOL
PHYTON	PICARA	PICARO	PICENE	*PICKINg*	*PICONG*	PIDGIN	PIGGINg	PIGNUT
PIGSNY+	PILLAU	PILULAe	PILULAr	PILULE	PIMENTo	PINANG	PINATA	*PINDAN*
PINENE	PINOLE	PINTLE	PINYON	PIRANA	PIRAYA	PISTIL	*PISTOU*	PITARAh
PITAYA	PITSAW	PITURI	PLAICE	PLATANe	PLEIAD	PLENCH+	PLEURAe	PLEURAl
PLINTH	PLISKY+	PLOIDY+	PLUTON	PNEUMA	POCHAY	PODSOL	*POHIRI*	*POITIN*
POLLAN	POLONY+	*POLYOL*	POMACE	POMATO+	POMELO	POMROY	PONDOK	PONTILe
PONTON	POOGYE	POONAC	*PORINA*	POSADA	POSEUR	*POSOLE*	POSTINg	*POTALE*
POTBOY	POTGUN	POTTLE	POUDRE	PRAWLE	PREFAB	PRELIM	PREMED	PREWYN

```
PROLAN  PROTYLe PRUINA  PSYLLA  PTERIN  PTISAN  PUCKLE  PUEBLO  PUGGRY+
PUISNE  PULKHA  PULTAN  PULTON  PULTUN  PUMELO  PUNCTO  PUNKIN  PURANA
PURIRI  PURLINe PURLINg PUTELI  PUTLOG  PUTSCH+ PUTURE  PYCNON  PYGARG
PYRENE  PYROLA  PYRONE  PYRROLe
```

```
RACEMEd RACINO  RACOON  RADIANt RADOME  RADULAe RADULAr RAFALE  RAGBAG
RAGINI  RAGLAN  RAGTAG  RAGTOP  RAILLY+ RAIYAT  RAMADA  RAMBLA  RAMCAT
RAMONA  RAMSON  RAMTIL  RANDAN  RANDEM  RANDON  RANSEL  RANULAr RASURE
RATLINe RATLINg RATTAN  RATTON  RAWARU  REAGIN  REBATO  REBATO+ RECEPT
REDBAY  REDBUD  REDBUG  REDCAP  REDEYE  REDFIN  REDLEG  REDOWA  REDTOP
REEBOK  REGINAe REGINAl REGULO  RELEVE  REMORA  REMUDA  RENNINg RESEAUx
RESEDA  RETAMA  RETENE  REVEUR  REVERSe REVERSi REVERSo RHEBOK  RHYTON
RIALTO  RIANCY+ RIBAND  RIBAUD  RIBEYE  RIDGIL  RIFLIP  RIGLINg RIMAYE
RIOTRY+ RIPECK  RISTRA  RITARD  RIVLIN  ROADEO  ROBALO  ROBAND  ROESTI
ROGNON  RONYON  ROSACEa ROSBIF  ROSCOE  ROSULA  ROTOLO  ROTTAN  ROTULAe
ROUBLE  ROUCHE  ROUCOU  ROUNCY+ RUBACE  RUBATO  RUBIGO  RUCOLA  RUELLE
RUGOLA  RUGOSA  RUMAKI  RUMKIN  RUNDLEd RUNDLEt RUNNEL  RUSTREd RYOKAN
RYPECK
```

```
SABKHAh SABKHAt SACBUT  SACHEM  SADDHU  SAFROLe SAGBUT  SAGOIN  SAGUIN
SAIKEI  SAIMIN  SAKIEH  SALINA  SALLAD  SALOOP  SALUKI  SAMAAN  SAMARA
SAMBUR  SAMECH  SAMFOO  SAMIEL  SAMITI  SAMPAN  SANCAI  SANDEK  SANDHI
SANGHAt SANNOP  SANPAN  SANPRO  SANTIR  SANTUR  SAPEGO+ SAPELE  SAPOTA
SAPOTE  SARAPE  SARDEL  SATANG  SATARA  SATORI  SATRAPy SAULGE  SAUREL
SAWFLY+ SAWLOG  SCAMTO  SCARAB  SCHELM  SCHEMA  SCHLUB  SCHORL  SCHRIK
SCHROD  SCHTIK  SCHUYT  SCILLA  SCLERAe SCLERAl SCLERE  SCOOBY+ SCOWTH
SCROBE  SCRORP  SCROTE  SCRUNTy SCRUTO  SCRYNE  SEABAG  SEABED  SEADOG
SEAHOG  SEALCH  SEALGH  SEANCE  SEARAT  SEAWANt SEAWAY  SECKEL  SECKLE
SEGHOL  SEICHE  SEIDEL  SEITAN  SENECA  SENEGA  SERANG  SERAPE  SERAPH
SERDAB  SEREIN  SERIPH  SEROON  SETULE  SHADUF  SHAIRD  SHAIRN  SHALOM
SHALOT  SHANNY+ SHANTIh SHARIF  SHEEVE  SHEKEL  SHELTA  SHELTY+ SHERIFf
SHEWEL  SHINDYs SHINDY+ SHIVOO  SHLOCKy SHMOCK  SHMUCK  SHNOOK  SHOGUN
SHOLOM  SHOORA  SHORAN  SHTETL  SHTICKy SHTOOK  SHTUCK  SHUFTI  SHUFTY+
SHYPOO  SIALON  SIDDHA  SIDDHI  SIDDUR  SIECLE  SIENNA  SIERRAn SIFAKA
SIMIAN  SIMKIN  SIMLIN  SIMNEL  SIMONY+ SIMOON  SIMORG  SIMPAI  SIMURGh
SINDON  SITCOM  SITREP  SKATOLe SKOLLY+ SKYCAP  SKYLAB  SLUTCHy SMEETH
SMRITI  SOLDAN  SOLUTE  SONERI  SONTAG  SORGHO  SORREL  SOUARI  SOUDAN
SOVRAN  SPATHEd SPAYAD  SPETCH+ SPIGOT  SPLAKE  SPLENT  SPLORE  SPUNGE
SPURRY* SPYCAM  SRADHA  STACTE  STADDA  STAITHe STALAG  STANOL  STATINg
STATTO  STATUA  STAYRE  STEROL  STIGME  STIRRAh STOLON  STORGE  STOTIN
STOWRE  STRATH  STRENE  STRICH+ STRIFT  STROMB  STROND  STROOKe STROUD
SUBLOT  SULDAN  SUNBOW  SUNDEW  SUNDOG  SUNDRA  SUNDRI  SUNRAY  SUPAWN
SURIMI  SWIPLE  SYLVINe SYNCOM  SYNROC  SYNTAN
```

```
TABARD  TABULI  TAGRAG  TAGUAN  TAHINA  TAHINI  TAHSIL  TAIAHA  TAILLE
TAILYE  TAISCH+ TAKAHE  TALBOT  TALLAT  TALLOL  TALWEG  TAMANU  TAMARAo
TAMARAu TAMARIn TAMBAC  TAMBAK  TAMBURa TAMEIN  TAMPAN  TANGUN  TANNINg
TANREC  TANUKI  TAONGA  TAPALO  TARAMA  TARAND  TARBOY  TARCEL  TARMAC
```

TARPAN	TARPON	TARSEL	*TASBIH*	TATAMI	*TATSOI*	*TAUHOU*	*TAUIWI*	TAUTOG
TAWHAI	*TEABAG*	TEAPOY	TECHNO	TECKEL	*TEFLON*	*TEHSIL*	TELEDU	TELEGA
TELLINg	TELOME	TELSON	TEMPEH	TENACE	TENAIL	TENDRE	TENREC	TENSON
TENUTO	TEOPAN	TEPHRA	TERCIO	TEREDO	TERETE	TERMLY+	TESTON	TETANY+
TETRYL	TEWART	THAIRM	THANNAh	THIBLE	THIRAM	THIVEL	THOWEL	THRAVE
THRENE	THUGGO	THYMOL	THYRSE	TIERCEd	TIERCEl	TIERCEt	TIETACk	TIGLON
TIMBREl	TIPCAT	TIPULA	*TIPUNA*	*TIRITI*	TISICK	TITIAN	TITOKI	TOCSIN
TOECAP	TOETOE	TOISON	TOITOI	TOLSEL	TOLUOLe	TOLUYL	TOMBACk	TOMBAK
TOMBOC	TOMCOD	TONEME	TONNAGe	TOOART	TORERO	TORULAe	TOTARA	*TOWKAY*
TOWMONd	TOWMONt	TRANNY+	TRICOT	TRIENE	TRILBY+	TRILBYs	TRIODE	TRIPOS+
TRISULa	TRITONe	TRIUNE	TROCHEe	TROELY+	TROGON	TROIKA	TROPINe	TROPINg
TROTYL	*TROUCH+*	*TUATUA*	TUBULE	TUCHUN	TUGHRA	TUGRIK	TUILLE	*TUKTOO*
TULADI	TULBAN	TUMPHY+	TUNDUN	TUPELO	*TUPUNA*	TURACOu	*TURNON*	TUSCHE
TUTSAN	TWIBILl	TYLOTE	TYMPANa	TYMPANi	TYMPANo	TYMPANy	TYPHON	
UAKARI	UBERTY+	UBIETY+	*UBUNTU*	ULICON	ULIKON	ULLING	ULTIMA	UMBRIL
UMWELT	UNEASE	UNFACT	UNIPED	UNIPOD	UNRULEd	UNWARE	UPCOME	UPGANG
UPHROE	UPLAND	UPMAKEr	UPTICK	UPTIME	URACIL	URANIN	URANYL	UREIDE
UROPOD	URTICA	USANCE						
VAHANA	VAKEEL	VALKYR	VALUTA	VARROA	VAUDOO	*VELCRO*	VELETA	VELLON
VENENE	VENEWE	VENIRE	VENNEL	VENTIL	VENULE	VERDIN	*VERLAN*	VERREL
VERSINe	VERSINg	VIBRIOn	VICUNA	VIDAME	VIELLE	VIHARA	VIKING	VIMANA
VINTRY+	VIRAGO	VIRAGO+	VIRINO	VISARD	VISCIN	VISILE	VOCULE	VOLOST
VOLUTEd	VOMICAe	VORAGO+	*VOUDON*	VOULGE	VULCAN			
WABAIN	WABOOM	WADMEL	WADMOLl	*WAIATA*	*WAIRUA*	*WAKAME*	WANDOO	WANGAN
WANGUN	WAPITI	*WARAGI*	WARDOG	WASABI	*WASHING*	WASTRY+	*WEAKON*	WEANEL
WEASON	*WEBCAM*	*WEBLOG*	WELKINg	WESAND	*WHANAU*	WHARVE	*WHENUA*	WHERVE
WICOPY+	WIGEON	WINDAC	WINDAS+	WINNLE	WISARD	WISENT	WITGAT	WITTOL
WOGGLE	WOMERA	WONING	WONTON	WOOBUT	WORMIL	WORREL	WORTLE	WRAITH
WROATH	WYVERN							
YAOURT	YAPOCK	YARPHA	*YARRAN*	YASMAK	YAUPON	YEELIN	*YIDAKI*	YNAMBU
YOUPON	YUKATA							

6.3.8 OTHER NON-PLURALS

AARRGHh	ABEIGH	ACKNEW	ACULEI	AEFALD	AFAWLD	AGAPAE	AGAPAI	AGOROTh
AGUNOT	AIKONA	ALIBLE	ALIYOS	ALIYOTh	ALLONS	*ALLYOU*	ALSOONe	ALUMNAe
ALUMNI	AMARNA	ANCILE	ANCORA	*ANELLI*	ANENST	ANGOLA	ANOUGH	ARCANE
ARCHEI	ARGULI	ARGUTE	*ARIARY*	ARILLI	ARIOSI	ARRECT	*ARRIBA*	ARSENO
ARSINO	*ASHRAF*	AWHILE	AWLESS	AWSOME				
BAALIM	BACULA	*BAKGAT*	BATEAUx	BEDIDE	BEDYDE	BEFELD	BEGILT	BEGIRT
BEGONE	BELIKE	BELIVE	BEMATA	BESANG	BESPATe	BESTAD	BESUNG	*BETCHA*

BETOOK	BETROD	BEWEPT	BIFOLD	BIFORM	BINOCS	BISSON	BLAISE	BOLETI
BORRELl	BOSHTA	BOSKER	BOTONEe	BUMALO	BYLIVE	BYPAST		

CADEAUx	CALAMI	CAMSHO	CANTHI	CAPITAl	CAPITAn	*CARDAN*	*CARRON*	CARTOP
CASINI	CENDRE	*CENTAI*	*CENTAS*	CENTRAl	CERULE	CESTOId	CHADRI	CHAETAe
CHAETAl	CHALOTh	CHOANAe	CHYLDE	CLAMBEr	COINOP	COLOBId	COMADE	COMODO
COMPASs	*COMPASt*	CONGII	COTEAUx	CRIBLE	CRISSAl	CRISTAe	CUMULI	CUPULAe
CUPULAr	CURULE	*CUSHTY*	CUSTOS	CYATHIa	CYTISI			

DAWNEY	DAYGLOw	DEBILE	DECANI	DEDANS	DEFASTe	DEGAGE	DEGRAS	DEMISS
DEMODEd	DIAMYL	DIARCHy	DIPSAS	DREICH*	DREIGH*	DRIEGH	DROMOI	DROMOS
DUELLI	*DUMELA*	DYABLE						

EASSEL	EASSIL	ECHINI	EFTEST	EKUELE	ELYTRAl	EMBOLIc	EMBOST	*EMLETS*
ENGILT	ENGIRT	ENLEVE	ENNUYEd	ENNUYEe	ENRAPT	ENTETEe	*EOCENE*	EOLIAN
EONIAN	EPHEBIc	EPUISEe	ERENOW	*ERUVIM*	*ERUVIN*	EURIPI		

FACEUP	FACILE	FACULAe	FACULAr	FAMULI	FARAND	*FECKINg*	FECUND	FEMORAl
FILTRE	*FINITO*	FINSKO	FLEURY	FODGEL	FORANE	FORBADe	FOREBYe	FORGAT
FORRAD	FORWHY	FRAENA	FULCRA	FUMULI	FUNEST	FURDER	*FUSUMA*	

GAMGEE	*GATVOL*	GAUCHE*	GEASON	GEMINI	GEMONY	GENERAl	GENTILe	GIDDAP
GIDDAY	GIDDUP	*GITTINg*	GNOMAE	GOBONY	GRASTE	GRIESY	GRIPLE	

HABILE	HAMULI	HANGUL	HANIWA	HELIAC	HEREAT	HEREOF	HEREON	HERETO
HOOROO	HORARY	HUDDUP	HUMERI					

IBADAH	*IBADAT*	IBIDEM	*IDEATA*	*IDOLON*	INBORN	INCAVI	INCAVO	INCONY
INCUBI	INCULT	INDIGN	INFELT	*INFIMA*	INFULAe	INGRAM	INMOST	INSULAe
INSULAr	INTIME	INTIRE	INTOWN	INWORN	INWOVEn	ISTHMIc		

KOUROI	KOUROS	KRONOR	KRONUR

LABARA	LABILE	LEETLE	LIEDER	LIFULL	LIKUTA	LIMINAl	LIMULI	LISSOMe
LOBULI	LOMATA	LOUCHE*	LOUNGY	*LUCHOTh*	LUMINAl	LUNULAe	LUNULAr	LUSTRAl
LYFULL								

MAKUTA	*MALIBU*	MALLEI	MALOTI	MAUNNA	*MAWGER*	MAYEST	MAYHAP	MEGARAd
MEIKLE	*MESIAD*	MESIAN	*MIDCAP*	*MIKVOS*	*MIKVOTh*	*MIRCHI*	MISUST	MODICA
MODULI	MODULO	MONACT	*MONTANe*	*MONTANt*	*MORYAH*	MOSHAV	MUSIVE	MYTHOI
MYTHOS								

NACHAS	*NADORS*	NATURAe	NATURAl	NEFAST	NIELLI	NOGAKU	NOMINAl	NONARY
NONFAT	NOSTOI	NOSTOS	*NOSTRO*	NOTOUR	NOWISE	NUBILE	NUCLEIc	NUCLEIn
NUMINA								

OBTECT	OCHONE	OCTOPI	*OMIGOD*	ONAGRI	OPTIMAl	OSCULAr	OUTHER	OUTSAT
OUTSAW	OUTWON	OUVERTe	OVERBY	OWERBY				

PADKOS	PALAMAe	*PANINO*	PARDEE	PASSIM	PEASON	PENILE	*PENILL*	PERAEA
PERFAY	PERFET	PERITI	*PERNIO*	PHALLIc	PHALLIn	PHOLAS	*PHOSSY*	PHYLON
PINETA	PINYIN	PITHOI	PITHOS	PLUTEI	POISHA	*POTHOS*	*PRELAW*	*PROGUN*
PROTEId	PROTEIn	PRUTOTh	*PTOOEY*	PUISNY	*PUNANI*	*PUNANY*	PUNCTA	PYLORIc

RACKLE	RAMULI	RAPHAE	RAPINI	RAUCLE*	*README*	RECKAN	REFLEW	REGAVE
REGILT	REGREW	REGULAe	REGULAr	REGULI	*RELATA*	REMOUD	REPAND	RESHOD
RESHOT	RETOOK	RETORE	RETORN	RETUSE	REWOKEn	*REWORE*	*REWORN*	REWOVEn
ROSTRAl	ROUPET	RUBATI	RUMINAl					

SALEWD	SANCTA	SATIVE	SAYEST	SBIRRI	SBIRRO	SCROTAl	SCRYDE	SCYPHI
SECUND	SEMINAl	SEMINAr	SEMPER	SEMPLE*	SEMPRE	SENITI	SENRYU	SEPMAG
SHAMOS	*SHARON*	SHNAPS	SHTOOM	*SIFREI*	SIGLOI	SIGLOS	SISTRA	SITULAe
SKEIGH*	SODAINe	SOEVER	SOIGNEe	SOLGEL	SOLITOn	SOMATA	*SOMONI*	SOWANS
SOWENS	SPRACK	STANCK	STATIM	STIEVE*	STRANG*	STRANGe	STRATI	STROMAl
STROOKe	SUABLE	SUBITO	SUBSEA	SUBTIL*	SUBTILe	SURBET	SVELTE*	SYNURAe

TABULAe	TABULAr	*TAIHOA*	TEGULAe	TEGULAr	TELARY	TEMENE	TENUTI	TERAPH
TERATA	TEREFAh	THALLIc	THOLOI	THOLOS	THROVE	THYRSI	TIFOSI	TIFOSO
TITULI	TOFORE	TORULIn	TRIENS	TROCHIl	TROGGS	TROPHIc	*TRYPAN*	TUFOLI
TUMULI								

UCKERS	UGSOME	ULTIMO	UNAKINg	UNBORE	UNBUSY	*UNCAST*	UNCINI	UNCLAD
UNCOOL	UNDEAD	UNDREW	UNFELT	UNFIRM	UNFOND	UNGAIN	UNGILT	UNGIRTh
UNGLAD	UNGORD	UNGULAe	UNGULAr	UNHEWN	UNHUNG	UNKEND	UNKEPT	UNLASTe
UNLICH	UNLOST	UNMARD	UNMEEK	UNMEET	UNMIRY	UNPURE	UNROVEn	UNRUDE
UNSAWN	UNSHOD	UNSHOT	UNSOFT	UNSOWN	UNSPUN	UNSUNK	UNTORN	UNTROD
UNWEPT	UNWIST	UNWOVEn	UPBLEW	UPBORE	UPDOVE	UPDREW	UPGIRT	UPGONE
UPGREW	UPHAND	UPHILD	UPHOVE	UPHUNG	UPMOST	UPRYST	*UPSOLD*	UPTOOK
UPTORE	UPTORN	URACHI						

VAGROM	VEDUTA	VEDUTE	VEGETE	VELOCE	VERDOY	VERLIG	VERREY	VESICAe
VESICAl	*VIENNA*	VIMINAl	VOLAGE	VOLENS	*VOSTRO*			

WANDLE	WANNEL	*WASSUP*	WEYARD	WHATNA	WHENAS	WHILOM	WHOMSO	*WOOHOO*
WOTCHA								

6.4 LESS FAMILIAR BUT LESS PROBABLE NON-HOOK SIXES

CONTAINING BB

ABBACY+	**ABDABS**	BABACO	BABLAH	BALBOA	**BARBAL**	BARBIE	BARBUT	BATBOY
BAUBEE	BAWBEE	BAWBLE	BEBUNG	BEEBEE	BEMBEX+	BEMBIX+	*BIBFUL*	BICARB
BIMBLE	BLOWBYs	*BOBLET*	BOBWIG	BOMBAX+	BOMBYX+	*BONOBO*	BOOBIE	BOSBOK
BOUBOU	*BUBKES*	*BUBKIS*	**BUBOED**	*BUIBUI*	**BULBAR**	BULBEL	BULBIL	BULBUL
BURBLEr	**BURBLY***	BURBOT	BUSBAR	BUSBOY	**CLUBBY***	DABBER	DIBBER	DIBBLEr
DIBBUK	DOBBIE	DOBBINg	**DRABBY***	DUBBER	DUBBINg	DYBBUK	EARBOB	GABBER

6. Six-Letter Words

GABBRO	GIBBET	GOBBET	**GRABBY***	GUBBAH	HABOOB	*HOBBER*	HOBJOB>	HOBNOB>
HUBBLY	JABBLE	JIBBER	*JILBAB*	JOBBERy	JOBBIE	JUBBAH	KEBBIE	KIBBLE
LABLAB	LEBBEK	LIBBER	LIBLAB	LOBBER	LUBBER	MOBBER	MOBBIE	MOBBLE
NABBER	NEBBUK	**NOBBUT**	NUBBINg	NUBBLE	**NUBBLY***	NYBBLE	**PLEBBY***	RABBET
RIBBER	RIBIBE	ROBBINg	**RUBBET**	**RUBBIT**y	**RUBBLY***	SABBATh	SKIBOB>	**SLABBY***
SNEBBE	SNUBBEr	SOBBER	SUBBIE	SUBDEB	SWABBY+	TABBIS+	TEBBAD	TUBBER
WABBIT	WABBLEr	**WABBLY***	*WEBBIE**	WIBBLE	YABBER			

CONTAINING CC

ACCEND	ACCITE	ACCLOY	ACCOIL	ACCREW	**ACETIC**	ALCAIC	*ANICCA*	*ARCSEC*
BUCCAL	CACHOU	CACOON	**CADMIC**	CADUAC	**CAECUM**	CAIMAC	CALCAR	**CALCED**
CALCES	CANCHA	**CAPRIC**e	CARACK	CARACT	CARCEL	CAROCH+	CAROCHe	**CASEIC**
CATCON	**CECILS**	CECITY+	CELIAC	**CERCAL**	**CERCUS**	CHACMA	CHEBEC	CHIACK
CHICLE	**CHICLY**	CHINCH+	CHOCHO	**CHORIC**	CHYACK	**CHYMIC**	CICALA	**CICALE**
CICELY+	CICERO	CICUTA	CILICE	**CISTIC**	**CITRIC**	**CLECHE**	CLITIC	CLOACAe
CLOACAl	CLOCHE	**CLONIC**	**COBRIC**	COCAINe	COCHIN	COCKET	COCKUP	**COOCOO**
COOTCH	COPECK	CORSAC	COUCAL	CRETIC	**CRISIC**	CROCUS+	CROCHEt	**CRUCES**
CULTCH+	**CUPRIC**	CURACY+	CUSCUS+	**CYANIC**	*CYCLIN*g	CYCLUS+	**CYSTIC**	DECCIE
DECOCT	*ECESIC*	**ECHOIC**	*ERUCIC*	ESCROC	**FLOCCI**	IPECAC	KACCHA	*KUCCHA*
MACACO	MOCOCK	MOCUCK	MUCLUC	*OCICAT*	**PECTIC**	**PICRIC**	**PYCNIC**	RICRAC
ROCOCO	**SACCOI**	SACCOS+	SCIROC	SCONCE	**SICCAN**	**SICCAR**	SPECCY+	SUCCAH
SUCCESs	SUCCORy	**SUCCOS**	**SUCCOT**h	SUCCUSs	TICTAC&	TICTOC&	**UNCHIC**	**ZINCIC**

CONTAINING FF

AFFEARd	AFFEARe	AFFEER	AFFINEd	AFFLUX+	AFFRAP>	AFFRAY	AFFRET>	**AFFYDE**
BIFFER	BIFFINg	BOUFFE	*BUYOFF*	CHAUFF	COFFLE	COIFFE	CUFFINg	CUFFLE
DEFFLY	*DIEOFF*	DUFFEL	DUFFLE	EFFACEr	EFFEIR	EFFERE	**EFFETE**	EFFLUX+
EFFRAY	EFFUSE	*FANFIC*	FARFAL	FARFEL	**FARFET**	FILFOT	FORFEX+	FURFUR
FYLFOT	GUFFIE	HAFFET	HAFFIT	*HUFFER*	INFEFT	KAFFIR	KEFFEL	LOGOFF
MAFFIA	**NAFFLY**	NEAFFE	NIFFER	NUFFIN	**OFFKEY**	OFFPUT	PIAFFEr	POFFLE
RAFFIA	RIFFLEr	RUBOFF	RUFFINg	**RUFFLY***	SCLAFF	SETOFF	SHROFF	SIFFLE
SKLIFF	SOFFIT	SPLIFF	**SPOFFY**	STRAFF	TAFFIA	TIFFINg	WAFFIE	**WAFFLY***
YAFFLE	ZAFFAR	ZAFFER	ZAFFIR	ZAFFRE				

CONTAINING HH

AHCHOO	**APHTHA**e	*BHIKHU*	CHALAH	CHALEH	CHETAH	CHINCHy	CHOCHO	CHOUSH+
DUHKHA	**HACHIS**	HADITH	HAINCH	HALLAH	**HEISHI**	HOORAH	HOOTCH+	HOUDAH
HOWDAH	HUMHUM	HUPPAH	JUBBAH	*PHWOAH*	RHAPHE	*SHAHID*	SHAIKH	*SHEESH*
SHIBAH	SHTCHI	**SHYISH**	THETCH	WHEECHs	WHEESHt	WHIDAH	WHYDAH	

CONTAINING MM

AMMINE **AMMINO** AMTMAN AMYLUM BAMMER *BOMMIE* BUMMEL BUMMLE *CAMMIE*
CHEMMY+ COMMERe COMMIE **COMMIS** COMMIXt CUMMER CUMMIN DAMMAR **DAMMIT**
DHAMMA *DHIMMI* DUMDUM **GEMMEN** GIMMAL GIMMIE GIMMOR GRAMMAr GRAMME
GREMMY+ GUMMER GYMMAL HAMMAL HOMMOS+ HUMHUM HUMMEL HUMMER **HUMMLE**
HUMMUS+ **IMMANE** JAMMER JEMIMA *JIMMIE* KIMMER KUMMEL LAMMER LAMMIE
LIMMER LUMMOX+ *MADTOM* MAHMAL MAIHEM MALLAM MALMAG *MAMAKO* *MAMAKU*
MAMLUK MAMZER MANDOM *MAOMAO* MARMOT MARRAM MARRUM MAUMET MAWMET
MAZUMA MEEMIE MEGOHM MEGRIM **MENTUM** **MERMAN** **MERMEN** MEROME *MESTOMe*
METUMP MIMOSAe **MIMSEY*** MINIUM MIOMBO MISHMI **MISMET** **MNEMIC** MNEMON
MOMSER MOMZER *MONEME* MONISM MOTMOT MOUSMEe MULMUL1 MULTUM **MUMBLY***
MUMPER MUSMON MUTUUM MUUMUU MYXOMA NIMMER NOMISM **OMASUM** OMNIUM
OSMIUM **POMMEE** POMMELe POMMEL> POMMIE *RAMMEL* RAMMER *RAMMLE* RIMMER
ROMCOM SEMEME SEMMIT SEMSEM SHIMMY SIMOOM SMEGMA SPAMMY* STEMMA
STEMMEr **STEMMY*** **SWIMMY*** TAMMAR TAMMIE **TOMIUM** *WAMMUL* WAMMUS+ WAMPUM
WHAMMO **WHIMMY*** *WIMMIN* *WOMMIT* YAMMER ZYMOME

CONTAINING PP

APEPSY+ **APPAID** APPAIR APPORT APPOSEr BOPEEP BUPPIE CAPPER *CHUPPAh*
CIPPUS COPPINg COPPLE COPPRA CROPPY+ DIPPER DOPPER DOPPIE *DOPPIO*
DRAPPY+ **DRIPPY*** EPOPEE FIPPLE **FLAPPY*** *GAPPER* GIPPER GRAPPA GRIPPEr
GRIPPY* GYPPER GYPPIE HIPPEN **HIPPIC** HIPPINg HIPPUS+ HOPPLEr HUPPAH
HOPPUS **HUPPOTh** JOYPOP> **KEPPEN** **KEPPIT** **KIPPEN** KOPPIE LAPPER LAPPET
LAPPIE LIPPEN LIPPER LIPPIE* **LUPPEN** MAYPOP MOPPER MOPPET *MUPPET*
NAPPIE* OPPUGN **PALPAL** **PALPUS** PAPACY+ PAPAIN PAPIST **PAPULAe** **PAPULAr**
PAPULE **PAPYRI** PARAPH PEAPOD PEEPUL **PEPFUL** PEPINO PEPLOS+ PEPLUM
PEPLUS+ PEPSINe PEPTIDe PETNAP> *PIOPIO* PIPAGE PIPKIN PIUPIU *POEPOL*
POMPEY POMPOM POMPON *POOPER* POPERY+ **POPISH** POPJOY POPLIN **POPRIN**
POPSIE *POSTOP* POTPIE PREAMP *PRENUP* **PRIAPIc** PROPYLa PULLUP **PULPAL**
PULPER PUMPER PUPATE PURPIE **PURPLY*** PYROPE QUIPPU **QUIPPY*** **RIPPLY***
RIPRAP> SAPPAN SHOPPEr SIPPER SIPPET SIPPLE **SKIPPY*** STEPPEr TAPPER
TAPPIT *TIPPEE* TIPPET TOPPER **TRAPPY*** **TRIPPY*** UNPOPE **UPPISH** **UPPITY**
UPWRAP WAPPER WIPPEN YAPPER YAPPIE* **YIPPEE** YIPPER YIPPIE YUPPIE
ZIPTOP

CONTAINING SS

ADMASS+ BADASS+ BAGASSe BOSSER *BOSSET* BYSSUS+ CASSIA CASSIS+ CESTOS+
CESTUS+ CISSUS+ CISTUS+ COSMOS+ COSSIE COSTUS+ CUISSEr CUSSER DASSIE
DOSSAL DOSSEL DOSSER DOSSIL ECESIS+ ENOSIS+ ESSIVE ESSOIN ESTRUS+
FOSSOR FOUSSA FUSSER GASSER GNEISS+ GOSSAN GOSSIB HASSAR HASSEL
HISSER HUSSAR HUSSIF HYSSOP JASSID JESSIE JISSOM JOSSER KAROSS+
KISSEL KOSMOS+ KOUSSO KUMISS+ LAISSE LAPSUS+ MASSIF MEGASSe MESSAN
MISSEL MISSISh MISSUS+ MOSSER MOSSIE* MYSOST NOESIS+ OSSEIN PASSUS+
PASTIS+ PISSER PLISSE POSSIE POTASSa POUSSE PUSSEL PUSSER PUSSLY+

RHESUS+ ROSSER RUSCUS+ RUSSIA SALTUS+ SAMOSA SAMSHU SANSEI SARSAR
SARSEN *SASTRA* SCOUSEr SECESH+ SEISINg SEISOR SELSYN **SEPSIS** **SEPSES**
SEROSAe SEROSAl SESELI SESTETt SESTON SHAMUS+ SHIKSA SHIKSEh SISKIN
SISSOO SIZISM SIZIST SNASTE SOLEUS+ SORBUS+ SPEISS+ SPENSE **STASES**
STASIS SUDSER SUSLIK SYNGAS+ SYNGAS> TASSIE TISWAS+ TSETSE TSOTSI
TSURIS+ *TUSSAC* TUSSAH TUSSAR TUSSEH TUSSER *TUSSES* TUSSIS+ TUSSORe
TUSSUR VOWESS+ WHOSIS+

CONTAINING VV

BOVVER *CHAVVY** CHIVVY DEVVEL> EVOVAE LUVVIE SAVVEY **SPIVVY** **VALVAL**
VALVAR VISIVE VIVACE VIVARY+ **VIVELY** VIVIFY **VIVRES** VOLVOX+ VOTIVE

CONTAINING WW

BOWSAW GEWGAW QAWWALi SWOWND SWOWNE WARSAW *WHENWE* WIGWAG>

CONTAINING YY

BAYYAN BYPLAY *DAYBOY* DOYLEY FLYBOY FLYWAY GLYCYL **GRAYLY** **GREYLY**
GRYESY GYNNEY HEYDEY HYDYNE KEYWAY *NAYSAYd* SAYYID **SPRYLY** SYZYGY+
YARELY YOWLEY

6.5 VERY IMPROBABLE LESS FAMILIAR SIXES

AKEAKE AMOMUM **BABBLY** *BAKKIE* BAOBAB BAZAZZ+ BEZAZZ+ BEZZLE BIBBERy
BIBBLE BIKKIE BIZAZZ+ **BLABBY** **BLEBBY** *BLOBBY** BOBBERy BOBBINg BOBBLE
BOBBLY BOWWOW *BREKKY+ **CALCIC** CHOCCY** CHUKKAr **COCCAL** **COCCIC** COCCID
COCCUS COCCYX+ *CUZZIE* DIKDIK DIKKOP *DUKKAH* *DUKKHA* FIZZEN FLYOFF
FUZZLE GIZZEN GOZZAN *HAJJAH* HAMMAM HAZZAN HUMMUM HUBBUB HUZZAH
IZZARD *JAZZBO* JAZZER **JEJUNAl** **JEJUNE** JIGJIG> JIMJAM JOJOBA JUJUBE
KABAKA KABIKI KABUKI KAIKAI KAKAPO *KAKURO* KALPAK *KALUKI* KANAKA
KANUKA *KAPUKA* KARAKA KATHAK KECKLE KECKSY+ KEEKER *KEKENO* KEKSYE
KICKUP *KIEKIE* KIKUYU KINKLE KISHKA KISHKE **KNACKY** **KNICKS** *KOKAKO*
KOKIRI *KOKOPU* KOLKOZy *KONAKI* *KONEKE* **KOOKIE** KOPECK KORKIR *KOTUKU*
KRAKEN *KUDLIK* **KULAKI** KUNKAR KUNKUR *LEKKER* LEZZIE *LIZZIE* **MAMMAE**
MAMMEE MAMMER MAMMET MAMMEY MAMMIE MAMMON MARKKAa *MARMEM* MAXIXE
MEZUZAh MIZZEN MIZZLE **MIZZLY** MOMISM MOMMET MOZZIE MOZZLE MUKLUK
MUKTUK MUMMIA NOZZER NUZZER *PAKOKO* PAPPUS+ PAXWAX+ PAZAZZ+ PIAZZA
PIAZZE PIKAKE PIPPINg PIZAZZy *PIZZAZ+ PIZZLE POPPER POPPET POPPIT
POPPLE **POPPLY** **POWWAW** **PREPPY** PUKEKO PUZZEL *QUAZZY** QUOKKA RAZZIA
RAZZLE RIZZARt RIZZER RIZZOR ROZZER **SAKKOI** SAKKOS+ *SCOZZA* **SCUZZY**
*SKANKY** *SKRIKE* SKRONK **SKUNKY** **SOZZLY** SUKKAH **SUKKOS** **SUKKOTh** *TEKKIE*
TSKTSK TZETZE UNKINK UPPROP> VIZZIE= WAKIKI *WHIZZO* **WHIZZY** WIZZEN
WUKKAS WUZZLE YAKKER YIKKER **ZIZITH** ZIZZLE ZOOZOO *ZUZZIM*

7. SEVEN-LETTER WORDS

7.1. FAMILIAR SEVENS

7.1.1 VERBS IN COMMON USE

ABANDON	ABOLISH	ABRIDGEr	ABSCOND	ABSOLVEr	ABSTAIN	ACCLAIM	ACCOUNT
ACHIEVEr	ACIDIFY	ACQUIREe	ACQUIREr	ADDRESS	ADJOURN	ADJUDGE	ADVANCEr
AFFLICT	AGITATE	AGONISE	AGONIZE	AMPLIFY	ANALYSEr	ANIMATEr	APPEASEr
APPLAUD	APPOINT	APPROVEr	ARRAIGN	ARRANGEr	ASSAULT	ASSUAGEr	ASTOUND
ATOMISEr	ATOMIZEr	ATTEMPT	ATTRACT	AUCTION	AUGMENT	AVERAGE	

BALANCEr	BANDAGEr	BAPTISEr	BAPTIZEr	BARRACK	BEGRIME	BEGUILEr	BELIEVEr
BENEFIT	BENEFIT>	BESEECH	BESIEGEr	BETROTH	BEWITCH	BLACKEN	BLUSTERy
BOLSTER	BOMBARDe	BOYCOTT	BREATHEr	BROADEN	BURGEON		

CANVASS	CAPSIZE	CAPTAIN	CAPTUREr	CAROUSEl	CAROUSEr	CAUTION	CENSUREr
CERTIFY	CHARTER	CHASTEN	CHATTERy	CHEAPEN	CHERISH	CHORTLEr	CHUCKLEr
CHUNDER	CLAMBER	CLAMOUR	CLARIFY	CLEANSEr	CLOBBER	CLUTTERy	COEXIST
COHABIT	COLLATE	COLLECT	COLLIDEr	COLLUDEr	COMBINEr	COMFORT	COMMAND
COMMEND	COMMENT	COMMUTEr	COMPACT	COMPAREr	COMPERE	COMPETE	COMPILEr
COMPOSEr	COMPUTEr	CONCEAL	CONCEDEr	CONCERN	CONCOCT	CONCUSS	CONDEMN
CONDONEr	CONDUCTi	CONFESS	CONFIDEr	CONFINEr	CONFIRM	CONFORM	CONFUSE
CONGEAL	CONGEST	CONJUREr	CONNECT	CONNIVEr	CONQUER	CONSENT	CONSIGN
CONSIST	CONSOLEr	CONSORT	CONSULTa	CONSUMEr	CONTACT	CONTAIN	CONTEND
CONTEST	CONTORT	CONTROL>	CONTROLe	CONVENEr	CONVERT	CONVICT	CORRECT*
CORRODEr	CORRUPT*	COUNSEL	COUNSEL>	COUNTER	CRACKLE	CREMATE	CRINKLE
CRIPPLEr	CRUCIFY	CRUMBLE	CRUMPLE	CURTAIL	CURTSEY		

DEBRIEF	DECEIVEr	DECLAREr	DECLINEr	DEFLATEr	DEFLECT	DEFRAUD	DEFROCK
DEFROST	DEGRADEr	DELIGHT	DELIVERy	DELOUSEr	DEPLETEr	DEPLOREr	DEPOSIT
DEPRESS	DEPRIVEr	DESCEND	DESERVEr	DESPAIR	DESPISEr	DESTROY	DETRACT
DEVALUE	DEVELOPe	DEVIATE	DIARISE	DIARIZE	DICTATE	DIGNIFY	DIGRESS
DISABLEr	DISBAND	DISCARD	DISCERN	DISCUSS	DISGUST	DISLIKEn	DISLIKEr
DISMISS	DISOBEY	DISPLAY	DISPOSEr	DISPUTEr	DISROBEr	DISRUPT	DISSECT
DISTILL	DISTORT	DISTURB	DIVERGE	DIVORCEe	DIVORCEr	DIVULGEr	DRAUGHTy
DRIBBLEr	DRIBBLEt	DWINDLE					

EDUCATE	ELEVATE	EMANATE	EMBRACEr	EMBROIL	EMPOWER	EMULATE	ENAMOUR
ENCHANT	ENCLOSEr	ENCRYPT	ENDORSEe	ENDORSEr	ENFORCEr	ENGORGE	ENGRAVEn
ENGRAVEr	ENGROSS	ENHANCEr	ENLARGEn	ENLARGEr	ENLIVEN	ENQUIREr	ENSLAVEr
ENSNAREr	ENTHRALl	ENTHUSE	ENTITLE	ENTREATy	ENTRUST	ENTWINE	ENVELOPe
ESPOUSEr	EXAMINEe	EXAMINEr	EXCLAIM	EXCLUDEe	EXCLUDEr	EXCRETEr	EXECUTEr
EXHAUST	EXHIBIT	EXPLAIN	EXPLODEr	EXPLOIT	EXPLOREr	EXPRESSo	EXTRACT

FALSIFY	FEATURE	FERMENT	FINANCE	FLATTEN	FLATTER	FLAVOURy	FLICKERy
FLITTERn	FLUMMOX	FLUSTERy	FLUTTER	FORBODE	FORESEEd	FORESEEn	FORESEEr
FORFEIT	FORGIVEd	FORGIVEn	FORGIVEr	FORSAKEd	FORSAKEn	FORSAKEr	FORTIFY
FORWARD*	FOSSICK	FRAZZLE	FRESHEN	FURNISH			

7. Seven-Letter Words

GARNISH GAROTTEr GESTATE GLADDEN GLIMPSEr GLISTEN GLITTERy GLORIFY
GRAPPLEr GRATIFY GRIMACEr GRIZZLEr GRUMBLEr

HARNESS HARPOON HARVEST HEARTEN HENPECK HORRIFY HOTFOOT HYDRATE

IDOLISEr IDOLIZEr IMAGINEr IMITATE IMMERSEr IMPANEL IMPANEL> IMPEACH
IMPERIL IMPERIL> IMPINGEr IMPLANT IMPLODE IMPLOREr IMPOUND IMPRESSe
IMPROVEr INCENSEr INCLUDE INDULGEr INFLAMEr INFLATEr INFLICT INHABIT
INHERIT INHIBIT INQUIREr INSPECT INSPIREr INSTALL INSTILL INTRUDEr
INVOLVEr ISOLATE ITEMISEr ITEMIZEr ITERATE

JAYWALK JOURNEY JUSTIFY

KIBBITZ

LACTATE LAIRISE LAIRIZE LAUNDER LECTUREr LICENSEe LICENSEr LIGHTEN
LIQUEFY

MAGNIFY MARSHALl MASSAGEr MEANDER MEASUREr MEDIATE MENTION MIGRATE
MISDIAL MISDIAL> MISFILE MISHEARd MISHEARd MISLEADd MISNAME MISREADd
MISTAKEd MISTAKEn MISTAKEr MISTIME MISTYPE MOISTEN MONITORy MORTIFY
MYSTIFY

NARRATEr NEGLECT NITPICKy NOURISH NULLIFY NURTUREr

OBSCURE* OBSERVEr OBVIATE OFFLOAD OPERATE OPPRESS OUTCROP> OUTDATE
OUTGROWd OUTGROWn OUTJUMP OUTLAST OUTLEAPt OUTLINEr OUTLIVEr OUTPACE
OUTPLAY OUTRACE OUTRANK OUTRATE OUTRIDEd OUTRIDEr OUTSELLd OUTSTAY
OUTSWIMd OUTSWIM> OUTTALK OUTVOTEr OVERACT OVERBIDd OVERBID> OVEREATd
OVERLAP> OVERLAYd OVERLIEd OVERLIEr OVERPAYd OVERRUNd OVERRUN> OVERSEEd
OVERSEEn OVERSEEr OVERTAX OVULATE OXIDISEr OXIDIZEr

PARTAKEd PARTAKEn PARTAKEr PERFECT* PERFECTa PERFECTi PERFECTo PERFORM
PERJUREr PERPLEX PERSIST PERTAIN PERTURB PERVADEr PETRIFY PICTURE
PILLAGEr PILLORY PLACATEr PLUMMET PLUNDER POLEAXE POLLUTEr PORTEND
PORTRAY PRATTLEr PREBOOK PRECEDE PRECOOK PREDATE PREDICT PREEMPT
PREFACEr PREHEAT PREPACK PREPAREr PREPLAN> PREPLANt PRESENT PRESIDEr
PRESORT PRESUMEr PRETEND PREVAIL PREVENT PREVIEW PREWRAP> PRICKLE
PROCEED PROCESS PROCUREr PRODUCEr PROFESS PROGRAM PROGRAM> PROJECT
PROLONGe PROMISEe PROMISEr PROMOTEr PROPOSEr PROSPER PROTECT PROTEST
PROVIDEr PROVOKEr PUBLISH PULSATE PURLOIN PURPORT PUTREFY

QUALIFY QUARREL QUIBBLEr QUICKEN QUIETEN

RADIATE RANSACK READAPT READMIT> READOPT REALIGN REALISEr REALIZEr
REALLOT> REAPPLY REARGUE REARISEd REARISEn REBOARD REBUILD RECEIVEr
RECHECK RECLAIM RECLINEr RECOUNT RECOVERy RECRUIT RECTIFY RECYCLEr
REDRESS REDRILL REELECT REENACT REENTER REEQUIP> REFLECT REFRAIN
REFRAME REFRESH REGRADE REGRESS REGROUP REHOUSE REINDEX REISSUEr

REJOICEr RELABEL RELABEL> RELEARNt RELEASEe RELEASEr RELIEVEr REMARRY
REMODEL REMODEL> REMOUNT RENEGUEr REOCCUR> REORDER REPAINT REPATCH
REPLACEr REPLANT REPRESS REPRINT REQUEST REQUIREr REQUOTE REROUTE
REROUTE= RESCIND RESCORE RESERVEr RESHAPEr RESOLVEr RESOUND RESPECT
RESPOND RESPRAY RESTACK RESTAFF RESTART RESTOCK RESTOREr RETHINKd
RETRACEr RETRACT RETRAIN RETREAT REUNITEr REVALUE REVERSEr REVISIT
REVOLVEr REWEIGH REWRITEd REWRITEr ROLLICKy ROUGHEN RUMMAGEr RUPTURE

SALVAGEe SALVAGEr SATISFY SAUNTER SCAMPER SCATTERy SCRATCHy SCREECHy
SCRUNCHy SCUFFLEr SCUTTLEr SECLUDE SECRETE* SERVICEr SHACKLEr SHARPEN
SHATTERy SHELTERy SHIMMERy SHORTEN SHRIVEL SHRIVEL> SHUDDERy SHUFFLEr
SIGNIFY SILENCEr SITUATE SKITTLE SKYDIVEr SKYLARK SLACKEN SLANDER
SLITHERy SLOBBERy SLUMBERy SMARTEN SMOTHERy SMUGGLEr SNAFFLE SNIFFLEr
SNIGGER SNORKEL SNORKEL> SNUFFLEr SNUGGLE SOLICITy SPARKLEr SPARKLEt
SPATTER SPECIFY SPLURGEr SPONSOR SQUEEZEr SQUELCHy STAGGERy STAMMER
STARTLEr STIFFEN STRETCHy STUMBLEr STUPEFY STUTTER STYLISEr STYLIZEr
SUBJECT SUBSIDEr SUBSIST SUBVERT SUCCEED SUCCUMB SUFFICEr SUGGEST
SUNBAKE SUPPORT SUPPOSEr SURFACEr SURMISEr SURPASS SURVIVEr SUSPECT
SUSPEND SUSTAIN SWADDLEr SWAGGER SWALLOW SWEETEN SWELTER SWINDLEr

TARNISH TERRIFY TESTIFY THICKEN TIGHTEN TORMENTa TORTUREr TOUGHEN
TRAIPSE TRAMPLEr TREMBLEr TRICKLEt TROUBLEr TROUNCEr TRUNDLEr TWIDDLEr
TWINKLEr TWITTERy TYPESETd TYPESET>

UNBLOCK UNCHAIN UNCHOKE UNCLAMP UNCOVER UNDERDOd UNDERDOg UNDERGOd
UNDERGOd UNDRESS UNEARTH UNHITCH UNLATCH UNLEARNt UNLEASH UNNERVE
UNPLAIT UNRAVEL UNRAVEL> UNSCREW UNSTRAP> UNTWIST UPGRADEr UPSTAGEr
URINATE UTILISEr UTILIZEr

VENTUREr VIBRATE VIOLATEr

WELCOMEr WHIMPER WHISPERy WHISTLEr WHITTLEr WITNESS WORSHIP WORSHIP>
WRANGLEr WRESTLEr WRIGGLEr WRINKLE

7.1.2 VERBS MORE OFTEN USED IN OTHER PARTS OF SPEECH

ABSCESS AFFRONTe AIRDROP> AIRLIFT AIRMAIL AMNESTY ANGUISH ANTIQUEr
ANTIQUEy APPAREL APPAREL> ARCHIVE ARMLOCK ARTICLE ASKANCE ASPHALT
ASSAGAI ASSEGAI ATROPHY ATTACHEr AUDIBLE AUTOPSY

BACKHOE= BACKLOG> BAGPIPEr BALLAST BALLOON BANQUET BARGAIN BARRAGE
BARRIER BAYONET BAYONET> BEELINE BEESWAX BICYCLEr BIGFOOT BIVOUAC&
BLANKETy BLARNEY BLEMISH BLINKER BLISTERy BLITHER BLOSSOMy BLUBBERy
BLUNDER BOBSLED> BOBTAIL BOMBAST BOOTLEG> BOULDERy BRACKET BRAILLEr
BRAMBLE BRANDER BRAVADO BRAVADO+ BRIGADE BRIQUET BRISTLE BRITTLE*
BROCADE BROTHER BUFFALO BUFFALO+ BULLDOG> BULLOCKy BULWARK BURGLARy
BUTCHERy BUTTOCK

CABBAGEy CADENCE CALIPER CALLOUS CAPSULE CAPTION CAPTIVE CARAMEL>
CARAVAN CARAVAN> CARCASE CARCASS CARJACK CARPOOL CARTOONy CASCADE
CASHIER CATALOG CATCALL CHAGRIN CHAGRIN> CHAMBER CHANNEL CHANNEL>
CHAPTER CHARIOT CHEQUER CHICKEN CHIMNEY CHINWAG> CHIPPER CHOPPER
CHOWDER CIRCUITy CLAPPER CLATTERy CLIMATE CLOSURE CLUSTERy COLLAGEn
COMMUNEr COMPANY COMPASS COMPLEX* COMPOST CONCAVE CONCEITy CONCERTi
CONCERTo CONCISE* CONCORD CONTENT CONTOUR CONVENT COPYCAT> CORNICE
COSTUMEr COSTUMEy COTTAGEr COTTAGEy COURIER COWHIDE CRICKET CRIMSON
CROCHET CROQUET CROWBAR> CRUSADEr CURETTE CURTAIN CUSHIONy CYANIDE

DEADPAN> DEFAULT DEFENCE DEFENSE DEMAGOGy DEMERIT DENIZEN DERRICK
DESPITE DIAGRAM DIAGRAM> DIAMOND DIFFUSEr DIPLOMAt DISCORD DISDAIN
DISEASE DISSENT DIVERSE DOGGONE* DRAGOON DRAPERY DRIZZLE DUCHESSe
DUNGEON

EARMARK ECHELON ECLIPSEr ECSTASY EDITION EMBARGO EMBARGO+ ENCLAVE
ENGLISH ENTRAIL EPISTLEr EPITAPH EPITHET ESQUIRE EXAMPLE EXCERPTa
EXPENSE EXTINCT EYEBALL EYEBROW

FANFARE FANFOLD FANTASY FASHIONy FATIGUE FEATHERy FIBROSE FILMSET>
FINESSEr FISSION FISSURE FLANKER FLANNEL FLANNEL> FORBEARd FOREARM
FORTUNE FOUNDER FOXHUNT FOXTROT> FRAUGHT* FRECKLE FREIGHT FRITTER
FURNACE FURTHER

GALLANT* GALLERY GARLAND GARMENT GAZETTE GENERAL> GENERALe GESTUREr
GIMMICKy GLAMOUR GLIMMERy GODDAMN GRANNIE= GRIDDLE

HACKSAWn HAMBONE HANDBAG> HARBOUR HISTORY HOBNAIL HOLIDAY HOLSTER
HUSBAND HUSHABY

IMPRINT IMPULSE INBOUND INCLINEr INFIGHTd INITIAL INITIAL> INVALID
INVERSE INVOICE

JAVELINa JAWBONEr JEALOUSe JEALOUSy JOURNAL JOURNAL> JOYRIDEd JOYRIDEr

KEYNOTEr KITCHEN KNEECAP> KNUCKLEr

LACQUER LAMPOON LANTERN LATERAL LATERAL> LAYBACK LEAFLET LEAFLET>
LEATHERn LEATHERy LEISURE LICENCEe LICENCEr LIGHTER LIGHTLY LIQUEUR
LOBSTER LULLABY

MACHINE MANACLE MANDATE MASCARA MESSAGE MIDWIFE MISCALL MISCASTd
MISDEALd MISDEALt MISDRAWd MISDRAWn MISFEEDd MISKICK MISSION MONSTERa
MONTAGE MORTICEr MOULDER MUDLARK

NETWORK NITRATE NITRIDE

OBLIQUE* OFFICER OUTCASTe OUTLOOK OUTRAGE OUTTAKEd OUTTAKEn OVERARM
OVERUSE OVERWET>

```
PACKAGEr PADDOCK  PADLOCK  PANCAKE  PARABLE  PARAGON  PARTNER  PASSAGEr
PASSION  PASTUREr PATIENT* PATTERN  PENANCE  PENSIONe PERFUMEr PERVERT
PIGMENT  PILLION  PINBALL  PIONEER  PIPETTE  PLACARD  PLANISH  PLASTERy
PLATEAUx PLATOON  PLOTTER  POLITIC& POLITICk POLITICo PONTOON  PORTION
POSTUREr POTHOLEr PRECASTd PRECISE* PRELUDEr PREMIERe PREMISE  PRESAGEr
PRETEXT  PROBATE  PROFANE* PROFILEr PROVERB  PURPOSE  PYRAMID
```

```
QUARTERn
```

```
RACQUET  RAMPAGEr RAMPART  RAPTURE  RATCHET  RAWHIDE  REBOUND  RECEIPT
REFEREE  REFOUND  RELAPSEr REMATCH  REPLETE  RESPITE  RETREAD  REVENGEr
RHUBARBy RIPOSTE  ROMANCEr RUBBISHy RUFFIAN
```

```
SANDBAG> SARDINE  SAWDUSTy SCALLOP  SCANDAL  SCANDAL> SCARLET  SCEPTRE
SCISSOR  SCOLLOP  SCOURGEr SCROOGE  SCRUPLEr SECTION  SEGMENT  SERVANT
SHALLOW* SHAMPOO  SHINGLEr SHOTGUN> SHUTTER  SHUTTLEr SHYLOCK  SIAMESE
SIAMEZE  SIRNAME  SKELTER  SKIPPER  SLATHER  SLIPPERy SNAPPER  SNOOKER
SOAPBOX  SOJOURN  SOLDIERy SOOTHER  SPACKLE  SPANGLEr SPANGLEt SPANIEL>
SPECKLE  SPINDLEr SPLOTCHy STATION  STAUNCH* STEALTHy STEAMER  STEEPLE
STENCIL  STENCIL> STEWARD  STICKER  STOMACHy STOPPER  SUBLIME* SUBSOIL
SUCTION  SUICIDE  SULPHURy SUMMONS  SUNBURNt SUNDOWN  SURFEIT  SURNAMEr
SURPLUS  SURPLUS> SWATTER  SYRINGE
```

```
TEARGAS> TEMPEST  TENSION  TERRACE  TEXTURE  THIMBLE  THUNDERy TOENAIL
TOPLINEr TOPSOIL  TORPEDO  TORPEDO+ TOURNEY  TRAFFIC& TRAILER  TRANSIT
TRAPEZE  TRAVAIL  TREACLE  TREADLEr TRELLIS  TRIGGER  TRINKET  TRIUMPH
TROLLEY  TROLLOPy TROUSER  TRUFFLE  TRUMPET  TRUSTEE  TURMOIL  TWADDLEr
```

```
UMBRAGE  UNHAPPY* UNIFORM* UNNOBLE  UPRIGHT  UPSTART  UPSURGE  UPSWINGd
```

```
VAMOOSE  VAMPIRE  VANTAGE  VARNISHy VESTUREr VICTUAL  VICTUAL> VINEGARy
VINTAGEr VIOLENT  VITRIOL  VITRIOL> VOUCHER
```

```
WARFAREr WARRANTy WEATHER  WEEKEND  WILDCAT> WRAPPER
```

7.1.3 NOUNS IN COMMON USE

```
ABALONE  ABDOMEN  ABILITY+ ABSENCE  ABSINTHe ACADEMY+ ACCRUAL  ACCUSAL
ACCUSER  ACETATEd ACETONE  ACIDITY+ ACREAGE  ACROBAT  ACRONYM  ACTRESSy
ACTUARY+ ADAPTOR  ADENOID  ADJUNCT  ADMIRAL  ADMIRER  ADVISORy AERATOR
AEROSOL  AGILITY+ AILMENT  AIRBASE  AIRCREW  AIRDROP  AIRFARE  AIRFLOW
AIRHOLE  AIRLINEr AIRLOCK  AIRPLAY  AIRPORT  AIRSHIP  AIRTIME  AIRWAVE
ALCOHOL  ALFALFA  ALGEBRA  ALIMONY+ ALLERGY+ ALMANACk ALUMINA  AMATEUR
AMENITY+ AMMETER  AMMONIAc AMNESIAc AMPHORAe AMPHORAl AMPUTEE  ANAEMIA
ANAGRAM  ANALOGY+ ANALYST  ANARCHY+ ANATOMY+ ANCHOVY+ ANEMONE  ANISEED
ANNUITY+ ANNULUS+ ANOMALY+ ANTENNAe ANTENNAl ANTHILL  ANTIGENe ANTONYMy
ANTHRAX+ ANXIETY+ APOLOGY+ APOSTLE  APRICOT  APTNESS+ AQUIFER  ARBITER
ARCHERY+ ARCHWAY  ARMBAND  ARMHOLE  ARMLOAD  ARMOURY+ ARMREST  AROUSAL
```

ARRIVAL ARSENAL ARSENIC ARTISAN ARTWORK ASHTRAY ASPIRINg ATHEISM
ATHEIST ATHLETE AUDITORy AUREOLAe AUSPICE AUTOCUE AVARICE AVENGER
AVIATOR AVOCADO AVOCADO+ AZIMUTH

BADNESS+ BAGGAGE BAILIFF BALCONY+ BALONEY BAMBINO BAPTISM BAPTIST
BARMAID BARONET BARROOM BASINET BASSOON BASTARDy BASTION BATHMAT
BATHTUB BATTERY+ BATTLER BAUXITE BAZOOKA BEANBAG BEARHUG BEATNIK
BEDGOWN BEDLAMP BEDMATE BEDOUIN BEDPOST BEDRAIL BEDROCK BEDROLL
BEDROOM BEDSIDE BEDSORE BEDTIME BEEHIVE BEGONIA BELLBOY BELLHOP
BENZENE BEQUEST BIGOTRY+ BILLION BIOLOGY+ BIPLANE BISCUITy BISMUTH
BITTERN BITUMEN BLADDERy BLASTER BLEEDER BLEEPER BLENDER BLOCKER
BLOOMERy BLOOPER BLOWFLY+ BLOWOUT BLUDGER BLUFFER BLUSHER BOARDER
BOASTER BOATFUL BOILERY+ BOMBORA BONANZA BONDAGEr BONFIRE BOOKEND
BOOKLET BOOSTER BOREDOM BOROUGH BOTTLER BOUDOIR BOUNCER BOUQUET
BOURBON BOWLFUL BOYHOOD BRACKEN BRAGGER BRAVERY+ BRAWLER BREADTH
BREAKER BREAKUP BREEDER BREVITY+ BREWERY+ BRIBERY+ BRINGER BROMIDE
BROMINE BROODER BROTHEL BROWNIE* BROWSER BRUISER BUBBLER BUFFOON
BUGBEAR BUGGERY+ BUILDER BUILDUP BULLION BUMPKIN BUNGLER BURETTE
BURNOUT BUSLOAD BUSTARD BUYBACK BUZZARD

CABARET CABINET CABOOSE CADENZA CADMIUM CAFFEINe CALCIUM CALIBREd
CALORIE CALYPSO CALYPSO+ CAMPHOR CANASTA CANDOUR CANNERY+ CANTEEN
CANTINA CAPITAL CAPSTAN CARAWAY CARBINE CARIBOU CARLOAD CARNAGE
CARPORT CARRIER CARRION CARVERY+ CARWASH+ CASETTE CASHBOX+ CASSATA
CASTOFF CATCHER CATERER ATFISH+ CATHEAD CATHODE CATWALK CAVALRY+
CAYENNEd CELLIST CENTURY+ CESSPIT CHALICEd CHARADE CHARGER CHARITY+
CHARMER CHATEAUx CHECKER CHECKUP CHEERER CHEETAH CHEMIST CHICORY+
CHIFFONy CHOLERA CHUTNEY CIRCLIP CISTERNa CITADEL CITIZEN CLANGER
CLARITY+ CLASSER CLASSICo CLEANER CLEANUP CLEAVER CLIMBER CLINGER
CLIPPER CLOCKER COACTOR COASTER COBBLERy COCAINE COCKPIT COCONUT
COINAGE COLLEGEr COLLIERy COLOGNEd COLONEL COMMODE COMRADE CONCEPTi
CONIFER CONTEXT COOKERY+ COOKTOP COOLANT COPILOT CORDIAL CORKAGE
CORONER CORONET CORTEGE COSSACK COTERIE COUNCIL COUNTRY+ COURAGE
COURTER COVERUP COWBELL COWGIRL COWHAND COWPOKE COWSHED COWSLIP
COYNESS+ CRACKER CRAMMER CRANIUM CRASHER CRAWLER CREATOR CREEPER
CREVICEd CRITTER CROONER CROPPER CROUTON CRUDITY+ CRUELTY+ CRUISER
CRUMPET CRUSHER CRYBABY+ CRYSTAL CUBICLE CUISINE CULPRIT CULTUREd
CULVERT CUPCAKE CURATORy CURRANTy CURRENT CUSTARDy CUSTODY+ CUTAWAY
CUTBACK CUTLASS+ CUTLERY+ CYCLIST CYCLONE CYPRESS+

DABBLER DAGWOOD DARLING DAWDLER DAYTIME DAZZLER DEADEYE DEBACLE
DEBATER DECAGON DECENCY+ DECIBEL DECIDER DECIMAL DECODER DECORUM
DEFICIT DEMIGOD DENSITY+ DENTIST DENTURE DESCENT DESKTOP DESSERT
DESTINY+ DEVIANT DEVOTEE DEWDROP DIALECT DIARIST DICTION DIEHARD
DIGNITY+ DILEMMA DIMNESS+ DINGBAT DIOCESE DIOXIDE DISHRAG DIVIDER
DOLPHIN DOODLER DOORMAT DOORWAY DOSSIER DOUBTER DOWAGER DRAGNET
DRAINER DRAPERY+ DREAMERy DRESSER DRIFTER DRILLER DRINKER DROPLET
DROPOUT DROPPER DROUGHTy DRUMMER DRYNESS+ DULLARD DURESSE DUSTBIN
DUSTPAN DWELLER DYNASTY+

EARACHE EARDROP EARDRUM EARLOBE EARMUFF EARPLUG EARRING EARSHOT
ECHIDNAe ECOLOGY+ ECONOMY+ EDIFICE EGGHEAD EGOTISM EGOTIST ELATION
ELECTOR ELEMENT ELITISM ELLIPSE EMBASSY+ EMERALD EMIRATE EMOTION
EMPATHY+ EMPEROR EMPRESSe ENDGAME ENQUIRY+ ENTRANT EPICURE EPIGRAM
EPISODE EPITOME EPSILON EQUATOR EQUINOX+ EROSION ESCAPEE ESSENCE
ESTUARY+ ETHANOL EVACUEE EVASION EXPANSE EYELASH+ EYESORE

FACTION FACTORY+ FACULTY+ FAILURE FAIRWAY FALLACY+ FALLOUT FALSITY+
FANATIC FARRIERy FASCISMi FASCISMo FASCISTa FASCISTi FATHEAD FEEDLOT
FERNERY+ FERVOUR FIANCEE FICTION FIDDLER FIELDER FIFTEEN FIGHTER
FIGMENT FIREARM FIREBUG FIREFLY+ FISHERY+ FISHNET FISTFUL FITNESS+
FIXTURE FLEABAG FLIPPER FLOATER FLOOZIE FLORIST FLOTSAM FLUENCY+
FLYOVER FLYPAST FLYTRAP FOGHORN FOLIAGEd FONDLER FOOTAGE FOOTWAY
FORAGER FORELEG FORGERY+ FORMULAe FORMULAr FOUNDRY+ FOXHOLE FRAILTY+
FREEDOM FREESIA FREEWAY FREEZER FRETSAW FRETTER FRIGATE FUCHSIA
FULCRUM FUMBLER FUNERAL FUNFAIR FURLONG FUSSPOT

GALLEON GAMBLER GANGWAY GARBAGEy GATEWAY GAZELLE GEARBOX+ GENTILE
GEOLOGY+ GESTAPO GETAWAY GHERKIN GIGATON GIRAFFE GIZZARD GLACIER
GLAZIERy GLOATER GLOBULEt GLUCOSE GLUTTONy GOBBLER GODDESS+ GODSEND
GONDOLA GOODBYE GORILLA GOSLING GOULASH+ GOURMET GRAFTER GRAMMAR
GRANDMA GRANDPA GRANITE GRANULE GRAVITY+ GRAZIER GREASER GREENIE*
GREMLIN GRENADE GRIEVER GRILLERy GRINDERy GRINNER GRISTLE GROANER
GROCERY+ GROOVER GROUPIE GROWLERy GROWNUP GRUBBER GUMBOOT GUMTREE
GUNBOAT GUNFIRE GUNSHIP GUNSHOT GUYLINE GUZZLER GYMNAST

HABITAT HADDOCK HAGGLER HAIRCUT HAIRNET HAIRPIN HALFWIT HALLWAY
HALOGEN HAMMOCK HAMSTER HANDFUL HANDGUN HANDLER HANDOUT HANDSAW
HANDSET HANGOUT HARDHAT HARELIP HARMONY+ HARPIST HARRIER HASHISH+
HATBAND HATCHETy HATRACK HAULAGE HAYLOFT HAYRICK HAYRIDE HAYSEED
HEADSET HEADWAY HEATHEN HEATHERy HECKLER HECTARE HEIRESS+ HELIPAD
HEMLINE HEMLOCK HEROINE HEROISM HERRING HEXAGON HICKORY+ HIDEOUT
HIGHWAY HILLOCKy HILLTOP HINDLEG HIPBONE HOARDER HOGWASH+ HONESTY+
HOODLUM HORIZON HORMONE HOSIERY+ HOSPICE HOSTAGE HOSTESS+ HOTCAKE
HOTHEAD HOTLINE HOTSHOT HUMDRUM HUNDRED HURDLER HUSTLER HYDRANTh
HYGIENE

ICEBERG ICEPACK ILLNESS+ IMAGERY+ IMPASSE IMPETUS+ INANITY+ INCISORy
INDEXER INERTIAe INERTIAl INFANCY+ INFERNO INFIDEL INFIELD INGROUP
INHALER INKSPOT INKWELL INQUEST INQUIRY+ INSIDER INSIGHT INSTANT*
INSULIN INSURER INSWING INTEGER INTERIM INVADER INVITEE ISOTOPE
ISTHMUS+

JACKASS+ JACKPOT JANITOR JASMINE JAWLINE JAYBIRD JOINERY+ JONQUIL
JOUSTER JUBILEE JUGGLERy JUKEBOX+ JUNIPER JUSTICEr

KARAOKE KASHMIR KAYAKER KESTREL KETCHUP KEYCARD KEYHOLE KEYWORD
KICKOFF KILLJOY KILOBAR KINGDOM KINGPIN KINSHIP KNEEPAD KNITTER
KNOCKER KNOWHOW KRYPTON

```
LABORER   LADYBUG   LANEWAY   LANOLINe  LANTANA   LARCENY+  LASAGNA   LATRINE
LATTICEd  LAUNDRY+  LAWBOOK   LAWSUIT   LEAKAGE   LEARNER   LECHERY+  LECTERN
LEGROOM   LEGWORK   LEMMING   LEOPARD   LEOTARD   LEPROSY+  LESBIAN   LETDOWN
LETTUCE   LEXICON   LIAISON   LIBERTY+  LIBRARY+  LIFTOFF   LIGNITE   LINSEED
LIONESS+  LITHIUM   LOCKJAW   LOGBOOK   LOOKOUT   LOTTERY+  LOWDOWN   LOWLAND
LOWLIFEr  LOYALTY+  LOZENGEd  LUCERNE   LUGGAGE   LUMBAGO   LUNATIC

MACHETE   MACRAMI   MADNESS+  MADONNA   MAESTRO   MAGENTA   MAGNATE   MAGNETOn
MAHJONGg  MAILBAG   MAILBOX+  MAILVAN   MAJESTY+  MALAISE   MALARIAl  MALARIAn
MAMMOTH   MANAGER   MANHOLE   MANHOOD   MANHUNT   MANSION   MARCHER   MARINERa
MARQUEE   MARTINI   MASSEUR   MASTERY+  MATADORa  MATADORe  MATCHUP   MATILDA
MATINEE   MATTOCK   MAXIMUM   MAYPOLE   MEDDLER   MEGATON   MEMENTO   MENTHOL
MERCURY+  MERMAID   MESSIAH   METHANE   MICROBE   MIDRIFF   MIGRANT   MILEAGE
MILITIA   MILLION   MIMICRY+  MINDSET   MINERAL   MINGLER   MINIBAR   MINIBUS+
MINICAB   MINICAR   MINIMUM   MINIVAN   MIRACLE   MISSILE   MISSIVE   MIXTURE
MOBSTER   MOCKERY+  MODESTY+  MODICUM   MOLLUSCa  MONARCHy  MONGREL   MONOCLEd
MONOLOGy  MONSOON   MOOCHER   MOORHEN   MOPHEAD   MORAINE   MORNING   MOURNER
MUDBATH   MUDDLER   MUDFLAP   MUDFLAT   MUDPACK   MUFFLER   MUGSHOT   MUMBLER
MUSICALe  MUSTANG   MUSTARDy  MYSTERY+

NAIVETY+  NAMETAG   NECKTIE   NEGRESS+  NETBALL   NEURONE   NEUTRON   NEWNESS+
NEWSBOY   NIGHTIE   NIRVANA   NOMINEE   NOSTRIL   NOTEPAD   NOVELTY+  NUCLEUS+
NUMERAL   NUNNERY+  NURSERY+  NUTCASE   NUTMEAL   NYMPHET

OATMEAL   OBELISK   OBESITY+  OCARINA   OCTAGON   OCTOPUSh  ODDBALL   ODYSSEY
OFFENCE   OFFRAMP   OILSEED   OILSKIN   OMNIBUS+  OPINION   OPPOSER   OPTIMUM
ORATION   ORATORY+  ORCHARD   ORDERER   OREGANO   ORIFICE   ORIGAMI   OSTRICH+
OUTBACK   OUTCOME   OUTDOOR   OUTFALL   OUTPOST   OUTSIDEr  OVATION

PADDLER   PAGEANT   PAGEBOY   PAINTER   PANACHE   PANTHER   PAPRIKA   PARADOXy
PARASOL   PARKWAY   PARLOUR   PAROLEE   PARSLEY   PARSNIP   PASSOUT   PASTIME
PATHWAY   PATRIOT   PAUCITY+  PAVLOVA   PAYBACK   PAYLOAD   PAYMENT   PAYROLL
PAYSLIP   PEACOCKy  PEARLER   PEASANTy  PEDDLERy  PELICAN   PENALTY+  PENDANT
PENGUIN   PENNAME   PENNANT   PERGOLA   PERJURY+  PERSONAe  PERSONAl  PERUSAL
PETUNIA   PHALANX+  PHALLUS+  PHANTOMy  PHARAOH   PHOENIX+  PIANISTe  PICADOR
PICCOLO   PIGGERY+  PIGSKIN   PIGTAIL   PIKELET   PILGRIM   PILLBOX+  PILLOCK
PINHEAD   PINHOLE   PITCHER   PITFALL   PLACEBO   PLACEBO+  PLANNER   PLANTER
PLATTER   PLAUDITe  PLAYBOY   PLAYOFF   PLAYPEN   PLEADER   PLEASER   PLIANCY+
PLODDER   PLUCKER   PLUGGER   PLUMAGEd  PLUMBERy  PLUNGER   PLYWOOD   POACHER
POINTER   POLECAT   POLYGONy  POLYMERy  PONTIFF   POOFTER   POPCORN   PORTENT
POSTAGE   POSTBOX+  POSTBOY   POTENCY+  POTLUCK   POTSHOT   POTTERY+  POULTRY+
POUNDER   POVERTY+  PRAIRIEd  PRAISER   PRAWNER   PREFECT   PRELATE   PREMIUM
PRETZEL   PRIMATE   PRINTERy  PRIVACY+  PROBITY+  PROBLEM   PRODDER   PRODIGY+
PRODUCT   PROGENY+  PRONOUN   PROPANE   PROPHET   PROTEGEe  PROTEIN   PROVISOr
PROVISO+  PROWESS+  PROWLER   PUBERTY+  PUDDINGy  PUMPKINg  PUNCHER   PURITAN
PURSUIT   PUZZLER

QUAFFER   QUALITY+  QUARTETt  QUICKIE   QUININE   QUINTETt  QUITTER
```

```
RACCOON  RACEWAY  RAGTIMEr RAILBUS+ RAILWAY  RAIMENT  RAINBOWy RAMBLER
RANCHERo RANCOUR  RAPPORT  RAREBIT  RATFINK  RATTLER  RAVIOLI  REACTOR
READOUT  REAGENT  REALISM  REALIST  REALITY+ REALTOR  REBIRTH  RECITAL
RECLUSE  RECTORY+ REDBACK  REDHEAD  REDNECK  REDSKIN  REDWOOD  REENTRY+
REFINERy REFUGEE  REFUSAL  REGATTA  REGENCY+ REGIMENt REMNANT  REMORSE
REMOVAL  RENEWAL  REPLICA  REPTILE  REQUIEM  ESCUER   RESIDUE  RETINUEd
RETIREE  RETRIAL  RETSINA  REUNION  REVELER  REVELRY+ REVENUEd REVENUEr
REVERIE  REVIVAL  REVIVER  RHOMBUS+ RIBCAGE  RINGLET  RISSOLE  RIVALRY+
RIVIERA  RIVULET  ROADWAY  ROASTER  ROBBERY+ ROCKERY+ ROOFTOP  ROOMFUL
ROOSTER  ROSEBUD  ROSTRUM  ROTUNDA  ROUNDUP  ROUTINE  ROWBOAT  ROYALTY+
RUBDOWN  RUNAWAY  RUSTLER

SABBATH  SADDLERy SADNESS+ SAFFRONy SAMURAI  SANCTUM  SANDBAR  SANDFLY+
SANDPIT  SANGRIA  SAPLING  SARCASM  SATCHEL  SAUSAGE  SAVANNAh SAVELOY
SAVIOUR  SAWMILL  SCALPEL  SCALPER  SCANNER  SCENERY+ SCHEMER  SCHOLAR
SCIENCEd SCOFFER  SCOOTER  SCOURER  SCRAPER  SCROTUM  SCULLERy SCUMBAG
SEABIRD  SEAFOOD  SEAGULL  SEALANT  SEAPORT  SEASIDE  SEAWEED  SECRECY+
SEDUCER  SEEDBED  SEEDBOX+ SEEDPOD  SEEPAGE  SEIZURE  SELLOUT  SEMINARy
SENATOR  SENDOFF  SERPENT  SERVERY+ SESSION  SETBACK  SETTLER  SEVENTH
SEVENTY+ SEXTANT  SHAKEUP  SHALLOT  SHEARER  SHELLER  SHERBET  SHERIFF
SHIFTER  SHINDIG  SHIPPER  SHOCKER  SHOOTER  SHOPPER  SHOUTER  SHOWOFF
SHUNTER  SHUTEYE  SHYNESS+ SHYSTER  SIBLING  SICKBAY  SICKBED  SIDEARM
SIDECAR  SIGNAGE  SILICONe SINGLET  SIRLOIN  SIXTEEN  SIZZLER  SKEPTIC
SKINNER  SKYLINE  SKYWARD  SLAMMER  SLASHER  SLAVERY+ SLEDGER  SLEEPERy
SLEIGHT  SLINGER  SLOGGER  SLIPWAY  SLYNESS+ SMASHER  SMASHUP  SMELTERy
SNEAKER  SNIFFER  SNIPPER  SNIPPETy SNOOPER  SOAKAGE  SOCIETY+ SOLOIST
SOLVENT  SOPRANO  SORCERY+ SORGHUM  SOUFFLEd SPANNER  SPARROW  SPATULAr
SPEAKER  SPECTRE  SPELLER  SPENCER  SPENDER  SPINACHy SPINNERy SPINOFF
SPITTLE  SPOILER  SPONGER  SPOTTER  SPRAYER  SPUTNIK  SPYHOLE  SQUALOR
STACKER  STACKUP  STADIUM  STAFFER  STALKER  STAMINAl STANDBYs STAPLER
STARDOM  STARLET  STARTER  STATUREd STATUTE  STEERER  STEPSON  STERNUM
STEROID  STICKUP  STINGER  STINKER  STIRRER  STIRRUP  STOMPER  STOPOFF
STORAGE  STRIKER  STRUDEL  STUBBLEd STUDENTy STUDIER  STUNNER  STYLIST
SUBDEAN  SUBPLOT  SUBSIDY+ SUCCESS+ SUCKLER  SULLAGE  SULTANA  SUMMARY+
SUNBEAMy SUNDECK  SUNDIAL  SUNLAMP  SUNRISE  SUNROOF  SUNROOM  SUNSPOT
SUPREMO  SURGEON  SURGERY+ SWEARER  SWEATER  SWEEPER  SWEETIE  SWIMMER
SWINGER  SWOTTER  SYMPTOM  SYNAGOG  SYNERGY+ SYNONYMe SYNONYMy

TABLOIDy TABOULI  TACKLER  TADPOLE  TAKEOFF  TANGENT  TANKARD  TANKFUL
TANNERY+ TANTRUM  TAPIOCA  TAVERNA  TAXICAB  TEACAKE  TEACHER  TEAROOM
TEATIME  TEMPTER  TEMPURA  TENANCY+ TENDRIL  TEQUILA  TERMITE  TERRAIN
TERRIER  TETANUS+ TEXTILE  THANKER  THEATRE  THEOREM  THERAPY+ THERMOS+
THICKETy THINKER  THISTLE  THOUGHT  THROWER  THUMPER  TIDDLER  TIGRESS+
TIMEOUT  TINFOIL  TIPSTER  TOASTER  TOBACCO  TODDLER  TOEHOLD  TOLLWAY
TONNAGE  TOOLBAG  TOOLBAR  TOOLBOX+ TOOLKIT  TOPSIDEr TOPSPIN  TORNADO
TORNADO+ TORRENT  TOSSPOT  TOUCHUP  TOURISM  TOURISTa TOURISTy TOWLINE
TOWROPE  TOYSHOP  TRACKER  TRACTOR  TRAGEDY+ TRAINEE  TRAINER  TRAITOR
TRAMWAY  TRANNIE  TRAPPER  TRAWLER  TREADER  TREASON  TREETOP  TREKKER
```

```
TRESTLE   TRIBUNE   TRIBUTEr  TRIDENT   TRILOGY+  TRINITY+  TRIPLET   TRISHAW
TROOPER   TROTTER   TRUANCY+  TRUCKER   TRUCKIE   TSARINA   TSUNAMIc  TUGBOAT
TUITION   TUMBLER   TURBINEd  TURNKEY   TURNOFF   TURNOUT   TUSSOCKy  TWELFTH
TWIRLER   TWISTER   TWOSOME   TYPHOID   TYPHOON   TYRANNY+

UKELELE   UNICORN   UNTRUTH   UPDRAFT   URANIUM   URETHRAe  URETHRAl  URGENCY+
UROLOGY+  UTENSIL   UTILITY+

VACANCY+  VACCINEe  VAGRANT   VALENCY+  VANILLA   VARIANT   VARIETY+  VARMINT
VARSITY+  VAULTER   VEHICLE   VENISON   VENTURI   VERANDAh  VERDICT   VERSION
VERTIGO   VERTIGO+  VESTIGE   VETERAN   VIADUCT   VICEROY   VICTORY+  VILLAGEr
VILLAINy  VISITOR   VITAMINe  VOLCANO   VOLCANO+  VOLTAGE   VOYAGER   VULTURE

WAFFLER   WAGTAIL   WALKOUT   WALKWAY   WALLABY+  WARATAH   WARBLER   WARHEAD
WARLOCK   WARLORD   WARPATH   WARRIOR   WARSHIP   WARTHOG   WARTIME   WASHOUT
WASHTUB   WASTAGE   WATCHER   WATERER   WAYSIDE   WEBSITE   WEDLOCK   WEEKDAY
WELFARE   WETLAND   WETNESS+  WHINGER   WHIPPET   WHISKERy  WHISKEY   WIDOWER
WINDBAG   WINGTIP   WIPEOUT   WOODBINd  WOODBINe  WOOMERA   WORKOUT   WORKTOP
WORRIER   WRECKER   WRINGER

YACHTIE   YARDAGE   YARDARM   YEAREND   YEARNER   YODELER   YOGHURT

ZILLION
```

7.1.4 NOUNS MORE OFTEN USED IN OTHER PARTS OF SPEECH

```
ACRYLIC   ADAMANT   ADIPOSE   ADJOINT   AEROBIC   ALLEGRO   AMBIENT   ANCIENT*
ANEROID   ANYBODY+  AQUATIC   ASEPTIC   ASSURED   AZURINE
BAROQUE   BEGUINE   BELOVED   BERSERK   BESTIAL   BETWEEN   BIFOCAL   BIZARRE
BLINDER   BOTANICa  BRAATAS+  BRAIDER   BRIEFER   BRINDLEd  BUSTIER   BUTTERY*
BUYABLE
CALORIC   CARDIAC   CAUSTIC   CENTRAL*  CERAMIC   CHEERIO   CHILLER   CHRONIC
CLEARER   COCKSHY+  COGNATE   COLONIC   COLORED   CRINKLY*  CRISPER   CROSSER
CRUMBLY*  CRUNCHY*  CUNNING*
DEAREST   DEFUNCT   DIETARY+  DIGITAL   DIURNAL   DIVINER   DORMANT   DRABBER
DRASTIC   DURABLE   DYNAMIC
EARNEST   EARTHLY*  EATABLE   ELASTIC   ELATIVE   ELDERLY+  ELEVENS+  ELITIST
EMPIRIC   EMPTIER   ENDEMIC   ERECTER   ERRATIC   ERUDITE   ETERNAL   ETHICAL
EVIDENT   EXACTER   EXTREME*
FAINTER   FANCIER   FEDERAL   FLASHER   FLATBED   FLUIDIC   FLUSHER   FORCEPS+
FOREVER   FORLORN*  FRANKER   FRESHER   FRONTAL   FROSTED   FURRIERy
GALLOWS+  GENERIC   GENETIC   GENITAL   GLACIAL   GRADUAL   GRAPHIC   GREENERy
GRITTER   GRIZZLY*  GROSSER   GROUSER
HAGGARD   HALCYON   HAYWIRE   HEARSAY   HERETIC   HESSIAN   HOPEFUL   HOSTILE
HUMBLER
ILLEGAL   INBOARD   INSULAR   INSURED
JOLLIER   JUGULAR
KINDRED   KINETIC   KINFOLK
```

LAMPERS+	LEEWARD	LEFTIST	LEGWEAR	LENIENT	LIBERAL	LIMITED	LINGUAL
LITERAL	LOATHER						
MANKIND	MARRIED	MARTIAL	MASSIVE	MATURER	MEDICAL	MELODICa	MENFOLK
MIDNOON	MIDTERM	MIDTOWN	MIDWEEK	MIDYEAR	MINIMAL	MODULAR	MONTHLY+
MOSTEST	MOVABLE						
NATURAL	NAUGHTY*	NEEDFUL	NEUTRAL	NEWBORN	NOMINAL	NONSTOP	NOTABLE
NOTHING	NOWHERE	NUMERIC	NUPTIAL				
OFFBEAT	OFFSIDEr	ONGOING	OPALINE	ORBITAL	ORDERLY+	ORGANIC	OUTSHOT
OUTWARD	OVERAGEd	OVERALL					
PARTIAL	PASSIVE	PAYABLE	PERCENT	PERHAPS+	PIEBALD	PIGFEED	PLASTIC
PLUMPER	POPULAR	POTABLE	PREDAWN	PREDUSK	PRIMARY+	PRIMMER	PRIVATE*
PSYCHIC							
QUANTUM	QUIETER						
RADIANT	RADICAL	RATABLE	REGALIAn	REGULAR	RIGHTER	ROBOTIC	ROCKIER
ROUGHER	ROUNDER	RUNDOWN					
SALIENT	SALTIER	SAUCIER	SAVOURY*	SCHNAPS+	SCIATICa	SECULAR	SECURER
SERVILE	SEVERAL	SHARPER	SIMPLER	SLACKER	SLEEKER	SLICKER	SLIMMER
SOLUBLE	SOMEONE	SOUNDER	SPARKLY*	SPARTAN	SPASTIC	SPECIAL*	SPHERIC
SQUARER	STABLER	STANDUP	STARKER	STEEPER	STILLER	STOPGAP	STRANGE*
SUPREME*	SURREAL	SWANKER	SWELLER	SWIFTER	SWISHER		
TARRIER	TAXABLE	TEENAGEd	TEENAGEr	TENFOLD	THERMAL	THINNER	TITULARy
TONIGHT	TORQUES+	TRICEPS+	TRIMMER	TWOFOLD			
UNAWARE	UNEQUAL	UNKNOWN	UPRIVER	UPSTATEr	URINARY+	UTOPIAN	UTTERER
VALIANT	VIBRANT	VISIBLE					
WESTERN	WHATNOT	WHEREAS+	WHOOPEE	WITHOUT	WOOLLEN	WORSTED	WRINKLY*
WRONGER							
YOUNGER							

7.1.5 NOUNS IN COMMON USE WHICH ARE VERB FORMS ENDING IN 'ING'

BACKING	BASHING	BEARING	BEATING	BEDDING	BELTING	BOOKING	CALLING
CEILING	COATING	CRAVING	CURLING	CUTTING	DEALING	DECKING	DIGGING
DRAWING	DUCTING	EARNING	ETCHING	EVENING	FAILING	FEELING	FILLING
FINDING	FITTING	FOOTING	GELDING	GRATING	HANGING	HEADING	HEARING
HELPING	HOLDING	HOUSING	INKLING	JOTTING	KERBING	KILLING	LANDING
LEANING	LEGGING	LICKING	LISTING	LOADING	LODGING	MAILING	MARKING
MEANING	MEETING	MOORING	MUGGING	NESTING	OPENING	PADDING	PAIRING
PARTING	PASTING	PEELING	PICKING	PLACING	POSTING	PRICING	PRUNING
RAILING	RANKING	READING	RIGGING	SACKING	SEEDING	SERVING	SETTING
SHAVING	SITTING	SOAKING	SPACING	TAILING	TASTING	TOPPING	TRACING
UNDOING	VIEWING	WARNING	WASHING	WEBBING	WEDDING	WHITING	WINNING
WORDING	WORKING	WRITING					

7.1.6 OTHER NOUNS WHICH ARE VERB FORMS ENDING IN 'ING'

```
ABIDING  AISLING  AMBLING  ANGLING  ARCHING  ARCKING  AWAKING
BAGGING  BAITING  BALKING  BALLING  BANDING  BANKING  BANTING  BARRING
BASTING  BATTING  BAWLING  BEADING  BEAMING  BEGGING  BELLING  BENDING
BETTING  BIASING  BIDDING  BIGGING  BILLING  BINDING  BIRDING  BIRLING
BITTING  BLADING  BLOWING  BLUEING  BOATING  BOILING  BOLTING  BOMBING
BONDING  BONKING  BOOMING  BOOZING  BOSSING  BOWLING  BRACING  BREWING
BROKING  BRUTING  BUCKING  BUDDING  BUFFING  BUGGING  BULKING  BULLING
BUMPING  BUNTING  BURNING  BUSHING  BUSKING  BUSSING  BUSTING  BUZZING

CABLING  CALKING  CALMING  CAMPING  CANNING  CANTING  CAPPING  CARDING
CARPING  CASTING  CEASING  CHASING  CHIDING  CIELING  CLONING  CLOSING
COGGING  COINING  COLLING  COMBING  CONNING  COOKING  COOLING  CORDING
COSTING  COWLING  CUBBING  CULLING  CUPPING  CURBING  CURSING  CYCLING

DAFFING  DAGGING  DAMPING  DANCING  DARNING  DAUBING  DAWNING  DIALING
DICKING  DIETING  DILLING  DIMMING  DIPPING  DISHING  DOATING  DOCKING
DODGING  DOGGING  DOPPING  DRIVING  DROVING  DUBBING  DUCKING  DUFFING
DUMPING  DUNNING  DUSTING

EASTING  EDITING  EMPTING  ENVYING

FABLING  FAGGING  FAIRING  FALLING  FANNING  FARCING  FARDING  FARMING
FASTING  FAWNING  FEEDING  FEERING  FELLING  FELTING  FENCING  FEUDING
FISHING  FIZZING  FLUTING  FLYTING  FOAMING  FOILING  FOLDING  FOOLING
FORGING  FORMING  FOULING  FOWLING  FRAMING  FRAYING  FUCKING  FUNDING
FURRING

GAFFING  GAINING  GANGING  GAPPING  GASPING  GASSING  GAUGING  GEARING
GETTING  GILDING  GINNING  GIRDING  GLAZING  GLEYING  GLIDING  GLOVING
GLOZING  GNAWING  GOLFING  GRADING  GRAVING  GRAZING  GREYING  GRICING
GROWING  GUIDING  GUISING  GUMMING  GUNNING

HACKING  HAINING  HALTING  HARLING  HARPING  HASHING  HASTING  HATTING
HAWKING  HEALING  HEATING  HEAVING  HEDGING  HEELING  HILLING  HINTING
HIPPING  HISSING  HOGGING  HOPPING  HORNING  HORSING  HOSTING  HOTTING
HOUTING  HOWLING  HUFFING  HUMMING  HUNTING  HURLING  HUSKING  HUTTING

IMAGING  IRONING  ITCHING

JACKING  JAMMING  JARRING  JEERING  JERKING  JESTING  JIBBING  JIGGING
JOBBING  JOGGING  JOINING  JUGGING  JUMPING

KAYOING  KEELING  KEENING  KEEPING  KEMPING  KENNING  KERNING  KILTING
KIRKING  KISSING  KNIFING  KNOWING*

LAGGING  LALLING  LAMBING  LAMMING  LAMPING  LAPPING  LASHING  LASTING
LATHING  LEADING  LEASING  LEAVING  LEERING  LEKKING  LENDING  LETTING
LIGGING  LIMPING  LIPPING  LISPING  LOAFING  LOANING  LOCKING  LOGGING
LONGING  LOOPING  LOOSING  LOOTING  LOPPING  LORDING  LOURING  LUGEING
LURKING
```

MAIMING	MALLING	MALTING	MAPPING	MARLING	MASHING	MASKING	MATTING
MELTING	MENDING	MERGING	MESHING	MICHING	MILKING	MILLING	MINDING
MISTING	MOANING	MOBBING	MOCKING	*MODDING*	MOLDING	MOOTING	MOSHING
MOUSING	MUMMING						

NAGGING	NAILING	NECKING	NERVING	NETTING	NODDING	NOGGING	NOONING
NULLING	NURSING	NUTTING					

PACKING	PANNING	PANTING	PARGING	PARKING	PARSING	PASSING	PAUSING
PECKING	PEGGING	PELTING	PETTING	PHASING	PIECING	PIGGING	PILLING
PIMPING	PINKING	PINNING	PIONING	PITTING	PLATING	POLLING	POURING
POUTING	PRATING	PRAYING	PRIMING	PROSING	PROVING	PUBBING	PUFFING
PUGGING	PUMPING	PUNNING	PURGING	PURLING	PURRING	PUTTING	

QUAKING	QUEUING

RACKING	RAFTING	RAGGING	RAIDING	RAISING	RAMPING	RANGING	RANTING
RAPPING	RASPING	RATTING	REDDING	REEDING	REEFING	REELING	RENNING
RENTING	REPPING	RESTING	RIBBING	RIDGING	RIFLING	RIMMING	RINGING
RINSING	RIOTING	RIPPING	RISPING	ROAMING	ROARING	ROCKING	RODDING
ROLFING	ROLLING	ROOFING	ROOTING	RORTING	ROUTING	RUBBING	RUCHING
RUGGING	RUINING	RUNNING	RUSHING	RUSTING	RUTTING		

SABBING	SAGGING	SAILING	SALTING	SALVING	SANDING	SCALING	SCORING
SCRYING	SEALING	SEAMING	SEARING	SEATING	SEELING	SEEMING	SEINING
SEISING	SEIZING	SELFING	SELLING	SENDING	SENSING	SERGING	SHADING
SHAKING	SHAPING	SHARING	SHOEING	SHORING	SHOVING	SHOWING	SIFTING
SIGNING	SINDING	SINGING	SINKING	SKATING	SKIVING	SLATING	SLICING
SLIDING	SLOWING	SMILING	SMOKING	SNARING	SNIPING	SNORING	SOARING
SOBBING	SOGGING	SOILING	SOOPING	SOPPING	SORNING	SORTING	SOSSING
SOTTING	SOUMING	SOURING	SOUSING	SPAEING	SPILING	STAGING	STARING
STEWING	STONING	STOPING	STOVING	STOWING	STYLING	SUBBING	SUCKING
SUITING	SUMMING	SURFING	SURGING	SWALING	SWAYING	SYNDING	

TABLING	TACKING	TAGGING	TALKING	TAMPING	TANKING	TANNING	TAPPING
TARRING	TASKING	TATTING	TEAMING	TEASING	TELLING	TENTING	TESTING
TEXTING	THAWING	TICKING	TIFFING	TILLING	TILTING	TINNING	TINTING
TIPPING	TITHING	TITLING	TOILING	TOLLING	TOOLING	TOSSING	TOTTING
TOURING	TOUSING	TRADING	TUBBING	TUFTING	TUGGING	TUNNING	TURFING
TURNING	TUSKING	TUTTING	TWINING				

UNITING	UNTYING	UPGOING

VAMPING	VANNING	VARYING	VEILING	VEINING	VEERING	VENDING	VENTING
VERSING	VESTING	VETTING	VOGUING	VOICING	VOIDING		

WADDING	WAFTING	WAILING	WAITING	WALKING	WALLING	WARDING	WARMING
WARPING	WASTING	WAULING	WAWLING	WEANING	WEARING	WEAVING	WEDGING
WEEDING	WEEPING	WELLING	WELTING	WESTING	WETTING	WHALING	WHINING
WICKING	WIGGING	WILDING	WINCING	WINDING	WINKING	WISHING	WITTING
WOLFING	WOLVING	WONNING					

YARDING	YAWNING	YAWPING	YELLING	YELPING	YOWLING

7.1.7 NON-PLURALS IN COMMON USE

ABREAST	ABUSIVE	ABYSMAL	ACUTELY	ADDENDA	ADEPTLY	ADVERSE*	AFFABLE
AGAINST	AGELESS	AGILELY	AGROUND	AIMLESS	AIRLESS	AIRSICK	ALOOFLY
ALREADY	ALRIGHT	AMIABLE	AMIABLY	AMONGST	AMOROUS	ANAEMIC	ANGELICa
ANGRILY	ANGULAR	ANOTHER	ANXIOUS	ANYTIME	APLENTY	AQUEOUS	ARCHAIC
ARDUOUS	ARTLESS	ASEXUAL	ASININE	ASTRIDE	ASUDDEN	ASUNDER	AUDIBLY
AUSTERE*	AWESOME	AWFULLY	AWKWARD*				

BABYISH	BALEFUL	BASEMAN	BASEMENt	BASHFUL	BATSMAN	BATSMEN	BEASTLY
BECAUSE	BENEATH	BIGGISH	BIGOTED	BILIOUS	BIPOLAR	BLANDLY	BLANKLY
BLATANT	BLEAKLY	BLESSED*	BLINDLY	BLOTCHY*	BLUNTLY	BONKERS	BRALESS
BRASHLY	BRAVELY	BRIEFLY	BRISKLY	BRISTLY*	BROADLY	BROUGHTa	BUBONIC
BULBOUS	BULLISH	BUOYANT	BUSHMAN	BUSHMEN			

CAPABLE*	CAPABLY	CAREFUL^	CARLESS	CARSICK	CAVEMAN	CAVEMEN	CERTAIN*
CHAOTIC	CHASSIS	CHEAPLY	CHIEFLY	CIVILLY	CLEANLY	CLEARLY	CLOSELY
CLUBMAN	CLUBMEN	COASTAL	COCKILY	COCKSHY	COLDISH	COLICKY*	COMICAL
COOLISH	COPIOUS	CRACKLY*	CRAZILY	CREWMAN	CREWMEN	CRISPLY	CROOKED*
CRUCIAL	CRUDELY	CRUELLY	CRYPTIC	CURABLE	CURIOUS*	CURSORY	CYNICAL

DARESAY	DARKISH	DEATHLY*	DEFIANT	DEMONIC	DENSELY	DEVIOUS	DISTANT
DITHERY*	DODDERY*	DOLEFUL*	DOORMAN	DOORMEN	DRIZZLY*	DRUNKEN	DRYLAND
DUBIOUS	DUCTILE	DURABLY	DUSTMAN	DUSTMEN	DUTIFUL		

EAGERLY	EARTHEN	EASTERN	ELEGANT	ELUSIVE	EMINENT	EMOTIVE	ENDLESS
ENVIOUS	EQUABLE	EQUABLY	EQUALLY	ERECTLY	EROSIVE	EROTICAl	ERRATUM
EVASIVE	EXACTLY						

FACTUAL	FAINTLY	FAIRISH	FALSELY	FARTHER	FATALLY	FATEFUL	FATUOUS
FEARFUL	FERTILE*	FERVENT*	FESTIVE	FIDGETY*	FIFTHLY	FINALLY	FINICKY*
FIREMAN	FIREMEN	FIRSTLY	FIXABLE	FIXEDLY	FLACCID*	FLIGHTY*	FLOWERY*
FLUVIAL	FOOLISH*	FOOTMAN	FOOTMEN	FORBADE	FOREIGN	FOREMAN	FOREMEN
FORESAW	FORGAVE	FORGONE	FORSOOK	FORWENT	FRAGILE*	FRANKLY	FRANTIC
FRECKLY*	FRESHLY	FRETFUL	FRIABLE	FROGMAN	FROGMEN	FULSOME*	FUNNILY
FURIOUS	FURTIVE	FUSSILY					

GASEOUS	GASTRIC	GENESES	GENESIS	GENTEEL*	GENUINE	GERMANE	GHASTLY*
GHOSTLY*	GINGERY	GIRLISH	GLEEFUL	GODLESS	GRAVELY	GREATLY	GROSSLY
GROUCHY*	GRUFFLY	GRUMBLY*	GUTLESS				

HALFWAY	HANGMAN	HANGMEN	HAPLESS	HAPPILY	HARDISH	HARMFUL	HARSHLY
HASTILY	HATEFUL	HAUGHTY*	HEALTHY*	HEAVILY	HEEDFUL	HEINOUS	HELLISH
HELPFUL	HERSELF	HIDEOUS	HIMSELF	HIRSUTE	HOTTISH	HOWEVER	HUFFILY
HUMANLY	HURTFUL						

IDEALLY	IDIOTIC	IGNEOUS	IGNOBLE*	ILLICIT	IMMENSE*	IMMORAL	INANELY
INBUILT	INDICES	INEPTLY	INEXACT	INGROWN	INHUMANe	INNARDS	INSIPID
INSTEAD	INTENSE*	IRATELY	IRKSOME				

JITTERY* JOBLESS JOCULAR JOINTLY JOYLESS

KIBBUTZ KINSMAN KINSMEN

LACONIC LANGUID LARGELY LAWLESS LEGALLY LEGIBLE LEGIBLY LEGLESS
LENGTHY* LEONINE LIKABLE LINEMAN LINEMEN LISSOME* LOCALLY LOGICAL
LONGISH LOOSELY LOUDISH LOUSILY LOUTISH LOVABLE LOYALLY LUCIDLY
LUCKILY LUSTFUL LYRICAL

MACABRE MAGICAL MAILMAN MAILMEN MANMADE MARITAL MASONIC MAUDLIN
MAYORAL MERRILY MESSILY MIDLIFEr MILKMAN MILKMEN MINDFUL MISERLY*
MISLAID MISTOOK MOONLIT MORALLY MORONIC MUNDANE*

NAIVELY NASTILY NEITHER NEMESES NEMESIS NERVOUS NEWSMAN NEWSMEN
NIGHTLY NINTHLY NODULAR NOISILY NOMADIC NONSLIP NOTABLY NOXIOUS
NUCLEAR NUGGETY

OARSMAN OARSMEN OBSCENE* OBVIOUS OCEANIC OFFHAND OFFLINE OFFPEAK
OMINOUS ONBOARD ONEROUS ONESELF ONETIME ONSHORE OPTICAL OPTIMAL
OPULENT OURSELF OUTDONE OUTGREW OUTLAID OUTRODE OUTSOLD OUTSWAM
OUTSWUM OVARIAN OVERATE OVERDID OVERDUE OVERFED OVERRANk OVERSAW
OVERTLY

PACIFIC PAINFUL^ PANICKY* PARTOOK PARTWAY PECKISH PENSIVE PEPPERY*
PHALLIC PIOUSLY PIQUANT PITEOUS PITIFUL* PIVOTAL PLAINLY PLAYFUL
PLIABLE POMPOUS POSTMAN POSTMEN POSTWAR POWDERY* PREPAID PRICKLY*
PROFUSE* PROUDLY PRUDENT PRUDISH PUERILE PUNGENT

QUEERLY QUICKLY QUIETLY

RAGGEDY* RAMPANT RAPIDLY RAUCOUS RAUNCHY* READILY REAROSE REBUILT
REDDISH REDEALT REDRAWN REHEARD RELIANT RESTFUL^ REWOUND REWROTE
RICKETY* RIGHTLY RIGIDLY ROUGHLY ROUNDLY ROWDILY RUBBERY* RUNLESS

SAINTLY* SANDMAN SANDMEN SATANIC SCARVES SCRAGGY* SCRAPPY* SCRAWLY*
SCRAWNY* SCRUBBY* SCRUFFY* SEASICK* SEISMIC SELFISH SENSORY SENSUAL
SERIOUS SHADOWY* SHAKILY SHAPELY* SHARPLY SHORTLY SHOWERY* SHOWMAN
SHOWMEN SIMILAR SINCERE* SIXTHLY SKETCHY* SKILFUL SLENDER* SLOWISH
SMARTLY SMITTEN SNOWMAN SNOWMEN SOBERLY SOLIDLY SOMEDAY SOMEHOW
SOULFUL SOUNDLY SPATIAL SPINDLY* SQUALID* SQUALLY* SQUAWKY* SQUEAKY*
STARLIT STATELY* STEEPLY STELLAR STERILE STERNLY STIFFLY STREAKY*
STRINGY* STRIVEN STROPPY* STYLISH SUMMERY* SUNLESS SWAGMAN SWAGMEN
SWARTHY* SWEETLY SWIFTLY SWOLLEN

TABULAR TACTFUL TACTILE TEARFUL TEDIOUS TEENAGEd TENABLE TENSELY
TENTHLY TENUOUS TERSELY TEXTUAL THEREBY THEREIN THIRDLY THIRSTY*
THISTLY* THRIFTY* THROUGH TIGHTLY TIMIDLY TIREDLY TITANIC TOPICAL
TOPLESS TOTALLY TOTTERY TRIVIAL TRODDEN TUBULAR TUNEFUL TWITCHY*
TYPICAL

UMPTEEN	UNAIDED	UNAIRED	UNALIKE	UNBOUND	UNBUILT	UNCANNY*	UNCLEAR*
UNCODED	UNCOUTH*	UNDEALT	UNDATED	UNDYING	UNEATEN	UNFAZED	UNFOUND
UNGODLY*	UNHEARD	UNIDEAL	UNKEMPT	UNLOVED	UNLUCKY*	UNMANLY*	UNMOVED
UNNAMED	UNOILED	UNOWNED	UNPAVED	UNRACED	UNRATED	UNREADY*	UNRULED
UNSAVED	UNSHORN	UNSOUND*	UNSPENT	UNSTUCK	UNSWEPT	UNTAKEN	UNTRIED
UNTRULY	UNUSUAL	UNWOUND	UPFIELD	UPFRONT	UPTIGHT*	USEABLE	USELESS
USUALLY	UTTERLY						

VAGINAL	VAGUELY	VARIOUS	VERBOSE*	VERDANT	VICIOUS	VIRTUAL	VISIBLY
VITALLY	VIVIDLY						

WARMISH	WAYLAID	WAYWARD	WEALTHY*	WEARILY	WEIGHTY*	WHEREBY	WHEREIN
WHETHER	WHITISH	WHOEVER	WILLING*	WINLESS	WINSOME*	WINTERY*	WISHFUL
WISTFUL	WITLESS	WITTILY	WOMANLY	WORKMAN	WORKMEN	WORLDLY*	WRIGGLY*
WRITTEN	WRONGLY	WROUGHT					

ZEALOUS	ZESTFUL

7.2 LESS FAMILIAR SEVENS WHICH ARE HOOK WORDS

7.2.1 FRONT HOOKS OF SIXES TO MAKE SEVENS

FRONT HOOKS WITH VOWELS

ABETTER	ABETTOR	**ABIDDEN**	**ABIOTIC**	**ABOUGHT**	**ABROACH**	ABUTTER	**ABYSSAL**
ACANTHIn	ACAUDAL	ACERATEd	ACEROUS	*ACHIRAL*	ACLINIC	ACORNED	ADHARMA
AEOLIAN	AEONIAN	AGAMETE	AGENTRY+	AGINNER	**AGRASTE**	AHEIGHT	AHUNGRY
ALENGTH	**ALONELY**	ALUMINE	AMENAGE	AMENDER	**AMENTAL**	**AMENTUM**	AMERCER
AMOTION	**AMUSIVE**	**ANOESES**	**ANOESIS**	**ANOETIC**	APHASIC	**APHESES**	APHONIC
APHOTIC	APOSTIL	**APTERIA**	**APTOTIC**	**AQUIVER**	ARACHIS+	**AREALLY**	**ARIPPLE**
AROUSER	ARUGOLA	*ASCARED*	**ASCONCE**	ASCRIBE	**ASEPSES**	**ASEPSIS**	**ASHIVER**
ASKLENT	ASOCIAL	ASPERSEr	**ASPRAWL**	**ASPREAD**	**ASPROUT**	**ASQUINT**	**ASTABLE**
ASTATIC	**ASTELIC**	**ASTRAND**	ASTRICT	**ASTYLAR**	**ATACTIC**	**ATHIRST**	**ATHRILL**
ATHWART	**ATINGLE**	ATROPINe	AVENTRE	*AVIATIC*	AVOIDER	AWAITER	AWARDER
AZYMITE							
EBAYING	EBONIST	ECOTYPE	**EDENTAL**	EIDOLON	**EIRENIC**	ELEGIST	*EMAILER*
EMENDER	EMICATE	**EMONGST**	ENATION	**EPERDUE**	EPICENE	**EQUITES**	ERASURE
ERECTOR	ERODENT	ESCRIBE	ESCROLL	ESERINE	ESTOVER	ESTRICH+	ETAMINE
EUPHROE	EVANISH	EVENTER	EVICTOR	EVOLUTE			
IMAGISM							
OBOVATE	**OCELLAR**	**OCREATE**	ODONATE	*ODORISE*	ODORIZE	**OESTRAL**	OESTRIN
OESTRUM	OESTRUS+	OKIMONO	**OMENTAL**	OMENTUM	OMICRON	OMIKRON	ONANISM
OPACIFY	OPOSSUM	**OROTUND**	OUAKARI	**OUTMOST**	OVERSETd	OZONATE	
UNEARED	UPLIGHT	UPLYING	UPRAISEr	UPREACH	**UREDIAL**		

FRONT HOOKS WITH CONSONANTS

BADLAND	*BADWARE*	BALLIUM	**BANALLY**	**BANGLED**	*BARISTA*	BASSIST	***BEERILY***
BHISTIE	BLAGGER	BLATHER	BLATTER	BLESSER	*BLINGER*	*BLITTER*	*BLOGGER*
BLOTTER	**BLOWSED**	BLUNGER	BLUNKER	BOBECHE	BOILERY+	**BOOZILY**	BORDURE
BOXLIKE	BRACHET	BRATTLE	BRAUNCH	BRICKLE*	BRIMING	BRIMMER	**BRINDED**
BROCKED	BROCKET	BROOKIE	BRONZER	**BRUCKLE**	BRUMMER	BRUSHER	

CACUMEN	**CAIRNED**	CAMELIA	CARABINe	***CARIOSE***	CARLING	CARRACK	CARRECT
CARTFUL	**CASTRAL**	**CEROTIC**	CHALLAH	CHALLAN	**CHALLOT**h	CHALUTZ+	CHAMLET
CHAMPER	CHANGER	CHEATERy	**CHIDDEN**	CHIPPIE*	CHITTER	CHOCKER	CHOUSER
CHUGGER	CHUNTER	CHUPPAH	CHUTZPAh	**CILICES**	CLACKER	CLADDER	*CLADDIE*
CLAMMER	CLAMPER	CLASHER	**CLASSIS**m	**CLASSIS**t	CLICKER	**CLIFTED**	CLINKER
CLIPPIE	CLITTER	**CLIVERS**	CLOGGER	CLOTTER	CLUBBER	CLUMBER	CLUMPER
CLUNKER	CORACLE	COUVERT	***CRABBIT***	*CRACKET*	*CRAFTER*	**CRAGGED**	*CRAMPER*
CRANKLE	**CRANKLY**	CRAPPER	CRAUNCH	CREAMERy	CRIBBER	**CRICKEY**	CRIMMER
CRIMPLE	CRINGER	CROCKET	CROSIER	CRUDDLE	**CRUMPLY***	CRUNKLE	**CULICES**

DANGLER	DAUNTER	**DEJECTA**	DELAPSE	DELUDER	DEMERGEr	DEVOLVE	**DIREFUL**
DJIBBAH	DRABBET	DRABBLEr	DRAFTER	DRAGGLE	DRAPIER	DREADER	DRIBBER
DRIBLET	DRIPPER	DRUBBER	DRUGGER	DRUMBLE	DUBIETY+	**DULOSES**	**DULOSIS**
DYESTER							

FACTIVE	FACTURE	**FAIRILY**	FALCADE	**FARRANT**	FASHERY+	FEASTER	FETCHER
FINCHED	FLACKERy	FLAGGER	FLANGER	FLAPPER	FLASKET	FLAUNCH	FLINGER
FLOGGER	FLOOSIE	FLOPPER	FLUBBER	FLUNKER	FLUTIST	FORPINE	FOULDER
FOXLIKE	FOXTAIL	**FRABBIT**	**FRAILLY**	*FRANGER*	**FRAPPEE**	FRIGGER	FRIPPERy
FRISKER	FROMAGE	**FRONTES**	*FROTHERy*	**FROUGHY***	FROUNCE	FRUMPLE	FULLAGE

GALLIUM	GASEITY+	GASKING	**GASTRAL**	**GAUNTLY**	GENLOCK	**GIRONIC**	GLADDIE
GLANCER	**GLANDES**	GLASSIE*	***GLAZILY***	GLEANER	GLISTER	**GLOBATE**d	**GLOBOSE**
GLUTEAL	**GOLDISH**	GOUTFLY+	GRABBLEr	GRACKLE	GRANGER	GRANTER	GRASPER
GRATINEe	GRAUNCH	***GREEKED***	GREGALE	***GRIDDED***	GRIDDER	GRIPPER	GRIPPLE
GROCKED	GROOMER	GROUTER	GRUBBLE	*GRUNDLE*	**GUNLESS**	GUNLOCK	

HABDABS	HAGGADAh	HALBERT	HAPLITE	HAUNTER	HAUTEUR	HEUREKA	**HEXARCH**y
HIDLING	HOSTLER						

JANGLER	JAUNTIE*	***JAWLESS***	JOSTLER	JUNCATE

KENOSES	KENOSIS+	KHANJAR	KLISTER	KNAPPER	KNOBBLE	KNUBBLE	**KNUBBLY***
KRIMMER	**KVETCHY***						

LEERILY	**LEMURES**	LEUGHEN	LIGNIFY	LIONISEr	LIONIZEr	LOBELIA	**LOCULAR**
LOCULUS	**LOMENTA**	**LOVERED**	**LOVERLY**	LOXYGEN			

MALISON	MARGENT	**MARROWY**	**MASHMAN**	**MASHMEN**	MAXILLAe	MAXILLAr	***MEMETIC***
METHOXYl	**METTLED**	**MOMENTA**	MONEYER	**MORPHIC**	MORRICE	MOUTHER	**MUSEFUL**

147

NAPHTHA **NASCENT** NATRIUM NAYWORD *NEDDISH* NEOLITH NOOLOGY+ **NUMBLES**
NUNDINE NUNHOOD **NUNLIKE** NUNSHIP

PACTION PAEONIC PALLIUM PANTLER PARPENT PARTIER PASTERN PATRIAL
PEATERY+ **PENATES** PENFOLD **PENSILE** PENTICE PEONISM *PICKILY* PIMPLED
PINCHER PINCASE *PINFALL* PINFOLD **PINNATE**d PINWORK **PLANATE** PLASHER
PLATINA PLEDGER PLESSOR PLINKER PLOWBOY PLUMPEN PLUNKER **PLUSHLY**
PLUTEAL **PORCINE** PORTHOS+ POULDER POUTHER PRABBLE PRANKLE PREAVER
PREBILL PREBIND**e** PREBOIL **PREBORN** PRECENT PRECEPT PRECESS PRECIPE
PRECODE **PRECOUP** PRECURE PREDIAL PREEDIT PREFILE PREFIRE PREFORM
PREFUND *PRELOAD* **PREMADE** **PREMEET** PREMISS **PREMIXT** PREMOLD PREMOVE
PRENAME *PREPAVE* PREPONE PREPOSE PRESALE PRESELL**e** *PRESHIP>* PRESHOWn
PRESIFT PRESOAK **PRESOLD** PRESTER PRETAPE *PRETELL**e*** PRETEST **PRETOLD**
PRETRIM> PRETYPE PREVERB PREVISE PREWARM PREWASH *PREWIRE* PREWORK
PREWORN PRICKER PRICKET PRIGGERy PROBAND PROLLER PROOFER **PROSILY**
PRUDERY+ **PRUNTED** PSALTERy **PURANIC**

RAMENTA **RASPISH** RATTRAP RECLOSE **REGALLY** REGENCE RELATER REMERGE
REPRISE RESTATE REVILER REVOKER RHACHIS+ **RONNING** ROUSTER ROYSTER

SALTERN SAMPLERy SARKING **SCALLED** SCANTLE SCARPER SCOLDER SCOOPER
SCOOTCH SCOPULAe SCORNER SCOURIE SCOURSE SCOUTER SCOWRIE SCRANCH
SCRANNY* **SCREAKY*** **SCRIMPY*** **SCROGGY*** **SCROTAL** **SCRUMMY*** SCRUMPY+ SCUDDLE
SCULTCH+ SCUMBER SCUMMER SCUNNER SCUPPER SCUTTER SENSATE **SENSILE**
SEXPERT SHAFTER SHAMBLE SHAMMER **SHEATHY*** SHIDDER SHIPPEN *SHIPPIE*
SHODDEN *SHUSHER* SIGNORE SIMPLEX+ **SIRENIC** SJAMBOK SJAMBOK> SKEGGER
SKIDDER SKIMMER SLANGER SLAPPER SLATTERn SLATTERy **SLAVISH** **SLIMPSY***
SLINKER SLINTER SLITTER SLOTTER SLUBBER SLUGGER SMATTER SMIRKER
SMOLDER SMOUSER SMUDGER SNICKER SNIGGLEr SOUTHERn SPARKER SPARKIE*
SPATHED **SPATHIC** SPATTEE SPAWNER SPEELER SPELTER **SPHENIC** SPINNET
SPITTEN SPITTER **SPLASHY*** SPLODGE SPODIUM SPOOLER SPOORER SPORTER
SPOUTER SPUDDER *SPUDDLE* SPUNKIE* SPUTTERy SQUITCH+ STACKET STAMPER
STANNIC **STARTLY** **STATUED** STEMPLE **STERNAL** **STIBIAL** STICKLEr STILTER
STINTER STIPPLEr STODGER *STOMIUM* STONISH STONKER STOOLIE STOPPLE
STOTTER *STOTTIE* **STOURIE*** STOWAGE **STRAPPY*** **STRIPEY*** STUSHIE SUNBELT
SUNLIKE SUNSUIT **SUNWISE** **SURGENT** *SWADDIE* SWALLET SWAPPER SWARMER
SWASHER SWIGGER SWILLER SWINERY+ **SWINISH** *SWINKER* **SWITCHY*** SWITHER

TACNODE TACTION **TACTUAL** TALIPED TANGLER TANTARA TARSIER *TARTILY*
TAUNTER **TENSILE** TERBIUM TESTATE **TETCHED** THEATER **THELVES** **THEREAT**
THEREOF **THEREON** **THERETO** **THERMAE** *THERMITe* **THETHER** *THICKIE* **THIGHED**
THILLER **THITHER** TILLITE TINWORK *TIRONIC* **TOFFISH** **TOMENTA** **TOUGHLY**
TRAMMEL TRAMMEL> TRAMPER TRANSOM TRANTER *TRASHER* TREDDLE TRENAIL
TRENTAL TRIBLET TRICKERy **TRICKLY*** TRIFLER TRIPPERy TRIPPLEr TROLLER
TROUTER TRUCKLEr TRUNNEL TUMBREL TUMBRIL **TUNABLE** **TURGENT** **TWADDLY***
TWANGLEr TWATTLEr *TWEAKER* *TWEENIE* TWEETER *TWIGLET* TWIGGER TWINTER
TZADDIK

VACUATE	VACUITY+	**VALGOID**	VASSAIL	VAUNTERy	**VAUNTIE**r	VELATED	**VELITES**
VENATIC	VENTAILe	**VESTRAL**	VIBICES	*VLOGGER*	VOCULAR		

WANGLER	**WAPPEND**	WASHERY+	**WASPISH**	WASSAIL	**WAXLIKE**	WHACKER	WHEELER
WHEREAT	**WHEREOF**	**WHEREON**	**WHERETO**	WHIDDER	WHIPPER	WHITHER	WHITTER
WHOLISM	WHOLIST	WHOOPER	WHOOPLA	WHOPPER	WHUMMLE	**WIMPISH**	WINCHER
WINDIGO	WOORALI	**WOOZILY**	WOURALI	WRASSLE	WRESTER		

XEROSES	**XEROTIC**

YCLEPED	YEARNER	**YMOLTEN**	**YPLIGHT**	**YSLAKED**

ZINCITE	ZOOGAMY+	ZOOGENY+	**ZOOIDAL**	ZOOLITE	ZOOLITH	ZOOLOGY+	*ZORBING*

7.2.2 END HOOKS OF SIXES TO MAKE SEVENS

END HOOKS WITH VOWELS

END HOOKS WITH 'A'

ABOMASAl	ACANTHAe	**ANALOGA**	ANONYMA	ARABICA	ASHRAMA	**BUZUKIA**	CANDIDAl
CANTALA	**CEMENTA**	CHIASMAl	CHIMERA	**CHRISMA**l	CODEINA	*CORTINA*	COTINGA
CROTALA	**CURIOSA**	**CYATHIA**	**DEJECTA**	DEODARA	DRACHMAe	DRACHMAi	**EMBLEMA**
EXOTICA	FAVELLA	*FORMICA*	GALLETA	*GALLICA*n	**GERMINA**l	GRAVIDAe	GUNNERA
INFANTA	**INGESTA**	KHALIFAh	KHALIFAt	LAVOLTA	**LOCUSTA**e	**LOCUSTA**l	LOMENTA
MADRASAh	MANDIRA	MANIOCA	MICELLAe	MICELLAr	**MOMENTA**	NANDINA	OSMUNDA
PAISANA	**PLACITA**	POTASSA	**PROPYLA**	QUININA	ROBUSTA	ROSACEA	SCHISMA
SECRETA	*SELECTA*	SENHORA	**SEQUELA**e	SERINGA	*SHEESHA*	SHEIKHA	SIGNORA
SQUILLAe	TAMBURA	TARTANA	TEMPERA	TRISULA	**TYMPANA**l	**VIATICA**l	

END HOOKS WITH '(A)E'

ABOLLAE	**ALUMNAE**	**AMOEBAE**	**ANTLIAE**	**APHTHAE**	**AREOLAE**	**ARISTAE**	**AURORAE**
AXILLAE	**CAMERAE**	**CANULAE**	**CARDIAE**	**CARINAE**	**CATENAE**	**CESURAE**	**CHAETAE**
CHOANAE	**CHORDAE**	**CICADAE**	**CLOACAE**	**CONCHAE**	**COPULAE**	*CORNEAE*	**CORONAE**
CRISTAE	**CRUSTAE**	**CUPULAE**	**EXEDRAE**	**EXUVIAE**	**FACULAE**	**FASCIAE**	**FECULAE**
FERULAE	**FIBULAE**	**GLOSSAE**	**HERNIAE**	**HYDRIAE**	**INFULAE**	**INSULAE**	**INTIMAE**
LACUNAE	**LAMINAE**	**LIGULAE**	**LINGUAE**	**LORICAE**	**LUNULAE**	**MACULAE**	**MEDUSAE**
MIMOSAE	**MORULAE**	**MUCOSAE**	**NATURAE**	**NEBULAE**	**NOVENAE**	NYMPHAEa	**OCHREAE**
PALAMAE	**PAPULAE**	**PATERAE**	PATINAEd	*PILULAE*	*PLANTAE*	**PLEURAE**	**RADULAE**
REGINAE	**REGULAE**	**RETINAE**	*ROTULAE*	**SCLERAE**	**SCORIAE**	**SEROSAE**	**SITULAE**
SQUAMAE	**STRIGAE**	**STRUMAE**	**SYNURAE**	**TABULAE**	**TAENIAE**	**TEGULAE**	**TORULAE**
TUNICAE	**UNGULAE**	**VAGINAE**	**VESICAE**	**VOMICAE**	**ZONULAE**		

OTHER END HOOKS WITH 'E'

ACQUITEd	ADONISE	ADVISEE	AFFAIRE	AFFEARE	ALANINE	ALEXINE	ALIDADE
ALSOONE	ALTERNE	ALUMINE	AMIDINE	ANATASE	ANILINE	**ANTICKE**d	ARABISE
ARSHINE	ARTISTE	ASPERSEr	ATTRITE	AUGUSTE*	BAGASSE	BAILLIE	BALLADE
BELDAME	BENZINE	BENZOLE	BERLINE	**BESPATE**	BETEEME	BHISTIE	BICORNE
BLINTZE	**BOTONEE**	BOUCHEE	*BOUCLEE*	**BREVETE**d	BRUCINE	BUGGANE	CAGOULE

7. Seven-Letter Words

CAPRICE	CARLINE	CAROCHE	CARPALE	CASERNE	CAVIARE	CELLOSE	CHIMERE
CHINESE	CHOPINE	CHORALE	CINEOLE	CITRINE	CODEINE	COELOME	COMMERE
COMMOTE	COMPOTE	*COSMINE*	COUCHEE	CYANINE	**DEFASTE**	DEMAINE	DEMEANE
DENTINE	DÉTENTE	DETENUE	DEVISEE	DHOOTIE	DIAMINE	DIAZINE	DILUTEE
DIOXANE	***DOLENTE***	*DOMAINE*	DOMINEEr	EMETINE	EMPLOYEe	EMPLOYEr	***ENGAGEE***
ENNUYEE	**ENTETEE**	**EPERDUE**	EPIGONE	EPIMERE	**EPUISEE**	ETAMINE	EUCAINE
EXTERNE	FETICHE	**FITCHEE**	FLAMBEE=	FLAVINE	**FOLIOSE**	**FOREBYE**	FORMATE
FRAPPEE	FRIANDE	FRIJOLE	GALOSHE	GANOINE	GARROTEr	GLYCINE	GOLOSHE
GOUGERE	GRADINE	GRANDEE	**GRATINE**e	GUANASE	GUANINE	HALTERE	HAPTENE
HARMINE	HYALINE	HYDRASE	HYDRIDE	INFANTE	INGENUE	INTERNEe	INTERNEt
INULASE	ISATINE	ISOBARE	ISOGONE	ISOMERE	JAGHIRE	KAGOULE	KAINITE
KAOLINE	LADRONE	LEASOWE	LEGATEE	LEUCINE	LURDANE	MARLINE	MATRICE
MAUVINE	MEGASSE	*MESTOME*	MICELLE	MODERNE*	MODISTE	MONTANE	*MOOLVIE*
MOUSMEE	MURRINE	MYELINE	NANDINE	NARCOSE	NITRILE	OBLIGEE	OCTETTE
OLEFINE	ORIGANE	**OUVERTE**	PAIOCKE	PAJOCKE	PANGENE	PARDALE	PARVISE
PENSILE	PEPSINE	PEPTIDE	**PESANTE**	PICKAXE	PICOTEE	PINKEYE	PISTOLEt
PLANCHEt	PLATANE	PLEDGEE	**POMMELE**d	PONTILE	PRANCKE	PRISERE	PROTYLE
PURLINE	PYRROLE	**RADIALE**	RATLINE	RECOUPEd	REQUITEr	ROSIERE	SAFROLE
SAVANTE	SCALARE	SCHOOLE	SCOURSE	SCROWLE	SDEIGNE	SECONDEe	SECONDEr
SHEATHEr	SIGNORE	SIXAINE	SKATOLE	**SODAINE**	**SOIGNEE**	SPARTHE	SPHAERE
SPHEARE	SPIREME	SPREDDEd	SPREDDEn	SPRINGEr	SPRINGE=	STAITHE	STATICE
STROOKEn	**SUBTILE***	SULFIDE	SUMMATE	SYLVINE	SYMBOLE	TARTANEd	TARTARE
TIMBALE	TOLUIDE	TOLUOLE	TRITONE	TROCHEE	TROPINE	TUSSORE	**UNBORNE**
UNLASTE	UNVAILE	VERDITEr	VERSINE	VISITEE	VOLANTE	WREATHEn	WREATHEr

END HOOKS WITH 'I'

ABOMASI	**ACANTHI**n	AFGHANI	*BANDARI*	**CHIASMI**c	**DACTYLI**c	DAKOITI	DEMENTIa
DENARII	**ELENCHI**c	**EPIGONI**c	**GRADINI**	HALLALI	HELLERI	JAMPANI	**OBLASTI**
PAESANI	QAWWALI	REVERSI	**RHYTHMI**c	**SECONDI**	SHIKARI	**SIGNORI**a	*SLOUGHI*
TYMPANIc							

END HOOKS WITH 'O'

BANDITO	BATTERO	BRACERO	BUDGEROw	CANTICOy	CYMBALOm	CYMBALO+	**GRADINO**
MOMENTO	**NITROSO**	PAESANO	PAISANO	PAMPERO	PIMENTOn	PRIMERO	PUMMELO
*RABBITO*h	REVERSO	*SCREAMO*	**SECONDO**	SERRANO	TAMARAO	**TYMPANO**	VERISMO
WHERESO							

END HOOKS WITH CONSONANTS

END HOOKS WITH 'D'

AFFEARD	**AFFINED**	**AGNAMED**	**ALCOVED**	**ANSATED**	**AURATED**	**BANGLED**	**BASQUED**
BISTRED	**BLOWSED**	**BLOWZED**	**CASQUED**	**CERATED**	CESTOID	**CLICHED**	COLLARD
COLOBID	COSTARD	**DECKLED**	**DEGREED**	**DEMODED**	**DISMAYD**	**DOTTLED**	DROMOND
EMERSED	**ENNUYED**	**ERMINED**	**FARCIED**	**GLAIVED**	**GOATEED**	**GOITRED**	GOLLAND
GOWLAND	**GRIECED**	**ICICLED**	**JUNGLED**	**KIRTLED**	LALLAND	**LANATED**	**LANGUED**
LOBATED	**LOCULED**	**LOUVRED**	**LUNATED**	**LYRATED**	**MASCLED**	MEGARAD	**METTLED**
NODULED	**NONAGED**	OUTWIND	**PALACED**	PARPEND	**PERUKED**	**PIMPLED**	*POLYPED*
PROTEIDe	PROVEND	**RACEMED**	**RUNDLED**	**RUSTRED**	SAGGARD	**SPATHED**	**STATUED**

STRAKED	TEMPLED	TIERCED	TOGATED	*TOUPEED*	TOWMOND	TURBAND	*UNLIKED*
UNSURED	VELATED	VISAGED	VOLUTED	WARRAND	ZONATED		

END HOOKS WITH '(A)L'

ADNEXAL	ALODIAL	AMENTAL	ANGINAL	APNOEAL	AURORAL	CAMBIAL	CAMERAL
CARINAL	CESURAL	CHAETAL	CHORDAL	CHOREAL	CHORIAL	CLOACAL	CONCHAL
CORNEAL	CORNUAL	CORONAL	CORYZAL	CRANIAL	CRESTAL	CRISSAL	CRUSTAL
CUBICAL	ELUVIAL	ELYTRAL	ENCINAL	ENTERAL	EPOCHAL	EXUVIAL	FASCIAL
FEMORAL	GLOSSAL	HEDERAL	HERNIAL	INTIMAL	ISCHIAL	LACUNAL	LAMINAL
LEXICAL	LIMINAL	LOCHIAL	LUMINAL	LUSTRAL	MAXIMAL	MEDUSAL	MIASMAL
MUCOSAL	NYMPHAL	OMENTAL	PALLIAL	PLEURAL	QUANTAL	QUINTAL	REGINAL
RETINAL	ROSTRAL	RUMINAL	SALIVAL	SATYRAL	SCLERAL	SCROTAL	SEMINAL
SEROSAL	STADIAL	STERNAL	STIGMAL	STRATAL	STROMAL	TAPETAL	TERTIAL
UREDIAL	VESICAL	VIMINAL	ZOARIAL				

OTHER END HOOKS WITH 'L'

BARBELL	**BORRELL**	BURRELL	CARRELL	CHANCEL	CHROMEL	DISMAYL	ESCROLL
ETHOXYL	FANNELL	FULFILL	GINGALL	JINGALL	MUCHELL	MULMULL	POINTEL
TASSELLy	THERMEL	TIERCEL	TIMBREL	**TOPFULL**	TRAMELL	TROCHILi	TWIBILL
WADMOLL	WOOSELL						

END HOOKS WITH 'N'

ABELIAN	ACKNOWNe	ALKALINe	AMOEBAN	**ANLAGEN**	**BETAKEN**	*BRAHMANi*	**BRONZEN**
CAPITANi	CAPITANo	CHALLAN	*CHIRREN*	CITHERN	COARSEN	CRYPTON	EMBRYON
ENVIRON	EPIZOAN	GELATINe	GELATINg	HOARSEN	HOMELYN	**INWOVEN**	**JIGSAWN**
LAMPERN	LETTERN	MEDUSAN	**MISSEEN**	MONERAN	NUCLEIN	ORARIAN	**OUTSEEN**
PAPAYAN	PASTERN	PHALLIN	POSTERN	PREWARN	PROTEAN	QUINTAN	**REFLOWN**
REGIVEN	**REGROWN**	**RERISEN**	**RESHOWN**	**RETAKEN**	REWAKEN	**REWOKEN**	**REWOVEN**
RIPSAWN	SALTERN	SHIPPON	**SHOTTEN**	SHRIVEN	**SIERRAN**	**SILVERN**	SMIDGEN
SOLITON	**STONERN**	**STROKEN**	TAMARINd	TERTIAN	TESTERN	**THRIVEN**	TORULIN
TRUDGEN	**UNDRAWN**	**UNLADEN**	UNROVEN	**UNWOVEN**	**UPBLOWN**	**UPDRAWN**	**UPGROWN**
UPRISEN	**UPTAKEN**	**URANIAN**	VIBRION	*VOUDOUN*	**WRITHEN**	**YESTERN**	ZITHERN

END HOOKS WITH 'R' OF VERBS

ABJURER	ABRADER	ACCEDER	ADDUCER	ADHERER	ADJURER	ADVISER	ALLEGER
ALLURER	AMENDER	AMERCER	APPOSER	AROUSER	ARRIVER	ASPIRER	ASSIZER
ASSUMER	ASSURER	BAFFLER	BEAGLER	BEETLER	BEHAVER	BLUNGER	BOGGLER
BOODLER	BRIDLER	BRONZER	BUCKLER	BUMBLER	BUNDLER	BURBLER	BUSTLER
BYLINER	CACKLER	CAJOLERy	CANDLER	CHANCERy	CHANGER	CHAUFER	CHOOSER
CHOUSER	CIRCLER	*COCKLER*	CODDLER	COERCER	COHERER	COMAKER	COUCHER
COUPLER	COURSER	CRADLER	CREASER	CRINGER	CUDDLER	CURDLER	CURRIERy
DAMAGER	DANDLER	DANGLER	DEBASER	DEBONER	DECREER	DEFACER	DEFAMER
DEFILER	DEFINER	*DEFUSER*	DELUDER	DENUDER	DEPOSER	DERIDER	DERIVER
DESIRER	DEVISER	DIBBLER	DIDDLER	DILATER	DILUTER	DOUBLER	DREDGER
DRUDGERy	EFFACER	EMPALER	ENABLER	ENCODER	ENDURER	ENGAGER	ENGINERy
ENROBER	ENSURER	ENTICER	ESCAPER	EVOLVER	EXCITER	EXCUSER	EXHUMER
EXPIRER	EXPOSER	FETTLER	FIGURER	FLANGER	FLEECER	FLENSER	FOOTLER
FOOZLER	FUDDLER	GABBLER	GARBLER	GARGLER	GIGGLER	GIRDLER	GLANCER
GOGGLER	GREETER	GRIPPER	GROUSER	GRUDGER	GUTTLER	HACKLER	HIGGLER

7. Seven-Letter Words

HOBBLER HOMAGER *HOPPLER* HUDDLER IGNITER IGNORER IMBIBER IMPALER
IMPEDER IMPOSER IMPUTER INCITER INDITER INDUCER INFUSER INHUMER
INJURER INTONER INVITER INVOKER *IODISER* IODIZER IONISER IONIZER
JANGLER JERQUER JINGLER JOGGLER JOSTLER JUMBLER KIDDIER KINDLER
LOCATER LOUNGER MANGLER MANURER MARBLER MENACER MIDDLER MISUSER
MOTTLER NEEDLER NEGATER NESTLER NETTLER NIBBLER NIGGLER NOBBLER
NOTICER OBLIGER OUTLIER PARADER PEOPLER PERUSER PHRASER PIAFFER
PICKLER PIDDLER PIERCER PIFFLER PINGLER PLAGUER PLEDGER *POLICER*
POTCHER POUNCER PRAISER PRANCER PUDDLER PUMICER *PURFLER* PURSUER
PUTTIER RABBLER RAFFLER RAVAGER REBATER REBUKER RECITER REDUCER
REFUSER REFUTER REGALER RELATER REMAKER REMOVER RENEGER REPINER
REPOSER RESIDER RESUMER RETAKER RETIRER REVERER REVILER REVISER
REVOKER RIDDLER RIFFLER RIPPLER RUFFLER RUMBLER SALUTER SAMPLERy
SCORSER SCRIBER SCYTHER SECEDER SEETHER SHELVER SHRIVER SLEEVER
SMOUSER SMUDGER SNEEZER SNOOZER SNUBBER SOLACER SPALLER SPARGER
SPARRER SPLICER SPURNER STARVER STEALER STEMMERy STEPPER STIFLER
STODGER STOOPER *STOOZER* STRAFER STRIDER STRIPER STRIVER STROKER
SUBDUER SWATHER SWERVER TANGLER TATTLER TEETHER THRIVER TICKLER
TINGLER TINKLER TIPPLER TOGGLER TOOTLER TORQUER TOUCHER TRIFLER
TROUPER TRUDGER TRYSTER TURTLER TWEEZER UNMAKER UPDATER UPRISER
VISITER WABBLER WADDLER *WAGGLER* WANGLER WARSLER WHEEZER WIGGLER
WINKLER WOBBLER WRITHER

OTHER END HOOKS WITH 'R'

ALNAGER **AREOLAR** *AXILLARy* *BLAGUER* ***CANULAR*** **CHILDER** CLAQUER CLAVIER
COPULAR CROUPER CUISSER **CUPOLAR** **CUPULAR** **FACULAR** **FIBULAR** GRANGER
GRUNGER INCOMER LACUNARy ***LAMINARy*** LEAGUER LEGATOR **LIGULAR** **LUNULAR**
MACULAR MASQUER MILLIER **MORULAR** **NEBULAR** NONUSER *ONLINER* **OSCULAR**
PAPULAR PAVISER **PILULAR** **PLANTAR** POTAGER QUINTAR **RADULAR** ***RANULAR***
RELIVER SCOUSER SOCAGER SWITHER **TEGULAR** **UNGULAR** UPMAKER **ZONULAR**

END HOOKS WITH 'T'

ACQUIST ALKANET ANIMIST ATTAINT **ATTASKT** BALLANT BARGEST BASSETT
BEDROPT BEIGNET **BELEAPT** **BEMEANT** **BEWRAPT** BORSCHT BOSQUET CALLANT
CANTLET *CHEVRET* CIRCLET **COMMIXT** **COMPAST** CONTRATe CORNETTi CORNETTo
COUPLET DECREET **DEWLAPT** DIPLONT DOUBLET DROGUET EPAULET FITCHET
GROSERT GURGLET HACKLET JINGLET *KENNETT* KINGLET LAMBERT LANGUET
MANCHET MANTLET MEDIANT **MIGHTST** **MISHAPT** **MISKENT** MOLINET MONTANTo
ORGIAST **OVERGOT** PALMIET PARPENT PELTAST PLEDGET **POLLENT** POUNCET
PREMIXT RACKETT RAGMENT **REWRAPT** RIPPLET ROOTLET RUNDLET SABKHAT
SANGHAT SEAWANT SENSIST SESTETTe SESTETTo SEXTETTe SHARIAT SHERIAT
SPAVIET SPRAINT STRAINT SUBPART **TAIVERT** TEMPLET TENNIST **THATCHT**
TIERCET TOWMONT TURBANT **UNCLIPT** **UPLEANT** **UPLEAPT** WADSETT WHEESHT
WOULDST ZONULET

END HOOKS WITH '(ER)Y' TO NOUNS

BEAVERY+ BINDERY+ BROKERY+ BUTLERY+ CAUTERY+ *CAMPERY*+ COOPERY+ COSHERY+
CYCLERY+ DAUBERY+ DEANERY+ DODGERY+ DOGGERY+ DUDDERY+ FARMERY+ FIBBERY+
FRATERY+ FULLERY+ *GAGGERY*+ GINNERY+ GULLERY+ GUNNERY+ HACKERY+ HELLERY+
HENNERY+ HOGGERY+ JAGGERY+ JOBBERY+ MAPPERY+ MERCERY+ MISTERY+ MONGERY+
MOUSERY+ NAILERY+ NOSHERY+ NUTTERY+ PEDLERY+ PICKERY+ PILFERY+ PUFFERY+
RATTERY+ RIFLERY+ ROGUERY+ SEALERY+ SPICERY+ SPIKERY+ STAGERY+ SUTLERY+
TOGGERY+ TRACERY+ TURNERY+ WAGGERY+ WASHERY+ WASTERY+ WEEDERY+ WHALERY+
WIGGERY+ WORMERY+

END HOOKS WITH 'Y' TO ADJECTIVES

BILLOWY* BRANCHY* BREATHY* CARROTY* CHANCEY* CHINCHY* CHINTZY* CHOOSEY*
CHURCHY* CLIQUEY* CREESHY* DOUGHTY* DROICHY* DROUTHY* FLAUNTY* FOUGHTY*
FRATCHY* FROWSTY* GROWTHY* KITSCHY* *KLUDGEY** KVETCHY* LATHERY* *LOUNGEY*
MAGGOTY* ORANGEY* PAUNCHY* PHLEGMY* PLAGUEY* PREACHY* PUCKERY* QUARTZY*
QUAVERY* QUEACHY* RACKETY* SCREAKY* SCRIMPY* SCRUNTY* SHEATHY* SHIVERY*
SHLOCKY SHRIEKY* SHRILLY* SHRIMPY* SHROUDY* *SHTICKY* SILVERY* SLEECHY*
SLOUCHY* SLOUGHY* *SLUTCHY* SMOOCHY* SMUTCHY* SNATCHY* *SNITCHY* SPIDERY*
SPLASHY* SPLEENY* SPRAWLY* SPRINGY* SQUASHY* SQUIFFY* SQUINTY* SQUIRMY*
SQUISHY* STARCHY* STENCHY* STREAMY* STREETY* STRIPEY* SWITCHY* THATCHY*
THREADY* THRILLY* THROATY* TIDDLEY* *TRANCEY** TRICKSY* UNHANDY* WILLOWY*
WREATHY* YELLOWY*

OTHER END HOOKS WITH 'Y'

ALMONDY AUTUMNY BALSAMY BEGGARY+ BIOGENY+ BLIGHTY+ *BOCKEDY* BURSARY+
BUTTONY CANKERY CASTORY+ CINDERY CIRCUSY CITRUSY CLOVERY CLUTCHY
COLOURY COPPERY COTTONY CRAMESY+ DACOITY+ DAKOITY+ DIARCHY+ DIDDLEY
DOWLNEY DYVOURY+ EPARCHY+ EPONYMY+ EUPHONY+ EXARCHY+ **FAGGOTY** FERRETY
FIDDLEY **FLAVORY** FURROWY GADGETY *GALANTY* *GARAGEY* GARGETY GLITCHY
GOSSIPY GRUMPHY+ *GRUNGEY* GUTTERY HERBARY+ **HICCUPY** ISOGONY+ *JARGONY*
JASPERY *JUDDERY* KITTENY KOLHOZY LADDERY LITTERY *LOLLOPY* MARROWY
MARTYRY+ **MATTERY** MEADOWY MELLOWY *MENSCHY* MILDEWY MORASSY MORTARY
MOTHERY MUTTONY NATTERY NECTARY+ NIGGERY OROGENY+ OVULARY PALMARY
PARROTY *PASTILY* PEDLARY+ PILLOWY PLOVERY POTHERY QUIVERY RABBITY
RAISINY RIBBONY *RUBBITY*+ RUSSETY **SALLOWY** *SALMONY* SATRAPY+ SCRUMPY+
SHINNEY SHLUMPY SIGNORY+ SINTERY SMOOTHY+ SPIRITY STARTSY STATUSY
SUCCORY+ SULFURY1 TACKETY TALLOWY TATTERY THRISTY TINDERY *TIMBERY*
TISSUEY TITTUPY TRIPODY+ *TURNIPY* TYMPANY+ UNTENTY VALLARY VAPOURY
VELVETY VERMILY+ VERMINY VILLANY+ **WEASELY** WEEVILY *WINDOWY*

OTHER END HOOKS

AARRGHH *AGGADAH* AGOROTH ALIYOTH ALKALIC AMTRACK ANIMISM BABOOSH+
BATEAUX BIBLESS *BILLYOH* BOOBOOK BUCKRAM **BUREAUX** BUSHWAH CADDISH
CADEAUX CALPACK **CAPLESS** CARLING CATLING CHALLAH **CHALOTH** CHAPESS+
CODLING **COTEAUX** CYMLING DAYGLOW DISBARK **EMBOLIC** EPHEBIC FILMISH
FINNACK FITCHEW **FOGLESS** GASKING **GATEAUX** GOPURAM GRAMASH+ GWEDUCK
HAGGISH HALALAH **HALLOTH** *HUPPOTH* HUTZPAH *IMPOSEX*+ **INKLESS** ISTHMIC
KERMESSe KOUMISS+ KOUMYSS+ LARGESSe LIMBECK LOWNESS+ *LUCHOTH* MANITOU
MANTRAM MANTRAP *MAPLESS* MASTICHe MATZOTH MEGILPH MERLING **MIKVOTH**

MILIEUX	MINIMAX	MISSEEM	**MISSISH**	MISTERM	MUNTING	*NUCLEIC*	OOMIACK
OUTBARK	**OUTRANG**e	**OUTRUNG**	OUTSINGd	OUTWING	**OUTWITH**	OVERDOG	**PARKISH**
PERFING	PITARAH	**POORISH**	POTHERB	PRECESS	PREWARM	**PRIAPIC**	**PRUTOTH**
PYLORIC	QABALAH	RATLING	**RAYLESS**	REPLUMB	**RESEAUX**	**RHOMBIC**	RIGLING
SABKHAH	SAHIBAH	SCHLEPPy	SCORIAC	SENSISM	SHANTIH	*SHARIAH*	*SHIKSEH*
SHINESS+	SIMPLEX+	SIMURGH	STIRRAH	SUBMENU	**SUCCOTH**	SUCCUSS	**TALLISH**
TALLITH	TAMARAU	**TEREFAH**	**THALLIC**	THANNAH	TIETACK	TOMBACK	TREPANG
TREVISS+	TRIPLEX+	**TROPHIC**	TURACOU	TURBITH	TZADDIQ	**UNAKING**	UNGIRTH
USURESS+	VENDISS+	ZEBRASS+					

7.3 LESS FAMILIAR NON-HOOK SEVENS

7.3.1 VERBS COMPRISED OF A COMMON PREFIX PLUS A VERB

BEBLOOD	BECHALK	BECHARM	BECLASP	BECLOAK	BECLOUD	BECLOWN	BECRAWL
BECRIME	BECROWD	BECRUST	BECURSE	BEDEVIL	BEDEVIL>	BEDIGHT	BEDIRTY
BEDIZEN	BEDRAPE	BEDWARF	BEFLECK	BEGLOOM	BEGROAN	BEHIGHTd	BEHOOVE
BEJEWEL	BEJEWEL>	BELABOR	BEMADAM	BEMEDAL	BEMEDAL>	BEMOUTH	BEPAINT
BEPEARL	BEPROSE	BEREAVEn	BEREAVEr	BERHYME	BESAINT	BESCOUR	BESHAME
BESHINEd	BESHOUT	BESHREW	BESLAVEr	BESLIME	BESMEAR	BESMILE	BESMOKE
BESPEAKd	BESPEEDd	BESPICE	BESPORT	BESPOUT	BESTAIN	BESTEAD	BESTICKd
BESTILL	BESTORM	BESTREWn	BESTROWn	BESWARM	BETHANK	BETHINKd	BETHORN
BETHUMB	BETHUMP	BETITLE	BETOKEN	BETREADd	BEVOMIT	BEWEARY	BEWHORE
BEWORRY							

COADMIT>	COANNEX	COCHAIR	CODRIVEd	CODRIVEn	CODRIVEr	COENACT	COERECT
COEXERT	COFOUND	COINFER>	COINTER>	COREIGN	CORIVAL>	COWRITEd	COWRITEr

DEBEARD	DEBRIDE	DECEASE	DECLAIM	DECLASSe	DECOLOR	DECROWN	DECURVE
DEFOCUS	DEFOCUS>	DEFORCEr	DEGLAZE	*DEINDEX*	DELEAVE	DELIMIT	DEMOUNT
DEORBIT	DEPAINT	DEPLANE	DEPLUME	*DEQUEUE*	DERANGEr	DESCALE	DESCANT
DESKILL	*DESNOOD*	DESPOIL	DESTAIN	*DESTOCK*	DESUGAR	DETRAIN	DEVOICE
DEWATER							

DISALLY	DISAVOW	DISCAGE	DISCANT	DISCASE	DISCIDE	DISCURE	DISEDGE
DISFORM	DISGOWN	DISHELM	DISHOME	DISHORN	DISJOINt	DISLEAF	DISLIMB
DISLIMN	DISLINK	DISLOAD	DISMASK	DISMAST	DISNEST	DISPACE	DISPARK
DISPART	DISPEND	DISPORT	DISPOST	DISRANK	DISRATE	DISROOT	DISSAVE
DISSEAT	DISTEND	DISTUNE	DISYOKE				

EMBATHE	EMBLAZEr	EMBLOOM	EMBOSOM	EMBOUND	EMBOWEL	EMBOWEL>	EMBOWER
EMBRAID	EMBRAVE	EMBREAD	EMBROWN	EMBRUTE	EMPANEL	EMPANEL>	EMPEACH
EMPERCE	EMPLACE	EMPLANE	EMPLUME				

ENCHAFE	ENCHAIN	ENCHARM	ENCHASEr	ENCHEER	ENCLASP	ENCLOUD	ENCRUST
ENFEVER	ENFLAME	ENFLESH	ENFRAME	ENGLOBE	ENGLOOM	ENGRACE	ENGRAFF
ENGRAFT	ENGRAIN	ENGRASP	ENGUARD	ENLIGHT	ENPLANE	*ENQUEUE*	ENRANGE

ENROUGH	ENROUND	ENSHELL	ENSNARL	ENSTAMP	ENSTEEP	ENSTYLE	ENSWEEPd
ENTRAIN	ENTWIST	ENVAULT	ENVENOM	ENWHEEL			

EXCURSE	EXPLANT	EXPOSIT	EXPOUND	EXPULSE	EXPURGE

FORFAIRn	FORFEND	FORHENTd	FORLENDd	FORPINE	FORSLOW	FORWARN

FORELAYd	FORELIEd	FORERUNd	FORESAYd

IMBATHE	IMBLAZE	IMBOSOM	IMBOWER	IMBROWN	IMBRUTE	IMMERGE	IMPAINT
IMPASTE	IMPEARL	IMPLATE	IMPLEAD	IMPOWER			

INBREEDd	INBRINGd	INCHASE	INCLASP	INCLOSEr	INCROSS	INCRUST	INCURVE
INDWELLd	INEARTH	INFORCE	INFRACT	INGLOBE	INGRAFT	INGRAIN	INGROSS
INJELLY	INJOINT	INNERVE	INQUIET	INSCULPt	INSHELL	INSINEW	INSNAREr
INSTATE	INTITLE	INTREAT	INTRUST	INTWINE	INTWIST	INWEAVE	

MISALLY	MISAVER>	MISBIAS	MISBIAS>	MISBILL	MISBINDd	MISCITE	MISCODE
MISCOIN	MISCOOK	MISCOPY	MISDATE	MISDEEM	MISEDIT	MISFALLd	MISFARE
MISFIRE	MISFORM	MISGIVEd	MISGIVEn	MISGROWd	MISGROWn	MISJOIN	MISKEEPd
MISKNOWd	MISKNOWn	MISLIKEr	MISLIVE	MISLUCK	MISMAKEd	MISMARK	MISMATE
MISMEETd	MISMOVE	MISPAGE	MISPART	MISPLAN>	MISPLANt	MISPLAY	MISRATE
MISRELY	MISRULE	MISSEAT	*MISSELLd*	MISSENDd	MISSORT	MISSTEP>	MISSTOP>
MISSUIT	MISTELLd	MISTEND	MISTUNE	MISWEEN	MISWEND	MISWORD	MISYOKE

OUTBAKE	OUTBAWL	OUTBEAM	OUTBRAG>	OUTBULK	OUTBURNt	OUTCOOK	OUTCROW
OUTDARE	OUTDRAG>	OUTDRAWd	OUTDRAWn	OUTDROP>	OUTDUEL	OUTDUEL>	OUTDURE
OUTEARN	OUTECHO+	OUTFACE	OUTFAST	OUTFAWN	OUTFEELd	OUTFINDd	OUTFIRE
OUTFISH	OUTFLOWn	OUTFOOL	OUTFOOT	OUTGAIN	*OUTGAZE*	OUTGIVEd	OUTGIVEn
OUTGLOW	OUTGNAWn	OUTGRIN>	OUTGUSH	OUTHEARd	OUTHEARd	OUTHIRE	OUTHOWL
OUTHUNT	OUTJEST	OUTJINX	OUTKEEPd	OUTKILL	OUTKISS	*OUTLEADd*	OUTLOVE
OUTMOVE	OUTNAME	OUTPASS	OUTPEEP	OUTPEER	OUTPITY	OUTPLAN>	OUTPLOD>
OUTPLOT>	OUTPOLL	OUTPOUR	OUTPRAY	OUTPULL	OUTPUSH	OUTRAVE	OUTREADd
OUTRINGd	OUTROAR	OUTROCK	OUTROLL	OUTROOT	OUTRUSH	OUTSAIL	OUTSOAR
OUTSPAN>	OUTSTEP>	OUTSULK	OUTTASK	OUTTELLd	OUTTROT>	OUTWAIT	OUTWALK
OUTWEARd	OUTWEARy	OUTWEED	OUTWEEPd	OUTWELL	OUTWICK	OUTWILE	OUTWILL
OUTWISH	OUTWORK	OUTYELL	OUTYELP				

OVERAWE	OVERBET>	OVERBUYd	OVERCUTd	OVERDRY	OVERDUB>	OVERDYE=	OVERDYEr
OVEREGG	OVEREYE	OVEREYE=	OVERFLY	OVERGETd	OVERHITd	OVERJOY	OVERLETd
OVERMAN>	OVERMANy	OVERMIX	OVERNET>	OVERPLY	OVERRED>	OVERRENd	OVERREN>
OVERSEWn	OVERSOWn	OVERSUP>	OVERTIP>	OVERTOP>			

PREBAKE	PRECOOL	PREDOOM	PREFADE	PREHEND	PREWARN

READORN	REAFFIX	REALTER	REAMEND	REANNEX	REAVAIL	REAWAKEn	REBADGE
REBEGINd	REBLEND	REBLOOM	REBRACE	*REBRAND*	REBREEDd	RECARRY	RECATCHd
RECENSE	RECHART	RECHEAT	RECLASP	RECLEAN	RECLIMB	RECOLOR	RECOURE
RECOWER	RECRATE	RECROSS	RECROWN	RECURVE	REDOUBT	REDRAFT	REDREAMt

155

```
REDRIVEd REDRIVEn REEDIFY  REEJECT  REENDOW  REENJOY  REERECT  REEVOKE
REEXPEL> REFENCE  REFIGHTd REFLOAT  REFLOOD  REFOCUS  REFOCUS> REFORGE
REFRACT  REFRONT  REGAUGE  REGLAZE  REGLOSS  REGORGE  REGRAFT  REGRANT
REGRATEr REGREEN  REGREET  REGRINDd REGROOM  REHINGE  REIMAGE  REINCUR>
REINTER> REJUDGE  RELIGHT  REMOULD  REOFFER  REPANEL  REPANEL> REPAPER
REPIQUE  REPLATE  REPLEAD  REPOINT  REPOSIT  REPOWER  REPRICE  REPRIME
REPRIZE  REPROBE  REPROOF  REPROVEr REPULSEr RERAISE  RESCALE  RESEIZE
RESHAVEn RESHINE  RESHOOTd RESIGHT  RESKILL  RESLATE  RESMELT  RESPACE
RESPADE  RESPEAKd RESPELL  RESPIRE  RESPLITd RESPOOL  RESTAGE  RESTAMP
RESTOKE  RESTUDY  RESTUFF  RESTUMP  RESTYLE  RESURGE  RETALLY  RETASTE
RETEACHd RETITLE  RETOTAL  RETOTAL> RETOUCH  RETRACK  RETWIST  REUNIFY
REUTTER  REVOICE  REWATER  REWEAVE  REWIDEN


UNBEGETd UNBLESS  UNBLIND  UNBOSOM  UNBRACE  UNBRAID  UNBRAKE  UNBUILDd
UNCHAIR  UNCHARM  UNCHECK  UNCHILD  UNCLASP  UNCLOAK  UNCLOSE  UNCLOUDy
UNCRATE  UNCROSS  UNCROWN  UNCURSE  UNDEIFY  UNDIGHTd UNDRAPE  UNFENCE
UNFLESH  UNFLUSH  UNFROCK  UNGLOVE  UNGUARD  UNHEART  UNHINGE  UNHOARD
UNHORSE  UNHOUSE  UNJOINT  UNLEVEL  UNLEVEL> UNLOOSEn UNMARRY  UNMITER
UNMITRE  UNMOULD  UNMOUNT  UNORDER  UNPAINT  UNPANEL> UNPAPER  UNPERCH
UNPLACE  UNPLUMB  UNPLUME  UNPURSE  UNQUEEN  UNQUIET* UNQUOTE  UNREAVE
UNREEVE  UNRIVET  UNROOST  UNROUND  UNSAINT  UNSCALE  UNSENSE  UNSHALE
UNSHAPEn UNSHELL  UNSHIFT  UNSHOOT  UNSHOUT  UNSIGHT  UNSINEW  UNSLINGd
UNSNARL  UNSNECK  UNSPEAKd UNSPELL  UNSPOOL  UNSTACK  UNSTATE  UNSTEEL
UNSTICKd UNSTOCK  UNSTRIP> UNSWEARd UNTEACHd UNTHINKd UNTRACE  UNTRACK
UNTREAD  UNTRUSS  UNTWINE  UNVISOR  UNVOICE  UNWATERy UNWEAVEd UNWITCH
UNWOMAN  UNWRITEd


UPBRAID  UPBREAKd UPBRINGd UPBUILDd UPBURSTd UPCATCHd UPCHEER  UPCHUCK
UPCLIMB  UPCLOSE  UPCURVE  UPFLINGd UPHEAVEr UPHOARD  UPHOIST  UPROUSE
UPSCALE  UPSHIFT  UPSHOOTd UPSKILL  UPSPEAKd UPSPEAR  UPSTANDd UPSTARE
UPSWEEPd UPSWELL  UPTHROWd UPTHROWn UPTRAIN  UPVALUE  UPWHIRL
```

7.3.2 OTHER VERBS

VERBS ENDING IN 'IZE' WITH 'ISE' EQUIVALENT

```
ADONIZE  AGATIZE  AGENIZE  ANODIZE  APPRIZEr ARABIZE  ATHEIZE  BROMIZE
COALIZE  COGNIZEr CYANIZE  CYCLIZE  DOCKIZE  DUALIZE  EBONIZE  ECHOIZE
EGOTIZE  ELEGIZE  EROTIZE  GALLIZE  GRECIZE  HEROIZE  ICONIZE  IRIDIZE
IRONIZE  KYANIZE  LAICIZE  LIONIZEr MYTHIZE  OBELIZE  PECTIZE  PEPTIZEr
POETIZEr UNITIZEr
```

OTHER VERBS CONTAINING HEAVY LETTERS

```
ABJOINT  ANALYZEr AZOTISE  BOXHAUL  CONJOINt DIALYZEr DISJECT  DOCQUET
EXPIATE  EXPUNCT  EXPUNGEr EXSCIND  EXTRUDEr INJUNCT  INQUERE  JALOUSE
JELLIFY  JEOPARDy JOLLIFY  LACQUEY  LIQUATE  LIQUIFY  OXALATE  OXIDATE
PARQUET  PASQUIL> PICQUET  POLLAXE  POSTFIX  QUACKLE  QUIDDLEr QUIESCE
QUINCHE  REJOURN  REQUERE  SCHMOOZe SCHMOOZy SHMOOZE  SNOOZLE  SPREAZE
SPREEZE  SPULZIE= SQUIDGE  SQUINCH  SQUINNY* SQUOOSHy TELEFAX  TRAJECT
TUILZIE= WHAIZLE  WHEEZLE  ZINCIFY  ZINKIFY  ZIPLOCK  ZOMBIFY
```

VERBS ENDING IN 'ISE' WHICH HAVE 'IZE' EQUIVALENTS

AGATISE	*AGENISE*	ANODISE	APPRISEr	ATHEISE	BROMISE	COALISE	COGNISEr
CYANISE	*CYCLISE*	DOCKISE	DUALISE	EBONISE	ECHOISE	EGOTISE	ELEGISE
EROTISE	GALLISE	*GRECISE*	HEROISE	ICONISE	IRIDISE	IRONISE	KYANISE
LAICISE	MYTHISE	OBELISE	OZONISEr	PECTISE	PEPTISEr	POETISEr	UNITISEr

OTHER VERBS ENDING IN 'IFY'

ACETIFY	ANGLIFY	BEATIFY	BRUTIFY	CAPRIFY	CARNIFY	COALIFY	*CORNIFY*
DAMNIFY	DANDIFY	DENSIFY	DULCIFY	ICONIFY	LITHIFY	*MATTIFY*	MERCIFY
METRIFY	MICRIFY	MOLLIFY	MUNDIFY	NIGRIFY	NITRIFY	PLEBIFY	PONTIFY
PROSIFY	RUSSIFY	SACRIFY	SCARIFY	SCORIFY	TACKIFY	THURIFY	TIPSIFY
TORRIFY	VERBIFY	VERSIFY	VITRIFY				

OTHER VERBS

ABREACT	ABROOKE	ABSCIND	ABSCISE	ACTUATE	ACYLATE	ADHIBIT	ADPRESS
ADULATE	AGGRACE	AGGRADE	AGGRATE	AGGRESS	ALIMENT	ALLEDGE	ALLEGGE
ARREEDEd	ASPERGEr	ASSEVER	ASSIEGE	ASSWAGE	ATTRIST	ATTUITE	AUREOLE
AUSFORM							

BACKFIT>	BARTEND	BATFOWL	BATTILL	BAUCHLE	BEDUNCE	BEKNAVE	*BELLOCK*
BENIGHT	BESEEKEd	BLETHER	BLOOSME	BOLLOCK	BRANGLE	*BREENGE*	*BREINGE*
BRISKEN	*BRODDLE*	BROIDERy	BROMATE	BURNISH	BURTHEN		

CAROMEL>	CASEATE	CHAMFER	CHAMOIS	CHAUNGE	CHELATE	CHIRRUPy	CHIVARI+
CHIVARI=	CHUNNER	CLANGOR	CLARION	CLAUGHT	CLOTURE	COHIBIT	COMBUST
COMPAND	COMPART	COMPEAR	COMPEER	COMPLOT>	COMPORT	CONDOLEr	CONFUTEr
CONGREE	CONGRUE	CONNOTE	CONSTER	*CONSPUE*	CONTEMN	CONTUND	CONTUSE
CONVOKEr	CORNROW	CORNUTE	CORRADE	COSTEAN	COTTISE	CRAMPON	CRISPEN
CROODLE	CUIRASS	CUITTLE					

DARRAINe	DARRAYN	DAUNDER	DAUNTON	DEBAUCH	DEBOUCHe	DECRYPT	DECUPLE
DEGAUSS	DEHISCE	DEMERSE	DEPRAVEr	DERAIGN	DESPOND	DESTINE	DETERGEr
DETRUDE	DIALYSEr	DIREMPT	DISCEPT	DISCERP	DISGEST	DISPONEe	DISPONEr
DISPREDd	DISPRED>	DISSERT	DISTAIN	*DIVULSE*	DOGSLED>	DOGTROT>	DRYBEATd
DRYWALL							

EARBASH	ELECTROn	ELOCUTE	EMBOGUE	EMPAIRE	EMPAYRE	*ENDPLAY*	ENFELON
ENGRAIL	ENGULPH	ENNOBLEr	ENOUNCE	ENRHEUM	ENTAYLE	EPILATE	EPURATE
ESCALOPe	ESCHEAT	ESLOYNE	ESTREAT	ESTREPE	EVIRATE	EVITATE	EVOCATE

FELLATE	FENAGLE	FERRULE	FESTOON	FILIATE	FINAGLEr	FLAUGHT	FLECKER
FLEHMEN	FLEMISH	FLORUIT	FLOUNCE	FLYBLOWd	FLYBLOWn	FOLIATE	FORSLOE=
FULMINE	FURBISH	FURCATE					

GADROON	GAINSAYd	GALOCHE	GALUMPH	GAMBADO	GAMBADO+	GANTLET	GAVOTTE
GHILLIE	GILLNET>	GITTERN	GODROON	GRADATE	GRADDAN	GREATEN	GRUNTLE
GUARISH	GUDGEON	GUERDON	GUESTEN	GUMSHOE=	GUTTATE		

HACKNEY	HAGRIDEd	HAGRIDEr	HANDSEL	HANDSEL>	HEARKEN	HOSANNAh

7. Seven-Letter Words

```
ILLAPSE   IMBURSE   IMPLETE   IMPREGN   INDORSEe  INDORSEr  INFLECT   INGULPH
INHAUST   INHERCE   INTHRAL>  INTHRALl  INTROFY   INVEIGH   IRISATE

KAMERAD   KARANGA   KNEVELL   KURBASH

LAMBASTe  LEISTER   LIBRATE   LICHTLY   LIPREADd  LOGROLL   LOUNDER   LOWBALL

MAISTER   MARCONI=  MAULGRE   MAUNDER   MEDEVAC   MEDEVAC&  MEDIVAC   MEDIVAC&
MIDWIVE   MINIATE   MINNICK   MINNOCK   MOBCAST   MOITHER   MONOSKI   MORDANT
MORTISEr  MOWBURNt  MULLION   MULTUREr  MURGEON   MURTHER   MYSPACE

NECROSE   NICTATE   NIGGARD   NONPLUS   NONPLUS>  NONPROS>  NONSUIT   NORTHERn
NOTCHEL   NOTCHEL>  NOURSLE   NOUSELL

OBTRUDEr  OCTUPLEt  OCTUPLEx  OLOGOAN   OUTHYRE   OUTMODE

PALAVER   PANTILE   PARBAKE   PARBOIL   PARROCK   PENTISE   PERCUSS   PERDURE
PERFUSE   PERIWIG>  PERMUTE   PERTAKEd  PERTAKEn  PHILTER   PHILTRE   PHONATE
PHRENSY   PICKEER   PLAYACT   PLENISH   PLICATE   PLOUTER   PLOWTER   PODCAST
POLLARD   PONIARD   PORLOCK   PORRECT   PORTAGE   POTBOIL   POURSEW   POURSUE
PRAUNCE   PREASSE   PRELECT   PREVENE   PROCTOR   PROLATE   PRONATE   PRORATE
PROSECT   PROTEND   PROVINE

RABATTE   RATTOON   REALLIE   RECOYLE   RECUILE   REDBAIT   REDLINEr  REDOUND
REFLATE   REGREDE   RELLISH   REMERCY   RENAGUE   REPLEVY   REPRIVE   REPRYVE
RETRATE   RIGHTEN   ROISTER   ROSETTE   RUBICON   RUINATE

SALTATE   SATIATE   SCAMBLEr  SCEDULE   SCEPTER   SCHLUMPy  SCHMEAR   SCHMEER
SCHMOOSe  SCHNORR   SCOWDER   SCRAIGH   SCRAUGH   SCREEVEr  SCREIGH   SCRIEVE
SCROUGEr  SCUMBLE   SEALIFT   SELVAGEe  SERIATE   SERRATE   SERUEWE   SERVEWE
SHEBEEN   SHELLAC&  SHELLACk  SHMOOSE   SHOGGLE   SHOOGIE=  SHOOGLE   SHRIEVE
SIGMATE   SINUATE   SKELDER   SKELLIE*  SKIDDOO   SKITTERy  SKREEGH   SKREIGH
SKRIECH   SKRIEGH   SKUTTLE   SKYSURF   SLEEKEN   SLICKEN   SLIDDERy  SLOCKEN
SMICKER   SMOODGE   SNIFTER   SNIRTLE   SNOTTERy  SOLVATE   SPAIRGE   SPANCEL
SPANCEL>  SPELDER   SPELUNK   SPLATCH   SPLOOSH   SPRIGHT   SPULYIE=  STARKEN
STEEPEN   STIDDIE=  STOITER   STOUTEN   STRAYVE   STRIATE   STRODLE   SUBDUCE
SUBCOOL   SUBDUCT   SUBEDIT   SUBJOIN   SUBLATE   SUBPENA   SUBSUME   SUBTEND
SUBVENE   SULFATE   SURBATE   SURVEIL   SURVIEW   SUSPIRE   SWINDGE   SWINGLE
SYNAPSE

TALLAGE   TALLYHO   TAMBOURa  TELPHER   TITRATE   TOMFOOL   TONSURE   TOPWORK
TORPEFY   TORREFY   TRACHLE   TRADUCEr  TRINDLE   TRISECT   TUILYIE=  TUMESCE
TUTOYER   TWEEDLEr  TYRANNE

ULULATE   UPHOORD   USUCAPT

VALANCE   VALUATE   VANDYKE   VARIATE   VERMEIL   VICIATE   VITIATE   VODCAST
```

WAMPISH	WARSTLEr	WAYFAREr	WAYMARK	WAYMENT	*WEBCAST*	WHAISLE	WHEEDLEr
WHEENGE	WHEEPLE	WHERRET	*WHERRIT*	WHICKER	WHIMPLE	WHIRRET	WHOMBLE
WIRETAP>	WRASTLE						

YCLEEPE	YELLOCH	YOUTHEN

7.3.3 NOUNS BY COMMON ENDINGS

ADE

BOUTADE	CHAMADE	COUVADE	ESTRADE	FOUGADE	GAMBADE	LIMEADE	*PARKADE*
PASSADE	ROULADE	SCALADE	TORNADE	TORSADE	TRIBADE		

AGE

ABUSAGE	AJUTAGE	APANAGEd	ARRIAGE	AULNAGEr	BEERAGE	BOSCAGE	BOSKAGE
BREWAGE	BROCAGE	BROKAGE	BULKAGE	BUOYAGE	BURGAGE	CARTAGE	CENTAGE
COMPAGE	CORDAGE	CORNAGE	CORSAGE	COWHAGE	CRANAGE	CUTTAGE	DOCKAGE
DRAYAGE	DUNNAGE	*ECOTAGE*	ESCUAGE	ETALAGE	FALDAGE	FARDAGE	FLOTAGE
FLOWAGE	FOGGAGE	GUIDAGE	GUNNAGE	HAYLAGE	HEADAGE	HERBAGEd	HIREAGE
KEELAGE	LAIRAGE	LASTAGE	LEAFAGE	LIGNAGE	LINEAGE	LINKAGE	LOCKAGE
MELTAGE	MILLAGE	MINTAGE	MOCKAGE	MOORAGE	MOULAGE	OUVRAGE	PANNAGE
PAWNAGE	PAYSAGE	PEERAGE	PEONAGE	PIERAGE	PLUSAGE	PONDAGE	PONTAGE
POTTAGE	PRIMAGE	PRISAGE	QUAYAGE	*RAILAGE*	REMUAGE	ROOTAGE	SACKAGE
SCALAGE	SCAVAGEr	SCUTAGE	*SEPTAGE*	SERFAGE	SINKAGE	SOILAGE	SONDAGE
SPINAGE	TANKAGE	TANNAGE	TENTAGE	THANAGE	THENAGE	TILLAGE	TOLLAGE
TRUCAGE	TUNNAGE	UNITAGE	VENDAGE	VENTAGE	VIDUAGE	VITRAGE	VORLAGE
WAFTAGE	WAINAGE	WANTAGE	WARPAGE	WATTAGE	*WEBPAGE*	WEFTAGE	WINDAGE
WORDAGE							

AL *excluding 'IAL'*

ABETTAL	ABUTTAL	ADRENAL	ALLHEAL	AMYGDALa	AMYGDALe	ARRAYAL	AUSTRAL
BEDERAL	BIMETAL	BORSTALl	BRINJAL	BUTYRAL	CAPORAL	CERAMAL	CHLORAL
COAEVAL	COEQUAL	DEISEAL	DEPOSAL	DEVISAL	DIEDRAL	*ETHANAL*	EXCUSAL
EXPOSAL	FRACTAL	*GLYPTAL*	GOMERAL	HUMERAL	JUVENAL	KURSAAL	LACTEAL
LANITAL	*MACERAL*	METICAL	MISTRAL	NAGMAAL	NARWHALe	ORDINAL	OVOIDAL
PALATAL	PASCHAL	PEDOCAL	PEREGAL	PEYTRAL	POUNDAL	PURSUAL	QUETZAL
QUITTAL	RECUSAL	REFUTAL	REPOSALl	RETIRAL	REVISAL	RORQUAL	RUDERAL
SAHIWAL	*SECONAL*	SHIMAAL	SPOUSAL	SUBDUAL	SUBGOAL	SYNODAL	*TARSEAL*
UPRISAL	VEGETAL	VENTRAL	VERONAL	WADMAAL			

AN *excluding 'IAN'*

ALLOXAN	*ANATMAN*	ATAGHAN	BARACAN	BARCHANe	BARKHAN	BODHRAN	BRECHAN
BROCHAN	CAPELAN	CATAPAN	CATERAN	CLAYPAN	COURLAN	DARSHAN	DECUMAN
DEXTRAN	DIPNOAN	DISHPAN	FIREPAN	*FREEGAN*	*FRUCTAN*	GAMELAN	HABITANt
HANUMAN	HARDPAN	HARIJAN	HEXOSAN	*HOUNGAN*	INDICANt	KNEEPAN	*LEGUAAN*
MOHICAN	OOLAKAN	ORTOLAN	OTTOMAN	OULAKAN	PEMICAN	PULLMAN	QUARTAN
SALTPAN	SARAFAN	SHAITAN	SHEBEAN	SHEITAN	SKIDPAN	SOROBAN	SOULDAN
SOYBEAN	SPORRAN	STEWPAN	SUBCLAN	SWANPAN	TAILFAN	TELERAN	*TRIPTANe*
TULCHAN	URETHANe	WANIGAN	XANTHAN	YAKHDAN	YATAGAN	ZYMOSAN	

7. Seven-Letter Words

ANE

ABTHANE COWBANE DOGBANE DOGVANE FLYBANE HENBANE HEPTANE HOGMANE
LINDANE MIRBANE MYRBANE PENTANE PHYTANE SOUTANE TERRANE TSIGANE
TZIGANE

ANT

ALICANT AMARANTh CALMANT COURANTe COURANTo ETCHANT FONDANT FORMANT
GARDANT GELLANT GEOMANT IMITANT INTRANT ODORANT OPERANT OXIDANT
PISSANT RESIANT SALTANT SPIRANT *TAGGANT* TITRANT VERSANT ZEALANT

AR

ALCAZAR ALLOBAR AMILDAR ANNULAR ANTBEAR AUTOCARp BOLIVAR CALAMARi
CALAMARy CHADDAR CHEDDARy CHOBDAR CHUDDAR COUGUAR CUDBEAR DAYSTAR
DRAWBAR ESCOLAR EYEWEAR *FACEBAR* FELSPAR FENITAR FLATCAR FOOTBAR
FORECAR GYROCAR HANDCARt HANDJAR *HEELBAR* JACAMAR JAMADAR JANIZARy
JEMADAR JEMIDAR KHADDAR KILOBAR KOFTGARi LASHKAR *LEQUEAR* LUPANAR
MAILCAR MEGABAR MOOKTAR MUKHTAR ORDINARy PALIKAR PATAMAR PHEAZAR
PICAMAR RAILCARd REALGAR *ROLLBAR* SAMBHAR SAMOVAR SEMITAR *SEROVAR*
SHALWAR SIDEBAR SIMITAR SIMULAR *SLIOTAR* SUBADAR SUBEDAR *SUNSTAR*
SYMITARe TANADAR *TASKBAR* TEMPLAR TOLLBAR TRAMCAR TROCHAR TUSHKAR
TUTELARy TWISCAR TYPEBAR *WEBINAR*

ARD *excluding 'WARD'*

BEEYARD BEGHARD BELGARD BOGGARD BOLLARD BROCARD DASTARDy FOULARD
GOLIARDy GUISARD GURNARD HALYARD INNYARD LAGGARD LANIARD LANYARD
MALLARD MANSARD POCHARD POCKARD POULARDe REYNARD TAILARD TANYARD
UNITARD *WINNARD*

ARY+

ALVEARY+ BILIARY+ BULLARY+ CALVARY+ DENTARY+ FEODARY+ FEUDARY+ GRAMARY+
GRAMARYe GRANARY+ JAGGARY+ LANIARY+ OSSUARY+ OSTIARY+ PEATARY+ PESSARY+
PETRARY+ PISCARY+ PLENARY+ QUINARY+ SCENARY+ SECTARY+ SIGNARY+ TERNARY+
TOPIARY+ TURBARY+ ZEDOARY+

ASE

AMIDASE AMYLASE APYRASE CASEASE *CASPASE* DIABASE DIAPASE ENOLASE
EUCLASE *FANBASE* ISOBASE LACTASE MALTASE OXIDASE PECTASE RENNASE
SUCRASE SURBASEd URICASE

ATE

AGEMATE AIRDATE AMIRATE CANTATE CAPRATE CAUDATEd CEDRATE CHOLATE
CILIATEd CITRATEd CYANATE DEALATEd DEODATE DOGEATE *ENDGATE* EXUDATE
FERRATE *FIBRATE* GALLATE INGRATE KHANATE LABIATEd LITHATE MALEATE
MURIATEd NEONATE NIOBATE OSMIATE OUTGATE PECTATE PHENATE PHORATE
PICRATEd RECHATE SOCIATE SORBATE STOMATE TANNATE TOLUATE VIRGATE
VULGATE ZINCATE

BOY
CALLBOY *DEADBOY* FOOTBOY GOWNBOY HAUTBOY HERDBOY HOMEBOY *LIFTBOY*
LINKBOY SANDBOY SHOPBOY TALLBOY

DOM
BOSSDOM CHEFDOM CZARDOM DOGEDOM DOLLDOM DUKEDOM EARLDOM FOGYDOM
GEEKDOM GURUDOM HALIDOMe HEIRDOM HOBODOM JARLDOM RHABDOMe SELFDOM
SERFDOM TSARDOM TZARDOM WIFEDOM

EAU
BANDEAUx CHAPEAUx CORBEAU MANTEAUx MOINEAU PONCEAUx ROULEAUx TABLEAUx
TONNEAUx

EE
ABORTEE ADOPTEE ALIENEE *AUDITEE* AWARDEE BANSHEE BHISTEE BOURREE
BUKSHEE CALIPEE CHORDEE CHUTNEE COWTREE DRAFTEE ELECTEE EVICTEE
FILAREE FREEBEE *FRISBEE* GALILEE GEECHEE GRANTEE GUARDEE HICATEE
HONOREE KILLDEEr KIMCHEE LEECHEE LIBELEE MACHREE MANATEE ORDINEE
PERIGEE PUGAREE PUGGREE QUASHEE RATAFEE SPONDEE STANDEE THUGGEE
VOUCHEE WHANGEE

EEN
ARSHEEN *BAWNEEN* BUCKEEN *CARBEEN* COLLEEN CRUBEEN DASHEEN DUDHEEN
GOMBEEN JACKEEN KAMSEEN NANKEEN NARCEEN PEEBEEN POSTEEN POTHEEN
POTTEEN PRETEEN RATTEEN SHONEEN SUBTEEN TERREEN

EL
AEROGEL *BILEVEL* *BIOFUEL* BURRHEL CALOMEL CAMBREL CARAVEL CHARNEL
CHATTEL CHESSEL CHUNNEL COLUMEL CORONEL COSTREL COWHEEL CUSTREL
DAMOSEL DAMOZEL DOGGREL DOTTREL DREIDEL EVANGELy FARTHEL FLOATEL
FRESNEL FUTCHEL GAMBREL GANGREL GOMEREL GRAPNEL GRAUPEL HAVEREL
JEZEBEL *KNEIDEL* LANGREL LIMACEL LIONCEL MANDREL MANTEEL *MICHAEL*
OENOMEL OINOMEL PEDICEL PEYTREL POITREL RADICEL RASCHEL ROUNDEL
SHTETEL SPIEGEL SPIGNEL STANIEL STANNEL STANYEL STEMPEL *STOKVEL*
SYNFUEL TINCHEL TRESSEL WASTREL WIMBREL

EN *excluding 'EEN'*
ACROGEN AGNOMEN ALBUMEN *AUTOPEN* *BREDREN* BULLPEN CERUMEN *CHORTEN*
CITHREN CRYOGENy DURAMEN ENDOGENy FLANNEN FORAMEN GREISEN GREYHEN
HEGUMENe HEGUMENy HUMOGEN INDIGENe INDIGENt IONOGEN KEROGEN LUCIGEN
LYSOGENy MITOGEN MUCIGEN MUTAGEN NETIZEN ONCOGENe *PARABEN* POCOSEN
PYROGEN RONTGEN SAMISEN SARSDEN STOLLEN SWIDDEN TWITTEN VAURIEN
WHEATEN WITCHEN WOODHEN XYLOGEN ZYMOGENe

ENT
ABLUENT ANTIENT AUDIENT BUTMENT CHOLENT COAGENT DILUENT EXIGENT
FITMENT HUTMENT MANRENT MORDENT PENDENT ODDMENT PSCHENT SAPIENT
SARMENTa SEQUENT SORBENT SUBRENT TALLENT TOTIENT UNGUENTa VARMENT

7. Seven-Letter Words

ER *extensions of verbs*

ABORTER	ADAPTER	ADORNER	AGISTER	ALIENER	ALIGNER	ALLAYER	ALTERER
AMASSER	ANNOYER	ARMORER	ARRAYER	ASSAYER	AUGURER	*AVERTER*	BATCHER
BAULKER	*BELAYER*	BELCHER	BENCHER	BEVELER	BLEATER	*BLITZER*	BLOATER
BLURTER	BOTCHERy	BOUNDER	BRANNER	BROILER	BRUITER	BURSTER	CAPERER
CAROLER	CAULKER	CAVILER	CHANTER	CHEEPER	CHIRPER	CHOMPER	CHURNER
CLAIMER	CLASPER	CLOUTER	COLORER	COMPTER	COUGHER	COVERER	COVETER
COZENER	CRIMPER	CROAKER	CROWDER	CROWNER	CRUMBER	CUPELER	DALLIER
DECAYER	DECOYER	DECRIER	DEIFIER	DELAYER	DIALLER	DISCOER	DITCHER
DOLLIER	DRAGGER	DRAWLER	DROWNER	DUELLER	EDIFIER	ELOINER	EMITTER
ENDOWER	ENJOYER	ENTERER	ESSAYER	EXALTER	FAGOTER	*FAITHER*	FAVORER
FECHTER	FEIGNER	FILCHER	FLEERER	FLESHER	FLIRTER	FLOODER	FLOORER
FLOSSER	FLOUTER	FOCUSER	FOISTER	FORAYER	FORGOER	FRILLER	FROWNER
FRUITERy	FUELLER	GLEAMER	GLOSSER	GNASHER	GRAINER	GRASSER	GRIFTER
GROUPER	GRUELER	GRUNTER	GUARDER	GUESSER	HEISTER	HOISTER	HONORER
HOUNDER	HOVERER	HURRIER	INLAYER	JEWELER	JOINTER	JOLLYER	KNEADER
KNEELER	KNOLLER	KNOTTER	KOTOWER	LABELER	LASSOER	LAUGHER	LEACHER
LEVELER	LIBELER	LIMITER	LIVENER	LUNCHER	LURCHER	LYNCHER	MARRIER
MATCHER	MISDOER	MITERER	MODELER	MOUCHER	MOULTER	MOUNTER	MUNCHER
NOINTER	NOTCHER	OMITTER	ORBITER	OUTDOER	OUTGOER	*PARRIER*	PARTYER
PATCHERy	PEACHER	*PEDALER*	PERCHERy	PIVOTER	PLAITER	PLEATER	PLONKER
POINDER	PREENER	PRESSER	PRINKER	PROGGER	PROULER	QUACKERy	QUASHER
QUELLER	QUERIER	QUESTER	QUILTER	QUOITER	RALLIER	RAVELER	RAVENER
REACHER	REIFIER	RELAXER	RENEWER	REPLIER	RESINER	RIPENER	RIVETER
ROSINER	SALLIER	SAVORER	SCALDER	*SCARFER*	SCAUPER	SCOWLER	SCREWER
SCUDDER	SCULKER	*SHAGGER*	SHARKER	SHEDDER	SHEETER	SHIRKER	SHUCKER
SHUNNER	SIGHTER	SKIRTER	*SLANTER*	SLEDDER	SLURPER	SMACKER	SMEARER
SMELLER	*SNACKER*	SNARLER	SNEERER	SNORTER	SPANKER	SPEARER	SPEEDER
SPIELER	SPILLER	SPOOFERy	SPURRER	*SPURTER*	STAINER	STANDER	STOCKER
STOOKER	*STORMER*	STRAYER	STREWER	STROWER	STROYER	STUMPER	*SUGARER*
SWAMPER	SWOONER	SWOOPER	SWORDER	TABORER	TALLIER	TAPERER	TENONER
THIGGER	TORCHERe	TREATER	TRILLER	TRUSSER	TRUSTER	TWANGER	UNIFIER
USURPER	VAPORER	VENOMER	VOMITER	WAGERER	WAGONER	WAISTER	WAKENER
WALTZER	WAULKER	WAVERER	WEIGHER	WELCHER	WELSHER	WENCHER	WHETTER
WHIRLER	WIDENER	WIELDER	WOOLDER	WOUNDER	WREAKER	YACHTER	YIELDER

ER *other, excluding 'IER' & 'STER'*

ACROTER	ALLOVER	ALMONER	AQUAFER	*APTAMER*	ARMIGERo	BACONER	BIGENER
BILAYER	BLUCHER	BOULTER	BOURDER	BOWLDER	BURGHER	BYWONER	CADAVER
CAGANER	CALIBER	CALIVER	CALOYER	CENTNER	CHALDER	CHANNER	*CHARVER*
CHAUMER	CHIGGER	CHUDDER	CLOWDER	COGENER	CORULER	COULTER	CROFTER
CRULLER	CUTOVER	DIETHER	DIMETER	DIOPTER	DRABLER	DROGHER	EXCIMER
FEMITER	FILACER	FILAZER	FLINDER	FUEHRER	GAULTER	GRANFER	*GRIEFER*
GRISTER	GUILDER	GUTCHER	HANAPER	INGENER	IONOMER	JOINDER	KEGELER
KLEZMER	KREUZER	KRULLER	*KRUMPER*	LAMETER	LAMIGER	LAMITER	LANDLER
LAYOVER	LEIDGER	LEISLER	*LIVEYERe*	LORIMER	LORINER	LUCIFER	LYMITER
MAHSEER	MAUTHER	MAWTHER	METAYER	MINEVER	MINIVER	MONIKER	MYNHEER
ODALLER	OSSETER	PARDNER	PILCHER	PILSNER	PORIFER	POUFTER	POULTER
PUTCHER	ROSAKER	ROTIFER	*ROWOVER*	RUNOVER	SCORPER	SCOWRER	SCUDLER

SELTZER	SHICKER	*SKANGER*	SKEETER	SKUDLER	SLENTER	SPADGER	SPECTER
STUIVER	STURMER	SUMPTER	*SWEDGER*	TANAGER	TUSHKER	*TWEENER*	*TWOCKER*
UDALLER	VELIGER	VENERER	VINTNER	VITAMER	VOCODER	WOOFTER	YOUNKER

ERY+

BEANERY+	BOOTERY+	CATTERY+	DUNCERY+	ESOTERY+	FAGGERY+	FIGGERY+	FOOLERY+
GAUDERY+	GOOSERY+	GRAPERY+	HUCKERY+	JOOKERY+	JOUKERY+	KNAVERY+	LEAFERY+
MICKERY+	MONKERY+	PLUMERY+	POOVERY+	PUGGERY+	RAGGERY+	RETTERY+	ROOKERY+
TRIPERY+	TUSHERY+	ZOOPERY+					

ET *excluding 'LET'*

ARBORETa	BACKSET	BEAUFET	BLUSHET	BONESET	BRASSET	BRISKET	BYCOKET
CALUMET	CHIPSET	CIGARET	CLAPNET	CRAMPET	CRESSET	CROWNET	*DARKNET*
DRUGGET	*EVERNET*	FLACKET	FLEURET	FRESHET	FRISKET	GUICHET	HAROSETh
IODURET	ISOHYET	JACONET	KEEPNET	KNESSET	LATCHET	LAZARET	LEVERET
LINCHET	*LOCKSET*	LYNCHET	*MATCHET*	MERCHET	MINARET	MINIVET	MISDIET
MOONSET	NAILSET	PLACKET	PLASHET	POMFRET	QUANNET	REMANET	RESOJET
RIVERET	ROCQUET	SAKERET	SALICETa	*SANGEET*	SARSNET	SATINET	SEAMSET
SKIRRET	SMICKET	SNICKET	SOLERET	TABARET	TABINET	TABORET	*TOOLSET*
TRAMPET	TWINJET	TWINSET	VILAYET	WATCHET	WHISKET	WHITRET	

ETTE

AILETTE	ARIETTE	AVIETTE	BLUETTE	BUVETTE	CUNETTE	CUVETTE	DINETTE
FOUETTE	FUMETTE	GALETTE	GENETTE	LADETTE	LAYETTE	LORETTE	LUNETTE
MINETTE	MOFETTE	MUSETTE	NAVETTE	*NEDETTE*	NONETTE	PALETTE	PROETTE
SYRETTE	TONETTE	VEDETTE	VIDETTE				

EUR

DANSEUR	DOUCEUR	FARCEUR	FLANEUR	FRISEUR	PRIMEUR	PRONEUR	REMUEUR
SABREUR	*TRACEUR*						

EY

BACKSEY	BOLONEY	CHANTEY	CHARLEY	CHIMLEY	CHUMLEY	COMFREY	*DOOBREY*
DOVEKEY	FLUNKEY	*FRAWZEY*	JEEPNEY	KOUPREY	LAMPREY	LANGLEY	*MOCKNEY*
ORPHREY	PAISLEY	PALFREY	PASSKEY	PIGSNEY	PUSSLEY	SHANTEY	SHAWLEY
SHEENEY*	SPINNEY	SPOONEY*	SPURREY	STEPNEY	SWANKEY*	SWEENEY	SWINNEY
TOCKLEY	TRAWLEY	WHIMSEY*	WOOLSEY				

FISH+

BATFISH+	BOXFISH+	CODFISH+	COWFISH+	DOGFISH+	GARFISH+	GEMFISH+	JEWFISH+
LUBFISH+	MUDFISH+	OARFISH+	PANFISH+	PIGFISH+	PINFISH+	RATFISH+	REDFISH+
SAWFISH+	SUNFISH+	TUBFISH+					

FLY+

BEETFLY+	*BUSHFLY*+	CORNFLY+	DEERFLY+	DROPFLY+	GALLFLY+	GLOWFLY+	SHADFLY+
SHOOFLY+	*TAILFLY*+	*WORMFLY*+					

7. Seven-Letter Words

FUL

BOOKFUL	CAGEFUL	CROPFULl	DISHFUL	GUTSFUL	*HEADFUL*	HORNFUL	KISTFUL
LOCKFUL	LUNGFUL	NESTFUL	*PAGEFUL*	PAILFUL	PALMFUL	POKEFUL	RACKFUL
SACKFUL	*SHEDFUL*	SHIPFUL	SHOPFUL	SKEPFUL	SKINFUL	TENTFUL	TRAYFUL
TUBEFUL	VIALFUL	WAMEFUL					

HEAD

AIRHEAD	*BEDHEAD*	BIGHEAD	BOWHEAD	CUPHEAD	GODHEAD	JARHEAD	JUGHEAD
NETHEAD	PITHEAD	POTHEAD	RAGHEAD	RAWHEAD	SAPHEAD	SUBHEAD	TOWHEAD
WEBHEAD							

HOOD

APEHOOD	CATHOOD	CUBHOOD	ELFHOOD	GODHOOD	*LADHOOD*	SONHOOD

IA

ABOULIA	ABROSIA	ACAPNIA	ACEQUIA	ACHOLIA	ACRASIA	ACTINIAe	ACTINIAn
ADIPSIA	*AGEUSIA*	AGNOSIA	*AKRASIA*	ALBIZIA	ALGESIA	AMENTIA	ANALGIA
ANERGIA	ANGARIA	ANOPSIA	ANOSMIA	APHAGIA	*APHAKIA*	APHASIAc	APHONIA
APLASIA	APRAXIA	ARCADIAn	ARGYRIA	ASTASIA	ASTERIA	ATRESIA	ATROPIA
AURELIAn	BANKSIA	*BARTSIA*	*BATAVIA*	BOHEMIAn	BOLIVIA	BONAMIA	BORONIA
BULIMIAc	*BUMELIA*	CAMISIA	CELOSIA	CLARKIA	COMITIAl	DAPHNIA	DATARIA
DAVIDIA	DECURIA	DEUTZIA	*DIANOIA*	*DIASCIA*	DOULEIA	DYSURIA	*ECTASIA*
ECTOPIA	ENTASIA	EPISCIA	EQUINIA	EUGENIA	EULOGIAe	*EUTAXIA*	EUTEXIA
EXURBIA	FELICIA	*FUNCKIA*	GALABIAh	GAZANIA	*GIARDIA*	GODETIA	*HRYVNIA*
HYPOXIA	IGNATIA	INDICIAl	LATAKIA	LEWISIA	*LIPEMIA*	*LIPURIA*	LOGANIA
MAHONIA	MALACIA	MELODIA	MEROPIA	MONILIAl	MORPHIA	MUDIRIA	MYALGIA
NEMESIA	NOTITIAe	OLEARIA	ONYCHIA	OPUNTIA	OTALGIA	PELORIAn	PENTHIA
POGONIA	POLYNIA	PYAEMIA	PYREXIAl	QUASSIA	RAOULIA	RATAFIA	ROBINIA
ROSALIA	RUELLIA	SCAGLIA	SCANDIA	SENOPIA	SEQUOIA	SHORTIA	SILESIA
SINOPIA	STHENIA	SYNOVIAl	TILAPIA	TITANIA	TOXEMIA	TUTANIA	URAEMIA
VALONIA	VEDALIA	VIREMIA	WOODSIA	XERASIA			

IAL

DECRIAL	GHARIAL	GREMIAL	PAIRIAL	PLUVIAL

IAN

CRUSIAN	CYPRIAN	DULCIANa	ETESIAN	FUSTIAN	GENTIAN	GRECIAN	HALLIAN
HASBIAN	MARTIAN	SALPIAN	SAURIAN	SUIDIAN	THERIAN	

IC

ALEMBIC	ALOETIC	AMNESIC	AUXETIC	AVIONIC	BALDRICk	BAUDRICk	BAWDRIC
BULIMIC	DEMOTIC	DEONTIC	EIDETIC	EKISTIC	ENTERIC	ERISTIC	EUGENIC
FLUERIC	GENOMIC	GEORGIC	GLYPTIC	GNOSTIC	HEDONIC	HEMATIC	HEPATICa
ILLOGIC	KENOTIC	KERAMIC	KINESIC	MELANIC	PARETIC	PELAGIC	PHRENIC
POLEMIC	PROOTIC	PSIONIC	PTARMIC	PYRRHIC	QUADRIC	QUANTIC	QUARTIC
QUINTIC	STYPTIC	TABETIC	*TELEPIC*	TETANIC	THEORIC	TONETIC	TRIADIC
TRIATIC	ZETETIC	ZYMOTIC					

ID *excluding 'OID'*

ANNELID	*ANOBIID*	ANTACID	ARANEID	ARCTIID	ASCARID	ASTERID	BRUCHID
CAMELID	CARABID	CAROTID	CEPHEID	CHLORIDe	*CHYTRID*	CLUPEID	*CORIXID*
DAPHNID	DIAGRID	DIAPSID	ENERGID	EPACRID	EPEIRID	FLUORIDe	GLOCHID
HOMINID	HYDATID	ICTERID	IGUANID	KATYDID	LEPORID	MONACID	NOCTUID
NONACID	OCEANID	OXYACID	PAGURID	PAROTID	PERACID	PEROXIDe	PHASMID
PHYLLID	PLASMID	PLASTID	PSYLLID	PYRALID	SATYRID	SCIARID	SCIURID
SEAMAID	SIGANID	SILURID	*SKIDLID*	SULPHIDe	SYLPHIDe	SYRPHID	TABANID
TRIACID	TRIOXIDe						

IDE

AIRSIDE	ALCAIDE	BASTIDE	BIOCIDE	CARBIDE	DAYSIDE	DEICIDE	DEPSIDE
DIAMIDE	EPOXIDE	FARSIDE	*LEGSIDE*	NUCLIDE	OVICIDE	OZONIDE	RAPHIDE
RIPTIDE	TRITIDE	URANIDE					

IE

BANSHIE	BEARDIE*	BEASTIE	BLASTIE*	*BLOCKIE*	BOLSHIE*	BRASSIE*	BRICKIE*
BRULYIE	BRULZIE	CAMOGIE	CHALLIE	CHANTIE	CHARLIEr	CHARPIE	CHEAPIE
CHINKIE*	CHOOKIE	*CHORRIE*	CLUDGIE	COONTIE	CREEPIE*	CROWDIE	CRUISIE
CRUIZIE	DHURRIE	DOMINIE	*DOOBRIE*	DOVEKIE	DRUGGIE*	*EATERIE*	*EUGARIE*
FEDARIE	*FLANNIE*	FLATTIE	*FLEECIE*	FLOSSIE*	*FLUNKIE*	FOOTSIE	FOUDRIE
FREEBIE	*FRESHIE*	GAUDGIE	GHOULIE	*GLEENIE*	INSANIE	JACKSIE	JOHNNIE
LITTLIE	*MUNTRIE*	NAGAPIE	NARTJIE	NITCHIE	NITERIE	PIGSNIE	PLISKIE
PLOTTIE*	POLONIE	POUSSIE	PREEMIE	PRESSIE	PROSSIE	PROSTIE	QUASHIE
QUEENIE*	QUEYNIE	RAMILIE	REALTIE	REMANIE	RIEMPIE	ROTCHIE	ROUGHIE
SCHEMIE	SCOTTIE	SCRAPIE	SHARPIE	SHAWLIE	SHEENIE*	SHELTIE	SHORTIE
SKOLLIE	SMARTIE	SMYTRIE	SNOTTIE*	*SOSATIE*	SPOTTIE*	STAGGIE*	STARNIE
STASHIE	STEAMIE*	STEELIE*	STISHIE	*STOMPIE*	*STOOKIE*	STUDDIE	SWAGGIE
SWANKIE*	*SWANNIE*	*SWIFTIE*	TAILLIE	TAILZIE	TOASTIE*	TOOTSIE	TOUGHIE
TROELIE	TROOLIE	TUMSHIE	*TWINKIE*	*TWOONIE*	WASTRIE	WEIRDIE	*WHARFIE*
WHEELIE*	*WHOOPIE*	*YUGARIE*					

IER *excluding extensions of verbs*

ATELIER	BOUVIER	BRASIER	BRAZIERy	BREVIER	COTTIER	CROZIER	EPICIER
FLYTIER	GAMBIER	*GURRIER*	HAULIER	HELLIER	JAMBIER	KLAVIER	LARMIER
LUTHIER	OUVRIERe	PANNIER	PERRIER	RENTIER	SUCRIER	TABLIER	VERNIER

ILE

ANDVILE	BASTILE	CENTILE	ESTOILE	FAVRILE	GENTILE	GRACILE	NARGILEh
SEXTILE	STABILE	SUBFILE	VERBILE				

IN *excluding 'KIN'*

ACRASIN	ACRIDINe	ACYLOIN	ADERMIN	ALBUMIN	ALLICIN	ANEURIN	ATABRINe
ATEBRIN	BALADINe	BEAUFIN	BEDAWIN	BENZOIN	BLUEFIN	BOTULIN	*BOURSIN*
BRAHMIN	*BREDRIN*	BUTYRIN	*CALPAIN*	CAPELINe	CAROTIN	CERASIN	CERATIN
CERESINe	CHAUVIN	CHITLINg	CHLORINe	CINERIN	CIPOLIN	CLARAIN	COALBIN
COMPLINe	CREATINe	CREATINg	CRISPINg	CUMARIN	CYSTEINe	DAUPHINe	DEXTRINe
DIGOXIN	DRUMLIN	DUCKPIN	DUMPBIN	EASTLINg	EISWEIN	ELASTIN	EMULSIN
EREPSIN	ERMELIN	ETIOLIN	FIBROIN	FIVEPIN	FLUORINe	FOLACIN	FUCHSINe

```
GALLEIN  GALOPINg  GASTRIN  GERMAINe  GHRELIN  GLAIRINg  GLIADINe  GLONOIN
GRAPLINe HALFLINg  HEADPIN  HEMATINe  HEPARIN  HIRUDIN   HOATZIN   HOMININe
HORDEIN  HUITAIN   INCHPIN  INDAMINe  INDULINe INHIBIN   ISOSPIN   JACOBIN
JALAPIN  KERATIN   KHAMSIN  KINCHIN   KINETIN  KREMLIN   LAMININ   LEGUMIN
LEVULIN  LIGROINe  LITTLINg LOBEFIN   LUPULINe MASHLIN   MAUVEINe  MECONIN
MELANIN  MONDAINe  MORPHINe MORPHINg  MUEDDIN  MULLEIN   MURLAIN   MURRAIN
NARCEINe NAVARIN   NICOTINe NINEPIN   OPSONIN  OUABAIN   PALADIN   PATULIN
PEARLINg PICOLINe  PINGUIN  PLASMIN   POCOSIN  POUSSIN   PRAWLIN   PTOMAINe
PTYALIN  QUASSIN   QUIBLIN  QUINTIN   QUODLIN  RATTLINe  RATTLINg  RAVELINg
RELAXINg RESILINg  SAGOUIN  SALICINe  SAPONINe SAVARIN   SCULPINg  SERAFIN
SERICIN  SEXTAIN   SIRTUIN  SKULPIN   SMIDGIN  SNAPTIN   SOLANINe  SOUPFIN
SPELDINg SPONGINg  STEARINe STEARINg  SUBERIN  SURAMIN   SURLOIN   TABORINe
TABORINg TAILFIN   TANGHIN  THEELIN   THIAMINe THIAZINe  THIONINe  TOLIDINe
TRIAZINe TRYPSIN   TUBULIN  TUNICIN   TURACIN  TYLOSIN   VILLEIN   VITRAIN
VOLUTIN  WESTLIN   XANTHINe XERAFIN   XYLIDINe
```

INE
```
ACARINE  ADENINE   ALEPINE  ARCHINE   ARCSINE  BETAINE   BOTTINE   BOWLINE
BULGINE  CARMINE   CASSINE  CHOLINE   CHORINE  CONIINE   CUTLINE   CYSTINE
DELAINE  DESMINE   DIETINE  DOUCINE   DOURINE  DYELINE   ENAMINE   ERRHINE
FANZINE  FASCINE   GUMLINE  HIPLINE   HOPBINE  HYACINE   ICEWINE   INOSINE
ISOLINE  KEYLINE   LAUWINE  LOGLINE   MIDLINE  MILLINEr  NERVINE   NEURINE
OLIVINE  OXAZINE   PANTINE  PEBRINE   PENNINE  PISCINE   POTLINE   POUTINE
PRALINE  PRIMINE   PROLINE  PROMINE   RHIZINE  ROMAINE   SALTINE   SEALINE
SESTINE  SETLINE   SORDINE  STANINE   STIBINE  SUBLINE   TACRINE   TAGLINE
TARTINE  TAURINE   TERRINE  THYMINE   TONTINEr UREDINE   URIDINE   VITRINE
WEBZINE  ZEBRINE
```

ING *excluding 'LING'*
```
CISSING  COAMING   DESKING  EEVNING   EILDING  ERLKING   FERNING   FIRRING
HILDING  HYLDING   INBEING  INGOING   KARTING  LAPWING   LOONING   NITHING
REDWING  ROADING   ROUMING  SACRING   SUBRING  SUGGING   UNBEING   VERBING
VISHING  WEBRING
```

ION
```
ABUSION  ALATION   ALERION  AMATION   ANTLION  CAMPION   CANTION   CESSION
CHORION  COITION   CULLION  ELISION   ELUSION  ELUTION   EMPTION   ERASION
EXOMION  FERMION   FLEXION  FLUXION   FRANION  FUSHION   GILLION   GRUNION
HALLION  HELLION   JILLION  LAMPION   LECTION  MERSION   MICTION   MIXTION
MORRION  MUNNION   MURRION  ORARION   PEREION  PLERION   PLOSION   PULSION
RAMPION  RECTION   RUCTION  RULLION   RUNNION  SUASION   SYMBIONt  TAMPION
TERNION  TERSION   TOMPION  TORDION   TORSION  TURDION   UNCTION   UNITION
WANNION
```

IRE
```
ARMOIRE  AVODIRE   PISMIRE  RAMPIREd  RIMFIRE  SALTIRE   SAMPIRE
```

IS+

ABATTIS+	CHALLIS+	CIDARIS+	COLITIS+	CORONIS+	EPACRIS+	FINALISe	FINALISm
FINALISt	GAPOSIS+	GLOTTIS+	ILEITIS+	*LIATRIS+*	LYCHNIS+	MARQUISe	PARULIS+
PHLOMIS+	PYRALIS+	PYRAMIS+	PYROSIS+	SHERRIS+	SINOPIS+	TITANISm	TRAVOISe
TSOURIS+	TURKOIS+	UVEITIS+	WHATSIS+	WHOOSIS+			

ISM

ABLEISM	ASTEISM	ATAVISM	BAALISM	*BARDISM*	*BIPRISM*	BOGYISM	BRUTISM
BRUXISM	CHARISMa	CHORISM	CLADISM	CLONISM	COPYISM	CRETISM	CULTISM
CZARISM	DADAISM	DIORISM	DODOISM	DONNISM	DUALISM	ECHOISM	ENTRISM
EPICISM	EROTISM	ETACISM	ETATISMe	EXOTISM	FADDISM	FALSISM	FATTISM
FAUVISM	FIDEISM	FOGYISM	FOODISM	GURUISM	*HANDISM*	HEURISM	HOBOISM
IDOLISM	ITACISM	KARAISM	*LADDISM*	LADYISM	LAICISM	LEFTISM	LEGGISM
LIONISM	LOCOISM	LOOKISM	NARCISM	NEURISM	OBELISM	ODYLISM	OGREISM
ORALISM	*ORPHISM*	PHAEISM	PHOBISM	PHOTISM	PIANISM	PIETISM	PLENISM
RANKISM	SELFISM	SIZEISM	SOPHISM	STATISM	TACHISMe	TACTISM	TROPISM
TSARISM	TYCHISM	TZARISM	URANISM	UTOPISM	ZANYISM		

IST

ABLEIST	AGONIST	ALTOIST	AMORIST	ANGLIST	ATAVIST	ATOMIST	BUNDIST
CAMBIST	CASUIST	CHEKIST	CHORIST	CHUTIST	CHYMIST	CLADIST	COPYIST
CORNIST	COSMIST	CULTIST	CZARIST	DADAIST	DIALIST	DIETIST	DUALIST
DUELIST	DUMAIST	ECHOIST	ELOGIST	ENTRIST	EPEEIST	EPICIST	EXODIST
FADDIST	FATTIST	FAUNIST	FAUVIST	FEUDIST	FIDEIST	FUGUIST	GAMBIST
GNOMIST	HERBIST	HORNIST	HYGEIST	HYLOIST	HYMNIST	IAMBIST	IDOLIST
IDYLIST	IMAGIST	IRONIST	IVORIST	JUDOIST	*LOOKIST*	METRIST	*MIDLIST*
MYALIST	MYTHIST	NARCIST	OCULIST	OLIGIST	OLOGIST	ONANIST	ORALIST
PALMIST	PHOBIST	PIARIST	PIETIST	PLENIST	PLUMIST	POLLIST	POLOIST
PROTIST	QUERIST	REVUIST	RHYMIST	SACRISTy	SELFIST	SIZEIST	SOPHIST
STATIST	*SUMOIST*	TACHISTe	TITLIST	TROPIST	TSARIST	TUBAIST	TZARIST
UNALIST	UTOPIST	VACUIST	VIOLIST				

IT

AQUAFIT	AQUAVIT	*BLUETIT*	BUSHTIT	CATSUIT	CHINDIT	COALPIT	*COLETIT*
CONDUIT	CRAMPIT	*DIPSHIT*	*DRYSUIT*	EXTRAIT	FLEAPIT	FROGBIT	*FUCKWIT*
GIGABIT	HAWKBIT	INCIPIT	INTROIT	KILOBIT	LIMEPIT	MEGABIT	MEGAHIT
MESQUITe	MEZQUITe	PARFAIT	QUIDDITy	REPUNIT	RETRAITe	RETRAITt	RINGBIT
RINGGIT	*ROOTKIT*	SUBUNIT	TRAYBIT	TREYBIT	*WETSUIT*	WHATSIT	

ITE

ACONITE	ALUNITE	AMOSITE	APATITE	ARENITE	AXINITE	AZURITE	BAINITE
BEDRITE	BIOTITE	BORNITE	BRUCITE	BURKITE	CHEDITE	COESITE	CORDITE
CRINITE	CUPRITE	CYANITE	DIORITE	DULCITE	DUNNITE	EBONITE	EGALITE
EREMITE	ERINITE	EUCRITE	*FANSITE*	FELSITE	FERRITE	GAHNITE	GOTHITE
GUERITE	HESSITE	HOPLITE	HYALITE	ICHNITE	INOSITE	JADEITE	KERNITE
KUNZITE	KYANITE	LEUCITE	LITHITE	LYDDITE	MANNITE	MARLITE	MELLITE
MULLITE	NACRITE	NEURITE	NIOBITE	NITRITE	PENLITE	PERLITE	PICRITE
PITTITE	PITUITE	PYCNITE	SIENITE	SORBITE	SPILITE	STYLITE	SUBSITE
SULFITE	SYENITE	SYLVITE	TECTITE	TEKTITE	TERGITE	THORITE	THULITE

7. Seven-Letter Words

THWAITE   TURFITE   TURGITE   ULEXITE   UNAKITE   URALITE   URANITE   YPERITE
ZEOLITE   ZEUXITE   ZOISITE   ZOONITE   ZORGITE

ITY+
AMINITY+ ANALITY+ ANILITY+ ARIDITY+ AUREITY+ AVIDITY+ CURVITY+ DUALITY+
EDACITY+ EGALITY+ EXILITY+ FATUITY+ FURMITY+ JOLLITY+ LAICITY+ NULLITY+
OMNEITY+ OPACITY+ ORALITY+ *OUTCITY*+ OVALITY+ PANEITY+ PIOSITY+ PRAVITY+
PRIVITY+ RAUCITY+ SUAVITY+ SURDITY+ TENSITY+ TENUITY+ UNICITY+ VASTITY+
VIDUITY+

IUM
ALODIUM   *BOHRIUM* CAESIUM   *DUBNIUM* ELOGIUM   ELUVIUM   ERODIUM   HAFNIUM
HASSIUM IRIDIUM   NIOBIUM   ORARIUM   OXONIUM   PLAGIUM   PROTIUM   PYTHIUM
RHENIUM   RHODIUM   STIBIUM   TAEDIUM   THORIUM   THULIUM   TRITIUM   TRIVIUM
YTTRIUM

IVE
CAITIVE   CORSIVE   CURSIVE   JUSSIVE   KHEDIVE   PLOSIVE   STATIVE

KIN
BARMKIN   BAWDKIN   BODIKIN   BOOMKIN   BRODKIN   CANAKIN   CANIKIN   CATSKIN
COWSKIN   CUTIKIN   DOESKIN   DOGSKIN   DOITKIN   FOXSKIN   GRISKIN   LADYKIN
LAMBKIN   LIMPKIN   LORDKIN   LUMPKIN   MANAKIN   MANIKIN   MINIKIN   RAMAKIN
RAMEKIN   *SHINKIN* SIMPKIN   WOLFKIN

LAND
BOGLAND   COTLAND   ELFLAND   FENLAND   HOLLAND   LAWLAND   MIDLAND   NORLAND
OUTLAND   RIMLAND   SUNLAND   TROLAND

LET
ANNULET   ARCHLET   BEAMLET   BENDLET   BOOMLET   CAPELET   CHAPLET   CORSLET
COVELET   *CUMULET* DEERLET   DEVILET   DOVELET   FLATLET   FONTLET   FORTLET
FROGLET   HARSLET   HERBLET   HOOKLET   HORNLET   LAKELET   LOBELET   MARTLET
MEDALET   MOONLET   NECKLET   NOTELET   OSSELET   PARTLET   *PICULET* PLAYLET
QUILLET   ROYALET   *SERVLET* SKILLET   *SNIGLET* STEMLET   STERLET   TARTLET
TOWNLET   TRIOLET   VEINLET   WAVELET   WINGLET

LING
DEVLING   EANLING   FATLING   FOPLING   GADLING   GODLING   HALLING   HERLING
HIRLING   KEGLING   KIDLING   KITLING   MADLING   MORLING   OAKLING   PIGLING
TANLING   WARLING   WITLING   YEALING   *YORLING*

NESS+
ALLNESS+ BIGNESS+ DUENESS+ DULNESS+ DUNNESS+ FARNESS+ FATNESS+ FEWNESS+
FEYNESS+ FULNESS+ GAYNESS+ HIPNESS+ HOTNESS+ ICINESS+ LAXNESS+ NOWNESS+
ODDNESS+ OLDNESS+ ONENESS+ OUTNESS+ PATNESS+ RAWNESS+ REDNESS+ RUMNESS+
TWONESS+ WAENESS+ WANNESS+ WOENESS+ WRYNESS+

ODE

ALAMODE	*BARCODE*d	CATHODE	CESTODE	CLADODE	CRUNODE	CUSTODE	KATHODE
PENTODE	SARCODE	SPINODE	SUBCODE	TETRODE	WAIVODE	ZINCODE	

OGY+

ANAGOGY+ ENOLOGY+ NEOLOGY+ OROLOGY+ OTOLOGY+ UFOLOGY+

OID

AGAMOID	AMBROID	AMYLOID	ANDROID	ASTROID	CHELOID	CHOROID	CISSOID
COLLOID	CRINOID	CYSTOID	DELTOID	DERMOID	DESMOID	DIPLOIDy	DISCOID
EMEROID	ETHMOID	EUPLOIDy	FACTOID	FIBROID	FUNGOID	GLENOID	GLOBOID
GOBIOID	HAPLOIDy	HYALOID	HYDROID	LABROID	LENTOID	MASTOID	MATTOID
NEGROID	OSTEOID	PERCOID	PLACOID	QUINOID	RHIZOID	SARCOID	SIGMOID
SPAROID	STYLOID	THYROID	XIPHOID				

ON *excluding 'ION' & 'OON'*

ACTINON	AGLYCONe	AILERON	ALENCON	ALEURONe	ANDIRON	AQUILON	*ARGONON*
BARYTONe	BENISON	*BENTHON*	BIOTRON	BLOUSON	BORAZON	BOURDON	CABEZONe
CAISSON	CALDRON	CAMARON	CARRYON	CAUDRON	CELADON	CHANSON	CHEVRONy
CHIGNON	CHRONON	CISTRON	*CLASSON*	CLOISON	CRESTON	CROUPON	DALAPON
DEMETON	DENDRON	DIATRON	DUDGEON	ECDYSONe	ENDERON	ENDIRON	ENTERON
EUDEMON	EXCITON	FAUCHON	*FAVICON*	FENURON	FLETTON	FLEURON	FOURGON
FRISSON	FRONTON	GLADDON	GRYPHON	HALLYON	HEBENON	*HEGEMON*y	HELICON
HYPERON	ISOTRON	*JOHNSON*	KEELSON	KILOTON	KIRIMON	KRYTRON	LIMACON
LINURON	LORGNON	LYRICON	*MADISON*	MEGARON	MENAZON	METOPON	MIDIRON
MOELLON	MONAXON	MONURON	MOUFLON	MYLODONt	NEGATON	NEPHRON	NEUSTON
NONAGON	NORIMON	NUCLEON	ORGANON	PAILLON	PARISON	*PELOTON*	PERAEON
PERIGONe	PHAETON	PIDGEON	PLASMON	*POCOSON*	POISSON	POLARON	POSITON
PULDRON	QUILLON	RIBSTONe	SABATON	SABAYON	SACATON	SADIRON	SALAMON
SERICON	SHALLON	SOREHON	SOUPCON	SPONSON	STEMSON	*STETSON*	SYNANON
SYNTHON	TACHYON	TARDYON	TELAMON	TENDRON	*THEOCON*	TORCHON	TRIAXON
UPSILON	VIDICON	*WAITRON*	WARISON	WAVESON	WIDGEON	YEALDON	YPSILON
ZACATON							

ONE

AMARONE	AMIDONE	CALZONE	CANZONEt	CASSONE	CHALONE	CHELONE	CHINONE
DAPSONE	DIPHONE	DRACONE	DUOTONE	ECOTONE	*ENDZONE*	ESTRONE	FLAVONE
HEMIONE	HISTONE	HYPNONE	ISOTONE	JAMBONE	LACTONE	MADRONE	MUSCONE
MUSKONE	OXYTONE	PADRONE	PALLONE	PAYFONE	PINBONE	QUINONE	REDBONE
SPUMONE	SUBTONE	SUBZONE	SULFONE	TRIZONE	VIOLONE	*WARZONE*	

OON

BARGOON	BRADOON	BRIDOON	CARDOON	EFTSOON	GALLOON	GORSOON	GOSSOON
JARGOON	LARDOON	MADZOON	MATZOON	PATROON	PULTOON	ROCKOON	TESTOON

OR

ABACTOR	ABLATOR	ADJUROR	AGISTOR	ALASTOR	ALIENOR	ANAPHORa	ASSUROR
ATHANOR	BICOLOR	BIOPHORe	CHADDOR	CHANTOR	CITATORy	DEBITOR	DELATOR
DEVISOR	DILATORy	DILUTOR	DIVISOR	DONATORy	EDUCTOR	EJECTOR	EMULSOR

7. Seven-Letter Words

ENACTORy EVERTOR EXACTOR EXCITOR FUNCTOR GENITOR GRANTOR GYRATORy
HERITOR HUMIDOR IGNITOR *IMPEDOR* ISOCHORe LANGUOR LAXATOR LEVATOR
LOCATOR MACHZOR MALODOR MARKHOR MIRADOR NEGATORy OBLIGOR PANDOOR
PARADOR PARITOR PLEDGOR PRAETOR PRESSOR QUESTOR QUITTOR RELATOR
REVISORy ROTATORy *SANTOOR* SEPTUOR SETTLOR SEXTUOR SIGNIORi SIGNIORy
SIMILOR STENTOR STERTOR STRIDOR TANDOORi TEMBLOR TRUSTOR TWISTOR
VENATOR ZELATOR

OSE
AGAROSE AMYLOSE CALLOSE CASEOSE DULCOSE GLYCOSE HEPTOSE HOGNOSEd
ISODOSE LACTOSE LIGNOSE MALTOSE MANNOSE PECTOSE PENTOSE SORBOSE
SUCROSE THYLOSE VISCOSE

OUR
ACATOUR BITTOUR DORTOUR *ECOTOUR* FAITOUR FULGOUR HAVEOUR HAVIOUR
MAINOUR PANDOUR *PARKOUR* PAVIOUR SANTOUR

OUT
BACKOUT BAILOUT BURGOUT *CAMPOUT* COOKOUT EELPOUT *FADEOUT* FOLDOUT
GRAYOUT HOLDOUT LOCKOUT MISSOUT *PUCKOUT* PULLOUT RAINOUT ROLLOUT
SHUTOUT SICKOUT SLIPOUT SPINOUT SURTOUT TAKEOUT WIDEOUT

RY+ *excluding 'ARY' & 'ERY'*
ABHENRY+ ABHENRYs ALMONRY+ AVOUTRY+ CAMELRY+ CANONRY+ CHANTRY+ CHIEFRY+
CHOLTRY+ DEMONRY+ DEVILRY+ DIANDRY+ *DRUIDRY+* EQUERRY+ FELONRY+ GAUNTRY+
GIANTRY+ GUILDRY+ HELOTRY+ HERONRY+ JEWELRY+ MAISTRY+ MASONRY+ NONJURY+
PHRATRY+ PLANURY+ PSALTRY+ ROBOTRY+ SHANDRY+ SOWARRY+ TAPSTRY+ TILBURY+

SHIP
DOGSHIP DONSHIP ENDSHIP FOXSHIP GODSHIP LUDSHIP MIDSHIP SIBSHIP
SONSHIP

STER *excluding extensions of verbs*
BUMSTER CLYSTER DABSTER DIASTER DIESTER FIBSTER FUNSTER GAGSTER
GYPSTER HEPSTER HIPSTER KEESTER KEISTER KEYSTER KIESTER LAMSTER
MAYSTER MEISTER MINSTER MUNSTER OLDSTER PENSTER PIASTER PUNSTER
RODSTER SHASTER TAPSTER WABSTER WEBSTER YAPSTER *YUPSTER*

ULE
AMPOULE BASCULE CELLULE CIBOULE DUCTULE *FAUNULE* *FLORULE* GUAYULE
NERVULE NOCTULE *PENDULE* PINNULE PLUMULE PUSTULEd SPATULE SPICULE
SPINULE SPORULE STIPULEd SUBRULE TRAGULE VEINULEt VIRGULE ZEBRULE

UM *excluding 'IUM'*
AGENDUM ALYSSUM ARCANUM BACULUM BLELLUM BLUEGUM CENTRUM CHETRUM
CHILLUM FRAENUM FRUSTUM GRASSUM LABARUM LADANUM LUSTRUM NOSTRUM
NOTAEUM ORGANUM PABULUM PANICUM PANTOUM RASTRUM SECULUM SISTRUM
SKELLUM SOLANUM SOLIDUM STANNUM STEWBUM STICKUM STRATUM TETOTUM
TRANKUM TRIDUUM TRINKUM VITREUM

UP

BRUSHUP	*CHELLUP*	*CLOSEUP*	*FLAREUP*	GILTCUP	INGROUP	KINGCUP	SCALEUP
SCREWUP	STARTUP	WICKIUP	WICKYUP				

URE

ABATURE	BRISURE	COENURE	COUPURE	COUTURE	DASYURE	FLEXURE	FRISURE
FRITURE	GARBURE	GRAVURE	GUIPURE	GYPLURE	LEASURE	MONTURE	MORSURE
NERVURE	PARTURE	PLEXURE	PULTURE	RONDURE	SEASURE	SEISURE	SEYSURE
SOILURE	VERDUREd	VOITURE	WAFTURE				

US+

ABORTUS+	ANGELUS+	ARBUTUS+	AUTOBUS+	BOLETUS+	BONASUS+	BULIMUS+	BURNOUSe
CAESTUS+	CARDUUS+	CAROLUS+	CHOREUS+	CHURRUS+	COLOBUS+	CORYLUS+	CUBITUS+
DATABUS+	DEDIMUS+	ECHINUS+	EMBOLUS+	EURIPUS+	FIDIBUS+	GLADIUS+	GRAMPUS+
HALITUS+	HELIBUS+	*HOUMOUS+*	ICTERUS+	ILIACUS+	INCUBUS+	JACOBUS+	KASHRUS+
LIMULUS+	LINCTUS+	MALLEUS+	PEGASUS+	PELORUS+	PETASUS+	PHOEBUS+	PLUTEUS+
PORTOUS+	POSTBUS+	PROTEUS+	PYLORUS+	QUIETUS+	REGULUS+	RHABDUS+	RHAMNUS+
RICINUS+	SARDIUS+	SEROPUS+	SOUKOUS+	STURNUS+	TERTIUS+	THALLUS+	THIASUS+
TOTANUS+	TRACTUS+	TRISMUS+	TROCHUS+	TROILUS+	TUMULUS+	URACHUS+	VAGITUS+
VIDIMUS+	VOMITUS+	*XENOPUS+*					

WARD

AIRWARD	BEDWARD	FROWARD	GODWARD	HAYWARD	HOGWARD	MANWARD	NAYWARD
NORWARD	SEAWARD	SUNWARD	VANWARD				

WAY

AREAWAY	BELTWAY	BIKEWAY	CARTWAY	FARAWAY	FISHWAY	FOLKWAY	LICHWAY
LIFEWAY	*PACEWAY*	PACKWAY	RINGWAY	RODEWAY	ROLLWAY	ROPEWAY	SHIPWAY
SIDEWAY	SKIDWAY	SOMEWAY	SPURWAY	TAXIWAY	THRUWAY	TIDEWAY	

WEED

BURWEED	CUDWEED	DYEWEED	GUMWEED	HOGWEED	MATWEED	MAYWEED	OARWEED
OREWEED	PIGWEED	PINWEED	RAGWEED	TARWEED			

WOOD

BARWOOD	BAYWOOD	BOGWOOD	BOXWOOD	CAMWOOD	DOGWOOD	DYEWOOD	ELMWOOD
FATWOOD	*FIRWOOD*	GUMWOOD	INKWOOD	LOGWOOD	NUTWOOD	SAPWOOD	

7.3.4 ADJECTIVES ENDING IN 'Y'

BAIRNLY*	BUIRDLY*	CHILDLY*	CLERKLY*	COURTLY*	FLESHLY*	FLOUNCY*	GIANTLY*
GRADELY*	GRISTLY*	LIMPSEY*	PAUGHTY*	QUEECHY*	QUEENLY*	SHAMBLY*	SHINGLY*
*SHMOOZY**	SHOGGLY*	SHOOGLY*	SHREDDY*	SIGHTLY*	SPANGLY*	SPLODGY*	SPLURGY*
SPRAYEY*	SPRIGGY*	SQUATTY*	SQUEEZY*	SQUIDGY*	STUMBLY*	SWELTRY*	TEENTSY*
TREACLY*	TREMBLY*	TWIDDLY*	*UNCOMFY**	UNFUNNY*	UNFUSSY*		

7.3.5 NON-PLURALS BY COMMON ENDINGS

ABLE

ACTABLE	ADDABLE	CITABLE	CODABLE	DATABLE	DOWABLE	DRYABLE	DUPABLE
DYEABLE	ERRABLE	EYEABLE	FADABLE	FINABLE	FLYABLE	*FRYABLE*	GELABLE
GETABLE	*GIVABLE*	HATABLE	HEWABLE	HIDABLE	HIRABLE	LINABLE	LIVABLE
LOSABLE	MAKABLE	MINABLE	MIRABLE	MIXABLE	MUTABLE	NAMABLE	OWNABLE
PACABLE	*POKABLE*	*POSABLE*	RIDABLE	ROPABLE	ROWABLE	RULABLE	SALABLE
SAVABLE	SAYABLE	SEEABLE	SEWABLE	SIZABLE	SKIABLE	SOWABLE	SUEABLE
TAKABLE	TAMABLE	TOTABLE	TOWABLE	TRIABLE	TYPABLE	UNHABLE	VATABLE
VOLABLE	VOTABLE	WADABLE	*WAXABLE*	WIRABLE			

ABLY

CURABLY	*LIKABLY*	LOVABLY	MOVABLY	MUTABLY	PLIABLY	RATABLY	SALABLY
SIZABLY	TAXABLY	TENABLY	TUNABLY	USEABLY	VOCABLY		

AL *excluding 'IAL'*

ACNODAL	ACTINAL	ALBINAL	ANCONAL	*ANTICAL*	APOGEAL	APSIDAL	APTERAL
AUGURAL	BALNEAL	BASINAL	BATHYAL	BENTHAL	BIMANAL	BIMODAL	BIPEDAL
BITONAL	BIZONAL	BURGHAL	CANTHAL	CENSUAL	CHASMAL	CLAUSAL	CLYPEAL
COMITAL	COTIDAL	CREEDAL	CRYPTAL	CUBITAL	DATIVAL	DECADAL	DECANAL
DEXTRAL	DIGONAL	DISLEAL	DOMICAL	ECTYPAL	EDICTAL	EPHORAL	EPIGEAL
EQUINAL	ESTIVAL	ESTRUAL	FEMINAL	FIGURAL	FINICAL	FLUIDAL	FRAMPAL
FUTURAL	GAMETAL	GEMINAL	GEOIDAL	GLAREAL	GLOTTAL	GNATHAL	GONADAL
HELICAL	HEMATAL	HUMORAL	HYMENAL	HYOIDAL	HYPURAL	INCISAL	INCUDAL
INDEXAL	INVITAL	IRIDEAL	LITORAL	LOESSAL	LUMENAL	MATINAL	MENSUAL
MONADAL	NADIRAL	NEMORAL	NODICAL	*NONORAL*	NUCLEAL	OBITUAL	OCTAVAL
OEDIPAL	OSCHEAL	OSMOLAL	PAGINAL	PALUDAL	PASCUAL	PERORAL	PHASEAL
PHRASAL	*PLEONAL*	PREANAL	PREMEAL	PREORAL	PROCTAL	PUBERAL	SCRIBAL
SEGETAL	SEISMAL	SERUMAL	SHRINAL	SIDERAL	SINICAL	*SOLUTAL*	SOMITAL
SORORAL	SPATHAL	SPHERAL	SPONSAL	STOICAL	SUBORAL	SUBOVAL	SUDORAL
SUTURAL	TETANAL	TIMBRAL	TISSUAL	TOXICAL	TROCHAL	TRUNCAL	TUMORAL
UMBONAL	UNCINAL	UNMORAL	UNROYAL	UNVITAL	UNVOCAL	VATICAL	VICINAL

ALLY

AURALLY	AXIALLY	BASALLY	DUCALLY	FOCALLY	FUGALLY	JURALLY	MESALLY
METALLY	MODALLY	NASALLY	NAVALLY	NODALLY	PENALLY	RURALLY	TIDALLY
TONALLY	VAGALLY	VENALLY	VIRALLY	VOCALLY	ZONALLY		

AN *excluding 'IAN' & 'MAN->MEN'*

AMEBEAN	ANTIMAN	APOGEAN	*ARCHEAN*	AVELLANe	AZUREAN	EPIGEAN	EXURBAN
FORERANk	LACTEAN	LETHEAN	LYNCEAN	PIGMEAN	PLEBEAN	PYGMEAN	REBEGAN
SLURBAN	SPELEAN	TAUREAN	TRIDUAN	*UILLEAN*	UNCLEAN*	UNHUMAN	

ANT

ABEYANT	AGACANTe	AMORANT	BRISANT	CLAMANT	*CREMANT*	EMANANT	EMICANT
EPATANT	FLOTANT	GESTANT	ISSUANT	ITERANT	JESSANT	LATRANT	PASSANT
PERSANT	POYNANT	PROVANT	PULSANT	REBOANT	REGNANT	REPTANT	ROUSANT
SEJEANT	STATANT	ULULANT	UNMEANT	URINANT	VERNANT		

AR

ANTICAR	ANTIWAR	BASILARy	BIFILAR	DIPOLAR	FABULAR	HAMULAR	INSOFAR
LOBULAR	MILITARy	MUDEJAR	MUTULAR	OSMOLAR	OVERFAR	PABULAR	RAMULAR
REDSEAR	SKIWEAR	*SOLUNAR*	SUBALAR	TUMULARy	UNDULAR	VENULAR	VITULAR

ARY

CILIARY	EPULARY	LACTARY	MANUARY	MILIARY	OBOLARY	OLIVARY	RETIARY
TRINARY	UNCHARY	UNITARY	UNSCARY	UNWEARY			

ATE

ARCUATEd	AUREATE	BISTATE	BULLATE	BURSATE	CIRRATE	CLAVATEd	CONNATE
CORDATE	COSTATEd	CRENATEd	CRINATEd	CUNEATEd	CURTATE	CURVATEd	CUSPATEd
DENTATEd	EBRIATEd	EXARATE	FALCATEd	FERMATE	FISSATE	FOSSATE	FOVEATEd
GALEATEd	HASTATEd	LARVATEd	LIMBATE	LINEATEd	NERVATE	OCULATEd	ODORATE
OSTIATE	*PALEATE*	PALMATEd	PELTATE	PENNATEd	PILEATEd	PLUMATE	PORTATE
QUINATE	QUORATE	ROSEATE	SCOPATE	SCUTATE	SEPTATE	SPICATEd	SPINATE
STYLATE	SULCATEd	TERNATE	THECATE	VALLATE	VITTATE		

EAU

BATTEAUx	BERCEAUx	COUTEAUx	JAMBEAUx	MORCEAUx	NOUVEAUx	RONDEAUx	TRUMEAUx

ED

ABLUTED	ALLEYED	AMBERED	ANTIRED	ARBORED	ARRASED	BASINED	BEGORED
BEINKED	BEMAZED	BETAXED	BITUMED	BOUGHED	BRACTED	BRAWNED	BRIARED
BRIERED	CEDARED	CHASMED	CORNFED	*CRUNKED*	DAISIED	*DENIMED*	*EASELED*
ENFILED	EPOXYED	*EXAPTED*	FIBERED	FRONDED	FRUCTED	FUCUSED	GESSOED
GOWANED	GRISLED	GRUFTED	*HANDFED*	INVEXED	*ISLETED*	IVORIED	*KAYLIED*
LAPELED	LETHIED	LOWBRED	MESELED	MISPLED	MOGULED	MONEYED	MOTTOED
MURALED	NIGHTED	NODATED	OSIERED	OUTBRED	OUTSPED	OVERBED	PANSIED
PENNIED	PETALED	PINNOED	PREAGED	*PRENEED*	RAGULED	RHEUMED	RIDERED
RIVERED	SEPALED	SERIFED	SHARDED	SLEIDED	STAIRED	SWACKED	TALONED
THONGED	TIARAED	TUTOYED	UDDERED	UMBELED	UNACTED	*UNADDED*	UNAIMED
UNASKED	UNBAKED	UNBASED	UNBATED	UNBOWED	*UNCARED*	*UNCEDED*	UNCITED
UNCURED	UNDRIED	UNENDED	UNFADED	UNFAKED	UNFAMED	UNFEUED	UNFILED
UNFIRED	UNFUMED	UNFUSED	*UNGATED*	*UNGAZED*	UNGORED	UNGULED	UNHIRED
UNHOPED	UNJADED	UNLOBED	UNMATED	UNMETED	UNMINED	UNNOTED	*UNOAKED*
UNPACED	UNPAGED	UNPARED	UNPOSED	UNRAZED	UNRIMED	UNSATED	UNSAWED
UNSIZED	UNSOWED	UNSPIED	*UNTIMED*	UNTIRED	UNTONED	UNURGED	UNVEXED
UNWAGED	UNWAKED	UNWAXED	UNWAYED	UNWIPED	UNWOOED	UNZONED	WHELKED
WHORLED	WONDRED	WOOLLED	WORLDED	WRIZLED			

EDLY

ADDEDLY	COWEDLY	DATEDLY	DAZEDLY	FADEDLY	JADEDLY	MAZEDLY	MIXEDLY
MUTEDLY	NAKEDLY	NOTEDLY	VEXEDLY				

EN excluding 'MAN -> MEN'

ANYWHEN	BEECHEN	BIRCHEN	*BITCHEN*	BOUNDEN	BRICKEN	*BRUSSEN*	BURSTEN
DRUCKEN	*EMACSEN*	ENRIVEN	FLANKEN	GLASSEN	GRUTTEN	HILLMEN	LARCHEN
LEUCHEN	LOKSHEN	MARCHEN	*MENSHEN*	MOULTEN	OVERMEN	PIROGEN	PUTAMEN

7. Seven-Letter Words

| SLIDDEN | STANDEN | STOODEN | STRAWEN | STUDDEN | SUDAMEN | TEGUMENt | TROCKEN |
| TWIGGEN | *UNGREEN* | UNOFTEN | UNRISEN | UNRIVEN | VELAMEN | WHATTEN | WRYTHEN |

ENT

ATTUENT	CANDENT	CLEMENT	CREDENT	CUMBENT	DISTENT	FORLENT	FORNENT
FULGENT	HORRENT	LAMBENT	MISSENT	MISWENT	OUTWENT	*REBLENT*	RINGENT
STUPENT	UNBLENT	UNSHENT					

ES

ABIOSES	ACHATES	ALGESES	AMBONES	ANNATES	APHIDES	APSIDES	ARBORES
ASCITES	AUXESES	BOONIES	BORACES	COJONES	CRUORES	DARBIES	DWARVES
ECDYSES	ECTASES	EIKONES	EMONGESt	*ENDYSES*	ENTASES	GLIOSES	HELICES
HEREDES	HOMINESs	HURDIES	HYRACES	INCUDES	ISOETES	JACALES	KINESES
KRYPSES	KYLICES	LAPIDES	LATICES	LIMITES	LIMOSES	LITOTES	LONGIES
MAATJES	MEIOSES	MERISES	MITOSES	MONADES	MONOSES	MURICES	MYCETES
MYCOSES	MYIASES	NAIADES	NOMBLES	*NOPALES*	ORDINES	OREADES	PARESES
PEDESES	PINONES	PRAESES	PYROSES	PYXIDES	RADICES	REMIGES	SCABIES
SENORES	SONTIES	SORITES	STIRPES	STOVIES	SYNAXES	TAGETES	TALIPES
TELESES	TRIONES	TRIPSES	TYLOSES	TYRONES	VARICES	*WALKIES*	XEROTES
ZYMOSES							

FUL

ARMSFUL	BAGSFUL	BANEFUL	BODEFUL	BRIMFULl	CANSFUL	CUPSFUL	DAREFUL
DEEDFUL	DERNFUL	DOOMFUL	DUREFUL	EASEFUL^	GAINFUL	GASHFUL	GAZEFUL
GLADFUL	GUSTFUL	HATSFUL	JARSFUL	JESTFUL	JUGSFUL	LISTFUL	MASTFUL
MAZEFUL	MISTFUL	MOANFUL	ODORFUL	PESTFUL	PITHFUL	PLOTFUL	POUTFUL
PREYFUL	PUSHFUL	RAGEFUL	RISKFUL	RUTHFUL	SIGHFUL	SONGFUL	SWAYFUL
TALEFUL	TEEMFUL	TEENFUL	TOILFUL	WAILFUL	WAKEFUL	WILEFUL	WILLFUL
WORKFUL	ZEALFUL						

IA

ACHENIAl	ACROMIAl	AECIDIAl	AEROBIA	ALLODIAl	ALLUVIAl	ANCILIA	APHELIAn
AQUARIAl	AQUARIAn	ASCIDIAn	ASPIDIA	BASIDIAl	BIENNIAl	BOTHRIA	BRACHIAl
CIBORIA	CIMELIA	CONARIAl	CONIDIAl	CONIDIAn	COREMIA	CYMATIA	DELIRIA
DILUVIAl	DILUVIAn	DOMATIA	EMPORIA	ENCOMIA	*EPYLLIA*	EXORDIAl	FILARIAe
FILARIAl	FILARIAn	FIMBRIAe	FIMBRIAl	*FUSARIA*	GANGLIAl	GANGLIAr	GONIDIAl
GYNECIA	HIMATIA	HYMENIAl	ILLUVIAl	IMPERIAl	INDUSIAl	LACINIAe	LIXIVIAl
MINUTIAe	MINUTIAl	MYCELIAl	MYCELIAn	NOVALIA	OOGONIAl	PATAGIAl	PECULIAr
PERIDIAl	PYGIDIAl	PYXIDIA	REFUGIA	ROSARIAn	SCHOLIA	SEDILIA	SILPHIA
SOLARIA	SOLATIA	SOREDIAl	SPLENIAl	SUDARIA	SYCONIA	TALARIA	ULNARIA
VELARIA	ZOOECIA						

IAL

ABAXIAL	ADAGIAL	ADAXIAL	*AKENIAL*	ANAXIAL	BIAXIAL	CERRIAL	CNEMIAL
COAXIAL	DIARIAL	EPAXIAL	FAUCIAL	IRIDIAL	MONDIAL	OVARIAL	RACHIAL
SOMNIAL	SPACIAL	TRUCIAL	UXORIAL				

IAN

ACARIAN	APICIAN	DIARIAN	ELYSIAN	EXILIAN	IRIDIAN	ORTHIAN	*PERMIAN*
PLUVIAN	PRIDIAN	STYGIAN	THALIAN	VERMIAN	*WARDIAN*		

IC

ABIETIC	ABOULIC	AGAPEIC	AGGADIC	AGNATIC	*AGNOSIC*	AGRAVIC	*AKRATIC*
ALBINIC	ALBITIC	ALETHIC	*ALGESIC*	*ALGETIC*	ALGINIC	ALKYLIC	ALLELIC
ALLYLIC	AMOEBIC	ANERGIC	ANIONIC	ANOSMIC	APHETIC	APLITIC	APNOEIC
APOGEIC	APRAXIC	APROTIC	ARGOTIC	ARKOSIC	*ATRESIC*	*ATRETIC*	AUGITIC
AUXINIC	BARYTIC	BASILICa	BATHMIC	BENEFICe	BENTHIC	BENZOIC	BIONTIC
BIOPSIC	BIOPTIC	BORONIC	*BOSONIC*	BUTYRIC	DATURIC	DEISTIC	DELPHIC
DELTAIC	DHARMIC	DIBASIC	DIMERIC	DINERIC	DIPLOIC	DIPODIC	DISOMIC
DRUIDIC	DRYADIC	DULOTIC	DUNITIC	DYSURIC	EDAPHIC	EIDOLIC	ELLAGIC
ENERGIC	ENTOMIC	ENTOPIC	ENTOTIC	ENZYMIC	EOSINIC	EPEIRIC	EPIGEIC
EPIZOIC	ERETHIC	ERGODIC	ERGOTIC	ETHERIC	ETHYLIC	EUPNEIC	EXOSMIC
EXTATIC	FARADIC	FATIDIC	*FJORDIC*	FLUORIC	FUMARIC	*FUSIDIC*	GALENIC
GAMETIC	GLOTTIC	GLYPHIC	GNATHIC	GONADIC	GONIDIC	GYRONIC	HAGADIC
HALAKIC	HEBETIC	HENOTIC	HEXADIC	*HEXYLIC*	*HOLONIC*	*HOMERIC*	HYAENIC
HYPOXIC	IDENTIC	IDYLLIC	ILLITIC	ISMATIC	JADITIC	JALAPIC	JURIDIC
KARSTIC	KETONIC	KETOTIC	LEVITIC	LEXEMIC	LIPIDIC	LITOTIC	*LOESSIC*
MALEFICe	*MALONIC*	MANTRIC	MEIOTIC	MEROPIC	MESONIC	METOPIC	MIRIFIC
MITOTIC	MONADIC	MONODIC	MOTIFIC	MOTIVIC	MOTORIC	MYALGIC	MYRRHIC
NEMATIC	NEPHRIC	NEPOTIC	NERITIC	*NEUSTIC*	NIMONIC	NORITIC	NYMPHIC
ODONTIC	OGHAMIC	OMNIFIC	ONEIRIC	OOLITIC	OOLOGIC	OPHITIC	OPSONIC
OSMATIC	OSMOTIC	OSSIFIC	OTALGIC	*OXYNTIC*	PALUDIC	PARODIC	PAROTIC
PEDETIC	PELITIC	PELORIC	PIRATIC	PLASMIC	*PLEONIC*	PLUMBIC	PODALIC
PODITIC	POTAMIC	PROSAIC	PRUSSIC	PSALMIC	PSOATIC	*PTEROIC*	PYAEMIC
PYRETIC	PYREXIC	PYRIDIC	PYRITIC	*PYRUVIC*	RHEUMIC	RUBIDIC	SARONIC
SATIRIC	SATYRIC	SEBASIC	SEBIFIC	SELENIC	SEMATIC	SIBYLIC	*SIMATIC*
SKALDIC	SOMATIC	SOMITIC	SORITIC	SPASMIC	SPERMIC	SPLENIC	STEARIC
STHENIC	STROBIC	SUBERIC	SYBOTIC	SYLPHIC	SYNODIC	TANTRIC	TAXEMIC
TAXITIC	TELOMIC	TEREBIC	THERMIC	THIOLIC	THIONIC	TONEMIC	TOTEMIC
TOYETIC	TOXEMIC	TRISMIC	TRYPTIC	TYRONIC	UMBONIC	URAEMIC	UVEITIC
VALERIC	VANADIC	VEGANIC	VELARIC	VENEFIC	VERIDIC	VINYLIC	VIREMIC
VOLATIC	VOLTAIC	XANTHIC	XYLONIC	ZEBRAIC	ZYGOTIC		

ID *excluding 'OID'*

BANDAID	BESTRIDe	FOREDID	FORSAID	IMPAVID	MISSAID	*NAYSAID*	NONPAID
NONSKID	OCTOFID	OUTCHIDe	*OUTSAID*	PINGUID	REMORID	SCABRID	SUBACID
SUBARID	TAXPAID	UNSOLID	UNSTAID				

IE

BOOKSIE*	BRAWLIE*	*CLOOTIE*	COUTHIE*	CUTESIE*	FEMININE	GRIESIE	GRUSHIE
HIRSTIE	INCONIE	PLOOKIE*	PLOUKIE*	PRENZIE	PRIMSIE*	REECHIE*	ROUTHIE*
SINOPIE	TEACHIE	*TOOSHIE*	TOUSTIE*	TRICKIE*	UNWARIE*	VAWNTIE*	

ILE

ABAXILE	AMABILE	CORTILE	FEBRILE	FICTILE	FISSILE	FLEXILE	INUTILE
SECTILE	TORTILE	UMWHILE	UNAGILE				

7. Seven-Letter Words

ILY *derived from adjectives*

BAGGILY	BALKILY	BALMILY	BAWDILY	BEADILY	BEAMILY	BEEFILY	BONNILY
BOSSILY	BULKILY	BUMPILY	BURLILY	BUSHILY	CAMPILY	CANNILY	*CANTILY*
CATTILY	CHARILY	CORNILY	CURLILY	CUSHILY	DANDILY	DEEDILY	DINGILY
DIRTILY	DOOMILY	DOTTILY	DOWDILY	DUMPILY	DUSKILY	DUSTILY	EMPTILY
FANCILY	FATTILY	FIERILY	FILMILY	FISHILY	FLAKILY	*FLUKILY*	FOAMILY
FOGGILY	FUGGILY	*FUNKILY*	FURRILY	FUSTILY	GASSILY	GAUDILY	GAUZILY
GAWKILY	GIDDILY	GODLILY	GOOFILY	GOUTILY	GRIMILY	GUSHILY	GUSTILY
GUTSILY	HANDILY	HARDILY	HEADILY	HEFTILY	HOARILY	HORNILY	HORSILY
HUSKILY	ITCHILY	JERKILY	JOLLILY	JOLTILY	JUICILY	JUMPILY	LANKILY
LEAKILY	LOFTILY	LOOBILY	*LOONILY*	*LOOPILY*	LOWLILY	LUMPILY	LUSTILY
MANGILY	MANLILY	MEATILY	MILKILY	MIRKILY	MISTILY	MOODILY	MOONILY
MOUSILY	MUCKILY	MUDDILY	MUGGILY	MURKILY	MUSHILY	MUSKILY	MUSSILY
MUSTILY	NATTILY	NEEDILY	NERVILY	NIFTILY	NUTTILY	PAWKILY	PERKILY
PESKILY	PETTILY	PHONILY	PITHILY	POCKILY	PODGILY	*PRICILY*	PRIVILY
PUDGILY	PURSILY	PUSHILY	QUAKILY	RAINILY	*RANDILY*	*RANGILY*	*RATTILY*
REEDILY	RISKILY	RITZILY	ROCKILY	ROOMILY	ROUPILY	RUDDILY	RUSTILY
RUTTILY	SALTILY	*SARKILY*	SAUCILY	SCARILY	SEEDILY	SHADILY	SHINILY
SHOWILY	SILKILY	SILLILY	SLIMILY	SMOKILY	SNAKILY	SNOWILY	SOAPILY
SOGGILY	SOOTILY	SORRILY	SPICILY	SPIKILY	STAGILY	STONILY	SULKILY
SUNNILY	SURLILY	TACKILY	TARDILY	TASTILY	TATTILY	TAWNILY	TEARILY
TECHILY	TESTILY	TINNILY	TIPSILY	TOSSILY	TUFTILY	WACKILY	*WASHILY*
WASPILY	WEEDILY	*WEEPILY*	WINDILY	WISPILY	WORDILY	*ZESTILY*	

INE

ANGUINE	BYSSINE	CAPRINE	CAULINE	CEDRINE	CERVINE	CORVINE	CRIMINE
CYPRINE	ELAPINE	HIRCINE	HYENINE	MILVINE	NARDINE	OTARINE	PARDINE
PERCINE	PHOCINE	PONTINE	RALLINE	SITTINE	TIGRINE	TURDINE	UTERINE
VESPINE	VULPINE						

IS

ABIOSIS	ALGESIS	APHESIS	ASCARIS	AUXESIS	*CALLAIS*	CHABLIS	COXITIS
CROQUIS	ECDYSIS	ECTASIS	*ENDYSIS*	ENTASIS	EPHELIS	GLIOSIS	*HAUBOIS*
KETOSIS	KINESIS	KRYPSIS	LIMOSIS	MAUVAISe	MEIOSIS	MERISIS	MILREIS
MITOSIS	MONOSIS	MYCOSIS	MYIASIS	PARESIS	PAROTIS	PEDESIS	PILOTIS
POROSIS	SHAMOIS	SYNAXIS	TELESIS	TRIPSIS	TSOORIS	TYLOSIS	VIROSIS
XEROSIS	ZYGOSIS	ZYMOSIS					

ISH

ALUMISH	BADDISH	BALDISH	BEAMISH	BEARISH	BEAUISH	*BLOKISH*	BLUEISH
BOARISH	BOGGISH	BOOKISH	BOORISH	BRINISH	BRUTISH	BUCKISH	CARLISH
CATTISH	CLAYISH	COLTISH	*CRONISH*	CULTISH	CURRISH	DAMPISH	DANKISH
DEAFISH	DOGGISH	DOLLISH	DOLTISH	DONNISH	*DORKISH*	DOVEISH	DRONISH
DULLISH	DUMPISH	DUNCISH	DUNNISH	DUSKISH	FADDISH	FALSISH	FASTISH
FATTISH	FENNISH	FINEISH	FOGYISH	FOLKISH	FULLISH	GAMPISH	GAWKISH
GNOMISH	GOATISH	GOODISH	GRAYISH	GREYISH	GULLISH	JIGGISH	*JOCKISH*
KERNISH	KIDDISH	KNAVISH	LADDISH	LADYISH	LARGISH	LARKISH	LAZYISH
LEFTISH	*LOGGISH*	LOMPISH	LUMPISH	LUSKISH	MADDISH	MAIDISH	MANNISH
MAWKISH	MINXISH	MONKISH	MOONISH	MOORISH	MOREISH	MUGGISH	MURKISH

NERDISH NICEISH NOIRISH NUNNISH *NURDISH* OGREISH PEAKISH PEEVISH
PERKISH PETTISH PIGGISH PINKISH PIXYISH PUCKISH PUGGISH PUNKISH
RANKISH RATTISH RIGGISH ROGUISH ROINISH ROMPISH ROOKISH ROYNISH
RUNTISH RUTTISH SADDISH SALTISH SERFISH SICKISH SNAKISH SNOWISH
SOFTISH SOTTISH SOURISH TANNISH TARTISH TIGRISH TITTISH TOADISH
TONNISH TOWNISH VAMPISH VOGUISH WAGGISH *WAIFISH* WANNISH WEAKISH
WEARISH WENNISH WETTISH WILDISH WISPISH *WOGGISH* WOLFISH WOLVISH
WORDISH WORMISH ZANYISH

IT
BACKLIT BAREFIT *BOOSHIT* BROCKIT CLEEKIT DROOKIT DROUKIT EXCUDIT
FIRELIT GLAIKIT HOWBEIT INVENIT *LAMPLIT* LIMELIT MISWRITe OUTWRITe
OVERFIT OVERLIT SEMIFIT SHILPIT SKELPIT SLEEKIT SNODDIT SPOTLIT
STEEKIT STICKIT *THANKIT* THIGGIT TRAIKIT UNSPLIT

IVE
AMATIVE COSTIVE FICTIVE FISSIVE FLUXIVE PREDIVE RESTIVE SUASIVE
TARDIVE TENSIVE TORSIVE TORTIVE TUSSIVE UNALIVE UNITIVE

LESS
AIDLESS ARMLESS AWELESS AWNLESS *BAGLESS* BARLESS BEDLESS BITLESS
BOWLESS BUDLESS *COXLESS* CUBLESS DEWLESS EARLESS EGGLESS EGOLESS
EYELESS FATLESS FEELESS FINLESS FLYLESS FURLESS *GAPLESS* GUMLESS
HATLESS HIPLESS HITLESS HUELESS ICELESS INNLESS IRELESS JAGLESS
KEYLESS KINLESS LIDLESS LIPLESS MANLESS MATLESS NAPLESS NETLESS
OARLESS *ORBLESS* PEGLESS RIBLESS RIMLESS RODLESS *TAGLESS* TAXLESS
TIELESS TIPLESS TOELESS TOYLESS TUGLESS VOWLESS WARLESS WAYLESS
WEBLESS WIGLESS ZIPLESS

LIKE
AIRLIKE ANTLIKE APELIKE ARMLIKE ASSLIKE *BAGLIKE* BATLIKE BEDLIKE
BEELIKE BOWLIKE BUDLIKE CATLIKE CUPLIKE DOGLIKE *EARLIKE* EELLIKE
ELFLIKE EYELIKE *FADLIKE* FANLIKE FATLIKE FINLIKE GEMLIKE GODLIKE
GUMLIKE GUTLIKE *HAGLIKE* HATLIKE HENLIKE HIPLIKE HOBLIKE HOELIKE
HOGLIKE HUTLIKE ICELIKE IVYLIKE *JAMLIKE* JAWLIKE JETLIKE *JIGLIKE*
LAWLIKE LEGLIKE LIPLIKE MANLIKE MAPLIKE NETLIKE NIBLIKE NUTLIKE
OARLIKE OATLIKE OWLLIKE PEALIKE PEGLIKE PIGLIKE PODLIKE POTLIKE
PUSLIKE RATLIKE RAYLIKE RIBLIKE RODLIKE RUGLIKE SACLIKE SAWLIKE
SICLIKE SONLIKE TAGLIKE TEALIKE TINLIKE TOELIKE TOYLIKE TUBLIKE
URNLIKE WARLIKE WEBLIKE WIGLIKE

LY *extensions of adjectives*
ACRIDLY ALERTLY BLACKLY BRITTLY BUXOMLY CRASSLY CROSSLY DOUCELY
FETIDLY FLEETLY GELIDLY GRANDLY GREENLY HUMIDLY IGNOBLY INERTLY
LEVELLY LITHELY LIVIDLY LOATHLY LURIDLY MOISTLY OBESELY PEARTLY
PRONELY RABIDLY SCANTLY SHEERLY SLACKLY SLEEKLY SLICKLY SNIDELY
SOOTHLY SPARELY SQUATLY STAIDLY STALELY STARKLY STOUTLY SUAVELY
TEPIDLY TEUGHLY THICKLY TRITELY UNFITLY VALIDLY VAPIDLY WEIRDLY
WHITELY

7. Seven-Letter Words

LY other

ACTORLY	ADULTLY	ALIENLY	ANGERLY	ANTICLY	APISHLY	BIFIDLY	*BOGUSLY*
BRUTELY	CHEERLY	CRUSILY	DEARNLY	DREADLY	EROSELY	FLUIDLY	FUSIBLY
FRIARLY	GIANTLY	GREISLY	GRIESLY	GRISELY	HARTELY	HAZELLY	HEARTLY
INAPTLY	INNERLY	LAIRDLY	LAITHLY	LICITLY	MAJORLY	MASCULY	NONOILY
NOVELLY	OCTUPLY	OVATELY	PRIMELY	PRIORLY	RAVELLY	RIANTLY	RISIBLY
SLANTLY	SMICKLY	SOLUBLY	SWITHLY	TACITLY	THEGNLY	TIGERLY	TUMIDLY
TWINKLY	UNAPTLY	VICARLY	VIXENLY	VOLUBLY	VOWELLY	WIGHTLY	WOFULLY

MAN->MEN

ADWOMAN	ARTSMAN	AUTOMAN	BEADMAN	BEDEMAN	BELLMAN	BELTMAN	BILLMAN
BIRDMAN	BOATMAN	BOGYMAN	BONDMAN	BOOKMAN	BYREMAN	CASEMAN	CASEMENt
CHAPMAN	COALMAN	DAYSMAN	*DEADMAN*	DESKMAN	DRAYMAN	FACEMAN	FLAGMAN
FREEMAN	GADSMAN	GATEMAN	GLEEMAN	GOODMAN	GOWNMAN	GRIPMAN	GUDEMAN
HACKMAN	*HARDMAN*	HEADMAN	HELIMAN	HERDMAN	HOODMAN	HOSEMAN	*IRONMAN*
ISLEMAN	JACKMAN	JARKMAN	JUNKMAN	JURYMAN	KEELMAN	LANDMAN	LEADMAN
LENSMAN	LIFTMAN	LINKMAN	LOCKMAN	LOCOMAN	ODDSMAN	*ORRAMAN*	*PACEMAN*
PACKMAN	PASSMAN	PASSMENt	PEATMAN	PIKEMAN	PLOWMAN	POLLMAN	PORTMAN
RAFTMAN	RAILMAN	REEDMAN	REELMAN	REPOMAN	RINGMAN	ROADMAN	RODSMAN
RUCKMAN	SAGAMAN	SEEDMAN	SHIPMAN	SHIPMENt	SHOPMAN	SIDEMAN	SOCKMAN
SOKEMAN	SONGMAN	SPAEMAN	SURFMAN	TAPSMAN	TAXIMAN	TELEMAN	TOLLMAN
TONGMAN	TOOLMAN	TOPSMAN	TRUEMAN	TURFMAN	WAKEMAN	WINGMAN	WIREMAN
WOODMAN	WOOLMAN	YARDMAN	YEGGMAN				

OID

ACAROID	AGATOID	AMEBOID	ANTHOID	ARCTOID	BYSSOID	CIRSOID	CORMOID
COSMOID	COTTOID	CTENOID	DENTOID	ERICOID	HAEMOID	HELCOID	HISTOID
HYENOID	HYPNOID	LIANOID	LITHOID	MUSCOID	MYELOID	NAEVOID	NEUROID
OBOVOID	OCELOID	OCHROID	*OIDIOID*	PHACOID	PHYTOID	PIGMOID	PYGMOID
SAUROID	SIALOID	SIMIOID	SPIROID	SPOROID	TENIOID	THEROID	TIGROID
TURDOID	VESPOID	VISCOID	ZEBROID	ZINCOID			

OSE

ACEROSE	ACETOSE	ACINOSE	ARENOSE	CARNOSE	CIRROSE	CRINOSE	EBRIOSE
GRUMOSE	HERBOSE	LABROSE	LEPROSE	MUSCOSE	OPEROSE	PANNOSE	PLUMOSE
RECHOSEn	SCAPOSE	SINUOSE	SPINOSE	TALCOSE	TITMOSE	TYPHOSE	UMBROSE
URINOSE	VENTOSE	VILLOSE					

OUS

ACETOUS	ACINOUS	ADIPOUS	AENEOUS	AGAMOUS	ANUROUS	APODOUS	ARENOUS
ATHEOUS	ATOKOUS	AZOTOUS	AZYGOUS	AZYMOUS	BADIOUS	BIVIOUS	BRUMOUS
BULLOUS	CARIOUS	CASEOUS	CEREOUS	*CESIOUS*	CHYLOUS	CHYMOUS	CIRROUS
CITROUS	CORIOUS	CORMOUS	CUPROUS	DUTEOUS	EMULOUS	ESTROUS	FEATOUS
FERROUS	FIBROUS	FOLIOUS	FULVOUS	FUNGOUS	FUSCOUS	GALLOUS	GEALOUSy
GLEBOUS	GLOBOUS	GRUMOUS	HERBOUS	HUGEOUS	HYDROUS	IMPIOUS	INVIOUS
LENTOUS	LEPROUS	LIMBOUS	LUTEOUS	NACROUS	NIMIOUS	NIOBOUS	NITROUS
NIVEOUS	NOCUOUS	OCHROUS	ODOROUS	ONYMOUS	OPACOUS	OSMIOUS	OZONOUS
PARLOUS	PERLOUS	PETROUS	PICEOUS	PILEOUS	PLUMOUS	RAMEOUS	RHODOUS
RIOTOUS	ROUTOUS	RUBIOUS	RUINOUS	SANIOUS	SARCOUS	SIMIOUS	SINUOUS

SPINOUS	SPUMOUS	TALCOUS	TIMEOUS	TYPHOUS	UBEROUS	UMBROUS	URANOUS
URINOUS	USUROUS	VACUOUS	VALGOUS	VEINOUS	VIDUOUS	VILLOUS	VISCOUS
VITIOUS	ZINCOUS						

SOME

BEESOME	EYESOME	GAYSOME	NOISOME	NOYSOME	TOYSOME	WAESOME	WAGSOME
WOESOME							

UM

CRISSUM	ELYTRUM	EXUVIUM	*IDEATUM*	ISCHIUM	JUGULUM	OSCULUM	PINETUM
PUNCTUM	*RELATUM*	TAPETUM	*TERTIUM*	UREDIUM	ZOARIUM	ZOECIUM	

US *excluding 'OUS'*

ACULEUS	ALUMNUS	ARCHEUS	ARGULUS	ARILLUS	CALAMUS	CANTHUS	CLYPEUS
COLONUS	CONATUS	CONGIUS	CUMULUS	CYATHUS	CYTISUS	EPHEBUS	FAMULUS
FRACTUS	FUMULUS	GLUTEUS	HABITUS	HAMULUS	HUMERUS	LOBULUS	MODULUS
OCELLUS	PERITUS	*PLUVIUS*	RAMULUS	SCYPHUS	SILENUS	SOLIDUS	STRATUS
THYRSUS	*TITULUS*	TORULUS	UNCINUS				

7.3.6 OTHERS CONTAINING HEAVY LETTERS

NOUNS CONTAINING 'J'

ALFORJA	APAREJO	BASENJI	BEJESUS+	BLUEJAY	CAJAPUT	CAJEPUT	CAJUPUT
CATJANG	CONJURY+	DEJEUNEr	DISJUNE	GJETOST	*HANDJOB*	IJTIHAD	JACINTHe
JACKDAW	JACKLEG	*JAMBART*	JAMBIYAh	JAMBOOL	JAMDANI	JANNOCK	JAWFALL
JAWHOLE	JELLABAh	JEOFAIL	JERREED	JESSAMY+	JETBEAD	JETFOIL	JETPORT
JIGABOO	JOANNES+	JOBNAME	JODHPUR	JOGTROT	JOYANCE	JUGGINS+	JUMBUCK
JUMELLE	KAJAWAH	KAJEPUT	*KIPUNJI*	MAJAGUA	MAJORAT	MANJACK	MOJARRA
MUNTJAC	MUNTJAK	NAARTJE	REJONEO	SAPAJOU	*WUDJULA*	ZANJERO	

NOUNS CONTAINING 'Q'

ACQUEST	ALFAQUIn	ALIQUOT	CHARQUId	COMIQUE	COQUINA	COQUITO	CUMQUAT
DAQUIRI	*DIQUARK*	GRECQUE	INQILAB	KUMQUAT	*LALIQUE*	MACAQUE	MADOQUA
MAQUILA	OBLOQUY+	OBSEQUY+	OQUASSA	PERIQUE	PIROQUE	PREQUEL	QUADRATe
QUAHAUG	QUAMASH+	QUERIDA	QUETSCH+	QUILLAIa	QUINELA	QUINNAT	QUIXOTE
QUOMODO	RELIQUE	SILIQUAe	SILIQUE	SQUADDY+	TSADDIQ	VAQUERO	

NOUNS CONTAINING 'X'

ABRASAX+	ABRAXAS+	*AIRPROX+*	ANOREXY+	ANTEFIXa	APTERYX+	ATARAXY+	*AXEBIRD*
AXOLOTL	AXONEME	BOSTRYX+	*BOXPLOT*	BOXROOM	BROADAXe	CARAPAX+	*CASEMIX+*
CELOTEX+	CHOENIX+	COALBOX+	CONFLUX+	COXALGY+	CURTAXE	*DISTRIX+*	*EDITRIX+*
EPITAXY+	*EXABYTE*	EXCHEAT	EXCIPLE	EXCLAVE	EXEGETE	EXEMPLE	EXERGUE
EXOCARP	EXODERM	EXOGAMY+	EXTREAT	*FAREBOX+*	FEEDBOX+	FIREBOX+	FOWLPOX+
FUNPLEX+	GRAVLAX+	HELLBOX+	HEXAPLAr	HEXAPODy	HEXEREI	HOMOSEX+	*HUMIDEX+*
INDOXYL	*KLEENEX+*	LOCKBOX+	MARTEXT	MAXWELL	*MEATAXE*	*MIXDOWN*	NARTHEX+
ORATRIX+	OXBLOOD	OXHEART	OXYPHILe	OXYSALT	OXYSOME	PACKWAX+	PANCHAX+
PAXIUBA	PHARYNX+	PLANXTY+	PRINCOX+	SALPINX+	SANDBOX+	SALTBOX+	SAXHORN

7. Seven-Letter Words

SAXTUBA   SEALWAX+   SEXFOIL   *SHOEBOX+*   SHOWBOX+   SONOVOX+   SPANDEX+   SUBTEXT
TALKBOX+   TELETEXt   TORTRIX+   *TREEWAX+*   TUBIFEX+   VICTRIX+   WAXBILL   WOODBOX+
WORKBOX+   XANTHAM   XYLENOL   XYLITOL   ZOOTAXY+

NOUNS CONTAINING 'Z'

ALCORZA   ALIZARIn   AZULEJO   BAZOUKI   BENZENE   BENZOYL   BEZIQUE   *BIZARRO*
BIZNAGA   BRITZKA   CANZONA   CAZIQUE   *CERVEZA*   CHALAZAe   CHALAZAl   *CHAMETZ+*
CHOMETZ+   CHORIZO   CRUZADO   CRUZADO+   CZARDAS+   CZARINA   *DANAZOL*   DIAZOLE
DOPIAZA   DOZENTH   EMPRIZE   EPAZOTE   FAHLERZ+   FAZENDA   FORZATO   GAZOOKA
GENIZAH   GUEREZA   ISOZYME   MAZURKA   MESTIZA   MESTIZO   MESTIZO+   MITZVAH
MOZETTA   ORGANZA   OUTSIZEd   RHIZOME   RIOTIZE   *ROMANZA*   ROZELLE   SAZERAC
SCHANZE   SCHERZO   SCHMALZy   SCHMELZe   SHIATZU   SHMALTZy   SOVKHOZy   SPATZLE
STARETZ+   THIAZOLe   TZARINA   TZIGANY+   WEAZAND   ZABTIEH   ZAITECH   ZAMARRA
ZAMARRO   ZAMBUCK   ZAMOUSE   ZANELLA   ZANJERO   ZAPATEO   ZAPTIAH   ZAPTIEH
ZAREEBA   ZARNICH   *ZEBRANO*   ZEBRINA   ZEBRULA   ZELKOVA   ZEMSTVO   ZENAIDA
ZIGANKA   ZIKURAT   ZOOGLEAe   ZOOGLEAl   ZOOGONY+   ZOONOMY+   ZOOTAXY+   ZOOTOMY+
ZOOTYPE   ZORILLA   ZORILLE   ZORILLO

NON-PLURALS

**ALFEREZ   ANTIJAM   ANTISEX   ANTITAX   ANZIANI   *APIEZON*   ARUSPEX   BAZOOMS
BETWIXT   BONJOUR   BRUSQUE*   CALZONI   CANZONI   CHAMOIX   DEFROZEn   ECTOZOAn
ENDOZOA   ENFROZEn   ENTOZOAl   ENTOZOAn   EPIZOON   EXCRETAl   EXEMPLAr   EXHEDRAe
EXTENSE   EXTREMAl   FORZATI   *GENIZOTh*   *GROZING*   HAZANIM   HIJINKS   JAMBEUX
JAUNTEE   JEEPERS   *JIBBONS*   *JIMPSON*   JIVEASS   *JONNOCK*   JOYRODE   *KUNJOOS*
LAYDEEZ   LOZENGY   MESQUINe   METAZOAl   METAZOAn   MIDSIZEd   MIXIBLE   MOZETTE
NONZERO   ODZOOKS   OVERLAX   OXYMORA   PARAZOAn   PERJINK   PHENOXY   PIROJKI
POLYZOAn   POSTTAX   PREJINK   PROXIMO   QUONDAM   RECTRIX   REFROZEn   RHIZOMA
RHIZOPI   SCHERZI   SHEGETZ   SHOWBIZ   SIXFOLD   SUBAQUA   SUBTAXA   SUBZERO
TAXWISE   TECTRIX   TENDENZ   *TOLARJI*   UNCRAZY   UNFROZEn   *UNISIZE*   VAUDOUX
VEXILLAr   VITRAUX   XERARCH   ZADDICK   ZAMPONE   ZAMPONI   ZEMSTVA   ZINGANI
ZINGANO   ZINGARA   ZINGARE   ZINGARI   ZINGARO   ZLOTYCH   ZOEFORM**

7.3.7 OTHER NOUNS

ABFARAD   ABIGAIL   ACADEME   ACALEPHe   ACEROLA   ACHARYA   ACHIOTE   ACOLYTE
ACOLYTH   ACUSHLA   ADENOMA   *AEROBAT*   *AEROBOT*   AEROSAT   *AGAMONT*   AGELAST
AIDANCE   AILANTO   AINSELL   AIRBOAT   AIRFOIL   AIRGLOW   AIRPARK   AIRPOST
AIRSHED   *AIRSHOT*   *AIRSHOW*   AIRSTOP   *AKIRAHO*   ALAMEDA   ALANNAH   ALCALDE
ALCAYDE   ALCHEMY+   ALCHERA   ALECOST   ALLONGE   ALLONYM   ALLSEED   ALMIRAH
ALPHORN   ALTESSE   ALTHAEA   ALTHORN   ALVEOLE   *AMANDLA*   AMANITA   AMBASSY+
AMBATCH+   AMBOINA   AMBOYNA   AMBSACE   AMESACE   AMNIOTE   *AMOKURA*   AMOROSA
AMOROSO   AMPASSY+   AMREETA   AMYLENE   ANAGOGE   *ANALYTE*   ANAPEST   ANCHUSA
ANCILLAe   ANCRESS+   ANDANTE   ANELACE   ANETHOLe   ANGIOMA   ANHINGA   *ANIMACY+*
ANISOLE   ANKLONG   ANKLUNG   ANNATTA   ANNATTO   ANNICUT   ANODYNE   ANOLYTE
ANTBIRD   ANTILOGy   APADANA   APAGOGE   APETALY+   APLANAT   APOGAMY+   APOLUNE
APOMICT   APOTHEM   APSARAS+   ARABESK   ARAROBA   ARBLAST   *ARBORIO*   ARCHFOE
ARDENCY+   ARDRIGH   ARIETTA   ARMILLAe   ARNATTO   ARNOTTO   ARRIERO   ARUGULA

ASHCAKE ASHFALL ASINICO ASSHOLE ASTATKI ASTHENY+ ASTHORE ASTILBE
ATALAYA ATEMOYA ATHLETA ATHODYD ATISHOO AUBERGE AUFGABE AURICLEd
AUROCHS+ *AUTARCHs* *AUTARCHy* AUTARKY+ AUTOMATa AUTOMATe AUTONYM *AUTOPUT*
AUTOVAC AWLBIRD

BAASKAP BACALAO BACKLOT BACKSAW BACLAVA BADMASH+ BAGARRE BAGWASH+
BAGWORM BAHADUR BAKLAVA BAKLAWA BALISTAe BALLUTE BANDANA BANDOOK
BANDORA BANDORE BANDROL *BANDSAW* BANDURA BANNOCK *BANSELA* BANTENG
BARDASH+ BARILLA BARKEEP *BARMPOT* BARONNE BARRACE BARRICO BARRICO+
BARWARE BASHLIK BASHLYK BASMATI BASOCHE *BATGIRL* BATISTE BATTUTA
BATTUTO BEARCAT BECASSE BEDTICK BEEFALO BEGINNEr BELLEEK BENOMYL
BENTHOS+ *BETTONG* BERDASH+ BERETTA BERGAMA BERGERE BERGYLT BERSEEM
BHANGRA BHEESTY+ BIDARKA BIGHORN BILSTED BILTONG BIMORPH BINOCLE
BIOCHIP *BIOFACT* *BIOFILM* BIOHERM BIOMASS+ BIONOMY+ BIOTECH BIOTOPE
BIOTYPE *BIRCHIR* *BIRDDOG* BIRETTA *BIRIANI* BIRLINN BIRYANI BISNAGA
BISTORT BITTOCK BIVINYL BLAWORT BLEWART BLEWITS+ *BLOKART* BLOWGUN
BLUECAP BOGGART BOLOGNA *BONIATO* BONNOCK *BONSELA* BORNEOL BORTSCH+
BOTARGO BOTHOLE BOTTEGA BOUILLI BOURKHA BOURLAW BOWKNOT BOWSHOT
BOWYANG BOYCHIK BRADAWL BRANSLE BRANTLE BRASERO BRAVURA BRECHAM
BREWSKI *BREWSKI+* BRICOLE BRIGAND BRIOCHE BRISTOL BRITSKA BROCOLI
BRONCHO *BUCARDO* BUCKEYE BUCKSAW BUDMASH+ BUDWORM BUGLOSS+ BUGSEED
BUGWORT BULGHUR BULLACE BULRUSHy *BUMFUCK* BUNDOOK BUNRAKU BURDASH+
BURDOCK BURGESS+ BURGHUL BURLESK BURRITO BURSEED BUSGIRL BUSHIDO
BUSHPIG *BUSUUTI* BUTANOL BYPLACE

CABILDO CADDYSS+ CADELLE CADRANS+ CAESURAe CAESURAl *CALALOO* CALDERA
CALLUNA CALOTTE CALTRAP CALTROP CALUMBA CALUMNY+ CAMBOGE CAMELOT
CAMOODI CAMORRA CAMPANA CAMPHOL CAMPONG CANBANK CANDELA *CANDIRU*
CANELLA CANNOLI CANNULAe CANNULAr CANTATA CANTDOG CANTRAP CANTRED
CANTREF CANTRIP CAPITOL CAPUERA CARABAO CARANNA CARAUNA CARBARN
CARBENE CARBORA CARFARE CARIAMA CARIERE CARIOLE CARITAS+ CASSABA
CASSAVA *CASSENA* *CASSENE* *CASSINA* CASSINO *CASSPIR* CATALPA CATARRH
CATASTA CATAWBA CATBIRD CATBOAT CATELOG CATFALL *CATFLAP* CATHOLE
CATMINT CATSPAW CATTABU CATTAIL CATTALO CATTALO+ CATWORM CAULOME
CAVALLA CAVALLY+ CAVETTO CEDILLA CEILIDH CELESTA CELESTE CEMBALO
CENTARE CENTAURy CENTAVO CENTIME CENTIMO *CERRADO* CHABOUK *CHAEBOL*
CHALUPA *CHAMISAl* CHAMISE CHAMISO CHAMPAK *CHANOYO* CHANOYU CHAPATI
CHAPATI+ CHARPAI CHARPOY *CHATBOT* CHAYOTE CHEMISE CHEROOT CHERVIL
CHESNUT CHETNIK CHEVIOT CHEWINK *CHIANTI* CHIBOUK CHIKARA CHILIAD
CHIMBLY+ CHINOOK CHLAMYS+ CHONDRE CHRISOM CHRISTY+ CHROMYL CHUPATI
CINEASTe CINEREAl CIPHONY+ CITHARA CITTERN CLARINO CLERISY+ CLIPART
CLOTBUR CODETTA CODILLA CODILLE COEHORN COLIBRI COLLINS+ COMATIK
COMPEND CONDYLE CONSEIL COONDOG COPAIBA COPAIVA COPIHUE CORANTO
CORANTO+ CORBEIL CORBINA CORDOBA CORELLA CORNUTO COROLLA CORPORAl
CORRIDA CORRODY+ CORSAIR CORSNED CORVINA CORYPHEe COTHURNi COTTOWN
COULOIR COULOMB COWBIND COWBIRD COWFLAP COWFLOP COWHERB COWHERD
COWPOKE CRANNOGe *CRAPAUD* *CRAPOLA* *CRATHUR* CRAWDAD *CREMINI* CREMONA
CREOSOL CRIMINI CRINGLE CRIOLLO CRITTUR CROTTLE CRUSADO CRUSADO+

7. Seven-Letter Words

```
CSARDAS+ CULOTTE  CUMSHAW  CUPGALL  CURRAGH  CURTANA  CURTESY+ CUTBANK
CUTDOWN  CUTWORK  CUTWORM  CYTOSOL

DADDOCK  DAGLOCK  DAIMOKU  DALGYTE  DAMBROD  DAMIANA  DANELAW  DARIOLE
DAROGHA  DASHEKI  DASHIKI  DASHPOT  DASYPOD  DAWBAKE  DAYBOAT  DAYBOOK
DAYCARE  DAYGIRL  DAYMARE  DAYMARK  DAYPACK  DAYROOM  DAYSACK  DAYTALEr
DAYWEAR  DAYWORK  DEASOIL  DEASIUL  DECALOG  DECAPOD  DECIARE  DECIDUAe
DECIDUAl DEMAYNE  DEMESNE  DEMIREP  DEMIVEG+ DEODAND  DEPECHE  DERVISH+
DETINUE  DEWANNY+ DEWFALL  DHANSAK  DHOURRA  DIABOLO  DIADROM  DIASTEMa
DICAMBA  DICHORD  DICKENS+ DICLINY+ DICOTYL  DIDAKAI  DIDAKEI  DIDICOI
DIDICOY  DIEBACK  DIETHYL  DIGICAM  DIGLYPH  DIGRAPH  DIMORPH  DINMONT
DIOPTRE  DIORAMA  DIPTERAl DIPTERAn DIPTYCA  DIPTYCH  DIRTBAG  DISEUSE
DISFAME  DISTICHs DISTOME  DISTYLE  DITTANY+ DOGBOLT  DOGCART  DOGFACE
DOGGESS+ DOGHOLE  DOGTOWN  DOMICILe DONGOLA  DOPATTA  DORHAWK  DORLACH
DORNECK  DORNICK  DORNOCK  DOVECOTe DOYENNE  DRACENA  DRAMADY+ DRAMEDY+
DREVILL  DROSERA  DROSHKY+ DROSTDYs DRYWELL  DUARCHY+ DUBSTEP  DUNNART
DUNNOCK  DUOPOLY+ DUPATTA  DURANCE  DURMAST  DUSTRAG  DUUMVIRi DUVETYNe
DVORNIK  DYSODILe DYSPNEAl

EARBALL  EARFLAP  EARLOCK  EARPICK  EARWORM  EBAUCHE  EBRIETY+ ECHELLE
ECLOGUE  ECTHYMA  ECUELLE  EELFARE  EELWORM  EGGMASS+ EGGWASH+ EIGHTVO
EINKORN  EKPWELE  ELDRESS+ ELFLOCK  ELLWAND  EMERITAe EMPRISE  ENCRATY+
ENDLEAF  ENDNOTE  ENDOPOD  ENOMOTY+ ENPRINT  ENTENTE  ENTROPY+ EOBIONT
EPAGOGE  EPERGNE  EPHEDRA  EPIBLEM  EPIBOLY+ EPICEDE  EPIDERM  EPIDOTE
EPISOME  EPITHEMa ERATHEM  EROTEMA  EROTEME  ERRANCY+ ESPARTO  ESSOYNE
ESTHETE  ESTRIOL  ETAERIO  ETAGERE  ETHINYL  ETHIOPS+ ETRENNE  EUGENOL
EUGLENA  EUPHORY+ EUPNOEA  EUSTACY+ EUSTASY+ EUSTELE  EUSTYLE  EUTROPY+
EYEBANK  EYEBATH  EYEBEAM  EYEBOLT  EYEFOLD  EYEHOLE  EYEHOOK  EYELIAD
EYELIFT  EYESHOT  EYESPOT  EYEWASH+ EYEWINK

FACIEND  FACONNE  FADAISE  FAHLORE  FAIENCE  FALBALA  FALCULAe FAMILLE
FANTAIL  FANTASM  FANTAST  FANTEEG  FANWORT  FARADAY  FARINHA  FARRAGO
FARRAGO+ FARRUCA  FARTLEK  FATBACK  FATBIRD  FAYENCE  FEEDBAG  FELWORT
FERMATA  FERRUGO  FETLOCK  FIBROMA  FIGWORT  FILABEG  FILASSE  FILBERD
FILBERT  FILEMOT  FILIBEG  FINBACK  FINDRAM  FINMARK  FINNOCK  FIREDOG
FIREPOT  FISHEYE  FISHGIG  FISTULAe FISTULAr FLATCAP  FLATTOP  FLOKATI
FLUENCE  FLUTINA  FLYBACK  FLYBELT  FLYBOAT  FLYBOOK  FLYHAND  FOLIOLE
FOLKMOTe FONTINA  FOOTBAG  FOOTPAD  FOREBAY  FOREGUT  FOREPAW  FORETOP
FORLANA  FOUMART  FOVEOLAe FOVEOLAr FOVEOLEt FOYBOAT  FRACTURe FRAKTUR
FROGEYEd FUNICLE  FURIOSO  FURLANA  FURMETY+ FUSAROLe FUSBALL  FUSILLI
FUTHARC  FUTHARK  FUTHORC  FUTHORK  FUTTOCK

GABELLEd GABELLEr GABFEST  GABNASH+ GADWALL  GALABEAh GALANGAl GALATEA
GALIPOT  GALLIOT  GALLNUT  GALLOOT  GAMBOGE  GANACHE  GANGSTA  GARBOIL
GARIGUE  GAROUPA  GARPIKE  GARVOCK  GASAHOL  GASOHOL  GASTREA  GEDECKT
GEEBUNG  GEELBEK  GEMCLIP  GEMSBOK  GENISTA  GENOISE  GENSENG  GEODESY+
GEODUCK  GEOFACT  GEOGENY+ GEOGONY+ GERBERA  GERENUK  GESTALT  GHILGAI
GILBERT  GINGELI  GINGELY+ GINGHAM  GINGILI  GINSENG  GINSHOP  GIRASOLe
GIRLOND  GIROLLE  GIROSOL  GISARME  GLUCINA  GLUEPOT  GOBURRA  GODSLOT
```

GOLDARN	GOLDBUG	GOLDEYE	GOLDURN	*GOLIATH*	GOMERIL	*GONOPOD*	GOOMBAH
GOOMBAY	GORCROW	*GORDITA*	GORMAND	GORSEDD	GOSHAWK	GOSPORT	GOUACHE
GOURAMI	GOURAMI+	GRANDAD	GRANDAMe	GRANITA	GRANNAM	*GRANNOM*	GRANOLA
GRAYLAG	GREENTH	GREYLAG	GROCKLE	GROGRAM	GRUYERE	GRYSBOK	GUANACO
GUARANA	GUARANI	GUARANI+	*GUMBALL*	GUMBOIL	GUMDROP	GUNPLAY	GUNPORT
GUNROOM	GUNWALE	GWINIAD	GWYNIAD	*GYMSLIP*	GYTRASH+		

HABITUE	HACKBUT	HADROME	HAEMONY+	HAFTARAh	HAGBOLT	HAGDOWN	HAIRCAP
HALBERD	HALIBUT	HALIMOTe	*HALOUMI*	HAMBURG	HANGDOG	HANGTAG	*HAPKIDO*
HAPLONT	*HARAMDA*	*HARAMDI*	*HARDASS+*	HARDOKE	HARDTOP	HARIANA	HARICOT
HARISSA	HARMALA	HARMOSTy	HASSOCKy	HATTOCK	HAUBERK	HAVARTI	HAWBUCK
HAYBAND	HAYFORK	HAYRACK	*HAYRAKE*	*HEADEND*	HEADRIG	HEELTAP	*HEITIKI*
HEKTARE	HELIAST	HELLCAT	HEMAGOG	HEMIOLA	*HEMIPODe*	HENCOOP	HERDESS+
HERSALL	HETAERAe	HETAIRAi	HEYDUCK	HIDALGA	HIDALGO	HINDGUT	HISTRIOn
HODADDY+	HOECAKE	HOEDOWN	HOGBACK	*HOKONUI*	HOLDALL	HOLIBUT	HOLYDAMe
HOMBURG	HOMOLOGy	HOOFROT	HOOLOCK	HOOSGOW	HOPBIND	HOPSACK	HOPTOAD
HORDOCK	*HORNBAG*	HORNBUG	HORNITO	*HOROEKA*	*HOTLINK*	*HOTSPOT*	HOTSPUR
HUANACO	HURLBAT	HUSWIFE	*HYDROMA*	HYDROPSy	*HYGROMA*	HYPONEA	

ICEBALL	ICEBOAT	ICEFALL	IDIOTCY+	IDLESSE	IGARAPE	IKEBANA	ILKADAY
IMPASTO	IMPIETY+	IMPRESA	IMPRESE	IMPREST	INBREAK	INBURST	INCONNUe
· INDRAFT	INFARCT	INFAUNAe	INFAUNAl	INGRESS+	INKBLOT	INKHORN	*INKHOSI*
INSCAPE	INTRADAy	IPOMOEA	ISAGOGE	*ISOAMYL*	ISOBATH	ISODONT	*ISOFORM*
ISOGAMY+	ISOGENY+	ISOGRAM	ISOGRIV	ISOKONT	ISOLEAD	*ISONOME*	ISONOMY+
ISOPACHs	ISOTACHs	ISOTOPY+	ISOTYPE	IVRESSE			

KABADDI	KACHERI	KACHINA	KADDISH+	KAHAWAI	KALIMBA	KAMICHI	KAMPONG
KANTELA	KANTELE	*KARENGO*	*KAROSHI*	KASHRUTh	KATCINA	KATORGA	*KATSURA*
KEITLOA	KELLAUT	*KERBAYA*	KERYGMA	*KETUBAH*	KHEDIVAl	KIDDUSH+	KILLCOW
KILORAD	KIRMESS+	KITENGE	KITHARA	KLATSCH+	KLAVERN	KLEAGLE	KLIPDAS+
KLOOTCH+	KNITTLE	KOLBASI	*KOROWAI*	KUFIYAH	*KULBASA*		

LADYCOW	LAETARE	*LAKEBED*	LAMBADA	LAMELLAe	LAMELLAr	LAMPUKA	LAMPUKI
LANGAHA	LAPSANG	*LAPTRAY*	LAPWORK	LASAGNE	LASSOCK	LATENCE	LATENCY+
LATILLA	LATITAT	LATOSOL	LAVROCK	*LAWFARE*	LAYLOCK	LAYTIME	LEAFBUD
LECHAIM	LECTURN	LECYTHI	LEGHORN	LEGITIM	LEHAYIM	LEMPIRA	*LENTISC*
LENTISK	LEPTOME	LEUCOMA	LEUKOMA	LEWDSBY+	LINALOL	LINECUT	LINGCOD
LINGULAe	LINGULAr	*LINKROT*	LINOCUT	LINSANG	*LIRIOPE*	LISPUND	LITURGY+
LIVELOD	LLANERO	LOBIPED	LOBWORM	LOCKNUT	LOCKRAM	LONGBOW	LORDOMA
LORRELL	LOVEBUG	LOWVELD	LUCARNE	LUGHOLE	LUGSAIL	LUGWORM	LUMBANG
LUTFISK	LUTHERN	LYCOPOD	LYMPHAD				

MACHAIR	MADDOCK	MADEIRA	MADRONA	MADRONO	MADWORT	MAFIOSO	MAGALOG
MAHUANG	MAILLOT	MAINTOP	MALANGA	MALARKY+	MALICHO	*MALWARE*	MANCALA
MANDALA	MANDIOCa	MANDOLA	MANDORA	MANDRILl	MANGABY+	*MANGEAO*	MANGOLD
MANIHOC	MANIHOT	MANILLA	MANILLE	MANIPLE	*MANKINI*	MANPACK	MANROPE
MANYATA	MARABOUt	MARANTA	MARASCA	MARCATO	MARGOSA	MARPLOT	MARRANO
MARSALA	MARYBUD	MASTABAh	MATELOTe	MATOOKE	MATRASS+	MATROSS+	MATSURI
MAWSEED	*MAYBIRD*	MAYBUSH+	MEDIACY+	*MEDIGAP*	MEDRESA	*MEDRESE*	MEDULLAe

MEDULLAr MEERCAT MEERKAT MEGAFOG MEGAPODe *MEGILLA*h MELANGE MELILOT
MELTITH MENDIGO MENORAH *MERANTI* MERFOLK MESCLUN MESHUGAh MESTESO
MESTESO+ MESTINO MESTINO+ *METATAG* METCAST METHINK METISSE MIDCULT
MIDSOLE MILFOIL MILKSOP MILLRUN MINEOLA MINILAB MINISKI MINORCA
MINUEND MISDEED MISEASE MISTBOW MISTICO MITSVAH MOCHELL MOCHILA
MOCKADO+ MODELLO MOIDORE *MOLASSE* MOLLUSK MONARDA MONOCOT MONOECY+
MONOFIL MONOPODe MONOPODy MONTERO MOONBOW MOONEYE MOORILL MOORLOG
MORELLE MORELLO MORICHE MORISCO MORISCO+ MORPHEW *MORRELL* MORRHUA
MORWONG *MOSELLE* MOUSAKA MOVIOLA MRIDANGa MUDFLOW MUDHOLE MUDHOOK
MUDROCK MUDSCOW MUDSILL MUDWORT MUGGINS+ MUGWORT MULATTA MULATTO
MULATTO+ MULLOCKy MURAENA *MURRAGH* MUSKRAT MUSPIKE *MYCELLA* MYOSOTE
MYOTUBE MYRINGA MYRRHOL

NACARAT NACELLE NAEBODY+ NAIVETE NAMASTE *NANOBOT* *NANODOT* NAPHTOL
NARCOMA NARGILY+ NASHGAB NAVARCHs NAVARCHy NAVARHO *NEATNIK* NEGLIGEe
NEGRONI NELUMBO *NEOSOUL* NEOTENY+ NEOTYPE *NETROOT* NETSUKE NEUROMA
NEURULAe NEURULAr *NGARARA* NIBLICK *NIDDICK* NIGELLA NIHONGA NILGHAI
NILGHAU NIMIETY+ NITINOL NOCTURNe NOMARCHy NOMBRIL NONBANK NONBODY+
NONBOOK NONCOLA NONETTO NONFACT NONHERO+ NONPAST NONPLAY NONSKED
NONSUCH+ NONUPLEt NONWORD NOONDAY NORTENA NORTENO NOSEBAG NOSEGAY
NOTAIRE NOURICE NOVELLAe NOYANCE NUDNICK NUNATAK NUTGALL NUTMEAT
NUTPICK NYLGHAI NYLGHAU

OAKMOSS+ OARLOCK OATCAKE OBVERSE OCTANOL OCTAPLA OCTOPOD ODALISK
OERSTED OILBIRD OILCAMP OILHOLE *OLESTRA* *OLICOOK* OLITORY+ OLOROSO
OLYCOOK OMNIETY+ ONDATRA ONSTEAD OOFTISH+ OOPHYTE OOSPERM OOSPORE
OPERAND OPHIURAn OPORICE OPUSCLE ORCINOL ORGANDY+ ORIENCY+ ORLEANS+
OROPESA ORTHROS+ *OSSETRA* OSSICLE OSTEOMA OSTIOLE OSTMARK OTOCYST
OTOLITH OUGUIYA OUSTITI *OUTCALL* OUTEDGE OUTHAUL OUTLASH+ OUTPART
OUTPORT OUTROOP OUTROPEr OUTSERT OUTSOLE OUTTURN OUTWASH+ OVERSEA
OVIDUCT OWRELAY

PACHISI PADELLA PAENULAe PAHLAVI PAKFONG PAKTONG PALABRA PALETOT
PALINKA PALMYRA PALOOKA PANACEAn PANDECT PANDORA PANDORE PANDURA
PANGAMY+ PANGRAM PANICLEd PANNICK PANOCHA PANOCHE PARACME PARADOS+
PARAFLE PARANYM PARATHA PAREIRA PARELLA PARELLE PARGANA PARONYMy
PARTITA PARVENUe PASSADO PASSADO+ PASSATA PASTINA PATBALL PATELLAe
PATELLAr PATENCY+ PATRICK PATRICO+ *PAVISSE* PAYLIST PEACOAT PEAFOWL
PEASCOD PEDAGOGy PEDICAB PEDICLEd PEDRAIL PEDRERO PEDRERO+ PEEKABOo
PEERESS+ PEISHWAh PELISSE PELLACH PELLACK PELLOCK PEMBINA PENICIL
PENOCHE PENTACT PENTENE PENUCHE PENUCHI PERCALE PEREIRA *PERENTY*+
PERFIDY+ PERIDOTe PERILLA PERIOST PERSALT PERSICOt PESAUNT PETASOS+
PETIOLEd PETRALE PFENNIGe PHELLEM PHONEME *PHORESY*+ PIANINO PIASABA
PIASAVA PIASTRE PIBROCH PICKMAW PIDDOCK PIEDISH+ PIEFORT *PIEHOLE*
PIEROGI+ PIERROT PIGBOAT *PIGFACE* PIGHTLE PIGMEAT PIGNOLIa PIGWASH+
PILCORN PILCROW *PILINUT* PINDARI PINDOWN PINITOL PINNACE PINNOCK
PINNULAe PINNULAr PINOCLE PINTADA PINTADO PINTAIL PINTANO PINWALE
PINWORM PIRAGUA PIRANHA PIROGUE PISCINAe PISCINAl *PISHEOG* PISHOGE
PISSOIR PITUITA PLAFOND PLECTRE PLEROMA PLEROME PLIMSOLe PLIMSOLl

PLUGOLA	PLUMCOT	*POBLANO*	POCHOIR	PODAGRAl	PODESTA	POETESS+	POINADO+
POLACRE	POLENTA	POLLACK	POLLICY+	POLLOCK	POLYCOT	POLYENE	POLYGAMy
POLYOMA	POMEROY	POOFTAH	PORCINI	PORRIGO	PORTESSe	PORTICO	PORTICO+
POSAUNE	POSEUSE	*POSITIF*	POSTBAG	POSTDOC	POTENCE	POTHOOK	POTICHE
POTLACHe	POTOROO	POUFTAH	POULDRE	*POUSADA*	POWHIRI	PREBEND	PREGAME
PRELACY+	PRELATY+	PRETERM	PRIMACY+	PRIMULA	PRIVADO	PRIVADO+	PROBANG
PRODRUG	PROSODY+	PROSOMAl	PROTHYL	PROTORE	PROVAND	PROVOST	PRURIGO
PUCELLE	PUDDOCK	PUDENCY+	PUGMARK	*PUKATEA*	PUNALUAn	PURLIEU	PURVIEW
PUSHROD	PUTCHUK	*PUTDOWN*	PUTLOCK	PUTTOCK	PYEBALD		

RABANNA	RACLOIR	RADIATA	RADICLE	RAGBOLT	RAGWORK	RAGWORM	RAGWORT
RAILBED	RAKSHASa	RAMPICK	RAMPIKE	RAMPOLE	RANGOLI	RANPIKE	RAPLOCH
RASBORA	RATATAT	RATHOLE	RATPACK	RATTAIL	*RAUPATU*	*RAURIKI*	RECLAME
REDBIRD	REDCOAT	*REDFOOT*	REDPOLL	REDROOT	REDTAIL	REDWARE	REEDBED
REGOSOL	REITBOK	RELACHE	RELIEVO	*RELLENO*	REMBLAI	REREDOS+	REREMAI
RETABLE	RETICLE	RETINOL	REVEUSE	RHATANY+	RHODORA	RHYTINA	RIBWORK
RIBWORT	RICKSHAw	RICOTTA	RIDOTTO	RIGGALD	RIKISHA	RIKSHAW	RIMROCK
RIMSHOT	RINGTAW	RIOTISE	RIPCORD	RIPIENO	RISIBLE	RISOTTO	RIVIERE
ROADBED	ROCKABYe	ROCKLAY	ROEBUCK	*ROGALLO*	ROKELAY	ROLLMOP	ROLLOCK
ROMAIKA	ROMAUNT	ROMNEYA	RONDINO	*ROOIKAT*	ROOINEK	*ROOTCAP*	ROSEBAY
ROSEHIP	ROSELLA	ROSELLE	ROSEOLAr	ROSINOL	ROSOLIO	ROUILLE	ROUNDLEt
ROWLOCK	RUBASSE	RUBELLAn	RUBEOLAr	RUDDOCK	RUDESBY+	RUFIYAA	RULLOCK
RUNANGA	RUNBACK	RUNDALE	RUNFLAT	RUSALKA	*RUSSULAe*	RYEPECK	

SABELLA	SABURRAl	SACKBUT	*SADHANA*	SAGATHY+	SAGITTAl	SAGUARO	SAHUARO
SAIMIRI	SAKIYEH	SAKSAUL	SALBAND	SALCHOW	SALFERN	SALIGOT	SALSIFY+
SALTCAT	SALVETE	SAMADHI	SAMBHUR	SAMBUCA	SAMBUKE	*SAMITHI*	*SAMOYED*
SAMSARA	SAMSHOO	SANDBURr	SANDDAB	SANDHOG	SANDLOT	SANGOMA	SANICLE
SANTERA	*SANTERO*	*SANYASI*	SAOUARI	SAPHENAe	SAPROBE	SAPSAGO	SARANGI
SARCINAe	SARCOMA	SARDANA	SASHIMI	SATIETY+	SATSUMA	SAUTOIRe	SAWBILL
SAWBUCK	SCALADO	SCAPULAe	SCAPULAr	SCATOLE	SCHANSE	SCHELLY+	SCHLONG
SCHNOOK	SCHTOOK	SCOTOMA	SCOTOMY+	SCRIENE	SCROYLE	SCYTALE	SEABANK
SEABOOT	SEAFOLK	SEAFOWL	SEAHAWK	SEAKALE	SEAMARK	SEAWALL	SEAWARE
SEAWORM	SEBUNDY+	SEEDLIP	SEMIPED	SEMIPRO	SENECIO	SENTIMO	SEPIOST
SEPTIME	SERIEMA	SERKALI	SERPIGO	SERPIGO+	SESTINA	SETUALE	SETWALL
SEVICHE	SEVRUGA	SFUMATO	SHADOOF	SHAKUDO	SHALLOP	*SHAMINA*	SHASLIK
SHASTRA	SHEBANG	*SHEMALE*	*SHERANG*	SHEREEF	SHEROOT	SHIATSU	SHICKSA
SHITAKE	SHITTIM	*SHIVITI*	*SHMATTE*	SHOEPACk	*SHOPBOT*	SHOTTLE	SIAMANG
SIEVERT	SILICLE	SILLOCK	SIMARRE	SINGULT	SIRGANG	*SITELLA*	SITFAST
SKYHOME	SKYSAIL	SLADANG	SMARAGDe	*SMOKEHO*	*SNOTRAG*	SNOWCAP	*SNOWCAT*
SOCKEYE	*SOFABED*	SOLDADO	SOLFEGE	SOLIPED	SONANCE	SONANCY+	SONDELI
SOROCHE	SOUBISE	SOUROCK	SOURSOP	SOUSLIK	SOWBACK	SOYMILK	*SPAMBOT*
SPERTHE	SPIRAEA	SPIRTLE	SPIRULAe	SPONDYL	SPREAGH	SPUMONI	SPURTLE
SPYWARE	SRADDHA	STACHYS+	STADDLE	STARETS+	STEMBOK	STENGAH	STENOKY+
STEWPOT	STIPEND	*STOMACK*	STRETTA	STRETTO	STRIGIL	STROBILa	STROBILe
STROBILi	STROPHE	STUDDLE	STYRENE	SUBAREA	SUBATOM	SUBCELL	SUBCULT
SUBECHO+	SUBFUSC	SUBFUSK	SUBIDEA	SUBITEM	SUBRACE	SUBSALE	SUBSECT
SUBSERE	SUBSONG	SUBTACK	SUBTASK	SUBTEST	SUBTYPE	SUMATRA	SUNBATHe

7. Seven-Letter Words

SUNBIRD	SUNDARI	SUNGLOW	SUNTRAP	SURANCE	SURCOAT	SWINGBYs	*SYLLOGE*
SYMBIOTe	SYNAPTE	SYNCARPy	SYNCHRO	SYNCOPE	SYNTAGMa	SYRINGA	SYSTOLE

TABRERE	TALAUNT	TALAYOT	TALIPAT	TALIPOT	TALOOKA	TAMANDUa	TAMASHA
TAMBALA	TAMPALA	TANAGRA	TANBARK	TANGELO	TANGRAM	TANIWHA	*TANKINI*
TANTIVY+	TANTONY+	TAPHOLE	TAPLASH+	TAPROOM	TAPROOT	*TARAIRE*	*TARAMEA*
TARBUSH+	TARROCK	TARTUFE	*TARTUFO*	TATOUAY	*TAUHINU*	*TAUPATA*	TAUTAUG
TAWHIRI	TEABOWL	TEACART	TEASHOP	TEAWARE	TELECOM	TELEOST	TELERGY+
TELFORD	TENTIGO	TERAOHM	TEREBRAe	TERPENE	TERRENE	*TERROIR*	TESTACY+
TESTRILl	TESTUDO	TETRACT	TEUCHAT	THALWEG	*THANGKA*	THEELOL	THEOLOGy
THEORBO	THERIACa	THEURGY+	THIONYL	THREAVE	THRENOS+	THRETTY+	THRIMSA
THRUPUT	THRYMSA	TIDERIP	TIEBACK	*TIKANGA*	TIMARAU	TIMOLOL	TIMOTHY+
TINAMOU	TINHORN	TINTACK	TINTYPE	TINWARE	TIPCART	TIRASSE	TITLARK
TOECLIP	TOESHOE	*TOFUTTI*	TOHEROA	TOHUNGA	TOISECH	TOLUENE	TOMBOLA
TOMBOLO	TONDINO	TONEARM	TONEPAD	TONNELL	TOPARCHs	TOPARCHy	TOPCOAT
TOPKNOT	TOPMAST	TOPONYMy	TOPSAIL	TORGOCH	TORTONI	TOSTADA	TOSTADO
TOURACO	TOWBOAT	TOWPATH	*TOWSACK*	TRACHEAe	TRACHEAl	TRANCHEt	TRANECT
TRANGAM	TRANGLE	TREAGUE	TREFOIL	TREHALA	TREILLE	TREMOLO	TRENISE
TRIARCHs	TRIARCHy	TRIBADY+	TRICLAD	TRICORNe	TRIDARN	*TRIELLA*	TRIFOLY+
TRIGAMY+	TRIGLOT	TRIGRAM	TRILITH	TRILOBEd	TRIMTAB	TRINGLE	TRIONYM
TRIPACK	TRIPOLI	TRIREME	TRISEME	TRISOME	TRISOMY+	TRITOMA	TROMINO
TROMINO+	TRYSAIL	TSADDIK	*TSANTSA*	*TSATSKE*	TUATARA	TUATERA	TUBFAST
TUGHRIK	TUNDISH+	TUNICLE	TURBETH	TURBOND	TURFSKI	TURISTA	TURKIES+
TURNDUN	TURPETH	TUSSUCK	TUTENAG	TUTRESS+	TUTWORK	TWANKAY	TWASOME
TWIGLOO	TYLOPOD						

UKULELE	UMBRERE	*UMLUNGU*	UNFAITH	*UNIBROW*	UNIFACE	UNRIGHT	UNTRUSTy
UNWORTHy	UPSTAIR	UPTREND	URGENCE	URODELE	UROLITH	UROMERE	UROSOME
USAUNCE	UTRICLE						

VACATUR	VACUOLE	VALENCE	VALONEA	VANESSA	VANITAS+	*VANLOAD*	VANPOOL
VAREUSE	VARIOLAr	VARIOLE	VELOUTE	VENDACE	VENTANA	VENTIGE	VERBENA
VERGLAS+	VERMELL	VERMUTH	VERRUCAe	VERRUGA	VESICLE	VESSAIL	VETTURA
VIBRATOr	VICOMTE	VICUGNA	VIHUELA	VILIACO	VILIACO+	VILIAGO	VILIAGO+
VINASSE	VIRANDA	VIRANDO	VIRELAI	VIRELAY	VIRETOT	VISNOMY+	VITESSE
VOCABLE	VOLPINO	VOLUSPA	VOTRESS+	VULTURN			

WAESUCK	WAKANDA	WALLABA	WALLEYEd	WAMEFOU	WANHOPE	*WANKSTA*	WANNABEe
WARBIRD	WARDROP	*WAREHOU*	WASHDAY	WASHPOT	WASHRAG	WATTAPE	*WAVICLE*
WAYBILL	WAYPOST	WEASAND	*WEBLISH+*	*WEBMAIL*	WEIGELA	WENDIGO	WERGELD
WERGELT	WERGILD	WESSAND	WETBACK	WHAMPLE	WHANGAM	WHIPCAT	WHIPRAY
WHIRTLE	WHORTLE	WICKAPE	*WILLIAM*	WINDGUN	WINDOCK	WINDORE	*WINESAP*
WINESOP	WINNOCK	*WIRILDA*	*WISEGUY*	WISTITI	WITLOOF	WOLFRAM	WOODCUT
WOODLOT	*WOODRAT*	WOOLFAT	WOOLHAT	WOORARA	WOORARI	WORKBAG	WORKDAY
WOSBIRD	WRYBILL	WRYNECK					

YAMALKA	YAMULKA	YARDANG	YASHMAC	YASHMAK	YESHIVAh	*YOHIMBE*	YOUNGTH

7.3.8 OTHER NON-PLURALS

ACHARNE	ACIFORM	ADDIBLE	ADDREST	AEFAULD	AFTMOST	AGELONG	*AGGADOTh*
AGITANS	AGITATOr	AGRAPHA	AIBLINS	AIRWISE	ALAMORT	ALBERGO	ALEWIFE
ALFREDO	ALIFORM	ALIUNDE	ALONGST	ALVEOLI	*AMADODA*	*AMAKOSI*	AMATORY
AMBITTY	AMEARST	AMORINI	AMORINO	AMPULLAe	AMPULLAr	ANESTRA	ANESTRI
ANGLICE	ANIMATOr	ANTIAIR	ANTIBUG	ANTIFAT	ANTIFLU	*ANTIFOG*	ANTIFUR
ANTIGAY	ANTIGUN	ANTIPOT	ANTISAG	ANYMORE	ANYROAD	ANYWISE	*APESHIT*
APICULI	*ARCHAEAl*	*ARCHAEAn*	ARCHAEI	ARRIERE	ASCAUNT	ATTABOY	ATTONCE
AVIFORM							

BACILLI	BACKARE	BATWING	BAUSOND	BAWSUNT	BECURST	BEDFAST	BEGORAH
BEGORRAh	BEKNOWN	BENEMPT	BESHONE	BESPAKE	BESPOKEn	BESTUCK	BETIGHT
BICHORD	BIGFEET	BIGGETY	BIGGITY	*BIGTIME*	BIODATA	BIPARTY	*BLIKSEM*
BONSOIR	*BOOTCUT*	BOSHTER	BOTTONY	*BRACHOT*	BRAVURE	BRONCHIa	BUCKSOM
BULLOSA	BURSERA	BUTTALS	BYNEMPT				

CABOVER	CAERULE	CALANDO	CALATHI	CALENDS	CAMAIEUx	CARAMBA	CAVETTI
CEMBALI	CEREBRAl	CHAMBRE	CHONDRIn	CHORAGIc	CHOREGIc	CINGULAr	CLARINI
COAGULA	COBLOAF	CODROVE	COENURI	COLOSSI	COMPONE	COMPONY	CONDIGN
CONFEST	CORALLA	CORTILI	COTYLAE	COULDST	COWROTE	CREMSIN	*CRETONS*
CRIMINAl	*CRIMINY*	CRIVENS	CRUELLS	*CULMINA*	CYPSELAe		

DAMFOOL	*DAYANIM*	DAYLONG	DEIFORM	DELEBLE	DELENDA	DELIBLE	DELPHIN
DERNIER	DEWFULL	DIALLEL	DIBUTYL	DIHEDRAl	DINITRO	DIPHASE	DISPRAD
DITHIOL	DIVISIM	DOCHMII	DOCIBLE	DODDARD	DOGMATA	*DOLOSSE*	DONNARD
DONNART	DONNERD	DONNERT	DORMICE	DUCDAME	DUODENAl		

EBONICS	EDEMATA	ELDRICH	ELKHORN	ELUSORY	ELYTRON	EMBASTE	EMBAYLD
EMERITI	EMPIGHT	EMPTINS	ENDARCHy	ENDLANG	ENDLONG	ENDMOST	ENDWAYS
ENDWISE	ENEMATA	ENSWEPT	ENTRALL	ENTROLD	ENWOUND	EPHEBOI	EPHEBOS
EPIGENE	EPINAOI	EPINAOS	ERELONG	EREMURI	ESPANOL	ETATISTe	ETOURDIe

FABLIAUx	FAGOTTI	FAGOTTO	FANWISE	FARMOST	FARRAND	*FAUNULAe*	FEDAYEEn
FEELBAD	FIASCHI	FINIKINg	FINNSKO	FLOREAT	*FLORULAe*	FLYBLEW	*FORBARE*
FORBORE	FORDONE	FORWORN	FOSSULAe	FRENULAr	FRONTER	FUMETTI	FUMETTO
FUNEBRE	FURCULAe	FURCULAr	FUSIBLE				

GALLOCK	*GARBAGY*	GATELEG	*GATLING*	*GEFILTE*	*GELANDE*	GERTCHA	GIDDYAP
GIDDYUP	GINGIVAe	GINGIVAl	GIOCOSO	*GIRONNY*	GLAIKET	GLOMERA	GLUTAEI
GOBONEE	*GOSPODAr*	GOYISCH	*GUELDER*				

HADARIM	*HADAWAY*	HADDEST	HAGBORN	HAGRODE	HARDSET	HELLOVA	HELLUVA
HERISSE	HIDLINS	*HIELAND*	HISSELF	HOLESOMe	*HUCKERY*	HYPOGEAl	HYPOGEAn

ICHABOD	IMBRAST	INCIVIL	INDRAWN	INDWELT	INEDITA	INFAUST	INLYING
INOCULA	INPHASE	INSHORE	INSIGNE	INSOOTH	INSULSE	INSWEPT	INTAGLIo
INTROLD	INWOUND	IRACUND	ISODICA	ISODOMA			

7. Seven-Letter Words

KALENDS KERCHOO *KETUBOT*h *KEYRING* KNAIDEL *KOHANIM* *KONGONI*

LABELLA LAMBOYS LAPHELD LAPILLI LASHINS LATERAD LEKYTHI LENTIGO
LICENTE LISENTE LISTETH *LITHOPS* LOGGETS LOWBORN LUSTICK LYOPHILe

MACABER MAESTRI MAFIOSI *MALTESE* MANWISE MAPWISE MARENGO MARRELS
MENISCI MESARCH METOPAE MIDDEST *MIDBAND* MIDRASH MILCHIG *MILCHIK*
MINCEUR *MIOCENE* MISBORN MISDREW MISDONE MISFELL MISGAVE MISGONE
MISGREW MISKEPT MISKNEW MISLAIN MISMADE MISSHOD *MISSOLD* MISTEUK
MISTOLD MODELLI MODIOLI MOLOSSI MONERON MORENDO MOUILLE *MUSCOVY*
MUTANDA

NAIVIST NATHEMO NAUPLII NAUTILI *NEOGENE* NEWCOMEr *NICOISE* NONCASH
NONCORE *NONDRIP* NONDRUG NONETTI NONFARM NONFOOD NONFUEL NONGAME
NONHEME NONHOME NONIRON NONLIFE NONMEAT NONNEWS NONPEAK NONPOOR
NONSELF *NONWAGE* *NONWOOL* NONWORK *NOPLACE* NOTANDA NOUMENA1 NOVELLE
NUCELLI NURAGHE NURAGHIc

OBELION OLDWIFE OMNIANA OMPHALIc ONEFOLD ONLIEST ONSTAGE OODLINS
OOTHECAe OOTHECA1 *OPGEFOK* OSTRACA OSTRAKA OUTDREW OUTFELT OUTFLEW
OUTGAVE OUTGONE OUTKEPT OUTLAIN OUTSANG OUTSUNG OUTTOLD OUTTOOK
OUTWEPT OUTWORE OUTWORN OVERAPT OVERBIG OVERCOY OVERFAT OVERHOT
OVERNEW OVERSAD OVIFORM OVIPARA

PADRONI PANDANI PARERGA PARODOI PARODOS PARTITE PATIBLE PATONCE
PENNILL *PENTITI* *PENTITO* PERCASE PERFUMY PERICON PERINEA1 PERTOOK
PERTUSEd PESSIMA1 PHILTRA *PICANTE* PIGNORA PIROGHI *PITIETH* PLANULAe
PLANULAr PLECTRA PLEURON PLUMULAe PLUMULAr POLYACT *PORANGI* PORCINO
PREBADE PREBOOM PRECAVAe PRECAVA1 PREFARD PRELIFE PRELUDIo PREMOLT
PREMUNE PRENOON PRERACE PRERIOT PREROCK PRESONG PRITHEE PROBALL
PROFACE PRONAOI PRONAOS PRONOTA1 PRYTHEE PTERION PTERYLAe PUDENDA1
PULVINI *PUNAANI* *PUNAANY*

RATBITE RAWBONEd REAWOKEn REBEGUN RECHOSEn REDROVE REGMATA RESHONE
RESIDUA1 RESPELT RESPOKEn RHOMBOId RHOMBOS RIKISHI RILIEVI RILIEVO
RIPIENI *RISORII* ROLLTOP *ROOIBOS* ROSETTY RULESSE

SACELLA *SAGRADA* SAIDEST SALTATO SANTIMI SANTIMS *SANTIMU* SAPIENS
SCALENE SCALENI SCEPTRY SCHNELL SCHTOOM SCIOLTO SCIRRHI SCOLION
SCURRILe SCYBALA SEAGIRT SEAWIFE SEDARIM SEEWING SEMEION SEMIDRY
SEMILOG SEMIRAW SENARII SERRATI SFERICS *SHEEPLE* *SHIURIM* SIEMENS
SIGNEUR SILVICS SINSYNE *SIROSET* SKOLION SKYBORNe SKYCLAD SKYDOVE
SKYPHOI SKYPHOS SLAINTE SLEEPRY SLUMBRY SMITTLE *SNUBFIN* SOKAIYA
SOMEWHY SOPRANI SORDINI SORDINO SPECTRA1 SPECULAr SPICULAe SPICULAr
SPINONE *SPINONI* SPINULAe SPLENII SPORTIF SPURIAE STAMNOI STAMNOS
STASIMA STELENE *STELLIO*n STICHOI STICHOS STIMULI STOMATA1 STRETTE
STRETTI STREWTH STRIATA *STYLOPS* SUASORY SUNBACK SUNBEAT SUNFAST
SUPREMA SURCULI SYLLABIc

TACHINA	TAGMATA	TEGMINAl	TEMENOS	TEMPORE	TERMINI	TESSERAe	TESSERAl
THALAMIc	THANKEE	THEMATA	THONDER	THROMBIn	THYSELF	TIMPANA	TIMPANI
TIMPANO	TITMICE	TONDINI	TOPMOST	TORMINAl	TOYLSOM	*TOYTOWN*	TRIFOLD
TRIFORM	TRIPART	TRYMATA	TWAFALD	TWIFOLD	TWYFOLD		

ULPANIM	*UNADEPT*	UNADULT	UNAGING	*UNAWAKE*d	UNBEGOT	UNBEGUN	UNBLEST
UNBLOWN	UNBROKEn	UNBULKY	UNBURNT	UNCIVIL	*UNCLEFT*	UNDREST	UNDRUNK
UNEAGER	UNFANCY	UNFILDE	UNGROWN	UNHARDY	UNHASTY	UNHEEDY	UNHERST
UNIBODY	UNMACHO	UNMERRY	UNNEATH	UNNOISY	UNPINKT	UNROUGH	UNSHARP
UNSHEWN	UNSHOWN	UNSHOWY	UNSLAIN	*UNSLICK*	UNSLUNG	UNSMART	UNSMOTE
UNSOBER	UNSONCY	UNSONSY	UNSOOTE	UNSPIDE	UNSPILT	UNSPOKEn	UNSTUFT
UNSTUNG	UNSUNNY	UNSWEET	UNSWORE	UNSWORN	UNTRIDE	UNWELDY	UNWHIPT
UNWHITE	UNWITTY	UNWROTE	UNWRUNG	UNYOUNG	UPBORNE	UPBOUND	UPBRAST
UPBROKEn	*UPCOURT*	UPBUILT	UPCOAST	UPFLUNG	UPSPOKEn	UPSTOOD	UPSWEPT
UPSWUNG	UPTHREW	UPWOUND	URCEOLI				

VASCULAr	VERITAS	VERSUTE	VIDENDA	VINCULA	VISCERAl	VITELLIn	VITRAIL
VOETSAK	*VOETSEK*	VOLUBIL	VOLUBLE	*VONGOLE*			

WAYGONE	WEBFEET	WEBFOOT	WHILERE	WHYEVER	WORKSHY	WOTCHER	WOTTEST
WOTTETH							

7.4. LESS FAMILIAR BUT LESS PROBABLE NON-HOOK SEVENS

CONTAINING BB

ABBOTCY+	**BABALAS**	BABASSU	BABESIA	BABICHE	BABUCHE	BABUDOM	BABUISM
BABYSAT	*BABYSITe*	*BABYSIT>*	**BACKBITe**	**BAMBINI**	BANDBOX+	**BARBATEd**	BARBOLA
BARBULE	**BATABLE**	*BEATBOX+*	BEBEERU	*BEDBATH*	*BERBERE*	**BERBICE**	**BEROBED**
BIBASIC	BIBCOCK	BIBELOT	**BIBLIKE**	BIBLIST	**BILIMBI**	BILLBUG	**BILOBAR**
BILOBED	*BIOBANK*	**BITABLE**	BLAUBOK	BLESBOK	BLOUBOK	BLOWJOB	*BOBOTIE*
BOBSTAY	*BOERBUL*	BOGBEAN	BOMBLET	*BOOBIRD*	**BOOBISH**	BOOMBOX+	BOSHBOK
BOSSBOY	**BOWBENT**	*BOXBALL*	**BRAMBLY***	BREWPUB	BUBALIS+	BUBINGA	BUBUKLE
BUGABOO	BUGBANE	BULBLET	BULLBAT	BUMBAZE	BUMBOAT	**CABBAGY**	CABBALAh
CABOMBA	CLABBER	CRABBER	CRIBBLE	**CUBBISH**	DABBITY+	**DRIBBLY***	**EBBLESS**
FLUBDUB	FRIBBLEr	FUBBERY+	GABBARD	GABBART	**GIBBOSE**	**GIBBOUS**	GRABBER
GRIBBLE	GUBBINS+	**HOBBISH**	*JALABIB*	JIBBOOM	KABBALAh	KNOBBER	**KNOBBLY***
LIBBARD	LOBBYER	LUBBARD	LULIBUB	**MOBBISH**	*MOBBISM*	NEBBICHs	NEBBISHe
NEBBISHy	**NOBBILY**	PRIBBLE	RABBONI	RIBBAND	RIBIBLE	RUBABOO	*RUBBIDY+*
SCABBLE	SHABBLE	**SHRUBBY***	SLABBERy	SNABBLE	SNUBBER	**SQUABBY***	STABBER
STIBBLEr	*STUBBIE***	**STUBBLY***	SUBBASE	SUBBASS+	SWABBER	SWABBIE	SWOBBER
TRIBBLE	**TUBBISH**	WHOOBUB	YOBBERY+	**YOBBISH**	YOBBISM		

CONTAINING CC

ACCABLE	ACCIDIA	ACCIDIE	ACCINGE	ACCOAST	**ACCOIED**	ACCOMPT	ACCOURT
ACCOYLD	ACCRETE	ACCURSE	**ACCURST**	**ACERBIC**	ACICULAe	ACICULAr	**ACMATIC**
ACOUCHI	ACOUCHY+	**ACRATIC**	**ACRONIC**	**ACROTIC**	**ACTINIC**	*ALPACCA*	ASCETIC
ASCITIC	BACCARAt	**BACCARE**	**BACCATEd**	**BACCHII**	*BACHCHA*	BAROCCO	BAWCOCK
BIBCOCK	**BORACIC**	**BRACCIA**	**BRACCIO**	BRECCIAl	BUCCINA	BUCOLIC	BYCATCH+
CACHEXY+	CACIQUE	CACODYL	CACOEPY+	CACOLET	*CACONYMy*	**CACTOID**	CADDICE

CADENCY+ **CADUCEI** CALCIFY CALCINE CALCITE **CALCULI** CALECHE **CALICES**
CALICHE CALICLE **CALYCES** CALYCLEd CAMBRIC CANDOCK CANNACH **CANONIC**
CANOPIC CAPOUCH+ CAPROCK **CAPROIC** CAPUCHEd CARACAL CARACOLe CARACOL>
CARACUL CARCAKE CARDECUe **CARICES** CARIOCA CARLOCK CAROACH+ CARRACT
CARRICK CARROCH+ CASCARA *CASEVAC* CASSOCK CASTOCK **CATCHEN** CATCHUP
CATCLAW CATECHU CATFACE **CATHECT** **CECALLY** CECITIS+ *CELOMIC* CENACLE
CENTRIC CEVICHE *CHACHKA* CHALCID CHAMPACa CHANCRE CHARACT **CHASMIC**
CHAUNCE CHECHIA CHICANA CHICANEr CHICANO CHICKEE **CHLORIC** CHOCTAW
CHOREIC **CHROMIC** *CHUCKER* CHUCKIE CICHLID CICOREE **CIMICES** CLACHAN
CLASTIC CLAUCHT CLERUCHs CLERUCHy CLICKET COACHEE COACHER COCHLEAe
COCHLEAr COCKADEd COCKEYEd **COCKISH** COCKNEY COCOMAT COCOPAN COCOTTE
COCOYAM **COCTILE** COCTION **CODICES** CODICIL COELIAC COGENCE COGENCY+
COLICINe **COLITIC** **COMATIC** **COMEDIC** **COMETIC** CONACRE **CONCEDO** CONCENT
CONCHIE CONCREW CONCUPY+ CONDUCEr CONFECT **CONICAL** CONJECT CONTECK
CONVECT COONCAN COPPICE CORCASS+ CORNCOB COWITCH+ COWLICK COXCOMB
CRACKUP CRACOWE CREANCE **CREATIC** *CREWCUT* CRICOID CROCEINe **CROCINE**
CROMACK *CROMBEC* CRUCIAN CRYONIC **CUBICLY** *CUCKING* CUCKOLD CULCHIE
CULICID **CUMARIC** CURACAO CURACOA *CURCHEF* CURCUMA CURRACHs CUSTOCK
CUTICLE CYCASIN CYCLASE CYCLOID **CYCLOPS** **CYLICES** DAWCOCK DEICTIC
DICYCLY+ **DOCETIC** ECBOLIC **ECCRINE** *ECDEMIC* ECOCIDE ECORCHE **ECTATIC**
ECTOPIC FACTICE FELUCCA **FLOCCUS** **GNOCCHI** GORCOCK **GYNECIC** HAYCOCK
ICHTHIC ICTERIC JACCHUS+ **KACHCHA** **KUCHCHA** LUCENCE LUCENCY+ **MACCHIA**
MACCHIE MALACCA MEACOCK **MECONIC** MEDACCA *MOCCIES* MOROCCO **MYCOTIC**
OBCONIC OCCIPUT OCCLUDEr **OCTADIC** **ORECTIC** PACHUCO **PECCANT** PECCARY+
PECCAVI **PERCOCT** PETCOCK PICACHO *PICCATA* PLACCATe POLACCA PRACTICe
PRACTICk PUCCOON **RACEMIC** RECENCY+ SACCADE **SACCATE** SACCULE **SACCULI**
SCALDIC **SCANDIC** SCEPTIC SCHLICHs SCHLOCKy SCHMECK *SCHMICK** SCHMOCK
SCHMUCK SCHTICK SCHTUCK SCRAICH SCRAUCH SCREICH SCRIECH SCRITCH
SCROOCH SCUCHIN SEACOCK **SEBACIC** SICCITY+ **SILICIC** SIROCCO **SMECTIC**
SOCCAGE SQUACCO **STICHIC** SUCCADE **SUCCISE** **SUCCOSE** SUCCOUR **SUCCOUS**
SUCCUBAe **SUCCUBI** TECHNIC TOCCATA **TOCCATE** TWOCCER **UNCOMIC** VACANCE
VACCINAl VOCALIC ZECCHINe ZECCHINi ZECCHINo ZIMOCCA ZOCCOLO

CONTAINING FF

AFFABLY AFFIANT AFFICHE **AFFINAL** **AFFIXAL** AFFIXER AFFOORD AFFORCE
AGRAFFE *BAKEOFF* *BANOFFI* BEFFANA BLOWOFF **BLUFFLY** BOFFOLA BOILOFF
CAFFILA CAITIFF CHAFFERy **CLIFFED** COFFRET *COOKOFF* **DAFFILY** **DIFFORM**
DISTAFF DUSTOFF **EFFABLE** EFFENDI EFFORCE EFFULGE **FACTFUL** FALAFEL
FANCIFY FARCIFY FELAFEL FIEFDOM FINFISH+ FINFOOT **FISHFUL** FISHIFY
FIXATIF FLAMFEW **FLYLEAF** **FOODFUL** FORKFUL **FORMFUL** FOXFIRE FOXFISH+
FRITFLY+ FRUTIFY *FUNFEST* FURFAIR GAUFFER GRIFFIN GRIFFON HAFFLIN
HANDOFF **HUFFISH** HUFFKIN JUMPOFF LEADOFF **LIFEFUL** LOOFFUL MAFFICK
MAFFLED MAFFLINg MASTIFF **MIFFILY** **MUFFISH** OFFCAST OFFENSE OFFEREE
OFFERER OFFEROR OFFSCUM OFFTAKE PICKOFF PIFFERO PROFFER **PUFFILY**
RAFFISH RAKEOFF **RESTIFF** *RIFFAGE* RIFFOLA SAFFIAN SCAFFIE *SCUFFER*
SELLOFF SHUTOFF SKIFFLE *SNIFFLY** SNUFFER **SNUFFLY** STIFFIE STUFFER
SUFFARI **SUFFECT** SUFFETE SUFFUSE *SWOFFER* TAFFETA **TAFFETY** TIFFANY+
TRIFFIC TRIFFIDy TROFFER **UNRUFFE** WAVEOFF WHIFFER WHIFFET WHIFFLEr
ZIFFIUS+ **ZUFFOLI** **ZUFFOLO**

CONTAINING HH

AARRGHH	BACHCHA	BHISHTI	BORSHCH+	BRACHAH	BRUHAHA	CHACHKA	CHARKHA
CHAVISH	CHECHIA	CHIKHOR	CHUDDAH	CHUMASH+	CHUPPAH	DOBHASH+	HACHURE
HADEDAH	HAGBUSH+	HAGFISH+	HAHNIUM	HAIMISH	HALACHA	HALAKAH	HALAKHAh
HALAVAH	HARSHEN	HARUMPH	HATCHEL	HATCHEL>	HATCHERy	HAWKISH	HEIMISH
HENNISH	HERSHIP	HIBACHI	HICKISH	HIGHBOY	HIGHMAN	HIGHMEN	HIGHTOP
HIPPISH	HIPSHOT	HITCHER	HOBBISH	HOGFISH+	HOGGISH	HOGHOOD	HOOCHIE
HOPHEAD	HORNISH	HOUHERE	HUFFISH	HUNNISH	HUSHFUL	HUTCHIE	ICHTHIC
ICHTHYS+	KACHCHA	KHOTBAH	KHOTBEH	KHUTBAH	KUCHCHA	NAPHTHA	PADSHAH
RHAPHAE	RHAPHIS	RHONCHI	SCHLICHs	SHABASH+	SHAHADA	SHAHEED	SHAHDOM
SHEHITAh	SHITTAH	SHOCHET	SHOPHAR	SHOWGHE	SHRIECH	SHRIGHT	SHRITCH
THOTHER	THRUTCH	TOSHACHs	WHEYISH	WHORISH			

CONTAINING MM

ALMEMAR	ALMSMAN	ALMSMEN	ALUMIUM	AMALGAM	AMMIRAL	AMMONAL	AMMONIC
AMORISM	ATOMISM	BROMISM	BROMMER	BUMMALO	BUMMOCK	CAMBISM	CAMBIUM
CHEMISM	CHOMMIE	COMMATA	COMMODO	COMMOVE	COMSYMP	COSMISM	CRUMBUM
CRUMMIEr	DIGAMMA	DIMMISH	EDAMAME	EMPYEMA	FERMIUM	FILMDOM	GAMMOCK
GEMMATE	GEMMERY+	GEMMILY	GEMMULE	GREMMIE	GROMMET	GRUMMET	GUMMATA
GUMMILY	GUMMITE	GUMMOSE	GUMMOUS	HAMMADA	HAMMILY	HOLMIUM	HOMMOCK
HOMONYMy	HOUMMOS+	HUMMOCKy	IMAMATE	INFIMUM	JIMMINY	LEMMATA	MACADAM
MACRAME	MACUMBA	MAGMATA	MAGSMAN	MAGSMEN	MAHATMA	MAIDISM	MALMSEY
MALTMAN	MALTMEN	MAMAGUY	MAMAKAU	MAMELON	MAMEYES	MAMILLAe	MAMILLAr
MAMPARA	MAMPOER	MANUMEA	MANUMIT>	MAORMOR	MARIMBA	MARKMAN	MARKMEN
MARMITE	MARMOSEt	MASHLAM	MASHLIM	MASHLUM	MAXIMIN	MAXIMUS+	MEATMAN
MEATMEN	MELAMED	MELISMA	MELTEMI	MEMBRAL	MERONYMy	MESCLUM	MESEEMS
MESSMAN	MESSMEN	METAMERe	METONYMy	MIASMIC	MICROHM	MIDMOST	MILLDAM
MILLIME	MIMESES	MIMESIS	MIMETIC	MIMICAL	MIMULUS+	MINICAMp	MINICOM
MINIMUS+	MISHMEE	MITUMBA	MOBBISM	MOBSMAN	MOBSMEN	MOHALIM	MOHELIM
MOLIMEN	MONOMER	MONONYM	MOORMAN	MOORMEN	MOOTMAN	MOOTMEN	MORMAOR
MUDROOM	MUGWUMP	MUMPISH	MUONIUM	MUSIMON	MWALIMU	MYALISM	MYELOMA
MYOGRAM	MYOMATA	MYOTOME	MYTHISM	NUMMARY	OMMATEA	PLUMBUM	POMATUM
PROMMER	PSAMMON	RAMMISH	RAMSTAM	RUMMILY	RUMMISH	SCAMMER	SEMEMIC
SEMIMATt	SHAMMASh	SHAMMES	SHAMMOS	SHIMMEY	SKIMMIA	SKUMMER	SLUMGUM
SLUMISM	SLUMMER	SMEDDUM	SPAMMER	SPAMMIE*	STAMMEL	STUMMEL	SUMMAND
SUMMIST	TAGMEME	THRUMMY*	TRAMMIE	TROMMEL	TSIMMES	TUMMLER	TZIMMES
WHEMMLE	WHOMMLE	WOMMERA					

CONTAINING PP

AGITPOP	ALCOPOP	APEPSIA	APOCARPy	APOCOPE	APOPLEXy	APPALTI	APPALTO
APPARAT	APPEACH	APPERILl	APPLIER	APPRESS	APPRISEr	APPRIZEr	APPROOF
APPULSE	APROPOS	CHAPPAL	CHAPPIE*	CHUPPOTh	COPEPOD	COPPICE	COPSHOP
COWPLOP	CRAPPIE*	CROPPIE	CRUPPER	DRAPPIE	DROPPLE	ECHAPPE	EPICARP
EPITOPE	EUPEPSY+	EUROPOP	FOPPERY+	FOPPISH	FRIPPET	GENAPPE	GENIPAP
HIPPISH	JALOPPY+	JIPYAPA	KAUPAPA	KIPPAGE	KNAPPLE	KNOPPED	MAPPIST
NIPPILY	OPPIDAN	PAKAPOO	PALMTOP	PALPATE	PALSHIP	PAMPEAN	PAMPOEN
PANOPLY	PAPABLE	PAPADAM	PAPADOM	PAPADUM	PAPALLY	PAPAUMA	PAPERER

191

PAPHIAN	PAPILIO	**PAPILLA**e	**PAPILLA**r	PAPOOSE	PAPRICA	**PAPYRAL**	PAPYRUS+
PARAPET	PARPANE	PARSNEP	PASTEUP	*PEKEPOO*	PEMPHIX+	*PEPTALK*	PEPTONE
PERCEPT	PERIAPT	PERPEND	PERPENT	*PERSPEX+*	PINESAP	PIPEAGE	PIPEFUL
PIPERIC	**PIPLESS**	PITAPAT>	**PLATYPI**	PLENIPO	PLEOPOD	**PLUMPIE***	**PLUMPLY**
POCKPIT	POGONIP	POLYPODy	POLYPUS+	POMPANO	POMPELO	**POMPIER**	POMPION
POMPOON	POPADUM	POPEDOM	POPERIN	*POPETTE*	**POPEYED**	POPOVER	*POPSOCK*
POPSTER	PORKPIE	PORPESSe	POTSHOP	**PREPILL**	PREPREG	PREPUCE	**PRERUPT**
PRIAPUS+	PROCARP	PROPAGE	PROPALE	PROPEND	PROPENE	PROPINE	PROPJET
PROPMAN	**PROPMEN**	PROPONE	**PROPRIA**	PULPIFY	**PULPILY**	**PULPOUS**	PUMPION
PUPARIAl	PUPFISH+	**PUPILAR**y	PUPUNHA	PURPURA	PURPURE	PUSHPIN	*PUSHPIT*
PYROPUS+	QUIPPER	**RAPPINI**	RIPPIER	RIPSTOP	SAPPHIC	**SAPPILY**	SCAPPLE
SCHAPPE=	SEPPUKU	SHAPEUP	SHIPLAP>	**SHNAPPS**	SKIPPET	**SOPPILY**	SPEEDUP
STAPPLE	**STEEPUP**	*SUIPLAP*	SUPPAWN	SWIPPLE	SWOPPER	TAPPICE	TRIPPET
UPSLOPE	**UPSPAKE**	UPTEMPO	WHAPPER	YUPPIFY	*ZEPPOLE*	**ZEPPOLI**	

CONTAINING SSS

ABSCISSa	ABSCISSe	**ASCESES**	**ASCESIS**	**ASHLESS**	**ASKESES**	**ASKESIS**	BOSSISM
GASLESS	MESSIAS+	**MISSISH**	OSMOSES	OSMOSIS	OSSEOUS	**OSTOSES**	OSTOSIS+
SACLESS	**SAPLESS**	SASSABY+	**SASSILY**	SCEPSIS+	SCHLOSS+	SCISSEL	SCISSILe
SEERESS+	**SESSILE**	SETNESS+	**SEXLESS**	SINLESS	SKEPSIS+	*SKYLESS*	SONLESS
SOROSES	SOROSIS+	STYPSIS+	SUBBASS+	**SUBMISS**	**SUMLESS**	SUSPENSe	**SYCOSES**
SYCOSIS	**SYNESES**	SYNESIS+	WISEASS+				

CONTAINING VV

AKVAVIT	BIVALVEd	CONVIVE	DVANDVA	FLIVVER	REVIVOR	*SAVVILY*	VAIVODE
VALVATE	**VALVULA**e	**VALVULA**r	VALVULE	VAVASORy	VERVAIN	VETIVERt	**VIVARIA**
VIVENCY+	VIVERRA	**VIVIFIC**	VOIVODE	**VOLVATE**	**VOLVULI**	VOUVRAY	**VULVATE**

CONTAINING WW

AWLWORT	DEWCLAW	DOWNBOW	LOWBROW	**NEWMOWN**	TOWAWAY	WAIWODE	WARWOLF
WARWORK	**WARWORN**	WAXWEED	WAXWING	WAXWORK	WAXWORM	WAYWODE	**WAYWORN**
WEBWORK	WEBWORM	**WELAWAY**	WERWOLF	WETWARE	**WEYWARD**	WHIPSAWn	WHITLOW
WHITTAW	WINDROW	WINDWAY	WINGBOW	WIREWAY	WITWALL	WOADWAX+	WOIWODE
WOODWAX+							

CONTAINING YY

ACRYLYL	ALCHYMY+	APHYLLY+	ASPHYXY+	*AWAYDAY*	BUTYRYL	BYRLADY+	CHYLIFY
CHYMIFY	COPYBOY	DAYLILY+	DICYCLY+	DYARCHY+	**DYINGLY**	DYSLOGY+	EPIGYNY+
ETHYNYL	EURYOKY+	FLYAWAY	GRAYFLY+	**GRYSELY**	**GYRALLY**	**GYRONNY**	HOLYDAY
HRYVNYA	HYDROXYl	HYMNARY+	HYMNODY+	HYPONYMy	*LADYBOY*	LADYFLY+	LAYAWAY
LYINGLY	MYOLOGY+	**NYMPHLY**	**PAYABLY**	PLAYDAY	POLYNYA	**POLYNYI**	**ROYALLY**
SYNGAMY+	*SYNTENY+*	SYNTONY+	SYSTYLE	**SYZYGAL**	**VYINGLY**	YOBBERY+	**YOUNGLY**
YOUTHLY	YUPPIFY	ZYMURGY+					

7.5. VERY IMPROBABLE LESS FAMILIAR SEVENS

ABUBBLE	**ACYCLIC**	ALTEZZA	ANGAKOK	ANGEKOK	AZOTIZE	BABBITT	BABBLER
BACCHIC	BANGKOK	*BAZZAZZ+*	BEZZANT	*BEZZAZZ+*	BIBBERY+	BLABBER	BOBBERY+
BOBBISH	BOBBITT	BRABBLEr	*BUKKAKE*	*BUZZCUT*	BUZZWIG	*CACHACA*	CHAZZAN
CHAZZEN	CHUKKAR	CHUKKER	COCCOID	**COCCOUS**	DIZZARD	**DIZZILY**	ENFEOFF
FALLOFF	FEOFFEE	FEOFFER	FEOFFOR	FIZZGIG	FLAFFER	*FLUFFER*	FRIZZER
FRIZZLEr	**FRIZZLY***	*FUCKOFF*	*FUZZBOX+*	**FUZZILY**	HEIGHTH	**HIGHISH**	HUMBUZZ+
HUMMAUM	INFEOFF	**INKLIKE**	JACUZZI	**JAZZILY**	**JAZZMAN**	**JAZZMEN**	**JEJUNAL**
JEJUNUM	JIGAJIG>	JIGAJOG>	JINJILI	JUJITSU	JUJUISM	JUJUIST	JUJUTSU
JUKSKEI	KAKODYL	*KALOOKIe*	*KARAKIA*	KARAKUL	KEBBOCK	KEBBUCK	KHIRKAH
KIBITKA	*KICKBOX*	*KICKOUT*	**KIDLIKE**	KIDSKIN	KIKUMON	KILLICK	KILLOCK
KINKILY	KIPSKIN	**KIRKMAN**	**KIRKMEN**	KIRKTON	KLINKER	KNACKERy	KNICKER
KNUCKLY*	*KOEKOEA*	KOKANEE	*KOKOBEH*	*KOKOWAI*	**KOLACKY**	KOLKHOSy	KOLKHOZy
KOLKOZY	KOMATIK	*KOOKILY*	*KOPIYOK*	*KOPIYKA*	*KRUNKED*	**MAMMARY**	**MAMMATE**
MAMMATI	MAMMOCK	MAREMMA	**MAREMME**	**MARKKAA**	MAZZARD	MEZUZAH	**MEZUZOTh**
MIMMICK	MIZMAZE	MUEZZIN	MUMMERY+	MUMMIFY	MUMMOCK	**MUZZILY**	MUZZLER
NUZZLER	**OAKLIKE**	OLYKOEK	OUTKICK	OZONIZEr	**PALAZZI**	PALAZZO	PANPIPE
PAPPOSE	**PAPPOUS**	*PAZZAZZ+*	**PEPPILY**	PITPROP	**PIZAZZY**	*PIZZAZZy*	**POPPIED**
POPPISH	PREPPIE*	*PREPUPAe*	*PREPUPAl*	PREZZIE	QUIZZER	RIZZART	**ROKKAKU**
SCHIZZY*	SCHNOZZ+	SHIKKER	*SKANKER*	SKINKER	**SKOOKUM**	SKULKER	SKYHOOK
SKYJACK	*SKYLIKE*	SKYWALK	SNUZZLE	*SONGKOK*	**SUKKOTH**	SWAZZLE	SWIZZLEr
SWOZZLE	*TAKKIES*	TOKAMAK	TOKOMAK	TOPKICK	TWIZZLE	**TZITZIS**	**TZITZITh**
VETKOEK	*WAZZOCK*	WHIZZER	**ZAKUSKA**	**ZAKUSKI**	ZIZANIA	ZYZZYVA	

8. EIGHT-LETTER WORDS

8.1 FAMILIAR EIGHTS

8.1.1 VERBS IN COMMON USE

ABDICATE	ACCREDIT	ACCUSTOM	ACQUAINT	ACTIVATE	ADMONISH	ADVOCATE
ALIENATE	ALLOCATE	AMPUTATE	ANNOTATE	ANNOUNCEr	APPETISEr	APPETIZEr
APPRAISEe	APPRAISEr	APPROACH	ASSEMBLEr	ASTONISH	AUTOMATE	

BACKDATE	BACKFILL	BACKFIRE	BACKSTAB>	BADMOUTH	BARBECUEr	BEAUTIFY
BEDAZZLE	BEFRIEND	BEFUDDLE	BEGRUDGEr	BELITTLEr	BEQUEATH	BESMIRCH
BEWILDER	BLUDGEON	BODYSURF	BRANDISH	BRIGHTEN	BULLDOZEr	

CANONISEr	CANONIZEr	CANOODLEr	CASTRATEr	CHASTISEr	CHRISTEN	CIVILISEr
CIVILIZEr	CLASSIFY	COALESCE	CODIRECT	COGITATE	COINCIDE	COLLAPSE
COLONISEr	COLONIZEr	COMMENCEr	COMPLAINt	COMPLETE*	COMPOUND	COMPRESS
COMPRISE	CONCEIVEr	CONCLUDEr	CONDENSEr	CONFOUND	CONFRONTe	CONSERVEr
CONSIDER	CONSPIREr	CONSTRUEr	CONTINUEr	CONTRIVEr	CONVERGE	CONVINCEr
CONVULSE	COPULATE					

DAYDREAMt	DAYDREAMy	DECIMATE	DECIPHER	DECORATE	DECREASE	DEDICATEe
DEFECATE	DEFLOWER	DEGREASEr	DELEGATEe	DEMOLISH	DEMONISE	DEMONIZE
DENOUNCEr	DEPUTISE	DEPUTIZE	DESCRIBEr	DESPATCH	DESTRUCTo	DETHRONEr
DETONATE	DIAGNOSE	DIGITISEr	DIGITIZEr	DIMINISH	DISAGREE	DISALLOW
DISCLOSEr	DISCOLOR	DISCOVERt	DISCOVERy	DISGORGEr	DISGRACEr	DISGUISEr
DISHEVEL	DISHEVEL>	DISLODGE	DISMOUNT	DISPENSEr	DISPERSEr	DISPLACEr
DISPROVEn	DISPROVEr	DISSOLVEr	DISTRACT	DIVEBOMB	DOMINATE	DOMINEER
DOVETAIL	DOWNLOAD	DOWNPLAY	DOWNSIZEr			

ELONGATE	EMACIATE	EMBATTLE	EMBEZZLEr	EMBITTER	EMBLAZON	EMIGRATE
ENCIRCLE	ENCROACH	ENCUMBER	ENDANGER	ENERGISEr	ENERGIZEr	ENGENDER
ENSHRINEe	ENTANGLEr	ENTHRALL	ENTHRONE	ENTRENCH	ENVISAGE	ENVISION
EQUALISEr	EQUALIZEr	ESCALATE	ESTIMATE	ESTRANGEr	EULOGISEr	EULOGIZEr
EVACUATE	EVALUATE	EXCAVATE	EXCHANGEr	EXERCISEr	EXORCISEr	EXORCIZEr
EXPEDITEr						

FAREWELL	FINALISEr	FINALIZEr	FLOUNDER	FLOURISHy	FOREBODE	FORECAST
FORETELLd	FOREWARN	FRACTUREr	FREELOAD	FREQUENT*	FRIGHTEN	FUMIGATE
FUNCTION						

GALAVANT	GENERATE	GRADUATE

HANDCUFF	HANDICAP>	HANDPICK	HARANGUEr	HEADHUNT	HEIGHTEN	HESITATEr
HIGHTAIL	HOODWINK	HOUSESITd	HOUSESIT>	HUMIDIFY		

195

IDEALISEr	IDEALIZEr	IDENTIFY	IMMUNISEr	IMMUNIZEr	IMPRISON	INCREASEr
INCUBATE	INDICATE	INFRINGEr	INITIATE	INNOVATE	INSCRIBEr	INSTRUCT
INSULATE	INTERACT	INTERMIX	INTRIGUEr	INUNDATE	IRRIGATE	IRRITATE

JETTISON

LACERATE	LAMINATE	LANGUISH	LEGALISEr	LEGALIZEr	LENGTHEN	LEVITATE
LIBERATE	LITIGATE	LOCALISEr	LOCALIZEr			

MAINTAIN	MALINGERy	MARINATE	MARSHALL	MASSACREr	MAXIMISEr	MAXIMIZEr
MEDICATE	MEDITATE	MEMORISEr	MEMORIZEr	MINIMISEr	MINIMIZEr	MISCARRY
MISCOUNT	MISFIELD	MISJUDGEr	MISPLACE	MISQUOTEr	MISSPELL	MISSPENDd
MISTREAT	MITIGATE	MOBILISEr	MOBILIZEr	MODERATE	MORALISEr	MORALIZEr
MOTIVATE	MOTORISE	MOTORIZE	MULTIPLY	MUTILATE		

NAUSEATE	NAVIGATE	NOMINATE

OBLIGATE	OBSTRUCT	OPTIMISEr	OPTIMIZEr	ORGANISEr	ORGANIZEr	OUTBLUFF
OUTCLASS	OUTDRESS	OUTDRINKd	OUTFIGHTd	OUTPOINT	OUTPUNCH	OUTSCORE
OUTSKATE	OUTSMART	OUTSTRIP>	OUTWEIGH	OVERBOOK	OVERCALL	OVERCOMEd
OVERCOMEr	OVERCOOK	OVERDRAWd	OVERDRAWn	OVERFEEDd	OVERFILL	OVERFISH
OVERFLOWn	OVERHANGd	OVERHAUL	OVERHEARd	OVERHEARd	OVERHEAT	OVERLOAD
OVERLOOK	OVERMINE	OVERRATE	OVERRIDEd	OVERRIDEr	OVERRULEr	OVERSTAY
OVERSTEP>	OVERTAKEd	OVERTAKEn	OVERTURN	OVERTYPE	OVERWINDd	OVERWORK

PARALYSEr	PARALYZEr	PENALISE	PENALIZE	PERCEIVEr	PERMEATE	PERSPIRE
PERSUADEr	PINPOINT	POLARISEr	POLARIZEr	POPULATE	POSITION	POSTPONEr
PRACTISEr	PRECLUDE	PREJUDGEr	PREORDER	PRESERVEr	PRESSURE	PROCLAIM
PROGRESS	PROHIBIT	PROSPECT	PROTRUDE	PUNCTUREr	PURCHASEr	

QUANTIFY	QUESTION

READJUST	READVISE	REAFFIRM	REAPPEAR	REARREST	REASSERT	REASSESS
REASSIGN	REASSUME	REASSUREr	RECHARGEr	RECREATE	REDEFINE	REDEPLOY
REDESIGN	REDIRECT	REEMPLOY	REENGAGE	REENLIST	REENROLL	REFORMATe
REFORMAT>	REGISTER	REGULATE	REHEARSEr	REIGNITE	REINFECT	REINFORM
REINJECT	REINJURE	REINSERT	REINSUREr	REINVADE	REINVENT	REINVEST
REINVITE	REKINDLE	RELEGATE	RELOCATEe	REMEMBER	RENOUNCEr	RENOVATE
RENUMBER	REOCCUPY	REOFFEND	REORIENT	REPHRASE	REPOLISH	RERECORD
RESAMPLE	RESEARCH	RESEMBLEr	RESETTLE	RESONATE	RESTRAIN	RESTRICT
RESTRINGe	RESUBMIT>	RESURVEY	RETRENCH	RETRIEVEr	RICOCHET	RIDICULEr
RINGBARK						

SABOTAGE	SALIVATE	SANCTION	SANITISEr	SANITIZEr	SATIRISEr	SATIRIZEr
SATURATEr	SCAFFOLD	SCAVENGEr	SCHEDULEr	SCRAMBLEr	SCRIBBLEr	SCROUNGEr
SENTENCEr	SEPARATE	SERENADEr	SHOPLIFT	SHOWCASE	SIDESTEP>	SIGHTSEEd
SIGHTSEEn	SIGHTSEEr	SIMPLIFY	SIMULATE	SMOULDER	SODOMISE	SODOMIZE
SOLIDIFY	SPLATTER	SPLUTTERy	SPRINKLEr	SQUABBLEr	SQUANDER	STAGNATE

STAMPEDEr	STARGAZEr	STARGAZEy	STRADDLEr	STRAGGLEr	STRANGLEr	STRUGGLEr
SUBMERGE	SUBTRACT	SUNBATHEr	SUPPRESS	SURPRISEr	SURROUND	
TABULATE	TAILGATEr	TELEVISEr	THEORISEr	THEORIZEr	THREATEN	TOLERATE
TRANSFER	TRANSFIXt	TRANSMIT>	TRAVERSEr	TRESPASS	TRUNCATE	TYPECASTd
ULCERATE	UNBUCKLE	UNBURDEN	UNBUTTON	UNDERBIDd	UNDERBID>	UNDERCUTd
UNDERCUT>	UNDEREATd	UNDERLIEd	UNDERLIEr	UNDERPAY	UNDERPIN>	UNDULATE
UNFASTEN	UNSADDLE	UNSETTLE	UNSTITCH	UNTANGLE	UNTETHER	UNTHREAD
VALIDATE	VANQUISH	VAPORISEr	VAPORIZEr	VEGETATE	VOCALISEr	VOCALIZEr
WATERLOG>	WINDSURF	WITHDRAWd	WITHDRAWn	WITHHOLDd	WOMANISEr	WOMANIZEr

8.1.2. VERBS MORE COMMONLY USED IN OTHER PARTS OF SPEECH

ABSTRACT*	ACCOLADE	AIRBRUSH	ALPHABET	AMBITION	ANCESTOR	ANTIDOTE
ASTERISK	ATTORNEY	AUDITION				
BACKCHAT>	BACKDROP>	BACKDROPt	BACKHAND	BACKLASH	BACKPACK	BACKSTOP>
BACKWASH	BALLYHOO	BANKROLL	BANKRUPT	BLANDISH	BLOCKADEr	BOLLOCKS
BOOKMARK	BULLETINg	BULLSHIT>	BUSHWALK	BUSYBODY	BUTTRESS	
CALENDAR	CAMPAIGN	CANISTER	CATAPULT	CAUSEWAY	CAVALIER	CHAINSAW
CHAIRMAN	CHAIRMAN>	CHAMPION	CHARCOALy	CHITCHAT>	COCKTAIL	CONCRETE
CONFLICT	CONGRESS	CONTRACT	CONTRARY	CONTRASTy	CONVERSEr	CORDUROY
COURTESY	COVENANT	COXSWAIN	CREVASSE	CRITIQUE	CROSSCUTd	CROSSCUT>
CUPBOARD	CYLINDER					
DATABASE	DATELINE	DAYLIGHT	DEADHEAD	DEADLINE	DEADLOCK	DECENTER
DECISION	DESOLATEr	DIALOGUEr	DINGDONG	DISARRAY	DISCIPLE	DISCOUNT
DISFAVOR	DISHONOR	DISORDER	DISQUIET	DISTANCE	DISTASTE	DISTRESS
DISTRICT	DISTRUST	DOCUMENT	DOGFIGHTd	DOORSTEP>	DOUGHNUT>	DYNAMITEr
EMPHASISe	ENDEAVOR	ENGINEER	ENTRANCE	ENVELOPEr	EPIGRAPHy	EPILOGUE
EVIDENCE						
FIREBOMB	FISHTAIL	FOOTNOTE	FORKLIFT	FORTRESS	FOUNTAIN	FRACTION
FRAGMENT	FRONTIER	FURLOUGH				
GANGBANG	GANGRENE	GARRISON	GAUNTLET	GRIDIRON	GRIDLOCK	GUNFIGHTd
HALLMARK	HANDBALL	HEADLINEr	HICCOUGH	HIGHBALL	HOTHOUSE	
INNUENDO	INSTANCE	INTENDER	INTEREST	INTIMATEr		
JACKAROO	JACKEROO	JAUNDICE	JEOPARDY			
KANGAROO	KERCHIEF	KEYBOARD	KEYSTONE			
LANDFILL	LANDMARK	LANGUAGE	LAUREATE	LAVENDER	LEAPFROG>	LEVERAGE
LIPSTICK	LOOPHOLE	LOWLIGHT	LUNCHEON			
MANICURE	MANIFESTo	MANIFOLD	MARINADE	MASTHEAD	MAVERICK	MEDICINEr
MERCHANT	MINISTER	MISCHIEF	MISMATCH	MISNOMER	MISPRINT	MISTRESS
MISTRUST	MONOGRAM	MONOGRAM>	MONOTONE	MORTGAGEe	MORTGAGEr	MOTHBALL
MUNITION	MUSHROOM	MUTINEER				
NECKLACE	NEGATIVE	NEIGHBOR	NEWSCAST	NICKNAMEr	NOSEDIVE	

8. Eight-Letter Words

OBDURATE	OBSOLETE	OCCASION	OFFSHORE	ORNAMENT	OUTBREAKd	OUTBURSTd
OUTSWINGd	OVERBUSY	OVERCAST	OVERDOSE	OVERKILL	OVERLAND	OVERLORD
OVERPASS	OVERSIZE	OVERTIMEr	OVERTURE	OVERWARM		
PARAFFINe	PARAFFINy	PARALLEL	PARALLEL>	PAVEMENT	PAVILION	PEDESTAL
PEDESTAL>	PEDICURE	PEROXIDE	PETITION	PINNACLE	PINPRICK	PIPELINE
PLATFORM	PLEASUREr	PORPOISE	PORTRAIT	POSTCARD	POSTCODE	POSTMARK
PRACTICEr	PREAMBLE	PREMIERE	PRIMROSE	PROLOGUE	PROPERTY	PROPHESY
PROTOCOL	PROTOCOL>					
QUAGMIRE						
RAILROAD	RECOURSE	REGIMENT	REPARTEE	REPRIEVEr	REPROACH	RESOURCE
ROULETTE						
SANDWICH	SANGUINE	SCABBARD	SCRABBLEr	SEDIMENT	SENTINEL	SENTINEL>
SEQUENCEr	SHANGHAI	SHEPHERD	SHOEHORN	SHORTCUTd	SHORTCUT>	SHOULDER
SHOWBOAT	SIDELINEr	SIGNPOST	SILICATE	SINGSONGy	SKIRMISH	SNOWBALL
SNOWPLOW	SOLUTION	SOUVENIR	SPLINTERy	SQUADRONe	SQUATTER	SQUEEGEE
SQUIGGLEr	SQUIRRELy	SQUIRREL>	STANCHER	STILETTO	STILETTO+	STOCKADE
STRAIGHT*	STRANGER	STUBBORN	SUBCLASS	SUBGROUP	SUBLEASE	SUBPOENA
SUBTITLE	SUBTOTAL	SUBTOTAL>	SULPHATE	SYLLABLE	SYNOPSISe	
TAILPIPE	TAPESTRY	TELECAST	TELEGRAM>	THROTTLEr	TIPPYTOE	TOBOGGAN
TOMAHAWK	TRAVESTY	TREASUREr	TRICYCLEr	TWILIGHT		
ULTIMATE	UMBRELLA	UNDERLAYd	UNSMOOTH	UNSTEADY*	UPSTREAM	UPTHRUST
VACATION	VAGABOND					
WAITRESS	WARDROBEr	WATCHDOG>	WHIPLASH	WINDBURNt	WINDLASS	WINDMILL
WIRELESS	WOODSHED>	WORKSHOP>				

8.1.3 NOUNS IN COMMON USE

AARDVARK	ABATTOIR	ABDUCTOR	ABEYANCE	ABLUTION	ABORTION	ABRASION
ABSENTEE	ACCIDENT	ACCURACY+	ACHIEVER	ACRIMONY+	ACTIVIST	ACTIVITY+
ADDITION	ADDITIVE	ADHERENT	ADHESION	ADJUTANT	ADOPTION	ADULTERY+
AERATION	AEROFOIL	AEROGRAM	AERONAUT	AFFINITY+	AIRFIELD	AIRLINER
AIRPLANE	AIRPOWER	AIRSPACE	AIRSPEED	AIRSTRIP	AISLEWAY	ALACRITY+
ALEHOUSE	ALLEGORY+	ALLELUIAh	ALLEYCAT	ALLEYWAY	ALLIANCE	ALTITUDE
ALUMINUM	AMBIENCE	AMETHYST	AMMONIUM	ANACONDA	ANCESTRY+	ANECDOTE
ANEURISM	ANNEXURE	ANOREXIA	ANTEATER	ANTELOPE	ANTIBODY+	ANTIMONYl
APERTUREd	APOPLEXY+	APPENDIX+	APPETITE	APPLAUSE	APPROVAL	APPROVER
APTITUDE	AQUALUNG	AQUANAUT	AQUARIUM	AQUEDUCT	ARACHNID	ARGUMENTa
ARMAMENT	ARMCHAIR	ARSONIST	ARTEFACT	ARTIFICEr	ARTISTRY+	ASBESTOS+
ASSASSIN	ASSEMBLY+	ASSESSOR	ASSIGNEE	ASTEROID	ATOMISER	ATOMIZER
ATROCITY+	ATTACKER	ATTENDEE	ATTITUDE	AUDACITY+	AUDIENCE	AUTOCRAT
AUTONOMY+	AVERSION	AVIATION				

BABYFOOD	BABYHOOD	BACHELOR	BACKACHE	BACKBEAT	BACKBONEd	BACKDOWN
BACKLIFT	BACKREST	BACKSEAT	BACKSIDE	BACKSPIN	BACKYARD	BAGPIPER
BALDNESS+	BALLGAME	BALLPARK	BALLROOM	BANDANNA	BANISTER	BANKBOOK
BANKCARD	BANKNOTE	BARBWIRE	BARITONE	BARNACLEd	BARNYARD	BARONESS+
BARSTOOL	BARTERER	BASEBALL	BASELINEr	BASEMENT	BASILICAe	BASILICAl
BASILICAn	BASSINET	BATHROBE	BATHROOM	BEANPOLE	BEDCOVER	BEDFRAME

BEDQUILT	BEEFCAKE	BEETROOT	BEGINNER	BEHAVIOR	BEHEADAL	BEHOLDER
BELIEVER	BELLBIRD	BELLYFUL	BETRAYAL	BEVERAGE	BIATHLON	BIGAMIST
BIGMOUTH	BILLIARD	BIRDBATH	BIRDCAGE	BIRDSEED	BIRTHDAY	BLACKOUT
BLIGHTER	BLIZZARDy	BLOCKAGE	BLOWHOLE	BLOWLAMP	BLUEBELL	BLUEBIRD
BOATLOAD	BODYLINE	BODYSUIT	BODYWORK	BOLDNESS+	BOOKCASE	BOOKSHOP
BOOKWORK	BOOKWORM	BOOTLACE	BORDELLO	BOREHOLE	BORROWER	BOTANIST
BOUNDARY+	BOUTIQUEy	BRACELET	BRAGGART	BREADBOX+	BREAKAGE	BREAKOUT
BREATHER	BRICKBAT	BRIGALOW	BROCCOLI	BROCHURE	BRUNETTE	BRUSHOFF
BULLDUST	BULLFROG	BULLRUSH	BUNGALOW	BUOYANCY+	BURGLARY+	BURGUNDY+
BURROWER	BUSHFIRE	BUSHLAND	BUSINESSy	BUSTLINE	BUTCHERY+	BUZZWORD
CABOODLE	CAFFEINE	CAKEWALK	CALAMARI	CALAMITY+	CALCULUS+	CALMNESS+
CAMELLIA	CAMPFIRE	CAMPSITE	CANNABIS+	CANNIBAL	CAPACITY+	CAPSICUM
CARDIGAN	CARDINAL	CARNIVAL	CAROUSEL	CAROUSER	CARRIAGE	CASEBOOK
CASHBOOK	CASHMERE	CASSETTE	CASTANET	CASTAWAY	CASUALTY+	CATACOMB
CATALYST	CATARACT	CATEGORY+	CATFIGHT	CATHETER	CAULDRON	CELIBACY+
CELLMATE	CEMETERY+	CENOTAPH	CENTROID	CEREMONY+	CESSPOOL	CHAPLAIN
CHARISMA	CHASTITY+	CHATLINE	CHECKOUT	CHEMICAL	CHESTNUT	CHIPMUNK
CHITCHAT	CHIVALRY+	CHLORIDE	CHLORINE	CHOIRBOY	CHROMIUM	CINNAMONy
CITATION	CIVILIAN	CIVILITY+	CLAIMANT	CLAPTRAP	CLARINET	CLEANSER
CLEARWAY	CLEAVAGE	CLEMATIS+	CLEMENCY+	CLINCHER	CLUBROOM	COALFACE
COALMINEr	COATRACK	COCKATOO	COCKEREL	CODRIVER	COEDITOR	COERCION
COHESION	COLANDER	COLDNESS+	COLESLAW	COLLAGEN	COLLIERY+	COLONIST
COLOSSUS+	COMEBACK	COMEDIAN	COMMANDO	COMMERCE	COMMUTER	COMPILER
COMPOSER	COMPUTER	CONCERTO	CONJUROR	CONNIVERy	CONQUEST	CONSUMER
CONTEMPT	CONVENOR	CONVEYOR	COOKBOOK	COOKWARE	COOLNESS	CORPORALe
CORRIDOR	COSINESS+	COTENANT	COUNTESS+	COVERAGE	COWORKER	CRABMEAT
CRACKPOT	CRAYFISH+	CREATION	CREATURE	CREDENCE	CREDITOR	CRESCENT
CREWNECK	CRIBBAGE	CRIMINAL	CROCKERY+	CROSSBAR	CROSSBOW	CROUPIER
CRUCIBLE	CRUCIFIX+	CRUNCHER	CRUSADER	CUCUMBER	CURRENCY+	CUSTOMER
CYCLEWAY	CYNICISM					
DAFFODIL	DAMPNESS+	DANDRUFFy	DARKNESS+	DARKROOM	DATABANK	DAUGHTER
DAYBREAK	DEADBEAT	DEADWOOD	DEAFNESS+	DEATHBED	DEBILITY+	DEBUTANTe
DECANTER	DECKHAND	DECLARER	DEFECTOR	DEFENDER	DEFERRAL	DEFIANCE
DEFTNESS+	DELETION	DELICACY+	DELIRIUM	DELIVERY+	DELUSION	DEMEANOR
DEMENTIAl	DEMISTER	DEMOCRATy	DEMOTION	DEPORTEE	DEPRIVAL	DERELICT
DERISION	DESERTER	DESIGNER	DETAILER	DETAINEE	DETECTOR	DEVIANCE
DEVOTION	DIAMETER	DIATRIBE	DICTATORy	DILATION	DILUTION	DINOSAUR
DIPLOMATa	DIPLOMATe	DIPSTICK	DIRECTORy	DISASTER	DISKETTE	DISPOSAL
DISUNITY+	DITHERER	DIVIDEND	DIVINITY+	DIVISION	DIVORCEE	DOCILITY+
DOCTRINE	DOGHOUSE	DOGSBODY+	DOMINION	DONATION	DOOMSDAY	DOORBELL
DOORKNOB	DOORSTOP	DOURNESS+	DOWNFALL	DOWNPIPE	DOWNPOUR	DOWNSIDE
DOWNTIME	DOWNTOWN	DOWNTURN	DRAGLINE	DRAGSTER	DRAINAGE	DRAWBACK
DRAWDOWN	DRIVEWAY	DROPKICK	DRUDGERY+	DRUGGIST	DRUMBEAT	DRUMROLL
DRUNKARD	DUCKLING	DULLNESS+	DUMBBELL	DUMPSTER	DUNGHILL	DUODENUM
DURATION	DYSLEXIA					

EARPHONE EASEMENT EDGINESS+ EDUCATORy EFFLUENT EGGPLANT EGGSHELL
EIGHTEEN EJECTION ELECTION ELECTRON ELEGANCE ELEPHANT ELEVATORy
ELEVENTH EMBALMER EMIGRANT EMINENCE EMINENCY+ EMISSION EMPLOYEE
EMPLOYER EMPORIUM ENGRAVERy ENORMITY+ ENQUIRER ENSEMBLE ENTIRETY+
EPIDEMIC EPILEPSY+ EQUALITY+ EQUATION ERECTION ERUPTION ESCAPADE
ESCAPISM ESCAPIST ESPRESSO ESSAYIST ETERNITY+ EUCALYPTi EUPHORIA
EVENNESS+ EVICTION EXAMINER EXCISION EXECUTORy EXERTION EXORCISM
EXORCIST EXPLORER EXPONENT EXPORTER EXPOSURE EXTERIOR EYEGLASS+
EYELINER EYEPIECE EYESHADE EYESIGHT

FACILITY+ FAIRNESS+ FALCONRY+ FARMHAND FARMLAND FARMWORK FARMYARD
FARTHING FASTENER FATALIST FATALITY+ FAVORITE FEEDBACK FEMINISM
FEMINIST FEROCITY+ FERVENCY+ FESTIVAL FIDELITY+ FIFTIETH FIGURINE
FILAMENT FINALIST FINALITY+ FINISHER FIREBALL FIRESIDE FIRETRAP
FIREWALL FIREWOOD FIREWORK FIRMNESS+ FISHBONE FISHBOWL FISHPOND
FIXATION FLAGPOLE FLAGSHIP FLAMENCO FLAMINGO FLAPJACK FLATHEAD
FLATMATE FLATNESS+ FLATTERY+ FLEABITE FLOTILLA FLUORIDE FLUORINE
FOCACCIA FOLKLORE FOLLICLE FOLLOWER FONDNESS+ FOOLSCAP FOOTBALL
FOOTHILL FOOTHOLD FOOTPATH FOOTRACE FOOTREST FOOTSTEP FOOTWORK
FOREBEAR FOREHAND FOREHEAD FOREPLAY FORESKIN FORESTER FORESTRY+
FORMWORK FORTIETH FOULNESS+ FOURSOME FOURTEEN FOXGLOVE FOXHOUND
FREEHOLD FRICTION FRONTAGEr FRUITION FUGITIVE FULLNESS+ FUSELAGE
FUTILITY+

GADABOUT GALLOPER GANGSTER GARDENER GARDENIA GARGOYLEd GASLIGHT
GASOLINE GATHERER GELATINE GEMSTONE GENOCIDE GEOMETRY+ GERANIUM
GIFTSHOP GIGABYTE GIRLHOOD GIVEAWAY GLADIOLAr GLASSFUL GLOSSARY+
GLOWWORM GLUTTONY+ GOALPOST GOLDFISH+ GOLLYWOG GOODNESS+ GOODWILL
GOVERNOR GRADIENT GRAFFITI GRANDDAD GRANDEUR GRANDSON GRAPHITE
GRATUITY+ GREENERY+ GRIZZLER GRUMBLER GUARDIAN GUERILLA GUERNSEY
GUIDANCE GUMPTION GUNPOINT GUNSMITH GYMKHANA GYRATION

HACKWORK HAIRBALL HAIRLINE HALFBACK HALFTIME HAMPSTER HANDBOOK
HANDGRIP HANDOVER HANDRAIL HANDWORK HANGOVER HARDBACK HARDENER
HARDNESS+ HARDSHIP HARDWARE HARDWOOD HATCHERY+ HATSTAND HAWTHORNy
HAYSTACK HAZELNUT HEADACHEy HEADBAND HEADGEAR HEADLAMP HEADLAND
HEADLOCK HEADREST HEADROOM HEADWIND HEDGEHOG HEDONIST HEIRLOOM
HELIPORT HELLHOLE HELPDESK HELPLINE HENHOUSE HERALDRY+ HEREDITY+
HERITAGE HIBISCUS+ HIDEAWAY HIGHLAND HIGHLIFE HIGHNESS+ HIGHROAD
HIGHSPOT HIJACKER HILARITY+ HILLSIDE HOBBYIST HOLINESS+ HOLOGRAM
HOMEBODY+ HOMELAND HOMESTAY HOMETOWN HOMEWORK HOMICIDE HONEYDEW
HONEYPOT HOOKWORM HOOLIGAN HOSPITALe HOTELIER HOUSEFUL HUMANISM
HUMANIST HUMANITY+ HUMIDITY+ HUMILITY+ HUMORIST HUMPBACK HYACINTH
HYDROGEN HYMNBOOK HYSTERIA

IDEALISM IDEALIST IDENTITY+ IDEOLOGY+ IDLENESS+ IGNITION ILLUSION
IMBECILE IMMUNITY+ IMPETIGO IMPORTER IMPOSTOR IMPROVER IMPUNITY+
IMPURITY+ INACTION INCIDENT INCISION INDUSTRY+ INEQUITY+ INFANTRY+
INFINITY+ INFORMER INIQUITY+ INSANITY+ INSIGNIA INSOMNIAc INSTINCT

INTERCOM INTERIOR INTERVALe INTIMACY+ INTRUDER INVASION INVENTORy
INVESTOR IRONBARK ISLANDER

JAILBIRD JAMBOREE JAPONICA JEALOUSY+ JETLINER JEWELLERy JILLAROO
JOYRIDER JOYSTICK JUDGMENT JUMPSUIT JUNCTION JUNCTURE JUNKYARD
JUSTNESS+ JUVENILE

KEENNESS+ KEEPSAKE KEROSENE KICKBACK KILOBYTE KILOGRAM KILOWATT
KINDNESS+ KNACKERY+ KNAPSACK KNOCKOUT KNOTHOLE

LABELLER LABOURER LABRADOR LACROSSE LADYBIRD LADYSHIP LAMBSKIN
LAMPPOST LANDFORM LANDLADY+ LANDLINE LANDLORD LANDMASS+ LANDSLIP
LARRIKIN LATENESS+ LATITUDE LAUGHTER LAUNCHER LAVATORY+ LAXATIVE
LAYABOUT LAZINESS+ LECTURER LEFTOVER LEGALITY+ LEMONADE LENIENCY+
LETHARGY+ LEUKEMIA LICENSEE LICORICE LIFEBELT LIFEBOAT LIFEBUOY
LIFELINE LIFESPAN LIFETIME LIGAMENT LIKENESS+ LIMERICK LIMPNESS+
LINGERIE LINGUIST LINIMENT LINOLEUM LISTENER LITERACY+ LITTERER
LOCALITY+ LOCATION LOCKDOWN LODGMENT LOITERER LOLLYPOP LOOSENER
LORDSHIP LORIKEET LOUDNESS+ LOVEBIRD LOVEBITE LUSHNESS+ LYREBIRD

MACARONIc MACAROON MACKEREL MADHOUSE MAGAZINE MAGICIAN MAGNOLIA
MAHOGANY+ MAILROOM MAINLAND MAINSTAY MAJORITY+ MAKEOVER MANDARINe
MANDOLINe MANGROVE MANPOWER MARATHON MARAUDER MARIGOLD MARRIAGE
MARZIPAN MATCHBOX+ MATERIAL MATESHIP MATTRESS+ MATURITY+ MAYORESS+
MEALTIME MEANNESS+ MEASURER MEATBALL MEATHEAD MECHANIC MEDALIST
MEDIATORy MEGABYTE MEGASTAR MEGAWATT MELANOMA MELTDOWN MEMBRANEd
MEMORIAL MENISCUS+ MERIDIAN MERINGUE METAPHOR MIDFIELD MIDNIGHT
MIDPOINT MIGRAINE MILDNESS+ MILEPOST MILKMAID MILLINERy MILLPOND
MINIBIKEr MINISTRY+ MINORITY+ MINSTREL MISTRIAL MOBILITY+ MOCASSIN
MOISTURE MOLECULE MOLEHILL MOLESKIN MOLESTER MOMENTUM MONARCHY+
MONEYBAG MONGOOSE MONOGAMY+ MONOLITH MONOPOLY+ MONORAIL MONOTONY+
MONUMENT MOONDUST MORALITY+ MORPHINE MORTUARY+ MOSQUITO MOTORCAR
MOTORIST MOTORWAY MOUNTAINy MOUSSAKA MOUTHFUL MOVEMENT MUDGUARD
MUDSLIDE MUDSTONE MULBERRY+ MULTIPLEt MULTIPLEx MURDERER MUSICIAN
MUSTACHEd MUSTERER MUTATION MYSTIQUE

NAMESAKE NARCOTIC NARRATORy NATIVITY+ NAUTILUS+ NEATNESS+ NECKLINE
NEGLIGEE NEPOTISM NEWCOMER NEWLYWED NEWSREEL NEWSROOM NICENESS+
NICKNACK NICOTINEd NIGHTCAP NINETEEN NITROGEN NOBILITY+ NONEVENT
NONSENSE NOTATION NOTEBOOK NOVELIST NUISANCEr NUMBERER NUMBNESS+
NUMERACY+ NUTHOUSE NUTRIENT NUTSHELL

OBITUARY+ OBLIVION OBSERVER OBSTACLE OCCUPANT OCCUPIER ODOMETER
OFFENDER OFFICIAL OFFSHOOT OFFSIDER OILFIELD OINTMENT OLEANDER
OMISSION ONCOLOGY+ ONLOOKER OPENNESS+ OPERATOR OPERETTA OPPONENT
OPTICIAN OPTIMISM OPTIMIST OPULENCE ORGANISM ORGANIST ORIGINAL
OUTFIELD OUTHOUSE OUTSIDER OVERCOAT OVERSEER OVERTONE OVERVIEW

```
PACIFISM   PACIFIST   PALAMINO   PALEFACE   PALENESS+  PAMPERER   PAMPHLET
PANCREAS+  PANELIST   PANORAMA   PANTSUIT   PAPERBOY   PARABOLA   PARADIGM
PARADISE   PARAKEET   PARANOIAc  PARASITE   PARKLAND   PARLANCE   PARTICLE
PARTISAN   PASSBOOK   PASSOVER   PASSPORT   PASSWORD   PASTRAMI   PATIENCE
PAWNSHOP   PEDIGREEd  PEEPHOLE   PEGBOARD   PENCHANT   PENDULUM   PENTAGON
PHARMACY+  PHEASANT   PHYSIQUEd  PILCHARD   PILLAGER   PINAFOREd  PINECONE
PITTANCE   PIZZERIA   PLACENTAe  PLACENTAl  PLANKTON   PLATELET   PLATINUM
PLATYPUS+  PLAYGIRL   PLAYLIST   PLAYMATE   PLAYROOM   PLAYSUIT   PLAYTIME
PLECTRUM   PLETHORA   PLEURISY+  PODIATRY+  POLARITY+  POLISHER   POLLUTER
PONYTAIL   POOLHALL   POOLROOM   POOLSIDE   POPULACE   POROSITY+  PORRIDGE
PORTHOLE   POTTERER   POWDERER   PREACHER   PRECINCT   PREDATORy  PRESENCE
PRESTIGE   PRETENSE   PRINCESSe  PRINTOUT   PRIORITY+  PRISONER   PRODUCER
PROFILER   PROMOTER   PROPHECY+  PROPOSAL   PROPOSER   PROSTATE   PROTEGEE
PROVIDER   PROVINCE   PRUDENCE   PUBLICAN   PULLOVER   PUNGENCY+  PUPPETRY+
PURIFIER   PUSHOVER   PUSSYCAT

QUADRANT   QUANDARY+  QUANTITY+  QUIBBLER   QUOTIENT

RABBITER   RACECARD   RACEGOER   RADIANCE   RADIATORy  RAILHEAD   RAINCOAT
RAINDROP   RAINFALL   RAPIDITY+  RARENESS+  RASHNESS+  REACTION   REASONER
REBUTTAL   RECEIVER   RECLINER   RECORDER   RECOVERY+  REFERRAL   REFINERY+
REFORMER   REGISTRY+  REGROWTH   REINDEER   RELATION   RELATIVE   RELIANCE
RELIGION   REMINDER   RENEGADE   REPAIRER   REPEATER   REPORTER   REPRISAL
REPUBLIC   RESELLER   RESIDENT   RESISTOR   RESPONSEr  RESTORER   RESTROOM
RETAILER   RETAINER   REVELLER   REVEREND   REVERSAL   REVIEWER   REVISION
REVOLVER   RHAPSODY+  RICHNESS+  RICKSHAW   RIESLING   RIGIDITY+  RINGSIDEr
RINGTAIL   RINGWORM   RIVERBED   ROADKILL   ROADSHOW   ROADSIDE   ROADWORK
ROCKFALL   ROCKFISH+  ROOFLINE   ROOMMATE   ROSEBUSH+  ROSEMARY+  ROTATION
ROUGHAGE   ROYALIST   RUCKSACK   RUDENESS+  RUDIMENT   RUNABOUT   RYEBREAD

SABOTEUR   SADDLERY+  SAFENESS+  SAILBOAT   SALEYARD   SALINITY+  SALTBUSH+
SAMENESS+  SANCTITY+  SANDBANK   SANDHEAP   SANDHILL   SANDPUMP   SANDSHOE
SANDSOAP   SAPPHIREd  SATIRIST   SAUCEPAN   SCARCITY+  SCENARIO   SCHOONER
SCIATICAl  SCORCHER   SCOREPAD   SCORPION   SCREAMER   SCREWTOP   SCRUTINY+
SCULPTOR   SEABOARD   SEAFLOOR   SEAFRONT   SEAHORSE   SEAPLANE   SEARCHER
SEASHELL   SEASHORE   SEAWATER   SECONDER   SECURITY+  SEDATION   SEDATIVE
SEEDLING   SELECTOR   SELENIUM   SEMESTER   SEMINARY+  SENILITY+  SENORITA
SERENITY+  SERGEANTy  SEVERITY+  SEWERAGE   SEXINESS+  SHAMROCK   SHEEPDOG
SHINBONE   SHIPMENT   SHOELACE   SHOOTOUT   SHOPGIRL   SHORTAGE   SHOWDOWN
SHOWGIRL   SHOWROOM   SHRAPNEL   SHREDDER   SHRIMPER   SHUFFLER   SHUTDOWN
SICKNESS+  SICKROOM   SIDEKICK   SIDEROAD   SIDESHOW   SIDEWALK   SILENCER
SILKWORM   SIXTIETH   SKELETON   SKETCHER   SKINHEAD   SKULLCAP   SKYDIVER
SKYLIGHT   SLEEPOUT   SLIPKNOT   SLIPPAGE   SLIPRAIL   SLOWNESS+  SLOWPOKE
SMALLPOX+  SMIDGEON   SMOOTHIE   SMUGGLER   SMUGNESS+  SNAPSHOT   SNATCHER
SNOBBERY+  SNOWDROP   SNOWFALL   SNOWLINE   SNOWMELT   SNUFFBOX+  SNUGNESS+
SOBRIETY+  SOFTBACK   SOFTBALL   SOFTENER   SOFTNESS+  SOFTWARE   SOFTWOOD
SOLARIUM   SOLENOID   SOLIDITY+  SOLITUDE   SOLVENCY+  SOMBRERO   SONGBIRD
SONGBOOK   SORCERER   SORENESS+  SORORITY+  SOURNESS+  SOURPUSS+  SOUVLAKIa
SPARKLER   SPARSITY+  SPEARGUN   SPECIMEN   SPECTRUM   SPEEDWAY   SPILLAGE
```

SPILLWAY	SPINIFEX+	SPINSTER	SPITFIRE	SPITTOON	SPLENDOR	SPLITTER
SPOONFUL	SPREADER	SPRINTER	SPROCKET	SPRUIKER	SPYPLANE	SQUEALER
STAIRWAY	STALLION	STANDARD	STANDOFF	STARDUST	STARFISH+	STARLING
STARSHIP	STICKLER	STINGRAY	STINKBUG	STITCHERy	STOCKCAR	STOCKIST
STOPOVER	STOPPAGE	STOWAWAY	STRAINER	STRAPPER	STRATEGY+	STREAKER
STREAMER	STRENGTH	STRIPPER	STROLLER	STUDFARM	SUBAGENT	SUBTLETY+
SUBURBIA	SUFFERER	SUITCASE	SUNLIGHT	SUNSHADE	SUNSHINE	SUPPLIER
SURENESS+	SURVEYOR	SURVIVAL	SURVIVOR	SUSPENSEr	SWASTIKA	SWIMSUIT
SWINDLER	SYLLABUS+	SYMMETRY+	SYMPATHY+	SYMPHONY+	SYNCLINE	SYNDROME
SYPHILISe						

TABLETOP	TAILBONE	TAILLAMP	TAILSPIN	TAILWIND	TAKEAWAY	TAKEOVER
TALISMAN	TANDOORI	TAPEWORM	TAXATION	TAXPAYER	TEAHOUSE	TEAMMATE
TEAMWORK	TEARDROP	TEASPOON	TEENAGER	TELETHON	TELLTALE	TEMERITY+
TEMPLATE	TENACITY+	TENDENCY+	TENEMENT	TENTACLEd	TERMINAL	TERMINUS+
TESTICLE	TEXTBOOK	THATCHER	THEOLOGY+	THEORIST	THINNESS+	THIRTEEN
THOUSAND	THRASHER	THRESHER	THRILLER	THROBBER	THUGGERY+	THUMBNUT
TIDEMARK	TIDINESS+	TIGHTWAD	TIMECARD	TIMELINE	TIMIDITY+	TITANIUM
TOILETRY+	TOKENISM	TOLLGATE	TOOLSHED	TOPOLOGY+	TOREADOR	TORTOISE
TORTURER	TOTALITY+	TOWNSHIP	TRACTION	TRADEOFF	TRAMLINEd	TRAPDOOR
TRASHCAN	TRAVELOG	TREASURY+	TREMBLER	TREVALLY+	TREVALLYs	TRIANGLEd
TRIBUNAL	TRICKERY+	TRIFECTA	TRILLION	TRIMARAN	TRIPLANE	TRIPWIRE
TROMBONE	TRUELOVE	TRUENESS+	TUCKSHOP	TUNGSTEN	TURNCOAT	TURNOVER
TURNPIKE	TUTORIAL	TYPEFACE				

UGLINESS+	UNDERDOG	UNDERTOW	UNIONISM	UNIONIST	UNIVERSE	UPHEAVAL
UPHOLDER	UPPERCUT	UPSTROKE	USHERESS+			

VAGRANCY+	VALIDITY+	VALUATOR	VANGUARD	VARIANCE	VASTNESS+	VELOCITY+
VENDETTA	VENTURER	VERANDAH	VESTMENT	VIBRANCY+	VIBRATORy	VICINITY+
VILLAGERy	VINEYARD	VIOLENCE	VIRILITY+	VIRTUOSO	VISCOUNTy	VITALITY+
VIVACITY+	VOCALIST	VOCATION	VOLITION			

WALKOVER	WALLOPER	WANDERER	WARHORSE	WARMNESS+	WARRANTY+	WASHBOWL
WASHROOM	WASPNEST	WATERBED	WATERHEN	WATERWAY	WEAKLING	WEAKNESS+
WEAPONRY+	WELLNESS+	WHISTLER	WHITECAP	WHITENER	WILDFIRE	WILDLIFE
WILDNESS+	WINDFALL	WINDPIPE	WINDSOCK	WINGSPAN	WISENESS+	WISHBONE
WISTERIA	WOODCHIP	WOODLAND	WOODWIND	WOODWORK	WOOLSHED	WORDBOOK
WORDGAME	WORDPLAY	WORKBOOK	WORKLOAD	WORKMATE	WRANGLER	WRECKAGE
WRESTLER	WRIGGLER					

YEARBOOK	YEARLING	YODELLER	YULETIDE

ZEPPELIN	ZUCCHINI

8.1.4 NOUNS MORE COMMONLY USED IN OTHER PARTS OF SPEECH

ABERRANT	ABNORMAL	ABRASIVE	ABSOLUTE*	ACADEMIC	ACOUSTIC	ADDENDUM
ADHESIVE	ADJACENT	ADVISORY+	AFFLUENT	AGNOSTIC	ALARMIST	ALLERGIC
ALLUVIAL	ALLUVIUM	ANALOGUE	ANALYTIC	ANATHEMA	ANOREXIC	ANTIRUST
ANYTHING	ANYWHERE	APPARENT	AROMATIC	ARTERIAL	ATHLETIC	AUDITORY+
AUTISTIC						
BACKWARD	BACTERIAl	BACTERIAn	BIANNUAL	BIENNIAL	BIOLOGIC	BISEXUAL
BIVALENT	BIWEEKLY+	BOHEMIAN	BURNABLE			
CATHOLIC	CELIBATE	CELLULAR	CEREBRAL	CESAREAN	CESARIAN	CIRCULAR
CLERICAL	COLONIAL	COLOURED	COMBINED	COMMONER	CONSTANT	CONSULAR
COPYBOOK	CORONARY+	CORPORAS+	COSMETIC	CREATIVE	CRUCIATE	
DECADENT	DELICATE	DIABETIC	DIAGONAL	DIETETIC	DOGMATIC	DOMESTIC
DOMINANT	DOUBTFUL	DOWNCAST	DOWNHILL	DOWNWARD	DRAMATIC	DREADFUL
DYSLEXIC						
EASTERLY+	ECLECTIC	ECONOMIC	ECSTATIC	ECUMENIC	EDUCABLE	ELECTIVE
ELECTRIC	ELEVATED	ELIGIBLE	EMERGENT	EMPHATIC	ERUPTIVE	ETCETERA
EVERYDAY	EXISTENT	EXPLICIT	EXTERNAL			
FAITHFUL	FALSETTO	FAMILIAR	FEMININE	FOOTWEARy	FORENSIC	FOREWARD
FRENETIC	FRIENDLY*					
GODSPEED	GRACIOUS+	GRADABLE	GREATEST	GUTTURAL		
HABITUAL	HALFPACE	HANDHELD	HANDSOME*	HARDCORE	HARMONICa	HOMESPUN
HOMEWARD	HONORARY+	HORRIBLE	HYGIENIC	HYPNOTIC	HYSTERIC	
IGNORANT	IMMATURE	IMMORTAL	IMPERIAL	IMPOTENT	INCOMING	INDIGENT
INEXPERT	INFERIOR	INFINITE	INFRARED	INNOCENT	INSOLENT	INTEGRAL
INTENDED	INTERNAL	IRONCLAD	IRRITANT			
KERBSIDE	KNITWEAR					
LAPIDARY+	LAVISHER	LITERATE	LOGISTIC	LONESOME	LONGHAND	LUGGABLE
MAGNETIC	MARGINAL	MEANTIME	MEDIEVAL	MENSWEAR	METALLIC	MILITANT
MILITARY+	MOLASSES+	MORALLER	MOVEABLE			
NATIONAL	NEARSIDE	NEUROTIC	NONGLARE	NONHUMAN	NONWHITE	NONWOVEN
NORTHERN						
OBSCURER	OFFSTAGE	ONCOMING	OPPOSITE	OPTIONAL	ORDINARY*	ORIENTAL
ORTHODOXy	OUTBOARD	OUTBOUND	OVENWARE	OVERHEAD	OVERSHOT	
PARANOIC	PARANOID	PASTORALe	PASTORALi	PATHETIC	PECTORAL	PECULIAR
PENITENT	PERSONAL	PHONETIC	PHYSICAL	PLATONIC	POETICAL	PORTABLE
POSITIVE*	POSSIBLE*	POTBELLY+	PRECIOUS+	PREHUMAN	PRENATAL	PROBABLE
PRODIGAL	PROFANER	PROFOUND*	PROFUSER	PROMPTER	PUREBRED	
RAINWEAR	RATIONALe	REGIONAL	RELIABLE	RESIDUAL	RESOLUTE*	RESONANT
REUSABLE	RHETORIC	RHYTHMIC	RIPARIAN	ROMANTIC	RUMINANT	RUSTICAL
SANITARY+	SCHIZOID	SEASONAL	SEMANTIC	SEMIBOLD	SENSIBLE*	SILVERER
SINGULARy	SIXPENCE	SLAPDASH+	SLIGHTER	SMOOTHER	SOCIABLE	SOLITARY+
SOMEBODY+	SOMETIME	SOMEWHAT	SOUTHERN	SPARABLE	SPECIFIC	SPURRIER
SQUINTER	STACCATO	STALWART	STANDOUT	STEADIER	STERLING	STORABLE
SUBHUMAN	SUBLIMER	SUBURBAN	SUPERIOR	SWIMWEAR	SYMBOLIC	SYSTEMIC
TALKBACK	TANGIBLE	TECTONIC	TEMPORAL	TENDERER	TENPENCE	TERRIBLE
TERTIARY+	THANKYOU	THEATRIC	THEMATIC	THICKSET	THOROUGH*	TOMORROW
TORCHIERe	TROPICAL	TRUEBLUE	TUPPENCE	TUPPENNY+	TWOPENCE	
ULTRARED	UNDERAGEd	UNDERARM	UNLEADED	UNWASHED	UPMARKET	

```
VALUABLE   VARIABLE   VARICOSEd VARIETAL   VERTICAL   VIRGINAL   VITREOUS+
VOLATILE   VOLCANIC
WANTONER   WASHABLE   WEARABLE  WESTERLY+  WESTWARD   WINDWARD
```

8.1.5 VERB FORMS ENDING IN 'ING' COMMONLY USED AS NOUNS

```
BLESSING   BOTTLING   BREEDING   BRIEFING   BUILDING   CHIPPING   CLADDING
CLEARING   CLIPPING   CLOTHING   COLORING   COVERING   CROSSING   CROWNING
DRESSING   DRILLING   DRIPPING   DROPPING   DROWNING   DRUBBING   DUMPLING
DWELLING   FLOGGING   FLOORING   GHOSTING   GREETING   GROUPING   HOARDING
KINDLING   LIGHTING   OFFERING   OUTGOING   PAINTING   PLANTING   PRESSING
PRINTING   RAMBLING   ROASTING   SCOLDING   SHEARING   SHEETING   SHILLING
SHIPPING   SHOOTING   SHOPPING   SIGHTING   SOUNDING   SPANKING   SPELLING
STABBING   STANDING   STOCKING   STUFFING   SWELLING   TEACHING   TOWELING
TRAPPING   TRIMMING   UPRISING   WATERING   WEIGHING   WHIPPING   WRAPPING
```

8.1.6 OTHER VERB FORMS ENDING IN 'ING' WHICH ARE NOUNS

```
ADVISING   AGENTING   ALLAYING   ARCADING   ASSAYING   ASSUMING   ATTIRING

BABBLING   BANDYING   BATCHING   BEAGLING   BECOMING   BELLYING   BERRYING
BIRTHING   BLABBING   BLACKING   BLAGGING   BLANKING   BLASTING   BLEATING
BLEEDING   BLENDING   BLINDING   BLOATING   BLOCKING   BLOODING   BLOTTING
BLURTING   BLUSHING   BOARDING   BOASTING   BOTCHING   BOULTING   BRAGGING
BRAIDING   BRANDING   BRAWLING   BREAKING   BRICKING   BRIDGING   BRIGUING
BRINGING   BRONZING   BROODING   BROWNING   BROWSING   BRUISING   BRUSHING
BUCKLING   BUMBLING   BUNCHING   BUNDLING   BUNGLING   BURBLING

CANOEING   CAROLING   CATCHING   CATERING   CAULKING   CENTRING   CHAFFING
CHANTING   CHEATING   CHILLING   CHOPPING   CHORDING   CHROMING   CHUMPING
CHUNKING   CHURNING   CINCHING   CIRCLING   CLANGING   CLANKING   CLAPPING
CLASHING   CLASPING   CLASSING   CLEANING   CLEAVING   CLECKING   CLICKING
CLIMBING   CLOCKING   CLOGGING   CLOTTING   CLOUDING   CLOWNING   CLUBBING
COACHING   COASTING   COBBLING   COCKLING   COUCHING   COUGHING   COUPLING
COURSING   COURTING   CRACKING   CRADLING   CRAWLING   CRESTING   CRIBBING
CRINGING   CROAKING   CROONING   CROPPING   CRUISING   CURRYING

DABBLING   DANGLING   DARKLING   DAZZLING   DEFAMING   DERATING   DEVILING
DIALLING   DIVIDING   DOUBLING   DOUBTING   DOWELING   DRAFTING   DRAGGING
DREAMING   DREDGING   DRINKING   DROLLING   DROOKING   DROUKING   DUELLING

EMAILING   EMPTYING   ENTERING   ENTICING   EVENTING

FAGOTING   FAINTING   FEASTING   FEIGNING   FETTLING   FIELDING   FIGHTING
FILCHING   FLAGGING   FLAPPING   FLASHING   FLATTING   FLEERING   FLESHING
FLIRTING   FLITTING   FLOATING   FLOCKING   FLOODING   FLOSSING   FLUSHING
FOCUSING   FONDLING   FOOTLING   FOOZLING   FOUNDING   FRAGGING   FREEZING
```

8. Eight-Letter Words

FRETTING   FRIGGING   FRILLING   FRISKING   FROCKING   FROGGING   FROSTING
FRUITING   FUDDLING

GABBLING   GAGGLING   GAMBLING   GARAGING   GARBLING   GIGGLING   GLANCING
GLEAMING   GLEANING   GLOOMING   GNASHING   GOGGLING   GRAFTING   GRAINING
GRASSING   GREENING   GRIEVING   GRILLING   GRINDING   GRINNING   GRITTING
GROANING   GROINING   GROOMING   GROUTING   GROWLING   GRUDGING   GRUELING
GRUNTING   GUESSING

HANDLING   HATCHING   HAUNTING   HAVERING   HECKLING   HIGGLING   HOBBLING
HOISTING   HUMBLING   HURDLING   HURRYING   HUSTLING

INDEXING   INLAYING   INTONING   INVITING

JANGLING   JERQUING   JOINTING   JOLLYING   JOSTLING   JUGGLING

KAYAKING   KECKLING   KNITTING   KNOCKING   KNOTTING   KNURLING

LAUGHING   LAYERING   LEACHING   LEARNING   LETCHING   LIBELING   LIMITING
LOATHING   LOBBYING   LOUNGING   LOWERING   LUSTRING   LYNCHING

MANTLING   MANURING   MARBLING   MARRYING   MEDDLING   MIDDLING   MINGLING
MISDOING   MIZZLING   MODELING   MORPHING   MOTORING   MOTTLING   MOULDING
MOULTING   MOUNTING   MOURNING   MUDDLING   MULESING   MUMBLING   MUSCLING

NEEDLING   NESTLING   NIBBLING   NIGGLING   NOODLING   NORTHING   NOTCHING
NURSLING

ORDERING

PADDLING   PANELING   PAPERING   PATCHING   PEARLING   PEBBLING   PEDDLING
PERCHING   PHRASING   PIERCING   PILOTING   PINCHING   PITCHING   PIVOTING
PLAIDING   PLAINING   PLAITING   PLANKING   PLANNING   PLASHING   PLATTING
PLEADING   PLEASING   PLINKING   PLODDING   PLONKING   PLOTTING   PLUGGING
PLUMBING   PLUNGING   POACHING   POINDING   POINTING   POLICING   POUNDING
PRAISING   PRANCING   PRANKING   PRICKING   PRIGGING   PRONKING   PROOFING
PROWLING   PUDDLING   PURFLING   PURSUING

QUAILING   QUEENING   QUERYING   QUESTING   QUEUEING   QUIETING   QUILLING
QUILTING   QUIZZING   QUOINING

RABBLING   RALLYING   RANCHING   RATTLING   RAVELING   RAVENING   REFINING
RENEWING   REPINING   REPUTING   RETAKING   REVILING   REVIVING   RIDDLING
RIGHTING   RIPPLING   RIVETING   ROGERING   ROUNDING   RUFFLING   RUMBLING
RUSTLING

SAMPLING   SCALDING   SCALPING   SCAMPING   SCANNING   SCARFING   SCARPING
SCARRING   SCATTING   SCENTING   SCHEMING   SCOFFING   SCOOPING   SCORNING
SCOURING   SCOUTING   SCRAPING   SCREWING   SCRIBING   SCULLING   SCUMMING

SEDUCING	SEETHING	SETTLING	SEWERING	SHAFTING	SHARKING	SHARPING
SHAWLING	SHEALING	SHEDDING	SHELLING	SHELVING	SHIELING	SHIFTING
SHIRRING	SHIRTING	SHOALING	SHOUTING	SHRIVING	SHUCKING	SHUNTING
SIMPLING	SINGLING	SIZZLING	SKANKING	SKELPING	SKILLING	SKIMMING
SKIPPING	SKIRLING	SKIRTING	SKULKING	SLAGGING	SLAMMING	SLANGING
SLAPPING	SLASHING	SLATTING	SLEDDING	SLEDGING	SLEEKING	SLEEPING
SLEEVING	SLICKING	SLIMMING	SLOSHING	SLUBBING	SLUMMING	SMACKING
SMASHING	SMELLING	SMELTING	SMOCKING	SMUDGING	SNAPPING	SNARLING
SNEERING	SNEEZING	SNIFFING	SNIPPING	SNORTING	SNUBBING	SNUFFING
SOOTHING	SOURCING	SOUTHING	SPALLING	SPAMMING	SPARRING	SPAWNING
SPEAKING	SPEEDING	SPEERING	SPEIRING	SPELDING	SPENDING	SPILLING
SPINNING	SPITTING	SPLICING	SPOOFING	SPOOLING	SPOTTING	SPOUTING
SPRAYING	SPUDDING	SPURNING	SPURRING	SQUARING	STABLING	STACKING
STAINING	STALKING	STALLING	STAMPING	STAPLING	STARRING	STARTING
STARVING	STEADING	STEALING	STEAMING	STEANING	STEELING	STEENING
STEERING	STEEVING	STEINING	STEMMING	STICKING	STIFLING	STILLING
STILTING	STINGING	STINTING	STIRRING	STOPPING	STORMING	STORYING
STRAYING	STREWING	STRIKING	STRIPING	STRIVING	STROBING	STROKING
STROWING	STUDDING	STUMPING	STUNNING	SUCKLING	SUGARING	SWANNING
SWAPPING	SWARMING	SWASHING	SWATTING	SWAYLING	SWEALING	SWEARING
SWEATING	SWEEPING	SWEETING	SWERVING	SWILLING	SWIMMING	SWINGING
SWISHING	SWOONING	SWOPPING	SWOTTING			
TACKLING	TANGLING	TAPERING	TATTLING	TAUNTING	TEETHING	TEMPTING
THANKING	THIEVING	THIGGING	THINKING	THINNING	THIRDING	THRIVING
THROWING	TICKLING	TINGLING	TINKLING	TOASTING	TONGUING	TOOTHING
TORCHING	TOUCHING	TRACKING	TRAINING	TRAMPING	TRAWLING	TREADING
TREATING	TREKKING	TRICKING	TRIFLING	TRILLING	TRIPLING	TRIPPING
TROLLING	TROTTING	TROUTING	TRUCKING	TRUDGING	TRUMPING	TRUNKING
TRUSSING	TUMBLING	TURTLING	TUTORING	TWANGING	TWEAKING	TWILLING
TWINNING	TWISTING	TWITTING				
UNIFYING	UNLADING	UNMAKING	USHERING	USURPING	UTTERING	
VALETING	VAPORING	VAULTING	VAUNTING	VENTRING	VISITING	VOGUEING
VOMITING						
WAFFLING	WAISTING	WAKENING	WALTZING	WAMBLING	WANGLING	WARBLING
WATTLING	WAVERING	WHACKING	WHARFING	WHEELING	WHEEZING	WHIFFING
WHIRLING	WHIRRING	WHIZZING	WHOOPING	WHOPPING	WHUPPING	WINDLING
WITCHING	WOBBLING	WOOLDING	WORRYING	WOUNDING	WRAXLING	WRECKING
WRITHING						
YACHTING	YEARNING	YIELDING				

8.1.7 NON-PLURALS IN COMMON USE

ABORTIVE	ABRUPTLY	ABSURDLY	ABUNDANT	ACCURATE	ACTIVELY	ACTUALLY
ADEQUATE	ADORABLE	AIRBORNE	AIRCRAFT	AIRTIGHT	ALDERMAN	ALDERMEN
ALFRESCO	ALKALINE	ALMIGHTY	ALTHOUGH	AMENABLE	AMICABLE	AMICABLY
ANALYSES	ANALYSIS	ANNUALLY	ARDENTLY	ARGUABLE	ARGUABLY	ARROGANT
ARTESIAN	ARTISTIC	ASTUTELY	ATYPICAL			

BACKLESS	BARBARIC	BAREBACK	BAREFOOT	BASALTIC	BASELESS	BEARABLE
BEATABLE	BEDSOCKS	BEFALLEN	BEGOTTEN	BENDABLE	BIBLICAL	BIDDABLE
BINDABLE	BITESIZE	BITTERLY	BLISSFUL	BLUSTERY*	BOASTFUL	BOGEYMAN
BOGEYMEN	BONELESS	BOOKABLE	BOOTABLE	BRACKISH	BRAZENLY	BRETHREN
BRIGHTLY	BROWNISH	BRUTALLY				

CANDIDLY	CAREFREE	CARELESS	CASHLESS	CASUALLY	CAUTIOUS	CERVICAL
CHAIRMEN	CHATTERY	CHEEKILY	CHEERFUL	CHILDISH	CHILDREN	CHINLESS
CLEVERLY	CLIMATIC	CLINICAL	CLUBFOOT	CLUELESS	CLUMSILY	COACHMAN
COACHMEN	COARSELY	COCKSURE	COHERENT	COHESIVE	COLORFUL	COLOSSAL
COMATOSE	COMMONLY	COMMUNAL	CONFETTI	CONTRITE	CORDLESS	COVERTLY
COWARDLY	CRAFTILY	CREDIBLE	CREDIBLY	CRITERIAl	CRITICAL	CULINARY
CULPABLE	CULPABLY	CULTURAL	CYCLONIC			

DEBONAIRe	DECENTLY	DECISIVE	DECREPIT	DEFINITE	DESIROUS	DEVILISH
DEVOUTLY	DIABETES	DIALYSIS	DILIGENT	DIRECTLY	DISCREET*	DISLOYAL
DISMALLY	DISTINCT	DIVINELY	DIVISIVE	DOGGEDLY	DOLDRUMS	DOWNWIND
DRACONIC	DRAUGHTY*	DREARILY	DRIVABLE			

ECOLOGIC	EFFUSIVE	EIGHTHLY	ELOQUENT	ENORMOUS	ENTIRELY	ENVIABLE
ERECTILE	EUPHORIC	EVENTFUL	EVENTUAL	EVERMORE	EVERYONE	EXPERTLY
EXULTANT	EYEDROPS	EYETEETH	EYETOOTH			

FABULOUS	FACELESS	FAINTISH	FALLIBLE	FAMOUSLY	FANCIFUL	FARCICAL
FATHERLY	FEARLESS	FEARSOME	FEASIBLE	FEASIBLY	FEATHERY	FERVIDLY
FEVERISH	FIENDISH	FIERCELY	FIFTYISH	FINDABLE	FISHWIFE	FITFULLY
FITTABLE	FLAGRANT	FLAWLESS	FLEXIBLE	FLIPPANT	FLOODLIT	FLUENTLY
FOGBOUND	FOODLESS	FOOTSORE	FORCEFUL	FORCIBLY	FOREGONE	FOREMOST
FORESEEN	FORETOLD	FOREWENT	FORGIVEN	FORMALLY	FORMERLY	FORMULAE
FORSAKEN	FORTYISH	FOURTHLY	FRAGRANT	FREAKISH	FREEHAND	FREEWILL
FRESHMAN	FRESHMEN	FRUITFUL	FRUMPISH			

GALACTIC	GENEROUS	GEOLOGIC	GERMFREE	GETTABLE	GHOULISH	GIGANTIC
GIMMICKY	GINGERLY	GLITTERY*	GLOBALLY	GLORIOUS	GOALLESS	GODCHILD
GORGEOUS	GRACEFUL	GRACIOUS	GRANITIC	GRANULARy	GRATEFUL	GRAVELLY
GREEDILY	GREENISH	GRIEVOUS	GROWABLE	GRUESOME*	GULLIBLE	

HAIRLESS	HALFLIFE	HANDLESS	HANDMADE	HANDYMAN	HANDYMEN	HANGABLE
HARMLESS	HEADLESS	HEADLONG	HEARTILY	HEATEDLY	HEAVENLY*	HEAVYSET
HELLBENT	HELMSMAN	HELMSMEN	HELPLESS	HENCHMAN	HENCHMEN	HERDSMAN
HERDSMEN	HEREWITH	HESITANT	HISTORIC	HITHERTO	HOMELESS	HOMEMADE
HOMESICK	HONESTLY	HOPELESS	HORMONAL	HORRIBLY	HORRIFIC	HORSEMAN
HORSEMEN	HOURLONG	HUMANELY	HUMOROUS	HUNGOVER	HUNTSMAN	HUNTSMEN
HYPNOSES	HYPNOSIS					

```
IMMINENT  IMMOBILE  IMMODESTy  IMPLICITy  IMPOLITE*  IMPROPER  IMPUDENT
INACTIVE  INCISIVE  INDEBTED   INDECENT*  INDIRECT   INDOLENT  INEDIBLE
INFAMOUS  INFORMAL  INHERENT   INHUMANE   INSANELY   INSECURE  INTENTLY
INTREPID  INVASIVE  INWARDLY   IRONICAL

JOKINGLY  JOYFULLY  JOYOUSLY   JUBILANT   JUDICIAL

KICKABLE  KNOWABLE

LADYLIKE  LAUDABLE  LAVISHLY   LAWFULLY   LEAFLESS   LIFELESS  LIFELIKE
LIFELONG  LIGHTISH  LIKEABLE   LIKEWISE   LINESMAN   LINESMEN  LISTLESS
LITERARY  LOCKABLE  LONGWAYS   LOPSIDED   LOVELESS   LOVESICK  LOVINGLY
LUCKLESS  LUKEWARM  LUMINOUS   LUSCIOUS

MAJESTIC  MANFULLY  MANUALLY   MAPPABLE   MARITIME   MARKEDLY  MARKSMAN
MARKSMEN  MASTERLY  MATERNAL   MATRONLY   MATURELY   MEATLOAF  MEDIOCRE
MENDABLE  MENTALLY  MERCIFUL   MERCURIC   MESDAMES   METEORIC  MIGHTILY
MINDLESS  MISDEALT  MISHEARD   MISSPELT   MISSPENT   MISTAKEN  MODESTLY
MONETARY  MONSIEUR  MOONLESS   MOREOVER   MORTALLY   MOTHERLY  MOURNFUL
MUSCULAR  MUTUALLY  MYSTICAL   MYTHICAL

NAMELESS  NARROWLY  NAUSEOUS   NAUTICAL   NEEDLESS   NEUROSES  NEUROSIS
NEWFOUND  NEXTDOOR  NITPICKY*  NOBLEMAN   NOBLEMEN   NONRATED  NONSTICKy
NORMALLY  NOWADAYS  NUMEROUS

OBEDIENT  OPENABLE  OPERABLE   OUTDRANK   OUTDRUNK   OUTGROWN  OUTLEAPT
OUTRIGHT  OVERCAME  OVERDONE   OVERDREW   OVERHUNG   OVERLAID  OVERLAIN
OVERLEAF  OVERPAID  OVERRIPEn  OVERRODE   OVERSEEN   OVERTOOK

PAINLESS  PALATIAL  PARENTAL   PARTAKEN   PASSABLE   PASSERBY  PATENTLY
PATERNAL  PEACEFUL^ PEDANTIC   PEERLESS   PENKNIFE   PERILOUS  PERIODIC
PERVERSE* PETULANT  PINTSIZEd  PITIABLE   PLAINISH   PLAYABLE  PLEASANT*
PLUMPISH  PLUTONIC  POIGNANT   POLITELY   POPULOUS   POSSIBLY  POWERFUL
PREGNANT  PREVIOUS  PRINCELY*  PRISTINE   PROBABLY   PROLIFIC  PROMPTLY
PROPERLY  PROVABLE  PUBLICLY   PUNCTUAL   PUNITIVE

QUAINTLY  QUOTABLE

RACIALLY  RAFTSMAN  RAFTSMEN   RAINLESS   RANDOMLY   RAVENOUS  REACTIVE
READABLE  REARISEN  RECENTLY   RECKLESS   REINSMAN   REINSMEN  RELEARNT
RELEVANT  RELIABLY  REMEDIAL   REMOTELY   RESTLESS   RETICENT  REVERENT
RICKETTY  RIFLEMAN  RIFLEMEN   RIGHTFUL   RIGOROUS   RISKLESS  ROUNDISH
RUBBISHY  RUTHLESS

SADISTIC  SALESMAN  SALESMEN   SARDONIC   SAVAGELY   SCANTILY  SCARCELY
SCORNFUL  SCRAGGLY* SCRATCHY*  SEAMLESS   SEATLESS   SECONDLY  SECRETLY
SECURELY  SEDATELY  SEEDLESS   SELDOMLY   SELFLESS   SELLABLE  SENSIBLY
SENSUOUS  SERENELY  SEVERELY   SEXUALLY   SHAMEFUL   SHARPISH  SHEEPISH
SHOELESS  SHREWDLY  SHRUNKEN   SILENTLY   SINISTER   SINKABLE  SISTERLY
SIXTYISH  SLIGHTLY  SLIPPERY*  SLIPSHOD   SLOPPILY   SLOTHFUL  SLOVENLY*
SLUGGISH  SMALLISH  SMOOTHLY   SNEAKILY   SNOBBISH   SNOWLESS  SOCIABLY
```

8. Eight-Letter Words

SOCIALLY	SOLEMNLY	SOMBRELY	SORDIDLY	SOULLESS	SPACIOUS	SPARSELY
SPEEDILY	SPITEFUL^	SPLENDID*	SPOONFED	SPORADIC	SPOTLESS	SPRITELY*
SPURIOUS	SQUARELY	SQUIGGLY*	STAGNANT	STARLESS	STATICKY	STEADILY
STEALTHY*	STIMULUS	STOCKMAN	STOCKMEN	STOREMAN	STOREMEN	STRICKEN
STRICTLY	STRIDENT	STRONGLY	STUDIOUS	STUNTMAN	STUNTMEN	STUPIDLY
STURDILY	SUCCINCT*	SUDDENLY	SUICIDAL	SUITABLE	SUITABLY	SULLENLY
SUNBURNT	SUPERBLY	SUPERMAN	SUPERMEN	SUREFIRE	SURFABLE	SURGICAL
SWEETISH	SYNOPSES					

TACTICAL	TACTLESS	TALENTED	TASTABLE	TASTEFUL	TEARLESS	TENDERLY
TERRIBLY	TERRIFIC	THANKFUL^	THATAWAY	THUGGISH	THUNDERY*	TICKLISH
TIGHTISH	TIMELESS	TIRELESS	TIRESOME	TOGETHER	TOLERANT	TOPNOTCH
TORRIDLY	TORTUOUS	TOURISTY	TRANQUIL*	TRANQUIL^	TREELESS	TRUTHFUL
TUBELESS	TUNELESS	TURNABLE				

ULTERIOR	UMTEENTH	UNAFRAID	UNAMUSED	UNBACKED	UNBANKED	UNBEATEN
UNBOOKED	UNBROKEN	UNCARING	UNCOMMON*	UNCOOKED	UNDERATE	UNDERDID
UNDERFED	UNDERWAY	UNDOABLE	UNDRIVEN	UNDUBBED	UNEASILY	UNEDIBLE
UNENDING	UNERRING	UNEVENLY	UNFAIRLY	UNFILLED	UNFORCED	UNFORMED
UNFRAMED	UNFROZEN	UNFUNDED	UNGAINLY*	UNGRADED	UNHARMED	UNHEATED
UNHEEDED	UNIRONED	UNJUSTLY	UNKINDLY*	UNLAWFUL	UNLEARNT	UNLEASED
UNLIKELY*	UNLISTED	UNMAPPED	UNMARKED	UNOPENED	UNPAIRED	UNPLAYED
UNPROVEN	UNRANKED	UNRENTED	UNREPAID	UNSALTED	UNSAVORY	UNSEEDED
UNSEEMLY*	UNSHAVEN	UNSIGNED	UNSOLVED	UNSORTED	UNSPOILT	UNSPOKEN
UNSTABLE*	UNSURELY	UNTAPPED	UNTESTED	UNTIMELY*	UNTIRING	UNTITLED
UNTOWARD	UNUSABLE	UNVIABLE	UNWANTED	UNWEDDED	UNWIELDY*	UNWISELY
UNWORTHY*	UPCOMING	UPPISHLY	UPWARDLY	URGENTLY	USEFULLY	

VASCULAR	VEHEMENT	VENOMOUS	VENEREAL	VERBALLY	VERBATIM	VIEWABLE
VIGILANTe	VIGOROUS	VIRTUOUS	VIRULENT	VISUALLY	VOTELESS	

WALKABLE	WANTONLY	WASTEFUL	WATCHFUL	WAVELESS	WEEDLESS	WEREWOLF
WHATEVER	WHENEVER	WHEREVER	WICKEDLY	WIFELESS	WILFULLY	WINDLESS
WINGLESS	WINNABLE	WITHDREW	WITHHELD	WOEFULLY	WONDROUS	WOODSMAN
WOODSMEN	WORDLESS	WORKABLE	WORKLESS	WRETCHED*	WRONGFUL	

YEARLONG	YOUNGISH	YOURSELF	YOUTHFUL

ZESTLESS

8.2 LESS FAMILIAR EIGHTS WHICH ARE HOOK WORDS

8.2.1 FRONT HOOKS OF SEVENS TO MAKE EIGHTS

FRONT HOOKS WITH VOWELS

ABATABLE	*ABEGGING*	ABRACHIA	ABUTMENT	ACANTHUS+	**ACAUDATE**	**ACAULINE**
ACENTRIC	**ACERATED**	**ACHROMIC**	ACOSMISM	ACOSMIST	**ADYNAMIC**	AESTHETE
AESTIVAL	AETHERIC	AFEBRILE	**AFLUTTER**	**AGENESES**	**AGENESIS**	**AGENETIC**
AGLIMMER	*AGLITTER*	*AGLOSSAL*	AGRAPHIC	**AKINESES**	**AKINESIS**	*AKINETIC*
ALOGICAL	**AMAZEDLY**	**AMEIOSES**	**AMEIOSIS**	**AMIDMOST**	AMIDSHIP	**AMISSING**
AMITOSES	**AMITOSIS**	**AMITOTIC**	**AMORALLY**	AMORTISE	AMUSETTE	**ANODALLY**
ANOINTER	APIARIST	**APLASTIC**	**APRACTIC**	**APYRETIC**	APYREXIA	**ASEISMIC**
ASEPTATE	ASHINESS+	**ASPARKLE**	**ASPHERIC**	ASPIRANT	**ASTERNAL**	ASTHENIA
ASTHENIC	ASYNERGY+	ASYSTOLE	**ATECHNIC**	**ATONALLY**	**ATREMBLE**	**ATROPHIC**
ATROPINE	ATROPISM	**ATWITTER**	AVENTAILe	AVENTURE	AVOUCHER	**AWANTING**
AWEARIED	**AWEATHER**					
ECAUDATE	**ECOSTATE**	EDENTATE	EMERSION	**EMETICAL**	EMICTION	**EMISSILE**
EMISSIVE	ENERVATE	EPHORATE	EQUIPPER	ERADIATE	ESCALADEr	ESCALADO+
ESCALIER	ESCALLOP	**ESPECIAL**	ESPOUSAL	**ETYPICAL**	EVERSION	**EVOCABLE**
EVULGATE						
ICONICAL	ISABELLA					
OECOLOGY+	**OEDEMATA**	OENOLOGY+	OESTRIOL	OESTRONE	**OESTROUS**	**OMISSIVE**
OOLOGIST	*OSTOMATE*	OUROLOGY+	OVARIOLE	**OVARIOUS**		
UPRAISER						

FRONT HOOKS WITH CONSONANTS

BAILMENT	BANALITY+	BARTISAN	**BASHLESS**	**BEARLIKE**	**BENDWAYS**	**BENDWISE**
BESPOUSE	BETACISM	**BITCHILY**	**BLADDERY**	BLEACHERy	BLIMBING	**BLITHELY**
BLOGROLL	**BLOUSILY**	BOARFISH+	**BOATLIKE**	BORDERER	**BOWLLIKE**	**BRAINILY**
BRANCHERy	BRATCHET	BRATLING	BRATPACK	BRATTISH	BREACHER	**BREGMATA**
BRIMLESS	BROADWAY	BROGUERY+	**BROGUISH**	*BRUSSELS*		
CANNULAR	**CAPSIDAL**	CAROUSAL	**CASTABLE**	CASTEISM	CENSURER	CENTRISM
CENTRIST	**CHADARIM**	**CHALLOTH**	CHANDLERy	**CHAPLESS**	**CHARMFUL**	CHAROSETh
CHAUNTER	**CHAZANIM**	**CHEWABLE**	CHICKORY+	*CHOLLERS*	*CHUPPOTH*	**CLAWLESS**
CLAWLIKE	**CLITORAL**	**CLOSABLE**	**CLOVERED**	**CLUMPISH**	COCREATE	**COULDEST**
COVERALL	COVERLET	**CRANKISH**	*CRAUNCHY* *	**CREMAINS**	CRIBWORK	CRIPPLER
CROOKERY+	**CROUPILY**	**CRUSTILY**	**CUMBROUS**	CUNIFORM		
DARRAIGNe	DELATION	**DELUSIVE**	**DELUSORY**	DEPILATE	DEPURATE	DJELLABAh
DOLOROSO	DONENESS+	DRABBLER	**DRAFFISH**	DREARING		
FALTERER	**FIRELESS**	**FLABELLA**	FLECTION	FLICHTER	FRACKING	**FREEDMAN**
FREEDMEN	*FRICKING*	FRIGIDLY	**FRISKFUL**	**FRISKILY**	*FUNHOUSE*	**FUSELESS**
GANGLING	**GEARLESS**	**GELASTIC**	GELATION	**GLABELLAe**	**GLABELLAr**	*GLAMPING*
GLANDERS	GLOAMING	**GLOBATED**	GLOBULAR	**GLUMPILY**	**GLUMPISH**	**GOATLIKE**

GONENESS+	GOUTWEED	GRABBLER	GRAYLING	GREEKING	*GROCKING*	GROUNDER
GRUMNESS+	GUNHOUSE	GUNMAKER	GUNPAPER	*GUNSIGHT*	GUNSTICK	GUNSTOCK

HAGGADAH	**HAGGADIC**	HAGGADOTh	**HAIRLIKE**	HAIRLOCK	HALATION	*HAPLITIC*
HARUSPEX	**HEATABLE**	HEXAMINE	HEXARCHY+	**HITCHILY**	HOROLOGY+	*HOVERFLY+*

KALEWIFE	KETAMINE	**KETCHING**	**KNIGHTLY***	*KRUMPING*	

LABILITY+	LAMBLING	*LANGERED*	LAZURITE	LEPIDOTE	LEVIRATE	**LIGNEOUS**
LINCHPIN	**LOCULATE**d	LOMENTUM	LONENESS+			

MACERATEr	**MADWOMAN**	**MADWOMEN**	MAGISTERy	**MAIDLESS**	**MAXILLAE**	*MAXILLAR*y
MEAGERLY	*MEMETICS*	MENOLOGY+	**MERISTIC**	METHANAL	METHANOL	**METHOXYL**
METHYLIC	MISOGAMY+	**MOATLIKE**	MORALISM	MORALIST	**MORATORY**	MUTTERER

NAINSELL	NOVATION

PAIRWISE	**PALIFORM**	PALIMONY+	PALTERER	PARTWORK	PENLIGHT	PENOLOGY+
PENTOMIC	*PHISHING*	*PINBOARD*	**PITCHILY**	PLAYBACK	*PLEATHER*	PLIGHTER
PLOWLAND	**PLUCKILY**	*PLUGHOLE*	PLUMBAGO	**PLYINGLY**	PORTOLANi	PORTOLANo
PRANKISH	PRATTLER	PREADAPT	PREADMIT>	PREADOPT	PREALLOT>	*PREALTER*
PREBIRTH	*PREBOARD*	**PREBOUND**	*PREBUILD*d	**PREBUILT**	PRECHECK	**PRECHOSE**n
PRECITED	PRECLEAN	*PREDRAFT*	PREDRILL	PREELECT	PREENACT	PREERECT
PREFIGHT	PREFOCUS	**PREFROZE**n	**PRELIVES**	**PREMORSE**	PREPLACE	**PREPLANT**
PREPRESS	PREPRICE	PREPRINT	PRESCIND	PRESCORE	PRESHAPE	**PRESHOWN**
PRESIDER	*PRESOLVE*	**PRESPLIT**	PRESTAMP	*PRESTORE*	PRETASTE	PRETRAIN
PRETREAT	PRETRIAL	PREUNION	PREUNITE	*PREVALUE*	*PREVISIT*	PREVISOR
PREWEIGH	**PRIGGISH**	PUNITION	PUTTERER			

RABIETIC	**RADULATE**	**RAMENTUM**	RAPTNESS+	REDUCTOR	REGALITY+	REJECTOR
REMITTER	REMOTION	**REVOLUTE**	**REVULSED**	**RHEMATIC**	RURALITE	

SASHLESS	SCANDENT	SCARIOSE	**SCARIOUS**	**SCARLESS**	SCATTERY	*SCATTILY*
SCHILLER	**SCOPULAE**	SCORIOUS	SCOUTHERy	SCRAPPER	SCRAWLER	SCRIMPER
*SCRUMMIE**	*SCRUMPLE*	SCRUNCHY*	SCULLION	SCURRIER	*SCUTWORK*	SEDITION
SEDUCTOR	SELECTEE	SELFHOOD	**SFORZATI**	SFORZATO	SHACKLER	SHADDOCK
SHEADING	SHEATHER	SHEILING	**SHIPLESS**	*SHITLESS*	*SIRONISE*	*SIRONIZE*
SKINLESS	**SLIPLESS**	*SMIRKILY*	**SMITHERS**	*SMOOCHER*	SNAILERY+	**SNAPLESS**
SNIGGLER	**SNIPPILY**	SNOBBILY	SOMNIFIC	**SPACEMAN**	**SPACEMEN**	**SPARKISH**
SPARLING	SPECTATE	SPIKELET	**SPIRATED**	**SPITCHER**	SPLASHER	SPONTOON
SPRATTLE	SPRIGGER	SPURLING	SQUASHER	STAKEOUT	STALLAGE	STANNATE
STARTISH	STILLAGE	STIPPLER	STOCCATA	STOOSHIE	**STOPLESS**	**STOWABLE**
STRAMMEL	STRICKLE	**STROPHIC**	STRUMPET	STUMBLER	**SUBEROUS**	SUNBLIND
SUNBLOCK	SUNCHOKE	SUNDRESS+	SWADDLER	SWAINING	**SWAMPISH**	**SWINGMAN**
SWINGMEN	SWISSING					

TACONITE	TAILERON	TALLNESS+	**TAPELIKE**	THICKISH	THORNILY	TOMENTUM
TRAVELER	TREACHERy	TRIPPLER	**TROSSERS**	**TRUCKMAN**	**TRUCKMEN**	TRUNNION

| TRUSTILY | TUBEROUS | TURGENCY+ | TWADDLER | TWANGLER | *TWEEDILY* | TWIGLESS |
| TWIGLIKE | TWINKLER | | | | | |

| VAGILITY+ | **VALLEYED** | VENATION | *VENOLOGY+* | VENTAYLE | **VERISTIC** | VERMINED |
| VICELESS | *VICELIKE* | VIRIDIAN | *VLOGGING* | | | |

| WAGELESS | WALLEYED | WANTHILL | **WARTLESS** | **WASTABLE** | WEANLING | *WHIPLESS* |
| WHIPLIKE | WHIPSTER | **WOULDEST** | **WRACKFUL** | | | |

| YATAGHAN | **YBOUNDEN** | YEANLING | | | | |

| ZONETIME | **ZOOLITIC** | **ZOOLOGIC** | ZOOPHYTE | ZOOSPERM | ZOOSPORE | |

8.2.2 END HOOKS OF SEVENS TO MAKE EIGHTS

END HOOKS WITH VOWELS

END HOOKS WITH 'A'

ABSCISSAe	**AMYGDALA**e	ANAPHORAl	ANGELICAl	**ANTEFIXA**e	**ANTEFIXA**l	ARBORETA
AUTOMATA	BOTANICAl	**BRONCHIA**l	*BROUGHTA*	*CHAMPACA*	**CISTERNA**e	**CISTERNA**l
CONSULTA	DIASTEMA	DULCIANA	**EPITHEMA**	**EXCERPTA**	**FASCISTA**	HEPATICAe
HEPATICAl	JAVELINA	MANDIOCA	MARCHESA	MARINERA	MATADORA	MELODICA
*MOLLUSCA*n	MONSTERA	MRIDANGAm	**NYMPHAEA**	PERFECTA	PIGNOLIA	QUILLAIA
RAKSHASA	**SALICETA**	SARMENTA	SIGNORIAl	**STROBILA**e	**STROBILA**r	SYNTAGMA
TAMANDUA	TAMBOURA	THERIACAl	**TORMENTA**	*TOURISTA*	**UNGUENTA**	

END HOOKS WITH '(A)E'

ACANTHAE	ACICULAE	ACTINIAE	AMPHORAE	AMPULLAE	ANCILLAE	ANTENNAE
ARMILLAE	AUREOLAE	BALISTAE	CAESURAE	CANNULAE	CHALAZAE	COCHLEAE
CYPSELAE	DECIDUAE	DRACHMAE	ECHIDNAE	EMERITAE	EULOGIAE	EXHEDRAE
FALCULAE	*FAUNULAE*	FILARIAE	FIMBRIAE	FISTULAE	*FLORULAE*	FOSSULAE
FOVEOLAE	FURCULAE	GINGIVAE	GRAVIDAE	HETAERAE	INERTIAE	INFAUNAE
LACINIAE	LAMELLAE	LINGULAE	LOCUSTAE	MAMILLAE	MAXILLAE	MEDULLAE
MICELLAE	MINUTIAE	NEURULAE	NOTITIAE	NOVELLAE	OOTHECAE	PAENULAE
PAPILLAE	PATELLAE	PERSONAE	PINNULAE	PISCINAE	PLANULAE	PLUMULAE
PRECAVAE	PTERYLAE	*RUSSULAE*	SAPHENAE	*SARCINAE*	SCAPULAE	SCOPULAE
SEQUELAE	SILIQUAE	SPICULAE	SPINULAE	SPIRULAE	SQUILLAE	SUCCUBAE
TEREBRAE	TESSERAE	TRACHEAE	URETHRAE	VALVULAE	VERRUCAE	ZOOGLEAE

OTHER END HOOKS WITH 'E'

ABSCISSE	ABSINTHE	ACALEPHE	**ACKNOWNE**	*ACQUIREE*	ACRIDINE	**AFFRONTE**d
AFFRONTEe	**AGACANTE**	AGLYCONE	ALEURONE	ALKALISEr	AMYGDALE	ANETHOLE
ANTIGENE	*ATABRINE*	ATROPINE	**AVELLANE**	BACKBITEd	BACKBITEr	BALADINE
BARCHANE	**BARGEESE**	BARYTONE	BENEFICE	BESTRIDEd	BIOPHORE	*BOMBARDE*r
BROADAXE	BURNOUSEd	CABEZONE	CAPELINE	CARABINEr	CARACOLEr	CARDECUE
CERESINE	CINEASTE	COLICINE	COMPLINE	**CONTRATE**	**CONTROLE**	CORYPHEE
COURANTE	CRANNOGE	CREATINE	CROCEINE	CURARISE	CYSTEINE	DARRAINE
DAUPHINE	DEBOUCHE	DECLASSEe	DEVELOPEr	DEXTRINE	DISPONEE	DOMICILE

8. Eight-Letter Words

DOVECOTE	DUCHESSE	DUVETYNE	DYSODILE	ECDYSONE	EMPRESSE	ENDORSEE
ESCALOPE	ETATISME	ETATISTE	**ETOURDIE**	EXAMINEE	EXCLUDEE	FOLKMOTE
FUCHSINE	FUSAROLE	**GENERALE**	GERMAINE	GIRASOLE	GLIADINE	GRAMARYE
GRANDAME	GRAPLINE	GRATINEE	HALIDOME	HALIMOTE	HEGUMENE	HEMATINE
HEMIPODE	**HOLESOME**	HOLYDAME	**HOMININE**	IMPRESSEr	INCONNUE	INDAMINE
INDIGENE	INDORSEE	INDULINE	INTERNEE	ISOCHORE	JACINTHE	JEALOUSE
KALOOKIE	KERMESSE	LAMBASTE	LANOLINE	LARGESSE	LICENCEE	LIGROINE
LIVEYERE	**LUPULINE**	**LYOPHILE**d	MALEFICE	MARCHESE	MARQUISE	MASTICHE
MATADORE	MATELOTE	**MAUVAISE**	MAUVEINE	MEGAPODE	**MESQUINE**	MESQUITE
METAMERE	MEZQUITE	MISWRITEd	MONDAINE	MONOPODE	MUSICALE	NARCEINE
NARWHALE	NEBBISHEr	NOCTURNE	ONCOGENE	OUTCASTE	OUTCHIDE	OUTRANGE
OUTWRITEd	OUVRIERE	OXYPHILE	PARVENUE	PENSIONEr	PERIDOTE	PERIGONE
PFENNIGE	PIANISTE	PICOLINE	PLACCATE	**PLAUDITE**	PLIMSOLE	PORPESSE
PORTESSE	PORTIEREd	POTLACHE	POULARDE	PROLONGEr	PROMISEE	PROTEASE
PROTEIDE	PTOMAINE	QUADRATE	RATTLINE	RELEASEE	RETRAITE	RHABDOME
RIBSTONE	ROCKABYE	SALICINE	SALVAGEE	SAPONINE	SAUTOIRE	SCHMELZE
SCHMOOSE	SCHMOOZEr	**SCISSILE**	**SCURRILE**	SECONDEE	SELVAGEE	SESTETTE
SEXTETTE	SILICONE	**SKYBORNE**	SMARAGDE	SOLANINE	STEARINE	STROBILE
SULPHIDE	SYLPHIDE	SYMBIOTE	SYMITARE	SYNONYME	TABORINE	TACHISME
TACHISTE	THERMITE	THIAMINE	THIAZINE	THIAZOLE	THIONINE	TOLIDINE
TORCHERE	TRAVOISE	TRIAZINE	TRICORNE	TRIOXIDE	TRIPTANE	URETHANE
VACCINEE	VENTAILE	VITAMINE	WANNABEE	WOODBINE	XANTHINE	XYLIDINE
ZECCHINE	ZYMOGENE					

END HOOKS WITH 'I'

BRAHMANI	**CAPITANI**	CONCEPTI	CONCERTI	CONDUCTI	CORNETTI	COTHURNI
DRACHMAI	DUUMVIRI	FASCISMI	FASCISTIc	HETAIRAI	KOFTGARI	**MARCHESI**
PARCHESI	**PERFECTI**	SIGNIORI	STROBILI	TROCHILIc	ZECCHINI	

END HOOKS WITH 'O'

ARMIGERO	CAPITANO	**CLASSICO**	**CORNETTO**	COURANTO	EXPRESSO	**FASCISMO**
INTAGLIO	**LEGGIERO**	MONTANTO	PEEKABOO	PERFECTOr	POLITICO	**PRELUDIO**
RANCHERO	SESTETTO	STAMPEDO	**VIGOROSO**	ZECCHINO		

END HOOKS WITH CONSONANTS

END HOOKS WITH '(E)D'

ACERATED	ACETATED	APANAGED	ARCUATED	AURICLED	BACCATED	BARBATED
BARCODED	BRINDLED	CALIBRED	CALYCLED	CAPUCHED	CAUDATED	CAYENNED
CHALICED	CILIATED	CITRATED	CLAVATED	COCKADED	COCKEYED	COLOGNED
COSTATED	CRENATED	CREVICED	CRINATED	CUNEATED	CURVATED	CUSPATED
DEALATED	DENTATED	EBRIATED	FALCATED	FOLIAGED	FOVEATED	FROGEYED
GABELLED	GALEATED	GLOBATED	HASTATED	HERBAGED	*HOGNOSED*	LABIATED
LARVATED	LINEATED	LOZENGED	MIDSIZED	MONOCLED	MURIATED	OCULATED
OUTSIZED	OVERAGED	OVERSEED	PALMATED	PANICLED	*PATINAED*	PEDICLED
PENNATED	PERTUSED	PETIOLED	PICRATED	PILEATED	PINNATED	PLUMAGED
PRAIRIED	PUSTULED	RAMPIRED	RAWBONED	RETINUED	REVENUED	ROSETTED
SCIENCED	SOUFFLED	SPICATED	STATURED	STIPULED	STUBBLED	SULCATED

SURBASED TARTANED TEENAGED TRILOBED TURBINED UNAWAKED VERDURED
WALLEYED

END HOOKS WITH '(A)L'

ABOMASAL	ACHENIAL	ACROMIAL	AECIDIAL	ALLODIAL	AMPHORAL	ANTENNAL
AQUARIAL	*ARCHAEAL*	BASIDIAL	BRACHIAL	BRECCIAL	CAESURAL	CANDIDAL
CHALAZAL	CHAMISAL	CHIASMAL	CHRISMAL	CINEREAL	COMITIAL	CONARIAL
CONIDIAL	DECIDUAL	DIHEDRAL	DILUVIAL	DIPTERAL	DUODENAL	DYSPNEAL
ENTOZOAL	EROTICAL	EXCRETAL	EXORDIAL	*EXTREMAL*	FILARIAL	FIMBRIAL
GALANGAL	GANGLIAL	GERMINAL	GINGIVAL	GONIDIAL	HYMENIAL	HYPOGEAL
ILLUVIAL	INDICIAL	INDUSIAL	INERTIAL	INFAUNAL	KHEDIVAL	LIXIVIAL
LOCUSTAL	MALARIAL	METAZOAL	MINUTIAL	*MONILIAL*	MYCELIAL	NOUMENAL
OOGONIAL	OOTHECAL	PATAGIAL	PERIDIAL	PERINEAL	PESSIMAL	PISCINAL
PODAGRAL	PRECAVAL	PRONOTAL	PROSOMAL	PUDENDAL	PUPARIAL	PYGIDIAL
PYREXIAL	SABURRAL	SAGITTAL	SOREDIAL	SPECTRAL	SPLENIAL	STAMINAL
STOMATAL	SYNOVIAL	TEGMINAL	TESSERAL	TORMINAL	TRACHEAL	TYMPANAL
URETHRAL	VACCINAL	VIATICAL	VISCERAL	ZOOGLEAL		

END HOOKS WITH 'N'

ACANTHINe	ACTINIAN	ALFAQUIN	ALIZARINe	**APHELIAN**	AQUARIAN	ARCADIAN
ARCHAEAN	ASCIDIAN	AURELIAN	**BEREAVEN**	**BESPOKEN**	**BESTREWN**	**BESTROWN**
CHONDRIN	**CODRIVEN**	**CONIDIAN**	**DEFROZEN**	**DILUVIAN**	DIPTERAN	DISLIKEN
ECTOZOAN	**ENFROZEN**	**ENGRAVEN**	ENLARGEN	ENTOZOAN	**FEDAYEEN**	**FILARIAN**
FLITTERN	**FLYBLOWN**	**FORFAIRN**	**GALLICAN**	*HACKSAWN*	HISTRION	**HYPOGEAN**
LEATHERN	MAGNETON	**MALARIAN**	METAZOAN	**MISDRAWN**	**MISGIVEN**	**MISGROWN**
MISKNOWN	**MYCELIAN**	OPHIURAN	**OUTDRAWN**	**OUTFLOWN**	**OUTGIVEN**	**OUTGNAWN**
OUTTAKEN	**OVERSEWN**	**OVERSOWN**	**PANACEAN**	PARAZOAN	**PELORIAN**	**PERTAKEN**
PIMENTON	POLYZOAN	**PRESHOWN**	**PUNALUAN**	QUARTERN	REAWAKEN	**REAWOKEN**
RECHOSEN	**REDRIVEN**	**REFROZEN**	**REGALIAN**	**RESHAVEN**	**RESPOKEN**	ROSARIAN
RUBELLAN	SLATTERN	**SPREDDEN**	STELLION	**STROOKEN**	THROMBIN	*UILLEANN*
UNLOOSEN	**UNSHAPEN**	**UPBROKEN**	**UPSPOKEN**	**UPTHROWN**	VITELLINe	**WHIPSAWN**
WREATHEN						

END HOOKS WITH 'R' OF VERBS

ABRIDGER	ABSOLVER	ACQUIRER	ADVANCER	ANALYSER	ANALYZER	ANIMATER
ANTIQUER	APPEASER	APPRISER	APPRIZER	ARRANGER	ASPERGER	ASPERSER
ASSUAGER	ATTACHER	BALANCER	BANDAGER	*BAPTISER*	BAPTIZER	BEGUILER
BEREAVER	BESIEGER	BICYCLER	BRAILLER	CAPTURER	CENSURER	CHICANERy
CHORTLER	CHUCKLER	*COGNISER*	COGNIZER	COLLIDER	COLLUDER	COMBINER
COMMUNER	COMPARER	CONCEDER	CONDOLER	CONDONER	CONDUCER	CONFIDER
CONFINER	CONFUTER	CONJURER	CONSOLER	CONVENER	CONVOKER	*CORRODER*
COSTUMERy	COTTAGER	*COWRITER*	CRIPPLER	DECEIVER	DECLINER	DEFLATER
DEFORCER	DEGRADER	DELOUSER	*DEPLETER*	DEPLORER	DEPRAVER	DEPRIVER
DERANGER	DESERVER	DESPISER	DETERGER	DIALYSER	DIALYZER	DIFFUSER
DISABLER	DISLIKER	DISPONER	DISPOSER	DISPUTER	DISROBER	DIVORCER
DIVULGER	DRABBLER	DRIBBLER	*ECLIPSER*	EMBLAZER	EMBRACERy	ENCHASER
ENCLOSER	ENDORSER	ENFORCER	ENHANCER	ENLARGER	ENNOBLER	ENSLAVER
ENSNARER	EPISTLER	ESPOUSER	EXCLUDER	EXCRETER	EXECUTER	EXPLODER
EXPUNGER	EXTRUDER	FINAGLER	FINESSER	FORESEER	FORGIVER	FORSAKER

FRIBBLER	GAROTTER	GARROTER	GESTURER	GLIMPSER	GRABBLER	GRAPPLER
GRIMACER	*HAGRIDER*	IDOLISER	IDOLIZER	IMAGINER	*IMMERSER*	IMPINGER
IMPLORER	INCENSER	INCLINER	INCLOSER	INDORSER	INDULGER	INFLAMER
INFLATER	INQUIRER	INSNARER	INSPIRER	INVOLVER	*ITEMISER*	ITEMIZER
JAWBONER	KEYNOTER	LICENCER	LICENSER	LIONISER	LIONIZER	MASSAGER
MISLIKER	MISTAKER	MORTICER	MORTISER	MULTURER	NARRATER	NURTURER
OBTRUDER	OCCLUDER	OUTLINER	OUTLIVER	OUTRIDER	OUTVOTER	*OVERDYER*
OVERLIER	OXIDISER	OXIDIZER	OZONISER	PACKAGER	PARTAKER	*PASSAGER*
PASTURER	*PEPTISER*	PEPTIZER	PERFUMERy	PERJURER	PERVADER	PLACATER
POETISER	POETIZER	POSTURER	POTHOLER	PRATTLER	PREFACER	PRELUDER
PREPARER	PRESAGER	PRESIDER	PRESUMER	PROCURER	PROMISER	PROVOKER
QUIDDLER	RAMPAGER	REALISER	REALIZER	RECYCLER	*REDLINER*	REGRATER
REISSUER	REJOICER	RELAPSER	RELEASER	RELIEVER	RENEGUER	REPLACER
REPROVER	REPULSER	REQUIRER	REQUITER	RESERVER	RESHAPER	RESOLVER
RETRACER	REUNITER	REVENGER	REVERSER	REWRITER	ROMANCER	RUMMAGER
SALVAGER	SCAMBLER	SCOURGER	SCREEVER	SCROUGER	SCRUPLER	SCUFFLER
SCUTTLER	SERVICER	SHACKLER	SHEATHER	SHINGLER	*SHMOOZER*	*SHUTTLER*
SNIFFLER	SNIGGLER	SNUFFLER	SPANGLER	SPINDLER	SPLURGER	SPRINGER
SQUEEZER	STARTLER	STIPPLER	STUMBLER	STYLISER	STYLIZER	SUBSIDER
SUFFICER	SUPPOSER	SURFACER	SURMISER	SURNAMER	SURVIVER	SWADDLER
TOPLINER	TRADUCER	TRAMPLER	TREADLER	TRIPPLER	TROUBLER	TROUNCER
TRUCKLER	TRUNDLER	TWADDLER	TWANGLER	TWATTLER	TWEEDLER	TWIDDLER
TWINKLER	*UNITISER*	UNITIZER	UPGRADER	UPHEAVER	UPRAISER	*UPSTAGER*
UTILISER	UTILIZER	VESTURER	VINTAGER	VIOLATER	WARFARER	WARSTLER
WAYFARER	WELCOMER	WHEEDLER	WHIFFLERy	WHITTLER	WREATHER	

OTHER END HOOKS WITH 'R'

ACICULAR	AGITATOR	**AMPULLAR**y	ANIMATOR	AULNAGER	<u>BESLAVER</u>	BONDAGER
CANNULAR	*CHARLIER*	*CINGULAR*	COCHLEARe	COLLEGER	DAYTALER	DEJEUNER
<u>DEMERGER</u>	EXEMPLARy	**FISTULAR**	**FORMULAR**y	**FOVEOLAR**	*FRENULAR*	**FURCULAR**
GABELLER	**GANGLIAR**	GOSPODAR	*GUYLINER*	**HEXAPLAR**	JUSTICER	KILLDEER
LAMELLAR	**LINGULAR**	LOWLIFER	**MAMILLAR**y	*MAXILLAR*y	MEDULLARy	**MICELLAR**
MIDLIFER	*NEURULAR*	OUTROPER	**PAPILLAR**y	**PASSAGER**	**PATELLAR**	**PINNULAR**
PLANULAR	**PLUMULAR**	PROVISORy	RAGTIMER	REVENUER	**ROSEOLAR**	**RUBEOLAR**
SANDBURR	SCAPULARy	SCAVAGER	**SPATULAR**	**SPECULAR**	**SPICULAR**	STIBBLER
TONTINER	TOPSIDER	TRIBUTER	UPSTATER	**VALVULAR**	**VARIOLAR**	VERDITER
VEXILLARy						

END HOOKS WITH 'T'

BACCARAT	CANZONET	CASEMENT	CLASSIST	<u>CONGREET</u>	**CONJOINT**	<u>DISJOINT</u>
DRIBBLET	**EMONGEST**	FOVEOLET	GLOBULET	HABITANT	HANDCART	INDICANT
INSCULPT	*INTERNET*	*JEHADIST*	*JIHADIST*	JUNGLIST	KHALIFATe	MARABOUT
MARMOSET	<u>MISPLANT</u>	**MOWBURNT**	MYLODONT	NONUPLET	OCTUPLET	**OUTBURNT**
<u>PASSMENT</u>	PERSICOT	PISTOLET	PLANCHET	**PREPLANT**	QUARTETTe	QUARTETTi
QUARTETTo	QUINTETTe	QUINTETTi	QUINTETTo	**REDREAMT**	RETRAITT	ROUNDLET
SAFARIST	**SEMIMATT**e	SPANGLET	SPARKLET	SYMBIONT	TEGUMENT	TELETEXT
TRANCHET	TRICKLET	UTOPIAST	VEINULET	VETIVERT		

END HOOKS WITH 'Y'

ACTRESSY	ANTILOGY+	*ANTIQUEY*	ANTONYMY+	APOCARPY+	AUTARCHY+	AXILLARY+
BASILARY	BASTARDY+	BISCUITY	BLADDERY	BLANKETY+	BLISTERY*	BLOOMERY+
BLOSSOMY*	BOTCHERY+	BOULDERY	*BRAZIERY+*	BROIDERY+	BULLOCKY+	BULRUSHY
CABBAGEY	*CACONYMY+*	CAJOLERY+	CALAMARY+	CANTICOY	CARTOONY	CENTAURY+
CHAFFERY+	CHANCERY+	CHATTERY	CHEATERY+	*CHEDDARY*	CHEVRONY	CHIEFERY+
CHIFFONY	CHIRRUPY	CIRCUITY+	CITATORY	CLATTERY	CLERUCHY+	CLUSTERY
CLUTTERY	COBBLERY+	CONCEITY	COSTUMEY	COTTAGEY	*CRAUNCHY**	CREAMERY+
CROOKERY+	CRYOGENY+	CURATORY	CURRANTY*	CURRIERY+	CUSHIONY	CUSTARDY
DASTARDY+	DEMAGOGY+	DILATORY	DIPLOIDY+	DONATORY+	DREAMERY+	DROLLERY+
DROUGHTY*	ENACTORY	ENDARCHY+	ENDOGENY+	ENGINERY+	ENTREATY+	EUPLOIDY+
EVANGELY+	FARRIERY+	*FASHIONY*	FEATHERY*	FLACKERY+	FLAVOURY	FLICKERY
FLUSTERY	FLUTTERY	FRIPPERY+	FROTHERY+	FRUITERY+	FURRIERY+	*GARBAGEY*
GEALOUSY+	GLAZIERY+	GLIBBERY	GLIDDERY	GLIMMERY	GOLIARDY+	*GRILLERY+*
GRINDERY+	GROWLERY+	GYRATORY	HAPLOIDY+	HARMOSTY+	HASSOCKY	HATCHETY
HEATHERY*	HEGEMONY+	HEGUMENY+	HEXAPODY+	HEXARCHY+	HILLOCKY	HOMOLOGY+
HOMONYMY+	HUMMOCKY	HYDROPSY+	INCISORY	INTRADAY	JANIZARY+	JUGGLERY+
LACUNARY	LAMINARY	LEATHERY*	LYSOGENY+	MERONYMY+	METONYMY+	MONITORY+
MONOLOGY+	MONOPODY+	MULLOCKY	MUSTARDY	NAVARCHY+	NEBBISHY	NEGATORY
NOMARCHY+	ORANGERY+	OUTWEARY	OVERMANY	PARADOXY+	PARONYMY+	PATCHERY+
PEACOCKY*	PEASANTY	PEDAGOGY+	PEDDLERY+	PERCHERY	PHANTOMY	PLASTERY
PLUMBERY+	POLYGAMY+	POLYGONY+	POLYMERY+	POLYPODY+	PRIGGERY+	PRINTERY+
PSALTERY+	PUDDINGY	PUPILARY	QUACKERY+	QUIDDITY+	RAINBOWY	REVISORY
RHUBARBY	ROLLICKY	ROTATORY	SACRISTY+	SAFFRONY	SAMPLERY+	SAVAGERY+
SAWDUSTY	SCATTERY	SCHLEPPY*	SCHLOCKY*	*SCHLUMPY**	SCHMALZY*	*SCHMOOZY**
SCREECHY*	SCRUNCHY*	SCULLERY+	SHATTERY	SHELTERY	SHIMMERY*	SHMALTZY*
SHUDDERY	SIGNIORY+	SKITTERY*	SLABBERY+	SLATTERY	SLEEPERY	SLIDDERY
SLITHERY*	SLOBBERY*	SLUMBERY	SMELTERY+	SMOTHERY	*SMUGGERY+*	SNICKERY
SNIPPETY*	SNOTTERY+	SNUGGERY+	SOLDIERY+	SOLICITY+	SOVKHOZY	SPINACHY
SPINNERY+	SPLOTCHY*	SPOOFERY+	SPUTTERY	SQUELCHY*	SQUOOSHY*	STAGGERY
STEMMERY+	STOMACHY	STRETCHY*	*STUDENTY*	SULPHURYl	SUNBEAMY	SYNCARPY+
TABLOIDY+	TASSELLY	THICKETY	TITULARY+	TOPARCHY+	TOPONYMY+	TRASHERY+
TRIARCHY+	TRIFFIDY	TRIPPERY	TROLLOPY	TUMULARY	TUSSOCKY	TUTELARY+
TWITTERY	UNCLOUDY	UNTRUSTY	UNWATERY	VARNISHY	VAUNTERY+	VAVASORY+
VILLAINY+	VINEGARY	WHISKERY*	WHISPERY			

OTHER END HOOKS

AGGADOTH	*ALMANACK*	AMARANTH	AMMONIAC	AMNESIAC	APHASIAC	APPERILL
AUTOCARP	BALDRICK	BANDEAUX	BATTEAUX	BAUDRICKe	BEGORRAH	BERCEAUX
BOERBULL	BORSTALL	BRIMFULLy	BUDGEROW	BULIMIAC	CABBALAH	CAMAIEUX
CHALLOTH	CHAPEAUX	CHARQUID	CHATEAUX	CHIASMIC	CHITLING	CHORAGIC
CHOREGIC	*CHUPPOTH*	CHUTZPAH	CLASSISM	COMBLESS	COUTEAUX	CROPFULL
CUFFLESS	CYMBALOM	DACTYLIC	EASTLING	ELENCHIC	EPIGONIC	FABLIAUX
FANGLESS	FINALISM	FINIKING	FOOTLESS	FORERANK	GALABEAH	GALABIAH
GAMINESS+	GARBLESS	*GENIZOTH*	HAFTARAH	HAGGADAH	HALFLING	HAROSETH
HOMINESS+	HOSANNAH	HURTLESS	HYDRANTH	HYDROXYL	INTHRALL	JAMBEAUX
JAMBIYAH	*JEHADISM*	JELLABAH	*JIHADISM*	KABBALAH	KASHRUTH	*KETUBOTH*
KHALIFAH	KINDLESS	KINGLESS	LITTLING	MADRASAH	MAFFLING	MAHJONGG
MANDRILL	MANTEAUX	MARQUESS+	MASTABAH	MEGILLAH	MESHUGAH	METHOXYL
MINICAMP	MORCEAUX	NARGILEH	*NOUVEAUX*	NURAGHIC	OCTOPUSH+	OCTUPLEX

OMPHALIC	*OUTCROWD*	**OUTHEARD**	**OVERRANK**	PEISHWAH	**PLATEAUX**	PLIMSOLL
POLITICK	**PONCEAUX**	PRACTICK	*PUMPKING*	*RABBITOH*	RAILCARD	*RANKLESS*
REPOSALL	RHOMBOID	**RONDEAUX**	**ROOTLESS**	**ROULEAUX**	**RUMPLESS**	**RUSTLESS**
SAGENESS+	SAVANNAH	**SCAMPISH**	**SHAMMASH**	SHELLACK	SHOEPACK	*SOUPLESS*
SQUIRESS+	**SUCKLESS**	SULFURYL	SYLLABIC	**TABLEAUX**	**TACKLESS**	**TAILLESS**
TAMARIND	TAMARISK	TESTRILL	**THALAMIC**	TITANISM	**TONNEAUX**	**TRUMEAUX**
TSUNAMIC	TYMPANIC	UNDERGOD	**WATTLESS**	WOODBIND	YESHIVAH	

8.3 LESS FAMILIAR NON-HOOK EIGHTS

8.3.1 VERBS COMPRISED OF A COMMON PREFIX PLUS A VERB

BECARPET	BECHANCE	BECLAMOR	BECLOTHE	BECOWARD	BECUDGEL	BECUDGEL>
BEDAGGLE	BEDARKEN	BEDEAFEN	BEDIAPER	BEDIMPLE	BEDRENCH	BEDRIVEL
BEFINGER	BEFLOWER	BEFRINGE	BEGIRDLE	BEGLAMOR	BEHAPPEN	BEJUMBLE
BEKNIGHT	BELABOUR	BELIQUOR	BEMADDEN	BEMINGLE	BEMUDDLE	BEMUFFLE
BEMURMUR	BEPESTER	BEPOMMEL>	BEPOWDER	BEPRAISE	BESCORCH	BESCRAWL
BESCREEN	BESHADOW	BESHIVER	BESHROUD	BESMOOTH	BESMUDGE	BESMUTCH
BESOOTHE	BESPREADe	BESTREAK	BETATTER	BETHRALL	BETHWACK	

COADMIRE	COANCHOR	COAPPEAR	COASSIST	COASSUME	COATTEND	COATTEST
COAUTHOR	CODERIVE	CODESIGN	COEMBODY	COEMPLOY	COENAMOR	COENDURE
COEQUATE	COEVOLVE	COEXTEND	*COINFECT*	COINHERE	COINSUREr	COINVENT
COLOCATE	COMANAGEr	COMEDDLE	COMINGLE	COPURIFY	COREDEEM	CORELATE
COROTATE	COSCRIPT					

DEAERATE	DEBRUISE	DECENTRE	DECLUTCH	DECOLOUR	*DECOMMIT>*	DECOUPLEr
DEFOREST	DEFREEZEe	DEGENDER	*DEIONISEr*	DEIONIZEr	DELIBATE	DELUSTER
DEMARKET	DENATURE	DENAZIFY	DENOTATE	DEPEINCT	*DEPEOPLE*	DEPOLISH
DERATION	DESCHOOL	DESCRIVE	DESELECT	DESILVER	DESULFUR	*DETANGLEr*
DETASSEL	DETASSEL>	*DETHATCH*				

DISABUSE	DISADORN	DISANNEX	DISANNUL>	DISAPPLY	DISBENCH	DISBOSOM
DISBOWEL	DISBOWEL>	DISCANDY	DISCLAIM	DISCOURE	DISCROWN	DISENDOW
DISENROL>	DISFLESH	DISFROCK	DISGAVEL>	DISGRADE	DISHABIT	DISHORSE
DISHOUSE	DISINTER>	DISINURE	DISLEAVE	DISPATCH	DISPLANT	DISPLUME
DISPRIZE	DISPURSE	DISSEISEe	DISSEIZEe	DISSERVE	DISSEVER	DISTRAINt
DISUNITEr	DISVALUE	DISVOUCH				

EMBOLDEN	EMBORDER	EMMARBLE	EMPACKET	EMPEOPLE	EMPERISH	EMPIERCE
EMPLEACH	EMPLONGE	EMPOISON	EMPOLDER	EMPURPLE		

ENCHARGE	ENCIPHER	ENCLOTHE	ENCOLOUR	ENCRADLE	ENCREASE	ENDAMAGE
ENFEEBLEr	ENFETTER	ENFLOWER	ENFOREST	ENFREEZEe	ENGENDER	ENGIRDLE
ENGRIEVE	ENGROOVE	ENHEARSE	ENHUNGER	ENKERNEL>	ENKINDLEr	ENLUMINE
ENRAUNGE	ENRAVISH	ENSAMPLE	ENSCONCE	ENSCROLL	ENSHEATHe	ENSHIELD
ENSHROUD	ENSILAGE	ENSPHERE	ENSWATHE	ENTENDER	ENVASSAL>	ENWALLOW
ENWREATHe						

FORJUDGE	FORSLACK	FORSPEAKd	FORSPENDd	FORSWEARd	FORSWINK	FORTHINKd
FORWASTE	FORWEARY					

FOREDATE	FOREDOOM	FOREFEELd	FOREFEND	FOREHENTd	FOREKNOWd	FOREKNOWn
FORELENDd	FORELIFT	FORELOCK	FOREMEANd	FOREMEANt	FOREPLAN>	FOREREADd
FORESHEWn	FORESHOWn	FORESLOW				

IMBITTER	IMBOLDEN	IMBORDER	IMMANTLE	IMMINGLE	IMPLEACH	IMPLEDGE
IMPLUNGE	IMPOCKET	IMPOLDER	IMPURPLE			

INCORPSE	INCUMBER	INDRENCH	INGATHER	INGROOVE	INHEARSE	INSCONCE
INSCROLL	INSHEATHe	INSHRINE	INSOLATE	INSPHERE	INSPIRIT	INSTRESS
INSWATHE	INTHRONE	INTITULE	INTRENCH			

INTERBED>	INTERCUTd	INTERCUT>	INTERLAP>	INTERLAYd

MISADAPT	MISALIGN	MISALLOT>	MISALTER	MISAPPLY	MISASSAY	MISATONE
MISAWARD	MISBEGINd	MISBRAND	MISBUILDd	MISCLAIM	MISCLASS	MISCOLOR
MISDOUBT	MISDRIVEd	MISDRIVEn	MISENROL>	MISENROL1	MISENTER	MISFEIGN
MISFOCUS	MISFRAME	MISGAUGE	MISGRADE	MISGRAFF	MISGRAFT	MISGUESS
MISGUIDEr	MISINFER>	MISINTER>	MISLABEL	MISLABEL>	MISLABOR	MISLEARNt
MISLIGHT	MISLODGE	MISMARRY	MISMETRE	MISORDER	MISPAINT	MISPARSE
MISPATCH	MISPLEAD	MISPOINT	MISPOISE	MISPRICE	MISPRISE	MISPRIZEr
MISRAISE	MISREFER>	MISROUTE	MISROUTE=	MISSHAPEn	MISSHAPEr	MISSOUND
MISSPACE	MISSPEAKd	MISSPENDd	*MISSTAMP*	MISSTART	MISSTATE	MISSTEER
MISSTYLE	MISTEACHd	MISTHINKd	MISTHROWd	MISTHROWn	MISTITLE	MISTOUCH
MISTRACE	MISTRAIN	MISTRYST	MISTUTOR	MISVALUE		

OUTARGUE	OUTBITCH	OUTBLAZE	OUTBLEAT	OUTBLESS	OUTBLOOM	OUTBLUSH
OUTBOAST	OUTBRAWL	OUTBRAVE	OUTBREEDd	OUTBRIBE	OUTBUILDd	*OUTBULGE*
OUTBULLY	OUTCAPER	OUTCATCHd	OUTCAVIL	OUTCAVIL>	OUTCHARM	OUTCHEAT
OUTCLIMB	OUTCOACH	OUTCOUNT	OUTCRAWL	OUTCROSS	OUTCURSE	OUTDANCE
OUTDODGE	OUTDREAMt	OUTDRIVEd	OUTDRIVEn	OUTDWELL	OUTFABLE	OUTFEAST
OUTFENCE	OUTFLANK	OUTFLASH	*OUTFLOAT*	OUTFLUSH	OUTFROWN	OUTGLARE
OUTGLEAM	OUTGROSS	OUTGROUP	OUTGUESS	OUTGUIDE	OUTHOMER	OUTHUMOR
OUTLAUGH	OUTLEARNt	OUTMARCH	OUTMATCH	OUTPAINT	OUTPITCH	OUTPLACEr
OUTPOWER	OUTPREEN	OUTPRESS	OUTPRICE	OUTPRIZE	OUTQUOTE	OUTRAISE
OUTREACH	OUTREIGN	OUTRIVAL	OUTRIVAL>	OUTSAVOR	OUTSCOLD	OUTSCOOP
OUTSCORN	OUTSERVE	OUTSHAME	OUTSHINEd	OUTSHOOTd	OUTSHOUT	OUTSLEEPd
OUTSLICK	*OUTSMELL*	OUTSMILE	OUTSMOKE	OUTSNORE	OUTSPEAKd	OUTSPEEDd
OUTSPELL	OUTSPENDd	OUTSPORT	OUTSTANDd	OUTSTARE	OUTSTART	OUTSTATE
OUTSTEER	OUTSTUDY	OUTSTUNT	OUTSWEARd	*OUTSWEEPd*	OUTSWELL	OUTTHANK
OUTTHINKd	OUTTHROB>	OUTTHROWd	OUTTHROWn	OUTTOWER	OUTTRADE	OUTTRICK
OUTTRUMP	OUTVALUE	OUTVAUNT	OUTVENOM	OUTVOICE	OUTWASTE	OUTWATCH
OUTWHIRL	OUTWORTH	OUTWREST	OUTYIELD			

OVERARCH	OVERBAKE	OVERBEARd	OVERBEATd	OVERBILL	OVERBLOWd	OVERBLOWn
OVERBOIL	OVERBRIM>	OVERBULK	OVERBURNt	OVERCLOY	*OVERCLUB>*	OVERCOOL
OVERCRAM>	OVERCROP>	OVERCROWd	OVERCURE	OVERDARE	OVERDECK	OVERDUST

219

8. Eight-Letter Words

OVEREDIT	OVERFALLd	OVERFEAR	OVERFOLD	OVERFUND	OVERGALL	*OVERGEAR*
OVERGILD	OVERGIRD	OVERGIVEd	OVERGIVEn	OVERGOAD	OVERGROWd	OVERGROWn
OVERHALE	OVERHAND	OVERHATE	OVERHEAP	OVERHENTd	OVERHOLDd	OVERHOPE
OVERHUNT	OVERHYPE	OVERJUMP	OVERKEEPd	OVERLADEn	OVERLARD	OVERLEAPt
OVERLENDd	OVERLIVE	OVERLOCK	OVERLOVE	OVERMAST	OVERMELT	OVERMILK
OVERNAME	*OVERPACK*	OVERPART	OVERPEER	OVERPLAN>	OVERPLANt	OVERPLAY
OVERPLOT>	OVERPOST	OVERPUMP	OVERRACK	OVERRAKE	OVERREADd	OVERRUFF
OVERSAIL	OVERSALT	OVERSAVE	OVERSELLd	OVERSKIP>	OVERSLIP>	OVERSLIPt
OVERSOAK	OVERSTIR>	OVERSUDS	OVERSWAY	OVERSWIMd	OVERSWIM>	OVERTALK
OVERTASK	OVERTEEM	OVERTIRE	OVERTOIL	OVERTRIM>	OVERTRIP>	OVERURGE
OVERVEIL	OVERVOTE	OVERWEARd	OVERWEARy	OVERWEEN	OVERWING	*OVERWRAP>*

PREBLESS	PRECHILL	PRECLEAR	PREEXIST	PREFRANK	*PREGUIDE*	PRELIMIT
PREPASTE	PREPUNCH	PRERINSE	PRESLICE			

REABSORB	REACCEDE	REACCENT	REACCEPT	REACCUSE	READDICT	READVISE
REANOINT	REANSWER	REAROUSE	REASCEND	REASSAIL	REASSORT	REATTACH
REATTACK	REATTAIN	REBELLOW	REBORROW	REBOTTLE	REBRANCH	REBUTTON
RECARPET	*RECEMENT*	*RECENSOR*	RECENTRE	RECHANGE	RECHOOSEd	RECIRCLE
RECLOTHE	RECODIFY	RECOMMIT>	*RECONFER>*	RECONVEY	RECOUPLE	REDAMAGE
REDECIDE	REDEFEAT	REDEFECT	REDEMAND	REDIGEST	REDISTIL>	REDISTILl
REDIVIDE	REDOUBLEr	REEMBARK	REEMBODY	REEMERGE	REEXPORT	REEXPOSE
REFASTEN	REFIGURE	REFILTER	REFINISH	REFLOWER	REFOREST	REFREEZEd
REFRINGE	REGATHER	REGELATE	REGROOVE	REHAMMER	REHANDLE	REHARDEN
REILLUME	REIMPORT	REIMPOSE	REINCITE	REINDICT	REINDUCE	REINDUCT
REINFUSE	*REINSTAL>*	*REINSTALl*	REINVOKE	REJACKET	REJIGGER	REJUGGLE
RELAUNCH	RELETTER	RELUMINE	REMARKET	REMASTER	REMODIFY	REMURMUR
RENATURE	RENOTIFY	REOBJECT	REOBTAIN	REOPPOSE	REORDAIN	REOUTFIT>
REPACIFY	REPEOPLE	REPERUSE	REPLEDGE	REPLUNGE	REPREEVE	REPURIFY
REPURSUE	REQUIGHT	REREMIND	REREPEAT	REREVIEW	REREVISE	RESADDLE
RESALUTE	RESCHOOL	RESCREEN	RESCRIPT	RESCULPT	RESEASON	RESECURE
RESELECT	*RESHOWER*	RESILVER	RESKETCH	RESMOOTH	*RESOFTEN*	RESOLDER
RESPLICE	RESPREADd	RESPRINGd	RESPROUT	*RESTABLE*	RESTITCH	RESTRESS
RESTRIKEd	RESTRINGe	RESTRIVEd	RESTRIVEn	RESUMMON	RESUPPLY	RETACKLE
RETAILOR	RETARGET	RETEMPER	RETHREAD	REVERIFY	REVIVIFY	

UNANCHOR	UNBESEEM	UNBISHOP	UNBONNET	*UNBOTTLE*	UNBREECH	UNBRIDLE
UNBUNDLEr	UNBURROW	UNCHARGE	UNCHURCH	UNCIPHER	UNCLENCH	UNCLINCH
UNCLOTHE	UNCLUTCH	UNCOFFIN	UNCOUPLEr	UNCREATE	*UNDELETE*	UNDOUBLE
UNFETTER	UNFREEZEd	UNFRIEND	UNHALLOW	UNHEARSE	UNKENNEL	UNKENNEL>
UNKNIGHT	UNLIMBER	UNMANTLE	UNMINGLE	UNMUFFLE	UNPEOPLE	UNPOISON
UNPOLISH	UNPRAISE	UNPREACH	UNPRIEST	UNPRISON	UNPUCKER	UNREASON
UNRETIRE	UNRIDDLEr	UNRUFFLE	UNSEASON	UNSHROUD	UNSLUICE	UNSOCKET
UNSOLDER	UNSPHERE	UNSTARCH	UNSTRING	UNSWATHE	UNTACKLE	UNTEMPER
UNTENANT	UNTHATCH	UNTHRONE	UNVIZARD	UNWEAPON	UNWEIGHT	

UNDERACT UNDERBUYd UNDERLAP> UNDERLETd UNDERLET> UNDERMAN> UNDERRUNd
UNDERRUN> UNDERSAYd UNDERSETd UNDERSET> UNDERTAX UNDERUSE

UPFOLLOW UPGATHER UPSPRINGd

8.3.2 OTHER VERBS

VERBS ENDING IN 'IZE' WITH 'ISE' EQUIVALENTS

ACTIVIZE	ALBITIZE	ALKALIZEr	AMORTIZE	ANNALIZE	ANTICIZE	APHETIZE
APHORIZEr	ARBORIZE	ARCHAIZEr	ATHETIZE	*ATTICIZE*	AVIANIZE	BANALIZE
BOTANIZEr	CALORIZE	CANALIZE	CAPONIZE	CHROMIZE	COLORIZEr	COMPRIZE
CREOLIZE	CURARIZE	CUTINIZE	DIMERIZE	DIVINIZE	DYNAMIZE	EBIONIZE
EMBOLIZE	EMPERIZE	ERGOTIZE	ETERNIZE	ETHERIZEr	ETHICIZE	EUPHUIZE
FABULIZE	FARADIZEr	FEMINIZE	FIBERIZE	FLUIDIZEr	FOCALIZE	*FRANCIZE*
GRAECIZE	HEBRAIZE	HEPATIZE	HOMINIZE	HUMANIZEr	INFAMIZE	JAPANIZE
JAROVIZE	JUMBOIZE	LATERIZE	LATINIZE	LOGICIZE	LYRICIZE	MACARIZE
MADERIZE	MELANIZE	MELODIZEr	METALIZE	MONETIZE	NASALIZE	NEBULIZEr
NODALIZE	NOMADIZE	NOTARIZE	NOVELIZEr	OPSONIZE	PAGANIZEr	PATINIZE
POLEMIZE	POLONIZE	PTYALIZE	PYRITIZE	PYROLIZE	QUANTIZEr	RACEMIZE
REGULIZE	RESINIZE	RIGIDIZE	RIVALIZE	ROBOTIZE	ROMANIZE	ROYALIZE
RURALIZE	SALINIZE	SIMILIZE	SIMONIZE	SINICIZE	SIRENIZE	SOBERIZE
SOLARIZE	SOLECIZE	SORORIZE	SUBERIZE	SUBITIZE	SURPRIZE	TETANIZE
TOTALIZEr	TUTORIZE	UNIONIZEr	URBANIZE	VALORIZE	VELARIZE	*VIRILIZE*
VITALIZEr	VOLUMIZEr	VOWELIZE				

OTHER VERBS CONTAINING HEAVY LETTERS

ACQUIGHTd	*AQUAFARM*	AQUATINTa	ATMOLYZE	AUTOLYZE	BEJESUIT	BRONZIFY
CATALYZEr	COLLOQUE	COLLOQUY	COQUETTE	*DOWNZONE*	EQUIPAGE	EXECRATE
EXHUMATE	EXTUBATE	EXUVIATE	GAZUNDER	HEMOLYZE	JACKBOOT	JACKROLL
JACULATE	JOINTURE	JUBILATE	JUGULATE	JULIENNE	LIQUESCE	*LONGJUMP*
MALAXATE	PEJORATE	REQUOYLE	SEXTUPLEt	*SHOWJUMP*	SPUILZIE	SQUABASH
SQUATTLE	SQUILGEE					

VERBS ENDING IN 'ISE' WHICH HAVE 'IZE' EQUIVALENTS

ACTIVISE	ALBITISE	ANNALISE	ANTICISE	APHETISE	APHORISEr	*ARBORISE*
ARCHAISEr	ATHETISE	*ATTICISE*	*AVIANISE*	BANALISE	BOTANISEr	*CALORISE*
CANALISE	CAPONISE	*CHROMISE*	*COLORISEr*	CREOLISE	CUTINISE	DIMERISE
DIVINISE	DYNAMISE	EBIONISE	*EMBOLISE*	EMPERISE	ERGOTISE	ETERNISE
ETHERISEr	ETHICISE	EUPHUISE	FABULISE	FARADISEr	FEMINISE	*FIBERISE*
FLUIDISEr	FOCALISE	*FRANCISE*	*GRAECISE*	*HEBRAISE*	HEPATISE	*HOMINISE*
HUMANISEr	INFAMISE	*JAPANISE*	JAROVISE	JUMBOISE	*LATERISE*	*LATINISE*
LOGICISE	LYRICISE	MACARISE	MADERISE	*MELANISE*	MELODISEr	METALISE
MONETISE	NASALISE	NEBULISEr	NODALISE	NOMADISE	NOTARISE	NOVELISEr
OPSONISE	PAGANISEr	*PATINISE*	POLEMISE	POLONISE	PTYALISE	PYRITISE
PYROLISE	QUANTISEr	RACEMISE	REGULISE	RESINISE	RIGIDISE	RIVALISE
ROBOTISE	ROMANISE	ROYALISE	RURALISE	*SALINISE*	SIMILISE	*SIMONISE*
SINICISE	SIRENISE	SOBERISE	SOLARISE	SOLECISE	SORORISE	SUBERISE
SUBITISE	TETANISE	TOTALISEr	TUTORISE	UNIONISEr	URBANISE	VALORISE
VELARISE	*VIRILISE*	VITALISEr	VOLUMISEr	VOWELISE		

OTHER VERBS ENDING IN 'IFY'

ALKALIFY	DETOXIFY	DIVINIFY	EMULSIFY	ESTERIFY	ETHERIFY	GENTRIFY
GLASSIFY	KARSTIFY	LAPIDIFY	MOISTIFY	OPSONIFY	PRETTIFY	REAEDIFYe
RESINIFY	RIGIDIFY	SANCTIFY	SANGUIFY	SAPONIFY	SILICIFY	STELLIFY
STRATIFY	STULTIFY	*TRENDIFY*	ZINCKIFY			

OTHER VERBS

ABERRATE	ABNEGATE	ABROGATE	ABSTERGE	ABSTRICT	ACERBATE	ACIERATE
AFTEREYE	AGGRIEVE	AIRPROOF	ALKYLATE	ALLIGATE	AMBULATE	ANGULATE
ANKYLOSE	ANTECEDE	ANTEDATE	ANTEVERT	APRICATE	ARMATURE	ARROGATE
ASPERATE	ASPIRATE	ASSEGAAI	ASSONATE	ASTRINGEr	ATCHIEVE	ATMOLYSE
ATTEMPER	AUTOLYSE	*AUTOSAVE*	AUTOTYPE			

BACKFLIP>	BACKHAUL	BACKLIST	*BACKLOAD*	BACKSLAP>	BADINAGE	BALLOCKS
BALLYRAG>	BENEFACT	BERASCAL	BIOASSAY	BIOGRAPHy	BIRDLIME	*BLONDINE*
BLOVIATE	*BOATLIFT*	BOLDFACE	BOOTLICK	BOURGEON	BRATTICE	BRETTICE
BULLWHIP>	BULLYRAG>	BUTYLATE				

CALAMINE	CALENDER	CALLIPER	CANULATE	CAPRIOLE	CARBURET	CARBURET>
CARETAKEd	CARETAKEr	CARILLON	*CARSHARE*	CATALYSEr	CATENATE	CAVITATE
CENTUPLE	CHIVAREE	CHOUNTER	CHUGALUG>	CLANGOUR	CLOISTER	CLUBHAUL
COHOBATE	COLLOGUE	COMPLISH	COMPRINT	COMPULSE	CONFLATE	CONGLOBE
CONSTATE	CONTANGO	CONTANGO+	CONTRIST	CONTROUL	COPYEDIT	COPYREADd
CORDELLE	CORONATE	CORVETTE	COUNTROL>	CRAWFISH	CREASOTE	CRENELLE
CREOSOTE	CUMULATE					

DAMASKIN	DEADLIFT	DEFILADE	DENUDATE	DEROGATE	DIAPAUSE	DISBURSEr
DISHABLE	DISHERIT	DISLOIGN	DISPENCE	DISPIRIT	DISPLODE	DISPONGE
DISPREADd	DISPUNGE	DISSUADE	DIVAGATE	DOWNLINK	DUBITATE	DUMFOUND

ELUVIATE	EMENDATE	EMPATRON	ENFIERCE	ENFILADE	ENSORCEL1	ENVEIGLE
ERUCTATE	ESPALIER	ESTIVATE	ETHYLATE	ETIOLATE	EVANESCE	

FABULATE	*FACEBOOK*	FATIGATE	FEDERATE	FIDDIOUS	FILAGREE	FILIGREE
FILTRATE	*FLATLINEr*	FLYSPECK	FOOTSLOG>	FORHAILE	FORHOOIE=	FREEBASEr
FREEBOOTy	FURBELOW					

GALIVANT	GALLUMPH	*GANGSHAG>*	GARROTTEr	GEMINATE	*GIFTWRAP>*	GLACIATE
GLADWRAP>	GLISSADEr	GRALLOCH	*GREYLIST*	GUARANTY	GUNKHOLE	

HANDFAST	*HANDFEEDd*	*HANDKNIT>*	*HANDPASS*	HARDWIRE	*HEADBANG*	HEBETATE
HELICOPT	HELILIFT	*HEMOLYSE*	HERNIATE	HOMEPORT	HOTPRESS	HUCKSTER

ILLUMINE	IMPANNEL>	INCHOATE	INDAGATE	INDURATE	INHUMATE	*INSOURCE*
INTERESSe	INTERMIT>	INTONATE	INTROMIT>	INTUBATE	INVEAGLE	INVEIGLE
INVOCATE	INVOLUTE	IODINATE	ISOGRAFT			

KALENDAR	KEELHALE	KEELHAUL	KEYPUNCH	KOURBASH	KREASOTE	KREOSOTE

LALLYGAG>	*LANDMINE*	LAPIDATE	LAVEROCK	LEVIGATE	LIGATURE	*LINOTYPEr*
LIPOSUCK	LIVETRAP>	LOCOMOTE	LOLLYGAG>	*LONGLIST*	LORICATE	LUSTRATE

MACULATE	MAILSHOT>	MAINLINEr	MALEDICT	MALLEATE	MALTREAT	MANEUVER
MATURATE	MILITATE	MISLEEKE	MODULATE	*MONOTASK*	MOONWALK	

NECROPSY	NUCLEATE	NUMERATE

OBTEMPER	OBTURATE	OPALESCE	ORDINATE	OSCITATE	OSCULATE	OUTNIGHT
OVERBROW	OVERCRAW	OVERYEAR	OVIPOSIT			

PAGINATE	PALISADE	PALLIATE	PANBROIL	*PARASAIL*	PARBREAK	PATINATE
PATRIATE	PECULATE	PERORATE	PERSWADE	PERVIATE	PETTIFOG>	PHANTASY
PICAROON	*PICOWAVE*	PIGSTICK	PINGUEFY	PINWHEEL	PIRLICUE	PLAISTER
POSTDATE	POSTFORM	POSTSYNC	POTLATCH	POULTICE	POURTRAYd	PRAELECT
PRATFALL	PRENTICE	PRODNOSE	PROGNOSE	PROGRADE	PROMULGE	PROROGUE
PROTRACT	PUMICATE	PURLICUE				

RACEWALK	RADICATE	RAINWASH	RAMPAUGE	REDARGUE	REDSHIRT	REMIGATE
RENFORCE	RENVERSE	REPLEVIN	RESINATE	RETROACT	RETROFIT>	ROTAVATE
ROTOTILL	ROTOVATE	ROUGHDRY	RUMINATE			

SAGINATE	SANITATE	SAVEGARD	SCLEROSE	SCOMFISH	SCOWTHER	SCRATTLE
SCRIGGLE	SCROWDGE	SCUMFISH	SELVEDGE	SEMINATE	SEROTYPE	SHIVAREE
SHUNPIKEr	SIBILATE	SIDERATE	SIDESLIP>	SKELLOCH	SKYWRITEd	SKYWRITEr
SLAISTER	SLIPFORM	SMOOTHEN	SNOWSHOE=	SNOWSHOEr	SOLIDATE	SOMERSET
SOMNIATE	SONICATE	SOOTHSAYd	SOULDIER	SOUTHSAYd	SPANGHEW	SPECIATE
SPOLIATE	SPRACKLE	SPRADDLE	SPRANGLE	SPREATHE	SPREETHE	SPURGALL
STABLISH	STANCHEL>	STRAITEN	STRAMASH	STRAUCHT	STRAUGHT	STRAVAGE
STRAVAIG	STREIGNE	STRIDDLE	STRINKLE	STRODDLE	STUPRATE	SUBMERSE
SUBSERVE	SUBTRUDE	SUBVERSE	SULFURET	SULFURET>	SUPERADD	SUPERATE
SUPERLIEd	SUPINATE	SURCEASE	SURMOUNT	SURPRINT	SURREBUT>	

TABOGGAN	TALLIATE	TEETOTAL	TEETOTAL>	TELEMARK	TELEPATHy	TELEPORT
TELESHOP>	*TELETYPE*	TELEVIEW	*TELEWORK*	TIDIVATE	*TIMEPASS*	TINCTURE
TINPLATE	TITIVATE	TITUBATE	TOBOGGIN	*TOPSCORE*	TRANSACT	TRANSECT
TRANSHIP>	TRANSMEW	TRANSUDE	TRANSUME	TRAPNEST	TRAUCHLE	TREPHINEr
TRITIATE	TUBULATE					

UNPANNEL>	UNPERSON	URTICATE	USUFRUCT

VAPULATE	*VARITYPE*	VENENATE	VENERATE	VERJUICE	VESICATE	VIGNETTEr
VILIPEND	VOLITATE	VOLPLANE	VOUSSOIR	VOUTSAFE		

WAINSCOT	WAINSCOT>	*WAITLIST*

8.3.3 NOUNS BY COMMON ENDINGS

AGE

ACIERAGE	ADJUTAGE	AGIOTAGE	ALIENAGE	ALTARAGE	AMPERAGE	BARONAGE
BERTHAGE	BLINDAGE	BRAKEAGE	BRASSAGE	BROCKAGE	CABOTAGE	CHANTAGE
CLEARAGE	CLOUDAGE	COZENAGE	CREEPAGE	DIALLAGE	DISUSAGE	DRESSAGE
DRIFTAGE	ENALLAGE	FERRIAGE	FLOATAGE	FLOORAGE	FOOTPAGE	FRAUTAGE
FRONDAGE	FROTTAGE	FRUITAGE	GRAFTAGE	GRAINAGE	GRILLAGE	GROUPAGE
GUARDAGE	HELOTAGE	*HOMEPAGE*	LANGRAGE	LAYERAGE	*LITREAGE*	MALAXAGE
MARITAGE	MESSUAGE	METAYAGE	METERAGE	MISUSAGE	MUCILAGE	NONIMAGE
PILOTAGE	*PINOTAGE*	PLANTAGE	PLOTTAGE	PLUSSAGE	POUNDAGE	PUCELAGE
SMALLAGE	SPOILAGE	SPOUSAGE	SQUIRAGE	STEALAGE	STEARAGE	STEERAGE
STERNAGE	*STOCKAGE*	STREWAGE	STUMPAGE	SUBSTAGE	THIRLAGE	TRACKAGE
TRUCKAGE	TRUQUAGE	TUTELAGE	TUTORAGE	UMPIRAGE	VAULTAGE	VAUNTAGE
VERBIAGE	VICARAGE	VICINAGE	WAGONAGE	WATERAGE	WEIGHAGE	WHARFAGE

AL *excluding 'IAL'*

ACQUIRAL	ASTRAGALi	BALMORAL	BESTOWAL	BIDENTAL	BONEMEAL	CAPSIZAL
CONVEYAL	CORNMEAL	CORRIVAL	CRUMENAL	CUSTUMAL	DECRETAL	DEFRAYAL
DEISHEAL	DEMURRAL	DESPISAL	DEVERBAL	EPIDURAL	ESCHEWAL	FALDERAL
FISHMEAL	FORBIDAL	GUNMETAL	HICKYMAL	HYMENEAL	ISOGONAL	LACRIMAL
LACRYMAL	LARYNGAL	LITTORAL	MADRIGAL	MEGADEAL	METHYLAL	MILLIGAL
NONEQUAL	NONLOCAL	NONMETAL	NONRIVAL	NONVOCAL	ORINASAL	OVERZEAL
PARIETAL	PETROSAL	PICTURAL	PRENASAL	PRIMATAL	PROCURAL	PROMETAL
RECEIVAL	REMITTAL	REPROVAL	REQUITAL	RESTORAL	REVIEWAL	RHODINAL
SAFRONAL	SELFHEAL	*SERVQUAL*	SPRINGALd	SURMISAL	SURROYAL	SURVEYAL
TETRONAL	TRIFOCAL	TURBINAL	UNIVOCAL	UPROOTAL	VARIETAL	VESPERAL
WARRAGAL	WARRIGAL	WOODMEAL				

AN *excluding 'IAN'*

ACARIDAN	*AGNATHAN*	BARRACAN	BARTIZAN	BERGHAAN	*BERRIGAN*	BILLYCAN
BRAINPAN	BRYOZOAN	BUSULFAN	*BUTSUDAN*	CERULEAN	CHITOSAN	CHLORDANe
CORDOVAN	COTQUEAN	DIOCESAN	DRAGOMAN	*ECHIURAN*	EMPYREAN	EULACHAN
FRAUGHAN	HARRIDAN	HIELAMAN	HOOLICAN	ISOPODAN	JAMBOLANa	JERRICAN
JERRYCAN	KALAMDAN	LANGSHAN	LARRIGAN	*LINKSPAN*	MACRURAN	*MESOZOAN*
MICHIGAN	MULLIGAN	NEOPAGAN	NONPAGAN	OOLACHAN	*PARMESAN*	PARTIZAN
PENTOSANe	PORTULAN	QALAMDAN	RAMBUTAN	RATAPLAN	SCALEPAN	SHWANPAN
SIALIDAN	SKEECHAN	SNEESHAN	STROUPAN	SUMPITAN	SUPERFAN	TARLATAN
TARLETAN	TRAGOPAN	TRUCHMAN	TURBOFAN	URODELAN	VENEREAN	WANNIGAN
YARRAMAN						

ANCE

ABIDANCE	ADAMANCE	AMBIANCE	AMORANCE	BRISANCE	BUOYANCE	EXITANCE
FEASANCE	ISSUANCE	ITERANCE	LAITANCE	NONDANCEr	ORDNANCE	OUTRANCE
PASTANCE	PIQUANCE	PORTANCE	RESIANCE	RIDDANCE	SORTANCE	TENDANCE
VALIANCE	VIBRANCE	VOIDANCE				

ANE

CAMPHANE	CAMSTANE	CATENANE	DUMBCANE	*ELASTANE*	FLEABANE	MARYJANE
PARAVANE	PRISTANE	PURSLANE	RATSBANE	SILOXANE	SKIPLANE	STEPHANE
TOWPLANE	WARPLANE					

ANT

ABRADANT	ADJUVANT	ALTERANT	AMBULANT	ASHPLANT	ASSONANT	COLORANT
CORYBANT	DEDICANT	DEPURANT	DILATANT	EVACUANT	EXCITANT	EXHALANT
EXPIRANT	EXSECANT	FAINEANT	FIGURANTe	FLOATANT	FUMIGANT	GENERANT
GRIEVANT	GUARDANT	INCITANT	INHALANT	INSULANT	INSURANT	JAZERANT
LIBELANT	LITIGANT	LUMINANT	*MEDICANT*	MOUNTANT	NAUSEANT	OBLIGANT
OLIPHANT	ORDINANT	PERMEANT	PLAINANT	PROVIANT	QUESTANT	REACTANT
RECREANT	RECUSANT	RELAXANT	RETIRANT	REVENANT	ROBORANT	SATURANT
SEMBLANT	SERJEANTy	SETENANT	SIBILANT	SIMULANT	SONORANT	TOXICANT
TULIPANT	URTICANT	VESICANT	VISITANT	WAXPLANT		

AR

ALVEOLAR	AUXILIARy	BEDEGUAR	CHOKIDAR	*CHURIDAR*	CINNABAR	COOLIBAR
CULTIVAR	*CYBERWAR*	EXAMPLAR	FELDSPAR	FOOTGEAR	GOODYEAR	HAVILDAR
HORSECAR	HOSPODAR	KILLADAR	KOMISSAR	LOADSTAR	LODESTAR	MACASSAR
MAGNETAR	MICROBAR	MILLIBAR	NAMASKAR	NECKGEAR	NECKWEAR	NENUPHAR
NIGHTJAR	NONSUGAR	PATTAMAR	POLESTAR	PREMOLAR	PULVINAR	RESALGAR
RISALDAR	SCIMETAR	SCIMITAR	SELICTAR	SILLADAR	SUBAHDARy	SUBVICAR
SUBSIZAR	SUPERCAR	SURBAHAR	TABERDAR	TALUKDAR	THANADAR	TORCULAR
TURBOCAR	WHEATEAR	*WORMGEAR*	ZAMINDARi	ZAMINDARy	ZEMINDARi	ZEMINDARy

ARY+

BALNEARY+	BESTIARY+	*BOONGARY+*	BREVIARY+	CATENARY+	CONGIARY+	COSTMARY+
DECENARY+	DONATARY+	EMISSARY+	FEDERARY+	FEMETARY+	JANISARY+	LEGATARY+
LUMINARY+	MILLIARY+	NOCTUARY+	NOVENARY+	OCTONARY+	PETCHARY+	PLAGIARY+
POTICARY+	SISERARY+	SPERMARY+	STANNARY+	STATUARY+	TEXTUARY+	VESPIARY+
VESTIARY+						

ASE

ALDOLASE	ANAPHASE	ARGINASE	CATALASE	DIASTASE	DIOPTASE	*DOORCASE*
ELASTASE	ESTERASE	FIREBASE	FUMARASE	GEARCASE	HEADCASE	*HELICASE*
IDOCRASE	KILOBASE	NOTECASE	NUCLEASE	PERMEASE	RHEOBASE	SEEDCASE
SLIPCASEd	SUBPHASE	*SYNTHASE*	TYPECASE			

ATE

ABLEGATE	ACRYLATE	ACULEATEd	AGUACATE	ALGINATE	AMEERATE	ANNULATEd
APHOLATE	APOSTATE	ARSENATE	BALDPATEd	*BANDMATE*	BEDPLATE	BENZOATE
BREVIATE	BUNKMATE	BUTYRATE	CALIFATE	CAPROATE	CASEMATEd	CHLORATE
CHORDATE	CHROMATE	CLODPATEd	COINMATE	CONEPATE	COPEMATE	CRANIATE
CREWMATE	DERIVATE	EMEERATE	ENDPLATE	FLUXGATE	FORMIATE	FUMARATE
HEADGATE	HELPMATE	*HOTPLATE*	HYLOBATE	KALIFATE	LEACHATE	LICHGATE
LIFTGATE	LYCHGATE	MAKEBATE	MALONATE	MECONATE	NIZAMATE	OMOPLATE
OPTIMATE	PLAYDATE	PLUMBATE	PRIORATE	PYRUVATE	RACEMATE	RAINDATE
RENEGATE	ROSINATE	RUNAGATE	SEATMATE	SEGOLATE	SELENATE	SERENATE

8. Eight-Letter Words

SHIPMATE	SORORATE	*SOULMATE*	SQUAMATE	STEARATE	SUBERATE	SUBSTATE
SURICATE	TARTRATEd	THIONATE	TITANATE	TOEPLATE	TRACTATE	TUNICATEd
UNGULATE	VALERATE	VAMPLATE	VANADATE	VEGELATE	VICARATE	VIZIRATE
XANTHATE	YOKEMATE					

ATION

ABLATION	ADNATION	AGNATION	CIBATION	CONATION	DOTATION	FETATION
HIMATION	IDEATION	ILLATION	IODATION	JOBATION	LAVATION	LAXATION
LEGATION	LIBATION	LIGATION	LIMATION	LOBATION	LUNATION	LUXATION
NATATION	NEGATION	NIDATION	*NIVATION*	NODATION	NUDATION	NUTATION
OBLATION	PACATION	POTATION	ROGATION	SOLATION	SUDATION	VEXATION
ZONATION						

BERRY+

COWBERRY+	DEWBERRY+	DOGBERRY+	FOXBERRY+	HAGBERRY+	INKBERRY+	NISBERRY+
PEABERRY+	SUNBERRY+	TEABERRY+	WAXBERRY+			

DOM

BIRTHDOM	BLOKEDOM	CHIEFDOM	CLERKDOM	DEVILDOM	DUNCEDOM	FAIRYDOM
FOGEYDOM	*GIPSYDOM*	HOTELDOM	LEECHDOM	LIEGEDOM	NOVELDOM	PACHADOM
PAGANDOM	PASHADOM	QUEENDOM	QUEERDOM	REBELDOM	SAINTDOM	SHEIKDOM
SWELLDOM	THANEDOM	THRALDOM	UNWISDOM	VILLADOM	WHOREDOM	

EE

ABDUCTEE	*ADMITTEE*	ALLOTTEE	ARRESTEE	AXLETREE	BALLOTEE	BIDARKEE
BILLETEE	BOORTREE	BOUNTREE	BOURTREE	BUCKSHEE	CALLIPEE	CAMPOREE
CHARIDEE	COLESSEE	CONFEREE	CORKTREE	DEPARTEE	DESIGNEE	DUNGAREEd
ENLISTEE	ENROLLEE	EXPELLEE	FRAILTEE	GAUNTREE	GREEGREE	HARAMBEE
HONEYBEE	*HONOUREE*	HYPNOTEE	INDICTEE	INDUCTEE	JAMPANEE	KEDGEREE
KIDNAPEE	LIBELLEE	MOONSHEE	MURDEREE	NECKATEE	OPTIONEE	PATENTEE
PENNYFEE	PHARISEE	PINDAREE	PUGGAREE	REJECTEE	REMITTEE	RETURNEE
ROOFTREE	SANGAREE	SCARABEE	SHIKAREE	SHIRALEE	SHOETREE	SLOETREE
SOWARREE	*SPHAIREE*	TIRRIVEE	TULLIBEE			

EN

ABORIGEN	ALLERGEN	AMIDOGEN	AMYLOGEN	ANDROGEN	ARMOZEEN	*BACLOFEN*
CARAGEEN	CISTVAEN	CLINAMEN	COGNOMEN	CULTIGEN	CYANOGEN	DAKERHEN
DIPLOGEN	DRISHEEN	ESTROGEN	FABURDEN	FLORIGEN	*FLUELLEN*	GLYCOGEN
GNATWREN	GRAVAMEN	GROSCHEN	HENEQUEN	HENIQUEN	HISTOGENy	HYALOGEN
KHAMSEEN	KISTVAEN	MAGDALENe	MENHADEN	MISCEGENe	OSTEOGENy	PARISHEN
PATHOGENe	PATHOGENy	PHOTOGENe	PHOTOGENy	POSHTEEN	POSTTEEN	PRENOMEN
PSORALEN	ROENTGEN	SEBESTEN	SENGREEN	SHAGREEN	SHAMISEN	*SHURIKEN*
SLEEVEEN	*SPALDEEN*	SQUIREEN	STARAGEN	*TAGAREEN*	VELSKOEN	YESTREEN

ENE

ARRASENE	BUTYLENE	CAMPHENE	CAROTENE	CHROMENE	CYMOGENE	DISTHENE
DRAISENE	ETHYLENE	FLUORENE	GASOGENE	GASOLENE	GAZOGENE	*GRAPHENE*
HEXYLENE	ISOPRENE	LIMONENE	LYCOPENE	MENTHENE	NEOPRENE	PHOSGENE

POLYGENE	PYROXENE	RETINENE	SQUALENE	STILBENE	TEREBENE	*TERYLENE*
VIROGENE	XANTHENE	ZYGOTENE				

ENT *excluding 'MENT'*

APERIENT	COPARENT	COREGENT	DECEDENT	DEFERENT	DEPONENT	DIVALENT
ESCULENT	EXHALENT	HATERENT	HIRRIENT	IMPONENT	INFLUENT	MISAGENT
MISEVENT	NESCIENT	QUITRENT	REASCENT	REFERENT	REMANENT	SENTIENT

ER *derived from verbs*

ABHORRER	ABSENTER	ACTIONER	ADJUSTER	ADMITTER	ADSORBER	ALLOTTERy
AMBUSHER	ANNEALER	ANSWERER	ARGUFIER	ARMOURER	ARRESTER	ASCENDER
ASSAILER	ASSENTER	ASSERTER	ASSIGNER	ASSORTER	ATTAINER	ATTENDER
ATTESTER	AWAKENER	BALLOTER	BANISHER	BANTERER	BASIFIER	BATTELER
BATTENER	BATTERER	BECKONER	BEFOULER	BEGETTER	*BEHEADER*	BELLOWER
BELONGER	BEMOANER	BESETTER	BESTOWER	BETRAYER	BEVELLER	BEWAILER
BEWRAYER	BICKERER	BILLETER	BLANCHER	BLAZONER	BLENCHER	BOTTOMER
BROACHER	*BRUNCHER*	BUDGETER	BURDENER	BUSHELER	BUTTONER	CABALLERo
CANALLER	CANVASER	CAREENER	CAREERER	CARESSER	CAROLLER	CATNAPER
CAVILLER	CAVORTER	CELLARER	CEMENTER	CHISELER	*CIPHERER*	CLAMORER
CODIFIER	COLEADER	COLOURER	COMBATER	COMPLIER	CONVEYER	COSHERER
COSIGNER	*CRAYONER*	CUDGELER	CUMBERER	CUPELLER	DAMPENER	DARKENER
DEADENER	*DEBARKER*	DEBUGGER	DEBUNKER	DEEPENER	DEFEATER	DEFERRER
DEFOAMER	DEFOGGER	DEFORMER	DEFRAYER	DEGASSER	DEHORNER	DEHORTER
DEMANDER	DEMURRER	DEPARTER	DEPICTER	*DEPLOYER*	*DEPORTER*	DERAILER
DETAINER	DETICKER	DESCRIER	DETACHER	DETECTER	DETERRER	DETESTER
DESALTER	DEVOURER	DEWORMER	DIALOGER	DIGESTER	DISARMER	DISOWNER
DIVERTER	DODDERER	DOGNAPER	DRENCHER	DRIVELER	DUPLEXER	ELOIGNER
EMBANKER	EMBODIER	EMBOSSER	ENAMELER	ENFOLDER	ENJOINER	ENLISTER
ENRICHER	ENROLLER	ENTAILER	ESCHEWER	EXCEEDER	EXHORTER	EXPANDER
EXPECTER	EXPELLER	EXPENDER	EXTENDER	EXTOLLER	EXTORTER	*FATHOMER*
FATTENER	FAVOURER	FERRETER	FETTERER	FIDGETER	FILTERER	FINGERER
FLAUNTER	FLAVORER	*FLENCHER*	FLETCHER	FLINCHER	FLOWERER	FODDERER
FOMENTER	FOREGOER	FOSTERER	FRESCOER	FRIVOLER	FROWSTER	FURROWER
GASIFIER	GAZUMPER	*GOLLOPER*	GOSPELER	GOSSIPER	GROVELER	GRUELLER
HALLOWER	HAMPERER	HANKERER	HARASSER	HARBORER	HARKENER	HARROWER
HASTENER	HAVOCKER	*HAZARDER*	HECTORER	HINDERER	HONOURER	HOVELLER
IMPACTER	IMPAIRER	IMPARTER	IMPELLER	IMPOSTER	IMPUGNER	INDENTER
INDICTER	INFECTER	INFERRER	INFESTER	INFOLDER	INPUTTER	INSERTER
INSETTER	INSISTER	INSULTER	INVENTER	INVERTER	JAPANNER	JUNKETER
KIBITZER	KIDNAPER	KVETCHER	LAMENTER	LARRUPER	LATHERER	LETTERER
LEVANTER	LEVELLER	LIBELLER	LINGERER	LINISHER	LUMBERER	MALIGNER
MARKETER	MAROONER	MISLAYER	MODELLER	MODIFIER	MOTIONER	MOUTERER
MUSICKER	NATTERER	NOTIFIER	OBTAINER	ONSETTER	ORDAINER	*ORIENTER*
OSSIFIER	OVERDOER	OYSTERER	PACIFIER	PANDERER	PARDONER	PARGETER
PARLEYER	PARROTER	PATTERER	PEDALLER	PENCILER	PERISHER	PESTERER
PHREAKER	PICKETER	PIECENER	PILFERER	PLOUGHER	POCKETER	POISONER
PONDERER	PROFITER	PUCKERER	PUNISHER	QUARRIER	QUAVERER	QUENCHER
QUIVERER	RACKETER	RANSOMER	RAREFIER	RATIFIER	RATOONER	RATTENER
RAVELLER	RAVISHER	REBELLER	REBUTTER	RECALLER	RECANTER	RECKONER

8. Eight-Letter Words

```
RECOILER   REDEEMER   REDRAWER   REFERRER   REFUNDER   REGAINER   REGARDER      |
REHEATER   REJECTER   RELOADER   REMARKER   RENDERER   RENOWNER   REOPENER
REPEALER   REPELLER   REPENTER   REROLLER   RESENTER   RESETTER   RESIGNER
RESISTER   RESORTER   RETARDER   RETELLER   RETORTER   RETURNER   REVAMPER
REVEALER   REVERTER   REVOLTER   REWARDER   REWINDER   ROCKETER   RUMOURER
SAVOURER   SCREEDER   SCREENER   SCRIPTER   SCROLLER   SEASONER   SERMONER
SHADOWER   SHIELDER   SHIVERER   SHOVELER   SHOWERER   SHRIEKER   SHRINKER
SHROOMER   SICKENER   SIGNALER   SIMPERER   SLALOMER   SLAVERER   SLEIGHER
SLIVERER   SLOUCHER   SMIRCHER   SNITCHER   SNIVELER   SOLDERER   SORROWER
SPRAWLER   SPRITZER   SQUAILER   SQUALLER   SQUAWKER   SQUEAKERy  SQUEGGER
SQUIRMER   SQUIRTER   STARCHER   STITCHERy  STRANDER   STREEKER   STRINGER
STRUTTER   SUBORNER   SUNDERER   SWITCHER   TABOURER   TAMPERER   TATTOOER
TEASELER   TEMPERER   THIRSTER   THREADER   THREAPER   THREEPER   THRUSTER
THWACKER   THWARTER   TINKERER   TITTERER   TOTTERER   TRENCHER   TROWELER
TUNNELER   TWITCHER   TYPIFIER   UGLIFIER   UNFOLDER   UNHAIRER   UNLOADER
UNMASKER   UNPACKER   UNREELER   UNVEILER   UNWINDER   UPBEARER   UPLIFTER
UPROOTER   UPSETTER   VANISHER   VAPOURER   VENEERER   VERIFIER   VILIFIER
VISIONER   VOLLEYER   WAGGONER   WEAKENER   WEASELER   WEIGHTER   WINTERER
WITHERER   WONDERER   WRENCHER
```

ER *other,* *excluding* *'IER',* *'OVER'* *&* *'STER'*
```
AVOUTRER   BARRATER   BAYADEER   BEDMAKER   BELLETER   BIJWONER   BILANDER
BIOMETER   BUPLEVER   BYLANDER   CALYPTERa  CAMELEER   CAPMAKER   CAPSOMERe
CARMAKER   CHAPITER   CLAVIGER   COHOLDER   COMETHER   CONGENER   CORDINER
COWINNER   CREUTZER   CUTWATER   CYMBALER   DATALLER   DERINGER   DIEMAKER
DIPLEXER   DONNIKER   DOUZEPER   DULCIMER   EBENEZER   ESSOINER   ETRANGERe
EVILDOER   EYEWATER   FAIRGOER   FALCONER   FELDSHER   FIGEATER   FILANDER
FILMGOER   FLYMAKER   FRAMPLER   FURRINER   FUSILEER   GENNAKER   GEOLOGER
GEOMETER   GOSSAMERy  GUNLAYER   HATMAKER   HAYMAKER   HEMIPTER   HOROPTER
HOSTELER   HOWITZER   ICEMAKER   IDOLATER   INCENTER   INHAULER   INHOLDER
INLANDER   JOLLEYER   KREUTZER   LARCENER   LARDERER   LATEENER   LAWGIVER
LAWMAKER   LOWRIDER   LUXMETER   MALANDER   MANRIDER   MASSETER   MICAWBER
MIJNHEER   MONICKER   MOUNSEER   MULETEER   NONOWNER   NONVOTER   NOVEMBER
OLIGOMER   OPIFICER   OROMETER   OSTREGER   OUTREMER   OXIMETER   OXPECKER
PARCENER   PEDALFER   PEWTERER   PHYSETER   PILSENER   PINSCHER   PLANKTER
PLAYGOER   POMANDER   POMWATER   PROSUMER   REDWATER   REGMAKER   SANDIVER
SCHLAGER   SCIMITER   SCUTIGER   SEAFARER   SECESHER   SHNORRER   SKIJORER
SITKAMER   SOLANDER   SUBORDER   SUCKENER   SYLVANER   TAUTOMER   TAVERNER
TEAMAKER   TERMINER   TETRAMER   TEUCHTER   THRONNER   THURIFER   TIMONEER
TOPMAKER   TRIMETER   UDOMETER   UPLANDER   UPTOWNER   VERDERER   VIAMETER
VRAICKER   WARMAKER   WARRENER   WELLDOER   WIGMAKER   YAWMETER   ZINGIBER
ZOOLATER
```

ERY+
```
BITCHERY+  CLOWNERY+  DIABLERY+  FREAKERY+  FROGGERY+  GROGGERY+  JAGGHERY+
LAMASERY+  LIENTERY+  PSEUDERY+  RAILLERY+  SHINNERY+  SLUTTERY+  SMITHERY+
SPOOKERY+  SWANNERY+  THIEVERY+  TRUMPERY+  WITCHERY+
```

ESS+ *excluding 'NESS'*

CATERESS+ CHIEFESS+ CLERKESS+ DEVILESS+ DOCTRESS+ DRUIDESS+ EDITRESS+
GIANTESS+ HUNTRESS+ LECTRESS+ ORATRESS+ PORTRESS+ PRIORESS+ RECTRESS+
RIVALESS+ TUTORESS+ VICARESS+ VICTRESS+ VOTARESS+ WARDRESS+

ET *excluding 'LET'*

ANCHORET ANTITHET BALCONET BALLONET BANNERET *BASCINET* BEDSHEET
BLANQUET BURGANET BURGONET BYSTREET CABERNET CELLARET COLLARET
CYANURET CYBERPET DOSSERET DRAGONET DUBONNET EARTHSET ELECTRET
EXTRANET FALCONET FLOWERET *FLYSHEET* HELPMEET INTRANET JIRKINET
LANNERET MARTINET *MICROJET* MOULINET MUSCADET MUSLINET PARAQUET
PAROQUET PARROKET PEETWEET PHOTOSET PULSEJET PULSOJET QUICKSET
SALMONET SARCENET SARCONET SARSENET SCRAMJET SERMONET SIPHONET
SOLLERET SUPERJET TABOURET *TIPSHEET* TOILINET TOUCANET TRAWLNET
TURBOJET *WATERJET* WHITTRET ZERUMBET

ETTE

AIGRETTE ANISETTE *BAGNETTE* BAGUETTE BARRETTEr *CHAVETTE* CREVETTE
DANCETTEe DRABETTE FAUVETTE *FLATETTE* FOSSETTE FRISETTE FRIZETTE
GRISETTE HACKETTE JEANETTE JOCKETTE MAQUETTE MOQUETTE NOISETTE
OMELETTE PALLETTE PALMETTE *PARKETTE* PIANETTE POCHETTE RACLETTE
REINETTE *RINGETTE* ROOMETTE ROQUETTE SEPTETTE SOCKETTE SPINETTE
STAGETTE SUEDETTE TOILETTE UMBRETTE

EUR

BATELEUR BLAGUEUR CHASSEUR CISELEUR CLAQUEUR ECRASEUR FROIDEUR
FRONDEUR FROTTEUR JONGLEUR LONGUEUR SECATEUR SEIGNEURy SIGNIEUR
TAILLEUR TROUVEUR TRUQUEUR VOYAGEUR

FISH+

BAITFISH+ *BANDFISH*+ BILLFISH+ BLOWFISH+ BLUEFISH+ BONEFISH+ CAVEFISH+
COALFISH+ DEALFISH+ DRUMFISH+ GOATFISH+ GRAYFISH+ JACKFISH+ KINGFISH+
LADYFISH+ LIONFISH+ LUMPFISH+ LUNGFISH+ MILKFISH+ MONKFISH+ MOONFISH+
NUMBFISH+ ROSEFISH+ SAILFISH+ SALTFISH+ SANDFISH+ SCARFISH+ STUDFISH+
SUCKFISH+ TILEFISH+ TOADFISH+ WALLFISH+ WEAKFISH+

FORM

COLIFORM IODOFORM PARAFORM PISIFORM PLANFORM UNCIFORM WAVEFORM

FUL

APRONFUL BASINFUL CHEEKFUL CHESTFUL *CRATEFUL* LADLEFUL NIEVEFUL
PLATEFUL POUCHFUL PRESSFUL PURSEFUL SCOOPFUL SHELLFUL SNOOTFUL
SPADEFUL STAGEFUL STICKFUL TABLEFUL TOOTHFUL TRAINFUL TRUCKFUL
TRUNKFUL WAGONFUL

HEAD

ACIDHEAD BALDHEAD BILLHEAD BLUEHEAD BOLTHEAD BONEHEAD *BOOFHEAD*
BULKHEAD BULLHEAD *BUTTHEAD* *CLUBHEAD* COKEHEAD DICKHEAD DOPEHEAD
DROPHEAD DRUMHEAD DUMBHEAD FORKHEAD *FUCKHEAD* *GEARHEAD* GILTHEAD

JOLTHEAD	*KNOBHEAD*	*LIONHEAD*	LONGHEAD	LUNKHEAD	NAILHEAD	*PIERHEAD*
PILLHEAD	PISSHEAD	PLOWHEAD	SLAPHEAD	SOFTHEAD	SOREHEAD	*STEMHEAD*
TOOLHEAD	WELLHEAD					

HOLE

FEEDHOLE	FUNKHOLE	KNEEHOLE	LAMPHOLE	PESTHOLE	SINKHOLE	WEEPHOLE
WOODHOLE	WORMHOLEd					

HOOD

AUNTHOOD	DOLLHOOD	IDLEHOOD	KINGHOOD	LADYHOOD	MAIDHOOD	MISSHOOD
MONKHOOD	PAGEHOOD	SERFHOOD	WIFEHOOD	WIVEHOOD		

IA

ACADEMIA	ACIDEMIA	ACIDURIA	ADULARIA	ADYNAMIA	AGENESIA	*AGLOSSIA*
AGRAPHIA	AGRYPNIA	AKINESIA	*ALOCASIA*	ALOPECIA	AMBROSIAl	AMBROSIAn
AMPHIBIAn	*ANIRIDIA*	ANOOPSIA	ANOXEMIA	APIMANIA	APOLOGIAe	APOSITIA
ARYTHMIA	*ASPERMIA*	ASPHYXIAl	ASTIGMIA	ATARAXIA	ATROPHIA	AUBRETIA
AUTOPSIA	AZOTEMIA	AZOTURIA	BAPTISIA	BATTALIA	BAUHINIA	BEDSONIA
BERGENIA	BERYLLIA	BIGNONIA	BOLTONIA	*BORRELIA*	BROMELIAd	BUDDLEIA
CALVARIAl	CALVARIAn	CAMBOGIA	CHOLEMIA	CHYLURIA	CONURBIA	COPREMIA
COXALGIA	DENTARIA	DIPLEGIA	*DYSLALIA*	DYSMELIA	DYSTAXIA	DYSTOCIAl
DYSTONIA	DYSTOPIAn	EGOMANIAc	ENCAENIA	ESTANCIA	ESTHESIA	EUPHOBIA
EUPHONIA	*EUTHYMIA*	FANTASIA	GALLABIAh	GALLERIA	GALTONIA	GAMBUSIA
GARCINIA	GEMATRIA	GERARDIA	GESNERIAd	GLOXINIA	*GLYCEMIA*	GLYCERIA
HAMARTIA	HATTERIA	HEMIOLIA	HEMIOPIA	HETAIRIA	HYDREMIA	HYPALGIA
HYPONOIA	INTARSIA	ISCHEMIA	ISCHURIA	IZVESTIA	KRAMERIA	LEUCEMIA
LIPAEMIA	LISTERIAl	LITHEMIA	MAGNESIAl	MAGNESIAn	MALVASIAn	METANOIA
MILIARIAl	MILTONIA	MONTARIA	MYOTONIA	*NOCTURIA*	*OLIGEMIA*	OLIGURIA
PANDEMIAn	PANMIXIA	PAROEMIAc	PAROEMIAl	*PAROSMIA*	PAROUSIA	PHACELIA
PHOTINIA	PHYSALIA	PLANARIAn	PLANURIA	PLUMERIA	POLYURIA	PROGERIA
RAPHANIA	*SANTERIA*	SAPREMIA	SAPUCAIA	SCOTOMIA	SCOTOPIA	SEMUNCIAe
SEMUNCIAl	SINFONIA	SORBARIA	STAPELIA	STOKESIA	STRONTIAn	SUBTOPIAn
SYNECHIA	SYNERGIA	TAQUERIA	*TIGRIDIA*	TITHONIA	*TOPALGIA*	TOXAEMIA
TRITONIA	URINEMIA	VALENCIA	VALLONIA	VERATRIA	VICTORIA	VIRAEMIA
VIRGINIA	*VISCARIA*	WEIGELIA	WISTARIA	YERSINIAe	YTTERBIA	ZIRCONIA
ZOIATRIA	ZOOMANIA	ZOONOMIA				

IAL

ARMORIAL	BINOMIAL	GERANIAL	PRAEDIAL	REBURIAL	SQUARIAL	TRIAXIAL
TROOPIAL	TROUPIAL					

IAN

AGRARIAN	APHIDIAN	APIARIAN	AULARIAN	BESONIAN	BEZONIAN	CONQUIAN
COUNTIAN	CREOLIAN	EGYPTIAN	ETHICIAN	HOMINIAN	IGUANIAN	ISTHMIAN
LEMURIAN	LOGICIAN	LUNARIAN	NICOTIANa	NUTARIAN	OBSIDIAN	OPHIDIAN
PAGURIAN	PELAGIAN	PICARIAN	PLEBEIAN	*QUARRIAN*	SIRENIAN	SYRPHIAN
THESPIAN	VALERIAN	VENETIAN				

IC

ANIMATIC	ANORETIC	ANTALGIC	ANTIPYIC	ATARAXIC	BIOETHIC	BIONOMIC
DALMATIC	DIOPTRIC	DIURETIC	*DOXASTIC*	DYSGENIC	ENTOPTIC	ENURETIC
ENZOOTIC	EPULOTIC	ESTHETIC	EUPHENIC	EXEGETIC	GEODESIC	GEODETIC
GEOPONIC	GNOMONIC	HAEMATIC	HERMETIC	HERPETIC	HEURETIC	HIDROTIC
HIERATICa	ISAGOGIC	ISOGONIC	KEPHALIC	LEUKEMIC	LITURGIC	MAIEUTIC
MONASTIC	NEOTERIC	NEURITIC	NONMUSIC	OPERATIC	ORTHOTIC	PANDEMIC
PASHALIC	PERIOTIC	PHENETIC	PHENOLIC	PHONEMIC	PHOTONIC	PHYLETIC
PREMEDIC	PROXEMIC	PULMONIC	SEMIOTIC	SILASTIC	SPAGYRIC	SPONDAIC
SUBTONIC	SUBTOPIC	SUBTUNIC	SYNOPTIC	TELESTICh	TOREUTIC	TRISOMIC
TURMERIC						

ID *excluding 'OID'*

ACETAMIDe	ANTHERID	BICUSPID	*BIOSOLID*	BONDMAID	BRACONID	*BRAEHEID*
CARANGID	CARYATID	CHIMERID	COLUBRID	COOKMAID	COVERLID	CYANAMIDe
CYPRINID	DIHYBRID	DISULFIDe	*DREPANID*	DYTISCID	ELATERID	*EUGLENID*
EUPATRID	FILARIID	GRANDKID	HANDMAID	HESPERID	HYDRACID	LACERTID
LAMPYRID	LIMNAEID	*LYCAENID*	MEDICAID	MONOACID	MURAENID	*MUSTELID*
NONFLUID	NONSOLID	OPHIURID	ORIBATID	PERIODIDe	PHORONID	POLYBRID
PROTOXIDe	REDUVIID	SALMONID	SCIAENID	SCLEREIDe	SCOLYTID	SCOMBRID
SCOPELID	*SERPULID*	SERRANID	SOLIQUID	SOLPUGID	SPHINGID	SYNAPSID
SYNERGID	TACHINID	TAILSKID	TETRACID	TETROXIDe	TRACHEIDe	*VANESSID*

IDE *excluding 'SIDE'*

ACTINIDE	ALGICIDE	ALKOXIDE	APHICIDE	ARSENIDE	*ASTATIDE*	BOURRIDE
CERAMIDE	CHROMIDE	*ETHOXIDE*	EVENTIDE	*FEMICIDE*	FETICIDE	FILICIDE
FREERIDE	HOLYTIDE	*MEDICIDE*	MITICIDE	MONOXIDE	NOONTIDE	NUCLEIDE
PULICIDE	RATICIDE	REGICIDE	SELENIDE	SILICIDE	SODAMIDE	SUBOXIDE
THIAZIDE	VATICIDE	VIRICIDE	VIRUCIDE	VITICIDE		

IE

AGACERIE	BATTERIE	BHEESTIE	*BOERTJIE*	BOISERIE	BONHOMIE	BOUDERIE
BRUILZIE	CAUSERIE	CAVIARIE	CHRISTIE	CREPERIE	CROSSTIEd	*CUDGERIE*
FANTASIEd	FISNOMIE	FLANERIE	FOEDARIE	GRUMPHIE	INTERTIE	JALOUSIEd
KILLOGIE	MALVESIE	METAIRIE	*NAARTJIE*	*NOSHERIE*	OBSEQUIE	ORGANDIE
PATOOTIE	*PERENTIE*	PLURISIE	POLLICIE	RAMILLIE	*SCHOOLIE*	*SCREENIE*
SHREWDIE	SQUADDIE	*STOUSHIE*	SWELCHIE	TIRRIVIE	VALKYRIE	VISNOMIE
WALKYRIE	WASTERIE	WHOOPSIE				

IER *excluding extensions of verbs*

BENITIER	BOURSIER	CAPONIERe	CATBRIER	CLOTHIER	COURTIER	DESTRIER
DOUANIER	FUSILIER	GASALIER	GASELIER	GASOLIER	HUISSIER	LAVALIERe
MOTELIER	NONSKIER	PEDALIER	QUARTIER	RECAMIER	ROTURIER	SABOTIER
SANGLIER						

ILE

BACKFILE	*ENOPHILE*	EOLIPILE	EOLOPILE	EREWHILE	LAETRILE	*METAFILE*
NAILFILE	NARGHILE	NEOPHILE	QUANTILE	QUARTILE	QUINTILE	SANDPILE
SERAFILE	SYMPHILE	WOODPILE	ZOOPHILE			

8. Eight-Letter Words

INE *excluding 'LINE'*

AEGIRINE	ALGERINE	AMANDINE	ANDESINE	ANSERINE	ARGININE	ARMOZINE
ASTATINE	ATHERINE	ATRAZINE	BAREGINE	BASQUINE	BULLGINE	CAMPHINE
COTININE	CURARINE	CYTIDINE	CYTISINE	CYTOKINE	CYTOSINE	DATURINE
DOPAMINE	DRAISINE	DUVETINE	EKTEXINE	ENDEXINE	EXOCRINE	*EYESHINE*
FREDAINE	GLASSINE	HYOSCINE	IBOGAINE	KEROSINE	KREATINE	LEMURINE
LINGUINE	LUSTRINE	MAZARINE	*MONOKINE*	MURRHINE	PALATINE	PELERINE
POITRINE	POULAINE	PROCAINE	PYRIDINE	PYRONINE	RABATINE	SANIDINE
SCIURINE	SEROTINE	SIMAZINE	SMALTINE	SOURDINE	SPERMINE	STOVAINE
SYCAMINE	TARWHINE	TELECINE	THEBAINE	TYRAMINE	TYROSINE	

ING *excluding 'LING'*

ALIASING	ANTIKING	BANXRING	*BEESTING*	BEESWING	BIRDWING	BITEWING
BLOGRING	*BLONDING*	BLUEWING	BULLRING	BUTCHING	*COFIRING*	CORKWING
CROFTING	DAIRYING	FOREKING	FOREWING	GREESING	GRESSING	HEADRING
HINDWING	LACEWING	LEGERING	MARAGING	NAETHING	NIDERING	NONBEING
OVERKING	PARAWING	PFENNING	SALADING	SALERING	SHOWRING	SKIORING
SMIRTING	*SMURFING*	SPONSING	TJANTING	TRITHING	*TWOCKING*	UPMAKING
WAYGOING	WINGDING	YELDRING	YOLDRING			

ION *excluding 'ATION'*

ADAPTION	ALLERION	ALLUSION	ALLUVION	ANNEXION	APHELION	AVOISION
AVULSION	COOPTION	DECURION	DILUVION	DISUNION	ECLOSION	EDUCTION
EGESTION	EMULSION	ENACTION	EPYLLION	ETHERION	EVECTION	EVULSION
EXACTION	FALCHION	FAUCHION	FENTHION	GANGLION	GNATHION	*GRILLION*
GUMPHION	ILLISION	INFIXION	INFUSION	INHESION	INUSTION	IRRISION
LENITION	LOCUTION	MELODION	MISUNION	MONITION	NOLITION	NONUNION
ORILLION	PANCHION	PRESSION	*QUARRION*	RECISION	REFUSION	SCALLION
SCANSION	SCONTION	SKILLION	*SKYRMION*	SORPTION	SPONSION	STICTION
STILLION	SWAPTION	THERMION	VOCALION	VOLUTION		

IS+

ADENITIS+	ALPHOSIS+	AORTITIS+	*BAVAROIS+*	BOTRYTIS+	BURSITIS+	CARDITIS+
CLITORIS+	COLPITIS+	CYSTITIS+	*DARTITIS+*	ECLIPSIS+	ENDEIXIS+	ENURESIS+
EUCHARIS+	*FASCITIS+*	KURTOSIS+	MASTITIS+	MEPHITISm	METRITIS+	MYELITIS+
MYOSITIS+	MYOSOTIS+	NEURITIS+	NOTORNIS+	ORCHITIS+	OSTEITIS+	OVARITIS+
PANMIXIS+	PARDALIS+	PHYLAXIS+	PHYLESIS+	PHYSALIS+	PYELITIS+	RACHITIS+
RECTITIS+	REVERSIS+	RHINITIS+	SAMNITIS+	SINUITIS+	SPARAXIS+	SUBCUTIS+
SYNTEXIS+	THELITIS+	TURQUOISe	TYRANNISe	UTERITIS+	UVULITIS+	

ISM

ACROTISM	ACTINISM	ACTIVISM	ALBINISM	ALGORISM	ALIENISM	ALLELISM
ALPINISM	ALTRUISM	APHORISM	APTERISM	ARCHAISM	ASTERISM	ATTICISM
AUTECISM	*BINARISM*	BOGEYISM	BOTULISM	BOYARISM	BULLYISM	CABALISM
CHARTISM	CLIQUISM	COLORISM	CRONYISM	CULLYISM	DANDYISM	DEVILISM
DIOECISM	DIRIGISMe	DITHEISM	DONATISM	DOWDYISM	DRUDGISM	DRUIDISM
DWARFISM	EBIONISM	ENTRYISM	EPIZOISM	ERETHISM	ERGOTISM	ETHERISM
ETHICISM	EUGENISM	EUPHUISM	FAIRYISM	FAKIRISM	FARADISM	FATALISM
FINITISM	FOGEYISM	FUTURISM	GIANTISM	HEDONISM	HELOTISM	HYLICISM

IDIOTISM	INCIVISM	IOTACISM	JINGOISM	*KABALISM*	*LABORISM*	LACONISM
LEGALISM	LOCALISM	LOGICISM	*LOOKSISM*	LOYALISM	LYRICISM	*NASALISM*
NATIVISM	NATURISM	NAVALISM	NEGROISM	NEPHRISM	NIHILISM	NOVELISM
OBEAHISM	OCKERISM	PAEANISM	PAGANISM	PALUDISM	PARECISM	PARTYISM
PELORISM	PETALISM	PEYOTISM	PHALLISM	PHRENISM	POLONISM	PRIGGISM
PROSAISM	PSELLISM	PSYCHISM	PTYALISM	PUGILISM	*QABALISM*	QUACKISM
QUIETISM	REGALISM	RIGHTISM	RIGORISM	ROBOTISM	ROWDYISM	ROYALISM
RURALISM	SAINTISM	SATANISM	SAVAGISM	SCIOLISM	SCRIBISM	SINAPISM
SOLARISM	SOLECISM	SOLIDISM	STOICISM	STRABISM	SWINGISM	SYBOTISM
TANTRISM	TERATISM	THUGGISM	TIGERISM	TOADYISM	TOTALISM	TRIADISM
TRIALISM	TROILISM	TUTORISM	ULTRAISM	UNDINISM	UNTRUISM	URBANISM
VEGANISM	VIRILISM	VITALISM	VOCALISM	VOLTAISM	*XANTHISM*	YAHOOISM

IST

ALIENIST	ALPINIST	ALTRUIST	ANNALIST	APHORIST	AQUARIST	ARBALIST
ARBORIST	ARCANIST	ARCHAIST	ARMORIST	ATTICIST	*AVANTIST*	AVIARIST
BANJOIST	BONGOIST	BURINIST	CABALIST	CALORIST	CANOEIST	CANONIST
CENTOIST	CERAMIST	CHARTIST	CIVILIST	COLORIST	CREOLIST	DEMONIST
DEMOTIST	DIALLIST	DIGAMIST	DITHEIST	DUELLIST	DUETTIST	DYNAMIST
ENTRYIST	ERRORIST	ETHERIST	ETHICIST	EUGENIST	EULOGIST	EUPHUIST
FABULIST	FIGURIST	FLAUTIST	FUTURIST	GARAGISTe	GROUPIST	HAGADIST
HALAKIST	HANDLIST	HOMILIST	HYGIEIST	HYLICIST	HYPOCIST	IDYLLIST
INTIMISTe	JINGOIST	*KABALIST*	*LABORIST*	LAPIDIST	LEGALIST	LIBELIST
LOCALIST	LOGICIST	LOYALIST	LUMINIST	LUNARIST	LUTANIST	LUTENIST
LUXURIST	LYRICIST	MELANIST	MELODIST	METALIST	MODALIST	MODELIST
MONODIST	MURALIST	NATIVIST	NATURIST	NEPOTIST	NIELLIST	NIHILIST
ODONTIST	OGHAMIST	OPTICIST	PAGANIST	PARODIST	PEYOTIST	PHALLIST
POLEMIST	PROSAIST	PSALMIST	PSYCHIST	PUCKFIST	PUGILIST	*QABALIST*
QUIETIST	RALLYIST	REGALIST	REVERIST	RIGHTIST	RIGORIST	RURALIST
SARODIST	SATANIST	SCIOLIST	SEMITIST	*SHITLIST*	SHOOTIST	SILURIST
SIMONIST	SIMPLISTe	SITARIST	SODALIST	SODOMIST	SOLARIST	SOLECIST
SOLIDIST	SOMATIST	TANGOIST	TENORIST	TOTALIST	TOTEMIST	TRIADIST
TRIALIST	TROILIST	ULTRAIST	URBANIST	VEGETIST	VISAGISTe	VITALIST
VOLUMIST	VOTARIST	*WOMANIST*				

ITE

ADAMSITE	AEGIRITE	AEROLITE	ALLANITE	AMBERITE	ANALCITE	ANDESITE
ANKERITE	APHANITE	ARGYRITE	ARSENITE	ARSONITE	AUTUNITE	AYENBITE
BACULITE	*BAKELITE*	BASANITE	BEAUXITE	BOEHMITE	BORACITE	BRAUNITE
BRONZITE	BROOKITE	CALAMITE	CATAMITE	CENOBITE	CERUSITE	CHEDDITE
CHLORITE	CHROMITE	CIMINITE	CIMOLITE	CLEVEITE	CRYOLITE	DATOLITE
DENDRITE	DOLERITE	DOLOMITE	*DUMPSITE*	ECLOGITE	EKLOGITE	ELVANITE
ENARGITE	EPITRITE	EPIZOITE	EPSOMITE	ERIONITE	ESSONITE	EUTAXITE
EUXENITE	FAYALITE	FLINKITE	FLUORITE	FUCHSITE	GALENITE	GNATHITE
GOBSHITE	GOETHITE	GYROLITE	HELLKITE	HEMATITE	HEPATITE	HOMESITE
ILMENITE	IODYRITE	JAROSITE	KALINITE	KAMACITE	KRYOLITE	LABORITE
LATERITE	LAZULITE	LEWISITE	LIMONITE	LIPARITE	LOCALITE	*MASONITE*
MEIONITE	MELANITE	MELILITE	MELINITE	*MENILITE*	MESOLITE	MONAZITE
MYLONITE	NEPHRITE	NOSELITE	ONYCHITE	OVERBITE	PARAKITE	PEARLITE

8. Eight-Letter Words

PERTHITE	PHENGITE	PHYLLITE	PICOTITE	PISOLITE	PLUMBITE	PREHNITE
PUMICITE	QUEENITE	RETINITE	RHYOLITE	ROBURITE	ROLAMITE	SAGENITE
SAPONITE	SAXONITE	SCAWTITE	SCLERITE	SEABLITE	SELENITE	SERICITE
SIDERITE	SINOPITE	SMALTITE	SMECTITE	SODALITE	SODOMITE	STANNITE
STEATITE	*STELLITE*	STERNITE	STIBNITE	STILBITE	SULPHITE	SYBARITE
TENORITE	TEPHRITE	TITANITE	TONALITE	TOTEMITE	TRICHITE	TRIPLITE
TROCHITE	TROILITE	UINTAITE	UMANGITE	URBANITE	*VEGEMITE*	VIRIDITE
WELLSITE	WURTZITE	XYLONITE	ZARATITE	ZYLONITE		

ITY+

ACERBITY+	ACRIDITY+	ADUNCITY+	ALGIDITY+	ALTERITY+	ASPERITY+	ASTUCITY+
AURALITY+	AXIALITY+	BASICITY+	BIFIDITY+	BOVINITY+	CALIDITY+	CANINITY+
CELERITY+	CUPIDITY+	DUMOSITY+	EQUINITY+	EXIGUITY+	FELICITY+	FELINITY+
FEMALITY+	FEMINITY+	FERACITY+	*FETIDITY+*	FLUIDITY+	FORTUITY+	FUGACITY+
FUMOSITY+	FURACITY+	FUTURITY+	GELIDITY+	GULOSITY+	HELICITY+	IDEALITY+
IDONEITY+	IMPARITY+	INTIMITY+	INVERITY+	IONICITY+	JOCOSITY+	LANOSITY+
LATINITY+	LEGERITY+	LIVIDITY+	LUCIDITY+	MEGACITY+	MINACITY+	MODALITY+
MOLALITY+	MOLARITY+	MORONITY+	MOROSITY+	MOTILITY+	MOTIVITY+	MUCIDITY+
MUCOSITY+	MULTEITY+	NASALITY+	NATALITY+	NIHILITY+	NODALITY+	NODOSITY+
NUBILITY+	OBTUSITY+	ORGANITY+	OTIOSITY+	PENALITY+	PERSEITY+	PILOSITY+
PUDICITY+	QUEERITY+	RABIDITY+	RAMOSITY+	RAPACITY+	RIMOSITY+	RIVALITY+
RUGOSITY+	RURALITY+	SAGACITY+	SALACITY+	SAPIDITY+	SATANITY+	SCANTITY+
SEDULITY+	SEROSITY+	SODALITY+	*SODICITY+*	SONORITY+	TEPIDITY+	TONALITY+
TONICITY+	TOROSITY+	TOXICITY+	TRIALITY+	TRIUNITY+	TUMIDITY+	UBIQUITY+
UNFIXITY+	URBANITY+	VAPIDITY+	VELLEITY+	VENALITY+	VENOSITY+	VINOSITY+
VERACITY+	VIRIDITY+	VOCALITY+	VORACITY+			

IUM

ACHENIUM	ACTINIUM	ALLODIUM	BDELLIUM	BIENNIUM	BOTHRIUM	CALADIUM
CORONIUM	DILUVIUM	ERYNGIUM	EULOGIUM	EUROPIUM	EXORDIUM	FRANCIUM
GRAPHIUM	HELENIUM	ILLINIUM	ILLUVIUM	INDICIUM	INGENIUM	LIXIVIUM
LUTECIUM	LUTETIUM	NEBULIUM	NOBELIUM	ONCIDIUM	ONYCHIUM	OOGONIUM
OPSONIUM	ORDALIUM	OSSARIUM	PERIDIUM	POLONIUM	PSYLLIUM	PYGIDIUM
RANARIUM	ROSARIUM	RUBIDIUM	SCANDIUM	SCHOLIUM	SILICIUM	SILPHIUM
SPLENIUM	THALLIUM	TRILLIUM	*UNUNBIUM*	VANADIUM	VENIDIUM	

IVE

ABESSIVE	ABLATIVE	ADESSIVE	AGENTIVE	ALLATIVE	AUDITIVE	CURATIVE
DONATIVE	DURATIVE	EJECTIVE	ERGATIVE	FIXATIVE	GENITIVE	ILLATIVE
INESSIVE	LENITIVE	LOCATIVE	OPTATIVE	QUIETIVE	TOTITIVE	

KIN

BAUDEKIN	BEARSKIN	BOOTIKIN	BRODEKIN	CALFSKIN	CANNIKIN	CAPESKIN
CIDERKIN	COONSKIN	COOTIKIN	CUITIKIN	DEERSKIN	DEVILKIN	DUNNAKIN
FISHSKIN	GOATSKIN	MANNIKIN	MOUSEKIN	MUNCHKIN	MUTCHKIN	PANNIKIN
PONYSKIN	SEALSKIN	SPILIKIN	SWANSKIN	THUMBKIN	TURNSKIN	WINESKIN
WOLFSKIN	WOODSKIN	WOOLSKIN				

LAND

BACKLAND	BOOKLAND	CLUBLAND	CORNLAND	CROPLAND	DOCKLAND	DOWNLAND
DUNELAND	EASTLAND	FILMLAND	FLATLAND	FOLKLAND	FORELAND	GANGLAND
LACKLAND	LAKELAND	MOORLAND	MOSSLAND	*PEATLAND*	PINELAND	PLAYLAND
PORTLAND	SCABLAND	SHETLAND	SLOBLAND	SNOWLAND	SOAPLAND	TIDELAND
TOWNLAND	WASHLAND	WILDLAND	YARDLAND			

LET

BANDELET	BARRULET	BRACTLET	BROOKLET	CAPELLET	CHAINLET	CHEVALET
CLOUDLET	CORSELET	COURTLET	CROSSLET	CROWNLET	DRUPELET	FLAMELET
FRONTLET	FRUITLET	GREENLET	GROUPLET	HEARTLET	HERBELET	LANCELET
MANTELET	MIQUELET	MURRELET	NERVELET	*PANTALET*	PLANTLET	PLUMELET
QUEENLET	RECOLLET	RONDELET	SEXTOLET	*SPIRELET*	*STATELET*	SWIFTLET
TERCELET	TROUTLET	UMBELLET	VERSELET	WRISTLET		

LINE

BALKLINE	*BASSLINE*	BELTLINE	BLUELINEr	BUNTLINE	CAMELINE	*CARELINE*
CONTLINE	COTELINE	FIGULINE	FISHLINE	GANTLINE	GIRTLINE	ISOCLINE
LOBELINE	LONGLINE	PEMOLINE	PLOTLINE	TAPELINE	*TIDELINE*	TRAPLINE
TROTLINE	TUMPLINE	*VASELINE*	ZIBELINE			

LING

ATHELING	BANTLING	BARDLING	BRISLING	CAGELING	CYMBLING	DEARLING
DUKELING	FLATLING	FROGLING	GNATLING	GOATLING	HIRELING	*HOTELING*
KINGLING	LORDLING	MORTLING	OUTFLING	PORKLING	QUISLING	RECKLING
REEDLING	RIDGLING	ROCKLING	SAIBLING	SANDLING	SNOBLING	SOFTLING
SPERLING	SPIRLING	TIRELING	TOWNLING	TWINLING	WHITLING	WILDLING
WISELING	WOLFLING					

MENT

ABETMENT	AGREMENT	ALAIMENT	ATRAMENT	AVERMENT	*BASHMENT*	BATEMENT
BODEMENT	CEREMENT	CLOYMENT	FAKEMENT	GAZEMENT	LAVEMENT	NEEDMENT
ORPIMENT	PARAMENTa	PEDIMENT	SEPIMENT	SORTMENT	VIREMENT	VIZAMENT
WARIMENT	WELDMENT					

NESS+

ACHINESS+	ACIDNESS+	AGEDNESS+	AIRINESS+	ALBINESS+	ARCHNESS+	ARIDNESS+
ARTINESS+	AVIDNESS+	AWAYNESS+	BARENESS+	BEINNESS+	BLUENESS+	BONINESS+
BOXINESS+	CAGINESS+	CAGYNESS+	*CAKINESS+*	CAMPNESS+	CANONESS+	COXINESS+
COZINESS+	CURTNESS+	CUTENESS+	DAFTNESS+	DANKNESS+	DEADNESS+	DEARNESS+
DEEPNESS+	DEMONESS+	DEWINESS+	DIRENESS+	DOPINESS+	DOWFNESS+	DOZINESS+
DRABNESS+	DUMBNESS+	EERINESS+	EVILNESS+	EYEDNESS+	FAINNESS+	FELLNESS+
FINENESS+	FOXINESS+	FOZINESS+	FREENESS+	GAMENESS+	GAMYNESS+	GLADNESS+
GLEGNESS+	GLIBNESS+	*GLUINESS+*	GLUMNESS+	*GOOINESS+*	GORINESS+	GRAYNESS+
GREYNESS+	GRIMNESS+	HALENESS+	HALFNESS+	HAZINESS+	HERENESS+	HOKINESS+
HUGENESS+	ICKINESS+	INKINESS+	IRONNESS+	JIMPNESS+	JOKINESS+	LACINESS+
LAMENESS+	LANKNESS+	LEANNESS+	LEWDNESS+	LIMINESS+	*LITENESS+*	LIVENESS+
LOGINESS+	LONGNESS+	LORNNESS+	*LOTHNESS+*	*LUNINESS+*	MALENESS+	MATINESS+
MAZINESS+	MEEKNESS+	MEETNESS+	MIRINESS+	*MOOTNESS+*	*MOPINESS+*	*MORENESS+*

8. Eight-Letter Words

MUCHNESS+ MUTENESS+ *NAIFNESS+* NEARNESS+ NEXTNESS+ NIGHNESS+ NUDENESS+
NULLNESS+ OILINESS+ OOZINESS+ OVALNESS+ PACKNESS+ PERTNESS+ PIEDNESS+
PINKNESS+ PIXINESS+ POKINESS+ POORNESS+ PORINESS+ PRIMNESS+ PUNINESS+
PURENESS+ RACINESS+ RANKNESS+ REALNESS+ RIFENESS+ RIMINESS+ RIPENESS+
ROPINESS+ TAMENESS+ TARTNESS+ TAUTNESS+ THATNESS+ TININESS+ TITANESS+
TRIGNESS+ TRIMNESS+ TWEENESS+ VAINNESS+ VILDNESS+ VILENESS+ VOIDNESS+
WARINESS+ WAVINESS+ WAXINESS+ WHATNESS+ WIDENESS+ WILINESS+ WIRINESS+
WOODNESS+ WORNNESS+ ZANINESS+

ODE
ANTINODE ANTIPODE ARILLODE CENTRODE NEMATODE PALINODE PHYLLODE
RHAPSODE THRENODE

OGY+
AEROLOGY+ AGROLOGY+ ALGOLOGY+ APIOLOGY+ ARCOLOGY+ AREOLOGY+ ATMOLOGY+
AUTOLOGY+ AXIOLOGY+ BATOLOGY+ CETOLOGY+ CHAOLOGY+ *CODOLOGY+* DEKALOGY+
DEMOLOGY+ DOSOLOGY+ DOXOLOGY+ ETHOLOGY+ ETIOLOGY+ FETOLOGY+ GEMOLOGY+
IDEALOGY+ KIDOLOGY+ MISOLOGY+ MIXOLOGY+ NOMOLOGY+ NOSOLOGY+ OINOLOGY+
ONTOLOGY+ OPTOLOGY+ OREOLOGY+ PARALOGY+ PEDOLOGY+ PELOLOGY+ PODOLOGY+
POMOLOGY+ POSOLOGY+ RHEOLOGY+ SEROLOGY+ SEXOLOGY+ SINOLOGY+ SITOLOGY+
TOCOLOGY+ TOKOLOGY+ VINOLOGY+ VIROLOGY+

OID
ACTINOID ALKALOID AMBEROID AUTACOID AUTOCOID BLASTOID CAMELOID
CARDIOID CATENOID CHORIOID CLUPEOID COTYLOID DORIDOID ECHINOID
EMBRYOID EMULSOID GROUPOID HELICOID HOMALOID HOMINOID HUMANOID
HYRACOID INDIGOID LEMUROID LIMULOID MEDUSOID MELANOID NUCLEOID
ODONTOID OMOHYOID PAROTOID PHYLLOID PINACOID PINAKOID PLASMOID
PRISMOID PSYCHOID PYRENOID RESINOID RETINOID RHABDOID SCAPHOID
SESAMOID SILUROID SINUSOID *SLEAZOID* SPHENOID SPHEROID THYREOID
TRENDOID TRIPLOIDy TROCHOID *VIRUSOID*

ONE *excluding 'STONE' endings*
AEROTONE *ALLOMONE* AQUATONE ARGEMONE BUTANONE *CAMPHONE* *CARPHONE*
CHINBONE CORNPONE *CUMARONE* DIAPHONE EDGEBONE *ETHONONE* GEOPHONE
HALAZONE HALFTONE *ISOPHONE* NALOXONE *REALTONE* RINGBONE *RINGTONE*
ROTENONE SEMITONE SULPHONE TRIPHONE *WOODTONE* XANTHONE ZABAIONE
ZABAJONE

OON
BIGAROON *BOSTHOON* CRAMPOON DOUBLOON DUCATOON FORENOON FRONTOON
GAMBROON GOMBROON OCTAROON OCTOROON POLTROON QUADROON RIGADOON
SHAGROON SHALLOON SPADROON TENOROON

OR
ACTUATOR ADDUCTOR ADJUSTOR ADULATORy *ALACHLOR* ARRESTOR ASPERSORy
ASSENTOR ASSERTORy ASSIGNOR ATTESTOR AVIGATOR BARRATOR BARRETOR
BISECTOR CANEPHORa CANEPHORe *CATAPHOR* CAVEATOR CHELATOR CODEBTOR
COFACTOR COLESSOR COLLATOR COPASTOR CREMATORy CURSITORy CUSPIDORe

236

DEFLATOR	DEPICTOR	*DETRUSOR*	DEVIATORy	DIGESTOR	ELICITOR	EMANATORy
EMBRASOR	EMULATOR	ENDORSOR	EPILATOR	EVOCATORy	EXCEPTOR	EXPANDOR
EXPIATORy	EXTENSOR	FELLATOR	GILLYVOR	HELIODOR	HYDRATOR	IDOLATOR
IMITATOR	IMPACTOR	IMPELLOR	INCENSORy	INCEPTOR	INDENTOR	INDICTOR
INDORSOR	INDUCTOR	INFECTOR	INFLATOR	INJECTOR	INVERTOR	IODOPHOR
ISOLATOR	KOMONDOR	KURVEYOR	LAUDATORy	LICENSOR	MAINDOOR	MANDATORy
MARKHOOR	MIGRATORy	NITRATOR	NONACTOR	NONCOLOR	NONJUROR	NONMAJOR
OBJECTOR	OBVIATOR	PARACHOR	PATENTOR	PISCATORy	PLEDGEOR	PRODITORy
PROMISOR	PROMOTOR	PRONATOR	PROVEDORe	PROVIDOR	PULMOTOR	PULSATORy
PURVEYOR	QUAESTOR	RECAPTOR	RECEPTOR	REDACTOR	REGRATOR	RELEASOR
REMITTOR	RONCADOR	SECRETORy	SECTATOR	SEIGNIORy	SERVITOR	SUBFLOOR
SUBPRIOR	TESTATOR	THRUSTOR	TITRATOR	TRADITOR	TRICOLOR	TRIMOTOR
URINATOR	UTILIDOR	VARACTOR	VARISTOR	VERDEROR	VIOLATOR	VITIATOR

ORY+

ALEATORY+	FERETORY+	FILATORY+	FUMATORY+	FUMITORY+	HERSTORY+	ISOSPORY+
LOCUTORY+	MIDSTORY+	NONSTORY+	OMNIVORY+	SEIGNORY+	SUDATORY+	VANITORY+
VOMITORY+	ZOOCHORY+					

OSE

ACARBOSE	ALBUMOSE	BLUENOSEd	BULLNOSE	BURNOOSEd	*CAMBOOSE*	CONENOSE
DEXTROSE	EXOSMOSE	FRUCTOSE	FURANOSE	HARDNOSEd	HAWKNOSE	HOOKNOSEd
KERATOSE	LEVULOSE	MEGADOSE	MUNGOOSE	PARCLOSE	PROTEOSE	PYRANOSE
RHAMNOSE	ROCKROSE	SECALOSE	STARNOSE	TORULOSE	TUBENOSE	TUBEROSE
WAYGOOSE						

OUT

BROWNOUT	BULLPOUT	CARRYOUT	CLOSEOUT	FLAMEOUT	FREAKOUT	HORNPOUT
PHASEOUT	PITCHOUT	RACAHOUT	SEASCOUT	SHAKEOUT	SPEAKOUT	STICKOUT
TACAHOUT	WATCHOUT	WHITEOUT				

OVER

BOILOVER	*COMBOVER*	*COMEOVER*	FLOPOVER	HOLDOVER	*LOOKOVER*	ROLLOVER
SLIPOVER	*STEPOVER*	WINGOVER	WRAPOVER			

RY+ *excluding 'BERRY', 'ARY', 'ERY' and 'ORY'*

ADVOUTRY+	BALLADRY+	BANDITRY+	BARRATRY+	BARRETRY+	BASKETRY+	BIOMETRY+
BISTOURY+	BLAZONRY+	BOTTOMRY+	BRAZENRY+	CALENDRY+	CANNONRY+	CHAPELRY+
CHAUNTRY+	CHOULTRY+	COQUETRY+	CORSETRY+	COUSINRY+	COWARDRY+	DEACONRY+
DEVILTRY+	ERRANTRY+	EXECUTRY+	FAGGOTRY+	GADGETRY+	GANNETRY+	GEOLATRY+
GOSSIPRY+	HARLOTRY+	HAZARDRY+	HERMITRY+	HOSTELRY+	IDOLATRY+	ISOMETRY+
JESUITRY+	LEGENDRY+	MANSONRY+	MISANDRY+	MISENTRY+	MISSILRY+	MONANDRY+
MUSKETRY+	NONENTRY+	NOOMETRY+	ODOMETRY+	OUTLAWRY+	PARROTRY+	PEDANTRY+
PIGEONRY+	PUNDITRY+	QUIXOTRY+	RACKETRY+	REINJURY+	REVESTRY+	RIBALDRY+
RIBAUDRY+	ROCKETRY+	SLOVENRY+	SUBENTRY+	TANISTRY+	TARTANRY+	TENANTRY+
TINSELRY+	TRUANTRY+	UDOMETRY+	VARLETRY+	VASSALRY+	WARDENRY+	WIZARDRY+
YEOMANRY+	ZEALOTRY+	ZOOLATRY+	ZOOMETRY+			

8. Eight-Letter Words

SHIP
BARDSHIP	CLANSHIP	DEANSHIP	DEMYSHIP	DOGESHIP	DUKESHIP	EARLSHIP
FIRESHIP	FORESHIP	GURUSHIP	KINGSHIP	LONGSHIP	MAGESHIP	RAJASHIP
SERFSHIP	TANKSHIP	TREESHIP	TWINSHIP	WARDSHIP	WINDSHIP	

SIDE
BANKSIDE	BURNSIDE	CURBSIDE	DIOPSIDE	DOCKSIDE	*FLIPSIDE*	FORESIDE
IRONSIDE	KINGSIDE	LAKESIDE	LANDSIDE	*OPENSIDE*	OVERSIDE	QUAYSIDE
SHIPSIDE	WEAKSIDE					

SOME
ACROSOME	AUTOSOME	CYTOSOME	ENDOSOME	*GONOSOME*	LIPOSOME	LYSOSOME
POLYSOME	PYROSOME	RIBOSOME				

STER *not derived from verbs*
BALUSTER	BANDSTER	BANGSTER	BIMESTER	BREWSTER	CADASTER	CANASTER
CYTASTER	DEEMSTER	DEMPSTER	DOOMSTER	DOPESTER	FILISTER	*FUNKSTER*
GAMESTER	GANISTER	GOADSTER	GONGSTER	HOOPSTER	*HYPESTER*	JOKESTER
LAMISTER	LEWDSTER	LINGSTER	LINKSTER	MALTSTER	MUENSTER	OLEASTER
PILASTER	PINASTER	POLLSTER	QUIPSTER	RIMESTER	RINGSTER	ROADSTER
SCAMSTER	SEAMSTER	SEMPSTER	SONGSTER	TEAMSTER	TONGSTER	WHITSTER

STONE
BURSTONE	CAMSTONE	CAPSTONE	EARSTONE	EYESTONE	FELSTONE	GUNSTONE
ICESTONE	INKSTONE	LAPSTONE	OILSTONE	POTSTONE	RAGSTONE	ROESTONE
RUBSTONE	SUNSTONE	TINSTONE	TOPSTONE			

ULE
AEDICULE	AMYGDULE	*DIGITULE*	FLOSCULE	FOOTRULE	FRUSTULE	GLANDULE
LODICULE	OPERCULE	OPUSCULE	PLANTULE	PUNCTULE	RADICULE	RETICULE
SILICULE	SPANSULE	SPHERULE	SQUAMULE	VAGINULE		

UM *excluding IUM*
ACONITUM	AGERATUM	ALBURNUM	ARGENTUM	ATHENEUM	BLACKGUM	CEREBRUM
COAGULUM	COLISEUM	CORUNDUM	DELUBRUM	DIESTRUM	ELECTRUM	FACTOTUM
FRENULUM	GALBANUM	GLUCINUM	GUAIACUM	GUAIOCUM	INOCULUM	LABDANUM
LABURNUM	LAUDANUM	NGULTRUM	OLIBANUM	ORIGANUM	PERINEUM	PLASTRUM
RESIDUUM	SAECULUM	SCALPRUM	SCHELLUM	SPECULUM	SPHAGNUM	STRIATUM
TANTALUM	TEETOTUM	TENENDUM	TESTATUM	*TILLICUM*	TRITICUM	VARIORUM
VASCULUM	VERATRUM	VIATICUM	VIBURNUM	VINCULUM		

URE
ARCATURE	CEINTURE	CISELURE	CUBATURE	CYNOSURE	DOUBLURE	ENACTURE
ENCOLURE	FILATURE	FIXATURE	GENITURE	*HUMITURE*	INCISURE	LINCTURE
OSSATURE	PAINTURE	REPOSURE	ROUNDURE	SCRIMURE	SINECURE	TAINTURE
TOURNURE	TRESSUREd	TUBULURE				

US+

ABOMASUS+ AMARACUS+ AMIANTUS+ AMPLEXUS+ ARQUEBUS+ CATHETUS+ CHORAGUS+
CHOREGUS+ COTTABUS+ CREPITUS+ DIANTHUS+ DIESTRUS+ DOCHMIUS+ ENCARPUS+
ENTELLUS+ EUONYMUS+ EVONYMUS+ EXCURSUS+ FREMITUS+ HEMIONUS+ INFLATUS+
LATHYRUS+ LIQUIDUS+ MICROBUS+ MODIOLUS+ MOTORBUS+ NUMINOUS+ OPINICUS+
OVERPLUS+ PANDANUS+ PERONEUS+ PODARGUS+ PORTEOUS+ POXVIRUS+ PROVIRUS+
PRURITUS+ REOVIRUS+ RHIZOPUS+ SCABIOUS+ SCIRRHUS+ SERRATUS+ SPHYGMUS+
SPIRITUS+ SPLENIUS+ STROMBUS+ SUBGENUS+ *SUBVIRUS+* SURCULUS+ TANTALUS+
TENESMUS+ TINNITUS+ TROLLIUS+ URCEOLUS+ VITELLUS+ *WATERBUS+*

WARD

BEARWARD EASTWARD GOALWARD *HEADWARD* HELLWARD HIVEWARD LANDWARD
LEFTWARD MOONWARD PARKWARD REARWARD REREWARD SELFWARD SIDEWARD

WARE

BAKEWARE CANEWARE *CAREWARE* CLAYWARE DISHWARE FIRMWARE FLATWARE
FREEWARE GIFTWARE *HOMEWARE* IRONWARE LIVEWARE SLIPWARE STEMWARE
TOLEWARE *TREEWARE*

WAY

CABLEWAY CARRAWAY *COLORWAY* CROSSWAY *DRANGWAY* FADEAWAY FALLAWAY
FLOODWAY FOLDAWAY GREENWAY GUIDEWAY HEREAWAY HOISTWAY HORSEWAY
HUNTAWAY LOCKAWAY MULLOWAY RIDGEWAY RIVERWAY ROCKAWAY ROLLAWAY
ROUTEWAY SLIDEWAY SOAKAWAY STERNWAY TEARAWAY TRACKWAY TRAINWAY

WEED

AGUEWEED BINDWEED BLUEWEED BULLWEED DANEWEED DEERWEED DUCKWEED
FIREWEED GOATWEED GULFWEED HEMPWEED IRONWEED ITCHWEED KNAPWEED
KNOTWEED LOCOWEED MILKWEED NECKWEED POKEWEED PONDWEED RICHWEED
ROCKWEED SILKWEED SNAPWEED SUMPWEED

WOOD

AGALWOOD BACKWOOD BASSWOOD BEARWOOD BEEFWOOD BENTWOOD BLUEWOOD
COLTWOOD CORDWOOD CORKWOOD *CRABWOOD* FUELWOOD HAREWOOD IRONWOOD
KINGWOOD LACEWOOD LATEWOOD MILKWOOD OVENWOOD *PEARWOOD* PINEWOOD
PORKWOOD ROSEWOOD SOURWOOD TEAKWOOD

WORK

BEADWORK BUHLWORK BUSYWORK CAGEWORK CAPEWORK CASEWORK DUCTWORK
FLATWORK FLUEWORK FRETWORK *GOLDWORK* HAIRWORK HEADWORK HORNWORK
IRONWORK LACEWORK LATHWORK LEADWORK LIFEWORK MESHWORK MILLWORK
OPENWORK PILEWORK RINGWORK ROPEWORK SALTWORK SEATWORK SLOPWORK
STUDWORK TIMEWORK TUBEWORK YARDWORK

WORT

BELLWORT COLEWORT DAMEWORT DANEWORT DROPWORT FLEAWORT GOUTWORT
HONEWORT HORNWORT LEADWORT LUNGWORT MILKWORT MODIWORT MOONWORT
MOORWORT PILEWORT PILLWORT SALTWORT SANDWORT SOAPWORT STARWORT

YARD

BALLYARD	BOATYARD	BONEYARD	COALYARD	DEERYARD	DOCKYARD	DOORYARD
FEEDYARD	FOREYARD	HAULYARD	KAILYARD	KALEYARD	MAINYARD	METEYARD
RICKYARD	SAVOYARD	SHIPYARD	SHOWYARD	TILTYARD	WHINYARD	WOODYARD

8.3.4 NON-PLURALS BY COMMON ENDINGS

ABLE

AGITABLE	ALLIABLE	AMUSABLE	ATONABLE	AVOWABLE	CALLABLE	CARTABLE
CASHABLE	CAUSABLE	CITEABLE	COINABLE	COOKABLE	*COPYABLE*	CUTTABLE
DAMNABLE	DATEABLE	DENIABLE	DIGGABLE	DRAPABLE	DRAWABLE	DUTIABLE
EDITABLE	ERASABLE	*ERODABLE*	EVADABLE	EVITABLE	*EXILABLE*	EXORABLE
EXPIABLE	FACEABLE	FARMABLE	FEEDABLE	FELLABLE	FILEABLE	*FILLABLE*
FILMABLE	FINEABLE	FIREABLE	FISHABLE	FOAMABLE	FOILABLE	FOLDABLE
FORDABLE	FORMABLE	FRAMABLE	FUNDABLE	FURLABLE	*GAGEABLE*	GAINABLE
GIVEABLE	GNAWABLE	GRAZABLE	GUIDABLE	GULLABLE	*HACKABLE*	HATEABLE
HEALABLE	HEARABLE	HELPABLE	HIREABLE	*HITTABLE*	HOLDABLE	HUGGABLE
HUNTABLE	IMITABLE	INARABLE	INSTABLE	INVIABLE	ISOLABLE	ISSUABLE
JAILABLE	JOINABLE	JUMPABLE	KEEPABLE	*KILLABLE*	KISSABLE	LAPSABLE
LEASABLE	LENDABLE	LETTABLE	LEVIABLE	LIENABLE	LIFTABLE	LINEABLE
LINKABLE	LIQUABLE	LISTABLE	LIVEABLE	LOANABLE	LOVEABLE	MAILABLE
MAKEABLE	MASKABLE	MELTABLE	MILLABLE	MINEABLE	MISSABLE	MOCKABLE
MOLDABLE	MOOTABLE	NAMEABLE	NESTABLE	NETTABLE	OATHABLE	OPINABLE
OVENABLE	OVERABLE	OXIDABLE	PACKABLE	PARSABLE	PAWNABLE	PEELABLE
PETTABLE	*PICKABLE*	PLACABLE	PLOWABLE	POSEABLE	*POTTABLE*	POURABLE
PRIZABLE	PRUNABLE	*RACEABLE*	RADIABLE	RAISABLE	RATEABLE	REAPABLE
REEFABLE	REELABLE	RENTABLE	RIDEABLE	RINSABLE	*ROCKABLE*	ROLLABLE
ROPEABLE	RUINABLE	RUNNABLE	RUSTABLE	*SACKABLE*	SAILABLE	SALEABLE
SALVABLE	*SANDABLE*	SATIABLE	SAVEABLE	SCALABLE	SEALABLE	SEISABLE
SEIZABLE	SENDABLE	SERVABLE	SHAKABLE	SHAMABLE	SHAPABLE	SHARABLE
SHAVABLE	SHEDABLE	SHOWABLE	*SIGNABLE*	SINGABLE	SIZEABLE	SLAKABLE
SLAYABLE	SLIDABLE	SMOKABLE	SOLVABLE	SORTABLE	STATABLE	*STEWABLE*
STONABLE	SWAYABLE	TAKEABLE	TALKABLE	TAMEABLE	TANNABLE	TAPEABLE
TEARABLE	*TEASABLE*	TELLABLE	TESTABLE	TILLABLE	TILTABLE	TITHABLE
TITRABLE	TOLLABLE	*TOTEABLE*	TRADABLE	TUNEABLE	TYPEABLE	VIOLABLE
VITIABLE	VOIDABLE	VOTEABLE	WADEABLE	WARHABLE	WELDABLE	WETTABLE
WILLABLE	WINDABLE	*WIPEABLE*	WRITABLE			

ABLY

ADORABLY	AMENABLY	AVOWABLY	DAMNABLY	DENIABLY	ENVIABLY	*FORMABLY*
GAGEABLY	GULLABLY	INVIABLY	ISSUABLY	KISSABLY	LAUDABLY	*LIKEABLY*
LOVEABLY	MOVEABLY	OPERABLY	PASSABLY	PITIABLY	PLACABLY	PORTABLY
PROVABLY	QUOTABLY	RATEABLY	READABLY	SALEABLY	SALVABLY	SATIABLY
SCALABLY	*SHAMABLY*	SIZEABLY	SORTABLY	TUNEABLY	UNUSABLY	VALUABLY
VARIABLY	VIOLABLY	*WORKABLY*				

AL *extensions of sixes*

ANARCHAL	ANCONEAL	ANTHERAL	APOLOGAL	ARGENTAL	ATOMICAL	AUTUMNAL
BIOTICAL	CALIPHAL	CANTONAL	CLIENTAL	COLUMNAL	CONOIDAL	CUBOIDAL

CUSPIDAL	DEIFICAL	DENTINAL	DIARCHAL	DOCTORAL	DOMAINAL	DROMICAL
ETHNICAL	EXARCHAL	FISTICAL	FORESTALl	FUCOIDAL	*FUSIONAL*	GESTICAL
GNOMICAL	GYROIDAL	HAPTICAL	HELIACAL	HEROICAL	IATRICAL	IRENICAL
KELOIDAL	LAGOONAL	LIPOIDAL	LUBRICAL	MANIACAL	MATRONAL	METRICAL
MOTIONAL	MUCOIDAL	NEURONAL	NONFATAL	NOTIONAL	OCTANTAL	ORPHICAL
PATRONAL	PECTINAL	PELLETAL	PERONEAL	PONDERAL	PREFIXAL	RECTORAL
REGENTAL	RUBRICAL	SATRAPAL	SECTORAL	SEPTICAL	SHOGUNAL	SILVICAL
SIPHONAL	SONANTAL	STATICAL	STERICAL	SYNDICAL	THETICAL	TOROIDAL
TRAGICAL	TRIGONAL	TRIPODAL	UNFORMAL	UNISONAL	UNLINEAL	URETERAL
UROPODAL	VISIONAL	ZENITHAL	ZODIACAL			

AL *other excluding 'IAL'*

ABAPICAL	ADUMBRAL	AGRESTAL	*AHEMERAL*	ANHEDRAL	ARBITRAL	ARBOREAL
ARCHIVAL	ARRHIZAL	AXONEMAL	BENTHOAL	BICAUDAL	BIMANUAL	BIMENSAL
BINAURAL	BIOCIDAL	BRACTEAL	CALENDAL	CATHODAL	CHONDRAL	CLIMATAL
CLITHRAL	COMPITAL	CONJUGAL	CRUNODAL	CURVITAL	DECLINAL	DEICIDAL
DEMERSAL	DENTURAL	DETRITAL	DIACONAL	DIANODAL	DIASTRAL	DICROTAL
DIOPTRAL	DITHECAL	DIVIDUAL	*DYARCHAL*	ECOTONAL	EMPYREAL	ENCRINAL
EPIFOCAL	EPIGAEAL	EPISODAL	EPISOMAL	EREMITAL	ETHEREAL	EXERGUAL
FISSURAL	FLEXURAL	FORNICAL	FULGURAL	FUNEBRAL	FUNEREAL	GESTURAL
GLUTAEAL	HAEMATAL	*HALLUCAL*	HIBERNAL	IMAGINAL	INCHMEAL	INFERNAL
INFRUGAL	INGUINAL	INIMICAL	KATHODAL	LONGEVAL	MACRURAL	MEDCINAL
MENISCAL	MENSURAL	MONACHAL	MONAURAL	MORAINAL	NEONATAL	NEUROSAL
NONFINAL	NONFOCAL	NONIDEAL	NONLEGAL	*NONLOYAL*	NONMODAL	NONMORAL
NONNASAL	NONNAVAL	NONROYAL	NONRURAL	NONTIDAL	NONTONAL	NONVIRAL
NONVITAL	NOVERCAL	NUNDINAL	NURTURAL	*ORONASAL*	OVICIDAL	OVIDUCAL
PARFOCAL	PASTURAL	PERIGEAL	PHRATRAL	PLASTRAL	POLLICAL	POLOIDAL
POSTANAL	*POSTICAL*	POSTORAL	POSTURAL	PREBASAL	PRELEGAL	PREMORAL
PRERENAL	PRIMEVAL	PROVIRAL	PROXIMAL	PUBERTAL	REVENUAL	SCEPTRAL
SEMIOVAL	SEPTIMAL	SHRIEVAL	SIDEREAL	SKELETAL	SOCIETAL	SOMEDEAL
SUBAURAL	SUBDURAL	SUBEQUAL	SUBNASAL	SUBNODAL	SUBTIDAL	SUBVIRAL
SUBVOCAL	SUBZONAL	SUPERNAL	SYNCOPAL	TELLURAL	TEXTURAL	THEATRAL
THORACAL	TRIAPSAL	TRILOBAL	TRINODAL	TRIPEDAL	TRITICALe	TRIZONAL
TURRICAL	UNFEUDAL	UNIALGAL	UNLETHAL	UNSEXUAL	*VARICEAL*	VESTURAL
VORTICAL	ZOOPERAL					

ALLY

ABORALLY	AERIALLY	ANIMALLY	APICALLY	ASTRALLY	BRIDALLY	CARNALLY
CAUDALLY	CAUSALLY	CHORALLY	CLINALLY	CLONALLY	COEVALLY	COITALLY
COSTALLY	DENTALLY	DISTALLY	DORSALLY	EPICALLY	FACIALLY	FAUNALLY
FESTALLY	FEUDALLY	FILIALLY	FISCALLY	FLORALLY	FRUGALLY	GENIALLY
JOVIALLY	LABIALLY	LAICALLY	LETHALLY	LINEALLY	MEDIALLY	MENIALLY
MESIALLY	NEURALLY	NOUNALLY	PLURALLY	POSTALLY	PRIMALLY	RADIALLY
RASCALLY	RECTALLY	RETRALLY	RITUALLY	SERIALLY	SIGNALLY	SPINALLY
SPIRALLY	TARNALLY	TRIBALLY	UNCIALLY	UNREALLY	VENIALLY	VERNALLY
VESTALLY						

8. Eight-Letter Words

AN *excluding 'IAN' and 'MAN/MEN'*

AMOEBEAN	ARBUTEAN	AUROREAN	BIOCLEAN	CONURBAN	EBURNEAN	EPIGAEAN
HERMAEAN	HYMENEAN	HYOIDEAN	INSECTAN	MISBEGAN	MORPHEAN	NONURBAN
NYMPHEAN	OEDIPEAN	PANHUMAN	PERIGEAN	PIGMAEAN	PYGMAEAN	SPELAEAN
SUBOCEAN	UNDERRAN					

ANT

ABDICANT	ABSONANT	ALIQUANT	*AVOIDANT*	BLATTANT	DIVIDANT	EQUITANT
EXCUBANT	EXIGEANTe	*FLOREANT*	HAURIANT	HEBETANT	INERRANT	INUNDANT
LACERANT	LATITANT	MITIGANT	NAISSANT	OBEISANT	OLEFIANT	OSCITANT
OSCULANT	PARAVANT	PERCEANT	PUISSANT	PURSUANT	RADICANT	RUTILANT
SEGREANT	TITUBANT	UNDULANT	UNPLIANT	VAGINANT	VEGETANT	VOLITANT

AR

ANOVULAR	ANTIWEAR	AVICULAR	BACILLARy	BILINEAR	BIOVULAR	CAPSULARy
CISLUNAR	COLINEAR	COLUMNAR	CONDYLAR	COPLANAR	DACTYLAR	*FIBRILAR*
INTERWAR	MODIOLAR	MULTICAR	NERVULAR	NONPOLAR	NONSOLAR	NUCELLAR
ORACULAR	OSTIOLAR	OVERDEAR	OVERNEAR	PENDULAR	PETIOLAR	PIACULAR
PLAYWEAR	PUSTULAR	SPORULAR	STIPULARy	SUBLUNARy	SUBPOLAR	SUBSOLAR
SUBTALAR	TISSULAR	TONSILAR	UMBELLAR	UNIFILAR	UNILOBAR	UNIPOLAR
UNVULGAR	VACUOLAR					

ARY

ARILLARY	CAVITARY	CINERARY	COMETARY	FUNERARY	LIMITARY	NUMERARY
OVERWARY	SALIVARY	SALUTARY	SOLIDARY	VICENARY		

ATE

ACERVATE	ADUNCATEd	AGMINATE	ANTLIATE	AREOLATEd	ARILLATEd	ARISTATE
BIFORATE	BIJUGATE	BREGMATE	CAPITATEd	CARINATEd	CLYPEATE	CRIBRATE
CRISPATEd	CRISTATEd	CRUSTATEd	CULTRATEd	CUPULATE	DEALBATE	DIGITATEd
DILATATE	ECHINATEd	ENTERATE	FASCIATEd	FIGURATE	FULCRATE	GLABRATE
GLADIATE	HAMULATE	IMPANATE	INAURATE	INCREATE	INCUDATE	INORNATE
LACUNATE	LIGULATEd	LOBULATEd	LUNULATEd	MOSCHATEl	MURICATEd	*MUTICATE*
OCELLATEd	OCHREATE	OVERLATE	PALAMATE	PUNCTATEd	ROSTRATEd	ROSULATE
SCYPHATE	SOMEGATE	STELLATEd	STRIGATE	SUBOVATE	SUBULATE	TAENIATE
TORQUATEd	TRABEATEd	TRISTATE	UMBONATE	UNCINATEd	UNORNATE	USTULATE
VAGINATEd						

ED *extensions of sixes*

ANTLERED	ARBOURED	AWNINGED	BADASSED	BIFORMED	BIKINIED	BISTERED
BLAZERED	BUSKINED	*CADDISED*	*CAFTANED*	CAMAILED	CARBOYED	CAUSEYED
COLUMNED	CORYMBED	CUSTOMED	DENTILED	DOLLARED	*DORMERED*	FENDERED
FINIALED	GABIONED	GALLUSED	*GAITERED*	GARRETED	*GOITERED*	GORGETED
GROTTOED	HAWKEYED	INTURNED	JERSEYED	KIMONOED	LANCETED	LEGIONED
LOUVERED	MANNERED	MITTENED	MUSLINED	NECTARED	NEWELLED	NIMBUSED
OBTECTED	PAJAMAED	PENNONED	*PONCHOED*	PORTALED	PURDAHED	PYJAMAED
RANCORED	RAPIERED	SACHETED	SPAVINED	STAMENED	STANZAED	STOREYED
SYSTEMED	TABARDED	TURBANED	TURRETED	TUXEDOED	ULSTERED	UNWONTED
VESSELED	WEEVILED	WICKERED				

ED *other*

ADDEBTED	ADDORSED	ALVEATED	ANGUIPEDe	ANTIWEED	BEDOTTED	BEFINNED
BEHATTED	BELFRIED	BEPLUMED	BERINGED	BEROUGED	BESOULED	BESUITED
BEUNCLED	BEWINGED	BIFORKED	BIPARTED	BLOODRED	BOUNTIED	CABOSHED
CAVITIED	CHEERLED	*COVERSED*	CYANOSED	DISMODED	DISORBED	DONNERED
DROPSIED	ENFESTED	ENGOULED	ENMOSSED	ENRIDGED	*FOUREYED*	INEDITED
INFLEXED	INVECKED	INVECTED	LINEBRED	LIVERIED	MALPOSED	*MURALLED*
OILFIRED	OPALISED	OPALIZED	ORIELLED	OVERBRED	PARSLIED	PETALLED
PRELOVED	*PREOWNED*	QUINSIED	SEPALLED	SHEETFED	STENOSED	TRUEBRED
TUNICKED	UMBELLED	UMBRATED	UNABATED	UNABUSED	UNADORED	*UNAGREED*
UNALLIED	UNAMAZED	UNANELED	*UNARCHED*	UNARGUED	UNATONED	UNAVOWED
UNBAITED	UNBANDED	UNBANNED	*UNBASTED*	UNBATHED	UNBILLED	UNBLAMED
UNBLOWED	UNBODIED	*UNBOILED*	*UNBONDED*	UNBRUSED	UNBUDDED	UNBURNED
UNBUSTED	UNCALLED	*UNCANNED*	*UNCARDED*	*UNCARVED*	UNCASHED	UNCASKED
UNCAUSED	UNCHEWED	*UNCLAWED*	UNCLOYED	UNCOATED	UNCOINED	UNCOMBED
UNCOOLED	UNCOYNED	*UNCREWED*	UNCULLED	UNCURBED	UNCURVED	UNDAMNED
UNDAMPED	UNDASHED	UNDEEDED	UNDEFIED	UNDENIED	*UNDENTED*	UNDINTED
UNDOOMED	UNDOTTED	UNDULLED	UNEARNED	UNEDITED	UNELATED	UNENVIED
UNERASED	UNESPIED	UNEVADED	UNFABLED	UNFANNED	UNFEARED	UNFELLED
UNFELTED	UNFILMED	UNFISHED	UNFLAWED	UNFLEXED	*UNFLUTED*	UNFOILED
UNFOOTED	UNFORGED	UNFORKED	UNFURRED	UNGAGGED	UNGALLED	*UNGARBED*
UNGAUGED	*UNGELDED*	UNGIFTED	UNGLAZED	UNGORGED	UNGRACED	UNGRAZED
UNGUIDED	UNHACKED	UNHAILED	UNHALSED	UNHALVED	UNHEDGED	UNHELPED
UNHUNTED	UNIDEAED	UNILOBED	UNIMBUED	UNINURED	UNISSUED	UNJOINED
UNJUDGED	*UNKEELED*	UNKENNED	UNLETTED	UNLEVIED	UNLICKED	UNLOOKED
UNMAILED	UNMARRED	UNMATTED	UNMELTED	UNMENDED	UNMILKED	UNMILLED
UNMINDED	UNMISSED	UNMOANED	UNMONIED	UNNEEDED	UNNETTED	UNOBEYED
UNPADDED	UNPAINED	UNPANGED	UNPARTED	UNPATHED	UNPEELED	UNPEERED
UNPINKED	UNPITIED	*UNPITTED*	UNPLOWED	UNPOISED	UNPOLLED	UNPOSTED
UNPOTTED	UNPRICED	UNPRIMED	UNPRIZED	UNPROBED	UNPROVED	UNPRUNED
UNPULLED	UNPURGED	UNRACKED	UNRAISED	UNREAPED	UNRECKED	UNRHYMED
UNRIFLED	UNRINGED	UNRINSED	UNROTTED	UNROUGED	UNROUSED	UNRUSHED
UNRUSTED	UNSAILED	UNSAINED	UNSASHED	UNSEARED	UNSEIZED	UNSERVED
UNSHADED	UNSHAKED	UNSHAMED	UNSHARED	UNSHAVED	UNSIFTED	UNSLAKED
UNSLICED	UNSMOKED	UNSOAKED	UNSOAPED	UNSOILED	UNSOURED	UNSPARED
UNSTAYED	UNSTONED	UNSUCKED	UNSUNNED	UNSWAYED	UNTAGGED	UNTAILED
UNTANNED	UNTARRED	UNTASTED	UNTENDED	UNTILLED	UNTILTED	UNTINGED
UNTRADED	UNTUFTED	UNUNITED	UNVALUED	UNVARIED	UNVEINED	UNVENTED
UNVERSED	*UNVESTED*	UNVETTED	UNVIEWED	UNWALLED	UNWARDED	UNWARMED
UNWARNED	UNWARPED	UNWASTED	UNWEANED	UNWEEDED	UNWEENED	UNWELDED
UNWETTED	UNWIGGED	UNWINGED	UNWOODED	UNWORDED	UNWORMED	UNYEANED
VANITIED	WHIMSIED	WRITHLED				

EDLY

ABASEDLY	AMUSEDLY	AVOWEDLY	BIASEDLY	CURVEDLY	CUSSEDLY	DEUCEDLY
ELATEDLY	FORCEDLY	FORKEDLY	GIFTEDLY	GORGEDLY	*HONIEDLY*	HUNTEDLY
JAGGEDLY	MASSEDLY	MATTEDLY	PETTEDLY	ROOTEDLY	SACREDLY	*SOTTEDLY*
STATEDLY	UNITEDLY	VARIEDLY	VEILEDLY	WINGEDLY	WONTEDLY	

8. Eight-Letter Words

EN *excluding 'MEN/MAN'*

BALLPEEN	BEHOLDEN	BOUGHTEN	DRAGOMEN	ENFROSEN	FOUGHTEN	GROUNDEN
INSUCKEN	*JEHADEEN*	*JIHADEEN*	MENSCHEN	MISEATEN	*MUSKOXEN*	NONGREEN
ONSCREEN	OUTEATEN	OVERKEEN	REBIDDEN	REBITTEN	REFALLEN	SELDSEEN
SEMIOPEN	SOMEWHEN	STRIDDEN	STRUCKEN	THREADEN	TRUCHMEN	UNARISEN
UNBIDDEN	UNBITTEN	UNCHOSEN	UNCLOVEN	UNDERMEN	UNFALLEN	UNGOTTEN
UNHIDDEN	UNHOLPEN	UNMOLTEN	UNRIDDEN	UNROTTEN	UNSHAKEN	UNSODDEN
UNWASHEN	UPHUDDEN	VERBOTEN	*YARRAMEN*			

ENT

ABDUCENT	ADDUCENT	BESPRENT	COVALENT	DEFLUENT	DESINENT	DIRIGENT
DIRIMENT	DORMIENT	EMULGENT	ERUMPENT	ESURIENT	FECULENT	FORELENT
FORSPENT	FRONDENT	HAURIENT	INSCIENT	LUCULENT	MUCULENT	OUTSPENT
OVERLENT	OVERWENT	PATULENT	PLANGENT	PRURIENT	PURULENT	REDOLENT
REFLUENT	RELUCENT	RENITENT	REVEHENT	SERVIENT	STREPENT	TEMULENT
UNDECENT	UNSILENT	VINOLENT				

ERLY

BADGERLY	BANKERLY	HUNGERLY	LATTERLY	LIMBERLY	LITHERLY	LUMBERLY
MANNERLY	PANDERLY	PORTERLY	READERLY	SICKERLY	SILVERLY	SOMBERLY
SOUTERLY	WINTERLY	WRITERLY				

ES *plurals of corresponding eights ending in 'IS'*

ACIDOSES	ADENOSES	ANABASES	*ANATEXES*	ANEMOSES	ANTHESES	ANURESES
APNEUSES	APODOSES	APOMIXES	BIOLYSES	CATHEXES	CENTESES	CHORISES
CONIOSES	CYANOSES	DIEGESES	DIERESES	DIPLOSES	DIURESES	EMPHASES
EMPTYSES	EMPYESES	ENCLISES	ENDEIXES	ENURESES	EPITASES	*EPITAXES*
EROTESES	EXEGESES	FETIALES	GEOTAXES	HAPLOSES	HELIOSES	HIDROSES
HOMEOSES	*HORMESES*	KURTOSES	KYLLOSES	KYPHOSES	LEUKOSES	LORDOSES
MATHESES	METHYSES	ORCHESES	ORTHOSES	PANMIXES	*PHERESES*	PHIMOSES
PHYLESES	PHYTOSES	PROTASES	PTILOSES	PYCNOSES	PYKNOSES	SUBCUTES
TENIASES	THLIPSES	XERANSES	ZOONOSES			

ES *extensions of sixes*

BASALTES	CONDORES	CURSORES	CUSPIDES	CYPRIDES	*DAEMONES*	DAIMONES
DOBLONES	HUIPILES	MAENADES	MENINGES	NEREIDES	PECTINES	PLEIADES
QUEZALES	SENHORES	*TALLITES*	VIATORES			

ES *other*

ALTRICES	ATLANTES	BEHALVES	BRITCHES	*BROEKIES*	CANITIES	CENTONES
CERASTES	*CNEMIDES*	CRUDITES	DIPSADES	DISTAVES	DOLMADES	DUXELLES
ENTREMES	EPULIDES	FAINITES	FLAMINES	FORCIPES	FORNICES	FRUTICES
GALOWSES	*GRUNDIES*	HAEREDES	HALLUCES	HUSWIVES	IMBRICES	*KEFTEDES*
KNEESIES	LARNAKES	LARYNGES	LOWLIVES	MIDLIVES	MUCRONES	MUNCHIES
NAYTHLES	NONLIVES	OFTTIMES	OLDWIVES	ORNITHES	OTITIDES	PARIETES
PHOLADES	POLLICES	PULMONES	RACHIDES	RHAGADES	SATELLES	SEAWIVES
SNUGGIES	SPADONES	SPHINGES	STAPEDES	STIPITES	*STYLOPES*	THORACES
TRIENTES	TUTRICES	UNNETHES	UNSELVES	VERTICES	VORTICES	

FORM
AERIFORM	ARCIFORM	AURIFORM	CONIFORM	CUBIFORM	ENSIFORM	GASIFORM
GRUIFORM	JANIFORM	LAVAFORM	LYRIFORM	NAPIFORM	NATIFORM	NUBIFORM
PEDIFORM	PICIFORM	PILIFORM	PIRIFORM	PYRIFORM	RANIFORM	RENIFORM
RETIFORM	ROTIFORM	SETIFORM	TUBIFORM	URSIFORM	VARIFORM	VASIFORM

FUL
AVAILFUL	BLAMEFUL	BLUSHFUL	CRIMEFUL	DEARNFUL	DEATHFUL	DIRGEFUL
DREAMFUL	GHASTFUL	GLOOMFUL	GROANFUL	GUILEFUL	HANDSFUL	HASTEFUL
HONEYFUL	HUMORFUL	LAUGHFUL	LIGHTFUL	LOATHFUL	MENSEFUL	MIGHTFUL
MIRTHFUL	MOISTFUL	NOISEFUL	ODOURFUL	PAILSFUL	PAUSEFUL	PLAINFUL
PRANKFUL	PRIDEFUL	PROUDFUL	SACKSFUL	SCENTFUL	SENSEFUL	SHEENFUL
SKILLFUL	SMILEFUL	SNEERFUL	SOOTHFUL	SPEEDFUL	SPELLFUL	SPOILFUL
SPORTFUL	STARTFUL	STORMFUL	SURGEFUL	TRADEFUL	TRISTFUL	TROTHFUL
TROUTFUL	TRUSTFUL	UDDERFUL	UNARTFUL	UNJOYFUL	UNMANFUL	UNSINFUL
UNUSEFUL	UNWILFUL	VAUNTFUL	VENGEFUL	VOICEFUL	WEARIFUL	WORTHFUL
WRATHFUL	WREAKFUL	WRECKFUL	WROTHFUL			

FULLY
AIMFULLY	ARTFULLY	IREFULLY	RUEFULLY	SINFULLY

IA
ACHAENIA	ANTHELIA	ANTHEMIA	ANTHODIA	BRANCHIAe	BRANCHIAl	CALDARIA
CARPALIA	CHALAZIA	COENOBIA	COLLEGIAl	COLLEGIAn	COLLUVIAl	COLLYRIA
CONTAGIA	CORMIDIA	CTENIDIA	CYMBIDIA	DECENNIAl	DENTALIA	DICHASIAl
EPICEDIAl	EPICEDIAn	EPIMYSIA	EXONUMIA	GELSEMIA	GYMNASIAl	GYNAECIA
GYNOECIA	HERBARIAl	HERBARIAn	HOSPITIA	IMPLUVIA	MANUBRIAl	MARSUPIAl
MARSUPIAn	MARTYRIA	MAZAEDIA	PALLADIA	PARHELIA	PETECHIAe	PETECHIAl
PHELONIA	POLLINIA	PRESIDIAl	PTERYGIAl	PYCNIDIAl	RADIALIA	REPTILIAn
RHIZOBIAl	SACRARIAl	SENSORIAl	SEPTARIAn	SPORIDIAl	SYMPODIAl	SYMPOSIAc
SYMPOSIAl	SYNANGIA	SYNEDRIAl	TENTORIAl	TERRARIA	TRAPEZIAl	TRIENNIAl
TRIFORIAl	TRIPUDIA	TROPARIA	UREDINIAl	UROPYGIAl	VESTIGIAl	ZOOCYTIA

IAL
AGENTIAL	BARONIAL	BIFACIAL	BIRACIAL	BIRADIAL	BISERIAL	DOMANIAL
ECDYSIAL	ENDEMIAL	ETHERIAL	EUSOCIAL	EXEQUIAL	FAMILIAL	FIDUCIAL
GONADIAL	INDUVIAL	LOESSIAL	MANORIAL	MANURIAL	MONAXIAL	MOTORIAL
NAUPLIAL	NOTARIAL	PARAXIAL	PELAGIAL	PRANDIAL	PREAXIAL	PROEMIAL
RASORIAL	REMIGIAL	RIPARIAL	SORORIAL	SOTERIAL	SUBAXIAL	SUTORIAL
TENURIAL	UNFILIAL	UNGENIAL	UNIAXIAL	UNSOCIAL	VICARIAL	VIZIRIAL

IAN
DEDALIAN	DEMONIAN	DEVONIAN	DIGYNIAN	FAUSTIAN	FAVONIAN	GAUSSIAN
GYPSEIAN	IDYLLIAN	MELANIAN	MILESIAN	MONECIAN	ORDALIAN	PAVONIAN
PRUSSIAN	RANARIAN	SALOPIAN	SELENIAN	SILURIAN	SUTORIAN	

IBLE

EDUCIBLE	ELIDIBLE	ELUDIBLE	ERODIBLE	EROSIBLE	EVADIBLE	EVASIBLE
EXIGIBLE	FORCIBLE	LAPSIBLE	MISCIBLE	PARTIBLE	PASSIBLE	RENDIBLE
RINSIBLE	RUNCIBLE	SUASIBLE	TENSIBLE	VINCIBLE		

IBLY

ELIGIBLY	FALLIBLY	FLEXIBLY	GULLIBLY	*INEDIBLY*	PASSIBLY	TANGIBLY
TENSIBLY	VENDIBLY	VINCIBLY				

IC *extensions of sixes*

ADENYLIC	*ALEXINIC*	ALUMINIC	AMNIONIC	AMULETIC	ANALOGIC	ANIMALIC
ANTHEMIC	AORISTIC	ARGENTIC	BALLADIC	BALLETIC	BALSAMIC	BARYONIC
BENZYLIC	BIOGENIC	BISTROIC	BROMIDIC	DAEDALIC	DAEMONIC	DAIMONIC
DALTONIC	DESERTIC	DESPOTIC	DIALOGIC	DIAPIRIC	DIATOMIC	*DOLMENIC*
DYNASTIC	EGOISTIC	ENNEADIC	EOLITHIC	EPILOGIC	EPIMERIC	EPONYMIC
EUPHONIC	GENTILIC	GERMANIC	GNEISSIC	HADRONIC	HAPTENIC	HERALDIC
HERMITIC	HOLISTIC	ISATINIC	ISOBARIC	ISOMERIC	JESUITIC	JURISTIC
KAOLINIC	KISMETIC	LEPTONIC	MAENADIC	MAGNESIC	METHODIC	MONISTIC
MYELINIC	MYOGENIC	NEKTONIC	NEURONIC	OLEFINIC	ORGASMIC	OXYGENIC
OROGENIC	PARSONIC	PENTADIC	PETROLIC	PHENYLIC	PHYTONIC	PLANETIC
PODSOLIC	PODZOLIC	POTASSIC	PROTONIC	PUNDITIC	PURISTIC	PYRROLIC
PYTHONIC	REAGINIC	SANTALIC	SERAPHIC	SERMONIC	SHAMANIC	SIPHONIC
SONANTIC	SOVIETIC	STANZAIC	STOLONIC	SULFURIC	SULTANIC	TALIONIC
TALMUDIC	TARTARIC	TELFERIC	TELSONIC	TETRADIC	THEISTIC	TRIGONIC
TRIMERIC	TRIPODIC	TYPHONIC	URANYLIC	URETERIC	VANDALIC	

IC *other*

AGRESTIC	AMNESTIC	AMNIOTIC	AMPHORIC	ANABATIC	ANABOLIC	ANAGOGIC
ANATOMIC	*ANIRIDIC*	ANODYNIC	ANORTHIC	ANOXEMIC	ANURETIC	APAGOGIC
APATETIC	APOGAEIC	APOGAMIC	*APORETIC*	APOSITIC	*ARENITIC*	ARYTHMIC
ASBESTIC	*ASPARTIC*	AUTARKIC	AUTOPSIC	AUTOPTIC	AZOTEMIC	BANAUSIC
BATHETIC	BAUXITIC	BEATIFIC	BIOLYTIC	BIOTITIC	BIOTYPIC	BIPHASIC
BORNITIC	*BUTANOIC*	DERMATIC	DEUTERIC	DIABASIC	DIABOLIC	DIALYTIC
DIATONIC	*DIEGETIC*	DIERETIC	DIHYDRIC	DIMETRIC	DIORAMIC	DIORITIC
DIPHASIC	*DIPLEGIC*	*DIPROTIC*	DYSMELIC	DYSPNEIC	DYSPNOIC	DYSTONIC
ELLIPTIC	EMPATHIC	ENDERMIC	ENDOZOIC	ENTASTIC	ENTHETIC	ENTOZOIC
ENTROPIC	EPAGOGIC	EPIBOLIC	EPIDOTIC	EPIGAMIC	EPIGENIC	EPINOSIC
EPISODIC	EPITAXIC	EPITOMIC	EPITONIC	EREMITIC	ERGASTIC	EROGENIC
EROTETIC	ESOTERICa	*ETHANOIC*	EUPHOTIC	EUPNOEIC	EUSTATIC	EUTROPIC
EXOERGIC	EXOGAMIC	EXOTERIC	FARADAIC	FELSITIC	FERRITIC	FIBROTIC
FULMINIC	GALVANIC	GAMBOGIC	GEOGONIC	GERONTIC	*GLUTAMIC*	*GUANYLIC*
GYMNASIC	HEMIOLIC	HEMIOPIC	HETAERIC	*HETAIRIC*	*HEXANOIC*	HOLOPTIC
HOLOZOIC	HOMEOTIC	HOPLITIC	*HORMETIC*	HORMONIC	HYDRONIC	HYDROPIC
HYLOZOIC	*IOPANOIC*	ISOGAMIC	ISOGENIC	ISONOMIC	ISOTONIC	ISOTOPIC
ISOTYPIC	ISOZYMIC	*JURASSIC*	KATHODIC	KLEPHTIC	*KYANITIC*	KYPHOTIC
LEPROTIC	LEUKOTIC	LIGNITIC	LIMNETIC	*LINOLEIC*	LITHEMIC	LORDOTIC
LYSERGIC	MAGNIFICo	MANDALIC	MANGANIC	MANNITIC	MARGARIC	MARLITIC
MASTITIC	MEDALLIC	MELLIFIC	MELLITIC	MEPHITIC	MESARAIC	*MESOZOIC*
METAZOIC	MOLYBDIC	MORAINIC	MORBIFIC	MORTIFIC	MURIATIC	MYOLOGIC

MYOTONIC	MYRISTIC	NEOLOGIC	NEOTENIC	NEPIONIC	NEUMATIC	NIRVANIC
NITROLIC	NOMISTIC	*NONANOIC*	NONBASIC	NONIONIC	*NONLYRIC*	NONOHMIC
NONTONIC	NONTOXIC	*OLIGEMIC*	*OLIGURIC*	OLIVINIC	OOPHYTIC	OOSPORIC
ORGASTIC	ORNITHIC	ORSELLIC	OSTEITIC	OTOTOXIC	OXIDASIC	*OXYTONIC*
PALLADIC	*PALMITIC*	PANGAMIC	PARHELIC	PELMATIC	PERLITIC	PETRIFIC
PHIMOTIC	PHRATRIC	PHREATIC	PLATINIC	PODAGRIC	POEMATIC	POLLINIC
POLYADIC	POLYENIC	POLYURIC	POLYZOIC	PONTIFICe	PORISTIC	PRELATIC
PRETONIC	PRIMATIC	PROSODIC	PROTATIC	PRURITIC	PSILOTIC	PULSIFIC
PYELITIC	PYKNOTIC	PYOGENIC	QUIXOTIC	*RETINOIC*	*RHINITIC*	RHIZOMIC
RHODANIC	RHOPALIC	RUTHENIC	SALVIFIC	*SAMSARIC*	SAPREMIC	SAPROBIC
SATURNIC	SIBYLLIC	SIGMATIC	SILVATIC	SOPHERIC	SORBITIC	SPAGERIC
SPAGIRIC	SPHYGMIC	SPILITIC	STENOTIC	STOMATIC	STRONTIC	STYLITIC
SUBOPTIC	SUBSONIC	SULFATIC	SULFITIC	SULFONIC	SYENITIC	SYLVATIC
SYNAPTIC	SYNDETIC	SYNERGIC	SYNGAMIC	*SYNGENIC*	*SYNTENIC*	SYNTONIC
SYSTOLIC	TANTALIC	TEKTITIC	TELERGIC	TELLURIC	TENESMIC	TERMITIC
TERPENIC	THEURGIC	TORNADIC	TOXAEMIC	TREMATIC	*TRIASSIC*	TRIBADIC
TRIBASIC	TRISEMIC	TRUISTIC	TUNGSTIC	TYRANNIC	UMBRATIC	UNEROTIC
UNEXOTIC	UNHEROIC	*UNIRONIC*	UNPOETIC	URALITIC	URANITIC	*URIDYLIC*
URINEMIC	UROLOGIC	*VALPROIC*	VAMPIRIC	VANILLIC	VIBRONIC	VILLATIC
VIRAEMIC	XERANTIC	YTTERBIC	ZEOLITIC	ZOOGENIC	ZOONITIC	ZOONOMIC
ZOONOTIC	ZOOTOMIC	*ZOOTOXIC*	ZOOTYPIC			

ID *excluding 'OID'*

ANTISKID	BACKSLIDe	*COMORBID*	FORELAID	FORESAID	GAINSAID	HYPOACID
ILLIQUID	INVISCID	LANDSLIDe	MULTIFID	NONRIGID	NONVALID	OBLIQUID
PELLUCID	POLYACID	PURTRAID	SEMIARID	SUBACRID	SUBFLUID	SUBHUMID
UNCANDID	UNFORBID	UNTURBID	ZYGAENID			

ILY *derived from adjectives*

BAULKILY	BLEARILY	BLOODILY	BLOWSILY	BLOWZILY	BLURRILY	BOTCHILY
BOUNCILY	BRASSILY	BRAWNILY	BREEZILY	BROODILY	BUNCHILY	CHATTILY
CHEERILY	CHEESILY	*CHESTILY*	CHILLILY	CHIRPILY	CHUNKILY	CLASSILY
CLOGGILY	CLOUDILY	COMELILY	CRAGGILY	CRANKILY	CREAKILY	CREAMILY
CREEPILY	CRISPILY	CROAKILY	DAINTILY	DRAFTILY	DREAMILY	DRESSILY
DROOPILY	DROWSILY	EARTHILY	FAULTILY	*FEISTILY*	FILTHILY	FLASHILY
FLEECILY	*FLESHILY*	FLIMSILY	FLINTILY	FLOSSILY	FOLKSILY	FREAKILY
FROSTILY	FROTHILY	FROWZILY	FRUITILY	FRUMPILY	GLASSILY	GLITZILY
GLOOMILY	GLOSSILY	GRASSILY	GREASILY	GRITTILY	GROGGILY	*GROOVILY*
GRUMPILY	GUILTILY	HOMELILY	HUNGRILY	JAUNTILY	KINDLILY	KNOTTILY
LIVELILY	LONELILY	LOVELILY	MOUTHILY	PALTRILY	PATCHILY	*PEACHILY*
PLAGUILY	PLUSHILY	PRETTILY	PRISSILY	PUNCHILY	QUEASILY	QUIRKILY
SAVORILY	SCURVILY	SHAGGILY	SHIFTILY	SHIRTILY	*SHITTILY*	SHODDILY
SICKLILY	SKIMPILY	SLANGILY	SLEAZILY	SLEEPILY	SLINKILY	SLUSHILY
SLUTTILY	SMEARILY	SMUDGILY	SMUTTILY	*SNARKILY*	SNOOPILY	SNOOTILY
SNOTTILY	SPARKILY	SPONGILY	SPOOKILY	SPOONILY	SPORTILY	SPOTTILY
SPUNKILY	STALKILY	STARRILY	STEAMILY	STICKILY	STINGILY	STOCKILY
STODGILY	STORMILY	STUMPILY	SULTRILY	SWANKILY	SWEATILY	TAWDRILY
TETCHILY	TOOTHILY	TOUCHILY	TRASHILY	TRENDILY	TRICKILY	UNHOLILY

8. Eight-Letter Words

UNTIDILY UNWARILY WATERILY WHEEZILY WHIMSILY WINTRILY WOOLLILY
WORTHILY WRATHILY

INE
ALCIDINE *ANTIMINE* APOCRINE AQUILINE BACULINE BERYLINE CAVATINE
DERACINE DIACTINE ELAPHINE HARDLINEr IANTHINE ICTERINE LEGATINE
LEPORINE LIMACINE MATUTINE *MONOLINE* MYRRHINE OSCININE OVERFINE
PALUDINE PAVONINE PETALINE QUERCINE REGULINE RESUPINE RIVERINE
SABULINE SEPALINE SLIMLINE SONATINE SORICINE STRIGINE STURNINE
SUILLINE SYLPHINE SYLVIINE THALLINE TOPAZINE UNDIVINE VIPERINE
VITULINE VOMERINE XENURINE

ING
ABORNING BATSWING *BLINGING* FATWAING *GULLWING* HOUSLING LEFTWING
NONCLING NONUSING PINDLING QUALMING *ROARMING* SEAGOING SIDELING
UNACHING UNAGEING UNBODING *UNBOWING* UNDARING UNFADING *UNGAZING*
UNGIVING UNMOVING UNSATING UNSEEING UNWANING WINDRING

INGLY
ACHINGLY BITINGLY BODINGLY BORINGLY BOWINGLY *CARINGLY* COOINGLY
DARINGLY DOTINGLY ERRINGLY FUMINGLY GAPINGLY GIBINGLY HOPINGLY
JAPINGLY JIBINGLY LIVINGLY LOSINGLY *LURINGLY* MOPINGLY MOVINGLY
MUSINGLY POSINGLY PULINGLY RAGINGLY RAVINGLY ROVINGLY SAVINGLY
TAKINGLY TAXINGLY UNKINGLY* URGINGLY VEXINGLY WOOINGLY

IOUS
CAESIOUS CAPTIOUS DIECIOUS EDACIOUS EXIMIOUS FACTIOUS FASHIOUS
ORAGIOUS PERVIOUS PLUVIOUS RUCTIOUS SPECIOUS STOCIOUS STOTIOUS
TENUIOUS TORTIOUS USURIOUS UXORIOUS YTTRIOUS

IS *having corresponding 'ES' plurals*
ACIDOSIS ADENOSIS ADIPOSIS ANABASIS *ANATEXIS* ANEMOSIS ANTHESIS
ANURESIS *APNEUSIS* APODOSIS APOMIXIS BIOLYSIS CATHEXIS CENTESIS
CHORISIS CONIOSIS CYANOSIS DIEGESIS DIERESIS DIPLOSIS DIURESIS
ELLIPSIS EMPTYSIS EMPYESIS ENCLISIS EPITASIS *EPITAXIS* EROTESIS
EXEGESIS FETIALIS FIBROSIS GEOTAXIS GRACILIS HAPLOSIS HELIOSIS
HIDROSIS HOMEOSIS *HORMESIS* KYLLOSIS KYPHOSIS LEUKOSIS LORDOSIS
MATHESIS METHYSIS NARCOSIS NECROSIS ORCHESIS ORTHOSIS *PHERESIS*
PHIMOSIS PHYTOSIS PROTASIS PTILOSIS PYCNOSIS PYKNOSIS TENIASIS
THLIPSIS THYLOSIS XERANSIS ZOONOSIS

IS *other*
BOREALIS CANTORIS GRISGRIS HALIOTIS HAUTBOIS METICAIS NARQUOIS

ISH
ACTORISH BAIRNISH BLACKISH BLEAKISH BLIMPISH BLOCKISH BLOKEISH
BLONDISH BLUNTISH BRAINISH BRISKISH BROADISH CAMELISH CEORLISH
CLANNISH CLERKISH CLIQUISH CLODDISH *CLOTTISH* CLOWNISH COARSISH
DANDYISH DOWDYISH DREGGISH DROLLISH DROOGISH DWARFISH *DWEEBISH*

FEEBLISH	FLATTISH	FLIRTISH	FOGEYISH	FRAILISH	*GIPSYISH*	GRUMPISH
IDIOTISH	JINGOISH	LEMONISH	LITTLISH	LIVERISH	NANNYISH	NINNYISH
NOVELISH	ORANGISH	PAGANISH	PIXIEISH	POKERISH	*POSERISH*	PROUDISH
PSEUDISH	QUACKISH	QUALMISH	QUEERISH	QUIRKISH	ROWDYISH	SAINTISH
SANDYISH	SKITTISH	SLANGISH	SLUTTISH	SMARTISH	SNEAKISH	SNOUTISH
SOLIDISH	SORRYISH	SPOOKISH	SQUARISH	SQUIRISH	STEEPISH	STILTISH
STOCKISH	STOUTISH	SWAINISH	SWELLISH	TIGERISH	TINGLISH	TOADYISH
TRAMPISH	TRICKISH	UNMODISH	VAGARISH	VAPORISH	VIPERISH	VIXENISH
WATERISH	WOMANISH	YOKELISH				

ISHLY

AGUISHLY	DUDISHLY	ELFISHLY	ELVISHLY	GARISHLY	IMPISHLY	JADISHLY
MODISHLY	MOPISHLY	MULISHLY	NEWISHLY	OAFISHLY	OGRISHLY	OWLISHLY
RAKISHLY	TONISHLY	TOYISHLY				

IUM

AECIDIUM	AEROBIUM	APTERIUM	ASCIDIUM	ASPIDIUM	BASIDIUM	BRACHIUM
CIBORIUM	CONARIUM	CONIDIUM	CYATHIUM	*DISODIUM*	*FUSARIUM*	GONIDIUM
GYNECIUM	INDUSIUM	PATAGIUM	PECULIUM	PYXIDIUM	REFUGIUM	SEDILIUM
SOLATIUM	SOREDIUM	SUDARIUM	SYCONIUM	VELARIUM	ZOOECIUM	

IVE

ADAPTIVE	ADOPTIVE	ALLUSIVE	CONATIVE	DELETIVE	DENOTIVE	DERISIVE
DILATIVE	DILUTIVE	EDUCTIVE	EGESTIVE	EMULSIVE	ENACTIVE	*EQUATIVE*
ERECTIVE	*EXAPTIVE*	EXCUSIVE	EXERTIVE	FRUCTIVE	FRUITIVE	IDEATIVE
ILLUSIVE	INFUSIVE	INNATIVE	LIGATIVE	MONITIVE	MUTATIVE	ORECTIVE
PLAUSIVE	POSTDIVE	PRACTIVE	PROCLIVE	PUTATIVE	ROTATIVE	SANATIVE
SEDUCIVE	SOLUTIVE	SORPTIVE	SPORTIVE	TAXATIVE	TRACTIVE	UNACTIVE
UNNATIVE						

LESS

BARKLESS	BATELESS	BATHLESS	BEAKLESS	BEAMLESS	BEATLESS	BEEFLESS
BELTLESS	BLOTLESS	BODILESS	*BOLTLESS*	*BONDLESS*	BOOKLESS	*BOONLESS*
BOOTLESS	BROWLESS	CALFLESS	CHADLESS	CLOYLESS	COALLESS	COATLESS
CODELESS	COOKLESS	CORELESS	CREWLESS	CROPLESS	CURBLESS	CURELESS
DATELESS	DEBTLESS	DEEDLESS	*DINTLESS*	DOORLESS	*DOWNLESS*	DRIPLESS
DUCTLESS	ECHOLESS	EDGELESS	EXITLESS	FADELESS	FAMELESS	FECKLESS
FEETLESS	FERNLESS	*FILMLESS*	FINELESS	FIRMLESS	FLAGLESS	FLAPLESS
FOAMLESS	FORDLESS	FORKLESS	FORMLESS	FRETLESS	FUMELESS	FUNDLESS
GAINLESS	*GAOLLESS*	GATELESS	GAUMLESS	GIFTLESS	GOLDLESS	GORMLESS
GRITLESS	HALTLESS	HATELESS	HEATLESS	HEEDLESS	HEELLESS	HEIRLESS
HELMLESS	HERBLESS	HIDELESS	HILTLESS	HIVELESS	HOLELESS	HOODLESS
HOOFLESS	HOOKLESS	HOOPLESS	HORNLESS	HUMPLESS	HYMNLESS	IDEALESS
IRONLESS	*JAILLESS*	*JURYLESS*	KEELLESS	KNOTLESS	LACELESS	LANDLESS
LEADLESS	LEAKLESS	LIMBLESS	LIMELESS	LINELESS	LINTLESS	LOAMLESS
LOBELESS	*LOCKLESS*	LOFTLESS	LORDLESS	*LUNGLESS*	MAILLESS	MAKELESS
MANELESS	MATELESS	MEALLESS	MEATLESS	MILKLESS	MOVELESS	NAILLESS
NATHLESS	NECKLESS	NORMLESS	NOTELESS	NOUNLESS	ODORLESS	*PANELESS*
PANGLESS	PATHLESS	PEAKLESS	*PELTLESS*	PILELESS	PITHLESS	PITILESS

8. Eight-Letter Words

PLANLESS	PLAYLESS	PLOTLESS	PLUGLESS	POETLESS	POLELESS	PORTLESS
RAILLESS	REDELESS	REINLESS	RIFTLESS	*RIMELESS*	RINDLESS	RINGLESS
RITELESS	ROADLESS	ROCKLESS	ROOFLESS	RULELESS	RUNGLESS	TAMELESS
TANKLESS	TAPELESS	TEEMLESS	TENTLESS	TERMLESS	TEXTLESS	THAWLESS
THEWLESS	THOWLESS	TIDELESS	TINTLESS	TOADLESS	TOILLESS	TOMBLESS
TONELESS	TOOLLESS	TOWNLESS	TRAMLESS	TURFLESS	TYRELESS	VANELESS
VEILLESS	VEINLESS	VENTLESS	VERBLESS	*VETOLESS*	VIEWLESS	*VINELESS*
WAKELESS	*WARDLESS*	WARELESS	WEETLESS	WELDLESS	*WICKLESS*	WINELESS
WITELESS	WONTLESS	WOODLESS	YOKELESS	*YOLKLESS*	ZEALLESS	ZONELESS

LIKE

AGUELIKE	AUNTLIKE	BALMLIKE	BARNLIKE	BEADLIKE	BEAMLIKE	BEANLIKE
BIRDLIKE	*BOLTLIKE*	BUSHLIKE	*CAGELIKE*	CALFLIKE	CAVELIKE	*CLAMLIKE*
CLAYLIKE	COMBLIKE	CORDLIKE	CORMLIKE	CRABLIKE	CULTLIKE	DAWNLIKE
DEERLIKE	DISCLIKE	DISHLIKE	DOMELIKE	DOVELIKE	*DOWNLIKE*	DRUMLIKE
DUNELIKE	DUSTLIKE	EPICLIKE	FANGLIKE	FAUNLIKE	FAWNLIKE	FELTLIKE
FERNLIKE	*FILMLIKE*	FISHLIKE	FOAMLIKE	FOOTLIKE	FROGLIKE	FUMELIKE
FUSELIKE	GAMELIKE	GATELIKE	*GERMLIKE*	GLENLIKE	GLUELIKE	GNATLIKE
GOADLIKE	GONGLIKE	GULFLIKE	HALOLIKE	HANDLIKE	HARELIKE	*HEADLIKE*
HEMPLIKE	HERBLIKE	HERDLIKE	HIVELIKE	HOMELIKE	HOODLIKE	HOOFLIKE
HOOPLIKE	HORNLIKE	*HOSELIKE*	*HUMPLIKE*	HYMNLIKE	IRONLIKE	*JADELIKE*
JUTELIKE	LACELIKE	LAMBLIKE	LARDLIKE	LATHLIKE	LAVALIKE	LEAFLIKE
LILYLIKE	LINELIKE	LIONLIKE	LOFTLIKE	LORDLIKE	*LYNXLIKE*	MASTLIKE
MAZELIKE	MOONLIKE	MOSSLIKE	MOTHLIKE	NESTLIKE	NOSELIKE	NOVALIKE
OVENLIKE	PALMLIKE	PINELIKE	PITHLIKE	PLAYLIKE	PLUMLIKE	POETLIKE
PUSSLIKE	QUAYLIKE	RASHLIKE	REEDLIKE	RINGLIKE	ROOFLIKE	ROOTLIKE
ROPELIKE	ROSELIKE	RUBYLIKE	RUNELIKE	RUSHLIKE	SALTLIKE	SANDLIKE
SCABLIKE	SCUMLIKE	SEALLIKE	SEAMLIKE	SEEDLIKE	SERFLIKE	SHEDLIKE
SIGHLIKE	SLABLIKE	*SLITLIKE*	SNAGLIKE	SNOWLIKE	SOAPLIKE	SONGLIKE
SOULLIKE	*SOUPLIKE*	SPARLIKE	STARLIKE	STEMLIKE	STEPLIKE	SUCHLIKE
SUITLIKE	SURFLIKE	SWANLIKE	TAILLIKE	TENTLIKE	TIDELIKE	TILELIKE
TOADLIKE	TOMBLIKE	TRAPLIKE	TREELIKE	TUBELIKE	TURFLIKE	VASELIKE
VEILLIKE	VEINLIKE	VESTLIKE	*VINELIKE*	VISELIKE	WAIFLIKE	*WANDLIKE*
WARTLIKE	WASPLIKE	WAVELIKE	WEEDLIKE	WHEYLIKE	WIFELIKE	WINGLIKE
WIRELIKE	WISPLIKE	WOLFLIKE	WOMBLIKE	WOOLLIKE	WORMLIKE	

LY *derived from adjectives, excluding 'ILY'*

ADROITLY	AUGUSTLY	BARRENLY	BENIGNLY	CHASTELY	CURSEDLY	DEMURELY
DOCILELY	FLORIDLY	*FOETIDLY*	FUTILELY	GAUCHELY	GOLDENLY	HOARSELY
HOLLOWLY	HORRIDLY	IMPURELY	INFIRMLY	MEAGRELY	MELLOWLY	MINUTELY
MODERNLY	MORBIDLY	MOROSELY	OBTUSELY	OPAQUELY	ORNATELY	PALLIDLY
PLACIDLY	PUTRIDLY	RAGGEDLY	RANCIDLY	ROBUSTLY	ROTTENLY	ROTUNDLY
RUGGEDLY	SALLOWLY	SPRUCELY	STANCHLY	STEEVELY	STIEVELY	STOLIDLY
SVELTELY	TORPIDLY	TURGIDLY	UNRIPELY	UNSAFELY	UNSTABLY	URBANELY
VULGARLY	WOODENLY					

LY *other, excluding 'EDLY', 'ERLY', 'ILY', 'INGLY' and 'ISHLY'*

ABJECTLY	ABSENTLY	ALPINELY	ARCANELY	ARGUTELY	ARRANTLY	AVERSELY
BEASTILY	BEGGARLY	BEHOVELY	BESEEMLY	BIHOURLY	BINATELY	BOVINELY

BROKENLY	COGENTLY	CONVEXLY	COUSINLY	CRAVENLY	CROUSELY	DATIVELY
DEMISSLY	DIVERSLY	DOCTORLY	DOTARDLY	DULCETLY	EQUINELY	ERRANTLY
FACETELY	FACILELY	FELINELY	FELLOWLY	FINITELY	FRENZILY	FROZENLY
GRAITHLY	GRAVIDLY	HECTORLY	HEROICLY	HIDDENLY	INDIGNLY	INNATELY
INTACTLY	JOCOSELY	JOCUNDLY	KERNELLY	LATENTLY	LEADENLY	LIMPIDLY
LINEARLY	LIQUIDLY	LISSOMLY	LOBATELY	LOUCHELY	LUCENTLY	LUMPENLY
LUNATELY	MAIDENLY	MALIGNLY	MEDIANLY	MOLTENLY	NATANTLY	NATIVELY
NOCENTLY	OBLATELY	OBLONGLY	OCULARLY	ODIOUSLY	ONWARDLY	OTIOSELY
OVERHOLY	OVERWILY	PASTORLY	PATRONLY	PEDATELY	PLIANTLY	POROUSLY
POTENTLY	PRIESTLY*	PROLIXLY	PROVENLY	RAMOSELY	*RAMOUSLY*	REFLEXLY
REMISSLY	REPANDLY	RIBALDLY	RIMOSELY	RUGOSELY	RUSTICLY	SAILORLY
SAVOURLY	SCRIGGLY*	SCRIMPLY	SEAMANLY	SECANTLY	SECUNDLY	SELECTLY
SENILELY	SEXTUPLY	SNIVELLY	SODDENLY	SOVRANLY	SQUIRELY	STRAGGLY*
STRAITLY	*SUNDRILY*	SUPINELY	TARTARLY	THRAWNLY	THWARTLY	TIMOUSLY
TINSELLY	TOWARDLY	*TRUANTLY*	TURBIDLY	UNCOMELY	UNCOSTLY	UNGENTLY
UNHOMELY	UNLIVELY	UNLORDLY	UNLOVELY*	UNMEETLY	*UNPURELY*	UNSUBTLY
UNWARELY	UNWIFELY*	UVULARLY	VACANTLY	VENOUSLY	VINOUSLY	VIRGINLY
VIRILELY	VISCIDLY	WEASELLY	WEEVILLY	WITTOLLY	WIZARDLY	WOUNDILY

MAN/MEN

AIRWOMAN	BAILSMAN	BANDSMAN	BANDYMAN	BANKSMAN	BARGEMAN	BATWOMAN
BEADSMAN	BEDESMAN	BLUESMAN	BOARDMAN	BOATSMAN	BONDSMAN	BOOGYMAN
BOTHYMAN	BRAKEMAN	BRIDEMAN	BRINKMAN	BUTTYMAN	*CANDYMAN*	CHAINMAN
CHESSMAN	*CHINAMAN*	CHOIRMAN	CHOREMAN	CLANSMAN	CLASSMAN	COLORMAN
CORPSMAN	CRAGSMAN	DAIRYMAN	DALESMAN	DOORSMAN	DRAGSMAN	DUTCHMAN
EARTHMAN	EVERYMAN	FERRYMAN	FOILSMAN	FORGEMAN	FRONTMAN	FUGLEMAN
FUNNYMAN	GANGSMAN	GAVELMAN	*GILDSMAN*	GLASSMAN	GOADSMAN	GOWNSMAN
HEADSMAN	HOASTMAN	HOISTMAN	HOTELMAN	HOUSEMAN	ISLESMAN	*KNIFEMAN*
LANDSMAN	LAYWOMAN	LEADSMAN	LIEGEMAN	LINKSMAN	LOCKSMAN	LODESMAN
LOFTSMAN	OVERSMAN	PENWOMAN	PETERMAN	PILOTMAN	PITCHMAN	PIVOTMAN
PLACEMAN	PLAIDMAN	PLATEMAN	POINTMAN	PRESSMAN	PRIZEMAN	PROSEMAN
PUNTSMAN	QUILLMAN	RADIOMAN	RANCHMAN	RIVERMAN	ROADSMAN	ROUTEMAN
SCENEMAN	SEAWOMAN	SEEDSMAN	SHAREMAN	SHEARMAN	SHEEPMAN	SHIREMAN
SHOREMAN	SIDESMAN	SONARMAN	SOUNDMAN	SPADEMAN	SPEARMAN	SQUAWMAN
STALLMAN	STEELMAN	STICKMAN	STILLMAN	SWAGSMAN	*SWEETMAN*	SWORDMAN
TACKSMAN	TALESMAN	TALLYMAN	TIDESMAN	TOWNSMAN	TOYWOMAN	TRACKMAN
TRAINMAN	TRASHMAN	TREWSMAN	VERSEMAN	WATCHMAN	WATERMAN	WEALSMAN
WEIGHMAN	WHALEMAN	WHEELMAN	WINCHMAN	YACHTMAN		

OID

AMOEBOID	ANCONOID	ARILLOID	ATHETOID	BOTRYOID	CERATOID	CHOREOID
CORONOID	DENDROID	ELYTROID	ERGATOID	GALENOID	GEOMYOID	GYNECOID
HEMATOID	HISTIOID	HYDATOID	ISTHMOID	KERATOID	LAMBDOID	LIGULOID
LYMPHOID	MANATOID	MUCINOID	MYCELOID	MYTILOID	NEMATOID	NEPHROID
NOCTUOID	*OCTOPOID*	ONISCOID	PETALOID	PHALLOID	PHELLOID	PITYROID
PYRANOID	RACEMOID	SCIUROID	SCLEROID	SEPALOID	SISTROID	SORICOID
SPONGOID	SQUALOID	STURNOID	TAENIOID	TAPIROID	TARSIOID	TERATOID
TETANOID	THALLOID	THYRSOID	TRICHOID	TUBEROID	*VARICOID*	VIBRIOID
VOLUTOID	YPSILOID					

8. Eight-Letter Words

ORY
ADDITORY	DECISORY	DELETORY	DERISORY	EMICTORY	ILLUSORY	INFUSORY
IRRISORY	JURATORY	LIBATORY	MINATORY	MUTATORY	NATATORY	NUGATORY
OBLATORY	PETITORY	POTATORY	PUNITORY	ROGATORY	SANATORY	VEXATORY

OSE
ACAULOSE	ANGINOSE	ANGULOSE	ANNULOSE	BARGOOSE	BIRAMOSE	BOOTHOSE
BOTRYOSE	CARGOOSE	CRIBROSE	CRUSTOSE	CUMULOSE	FARINOSE	FLEXUOSE
FRONDOSE	HAMULOSE	LACUNOSE	LAMINOSE	LITEROSE	LOBULOSE	MACULOSE
*MISCHOSE*n	NEBULOSE	NODULOSE	NUBILOSE	PALUDOSE	PLUVIOSE	PRUINOSE
RACEMOSE	RAMULOSE	RIVULOSE	RUGULOSE	SABULOSE	SETULOSE	SOPOROSE
SPATHOSE	SQUAMOSE	STRATOSE	STRIGOSE	STRUMOSE	SUBEROSE	TUBULOSE
TUMULOSE	UNDULOSE	VENENOSE	VENULOSE	VIRTUOSE		

OUS *extensions of fives*
ADUNCOUS	AMBEROUS	ANTICOUS	APTEROUS	ARBOROUS	ARSONOUS	ASPEROUS
COVETOUS	COVINOUS	CRANKOUS	CROUPOUS	DECOROUS	DIMEROUS	DOLOROUS
FELONOUS	FEVEROUS	*FRONDOUS*	GLAREOUS	GRISEOUS	ICHOROUS	INERMOUS
LIBELOUS	MUCINOUS	NIDOROUS	OCHEROUS	OCHREOUS	PETALOUS	PLUMBOUS
RESINOUS	ROSINOUS	RUMOROUS	SAPOROUS	SAVOROUS	SEPALOUS	SOPOROUS
SPERMOUS	STRUMOUS	SUDOROUS	TITANOUS	TUMOROUS	ULCEROUS	VALOROUS
VAPOROUS	VERTUOUS	VIPEROUS	VOMITOUS	WAVEROUS	WRONGOUS	

OUS *other, excluding 'IOUS'*
ACARPOUS	ACAULOUS	*ACOELOUS*	ANGINOUS	ANGULOUS	ANOUROUS	ANSEROUS
APHONOUS	ARACEOUS	ARANEOUS	ARSENOUS	ASTOMOUS	ATROPOUS	BIGAMOUS
BIJUGOUS	BIMANOUS	BIPAROUS	BIRAMOUS	BUTYROUS	CANOROUS	CARNEOUS
CERNUOUS	CHLOROUS	CHROMOUS	CITREOUS	CORNEOUS	CRIBROUS	CUMULOUS
CUPREOUS	DARTROUS	DEXTROUS	DIDYMOUS	DIGAMOUS	DIGYNOUS	DIOICOUS
DIPNOOUS	DITOKOUS	DIZYGOUS	ELYTROUS	ENGINOUS	EPIGEOUS	EUROKOUS
EXIGUOUS	FASTUOUS	FEATEOUS	FEATUOUS	FERREOUS	FLATUOUS	FLEXUOUS
FRABJOUS	GEMINOUS	GLABROUS	GLAUCOUS	GOITROUS	GYPSEOUS	HALITOUS
HAMULOUS	IDONEOUS	IMPOROUS	INCUBOUS	LACTEOUS	LAMINOUS	LEAPROUS
LUSTROUS	MELANOUS	MUTICOUS	MUTINOUS	NACREOUS	NEBULOUS	NEMOROUS
NODULOUS	NUBILOUS	OOGAMOUS	ORDUROUS	ORGULOUS	PABULOUS	PALUDOUS
PATULOUS	POACEOUS	PYRITOUS	PYRRHOUS	RACEMOUS	RAMULOUS	SABULOUS
SCABROUS	SCIOLOUS	SCLEROUS	SEDULOUS	SELENOUS	SETULOUS	SIBILOUS
SOMBROUS	SONOROUS	SQUAMOUS	STANNOUS	STRATOUS	TEMEROUS	THALLOUS
TIMOROUS	TUBULOUS	TUMULOUS	UNCTUOUS	UNDULOUS	UNFAMOUS	UNJOYOUS
VANADOUS	VENTROUS	VENULOUS	XANTHOUS			

SOME
BORESOME	CLOYSOME	DARKSOME	DOLESOME	DUELSOME	*FLAYSOME*	FLEASOME
FRETSOME	GLADSOME*	GLEESOME	GREWSOME*	HEALSOME	JOKESOME	LARKSOME
LIFESOME	LONGSOME	LOTHSOME	LOVESOME	PLAYSOME	TEDISOME	TOILSOME
TWIGSOME	WAILSOME	WORKSOME	*YAWNSOME*			

UM *excluding* `'IUM'`

ANESTRUM	CINGULUM	CORALLUM	CROTALUM	FURCULUM	HYPOGEUM	LABELLUM
NOTANDUM	OVERSWUM	PHILTRUM	PLACITUM	PRONOTUM	PUDENDUM	*PULLORUM*
SACELLUM	SCYBALUM	SECUNDUM	SPICULUM	VEXILLUM	VIDENDUM	

US *excluding* `'OUS'`

ALVEOLUS	ANESTRUS	APICULUS	ARCHAEUS	BACILLUS	BEJEEZUS	BRONCHUS
CALATHUS	CHIASMUS	CHONDRUS	COENURUS	DACTYLUS	DENARIUS	DETRITUS
ELENCHUS	EMERITUS	EPIGONUS	EREMURUS	GLUTAEUS	LAPILLUS	LECYTHUS
LEKYTHUS	NAUPLIUS	NUCELLUS	PULVINUS	*RISORIUS*	SCALENUS	SENARIUS
THALAMUS	THROMBUS					

WISE

ARCHWISE	COMBWISE	CRABWISE	DROPWISE	EDGEWISE	ELSEWISE	FLATWISE
LONGWISE	OVERWISE	PALEWISE	RINGWISE	SIDEWISE	SOMEWISE	STEPWISE
SUCHWISE	TEAMWISE	TENTWISE	THUSWISE			

8.3.5 OTHER EIGHTS CONTAINING HEAVY LETTERS

NOUNS CONTAINING 'J'

BENJAMIN	BLUEJACK	BOOTJACK	*CONJUNTO*	CUNJEVOI	DEMIJOHN	DISJUNCT
DOORJAMB	*FEIJOADA*	JACKSTAY	JACQUARD	*JAKFRUIT*	JAILBAIT	JALAPENO
JANITRIX+	JARARACA	JARARAKA	JARGONEL	*JATROPHA*	JELUTONG	JEREMIAD
JEREPIGO	JEROBOAM	JESTBOOK	JINGBANG	JOBSHARE	JOHANNES+	JOHNBOAT
JONCANOE	JORDELOO	JOVIALTY+	JUNKANOO	JURYMAST	KABELJOUw	KOMITAJI
LOGJUICE	MAHARAJAh	MAJOLICA	NINJITSU	NINJUTSU	QUILLAJA	SLAPJACK
STICKJAW	SUCURUJU	UNDERJAW	WHIPJACK			

NOUNS CONTAINING 'Q'

ADEQUACY+	AEQUORIN	AQUACADE	*AQUASHOW*	BRELOQUE	CHAQUETA	CINQUAIN
CLINIQUE	COQUILLA	COQUILLE	DAIQUIRI	DETRAQUEe	EMBUSQUE	EQUIVOKE
FILIOQUE	*GODSQUAD*	HAQUETON	HENEQUIN	HENIQUIN	HUAQUERO	JACQUARD
MAROQUIN	MBAQANGA	MORESQUE	MUSQUASH+	ODALIQUE	OLDSQUAW	PARAQUAT
PEQUISTE	PERRUQUE	PETANQUE	PIQUANCY+	*PIQUILLO*	POSTIQUE	PRATIQUE
QUAALUDE	*QUADPLAY*	QUADPLEX+	QUADRIGAe	QUANDANG	QUANDONG	QUANTONG
QUATORZE	QUATRAIN	QUENELLE	QUIDDANY+	QUIDNUNC	QUIETUDE	QUILLAJA
QUINCUNX+	QUINELLA	QUINIELA	QUINOLINe	QUINTAIN	RAMEQUIN	REMARQUEd
SEAQUAKE	SEQUENCY+	SEQUITUR	SQUAMULA	SQUARSON	SURQUEDY+	TEQUILLA
TOQUILLA	TURQUOISe	USQUABAE	USQUEBAE	VERQUERE	VERQUIRE	

NOUNS CONTAINING 'X'

ACETOXYL	*ALDOXIME*	ANATOXIN	ANTHELIX+	*AUXOCYTE*	AVIATRIX+	AXOPLASM
BATTLEAXe	BIOTOXIN	BOXTHORN	CARBOXYL	CARNIFEX+	CHRONAXY+	CINEPLEX+
CLANGBOX+	*COTURNIX+*	CREATRIX+	CURATRIX+	CURTALAXe	CYBERSEX+	*DOXAPRAM*
EARTHWAX+	ECONOBOX+	EPICALYX+	*EXAHERTZ+*	EXANTHEMa	EXIGENCE	EXIGENCY+
EXOPHAGY+	EXOPLASM	EXOSPORE	EXTERNAT	EXTRADOS+	FLAXSEED	FLEXAGON
FLEXTIMEr	FOURPLEX+	FOXSHARK	GENETRIX+	GENITRIX+	HERETRIX+	HERITRIX+
HEXAFOIL	HEXAGRAM	HOMEOBOX+	*HORSEBOX+*	HORSEPOX+	INTERSEX+	JANITRIX+

KETOXIME	LEXIGRAM	*LOOSEBOX+*	*LUNCHBOX+*	MAXICOAT	*MEGAPLEX+*	MICROLUX+
MILLILUX+	*NAPROXEN*	NEOTOXIN	NEURAXON	NITROXYL	OXAZEPAM	*OXIMETRY+*
OXTONGUE	OXYMORON	OXYTOCIN	*PAINTBOX+*	PARALLAX+	PAROXYSM	POLYAXON
QUADPLEX+	QUINCUNX+	SARDONYX+	SAUCEBOX+	SCRUMPOX+	SIXPENNY+	SIXSCORE
SMOKEBOX+	SOUNDBOX+	SPINTEXT	SUBINDEX+	SUBTAXON	SUPERFIX+	*SUPERMAX+*
SUPERSEX+	SUPERTAX+	SWEATBOX+	SWINEPOX+	TAXIARCH	TAXONOMY+	TEGUEXIN
TETRAXON	THYROXINe	TOADFLAX+	TOXOCARA	VIDEOTEXt	WATCHBOX+	WATERPOX+
WAXCLOTH	XANTHEIN	XANTHOMA	XENOGAMY+	XENOGENY+	XENOLITH	XENOTIME
XERAPHIN	XEROSERE	XYLOCARP	XYLOIDINe	ZELATRIX+	ZOOTOXIN	

NOUNS CONTAINING 'Z'

ALGUAZIL	*ALLOZYME*	BAROMETZ+	BENZIDINe	BOUZOUKIa	BRAZILIN	BRITZSKA
BRUNIZEM	*BUZKASHI*	*CALABAZA*	COENZYME	CREDENZA	CRUZEIRO	CZAREVNA
CZARITSA	*DAIDZEIN*	DIAZEPAM	DIAZINON	EPIZOOTY+	*EXAHERTZ+*	*FEMINAZI*
FORZANDO	GARBANZO	GAZPACHO	*GOHONZON*	GOLDSIZE	HOACTZIN	MANZELLO
MAZOURKA	*MECHITZA*	MESPRIZE	*METRAZOL*	MEZEREON	OXAZEPAM	PETUNTZE
PHENAZINe	*PYRAZOLE*	QUATORZE	RENDZINA	RHIZOPOD	RIBOZYME	SAMIZDAT
SARRAZIN	SCHANTZE	SCHIZONT	SCHMALTZy	*SHVARTZE*	SIEROZEM	SITZMARK
SOLONETZ+	SPAETZLE	SPETSNAZ+	SPRITZIG	STRELITZi	*SUNGAZER*	SUZERAIN
TERZETTA	TERZETTO	TRIAZOLE	TRISTEZA	TSARITZA	TZAREVNA	WHIZBANG
YAHRZEIT	YOKOZUNA	ZAMPOGNA	ZEBRINNY+	ZELATRIX+	ZIGGURAT	ZIRCALOY
ZOETROPE	*ZOLPIDEM*	ZOMBORUK	ZOOBLAST	ZOOCHORE	ZOOGLOEAe	ZOOGLOEA1
ZOOGRAFT	ZOOMANCY+	ZOOMORPHy	ZOOPATHY+	ZOOPHAGY+	ZOOPHILY+	ZOOPHOBE
ZOOPHYTE	ZOOSCOPY+	ZOOTHOME	ZOOTOXIN	ZOOTROPE	ZOPILOTE	ZUCHETTA
ZUCHETTO	ZWIEBACK					

NON-PLURALS

AFTERTAX	AMPHIOXI	BICONVEX	BIUNIQUE	BORDEAUX	*CHEQUING*	DIPLOZOA
ECTOZOON	ENDOZOON	ENTOZOON	EQUISETA	EXTRORSE	FORZANDI	GADZOOKS
GIAMBEUX	GOUJEERS	GRAZIOSO	HALUTZIM	HYDROZOAn	INTERREX	*JALFREZI*
JOGPANTS	KHAZENIM	LOQUITUR	LUSTIQUE	MAZELTOV	METAZOON	MIREPOIX
MITZVOTH	MULTIJET	NONQUOTA	OVERJUST	PARAZOON	PHORMINX	PIROZHKI
PIROZHOK	POLYZOON	PONTIFEX	PRECIEUX	PROTOZOA1	PROTOZOAn	QINDARKA
QINTARKA	QUADRANS	QUAGMIRY*	SAXATILE	*SAXICOLE*	SEXTARII	SHEQALIM
SHKOTZIM	SMORZATO	SPOROZOA1	SPOROZOAn	TERZETTI	*TOLARJEV*	TRACTRIX
TRAPEZII	UMQUHILE	UNEXPERT	UNSEXIST	VEHMIQUE	XENOPHYA	XEROMATA
XYLOMATA	ZADDIKIM	ZAIBATSU	ZASTRUGA	ZASTRUGI	*ZINDABAD*	ZOOPHORIc
ZYGANTRA	ZYGODONT	ZYGOMATA				

8.3.6 OTHER NOUNS

AASVOGEL	ABAMPERE	ABELMOSK	ABOIDEAUx	ABOITEAUx	ABORIGINe	ABSCISINg
ABUTILON	ACELDAMA	ACHILLEA	ACHROMAT	ACRODONT	ACROLEIN	ACROLITH
ACUPOINT	ADAMANCY+	ADHEREND	ADSCRIPT	ADVOCAAT	ADVOWSON	AEGLOGUE
AEGROTAT	AERODART	AERODUCT	AERODYNE	AEROLITH	AERONOMY+	AEROSTAT
AESCULIN	*AFTERSUN*	AGALLOCH	AGRIMONY+	AGRONOMY+	AIGUILLE	*AIRBOARD*
AIRBRICK	AIRBURST	AIRDROME	AIRFRAME	AIRGRAPH	AIRSCAPE	AIRSCREW
AIRSHAFT	AKARYOTE	ALASTRIM	ALBACORE	ALBICORE	ALCAHEST	ALCATRAS+

ALDEHYDE	ALDERFLY+	*ALDICARB*	ALEBENCH+	ALGAROBA	ALGUACIL	ALIGARTA
ALKAHEST	*ALKANNIN*	ALLERGIN	ALLOGAMY+	ALLOPATHy	ALLOSAUR	ALLOTYPE
ALLSPICE	ALMAGEST	ALTERNATe	ALUMROOT	AMADAVAT	AMANITIN	AMARELLE
AMARETTO	AMBERINA	AMBIVERT	AMELCORN	AMITROLE	AMORETTO	ANABAENA
ANABLEPS+	ANAEROBE	ANAGLYPHy	ANALCIME	ANALOGON	ANAPAEST	ANASARCA
ANATROPY+	ANCHUSIN	ANDESYTE	ANEURYSM	ANGKLUNG	*ANGLEDUG*	ANGLEPOD
ANGSTROM	ANTEPAST	ANTEROOM	ANTETYPE	ANTIARIN	ANTIATOM	ANTICULT
ANTIDUNE	ANTIHERO+	ANTIMASK	ANTIMERE	*ANTIMUON*	*ANTINOME*	ANTINOMY+
ANTINUKEr	ANTIPHONy	ANTIPOLE	ANTIPORN	ANTISNOB	ANTISTATe	ANTITYPE
ANTPITTA	ANVILTOP	APERITIF	APLUSTRE	APOLOGUE	APOSTACY+	APOSTASY+
APOTHECE	APOTHEGM	ARAPAIMA	ARAPONGA	ARAPUNGA	ARBALEST	ARBELEST
ARBUSCLE	ARCHDUKE	ARCHLUTE	ARETHUSA	ARGONAUT	ARMAGNAC	ARMONICA
ARPEGGIO	ARSEHOLEd	*ARTHOUSE*	ARTIFACT	ARVICOLE	*ASHTANGA*	ASPHODEL
ASSIENTO	ASSIGNAT	ATAMASCO	*ATENOLOL*	ATHANASY+	ATHEROMA	ATTENTAT
ATTERCOP	AUBRIETA	AURICULAe	AURICULAr	AUTOBAHN	AUTOCADE	AUTODYNE
AUTOGAMY+	AUTOGENY+	AUTOGIRO	AUTOGYRO	AUTOHARP	*AUTOTEST*	AUTOTOMY+
AUTOTUNE	AVIFAUNAe	AVIFAUNAl	AYURVEDA			
BAASKAAP	BAASSKAP	BACKFALL	BACKFLOW	BACKRUSH+	BACKSTAY	BACKVELD
BACKWORD	BACKWRAP	BACTERIN	BAGHOUSE	BAIDARKA	BAKEMEAT	BAKESHOP
BALEFIRE	BALISAUR	BALLADINe	BALLADINg	BALLCLAY	BALLHAWK	BALLISTAe
BALLONNE	*BANDEIRA*	BANDEROLe	BANDITTI	*BANGALAY*	*BANGALOW*	BANGTAIL
BANLIEUE	BANNEROL	BARATHEA	*BAREHAND*	BARESARK	BARGELLO	BARGHEST
BARGUEST	BARLEDUC	BAROGRAM	*BAROSAUR*	BAROSTAT	BAROUCHE	BARRANCA
BARRANCO	BASELARD	*BASILECT*	BASILISK	BASOPHILe	BASTILLE	BATHORSE
BAUDRONS+	BAYADERE	BEADROLL	BEAUCOUP	BECHAMEL	BEDCHAIR	BEDRIGHT
BEDSTAND	BEDSTEAD	BEDSTRAW	BEECHNUT	BEERHALL	BELLCOTE	BELLPULL
BENADRYL	BENEDICK	BENEDICT	BENISEED	BERCEUSE	BERDACHE	BERGAMOT
BERGFALL	BERGMEHL	BERNICLE	BERRETTA	BESOGNIO	BETATRON	BETELNUT
BETHESDA	BEVATRON	*BHELPURI*	BIACETYL	BICOLOUR	BIENNALE	BIGARADE
BIGEMINY+	BILLFOLD	BILLHOOK	BIMETHYL	BINNACLE	BIOMORPH	BIOPLASM
BIOPLAST	BIOSCOPE	BIOSCOPY+	*BIOTROPH*	BIPHENYL	BIRDCALL	BIRDFARM
BIRDFEED	BIRDSEYE	BIRDSHOT	BIRDSONG	BIRIYANI	BIRRETTA	BITSTOCK
BITTACLE	BLACKFIN	BLACKFLY+	BLACKLEG	BLACKTOP	BLASTEMAl	BLASTOMA
BLASTULAe	BLASTULAr	BLATANCY+	*BLINDGUT*	BLINKARD	*BLIPVERT*	BLOODFIN
BLOWHARD	BLUECOAT	BLUEGILL	BLUEGOWN	BLUESTEM	BLUETICK	BOATHOOK
BOATNECK	BOATTAIL	BOLLWORM	BOLTHOLE	BOLTROPE	BONGRACE	BONIFACE
BONSELLA	BONSPELL	BONSPIEL	*BOOGALOO*	BOOKLORE	BOOKREST	BOOMTOWN
BOONDOCK	BOOTLAST	BORACHIO	BORECOLE	BOSHVARK	BOSTANGI	*BOTTARGA*
BOUGHPOT	BOUILLON	BOUSOUKIa	BOWSPRIT	BRACIOLA	BRACIOLE	*BRAINIAC*
BRANCARD	BRANDADE	BRANDISE	BRANTAIL	BRASILIN	BRASSARD	BRASSART
BRASSICA	BREADNUT	BREASKIT	*BRESAOLA*	BRETESSE	BREVETCY+	BRINDISI
BROCATEL	BROCKRAM	BROMELIN	BROUGHAM	BRUCELLAe	BUCELLAS+	BUCKAROO
BUCKAYRO	BUCKEROO	BUCKHORN	BUCKSHOT	BUCKTAIL	BUGHOUSE	*BULLDYKE*
BULLHORN	BULLNECK	BULLSHOT	*BULWADDY+*	BUMALOTI	*BUNDWALL*	*BUNFIGHT*
BUNGHOLE	*BUNGWALL*	BURGRAVE	BURLETTA	*BURRAMYS+*	BURSICON	BUSHGOAT
BUSHMEAT	BUSHVELD					

8. Eight-Letter Words

CAATINGA	CABESTRO	CABRESTA	CABRESTO	CABRETTA	CABRILLA	CABRIOLEt
CABSTAND	CADASTRE	CALABASH+	*CALAMATA*	CALAMINT	CALANTHE	CALATHEA
CALIFONT	CALIPASH+	CALISAYA	CALLALOO	CALLIOPE	*CALLTIME*	CALOTYPE
CALTHROP	CALUTRON	CALVADOS+	CALYPTRA	CAMELEON	CAMISADE	CAMISADO
CAMISOLE	CAMPAGNA	CAMPHIRE	CAMSHAFT	CANAIGRE	CANAILLE	*CANEGRUB*
CANFIELD	*CANISTEL*	CANNABIN	CANNELONi	CANTHARId	CANTHOOK	CANTRAIP
CAPITAYN	CAPOEIRA	CAPONATA	CAPRIFIG	CAPYBARA	CARAGANA	CARASSOW
CARBAMYL	CARBARYL	CARBINOL	CARBONYL	CARDAMON	CARNAUBA	CARRIOLE
CARROTIN	CARRYALL	CARTLOAD	CARTROAD	CARYOTIN	CASELOAD	CASEWORM
CASIMERE	CASIMIRE	CASTRATOr	CATATONY+	CATHEDRAe	CATHEDRAl	CATHISMA
CATHOUSE	*CATOLYTE*	CATTLEYA	CAUDILLO	CAVALERO	CAVATINA	CAVESSON
CEMITARE	CENTIARE	CENTINELl	CENTONELl	CEPHALIN	CEROTYPE	CERULEIN
CERVELAS+	CERVELAT	CETYWALL	CHALDRON	CHALKPIT	CHAMBRAY	CHAMELOT
CHAMFRON	CHAMPART	CHANFRON	*CHANGEUP*	CHAPATTI	CHAPBOOK	CHAPERONe
CHAPTREL	*CHARANGA*	CHARANGO	CHARLADY+	CHASUBLE	*CHATROOM*	CHAWDRON
CHAYROOT	CHEEWINK	CHELIPED	CHEMURGY+	CHENILLE	CHENOPOD	CHERUBIM
CHERUBIN	CHEVEREL	CHEVERIL	CHEVERON	CHEVERYE	CHEVILLE	CHIGETAI
CHILDBED	CHILIASM	CHILIAST	CHILIDOG	CHILLADA	CHILOPOD	CHIMAERA
CHIMBLEY	*CHIMINEA*	CHINAMPA	CHINKARA	*CHIPOTLE*	CHIRAGRA	CHLOASMA
CHOLIAMB	CHORIAMBi	CHOWTIME	CHRESARD	CHRISMON	CHRISTOM	CHUPATTI
CHUPATTY+	CHURINGA	CHYMOSIN	CIABATTA	CILANTRO	CINNAMYL	CIRRIPEDe
CITRANGE	CITRININ	*CLADDAGH*	*CLAFOUTI*	CLAMBAKE	CLAPDISH+	CLAYBANK
CLAYMORE	CLERIHEW	CLODPOLE	CLODPOLL	CLOTPOLL	*CLUBFACE*	CLUBHAND
CLUBROOT	CLUBRUSH+	COALBALL	COALHOLE	COALSHED	COATROOM	COATTAIL
CODEBOOK	*CODENAME*	*CODEWORD*	*CODOMAIN*	COGNOVIT	COGWHEEL	COISTREL
COISTRIL	COKERNUT	COLESEED	COLISTIN	COLOBOMA	COLOPHONy	COLOTOMY+
COLUMNEA	COMEDOWN	COMPADRE	CONELRAD	CONEPATL	CONFERVAe	CONFERVAl
CONFRERE	CONODONT	CONSUMPT	CONTESSA	CONTINUO	CONTORNO	CONTRAIL
CONVERSO	COOKROOM	COOKSHOP	COOLABAH	COOLAMON	COOLDOWN	COOLIBAH
COPATRON	COPROSMA	COPYDESK	*COPYGIRL*	COPYHOLD	*COPYLEFT*	CORDWAIN
CORNBALL	CORNFLAG	CORNHUSK	CORNLOFT	CORNMILL	CORNMOTH	CORNWORM
CORTISOL	COTILLON	COULISSE	COUMARIN	COUMAROU	COUTILLE	COVETISE
COWGRASS+	COWHEARD	COWHOUSE	COYSTREL	COYSTRIL	CRAMOISY+	CRANEFLY+
CRANKPIN	CRASHPAD	*CRAYTHUR*	CREMORNE	*CRENSHAW*	CREODONT	CRETONNE
CREVALLE	CROMORNA	CROMORNE	CROSSARM	CROSTINI	CROUPADE	*CROWBOOT*
CROWFOOT	CROWSTEP	CRUMHORN	*CRYOBANK*	CRYOSTAT	CRYOTRON	CULVERIN
CUMBUNGI	CURASSOW	CUSSWORD	CUTGLASS+	CUTGRASS+	CUTPURSE	*CYNODONT*
DAHABIYAh	DAISHIKI	DALMAHOY	DAMASSIN	DAMBOARD	DAMNDEST	DAMOISEL
DANEGELD	DANEGELT	DANELAGH	DANSEUSE	DARNDEST	*DATACARD*	*DATAFLOW*
DATAGRAM	*DATEBOOK*	*DAYSHELL*	DEADBOLT	DEADFALL	DEATHCUP	DECAGRAM
DECEMVIRi	DECIGRAM	DEKAGRAM	DELEGACY+	DEMARCHE	DEMERARAn	DEMILUNE
DEMIURGE	DEMIVOLTe	DEMONIAC	DENTELLE	DENTICLE	*DEPRENYL*	DERRIERE
DESKFAST	*DESKNOTE*	DESPIGHT	DESPOTATe	DESYATIN	DEUDDARN	DEUTERON
DEVIANCY+	DEWPOINT	DIACETYL	*DIADOCHY+*	DIAGLYPH	DIAGRAPH	DIAMANTE
DIAPASON	DIAPENTE	DIAPHONY+	DIARRHEAl	DIASCOPE	DIASPORA	DIASPORE
DIASTOLE	DIASTYLE	DICENTRA	DIDACTYL	DIDDICOY	DIDRACHMa	DIELDRIN
DIELYTRA	DIESTOCK	*DIGESTIF*	*DIGIPACK*	*DIGITRON*	DIHEDRON	DIMETHYL
DINARCHY+	DIOBOLON	DIOLEFIN	DIPHENYL	DIPTERON	DIPTEROS+	DISPATHY+

DISPEACE	DISPROOF	DISSIGHT	DISTRAIL	DOCIMASY+	DOCKHAND	*DOCUSOAP*
DOGGEREL	DOGSLEEP	DOGWATCH+	*DOLCETTO*	DOLICHOS+	DOMESDAY	DOMINICK
DOOLALLY+	DOORNAIL	DOORPOST	DOORSILL	DORMANCY+	DOTTEREL	DOUGHBOY
DOUPIONI	DOWNBEAT	DOWNCOMEr	DOWNHAUL	DOWNRUSH+	*DOWNSPIN*	DOWNTICK
DOWSABEL	DRACAENA	DRAGROPE	DRAMSHOP	DRAWBORE	DRAWTUBE	DRIFTPIN
DRONKLAP	DROPSHOT	*DRUGLORD*	DRUMFIRE	DRYMOUTH	DRYPOINT	*DUATHLON*
DUCKBILL	DUCKMOLE	DUCKTAIL	DUECENTO	DUETTINO	DULCINEA	DULCITOL
DUMBSHIT	*DUMBSHOW*	DUMPCART	*DUNGHEAP*	DUNGMERE	DUOLOGUE	DUOPSONY+
DURUKULI	DUSTCART	*DUSTCOAT*	DUSTHEAP	DYNATRON	DYSCHROA	DYSPNOEAl
EARPIECE	EARTHNUT	EARTHPEA	EBENISTE	ECHOGRAM	ECLAMPSY+	ECOFREAK
ECOLODGE	ECTODERM	ECTOGENY+	ECTOMERE	EELGRASS+	EELWRACK	*EGGFRUIT*
EGGWHISK	EGLATERE	EINSTEIN	ELATERIN	*ELDORADO*	ELEGANCY+	ELEGIAST
ELKHOUND	EMERAUDE	EMOTICON	EMPANADA	ENCEINTE	ENCIERRO	ENDAMEBAe
ENDBRAIN	ENDOCARP	ENDOCAST	ENDODERM	ENDOGAMY+	ENDOSARC	ENDOSMOSe
ENDPOINT	ENHYDROS+	ENNEAGON	ENSIGNCY+	ENTAMEBAe	ENTHALPY+	ENTODERM
ENTREPOT	ENTRESOL	EOLIENNE	EPANODOS+	EPENDYMAl	EPHEDRINe	EPHEMERAe
EPHEMERAl	EPIBLAST	EPICOTYL	EPIFAUNAe	EPIFAUNAl	EPINASTY+	EPISEMON
EPISTASY+	EPISTOME	EPISTYLE	ERGOGRAM	ERIGERON	ERYTHEMAl	ERYTHRON
ESCARGOT	ESCAROLE	ESCHALOT	ESPUMOSO	ESTACADE	ESTRAGON	ESTRIDGE
ETHANOYL	ETHERCAP	*ETHNONYM*	*ETHOGRAM*	ETTERCAP	EUCARYON	EUCARYOTe
EUDAEMONy	*EUDAIMON*	EUKARYON	EUKARYOTe	EULACHON	EUONYMIN	EUPHRASY+
EUROBOND	EUROCRAT	*EURONOTE*	EURYBATH	EUTROPHY+	EVENFALL	EVENSONG
EYEBLACK	*EYEBLINK*	EYEPOINT	EYESTALK			
FACEDOWN	*FACEMAIL*	*FACEMASK*	FAHLBAND	FAIRLEAD	FALDEROL	FALDETTA
FALLBACK	FALTBOAT	FANDANGO	FANEGADA	FANLIGHT	FANTIGUE	FARCEUSE
FARNESOL	*FAROLITO*	FASCIOLA	FASCIOLE	FASTBACK	FASTBALL	FATSTOCK
FAUBOURG	FAUTEUIL	FEBLESSE	FEDELINI	FEDERACY+	FEEDHOLE	FELDGRAU
FELLATIOn	FEMERALL	FEMINACY+	FENCEROW	FENCIBLE	FENESTRAe	FENESTRAl
FENTANYL	*FERNALLY+*	FERNBIRD	FERNSHAW	FERRITIN	FETERITA	FIBRANNE
FILECARD	FILENAME	FILLIBEG	FILMCARD	FINITUDE	FINNMARK	FINOCHIO
FIREBACK	FIREBIRD	FIREBOAT	FIREBRAT	*FIREBUSH+*	FIRECLAY	FIREDAMP
FIREHALL	FIRELOCK	FIREMARK	FIREPINK	FIREPLUG	FIREROOM	FIREWORM
FISHBALL	FISHBOLT	*FISHCAKE*	*FISHKILL*	FISHPOLE	FISHWORM	FISSIPEDe
FISTMELE	FISTNOTE	FLAMBEAUx	FLANCARD	*FLAPERON*	FLASHGUN	FLATBACK
FLATBOAT	FLATIRON	FLATPACK	FLATWASH+	FLATWORM	FLAVANOL	FLAVONOL
FLESHPOT	*FLIPBOOK*	FLORENCE	FLUELLIN	FLUIDRAM	FLYPITCH+	FLYWHEEL
FOLDBACK	FOLDBOAT	FOLDEROL	FOLKMOOT	*FOLKSONG*	FOLKTALE	*FOLLOWUP*
FONTANEL	FONTANGE	*FOOSBALL*	FOOTBATH	FOOTMARK	FOOTPACE	FOOTPOST
FOOTROPE	FOOTWALL	FOOTWELL	FOREBITT	FOREBODY+	FOREBOOM	FOREDECK
FOREHOCK	FORELADY+	FORELIMB	FOREMAST	FOREMILK	FORENAME	FORENOON
FOREPART	FOREPEAK	FORESAIL	FORESTAY	FORETIME	FOREWIND	FOREWORD
FORKBALL	FORKTAIL	FORMALIN	FOUGASSE	FOULMART	*FOURBALL*	*FOURPLAY*
FRANKLIN	FRASCATI	FRAULEIN	FRESCADE	FRICADEL	FRITTATA	FROMENTY+
FROSTNIP	FRUMENTY+	*FRYBREAD*	FUGHETTA	FULGENCY+	FULLBACK	FUMAROLE
FUMEROLE	FUNBOARD	FUNGIBLE	FUNKHOLE	FURCRAEA	FURMENTY+	FURUNCLE
FUSSBALL						

GAIRFOWL	GALABIEH	GALABIYAh	GALAPAGO	GALLABEAh	GALLEASS+	GALLIARD
GALLIASS+	GALLIPOT	GALLIVAT	GALOPADE	GAMBESON	GAMBETTA	*GAMEPLAY*
GANGPLOW	GANTLOPE	GANYMEDE	*GAOLBIRD*	GAPESEED	GAPEWORM	GARBOARD
GARDYLOO	GAREFOWL	GARGANEY	GARRIGUE	GASFIELD	GASHOUSE	GASTRAEA
GASTRULAe	GASTRULAr	GATEFOLD	GATEPOST	GAVELOCK	GEEPOUND	GEMSBUCK
GEMSHORN	GENDARME	*GENOGRAM*	GENOTYPE	GENTRICE	GEOCARPY+	GEOGNOST
GEOGNOSY+	GEOMANCY+	GEOPHAGY+	GEOPHYTE	GEOPROBE	*GEOTHERM*	GERANIOL
GERBILLE	GEROPIGA	*GIFTABLE*	GIGAFLOP	GIGAWATT	GILDHALL	GILLAROO
GINGELEY	GINGELLI	GINGELLY+	GINGILLI	GINHOUSE	GIVEBACK	GLADIOLE
GLASNOST	GLAUCOMA	GLOBULIN	GLORIOLE	GLORIOSA	GLOSSEME	GLOSSINA
GLOWLAMP	GLUCAGON	*GLUEBALL*	GLUHWEIN	GLUMELLA	GLUTELIN	*GLUTENIN*
GLYCERINe	GLYCEROL	GOALBALL	GOATHERD	GOLCONDA	GOLFIANA	GOLGOTHA
GOLLIWOGg	GONDELAY	GONFALON	GONFANON	GONOCYTE	*GONODUCT*	GONOPORE
GOODSIRE	GOOFBALL	GOOSEGOB	GOOSEGOG	GORBELLY+	GORGERIN	GOSSYPOL
GOURMAND	GRACIOSO	GRADUAND	GRAMERCY+	GRAMOCHE	GRANDDAM	GRANDSIRe
GRAPHEME	GRATTOIR	GRAVITAS+	GRAVITON	GRAYBACK	GRAYMAIL	GREENBUG
GREENEYE	GREENFLY+	*GRENACHE*	*GREYBACK*	GRIDELIN	GRILLADE	GRIMOIRE
GRIPSACK	GROGSHOP	GROMWELL	GROSBEAK	GROSSART	GRUBWORM	GUACHARO
GUAIACOL	GUANIDINe	*GUARDDOG*	GUDESIRE	GUERIDON	GUIMBARD	GUITGUIT
GUMBOTIL	GUNFLINT	GUNNYBAG	GURDWARA	GURGOYLE	GUSTABLE	GYROSTAT

HABANERA	*HABANERO*	HABITUDE	HACIENDA	HACKBOLT	HAEMATIN	HAEREMAI
HAIRBAND	HAIRBELL	HAIRGRIP	*HAIRTAIL*	HAIRWORM	HALFBEAK	HALICORE
HALLALOO	HALLIARD	HALLOUMI	*HALOSERE*	HANDBELL	HANDBILL	HANDCLAP
HANDLOOM	HANDPLAY	*HANDROLL*	HANEPOOT	HANGBIRD	HANGFIRE	HANGNAIL
HANGNEST	HAPTERON	HARDBAKE	HARDBALL	HARDBEAM	HARDBOOT	HARDEDGE
HARDFACE	*HARDPACK*	*HARDROCK*	HARDTACK	*HARDTAIL*	HAREBELL	HARMALINe
HARTBEESt	HATGUARD	HAUSFRAU	HAVELOCK	HAWKBELL	HAWKBILL	HAYFIELD
HEADFAST	*HEADFUCK*	HEADMARK	HEADNOTE	HEADRACE	HEADRAIL	HEADROPE
HEADSAIL	HEADSTAY	*HEADWALL*	HEADWORD	HEARTPEA	HEATSPOT	*HEATWAVE*
HEBDOMAD	HEBETUDE	HECATOMB	HEDGEPIG	HEDGEROW	HEELBALL	HEELPOST
HEKETARA	HELIDECK	HELISTOP	HELLFIRE	HELLICAT	HEMATEIN	HEMOCOEL
HEMOCYTE	HEMOSTAT	HEMPSEED	HEPATOMA	HEPTAGON	HERCULES+	HERDWICK
HERISSON	HERONSEW	HICKWALL	*HICKYMAL*	HIELAMAN	HIERURGY+	*HILLFORT*
HINDCAST	HIRAGANA	HISTAMINe	HISTIDINe	HOGGEREL	HOGMANAY	HOGMENAY
HOLDBACK	*HOLDDOWN*	HOLDFAST	HOLLIDAM	HOLOGAMY+	HOLOTYPE	HOLSTEIN
HOMEBRED	*HOMEBREW*	*HOMEGIRL*	HOMOGENY+	HOMOGONY+	HOMOTONY+	HOMOTYPE
HOMUNCLE	HONEYBUN	HONORAND	*HOODMOLD*	HOOFBEAT	HOOSEGOW	HORNBEAK
HORNBEAM	HORNBILL	HORNBOOK	HORNGELD	HORNTAIL	HORNWORM	HOROLOGEr
HOROPITO	HORSEFLY+	HOTBLOOD	HOUSEBOY	HOUSEFLY+	HOUSETOP	*HOWLBACK*
HUMICOLE	HUMORESK	HYDRAGOG	*HYDRILLA*	HYDROGEL	HYDROMEL	HYDROSKI
HYDROSOL	HYPERGOL	HYPOBOLE	HYPODERMa			

ICEBLINK	ICEFIELD	ICEHOUSE	ICEKHANA	IDEOGRAM	*IDIOGRAM*	IDIOLECT
IDIOTYPE	IGNITRON	IGNOMINY+	IMITANCY+	IMPOLICY+	INCENTRE	INCHWORM
INDIGEST	INFOBAHN	*INFOTECH*	INGROWTH	INKSTAND	INOSITOL	INSTANCY+
INSTROKE	*INTEGRIN*	*INTERMAT*	*INTERWEB*	INTIFADAh	INTONACO	INTRADOS+
INVERTINg	IODOPSIN	IRENICON	IRISCOPE	ISARITHM	ISOBRONT	*ISOBUTYL*

ISOCHASM	ISOCHEIM	ISOCHIME	ISOCHRONe	ISOCRYME	ISOGRAPH	ISOLOGUE
ISOMORPH	ISOPHOTE	ISOPLETH	*ISOSTACY*+	ISOTHERE	ISOTHERM	ISOTROPY+
KAISERIN	*KALAMATA*	KALLIDIN	KALOTYPE	KALUMPIT	KALYPTRA	KAMAAINA
KAOLIANG	*KAREAREA*	KARYOTIN	KATCHINA	*KAUMATUA*	KEELBOAT	KEESHOND
KEIRETSU	KENOTRON	KEPHALIN	KERATOMA	KEYBUGLE	KHANSAMAh	KHILAFAT
KIDGLOVE	KIELBASA	KILLCROP	KILOBAUD	KILOGRAY	KILOMOLE	*KILOPOND*
KILOVOLT	KINGBIRD	KINGBOLT	KINGPOST	KIRIGAMI	KLYSTRON	KNEEHOLE
KOHLRABI	KOLBASSI	KORFBALL	KOTTABOS+	KRUMHORN	KRYOLITH	KYRIELLE
LACEBARK	LADYLOVE	LADYPALM	*LAEVULIN*	LAKEPORT	LAMANTIN	LAMBENCY+
LAMBKILL	LAMPASSE	LAMPHOLE	LANCEGAY	LANDDROSt	LANDFALL	LANDGRAB
LANDRACE	LANDRAIL	LANDSKIP	LANDWIND	LANGLAUF	LANGSPEL	LANGSYNE
LANTHORN	LANTSKIP	LAPBOARD	LARBOARD	LARKSPUR	*LASTBORN*	LATCHKEY
LATEWAKE	*LAVANDIN*	LAVATERA	*LAWCOURT*	*LAYSHAFT*	LAYSTALL	LEACHOUR
LEAFWORM	LECANORA	LECHAYIM	LECITHIN	LEEBOARD	*LEFTMOST*	LEGALESE
LEKGOTLA	LENIENCE	LENTICEL	LENTICLE	LEUCOSIN	LEVODOPA	LEWISSON
LEYLANDIi	LIBRAIRE	LIBRETTO	LICHANOS+	LICHENINg	LICHWAKE	LICKSPIT
LIFECARE	*LIFEHACK*	LIFTBACK	LILLIPUT	LIMEKILN	LIMEWASH+	LINALOOL
LINDWORM	*LINGUICA*	LINGUINI	*LINGUISA*	LINSTOCK	LINTSEED	LIPOCYTE
LIPOGRAM	*LIPSALVE*	LISPOUND	*LISTSERV*	LITHARGE	LITHOSOL	LIVELONG
LIVELOOD	LOANBACK	LOANWORD	LOBLOLLY+	LOBOTOMY+	LOBSTICK	LOCKSTEP
LOGBOARD	LOGOGRAM	LOGOMACHy	LOGOTYPE	LONGBOAT	LONGERON	LONGHAIR
LONGHORN	*LONGNECK*	LONGSPUR	LONGWALL	*LONGWORM*	LONICERA	LOOKDOWN
LOPGRASS+	*LOPOLITH*	LOPSTICK	LOTHARIO	*LOVEFEST*	LOVELOCK	*LOVESEAT*
LUDERICK	LUNANAUT	LUNGWORM	LUTEFISK	LUTEOLIN	LYNCHPIN	
MACAHUBA	MACKINAW	MACROPOD	MADRASSAh	MAESTOSO	*MAGAININ*	MAHARANI
MAIASAURa	MAILSACK	MAINSAIL	MAIOLICA	*MAIREHAU*	MAKEFAST	MALAPERT
MALARKEY	MALIHINI	*MALLCORE*	MALLECHO	MALODOUR	MALSTICK	MANCIPLE
MANDIBLE	MANDORLA	MANDRAKE	MANGABEY	*MANGANIN*	MANGONEL	MANNITOL
MANSHIFT	MANTILLA	MANTISSA	*MANUHIRI*	MANYATTA	MAPSTICK	MARAVEDI
MARCELLA	MARGARINe	MARGRAVE	MARIACHI	MARINARA	MARIPOSA	MARKDOWN
MAROCAIN	MARSPORT	MARTAGON	MARTELLO	MASCARON	MASOOLAH	MASSCULT
MASSICOT	MASSOOLA	*MASSTIGE*	MASTICOT	MASTODONt	MATERIEL	MATFELON
MATGRASS+	MATTRASS+	MEALYBUG	MEDICARE	MEGABUCK	MEGADYNE	MEGAFLOP
MEGALITH	MEGALOPS+	MEGAVOLT	*MEIOCYTE*	*MELITTIN*	MELODEON	MENARCHE
MERENGUE	MERGENCE	MERICARP	MEROGONY+	MERSALYL	MESCALINe	MESNALTY+
MESOCARP	MESOGLEAl	MESOPHYLl	MESOTRON	MESPRISE	*METABOLY*+	METEWAND
METHADONe	METOPRYL	MICRODOT	MICRURGY+	MIDBRAIN	MIDRANGE	MIDSPACE
MIDWATCH+	MIGNONNE	MILKSHED	MILLCAKE	MILLEPEDe	*MILLHAND*	MILLIARD
MILLIARE	MILLIPEDe	MILLRACE	MILLRIND	MILLTAIL	MINDFUCK	*MINIDISC*
MINIDISH+	MINIDISK	MINIPARK	MINIPILL	MINNEOLA	MINSHUKU	MIRLITON
MISARRAY	MISBIRTH	MISCREED	MISDREAD	MISERERE	MISFAITH	MISLETOE
MISTRUTH	MOBOCRAT	*MOCKTAIL*	MODERATOr	MOFUSSIL	*MOKOPUNA*	MOLDWARP
MOLECAST	MONELLIN	MONGCORN	*MONOBROW*	MONOCARP	MONOCRAT	MONOCYTE
MONOFUEL	MONOGENY+	MONOGLOT	MONOGONY+	MONOHULL	MONOKINI	MONOPOLE
MONOTINT	MONOTYPE	MONTEITH	MONTICLE	*MOONCAKE*	MOONFACEd	MOONPORT
MOONRISE	MOONROCK	MOONROOF	MOONSAIL	MOONSEED	MOONSHOT	*MOORBURN*

MOORFOWL	MOPBOARD	MOPEHAWK	MOPSTICK	MORDANCY+	MOREPORK	MORTBELL
MORTSAFE	MOSASAURi	MOSSBACK	MOTORAIL	MOUCHARD	MOUCHOIR	*MOUSEPAD*
MOVIEOKE	MOVIEOLA	MUCKHEAP	MUDIRIEH	MUIRBURN	MULLARKY+	MULTIFIL
MULTIPEDe	MUNDUNGO	MUNGCORN	MUSCADEL	MUSCADINe	MUSCATEL	*MUSKROOT*
MYOBLAST	MYOGRAPHy	MYOSCOPE	MYRIADTH	MYRIAPOD	MYRIOPOD	MYSTAGOGy

NAILFOLD	NAINSOOK	NAMETAPE	NANNYGAI	NANOGRAM	*NANOPORE*	*NANOTECH*
NANOTUBE	NANOWATT	*NANOWIRE*	NAPOLEON	NARGHILY+	NARICORN	NASTALIK
NAUMACHY+	NAVICERT	NAVICULAr	NEATHERD	NECKBAND	NECKBEEF	NEEDFIRE
NEGATRON	NENNIGAI	NEOBLAST	NEOMORPH	NEOMYCIN	NEOPHOBE	NEOPHYTE
NEOPLASM	NEPENTHE	*NETSPEAK*	NEUROPIL	NEUTRINO	*NEWSBEAT*	NEWSDESK
NEWSGIRL	NEWSPEAK	NIGROSINe	NINEBARK	NIRAMIAI	NITROSYL	NOBLESSE
NOCTILIO	*NOISENIK*	NOMOGENY+	NONADULT	NONBLACK	NONCLASS+	NONCRIME
NONESUCH+	NONGUEST	NONGUILT	NONISSUE	NONNOVEL	NONSTYLE	NONTRUTH
NOONTIME	*NOPALITO*	NORMALCY+	NOSEBAND	*NOTECARD*	NOUVELLE	NOVELESE
NOVERINT	NUCLEOLE	NUMSKULL	NUNCHAKU	NUNCHEON	NUTGRASS+	NUTSEDGE
NYSTATIN						

OBDURACY+	OBLIGATOr	OCEANAUT	OCHIDORE	OCOTILLO	OCTANGLE	OCTAPODY+
ODOGRAPH	ODONTOMA	OEILLADE	OENOPHILe	OENOPHILy	OERLIKON	OILCLOTH
OLDSTYLE	OLIGARCHy	OLYMPIAD	OMADHAUN	OMBRELLA	OMNIARCH	OMNIVORE
OMOPHAGY+	ONCOTOMY+	ONDOGRAM	*ONGAONGA*	ONTOGENY+	OOGAMETE	*OOMYCETE*
OOPHORON	OOSPHERE	OPERCELE	OPSIMATHy	OPULENCY+	OPUSCULE	ORATORIO
ORCHELLA	ORCHILLA	ORDINAND	*OREODONT*	*ORLISTAT*	ORSEILLE	ORTHICON
ORTHOEPY+	ORTHOPOD	OSNABURG	*OSSOBUCO*	OSTINATO	OSTRACODe	OTOSCOPE
OTOSCOPY+	OTTAVINO	OUISTITI	OULACHON	OUTCURVE	OUTGUARD	OUTSIGHT
OUTSKIRT	OVENBIRD	*OVERBANK*	*OVERBOOT*	OVERGANG	OVERHAIR	OVERSALE
OVERSHOE	OVERSOUL	OVERSPIN	OVERWASH+	OVERWORD	OWERLOUP	OWRECOME
OYSTRIGE						

PABOUCHE	PACHINKO	PACHOULI	PACKFONG	*PACKMULE*	PADERERO	PADUASOY
PAGEVIEW	*PAHAUTEA*	PAILLARD	PAITRICK	*PAKTHONG*	PALEBUCK	PALEOSOL
PALESTRAe	PALESTRAl	PALINODY+	PALLIARD	PALMETTO	PALMITIN	PALOMINO
PALSTAVE	PANATELA	PANCETTA	PANCHEON	PANDOWDY+	PANETELA	PANGOLIN
PANNICLE	PANNIKELl	*PANSTICK*	PANTABLE	PANTALONe	PANTHEON	PANTOFLE
PARABOLE	PARAFOIL	PARAGOGE	PARAGRAM	PARAMESE	PARAMOUR	PARANETE
PARANOEA	PARASANG	PARCHISI	PARFLESH+	*PARISHAD*	PAROCHINe	PARRIDGE
PARRITCH+	PARTERRE	PARVOLINe	PASHALIK	PASHMINA	PASSBAND	PASTICHE
PASTILLE	*PASTITSO*	PASTROMI	PATERERO	*PATHNAME*	PATRONNE	*PATTRESS*+
PATUTUKI	PAULDRON	PAVILLON	PAYGRADE	PEACENIK	PEARLASH+	PEARMAIN
PEASECOD	PECORINO	PEDERASTy	PEDERERO	PEDUNCLEd	PEIGNOIR	PELLAGRA
PELLICLE	PELLMELL	PEMBROKE	PENCRAFT	PENDENCY+	PENDICLEr	PENNEECH
PENNEECK	PENONCEL	PENSTOCK	PENTACLE	PENTANOL	PENTARCHy	PENTOSANe
PENTROOF	PENUCHLE	PENUCKLE	PENUMBRAe	PENUMBRAl	PERCOLIN	PEREGRINe
PERIAGUA	PERIANTH	PERIBLEM	PERIDERM	PERILUNE	PERISARC	*PERMATAN*
PERNANCY+	PESTHOLE	*PETABYTE*	PETALODY+	PETRONEL	PETUNTSE	PHALANGEr
PHANTASMa	PHANTAST	PHENETOLe	PHENOGAM	PHILABEG	PHILAMOT	PHILIBEG
PHILOMELa	PHILOMOT	PHINNOCK	PHISNOMY+	PHLEGMON	*PHONECAM*	PHOTOFIT
PHRYGANA	PHYLLOME	PIASSABA	PIASSAVA	PICAYUNE	PICHURIM	PICKADILl

PICKEREL	PICLORAM	PICOGRAM	PICOMOLE	PIECRUST	PIEDFORT	PIEDMONT
PIGSWILL	PILLWORM	PIMIENTO	PINCHBUG	PINCHGUT	PINGRASS+	PINKROOT
PINOCHLE	*PINSWELL*	PINTABLE	PIRARUCU	PISHOGUE	*PISOLITH*	PISTACHE
PITAHAYA	PITHBALL	PLANOSOL	PLANTAIN	PLASTRON	PLATANNA	PLATBAND
PLATEASM	PLATYSMA	PLAYBILL	PLAYBOOK	PLAYDOWN	PLECTRON	PLENARTY+
PLEONASM	PLEONASTe	PLEUSTON	*PLIOFILM*	PLIOSAUR	PLIOTRON	PLOWBACK
PLUGUGLY+	PODOMERE	POECHORE	POKEROOT	POLLIWIG	POLLIWOG	POLLYWIG
POLLYWOG	POLYGALA	POLYGLOTt	POLYMATHy	POLYSEME	POONTANG	POORTITH
POORWILL	POROGAMY+	PORTAGUE	*PORTFIRE*	PORTHORS+	PORTIGUE	PORTLAST
PORTOISE	POSITRON	POSTCAVAe	POSTCAVAl	POSTFACE	*POSTGRAD*	POSTHEAT
POSTHOLE	POSTICHE	POSTLUDE	POSTTEST	POTHOUSE	POTSHARD	POTSHARE
POTSHERD	POULDRON	POURSUIT	PRAEFECT	PREADULT	PREAUDIT	PRECURSE
PREDEATH	PREDELLA	PRESBYTEr	PRESIDIO	PRESSFAT	PRESSRUN	PRETENCE
PRETERITe	PRIEDIEUx	PRODROME	PROGGINS+	PROLAMINe	PROSTYLE	PROTAMINe
PROTENSE	*PROTEOME*	PRUNELLA	PRUNELLE	PRUNELLO	PSALMODY+	PSILOCIN
PSORALEA	*PUIRTITH*	PULLBACK	PULSIDGE	PULVILIO	PULVILLEd	*PUNCHBAG*
PUNCHEON	PUNGENCE	PURSLAIN	PUSHBALL	*PUSHBIKE*	PUSHCART	PUSHDOWN
PUTCHEON	PYENGADU	*PYINKADO*	PYODERMA	PYORRHEAl	PYROSTAT	

RACEPATH	RACHILLAe	RADDOCKE	RADIANCY+	RADICAND	RADWASTE	RAGWHEEL
RAILBIRD	RAINBAND	RAINBIRD	RAKEHELLy	RAMPANCY+	RAMSHORN	*RAMTILLA*
RANDLORD	*RANGIORA*	RAPESEED	RARERIPE	*RASMALAI*	*RATHOUSE*	RATHRIPE
RAVIGOTE	*RAWMAISH*+	RAYGRASS+	REAGENCY+	REAPHOOK	REDBELLY+	REDBRICK
REDDENDO	REDHORSE	REDSHANK	REDSHIFT	REDSTART	REEDBIRD	REEDBUCK
REFUSNIK	REGNANCY+	REGOLITH	REHOBOAM	REINFUND	REMOLADE	RENEGADO
RENMINBI	RENOGRAM	REPETEND	REPLICON	REPOUSSE	REPRIEFE	RESINATA
RESORCIN	RESPLEND	RETINULAe	RETINULAr	RETIRACY+	RETRAICT	*RETRONYM*
RETURNIK	*REUPTAKE*	REVANCHE	REVEILLE	RHEOCORD	RHEOSTAT	RHEOTOME
RHODAMINe	RIBGRASS+	RICEBIRD	RICHESSE	*RIDGETOP*	RIFAMPIN	RIGATONI
RIGAUDON	RILLMARK	RINGBOLT	RINGDOVE	RINGHALS+	RINGNECK	RINGTOSS+
RINGWOMB	RINKHALS+	*RIRORIRO*	RITENUTO	RITORNELl	RIVERAIN	ROCAILLE
ROLLBACK	*ROLLNECK*	RONDACHE	RONDAVEL	RONDELLE	RONGGENG	ROORBACH
ROORBACK	ROOTHOLD	*ROOTWORM*	ROPEWALK	ROSEBOWL	ROSEROOT	ROSESLUG
ROSOGLIO	ROTGRASS+	ROUGHLEG	ROUSSEAU	ROWNDELL	RUCKSEAT	RUMBELOW
RUNROUND	RUTABAGA	RYEFLOUR	RYEGRASS+	RYOTWARI		

SAFRANINe	SAGAMORE	SAGANASH+	SAILROOM	SAINFOIN	SALADANG	SALARIAT
SALEROOM	SALIENCE	SALIENCY+	SALPICON	SALSILLA	SAMPHIRE	SANDARACh
SANDSPUR	SANDWORM	SANNYASIn	SANSERIF	SANTALIN	SANTALOL	SANTONIN
SAPIENCE	SAPIENCY+	SARABANDe	SARDELLE	SARPANCH+	SARRASIN	SASARARA
SATINPOD	SATYRISK	*SAUCEPOT*	SAUFGARD	SAUROPOD	SAUTERNE	SAWBLADE
SAWBONES+	SAWHORSE	SAWSHARK	SAYONARA	SCABIOSA	SCALAWAG	SCARFPIN
SCARMOGE	SCELERATe	SCHAPSKA	SCHIEDAM	*SCHMATTE*	SCLEREMA	SCLEROMA
SCOINSON	SCOLIOMA	SCRANNEL	SCROFULA	*SCROGGIN*	SEABEACH+	SEACOAST
SEACRAFT	SEACUNNY+	SEADROME	SEAHOUND	SEALYHAM	SEAMOUNT	SEAPIECE
SEAROBIN	SEASCAPE	SEASPEAK	*SEATBACK*	*SEATBELT*	SEATRAIN	*SEATROUT*
SECODONT	SECRETINg	SEDERUNT	SEEDCAKE	SEEDTIME	SEICENTO	SELADANG
SELAMLIK	SEMIBULL	SEMIHOBO	*SEMILLON*	SEMILUNE	SEMITAUR	SEMOLINA
SENNIGHT	SEPALODY+	SEPTLEVA	SERAGLIO	SERAPHIM	SERAPHINe	SERENATA

8. Eight-Letter Words

SEROTINY+	SESTERCE	SETSCREW	SEWELLEL	SHABRACK	SHADBLOW	SHAGBARK
SHAMIANAh	SHANTUNG	SHEARLEG	*SHEDLOAD*	SHEEPCOTe	SHEERLEG	SHELDUCK
SHERBERT	SHERLOCK	SHERWANI	SHIGELLAe	SHIITAKE	SHILLALAh	SHINLEAF
SHIPLOAD	SHIPWORM	*SHITFACE*	*SHITLOAD*	SHLEMIEL	SHOEBILL	SHOPTALK
SHOWTIME	SIDALCEA	SIDEBAND	SIDEHILL	SIDELOCK	SIDENOTE	SIDEPATH
SIDESPIN	SIDEWALL	SILICULAe	SILKTAIL	SIMARUBA	SIMOLEON	SIMONIAC
SINCIPUT	SINKHOLE	SIRVENTE	*SITTELLA*	SKEWBALD	SKIAGRAM	SKIATRON
SKINCARE	SKINFOOD	*SKYBOARD*	SKYSCAPE	SLAPSHOT	*SLIMDOWN*	SLIPSOLE
SLOEBUSH+	SLOTBACK	SLOWBACK	SLUGABED	SLUGFEST	SLUGGARD	SLUGHORNe
SLUMLORD	*SMALLBOY*	SMALLSAT	SMILODON	SMOKEPOT	SMORBROD	*SNAKEPIT*
SNAPBACK	*SNAPLINK*	SNEAKEUP	SNEAKSBY+	SNEESHINg	SNOWBANK	SNOWBELL
SNOWBELT	SNOWBIRD	SNOWBOOT	SNOWBUSH+	*SNOWDOME*	SNOWMOLD	SNOWPACK
SNOWSHED	SNOWSLIP	SNOWSUIT	SOAPBARK	SOAPROOT	SOLIDAGO	SOLIDARE
SOLONETS+	SOLSTICE	SONATINA	SONGFEST	SONOBUOY	SONOGRAM	SOOCHONG
SORBITOL	SOUCHONG	SOURBALL	*SOURVELD*	SOUTACHE	SOUTHPAW	SOUTHRON
SOUTPIEL	SOVRANTY+	SOWBELLY+	SOWBREAD	*SPACELAB*	SPADILLE	SPADILLO
SPANDREL	SPANDRIL	SPANWORM	SPARERIB	*SPARTINA*	SPATFALL	SPATLESEn
SPECTRIN	SPEKBOOM	SPELDRINg	SPENDALL	SPICKNEL	SPINELLE	SPIRACLE
SPITBALL	*SPODOSOL*	SPRINGLEt	SPUMANTE	SPUNYARN	STAGGARD	STAGGART
STAGHORN	*STALAGMA*	STANDISH+	STANHOPE	STAROSTA	STAROSTY+	STARSPOT
STAUMREL	STAYSAIL	STEAPSIN	STEATOMA	STEELBOW	STEENBOK	STEGODONt
STEINBOK	STEMBUCK	STENLOCK	STENTOUR	STEPDAME	STEREOME	STERIGMA
STERNSON	STEWPOND	STICKPIN	STINKARD	STINKPOT	STOCKPOT	STOLPORT
STONEFLY+	STONERAG	STONERAW	STOPBANK	*STOPWORD*	*STOVETOP*	STRADIOT
STRAMONY+	STREIGHT	STREUSEL	STRONGYLe	STUDBOOK	STUNSAIL	STURGEON
SUBADULT	SUBCASTE	SUBCAUSE	SUBCHIEF	SUBCHORD	SUBCLAIM	SUBCLERK
SUBCRUST	SUBDEPOT	*SUBDWARF*	SUBEPOCH	SUBFIELD	SUBFRAME	SUBGENRE
SUBGRADE	SUBGRAPH	SUBIMAGO	SUBLEVEL	*SUBLIMITy*	SUBNICHE	SUBPANEL
SUBPRIME	SUBSCALE	SUBSHAFT	SUBSHELL	SUBSKILL	SUBSPACE	SUBSTYLE
SUBTENSE	SUBTHEME	SUBTILIN	SUBTILTY+	SUBTREND	SUBUCULA	SUBWORLD
SUCKHOLE	SUDDENTY+	SUIVANTE	SULFINYL	SULFONYL	SUMOTORI	SUNBURST
SUNGREBE	SUNPORCH+	SUNSCALD	SUPERBUG	*SUPERCOW*	SUPEREGO	SUPERGUN
SUPERHET	SUPERHIT	SUPERLOO	SURFBIRD	SURFBOAT	SURPLICEd	SURTITLE
SVASTIKA	SVEDBERG	SWAGSHOP	SWANHERD	SWANKPOT	*SWANSONG*	SWASTICA
SWAYBACK	*SWEETLIP*	SWEETSOP	*SWINGARM*	*SWINGBIN*	SWITCHEL	SYCAMORE
SYCOMORE	SYMPLAST	SYMPLOCE	SYNAPHEA	*SYNDETON*	SYNGRAPH	SYNTONIN
SYSADMIN						

TABASHIR	TABOOLEY	*TABOULEH*	TABOURINg	TAGALONG	TAGBOARD	TAGHAIRM
TAGLIONI	TAILBACK	TAILCOAT	TAILRACE	TAKEDOWN	TALAPOIN	*TALEGGIO*
TALKFEST	*TALKTIME*	TAMANOIR	TAMARACK	TAMBURIN	TAMWORTH	TANGENCE
TANGENCY+	TAPACOLO	TAPACULO	TAPADERA	TAPADERO	TAPENADE	TAPHOUSE
TARAKIHI	TARANTASs	TARBOOSH+	TARBOUSH+	TARRAGON	TARSIPED	TASTEVIN
TAUTONYMy	TEABOARD	*TEABREAD*	*TEALIGHT*	TEARDOWN	TELECHIR	TELEFILM
TELEGONY+	TELEPLAY	TELESALE	TELESEME	TELETRON	TELOMERE	TENAILLE
TENDENCE	TENEBRIO	TENOTOMY+	TEOCALLI	TEOSINTE	*TERABYTE*	TERAFLOP
TERAGLIN	TERAKIHI	TERAPHIM	TERATOMA	TERAWATT	TERIYAKI	TERPINOL
TERRAPIN	TERRELLA	TESTAMUR	TETRAGON	TETRAPLA	TETRAPODy	TETRARCHy
TEVATRON	THANATOS+	THEOCRAT	THEODICY+	THEOGONY+	THEONOMY+	THERBLIG

THEREMIN	THEROPOD	THINCLAD	THINDOWN	THINGAMY+	THIOTEPA	THIOUREA
THOLEPIN	THRENODY+	THRIDACE	THRISSEL	THRISTLE	THROSTLE	THUMBNUT
THUMBPOT	THURIBLE	THYMOSIN	TICKSEED	TIDEMILL	TIDEWAVE	*TIEBREAK*
TIECLASP	TIGEREYE	*TIGHTASS+*	TIMARIOT	TINSMITH	TIPSTOCK	TIRAMISU
TOADRUSH+	TOEPIECE	TOISEACH	TOKONOMA	TOLBOOTH	TOLLDISH+	TOLUIDINe
TOMALLEY	TOOLROOM	TOPCROSS+	TORNILLO	TORTILLA	*TOUCHPAD*	TOVARICH+
TOVARISH+	*TOWNHALL*	TOWNHOME	TOWNSKIP	TRACHOMA	TRACHYTE	*TRACKBED*
TRACKPAD	TRAHISON	TRAMROAD	TRANSEPT	TRANSIRE	TRAPBALL	*TRAPFALL*
TRAPROCK	TRAPUNTO	TREATISE	TRECENTO	TREDILLE	TREELAWN	TREENAIL
TRESSOUR	TRIBRACH	TRICHINAe	TRICHINAl	TRICHOME	TRICHORD	TRIDACNA
TRIGLYPH	TRIGRAPH	TRIMORPH	*TRIOLEIN*	TRIPTOTE	TRIPTYCA	TRIPTYCH
TRISCELE	TRISKELE	TRISTICH	TRIUMVIRi	TRIUMVIRy	TROCHISK	TROCHLEAe
TROCHLEAr	TROPHESY+	TROPONIN	TROTTOIR	TROUVERE	TRUDGEON	TSAREVNA
TSARITSA	TSUTSUMU	TUBERCLEd	*TUBEWORM*	TUBICOLE	TUCKAHOE	TUNBELLY+
TURLOUGH	TURNBACK	TURNDOWN	TURNHALL	TURNSOLE	TURNSPIT	TWELVEMO
TWOPENNY+						

ULTIMACY+	UMBRELLO	UMBRIERE	UNBELIEF	UNDERBUD	UNDERFUR	UNDERLIP
UNDERSEAl	UNDERSKY+	UNDERWIT	UNDESERT	UNITRUST	UNREPAIR	UNSAFETY+
UNSHADOW	UNTHRIFTy	UNVIRTUE	UPGROWTH	URNFIELD	*UROBILIN*	*UROBOROS+*
UROCHORD	UROSCOPY+	UROSTEGE	UROSTOMY+	UROSTYLE	URUSHIOL	*USERNAME*

VACHERIN	VAGOTOMY+	VAINESSE	VALIANCY+	*VALLHUND*	VAMBRACEd	VANILLIN
VARGUENO	VARLETTO	VARTABED	VASOTOMY+	VELATURA	VENDABLE	VENDANGE
VENDEUSE	VENDIBLE	VENOGRAM	*VENTOUSE*	VERATRINe	VERDANCY+	VERDELHO
VERGENCE	VERGENCY+	VERLIGTE	VERMOUTH	VERNACLE	VERNICLE	VERONICA
VERSICLE	VERTEBRAe	VERTEBRAl	VERTICIL	VIDEOFIT	VIEWDATA	VIGNERON
VIGORISH+	VILLAGIO	*VILLIACO*	*VILLIACO+*	VILLIAGO	VINDALOO	VINIFERA
VIOMYCIN	VIRTUOSA	VIRTUOSO	VITILIGO	VOCALESE	*VOORSKOT*	

WAGMOIRE	WAHCONDA	WALDHORN	WALKMILL	WALLAROO	WALLSEND	WANDEROO
WARCRAFT	WARDCORN	WARDMOTE	WARDROOM	WAREROOM	WARFARINg	WARMOUTH
WARRAGLE	WARRAGUL	WARRISON	WASHBALL	WASTELOT	WASTRIFE	WATCHEYE
WATERDOG	WATERLOO	*WATERSKI*	WATTHOUR	WAUKMILL	WAVEBAND	WAYBOARD
WAYBREAD	WAYLEAVE	*WAYPOINT*	*WEBISODE*	WEEPHOLE	WELLADAY	WELLCURB
WELLHOLE	WEREGILD	*WHAKAIRO*	*WHARENUI*	WHEYFACEd	WHIMBREL	WHINIARD
WHIPBIRD	WHIPCORDy	WHIPTAIL	WHIRLBAT	WHITEFLY+	WHITEPOT	WHITRACK
WHITRICK	WHODUNIT	WHORESON	WHORLBAT	*WHYDUNIT*	*WILDCARD*	*WINDBELL*
WINDBILL	WINDGALL	WINDSAIL	WINESHOP	WINGBACK	WINGBEAT	*WINGSUIT*
WIREHAIR	WISEACRE	WITBLITS+	*WITHEROD*	WOODCHAT	*WOODCHOP*	WOODHOLE
WOODLARK	WOODLORE	WOODNOTE	WOODROOF	WOODRUSH+	WOOLFELL	WOOLPACK
WOOLSACK	WORDLORE	WORKADAY	WORKBOAT	WORKFARE	WORKGIRL	*WORKHOUR*
WORKROOM	WORMCAST	WORMHOLEd	WORMROOT	WORMSEED		
YAKIMONO	YAKITORI	YARDBIRD	YARDWAND	YARMELKE	YARMULKA	YARMULKE
YELDROCK	YOGHOURT					

8.3.7 OTHER NON-PLURALS

AARDWOLF	ABDOMINAl	ABDUCENS	ABSTRUSE*	ACERVULI	ACOEMETI	ACROMION
ADESPOTA	AGNOMINAl	AGRAPHON	AGREMENS	AIRBOUND	AIRDRAWN	ALBERGHI
ALLNIGHT	ALLSORTS	AMARETTI	AMORETTI	ANALECTA	ANALECTS	ANECDOTAl
ANOESTRA	ANOESTRI	ANTENATI	ANTERIOR	*ANTIACNE*	ANTIBIAS	ANTIBOSS
ANTICITY	ANTICOLD	ANTIDORA	ANTIDRUG	ANTIFOAM	*ANTIGANG*	ANTILEAK
ANTILEFT	ANTILIFEr	ANTILOCK	ANTIMALE	ANTIPILL	ANTIRAPE	ANTIRIOT
ANTIROCK	ANTIROLL	ANTISERA	ANTISHIP	ANTISLIP	ANTISMOG	ANTISMUT
ANTISPAM	ANTITANK	ANTRORSE	ANYPLACE	*ARCHAEON*	ARMGAUNT	ARRAUGHT
ASPIRATAe	ASYNDETA	*ATTAGIRL*				

BACKDOOR	BACKMOST	BACKROOM	BAREHEAD	*BARELAND*	*BEESTUNG*	*BENCHTOP*
BERMUDAS	BESOUGHT	BESTADDE	BESTRODE	BICHROME	*BIGSTICK*	*BIRDLIFE*
BIRROTCH	*BISCOTTI*	*BISCOTTO*	BLEUATRE	BLONCKET	BONAMANI	BONAMANO
BOOKLICE	*BORLOTTI*	BOTONNEE	BOUTONNEe	BOWFRONT	*BUCATINI*	BUDGEREE
BULLSHAT	BUNODONT	BYRLAKIN				

CALATHOS	CAMPAGNE	CAPITULAr	CARETOOK	CAREWORN	CARGEESE	CASTELLAn
CASTRATI	CATWORKS	CELOMATA	CEPHALAD	CIABATTE	*CITRUSSY*	CITYWARD
CITYWIDE	CLAUSTRAl	CLAUSULAe	CLAUSULAr	CLITELLAr	CLUBFEET	CLUBFOOT
COLORADO	COMATULAe	COMPLEAT	CONFETTO	CONGRATS	*CONTEMPO*	CONTINUAl
CONTRAIR	CORAGGIO	CRAGFAST	*CRAMFULL*	CREDENDA	CREMOSIN	CRIBELLAr
CROSSBITe	*CROSTINO*	CROWFEET	CUNABULA			

DANCETTY	DARKMANS	DECUBITI	DEEPFELT	DEEPMOST	DIADOCHI	*DIATRETA*
DIGERATI	*DIKETONE*	DIPTEROI	DIRIMENT	DISBOUND	DISCLOST	DISCRETE*
DISTRAITe	DOGTEETH	DOGTOOTH	DORMOUSE	DOWNHOLE	DOWNMOST	DOWNTROD
DRAGONNE	DRICKSIE*	*DROPLOCK*	DRUTHERS	DRYSTONE	*DUCKFOOT*	DUPONDII
DURNDEST						

EARWIGGY	EASTMOST	EDGEWAYS	EGLOMISE	ELDRITCH	EMENDALS	ENAUNTER
ENCASTRE	ENCOMION	ENDODYNE	ENDOSTEAl	ENIGMATA	*EPITHECAe*	ESCAPADO
ESOPHAGI	ESPIEGLE	*EYELEVEL*				

FACETIAE	FANTOOSH	FAROUCHE	FARTHEST	FATTRELS	FEELGOOD	FELLAHIN
FERNINST	FEWTRILS	FIBRILLAe	FIBRILLAr	FINESPUN	FINICKINg	FINNESKO
FINNICKY	FISTIANA	FLAGELLAr	FLATLONG	FLATWAYS	FLEISHIG	*FLEISHIK*
FLOATCUT	FOODWAYS	FOOTWORN	FORAMINAl	FORBORNE	*FORDONNE*	FOREDONE
FOREKNEW	FORELAIN	FOREPAST	FOREWORN	FORINSEC	FORNENST	FORRADER
FORSOOTH	FORSPOKEn	FORSWATT	FORSWORE	FORSWORN	FORSWUNK	FOURCHEE
FRAMPOLD	FREEBORN	FRICANDO	FROLICKY	FROSTBITe	FUNICULI	FURIBUND

GADARENE	GAILLARDe	GARLICKY	GASTFULL	GASTIGHT	GASWORKS	GAYWINGS
GEFULLTE	*GERONIMO*	GILTWOOD	GINGLYMI	GLADIOLI	GLIOMATA	*GOLDTAIL*
GOLDTONE	GOODTIME	GOODWIFE	GORBLIMY	*GOSPELLY*	*GOSPODIN*	GRADATIM
GRAVLAKS	*GREENLIT*	GREGATIM	*GRISSINI*	*GRISSINO*	GUDEWIFE	*GUMLANDS*
GYNAECEA						

HAFTAROTh	*HAFTOROS*	HAFTOROTh	HANDSEWN	HANDWRITe	HARDCASE	HARIGALS
HEADMOST	HEREFROM	HEREINTO	HEREUNTO	HEREUPON	*HERPTILE*	HILLFOLK
HINDFEET	HINDFOOT	HINDMOST	HINDWARD	*HOLOCENE*	HOMEFELT	HOMODONT
HOMODYNE	HORDEOLA	*HORLICKS*	HORNFELS	HOUSESAT	HUSTINGS	HYPOGAEAl
HYPOGAEAn	HYPOGENE					

ICEBOUND	IGNORAMI	*INASMUCH*	INDEVOUT	INDOCILE	INDUCIAE	INDUVIAE
INFECUND	INFERIAE	INFICETE	INFLIGHT	INFOUGHT	*INGROUND*	INSOMUCH
INTERAGE	INTERROW	INTRINCE	INTRORSE	INURBANE	INVIRILE	ISODICON
ISODOMON						

KIELBASI	KIELBASY	KREPLACH	*KREPLECH*	*KUMBALOI*

LABRUSCA	LACKADAY	LANCIERS	LARGANDO	LASSLORN	LEKYTHOI	LEKYTHOS
LEMNISCI	LENTANDO	LEVOGYRE	LIBRETTI	LIFEHOLD	LIPOMATA	LITERATIm
LITERATOr	LOCKFAST	LODICULAe	*LONGCASE*	LONGLEAF	LONGTIME	LOTHFULL
LOVELORN	LUMBRICI	LYOPHOBE				

MADBRAIN	MALGRADO	MALLEOLI	MANCANDO	MANSUETE	MANSWORN	MANYFOLD
MATACHINa	MATACHINi	MAUSOLEAn	MAWBOUND	MENSTRUAl	MERCAPTO	MERCHILD
MESHUGGAh	MESHUGGE	*METADATA*	METAPLOT	MEUNIERE	MIGHTEST	*MINOTAUR*
MISBEGOT	MISBEGUN	MISBOUND	MISBUILT	MISDIGHT	MISDONNE	MISDROVE
MISFALNE	MISPROUD	MISSPOKEn	MISTHREW	MISWROTE	MITSVOTH	MONGEESE
MONODONT	MOONCALF	MORBILLI	MORIBUND	MOSLINGS	MOSTWHAT	MULTIAGE
MULTIDAY	MULTITONe	MULTIUSEr	*MURDABAD*			

NARCISSI	*NASSELLA*	NINEFOLD	NONBRAND	NONDAIRY	NONELECT	NONELITE
NONEMPTY	NONFATTY	NONHARDY	*NONINERT*	NONLABOR	NONLEAFY	*NONLEVEL*
NONMETRO	NONMONEY	*NONNOBLE*	NONOBESE	NONPARTY	NONPOINT	NONPRINT
NONTITLE	NONTRUMP	NONWOODY	NORMANDE	*NOSEDOVE*	NOTTURNI	NOTTURNO
NOUMENON	NOWHENCE	NUBECULAe	NUCLEOLI	NUDICAUL	NUTBROWN	NUTMEGGY

OBLIGATI	OBVOLUTEd	*OCKODOLS*	OILPROOF	OILTIGHT	OLYMPICS	OMNIVORA
OMPHALOS	ONSTREAM	OPENCAST	OPERCULAr	OPUSCULAr	*OSTINATI*	OSTRACON
OSTRAKON	OUTBROKEn	OUTBUILT	OUTCLOMB	OUTDROVE	OUTDWELT	OUTFOUND
OUTSHONE	OUTSLEPT	*OUTSMELT*	OUTSPELT	OUTSPOKEn	OUTSTOOD	OUTSWARE
OUTSWEPT	OUTSWORE	OUTSWORN	*OUTSWUNG*	OUTTHREW	OUTWOUND	OUTWROTE
OVERBLEW	OVERBOLD	OVERBORE	OVERBORNe	OVERCLAD	OVERCOLD	OVEREASY
OVERFAST	OVERFELL	OVERFLEW	OVERFOND	OVERFOUL	OVERFREE	OVERFULL
OVERGAVE	OVERGILT	OVERGIRT	OVERGLAD	OVERGONE	OVERGREW	OVERHARD
OVERHELD	OVERIDLE	OVERKEPT	OVERKEST	OVERKIND	OVERKNEE	OVERLEWD
OVERLONG	OVERLOUD	OVERLUSH	OVERMEEK	OVERMILD	OVERMUCH	OVERNEAT
OVERNICE	OVERPAGE	OVERPAST	OVERPERT	OVERRASH	OVERRICH	OVERRIFE
OVERRUDE	OVERSICK	OVERSLOW	OVERSOFT	OVERSOLD	OVERSOON	OVERSURE
OVERSWAM	OVERSWUM	OVERTAME	OVERTART	OVERTHINk	OVERWEAK	OVERWIDE
OVERWORE	OVERWORN					

PALEWAYS	PALISADO	PARABEMA	*PARASHOT*h	PARAVAIL	PARERGON	PARLANDO
PARLANTE	PECORINI	PEDICULI	PERACUTE	PERDENDO	PERFORCE	PERIBOLI

8. Eight-Letter Words

PERRADII	PERSAUNT	*PIGSTUCK*	PIROSHKI	*PITIKINS*	PLEASETH	*PLIOCENE*
POIGNADO	POLEWARD	POLTFEET	POLTFOOT	POLYARCHy	POLYTENE	PORRIDGY
PORTSIDE	POSTBASE	POSTBURN	POSTDRUG	POSTFIRE	POSTGAME	POSTNATI
POSTRACE	POSTRIOT	POSTSHOW	*POTBOUND*	PRATFELL	PRECEESE	PRECRASH
PREDELLE	PREFLAME	PREGGERS	PRELUNCH	*PRERADIO*	PRESCUTA	PRIMROSY
PROCHAIN	PROCHEIN	PRODROMIc	PROFORMA	PROLABOR	*PROTRADE*	PROUNION
PRYTANEA	PUDIBUND	PULICENE	PULVILLIo	PUNDONOR	PURBLIND	PURTRAYD
PUTAMINA	PYONINGS					

RAISONNE	RATPROOF	REALTIME	REARMICE	REARMOST	REBOUGHT	RECAUGHT
REDDENDA	REDSHARE	REDSHIRE	REDSHORT	REFOUGHT	REGROUND	REMEDIATe
RENFORST	RENVERST	REREMICE	RESOUGHT	RESPONSA	RESPRANG	RESPRUNG
RESTROVE	RESTRUCK	RESTRUNG	RETAUGHT	RETIARII	RETICULAr	RETRORSE
RISOLUTO	RISPETTI	RISPETTO	ROSTELLAr	RUBAIYAT	RUBICUND	*RUGALACH*
RUGELACH						

SALTANDO	SARTORII	SASTRUGA	SASTRUGI	SAWTEETH	SAWTOOTH	SCALDINI
SCALDINO	SCALPINS	SCEATTAS	SCHEMATA	SCHLIEREn	SCHOLION	SCIENTER
SCORDATO	SCRIMPIT	SCROGGIE*	SCROUNGY*	SCULPSIT	SCUTELLAr	SEABORNE
SEAMFREE	SELCOUTH	SELFSAME	SEMANTRA	SEMIBALD	SEMIDEAF	SEMIGALA
SEMIHARD	SEMINUDE	SEMISOFT	SEMIWILD	SEMPLICE	SENSILLAe	SEPARATA
SERIATIM	SHAGPILE	*SHEKALIM*	*SHEKELIM*	SHILINGI	SHOPWORN	SHORTARM
SHOULDST	SIDDURIM	SIDELONG	SIGHTSAW	SIGISBEI	SIGISBEO	SINFONIE
SITHENCE	SKYWROTE	SLYBOOTS	SMOULDRY	SNAKEBITe	SOARAWAY	*SOFTCORE*
SOLFEGGIo	SOMEDELE	SOPHERIM	SPAEWIFE	SPIRILLAr	SPRAUNCY*	STANDPAT
STAPEDII	STASIMON	STEDFAST	STICHERA	STIGMATA	STOMODEAl	STOTINKA
STOTINKI	*STOTINOV*	STOWLINS	STRAICHT	STRAUNGE	STRAWHAT	STROMATA
STUNKARD	SUBACUTE	SUBAUDIO	SUBCOSTAe	SUBCOSTAl	SUBDUPLE	SUBERECT
SUBMENTAl	SUBPHYLAr	SUBTRIST	SUBVERST	SUDAMINAl	SUNDROPS	SUNPROOF
SUNSHINY	SUPERBAD	SUPERFIT	SUPERHOT	SUPERLAY	*SURFSIDE*	SUSPENCE

TACITURN	TAIGLACH	TALEYSIM	TALLISIM	TALLITIM	*TALLITOTh*	TEENYBOP
TEFILLAH	TEFILLIN	TEGMENTAl	TEGUMINA	TEIGLACH	TENACULA	TENEBRAE
TENPENNY	TESSELLAe	TESSELLAr	THEMSELF	THEREFORe	THEREOUT	THESAURI
THISAWAY	THORNSET	THRAWARD	THRAWART	THREAPIT	THREEPIT	TIDYTIPS
TIMEWORN	TINSNIPS	TITMOUSE	TOILWORN	TOMATOEY	TOPLOFTY*	*TORTELLI*
TOWNFOLK	TRACTILE	TRAUMATA	TRIETHYL	TRIHEDRAl	TRIPHASE	TROWSERS
TRUEBORN	TRYWORKS	*TSITSITH*	*TWEENAGEr*	TWICHILD	TWINBORN	TWINIGHT

ULTIMATA	ULTRADRY	ULTRAHIP	ULTRAHOT	ULTRALOW	UMBILICI	UMPTIETH
UNBENIGN	UNBEREFT	UNBITTER	UNBLOODY	UNBOUGHT	UNBOUNCY	UNBRASTE
UNBRIGHT	UNCAUGHT	UNCHASTE*	UNCLASSY	UNDEFIDE	UNDERBITe	UNDERLIT
UNDEVOUT	UNDOCILE	UNDREAMT	UNDROSSY	UNFAULTY	UNFLASHY	UNFORGOT
UNFOUGHT	UNGENTLE	UNGREEDY	UNGROUND	UNGUILTY	UNHONEST	UNICOLOR
UNKOSHER	UNMELLOW	UNNANELD	UNPOLITE	UNPRETTY	UNSECRET	*UNSEELIE*
UNSELDOM	UNSHRUBD	UNSHRUNK	UNSICKER	UNSOLEMN	UNSONSIE	UNSOUGHT

UNSPRUNG	*UNSTARRY*	UNSTRUCK	UNSTRUNG	UNSUBTLE	UNTAUGHT	UNTENDER
UNTRENDY	UPADAISY	UPCAUGHT	URANISCI	UTRICULI		

VAGINULAe	VELAMINA	VERECUND	VERKRAMP	VERMOULU	VESICULAe	VESICULAr
VIBRISSAe	VIBRISSAl	VIRTUOSIc	VITICETA	*VOERTSAK*	*VOERTSEK*	VULSELLAe

WAKERIFE	WASTFULL	WAUKRIFE	*WAYLEGGO*	WEEKLONG	WELLBORN	WESTMOST
WETPROOF	WHEREFORe	WHEREOUT	WHOMEVER	WHOSEVER	WIDEBAND	WIDEBODY
WILLYARD	WILLYART	WOBEGONE	*WOODFREE*	WOODLICE	WOODMICE	*WORKSAFE*

YESHIVOTh YGLAUNST

8.4 LESS FAMILIAR BUT LESS PROBABLE NON-HOOK EIGHTS

CONTAINING BB

ABBATIAL	ABSORBER	**ABUSABLE**	AEROBOMB	***BAALEBOS***	BABELDOM	**BABELISH**
BABELISM	BABIRUSA	BABOUCHE	BABUSHKA	*BABYDOLL*	BACKBAND	BACKBEND
BACKBOND	*BACKBURN*	*BACKCOMB*	**BAILABLE**	BAILBOND	**BANKABLE**	***BANNABLE***
BARBASCO	BARBEQUEr	BARBERRY+	BARBETTE	BARBICAN	BARBICEL	BARBITAL
BARBLESS	BAREBOAT	BAREBONEd	**BARRABLE**	BASEBAND	**BASEBORN**	BATHCUBE
BAUBLING	BAYBERRY+	BEACHBOY	BEANBALL	**BEARABLY**	BEARBINE	BEBOPPER
BEDBOARD	**BEDDABLE**	BEEBREAD	**BEJABERS**	BELLBIND	BERBERINe	BERBERIS+
BERIBERI	*BERIMBAU*	BIBATION	**BIBULOUS**	**BIDDABLY**	BILABIAL	BILBERRY+
BILLABLE	BILLBOOK	BILLYBOY	**BILOBATE**d	BIMBASHI	BIMBETTE	BIOBLAST
BISTABLE	**BITEABLE**	BLACKBOY	**BLAMABLE**	**BLAMABLY**	BLESBUCK	BLOWBACK
BLOWBALL	BLOWTUBE	BLUEBACK	BLUEBALL	*BLUEBEAT*	BLUEBILL	BLUEBOOK
BLUEBUCK	*BLUEBUSH+*	*BLURBIST*	**BOATABLE**	BOATBILL	*BOBFLOAT*	BOBOLINK
BOBOWLER	BOBWHEEL	BOBWHITE	**BOILABLE**	BOMBESIN	BOMBLOAD	BOMBSITE
BOMBYCID	**BONDABLE**	BONIBELL	BONTEBOK	*BOOBHEAD*	**BOOBYISH**	BOOBYISM
BOSCHBOK	BOXBERRY+	BOXBOARD	BRAINBOX+	BROWBAND	BROWBEATd	**BUBALINE**
BUCKBEAN	**BUFFABLE**	**BULLBARS**	BULLYBOY	*BULNBULN*	BUNCOMBE	BUSHBUCK
CHUBBILY	**CLUBABLE**	*CLUBBILY*	**CLUBBISH**	CLUBBISM	CLUBBIST	**CRABBILY**
CURBABLE	DIBBUKIM	**DRABBISH**	**DYBBUKIM**	**FLABBILY**	*FLIBBERT*	**GABBROIC**
GABBROID	GIBBSITE	**GRUBBILY**	HOBBITRY+	HOBBYISM	JABBERER	LOBBYGOW
LOBBYISM	LOBBYIST	**LUBBERLY**	NABOBERY+	NABOBESS+	**NABOBISH**	NABOBISM
OBEYABLE	**OBVIABLE**	RABBINIC	RABBITRY+	REHABBER	RIBBONRY+	*RUBBOARD*
SABBATIC	**SCABBILY**	**SCRABBLY***	**SCRIBBLY***	*SCROBBLE*	SCRUBBER	**SHABBILY**
SILLABUB	SILLIBUB	**SLOBBISH**	SNOBBISM	**SNUBBISH**	**SORBABLE**	SQUABBER
STUBBILY	**SUBBASAL**	SUBBASIN	SUBBLOCK	SUBBREED	**SUBPUBIC**	SUBSHRUB
SUBTRIBE	**SUBURBED**	SYLLABUB	TABBINET	*TABBOULI*	*TIMEBOMB*	**UNBARBED**
UNRIBBED	UNRUBBED	**UNWEBBED**	ZAMBOMBA			

CONTAINING CC

ABRICOCK	***ABSCISIC***	ACCENTOR	ACCEPTEE	ACCEPTER	ACCEPTOR	ACCORAGE
ACCORDER	ACCOUTER	ACCOUTRE	ACCUSANT	ACESCENT	**ACETONIC**	**ACETYLIC**
ACICULUM	**ACIDOTIC**	**ACONITIC**	ACROLECT	ACROSTIC	ACUTANCE	ADVOCACY+
AIRCHECK	AIRCOACH+	**ALCHEMIC**	*ALCOLOCK*	**ALOPECIC**	**ANARCHIC**	**ANECHOIC**

ANICONIC	**APOCOPIC**	APRICOCK	ASCOCARP	**ASCORBIC**	BACCHANTe	**BACCHIAN**
BACCHIUS	BACKCAST	*BACKCOMB*	**BACTERIC**	BALLCOCK	BIOCYCLE	BISCACHA
BIZCACHA	BLACKCAP	BOYCHICK	**BRACCATE**	**BUCCALLY**	CABOCEER	**CABOCHED**
CABOCHON	CACAFOGO	CACHALOT	CACHEPOT	CACHEXIA	CACHOLOT	CACODOXY+
CACOLOGY+	CACOMIXLe	**CACUMINA**l	**CADUCEAN**	**CADUCEUS**	CADUCITY+	**CADUCOUS**
CAECALLY	CAECITIS+	**CAESURIC**	CAILLACH	CAIMACAM	**CALCANEA**l	**CALCANEA**n
CALCANEI	**CALCARIA**	CALCEATE	CALCRETE	CALCSPAR	CALCTUFA	CALCTUFF
CALCULARy	CALFLICK	CALLBACK	**CALYCATE**	**CALYCEAL**	**CALYCINE**	**CALYCOID**
CALYCULE	**CALYCULI**	**CAMSHOCH**	CANCELER	**CANCELLI**	*CANCERED*	**CANCRINE**
CANCROID	**CANNABIC**	CANSTICK	CANTICLE	CANTICUM	**CAPRYLIC**	CAPSICIN
CAPUCHIN	CARACARA	CARAPACEd	**CARBAMIC**	CARBOLIC	**CARBONIC**	CARCAJOU
CARCANET	**CARCERAL**	CARDCASE	**CARDITIC**	CARIACOU	CARJACOU	CARRITCH+
CARRYCOT	CARTOUCHe	CARUCAGE	CARUCATE	CARUNCLE	**CARYATIC**	CASCABEL
CASCABLE	CASCHROM	*CASHBACK*	CATCHALL	*CATCHCRY+*	CATCHFLY+	CATECHIN
CATECHOL	**CATHODIC**	**CATIONIC**	**CAUDICES**	CAUDICLE	CAULICLE	CAVICORN
CECROPIA	*CECROPIN*	CELERIAC	*CENOZOIC*	CEPHALIC	CERCARIAe	CERCARIA l
CERCARIAn	*CERCOPID*	**CEREBRIC**	**CERVICES**	*CERVICUM*	CETACEAN	CETERACH
CHACONNE	**CHALONIC**	**CHANCILY**	*CHAORDIC*	CHARACID	CHARACIN	CHARLOCK
CHARNECO	CHATCHKA	CHATCHKE	CHECHAKO	CHECKOFF	CHECKROW	CHECKSUM
CHERUBIC	**CHIASTIC**	*CHICHIER*	CHICKPEA	CHICNESS+	**CHIMERIC**	CHIPMUCK
CHOCKFULl	**CHOICELY**	**CHOLERIC**	CHOWCHOW	**CHTHONIC**	CHUBASCO	**CHURCHLY***
CICATRIX+	CICERONE	**CICERONI**	**CICHLOID**	CICINNUS+	**CICISBEI**	CICISBEO
CICLATON	*CICUTINE*	CINCHONA	CINCTURE	**CINNAMIC**	**CIRCITER**	**CIRCUSSY**
CIVICISM	CLACKBOX+	CLAMANCY+	CLARENCE	CLARSACH	CLAVECIN	CLAVICLE
CLAWBACK	*CLEARCUT*	**CLEIDOIC**	CLENCHER	**CLICHEED**	**CLITORIC**	CLOCHARD
COACHDOG	COACTION	**COACTIVE**	COAGENCY+	COALSACK	**COBALTIC**	COCINERA
COCKAPOO	COCKBILL	COCKBIRD	COCKBOAT	COCKLOFT	COCKNIFY	COCKSHOT
COCKSHUT	COCKSPUR	COCOANUT	COCOBOLA	COCOBOLO	COCOPLUM	CODPIECE
COELOMIC	*COENACLE*	COEFFECT	**COERCIVE**	COFACTOR	COGNOSCE	**COLCHICA**
COLDCOCK	**COLUMBIC**	COMPESCE	COMPLECT	COMPLICE	CONCAUSE	**CONCETTI**
CONCETTO	**CONCHATE**	CONCHOID	CONCLAVE	**CONCOLOR**	CONCOURSe	**CONFOCAL**
CONGENIC	*CONICINE*	CONICITY+	CONJUNCT	**CONOIDIC**	**COPREMIC**	COPRINCE
CORACOID	CORANACH	CORNACRE	CORNCAKE	CORNCRIB	CORNETCY+	CORNICHE
CORNICLE	**CORNIFIC**	COROCORE	COROCORO	CORONACH	**CORTICAL**	**CORTICES**
COSECANT	**COSMICAL**	**COUCHANT**	**COUMARIC**	COUSCOUS+	**COXALGIC**	CRACKJAW
CRACKNEL	**CRATONIC**	CREPANCE	**CRESCIVE**	**CRESYLIC**	CRICETID	**CROCEATE**
CROCEOUS	*CROCKPOT*	CROCOITE	CROMLECH	**CROPSICK**	CROSSCUT	**CROTCHED**
CROTCHETy	*CROTONIC*	CRUCIFER	CRUMMACK	CRUMMOCK	*CRUNCHIE***	CUBICITY+
CUBICULA	CUBISTIC	CUCURBIT	CULICINE	*CUMACEAN*	**CUNEATIC**	CURCULIO
CURCUMINe	CURLICUE	CURLYCUE	CURRICLE	CUTCHERY+	**CUTICULA**e	**CUTICULA**r
CYANITIC	**CYANOTIC**	CYCLAMEN	CYCLITOL	**CYCLONAL**	CYCLOPES	CYCLOSES
CYCLOSIS	**CYMATICS**	CYNANCHE	DABCHICK	*DANCICAL*	*DECANOIC*	DIACIDIC
DIARCHIC	DICACITY+	**DICASTIC**	**DICHOTIC**	**DICHROIC**	DICROTIC	DIDACTIC
DIPCHICK	**DISCINCT**	DOBCHICK	**DOCHMIAC**	**DUNCICAL**	**DYARCHIC**	ECCLESIAe
ECCLESIAl	**ECCRISES**	**ECCRISIS**	ECLIPTIC	**ECOCIDAL**	ECOTOXIC	ECOTYPIC
ECTOSARC	**ECTOZOIC**	**ECTROPIC**	EFFICACY+	**ELENCTIC**	ENCHORIC	ENCRINIC
ENCLITIC	EPICYCLE	**EUCRITIC**	EUTECTIC	*EXOCYTIC*	FASCICLEd	**FLOCCOSE**
FLOCCULE	**FLOCCULI**	GAMECOCK	GIMCRACK	**GLUCINIC**	GLUCOSIC	*GLYCEMIC*
GLYCERIC	**GLYCOLIC**	GLYCONIC	*HALACHIC*	HATCHECK	**HECTICAL**	**HECTICLY**

HICCATEE	**ICHTHYIC**	**ISCHEMIC**	ISOCRACY+	*ITACONIC*	JIMCRACK	*KAZACHOC*
LACTIFIC	**LACTONIC**	**LEUCEMIC**	**LEUCITIC**	LIBECCIO	LOCOFOCO	MACCABAW
MACCABOY	MACCOBOY	**MICROBIC**	*MICROCAP*	MICROCARd	MOCCASIN	MOORCOCK
MUCHACHA	MUCHACHO	NASCENCE	NASCENCY+	**NECROTIC**	**NICKELIC**	**NUCLIDIC**
NUMCHUCK	OCCIDENT	OCCIPITAl	**OCCLUSAL**	OCCLUSOR	OCCULTER	**OCCULTLY**
OCCUPATE	OCTARCHY+	OITICICA	**ORCHITIC**	ORICHALC	OXYTOCIC	PACHALIC
PASTICCIo	PAYCHECK	**PECCABLE**	PICCANIN	**PICNICKY**	**PICRITIC**	PINCHECK
PRINCOCK	PROCINCT	*PROSECCO*	PUTCHOCK	**PYCNOTIC**	**RACHITIC**	**RECTITIC**
RICERCARe	RICERCARi	**SACCULAR**	**SACCULUS**	**SACHEMIC**	**SARCODIC**	SCATBACK
SCENICAL	**SCHNECKEn**	**SCILICET**	SCINCOID	**SCOLECES**	SCOLECID	**SCOLICES**
SCOTOPIC	SCROOTCH	SCUTCHER	**SEECATCH**	SPICCATO	**STACCATI**	STICCADO
STICCATO	STOCCADO	STOPCOCK	STUCCOER	SUCCINYL	SUCCORER	SUCCUBUS+
SURUCUCU	**SYNCOPIC**	SYNECTIC	**THORACIC**	*TICKLACE*	TRICTRAC	TROCHAIC
TUCOTUCO	TUCUTUCO	*TUCUTUCU*	TURNCOCK	TWOCCING	*UNACIDIC*	**UNCATCHY**
UNCHANCY	**UNCHICLY**	UNICYCLE	VACCINIAl	VISCACHA	VIZCACHA	VULCANIC
WATCHCRY+	WOODCOCK	**ZIRCONIC**				

CONTAINING FF

AFFECTER	AFFERENT	AFFIANCE	**AFFINELY**	AFFIRMER	**AFFIXIAL**	**AFFLATED**
AFFLATUS+	AFFOREST	AFFRAYER	AFFRIGHT	AFFUSION	*BANOFFEE*	BEAUFFET
BLASTOFF	BOUFFANT	*BREAKOFF*	BUFFETER	CAFFEISM	CALCTUFF	CHAFFRON
CHAUFFER	CHECKOFF	COEFFECT	COIFFEUR	COIFFURE	*CUFFLINK*	DANDRIFF
DIFFRACT	DIFFUSOR	DYESTUFF	EFFECTER	EFFECTOR	EFFERENT	**EFFETELY**
EFFICACY+	EFFIERCE	**EFFIGIAL**	**EFFLUVIAl**	**EFFRAIDE**	EFFUSION	ETOUFFEE
FACELIFT	FALLFISH+	FANFARONa	*FARFALLE*	**FARMWIFE**	**FAULTFUL**	**FEASTFUL**
FEBRIFIC	FEVERFEW	FILEFISH+	**FILIFORM**	FIREFANG	**FIVEFOLD**	**FLATFEET**
FLATFISH+	FLATFOOT	FLIMFLAM	FLINTIFY	*FLIPFLOP>*	FLUIDIFY	FOALFOOT
FOGFRUIT	**FOLKLIFE**	FOOFARAW	FOOLFISH+	FOOTFALL	FOREFACE	**FOREFEET**
FOREFELT	**FOREFOOT**	FOREHOOF	FORFAULT	**FORKSFUL**	**FOUNTFUL**	**FOURFOLD**
FRAUDFUL	**FREAKFUL**	**FREEFORM**	FROGFISH+	FROUFROU	FRUCTIFY	FULLFACE
FURFURAL	FURFURAN	**FURFURES**	FURFUROLe	**FUSIFORM**	*GAFFSAIL*	GIRAFFID
GLIFFING	**GRAFFITO**	GREFFIER	**GRIEFFUL**	**GRUFFILY**	**GRUFFISH**	IFFINESS+
KAFFIYAH	KAFFIYEH	*KEFFIYAH*	KEFFIYEH	**MISGRAFF**	MOFFETTE	MOUFFLON
NAFFNESS+	**OFFISHLY**	OFFPRINT	**OFFTRACK**	PALSTAFF	PARAFFLE	PUFFBALL
PUFFBIRD	**RUFFLIKE**	SCLAFFER	SCOFFLAW	**SERIFFED**	SHELFFUL	SIFFLEUR
SNIFFILY	**SNIFFISH**	SNUFFILY	SOFFIONI	**SPIFFILY**	**SPOFFISH**	**SQUIFFED**
SQUIFFER	STAFFAGE	*STAFFMAN*	**STAFFMEN**	STIFFISH	**STUFFILY**	**SUFFIXAL**
SUFFLATE	SUFFRAGE	SURFFISH+	*SWOFFING*	TAFFAREL	TAFFEREL	TAFFRAIL
TARTUFFE	TIPSTAFF	**UNSTUFFY**	WOLFFISH+	WOODRUFF		

CONTAINING HH

APHTHOUS	BAKSHISH	BEHEMOTH	BROUHAHA	CACHUCHA	**CAMSHOCH**	CHATCHKA
CHATCHKE	**CHEAPISH**	CHECHAKO	*CHESHIRE*	**CHICHIER**	CHOWCHOW	**CHTHONIC**
CHUMSHIP	**CHURCHLY***	**CHURLISH**	DAHABEAH	DAHABIAH	DAHABIEH	*DISHDASHa*
ETHEPHON	**ETHERISH**	ETHNARCHy	FISHHOOK	**FRESHISH**	HABDALAH	HAFTORAH
HAILSHOT	**HALACHOTh**	*HALAKHIC*	**HALAKHOTh**	HALAKOTH	**HAMEWITH**	HANDHOLD
HANUKIAH	HAPHTARAh	HARDHACK	HARDHEAD	HARRUMPH	HASHMARK	HATBRUSH+
HATCHECK	HATCHWAY	HAVDALAH	*HAVDOLOH*	HAWFINCH+	HAWKMOTH	HAWKSHAW
HAZELHEN	**HEADACHY**	HEADFISH+	HEADSHIP	HEADSHOT	HEDGEHOP	HEIRSHIP

8. Eight-Letter Words

HELMINTH	HEPTARCHy	HERNSHAW	HEROSHIP	*HEUCHERA*	HIERARCHy	**HIGHBORN**
HIGHBRED	HIGHBROW	HIGHBUSH	HIGHJACK	**HIGHMOST**	*HIGHRISE*	*HIGHVELD*
HINAHINA	HINDHEAD	HIPPARCH	HOARHEAD	HOCKSHOP	HOGSHEAD	*HOLARCHY+*
HOTCHPOT	HUARACHE	HUARACHO	HUISACHE	HURCHEON	**HUSHEDLY**	HYPHEMIA
HYPHENIC	HYPOTHECa	**ICHTHYIC**	KACHAHRI	**MAHIMAHI**	*MASHGIAH*	*MASHIACH*
MASHLOCH	MISHMASH+	MISHMOSH+	*MUCHACHA*	MUCHACHO	NAPHTHOL	NAPHTHYL
NOHOWISH	NUTHATCH+	**NYMPHISH**	*OANSHAGH*	**OVERHIGH**	PADISHAH	PAHOEHOE
PARASHAH	PHOSHPIDe	PHOSPHINe	PHOSPHORe	PHOSPHORi	**PHTHALIC**	PHTHALIN
PHTHISES	PHTHISIC	**PHTHISIS**	PHYLARCHy	*PIHOIHOI*	***RHACHIAL***	RHAPHIDE
RHEOPHILe	RHONCHAL	**RHONCHUS**	**RHYTHMAL**	**RHYTHMED**	RHYTHMUS+	**RIGHTISH**
ROUGHHEWn	**ROUGHISH**	**SEMIHIGH**	SHADBUSH+	SHADCHAN	*SHADKHAN*	SHADRACH
SHASHLIK	*SHATOOSH+*	SHAUCHLE	**SHAUCHLY***	SHECHITAh	*SHEDHAND*	***SHIDDUCH***
SHITHEAD	SHITHOLE	*SHLOSHIM*	***SHOCHETS***	**SHOFROTH**	**SHORTISH**	SHOTHOLE
SHOUTHER	SHRADDHA	**SHREWISH**	*SHWESHWE*	**SUMPHISH**	**SYLPHISH**	THEARCHY+
TATAHASH+	THEOSOPHy	**THIEVISH**	**THINNISH**	THIOPHENe	**THIOPHIL**	THRESHEL
TOUGHISH	UNHEALTHy	***WASHHAND***	WHINCHAT	*WHOLPHIN*		

CONTAINING MM

ABOMASUM	ALARMISM	AMMOCETE	*AMMONATE*	*AXOLEMMA*	AMMONIFY	AMMONITE	AMMONOID
ANALEMMA	ARMYWORM	*AXILEMMA*	*AXOLEMMA*	BATHMISM	BUMMAREE	CAIMACAM	
CAMOMILE	CARDAMOM	CARDAMUM	CEMENTUM	CHUMMAGE	**CHUMMILY**	CIMBALOM	
CLAMMILY	CLAMWORM	COMEMBER	COMMERGE	COMMONEY	CONSOMME	**COREMIUM**	
CRUMMACK	CRUMMOCK	**CYMATIUM**	DEMONISM	DIDYMIUM	**DILEMMIC**	DIMERISM	
DIMMABLE	**DOMATIUM**	DOMINIUM	**DOOMSMAN**	**DOOMSMEN**	DRAMMACH	DRAMMOCK	
DRUMMOCK	DUMMERER	DUMMKOPF	DYNAMISM	EMBOLISM	**EMPYEMIC**	ENCOMIUM	
ENDEMISM	ENGRAMMA	ENGRAMME	EUMERISM	**EXEMPLUM**	**EXTREMUM**	FAMILISM	
FLAMMULE	FLIMFLAM	FLUMMERY+	**GAMESMAN**	**GAMESMEN**	GAMESOME	**GAMMADIA**	
GAMMATIA	GAMMONER	GAMODEME	**GEMMEOUS**	*GRAMMAGE*	**GUMMOSIS**	HAMMERER	
HEMATOMA	HOMEROOM	HOMOGAMY+	HUMANISM	**HUMMABLE**	HUMSTRUM	HYMENIUM	
IMBALMER	**IMMANELY**	**IMMANENT**	IMMANITY+	**IMMINUTE**	IMMOLATE	**IMMOTILE**	
IMPERIUM	**IMPRIMIS**	INTIMISM	**ISODOMUM**	*JAMMABLE*	KYMOGRAM	LAMMIGER	
LIMBMEAL	LUMINISM	LYMPHOMA	MACALLUM	MACARISM	MACHISMO	*MACHOISM*	
MAGMATIC	MAHIMAHI	**MAHZORIM**	MAILGRAM	MAINBOOM	MAINMAST	MAKIMONO	
MALAMUTE	MALAROMA	MALEMIUT	MALEMUTE	MALTWORM	MAMALIGA	MAMELUCO	
MAMELUKE	MAMSELLE	MANDAMUS	**MANIFORM**	MAPMAKER	**MARASMIC**	MARASMUS+	
MARCHMAN	**MARCHMEN**	MARIGRAM	MARJORAM	MASURIUM	MATAMATA	MAUMETRY+	
MAWMETRY+	MAXIMIST	MAXIMITE	MAZEMENT	MEALWORM	MECONIUM	MELAMINE	
MELANISM	**MEMBERED**	MEMSAHIB	MENOMINI	MENOPOME	MERYCISM	**MERESMAN**	
MERESMEN	MERIMAKE	MERISTEM	MEROSOME	**MERRYMAN**	**MERRYMEN**	**MESEEMED**	
MESMERIC	MESODERM	MESOMERE	MESOSOME	MESSMATE	*METAMALE*	***METAMICT***	
METASOMA	METOPISM	MEZEREUM	**MIASMATA**	**MIASMOUS**	MICROMHO	MIDMONTH	
MILESIMO	MILLIEME	MILLIMHO	MILLIOHM	MILLIREM	MIMESTER	MIMETITE	
MIMICKER	*MINIMART*	MINIMENT	MINIMILL	MINIMIST	*MINIMOTO*	**MINYANIM**	
MIROMIRO	**MISDEMPT**	MISHMASH+	MISHMOSH+	MITTIMUS+	MNEMONIC	MOCUDDUM	
MODALISM	MOKADDAM	**MOMENTLY**	MONADISM	**MONEYMAN**	**MONEYMEN**	MONIMENT	
MONOGERM	MONOMARK	MONOMIAL	**MONOMODE**	*MONOSEMY+*	MONOSOME	MONOSOMY+	
MOONBEAM	MORONISM	MORPHEME	MORTMAIN	**MOSHAVIM**	MOTORDOM	MOTORIUM	
MOTORMAN	**MOTORMEN**	*MOUSEMAT*	MOVIEDOM	MUCKWORM	MULTIGYM	MUNIMENT	
MUQADDAM	**MURIFORM**	**MURKSOME**	MURMURER	**MUTANDUM**	**MYCELIUM**	MYCETOMA	

MYOMANCY+ MYRMIDON *MYXAMEBAe* MYXEDEMA **MYXOMATA** NIMBYISM NOMADISM
NOMOGRAM NUMMULARy OHMMETER **OMNIFORM** **OMNIMODE** OPIUMISM PEMMICAN
PESSIMUM PHORMIUM PLUMBISM **POMMETTY** PSAMMITE PYGMYISM RACEMISM
RAMIFORM **RAMPSMAN** **RAMPSMEN** **ROOMSOME** SAMARIUM SCAMMONY+ SCHIMMEL
SCUMMILY SEISMISM SEMICOMA SEMIDOMEd *SEMIMILD* **SEMIMUTE** *SEMINOMAd*
SHAMOSIM SIMPLISM SIMULIUM **SLIMMISH** *SLOMMOCK* SLUMMOCK **SMALMILY**
SMARMILY SOMATISM **STEMMATA** STRUMMEL STRUMMER **SUMMABLE** **SUMMERLY**
SUMMITAL SUMMITRY+ SUMMONER SUPERMOM *SUPREMUM* **SWIMMILY** TAGMEMIC
TERMTIME THRUMMER *TIMEBOMB* TIMPANUM TOMMYROT TOMOGRAM TOTEMISM
TRILEMMA TYMPANUM **UNDIMMED** **UNMAIMED** **UNSUMMED** *WOMANISM* YAMMERER
ZAMBOMBA ZOMBIISM ZYMOGRAM

CONTAINING PP

AGITPROP AMPHIPOD ANTIPOPE ***APOAPSES*** **APOAPSIS** **APOCOPIC** APOGRAPH
APOPHONY+ APOPHYGE *APOPLAST* APOSPORY+ APPANAGEd APPEALER APPEARER
APPELLEE APPELLOR APPESTAT **APPETENT** APPLIQUE **APPOSITE** BEBOPPER
BEPIMPLE BLOWPIPE CHAPPATI CHAPPESS+ **CHOPPILY** CIOPPINO COPPERAH
COPPERAS+ CORNPIPE **DAPPERLY** DIDAPPER DIPLOPIA **DIPLOPIC** DIPLOPOD
DIPPABLE *DRIPPILY* DYSPEPSY+ ENDPAPER EOHIPPUS+ EPIPHANY+ EPIPHYTE
EPIPLOIC EPIPLOON **EPIPOLIC** EPISCOPE EPISCOPY+ EPISPERM EPISPORE
EPOPOEIA ESTOPPEL EUPEPSIA **EUPEPTIC** FIPPENCE *FLIPFLOP>* **FLOPPILY**
FLYPAPER *FOOTPUMP* **FRAPPANT** GRIPTAPE *HALFPIPE* HAPLOPIA HIPPARCH
HIPPURIC HIPPYDOM HORNPIPE HOSEPIPE HYPEROPE HYPOPNEA HYPOPYON
KIPPERER LAGNAPPE **LAPPETED** LIRIPIPE LIRIPOOP LOLLIPOP MALAPROP
MAYAPPLE **NONPAPAL** OILPAPER OPOPANAX+ **OPPILANT** OPPILATE OPPUGNER
OUTPUPIL PALMIPEDe **PALPABLE** **PALPABLY** PALPATORy PALPEBRAe PALPEBRAl
PAMPHREY **PANOPTIC** PANSOPHY+ PAPALISE PAPALISM PAPALIST PAPALIZE
PAPILLON PAPISHER **PAPISTIC** PAPISTRY+ **PAPULOSE** **PAPULOUS** **PAPYRIAN**
PAPYRINE PARADROP> *PARAPARA* PARPOINT PASPALUM PATTYPAN *PAUROPOD*
PAYPHONE PEATSHIP *PEEKAPOO* PEEPSHOW PEESWEEP PENPOINT PEPERINO
PEPERONI **PEPLUMED** PEPONIDA PEPONIUM **PEPTIDIC** **PEPTONIC** PEREOPOD
PERICARP PERICOPE PERIPETY+ PERIPLUS+ PERIPTERy **PERSPIRY** *PETAFLOP*
PETNAPER PHOSPHIDe PHOSPHINe PHOSPHORe PHOSPHORi PHOTOMAP> PHOTOPIA
PHOTOPIC PHOTOPSY+ PIEPLANT *PINGPONG* PINNIPEDe PIPECLAY PIPEFISH+
PIPELESS **PIPELIKE** PIPERINE PIPESTEM PIPEWORK PIPEWORT PIPINESS+
PIPINGLY *PLAYSLIP* PLUMIPED PODOCARP POETSHIP POLYPARY+ POLYPHONe
POLYPHONy POLYPIDE *POLYPILL* **POLYPINE** POLYPITE POLYPNEA **POLYPOID**
POLYPORE **POLYPOUS** POLYTYPE *POMPILID* POPEHOOD **POPELESS** POPELIKE
POPELING *POPESEYE* POPESHIP POPINJAY **POPISHLY** *POPLITEI* POPLITIC
POPSICLE POPSTREL POPULISM POPULIST PORPHYRY+ PORTAPAK **POSTCOUP**
POSTPAID POSTPOSE *POSTPUNK* PRAECIPE PRECEPIT PREPENSE ***PREPUBES***
PREPUBIS **PRESLEEP** **PRIAPEAN** PRIAPISM **PRINCIPE** PRINCIPIa PROLAPSE
PROPANOL *PROPENAL* PROPENOL **PROPENSE** **PROPENYL** PROPHAGE PROPHASE
PROPHESY PROPHYLL PROPOLIS+ PROPOUND ***PROPRIUM*** **PROPYLIC** PROPYLON
PROSOPON PROTOPOD PSEPHISM PSEPHITE PTEROPOD ***PUERPERAe*** *PUERPERAl*
PULPALLY **PULPITAL** **PULPITED** PULPITER PULPITRY+ PULPITUM **PULPLESS**
PULPMILL PULPWOOD PUMPHOOD **PUMPLESS** **PUMPLIKE** **PUPARIUM** PUPATION
PUPILAGE **PUPILLARy** **PURPLISH** **PURPURIC** PURPURIN **QUIPPISH** RAPPAREE
REPEREPE **RIPPABLE** *ROANPIPE* *RONEPIPE* SANDPEEP SAPPHISM SAPPHIST

271

SAPROPEL	SCHNAPPS+	SCRAPPLE	SCUPPAUG	*SEPTUPLEt*	SHLEPPER	***SLIPPILY***
SLIPSLOP	**SNAPPILY**	**SNAPPISH**	SPALPEEN	*SPANSPEK*	**STEEPEUP**	STROPPER
SUPERCOP	SUPERPRO	SUPERSPY+	**SUPPEAGO**	SUPPLANT	**SUPPLELY**	SUPPLIAL
SUPPOSAL	*SYNTHPOP*	**TAPPABLE**	TARPAPER	THRAPPLE	THROPPLE	**TIPPABLE**
TITTUPPY	TOPOTYPE	**TRAPPEAN**	**TRAPPOSE**	**TRAPPOUS**	TRIPPANT	**UNDIPPED**
UNHEPPEN	**UNLOPPED**	**UNPROPER**	**UNSAPPED**	**UNSUPPLE**	**UNTIPPED**	**UPSPRANG**
UPSPRUNG	WALDRAPP	WRAPPAGE				

CONTAINING SSS

ASBESTUS+	ASSISTER	ASSISTOR	BASENESS+	BASSNESS+	BIASNESS+	BONASSUS+
BRASSISH	**BUSHLESS**	BUSYNESS+	**CHAUSSES**	**COSMESES**	**COSMESIS**	**COSTLESS**
CROSSISH	**DISKLESS**	DUSKNESS+	**DUSTLESS**	**EASELESS**	EASINESS+	**ECSTASES**
ECSTASISe	ESQUISSE	**ESSAYISH**	**ESTHESES**	ESTHESIS+	FASTNESS+	**FESSWISE**
FISHLESS	FOSTRESS+	GASTNESS+	*GLOSSIST*	**GUSTLESS**	**ISLELESS**	ISOGLOSS+
ISOSTASY+	**LENSLESS**	*LOSSLESS*	LOSTNESS+	**LUSTLESS**	MASSEUSE	**MASSLESS**
MASTLESS	MISSENSE	**MOLOSSUS**	NESHNESS+	**NEWSLESS**	**NOSELESS**	NOSINESS+
OBSESSOR	**OSTEOSES**	OSTEOSIS+	**PASSLESS**	**PASTLESS**	PASTNESS+	POSHNESS+
PSILOSES	**PSILOSIS**	RASCASSE	**ROSELESS**	ROSINESS+	**SACKLESS**	**SAIKLESS**
SAILLESS	SAINTESS+	**SALTLESS**	SALTNESS+	*SANDLESS*	SANENESS+	SARGASSO
SASSOLIN	SASSWOOD	**SATELESS**	SATYRESS+	SAUCISSE	*SAWGRASS+*	SCHUSSER
SCISSION	SCISSURE	*SCUMLESS*	SEARNESS+	SEEDNESS+	**SEEMLESS**	SEISMISM
SELFNESS+	**SEMIOSES**	SEMIOSIS+	SESSPOOL	**SHUNLESS**	**SIGHLESS**	**SIGNLESS**
SIRIASES	**SIRIASIS**	**SISSYISH**	SIZINESS+	SKEWNESS+	**SKILLESS**	SLIMNESS+
SLITLESS	SMARTASS+	**SMOGLESS**	SNUBNESS+	**SOAPLESS**	SOAPSUDSy	**SOCKLESS**
SODALESS	**SOILLESS**	**SOLELESS**	SOLENESS+	**SONGLESS**	**SOOTLESS**	**SPANLESS**
SPINLESS	SPRYNESS+	**SPURLESS**	SPYGLASS+	**STAYLESS**	**STEMLESS**	**STENOSES**
STENOSIS	**STIRLESS**	STRESSOR	SUBSENSE	SUCHNESS+	**SUDSLESS**	SUITRESS+
SUNGLASS+	SUSURRUS+	**SYNAPSIS**	**SYNDESES**	SYNDESIS+	SYSSITIA	*TASKLESS*
THISNESS+	THUSNESS+	TSESSEBE	**TSORRISS**	**TUSKLESS**	UNSTRESS+	**VESTLESS**
WASTNESS+	**WISHLESS**					

CONTAINING VV

AVADAVAT	AVERSIVE	CONVOLVE	**CRIVVENS**	DIVIDIVI	**EVINCIVE**	**EVOLVENT**
LAVALAVA	LOVEVINE	**SLIVOVICa**	SPIVVERY+	TRIVALVEd	UNIVALVEd	VALVELET
VAVASOUR	VAVASSOR	VEGETIVE	VELVERET	VENVILLE	VESUVIAN	**VITATIVE**
VIVARIUM	VIVERRID	VIVIDITY+	VIVIFIER	VIVIPARA	VIVIPARY+	VIVISECT
VOCATIVE	VOLITIVE	VOLVULUS+	VOMITIVE	**VOTIVELY**	VULVITIS+	*VUVUZELA*

CONTAINING WW

BLOWDOWN	CHOWCHOW	CRAWLWAY	DOWNFLOW	DOWNWASH+	***GEWGAWED***	HAWKSHAW
HAWKWEED	KOWTOWER	NEWSHAWK	NEWSWIRE	*NEWWAVER*	OWREWORD	POWSOWDY+
REWAREWA	ROWDEDOW	ROWDYDOW	*SHWESHWE*	*SLOWDOWN*	SLOWWORM	STOWDOWN
TOWNWEAR	WALKAWAY	WALLOWER	WALLWORT	*WANTAWAY*	**WANWORDY**	WANWORTH
WARPOWER	**WARPWISE**	WARTWEED	WARTWORT	*WASHAWAY*	WASHBOWL	WASHWIPE
WASTEWAY	WAYWISER	WEBWHEEL	**WEFTWISE**	WELLAWAY	WHIPWORM	**WIDOWMAN**
WIDOWMEN	WIDTHWAY	WILDFOWL	WILDWOOD	WILLIWAU	WILLOWER	WINDBLOWn

WINDFLAW	WINNOWER	WIREDRAWn	**WIREDREW**	WIREWORK	WIREWORM	**WIREWOVE**
WIRRICOW	WITHWIND	WOODWALE	WOODWARD	WOODWORM	WOODWOSE	**WOOLWARD**
WOOLWORK	*WORKFLOW*	WORKWEAR	WORMWOOD	WORRICOW	WORRYCOW	

CONTAINING YY

ABEYANCY+	ALLOTYPY+	AUTOTYPY+	BAYBERRY+	BILLYBOY	**BIYEARLY**	**BOYISHLY**
BRYOLOGY+	BULLYBOY	**COYISHLY**	**CRYINGLY**	**CYMOSELY**	CYTOGENY+	CYTOLOGY+
DIDYNAMY+	DYSODYLE	DYSPATHY+	DYSPEPSY+	DYSPHAGY+	ENTRYWAY	EURYTHMY+
EVERYWAY	*FLYSPRAY*	GLYCERYL	GLYCOSYL	GYNANDRY+	GYNARCHY+	GYNIATRY+
GYPSYDOM	**GYPSYISH**	GYPSYISM	GYRODYNE	HOLOGYNY+	HOMOTYPY+	HYPERNYMy
HYPOPYON	**LAWYERLY**	LOGOTYPY+	*LYOLYSES*	*LYOLYSIS*	**LYRATELY**	LYSOZYME
MARTYRLY	MISOGYNY+	MONOGYNY+	MYCOLOGY+	MYOMANCY+	MYOPATHY+	*MYOPHILY+*
MYSTICLY	MYXOCYTE	NAYSAYER	PANEGYRY+	PAYNIMRY+	*PENNYBOY*	PERIGYNY+
PHYLLARY+	PHYLLODY+	**PHYSICKY**	POLYGENY+	POLYGYNY+	POLYONYMy	POLYPARY+
POLYSEMY+	POLYSOMY+	POLYTENY+	POLYTYPE	PORPHYRY+	**PRYINGLY**	**PYGMYISH**
PYGMYISM	PYROLOGY+	PYROLYSEr	PYROLYZEr	PYROXYLE	STAYAWAY	SYMPATRY+
SYMPHILY+	SYNANTHY+	SYNARCHY+	SYNASTRY+	**SYNCYTIA**l	*SYNKARYA*	**SYZYGIAL**
TAYBERRY+	**TOYISHLY**	**TRYINGLY**	TYPOLOGY+	WAYLAYER	XYLOLOGY+	XYLOTOMY+
YEASAYER	**YEASTILY**	**YELLOWLY**	**YEOMANLY**	YEOMANRY+	**YONDERLY**	ZYGOSITY+
ZYMOLOGY+						

8.5 VERY IMPROBABLE LESS FAMILIAR EIGHTS

ALBIZZIA	ANGEKKOK	*BABBELAS+*	*BABBITRY+*	**BACCHIAC**	BACKWORK	**BEAKLIKE**
BEDABBLE	BEMUZZLE	BEPEPPER	**BICYCLIC**	*BLEBBING*	**BLUBBERY***	BOBBINET
BOBBYSOX	BOCACCIO	*BOMBABLE*	BOOKRACK	**BOZZETTI**	**BOZZETTO**	BRABBLER
BRIBABLE	BUCKRAKE	BUCKSKIN	*BUMFLUFF*	*BURDIZZO*	*BUSHBABY+*	*BUZZBAIT*
BUZZKILL	**CACHEXIC**	CACHUCHA	**CALCIFIC**	**CALCITIC**	**CAPRICCI**o	CAPUCCIO
CHICCORY+	**COBWEBBY**	**COCCIDIA**	**COCCYGES**	COCKCROW	**COCKLIKE**	*COKELIKE*
CORKLIKE	*CRACHACH*	*CROZZLED*	CYCLECAR	CYCLICAL	**CYCLICLY**	**CYCLOPIC**
CZARITZA	**DICYCLIC**	**DISKLIKE**	DUCKWALK	ECCRITIC	**ENCYCLIC**	**EUCYCLIC**
EXOTOXIC	EXOTOXIN	**FLUFFILY**	**FOLKLIKE**	FOOTMUFF	**FORKLIKE**	**FRIZZILY**
FRIZZLER	*FUZZTONE*	GEFUFFLE	*HALAKHAH*	*HARAKEKE*	HASHEESH	HASHHEAD
HAWKLIKE	**HAZZANIM**	HIZZONER	**HOBNOBBY**	HOKYPOKY+	**HOOKLIKE**	*HOROKAKA*
HUBBUBOO	**HUSKLIKE**	HYPOGYNY+	HYPONYMY+	**IMMOMENT**	*INUKSHUK*	**JAZZLIKE**
JEJUNELY	JEJUNITY+	JICKAJOG	JIPIJAPA	JIUJITSU	JIUJUTSU	KAIMAKAM
KAKARIKI	KAKEMONO	KAKIEMON	KAMIKAZE	*KAMOKAMO*	KANTIKOY	KARATEKA
KATAKANA	KAVAKAVA	*KAWAKAWA*	**KAZACHKI**	**KAZACHOK**	**KAZATSKI**	**KAZATSKY**
KAZATZKA	**KEEPSAKY**	KEFUFFLE	**KENSPECK**	KERPLUNK	KHUSKHUS+	KICKBALL
KICKDOWN	*KICKFLIP*	KICKSHAW	**KILTLIKE**	KINAKINA	KINGKLIP	**KINGLIKE**
KINKAJOU	**KINSFOLK**	**KIRKWARD**	KIRKYARD	**KITELIKE**	KLONDIKEr	KLONDYKEr
KNACKISH	*KNEEJERK*	KNEESOCK	**KNOBLIKE**	KNOCKOFF	**KNOTLIKE**	KNOTWORK
KNUCKLER	KOFTWORK	*KOHEKOHE*	**KOLINSKI**	KOLINSKY+	**KOLKHOSY**	**KOLKHOZY**
KORIMAKO	*KOROMIKO*	KOUSKOUS+	KROMESKY+	*KRUMKAKE*	*KUMIKUMI*	*KUNEKUNE*
KUVASZOK	**LAKELIKE**	LIKEWAKE	LIKEWALK	LINKWORK	LOCKPICK	LYKEWAKE
LYKEWALK	**MAMMATUS**	MAMMETRY+	MAMMIFER	MAMMILLA	MAMMITIS+	**MAMZERIM**

8. Eight-Letter Words

MASKLIKE	MELAMDIM	**MEZUZOTH**	**MILKLIKE**	MINIMISM	*MOKOMOKO*	**MOMZERIM**
MOZZETTA	**MOZZETTE**	MUCKLUCK	<u>MUCKRAKEr</u>	MUDPUPPY+	**NECKLIKE**	<u>NIFFNAFF</u>
NOOKLIKE	OKEYDOKE	OMMATEUM	OZONIZER	PACKSACK	*PAPPADAM*	PAPPADOM
PAPPOOSE	**PARKLIKE**	**PEAKLIKE**	PECCANCY+	PEDIPALPi	PEPPERER	**PEZIZOID**
PIAZZIAN	PICKBACK	PICKLOCK	PICKWICK	***PIZZAZZY***	*PIZZELLE*	<u>POCKMARK</u>
POPPADOM	POPPADUM	POZZOLANa	<u>*PREAPPLY*</u>	**PREPPILY**	***PREPUPAE***	**PREPUPAL**
PROPPANT	PUPPODUM	PUPPYDOM	**PUPPYISH**	PUPPYISM	QAIMAQAM	QUIZZERY+
<u>QUIZZIFY</u>	RACKWORK	RAZMATAZ+	RICKRACK	RIFFRAFF	**ROCKLIKE**	ROCKWORK
RUBBABOO	**SACCADIC**	**SACKLIKE**	SCIROCCO	*SCUZZBAG*	SHEHITAH	SIKORSKY+
SILKLIKE	SKERRICK	SKEWBACK	**SKINLIKE**	SKIPJACK	SKOKIAAN	***SNAZZILY***
SPETZNAZ+	***STUKKEND***	SUBABBOT	**SUCCINIC**	SUKIYAKI	SWIZZLER	SYNONYMY+
TAKAMAKA	**TANKLIKE**	TASKWORK	TERRAZZO	<u>TICKTACK</u>	<u>TICKTOCK</u>	*TOKOTOKO*
TUBBABLE	**TUSKLIKE**	TZARITZA	TZATZIKI	**TZITZITH**	***UNBOBBED***	<u>UNDAZZLE</u>
<u>UNMUZZLE</u>	<u>UNPUZZLE</u>	WILLIWAW	WILLYWAW	WORKFOLK	WORKWEEK	***ZAKOUSKA***
ZAKOUSKI	***ZAMZAWED***	ZARZUELA	**ZIGZAGGY**	ZIKKURAT	ZIZYPHUS+	ZUGZWANG

9. NINE-LETTER WORDS

9.1 FAMILIAR NINES

9.1.1 VERBS IN COMMON USE

ADVERTISE	ADVERTIZE	AFFILIATE	AGGRAVATE	ALLEVIATE	ALTERNATE
ANGLICISE	ANGLICIZE	ANTIQUATE	APOLOGISE	APOLOGIZE	APPORTION
APPREHEND	AQUAPLANE	ARBITRATE	ASCERTAIN	ASSOCIATE	ATTRIBUTE
AUTHORISE	AUTHORIZE				

BACKTRACK	BACKPEDAL	BAMBOOZLE	BARNSTORM	BARRICADE	BEDRAGGLE
BENCHMARK	BLACKBALL	BLACKLIST	BLACKMAIL	BLASPHEME	BLINDFOLD
BRAINWASH	BROADCAST	BRUTALISE	BRUTALIZE		

CALCULATE	CALIBRATE	CAPTIVATE	CASTIGATE	CATALOGUE	CELEBRATE
CHALLENGE	CHAPERONE	CIRCULATE	COAGULATE	CONFIGURE	CONSCRIPT
CONSTRAIN	CONSTRICT	CONSTRUCT	COOPERATE	CRITICISE	CRITICIZE
CULMINATE	CULTIVATE	CUSTOMISE	CUSTOMIZE		

DECOMPOSE	DEFOLIATE	DEHYDRATE	DELINEATE	DEMYSTIFY	DENIGRATE
DESECRATE	DESIGNATE	DETERMINE	DEVASTATE	DEODORISE	DEODORIZE
DISAPPEAR	DISCHARGE	DISCOLOUR	DISCREDIT	DISEMBARK	DISENABLE
DISENGAGE	DISFIGURE	DISINFECT	DISLOCATE	DISMANTLE	DISMEMBER
DISORIENT	DISPARAGE	DISPLEASE	DISREGARD	DISSIPATE	DIVERSIFY
DOWNGRADE	DOWNSCALE	DRAMATISE	DRAMATIZE	DUMBFOUND	DUPLICATE

EAVESDROP	ECONOMISE	ECONOMIZE	EJACULATE	ELABORATE	ELECTRIFY
ELIMINATE	ELUCIDATE	EMBARRASS	EMBELLISH	EMBROIDER	EMPATHISE
EMPATHIZE	ENCOMPASS	ENCOUNTER	ENCOURAGE	ENDEAVOUR	ENLIGHTEN
ENRAPTURE	ENTERTAIN	ENUNCIATE	EPITOMISE	EPITOMIZE	ESTABLISH
EUTHANISE	EUTHANIZE	EVAPORATE	EVENTUATE	EXEMPLIFY	EXFOLIATE
EXONERATE	EXPURGATE	EXTRADITE	EXTRICATE		

FABRICATE	FASCINATE	FERTILISE	FERTILIZE	FLUCTUATE	FORECLOSE
FORESTALL	FORMALISE	FORMALIZE	FORMULATE	FORNICATE	FOSSILISE
FOSSILIZE	FRUSTRATE				

GALLIVANT	GALVANISE	GALVANIZE	GATECRASH	GERMINATE	GLAMORISE
GLAMORIZE	GLOBALISE	GLOBALIZE	GRAVITATE	GUARANTEE	

HAMSTRING	HANDCRAFT	HANDWRITE	HARMONISE	HARMONIZE	HIBERNATE
HIGHLIGHT	HITCHHIKE	HORSEWHIP	HUMILIATE	HYPHENATE	HYPNOTISE
HYPNOTIZE					

IMMIGRATE	IMPLEMENT	IMPLICATE	IMPROVISE	INDEMNIFY	INFATUATE
INFLUENCE	INFURIATE	INOCULATE	INSINUATE	INSTIGATE	INTEGRATE
INTENSIFY	INTERCEDE	INTERCEPT	INTERFERE	INTERJECT	INTERLINK

9. Nine-Letter Words

INTERLOCK	INTERLOPE	INTERPRET	INTERRUPT	INTERSECT	INTERVENE
INTERVIEW	INTRODUCE	IRRADIATE	ITALICISE	ITALICIZE	

LEGISLATE	LIQUIDATE	LUBRICATE	LUXURIATE

MAGNETISE	MAGNETIZE	MANHANDLE	MANOEUVRE	MECHANISE	MECHANIZE
MESMERISE	MESMERIZE	MISBEHAVE	MISDIRECT	MISHANDLE	MISINFORM
MISMANAGE	MISREPORT	MODERNISE	MODERNIZE		

NEGOTIATE	NORMALISE	NORMALIZE

OFFICIATE	ORIENTATE	ORIENTEER	ORIGINATE	OSCILLATE	OSTRACISE
OSTRACIZE	OUTFUMBLE	OUTMUSCLE	OUTNUMBER	OUTSOURCE	OUTSPRINT
OVERCROWD	OVERDRESS	OVERDRINK	OVERGRAZE	OVERPITCH	OVERPOWER
OVERPRICE	OVERREACH	OVERREACT	OVERSCORE	OVERSHOOT	OVERSLEEP
OVERSPEND	OVERSPILL	OVERSTAFF	OVERSTATE	OVERSTEER	OVERSTOCK
OVERTHROW	OVERTRAIN	OVERTRUMP	OVERVALUE	OVERWATER	OVERWHELM
OVERWRITE					

PATRONISE	PATRONIZE	PENETRATE	PERCOLATE	PERFORATE	PERSECUTE
PERSEVERE	PERSONIFY	PHOTOCOPY	PLURALISE	PLURALIZE	POLLINATE
POSTULATE	PREJUDICE	PREOCCUPY	PRERECORD	PRESCRIBE	PRESHRINK
PRIVATISE	PRIVATIZE	PROCREATE	PROGRAMME	PRONOUNCE	PROOFREAD
PROPAGATE	PROSECUTE	PUBLICISE	PUBLICIZE	PULVERISE	PULVERIZE
PUNCTUATE	PUSSYFOOT				

READDRESS	REAPPOINT	REARRANGE	REATTEMPT	REBALANCE	RECAPTURE
RECOGNISE	RECOGNIZE	RECOLLECT	RECOMBINE	RECOMMEND	RECOMPOSE
RECOMPUTE	RECONCILE	RECONFIRM	RECONNECT	RECONQUER	RECONVENE
RECONVERT	RECONVICT	REDEPOSIT	REDEVELOP	REDISCUSS	REDISPLAY
REEDUCATE	REENFORCE	REEXAMINE	REEXPLORE	REFASHION	REFINANCE
REFURBISH	REFURNISH	REHYDRATE	REIMBURSE	REINFLATE	REINFORCE
REINHABIT	REINSPECT	REINSTALL	REINSTATE	REINVOLVE	REITERATE
RELICENSE	REMEASURE	REMINISCE	REPACKAGE	REPLASTER	REPLENISH
REPLICATE	REPOSSESS	REPRESENT	REPRIMAND	REPROCESS	REPRODUCE
REPROGRAM	REPUBLISH	REPUDIATE	RESHUFFLE	RESURFACE	RESURRECT
RETALIATE	RETIGHTEN				

SACRIFICE	SAFEGUARD	SEGREGATE	SENSITISE	SENSITIZE	SERIALISE
SERIALIZE	SIDESWIPE	SLAUGHTER	SLEEPWALK	SOCIALISE	SOCIALIZE
SPEARFISH	SPECULATE	STABILISE	STABILIZE	STEAMROLL	STERILISE
STERILIZE	STIMULATE	STIPULATE	STOCKPILE	STONEWALL	SUBDIVIDE
SUBSCRIBE	SUBSIDISE	SUBSIDIZE	SUFFOCATE	SUMMARISE	SUMMARIZE
SUPERSEDE	SUPERVISE	SURRENDER	SYMBOLISE	SYMBOLIZE	

TANTALISE	TANTALIZE	TELEPHONE	TENDERISE	TENDERIZE	TERMINATE
TERRORISE	TERRORIZE	TITILLATE	TRANSCEND	TRANSFORM	TRANSFUSE
TRANSLATE	TRANSPIRE	TRANSPORT	TRANSPOSE		

UNCLUTTER	UNDERCOOK	UNDERFEED	UNDERLINE	UNDERMINE	UNDERPLAY
UNDERRATE	UNDERSELL	UNDERTAKE	UNHARNESS	UNINSTALL	UNSHACKLE
UPHOLSTER					

VACCINATE	VANDALISE	VANDALIZE	VENTILATE	VERBALIZE	VICTIMISE
VINDICATE	VISUALISE	VISUALIZE	VOLUNTEER	VOUCHSAFE	

WITHSTAND

9.1.2 VERBS MORE OFTEN USED IN OTHER PARTS OF SPEECH

ADVANTAGE	ADVENTURE	AGGREGATE	AUDIOTAPE	AUTOGRAPH	AVALANCHE
BACKLIGHT	BACKSPACE	BANDICOOT	BELLYACHE	BILLBOARD	BLACKBIRD
BLACKJACK	BLINDSIDE	BLOWTORCH	BLUEPRINT	BOBSLEIGH	BODYGUARD
BOMBPROOF	BOOMERANG	BOOTSTRAP	BREAKFAST	BRIQUETTE	BROADSIDE
BROWNNOSE	BUCCANEER	BURLESQUE	BUTTERFLY		
CARPENTER	CARPETBAG	CARTWHEEL	CAVALCADE	CHARACTER	CHARGRILL
CHAUFFEUR	CHECKMATE	CHRONICLE	COLLEAGUE	COMPANION	COMPOSITE
CONDIMENT	CONDITION	COPYRIGHT	CORKSCREW	CRESCENDO	CURVEBALL
DESTITUTE	DIAPHRAGM	DISHONOUR	DISTEMPER	DOCTORATE	DOWNTREND
EXCURSION	EXTROVERT				
FACSIMILE	FIREPROOF	FLASHBACK	FOOTFAULT	FORETASTE	FRAGRANCE
FREELANCE	FROSTBITE				
HONEYMOON	HOPSCOTCH	HORSESHOE	HYPERLINK		
INCARNATE	INSTITUTE	INTERFACE	INTERLUDE	INTERPLAY	INTROVERT
JITTERBUG					
KEYSTROKE					
LANDSCAPE	LANDSLIDE	LIMELIGHT	LOWERCASE		
MAILMERGE	MICROCHIP	MICROFILM	MICROWAVE	MINIATURE	MONOLOGUE
MOONLIGHT	MOONSHINE	MOTHPROOF	MOTORBIKE	MOTORBOAT	MOTORCADE
NEIGHBOUR	NIGHTCLUB	NURSEMAID			
OUTSPREAD	OVERCLEAN	OVERDRIVE	OVERNIGHT	OVERPRINT	
PANTOMIME	PARACHUTE	PARAGRAPH	PARTITION	PENTHOUSE	PHOSPHATE
PHOTOSTAT	PIECEMEAL	PIGGYBACK	PIROUETTE	PITCHFORK	PLACEKICK
POLYGRAPH	PREFLIGHT	PRELAUNCH	PRIVILEGE	PROFITEER	PROMENADE
PROSTRATE	PROTOTYPE				
QUADRUPLE	QUICKSTEP	QUINTUPLE			
RAINPROOF	REFERENCE	REPROBATE	RESERVOIR	ROADBLOCK	RUSTPROOF
SAILBOARD	SACRAMENT	SANDPAPER	SATELLITE	SCAPEGOAT	SCRIMMAGE
SCRUMMAGE	SCULPTURE	SELLOTAPE	SHARECROP	SHIPWRECK	SHORTLIST
SHORTWAVE	SIDETRACK	SIMULCAST	SNOWBOARD	SPACEWALK	SPARKPLUG
SPEARHEAD	SPOTLIGHT	STAIRCASE	STALEMATE	STARBOARD	STATEMENT
STRETCHER	STRONGARM	STRUCTURE	SUBMARINE	SUPERGLUE	SURCHARGE
SURFBOARD	SURROGATE	SUSPICION	SYNDICATE		
TELEGRAPH	TELESCOPE	TEMPERATE	TESTIMONY	TIMETABLE	TOPSTITCH
TRADEMARK					
UNDERCOAT	UNDERFOOT	UPPERCASE			
VESTIBULE	VIDEOTAPE				
WAISTCOAT	WAREHOUSE	WATERMARK	WISECRACK		

9.1.3 NOUNS IN COMMON USE

ABDUCTION	ABOLITION	ABORIGINE	ABSTAINER	ABUNDANCE	ACCESSORY
ACCORDION	ACETYLENE	ACQUITTAL	ACTUALITY	ACUTENESS	ADDICTION
ADDRESSEE	ADEPTNESS	ADHERENCE	ADJECTIVE	ADMIRALTY	ADMISSION
ADORATION	ADORNMENT	ADRENALIN	ADULATION	ADULTERER	ADULTHOOD
ADVERSARY	ADVERSITY	AERIALIST	AERODROME	AEROPLANE	AFFECTION
AFFIDAVIT	AFFLUENCE	AFTERGLOW	AFTERLIFE	AFTERMATH	AFTERNOON
AGGRESSOR	AGISTMENT	AGITATION	AGREEMENT	ALBATROSS	ALCOHOLIC
ALERTNESS	ALGORITHM	ALIGNMENT	ALLIGATOR	ALLOTMENT	ALLOWANCE
ALOOFNESS	ALTIMETER	ALUMINIUM	AMAZEMENT	AMBIGUITY	AMBULANCE
AMENDMENT	AMPERSAND	AMPHIBIAN	AMPLIFIER	AMPLITUDE	AMUSEMENT
ANARCHISM	ANARCHIST	ANCHORAGE	ANGIOGRAM	ANIMATION	ANIMOSITY
ANKLEBONE	ANNOTATOR	ANNOUNCER	ANNOYANCE	ANNULMENT	ANONYMITY
ANTHOLOGY	ANTIPATHY	ANTIQUITY	ANTISERUM	APARTHEID	APARTMENT
APPARATUS	APPENDAGE	APPLECART	APPLIANCE	APPLICANT	APPOINTEE
APPRAISAL	ARCHANGEL	ARCHENEMY	ARCHITECT	ARMISTICE	ARROGANCE
ARROWHEAD	ARTHRITIS	ARTICHOKE	ARTILLERY	ASCENDANT	ASPARAGUS
ASSAILANT	ASSERTION	ASSISTANT	ASSURANCE	ASTROLOGY	ASTRONAUT
ASTRONOMY	ATONEMENT	ATTENDANT	ATTENTION	ATTRITION	AUBERGINE
AUSTERITY	AUTHORESS	AUTHORITY	AUTOFOCUS	AUTOPILOT	AVOIDANCE
AWARENESS					

BACKBENCH	BACKSLASH	BACKSTAGE	BACKSWING	BACKWATER	BADMINTON
BALACLAVA	BALLERINA	BALLPOINT	BALSAWOOD	BANDSTAND	BANDWAGON
BANDWIDTH	BANNISTER	BARBARITY	BARGEPOLE	BAROMETER	BARRACKER
BARRACUDA	BARTENDER	BASKETFUL	BATHHOUSE	BATHWATER	BATTALION
BEACHGOER	BEANSTALK	BEDFELLOW	BEDSPREAD	BEEFSTEAK	BEEKEEPER
BEHAVIOUR	BETROTHAL	BICYCLIST	BILLABONG	BILLIONTH	BIOGRAPHY
BIOLOGIST	BIORHYTHM	BIOSPHERE	BIRDBRAIN	BIRTHMARK	BIRTHRATE
BLACKHEAD	BLACKNESS	BLANDNESS	BLASPHEMY	BLEAKNESS	BLINDNESS
BLOCKHEAD	BLOCKHOLE	BLOODBATH	BLOODLINE	BLOODLUST	BLOODSHED
BLUEBERRY	BLUNTNESS	BOARDROOM	BOARDWALK	BOATHOUSE	BOLSHEVIK
BOMBSHELL	BOOKMAKER	BOOKSTALL	BOOKSTAND	BOOKSTORE	BOOTMAKER
BOTTLEFUL	BOULEVARD	BOURGEOIS	BOWERBIRD	BOYFRIEND	BRASSERIE
BRASSIERE	BREADLINE	BREAKAWAY	BREAKDOWN	BREATHFUL	BRICABRAC
BRIEFCASE	BRIEFNESS	BRIGADIER	BRIMSTONE	BROADBAND	BROADLOOM
BROKERAGE	BROODMARE	BRUSHFIRE	BRUSHWORK	BRUTALITY	BUBBLEGUM
BUCKETFUL	BULLDOZER	BULLFIGHT	BUMBLEBEE	BUNKHOUSE	BUSHCRAFT
BUTTERCUP	BUTTERFAT	BUTTERNUT	BYSTANDER		

CABDRIVER	CADETSHIP	CAFETERIA	CANDIDATE	CANNISTER	CAPTAINCY
CAPTIVITY	CARBONATE	CARBUNCLE	CARDBOARD	CARDPUNCH	CARDSHARP
CARETAKER	CARJACKER	CARNIVORE	CARPENTRY	CARRYOVER	CARTILAGE
CARTRIDGE	CASSEROLE	CASSOWARY	CATACLYSM	CATAMARAN	CATCHMENT
CATHEDRAL	CELEBRANT	CELEBRITY	CELLPHONE	CENTENARY	CENTIPEDE
CENTURION	CERTAINTY	CESSATION	CHAIRLIFT	CHAMPAGNE	CHATTERER
CHEAPNESS	CHECKLIST	CHEEKBONE	CHEMISTRY	CHIEFTAIN	CHILBLAIN
CHILDHOOD	CHINSTRAP	CHIPBOARD	CHIROPODY	CHOCOLATE	CHOPSTICK
CIGARETTE	CIRCUITRY	CITIZENRY	CLASSMATE	CLASSROOM	CLEANSKIN

CLEARANCE	CLEARNESS	CLIENTELE	CLIPBOARD	CLOAKROOM	CLOSENESS
CLUBHOUSE	COACHLINE	COALFIELD	COALITION	COALMINER	COASTLAND
COASTLINE	COCKFIGHT	COCKHORSE	COCKROACH	COFOUNDER	COHERENCE
COLLATION	COLLECTOR	COLLISION	COLLUSION	COLONNADE	COLOSSEUM
COLUMNIST	COMBATANT	COMMANDER	COMMITTAL	COMMITTEE	COMMODITY
COMMODORE	COMMOTION	COMMUNION	COMMUNISM	COMMUNIST	COMMUNITY
COMPLAINT	COMPONENT	COMPOSURE	CONCIERGE	CONCOURSE	CONCUBINE
CONDUCTOR	CONFUSION	CONQUEROR	CONSENSUS	CONSIGNEE	CONSIGNER
CONSONANT	CONSTABLE	CONSULATE	CONTAINER	CONTENDER	CONTINENT
CONUNDRUM	CONVERTER	COOKHOUSE	CORIANDER	CORKBOARD	CORMORANT
CORNFIELD	CORNFLAKE	CORNFLOUR	CORPUSCLE	CORROSION	CORTISONE
COSMOLOGY	COSMONAUT	COUNTDOWN	COURTESAN	COURTROOM	COURTSHIP
COURTYARD	CRABSTICK	CRACKDOWN	CRACKHEAD	CRAFTWORK	CRANBERRY
CREMATION	CRICKETER	CRITICISM	CROCODILE	CROISSANT	CROSSBEAM
CROSSFIRE	CROSSHAIR	CROSSROAD	CROSSWIND	CROSSWORD	CRUDENESS
CUBBYHOLE	CURIOSITY	CURVATURE	CUSTODIAN		

DACHSHUND	DALLIANCE	DALMATION	DAMNATION	DANDELION	DAREDEVIL
DARTBOARD	DASHBOARD	DEBENTURE	DECADENCE	DECATHLON	DECEPTION
DECKCHAIR	DECORATOR	DEDUCTION	DEFEATISM	DEFECTION	DEFENDANT
DEFERMENT	DEFLATION	DEFORMITY	DEMEANOUR	DEMOCRACY	DENTISTRY
DEODORANT	DEPARTURE	DEPENDENT	DEPICTION	DEPLETION	DEPOSITOR
DEPRAVITY	DESERTION	DESPERADO	DESTROYER	DETECTION	DETECTIVE
DETENTION	DETERGENT	DETERRENT	DETONATOR	DETRACTOR	DETRIMENT
DEVELOPER	DEVIATION	DEXTERITY	DIARRHOEA	DICTATION	DIETITIAN
DIGESTION	DIGITISER	DIGITIZER	DIGNITARY	DILIGENCE	DIMENSION
DIPLOMACY	DIRECTION	DIRECTIVE	DIRECTORY	DISBELIEF	DISCLOSER
DISCOVERY	DISHCLOTH	DISHWATER	DISMISSAL	DISPARITY	DISPENSER
DISPERSAL	DISREPAIR	DISREPUTE	DISSENTER	DISTILLER	DIVERSION
DIVERSITY	DIZZINESS	DOLLHOUSE	DOMINANCE	DOMINATOR	DORMITORY
DRAGONFLY	DRAINPIPE	DRAMATIST	DRAWERFUL	DREADLOCK	DREAMBOAT
DREAMLAND	DREAMTIME	DRIFTWOOD	DROMEDARY	DRUGSTORE	DRUMSTICK
DUPLICITY	DUSTCOVER	DYSENTERY			

EAGERNESS	EARLINESS	EARTHLING	EARTHWORM	ECOLOGIST	ECONOMIST
ECOSYSTEM	EDITORIAL	EDUCATION	EGGBEATER	EGOMANIAC	EIDERDOWN
EIGHTIETH	ELBOWROOM	ELECTRODE	ELEVATION	ELOCUTION	ELOQUENCE
EMBEZZLER	EMERGENCE	EMERGENCY	EMULATION	ENCLOSURE	ENDOWMENT
ENDURANCE	ENERGISER	ENERGIZER	ENJOYMENT	ENROLMENT	ENTOURAGE
EPAULETTE	EPICENTER	EPICENTRE	EPIDERMIS	EQUALISER	EQUALIZER
EQUIPMENT	EROTICISM	ESCALATOR	ESPIONAGE	ESPLANADE	ESTIMATOR
ETHNICITY	ETIQUETTE	EUPHEMISM	EVERGREEN	EVOLUTION	EXCAVATOR
EXCEPTION	EXCLUSION	EXCREMENT	EXECUTION	EXECUTIVE	EXEMPTION
EXHIBITOR	EXISTENCE	EXPANSION	EXPERTISE	EXPLETIVE	EXPLOSION
EXPLOSIVE	EXPULSION	EXTENSION	EXTORTION	EXTRACTOR	EXTREMITY
EYESHADOW	EYESTRAIN				

FAINTNESS	FAIRYLAND	FAIRYTALE	FALSEHOOD	FALSENESS	FANCYWORK
FARMHOUSE	FATTINESS	FAVOURITE	FERRYBOAT	FERTILITY	FESTIVITY
FEUDALISM	FIELDWORK	FIFTEENTH	FIGHTBACK	FILMMAKER	FILMSTRIP

FINANCIER	FINGERTIP	FIREBREAK	FIREGUARD	FIRELIGHT	FIREPLACE
FIREPOWER	FIRESTORM	FIREWATER	FISTFIGHT	FLASHCUBE	FLATTERER
FLEXITIME	FLOODGATE	FLOODMARK	FLOTATION	FLOWCHART	FLOWERPOT
FLYWEIGHT	FOOTLIGHT	FOOTPRINT	FOOTSTOOL	FORECOURT	FOREFRONT
FOREIGNER	FORESHORE	FORESIGHT	FORMALITY	FORMATION	FORTITUDE
FORTNIGHT	FOSSICKER	FOXHUNTER	FRAGILITY	FRAILNESS	FRAMEWORK
FRANKNESS	FREEMASON	FREEPHONE	FREESTYLE	FREIGHTER	FREQUENCY
FRESHENER	FRESHNESS	FRIGIDITY	FRIVOLITY	FRONTLINE	FRUGALITY
FRUITCAKE	FUNGICIDE	FURNITURE	FUZZINESS		

GABARDINE	GALLANTRY	GALLSTONE	GANGPLANK	GATEHOUSE	GEARSHIFT
GELIGNITE	GENERATOR	GENIALITY	GEOGRAPHY	GEOLOGIST	GESTATION
GIBBERISH	GLADIATOR	GLASSWARE	GLOBALISM	GLYCERINE	GOALMOUTH
GODFATHER	GODLINESS	GODMOTHER	GODPARENT	GOLDFIELD	GOLDFINCH
GOLDMINER	GOLDSMITH	GONDOLIER	GONORRHEA	GOVERNESS	GRANDADDY
GRAPEVINE	GRASSLAND	GRASSROOT	GRATITUDE	GRAVEYARD	GREENBACK
GREENBELT	GREENHORN	GRENADIER	GREYHOUND	GRIEVANCE	GROUNDHOG
GROVELLER	GRUFFNESS	GUACAMOLE	GUARANTOR	GUARDRAIL	GUARDROOM
GUESSWORK	GUIDEBOOK	GUIDELINE	GUIDEPOST	GUITARIST	GUNPOWDER
GUNRUNNER	GUSTINESS	GYMNASIUM			

HAILSTONE	HAILSTORM	HAIRBRUSH	HAIRDRIER	HAIRDRYER	HAIRPIECE
HAIRSPRAY	HAIRSTYLE	HALFPENNY	HAMBURGER	HANDBRAKE	HANDIWORK
HANDLEBAR	HANDPRINT	HANDSHAKE	HANDSTAND	HANDTOWEL	HANDYWORK
HAPPINESS	HARMONICA	HARVESTER	HASTINESS	HATCHBACK	HAVERSACK
HEADDRESS	HEADLIGHT	HEADPHONE	HEADSPACE	HEADSTAND	HEADSTONE
HEADWATER	HEARTACHE	HEARTBEAT	HEARTBURN	HEARTLAND	HEARTWORM
HEAVINESS	HEPATITIS	HERBALIST	HERBARIUM	HERBICIDE	HERBIVORE
HESITANCY	HIERARCHY	HIGHCHAIR	HIGHFLIER	HILLBILLY	HINDRANCE
HINDSIGHT	HISTORIAN	HOLOCAUST	HOMEBUYER	HOMEMAKER	HOMEOWNER
HOMESTEAD	HONEYCOMB	HOOFPRINT	HOROSCOPE	HORSEMEAT	HORSEPLAY
HORSESHIT	HOSTILITY	HOURGLASS	HOUSEBOAT	HOUSEHOLD	HOUSEMAID
HOUSEMATE	HOUSEWORK	HUNCHBACK	HUNDREDTH	HURRICANE	HUSBANDRY
HYDRATION	HYDROFOIL	HYDROLOGY	HYDROXIDE	HYPNOTISM	HYPOCRISY

IDENTIKIT	IGNORAMUS	IGNORANCE	IMBALANCE	IMITATION	IMMENSITY
IMMERSION	IMMINENCE	IMPLOSION	IMPOTENCE	INABILITY	INCENTIVE
INCEPTION	INCIDENCE	INCLUSION	INCREMENT	INCURSION	INDECENCY
INDEMNITY	INDICATOR	INDIGNITY	INDOLENCE	INDUCTION	INEPTNESS
INERTNESS	INFECTION	INFERENCE	INFIELDER	INFIRMARY	INFIRMITY
INFLATION	INFLEXION	INFLUENZA	INFORMANT	INGENUITY	INITIATOR
INJECTION	INJUSTICE	INNERSOLE	INNKEEPER	INNOCENCE	INNOVATOR
INSERTION	INSOLENCE	INSOMNIAC	INSPECTOR	INSULATOR	INTEGRITY
INTELLECT	INTENSITY	INTENTION	INTESTINE	INTRICACY	INTRUSION
INTUITION	INVENTION	INVENTORY	INVERSION	IRONSTONE	IRRIGATOR
ISOLATION	ITCHINESS	ITINERARY			

JAILBREAK	JAILHOUSE	JAYWALKER	JELLYBEAN	JELLYFISH	JETSTREAM
JEWELLERY	JOBCENTRE	JOCKSTRAP	JOVIALITY	JUBILANCE	JUDGEMENT
JUDICIARY	JUICINESS	JUMPINESS			

```
KICKBOXER   KIDNAPPER   KILOHERTZ   KILOJOULE   KILOMETER   KILOMETRE
KIWIFRUIT   KNOCKDOWN   KNOWLEDGE


LABYRINTH   LACTATION   LAMEBRAIN   LAMINGTON   LAMPLIGHT   LAMPSHADE
LANDOWNER   LATECOMER   LAUNCHPAD   LAWNMOWER   LAYPERSON   LEASEBACK
LETTERBOX   LIABILITY   LIBRARIAN   LIFEBLOOD   LIFEGUARD   LIFESAVER
LIFESTYLE   LIGHTBULB   LIMESTONE   LIMOUSINE   LIQUIDITY   LIQUORICE
LITTERBUG   LIVESTOCK   LOCKSMITH   LODGEMENT   LOGARITHM   LOINCLOTH
LONGEVITY   LONGITUDE   LOUDMOUTH   LOVELIGHT   LOVEMAKER   LUBRICANT
LUNCHROOM   LUNCHTIME


MACADAMIA   MACHINERY   MACHINIST   MAGNESIUM   MAGNETISM   MAGNETITE
MAGNITUDE   MAINFRAME   MAINLINER   MANDARINE   MANGANESE   MANIFESTO
MANNEQUIN   MANNERISM   MARGARINE   MARIJUANA   MARMALADE   MARSHLAND
MARSUPIAL   MARTYRDOM   MASOCHISM   MASOCHIST   MATERNITY   MATRIARCH
MATRIMONY   MAYFLOWER   MEATINESS   MECHANISM   MEDALLION   MEDALLIST
MEDIATION   MEDITATOR   MEGAHERTZ   MEGAJOULE   MEGAPHONE   MEGASTORE
MELODRAMA   MENAGERIE   MENOPAUSE   MENTALITY   MERCENARY   MERRIMENT
MESSENGER   MESSINESS   METALWORK   METEORITE   METHADONE   METHODIST
MEZZANINE   MICROLITE   MIDWIFERY   MIGRATION   MILESTONE   MILITANCE
MILITANCY   MILKINESS   MILLIGRAM   MILLINERY   MILLIONTH   MILLIPEDE
MILLSTONE   MINCEMEAT   MINEFIELD   MINIBREAK   MINISKIRT   MISTINESS
MISTLETOE   MODERATOR   MODERNISM   MODERNIST   MODERNITY   MOISTENER
MONASTERY   MONOPLANE   MONSIGNOR   MOODINESS   MOONSCAPE   MOONSTONE
MORALISER   MORALIZER   MORBIDITY   MORTALITY   MORTGAGEE   MORTGAGOR
MORTICIAN   MOTIVATOR   MOUSETRAP   MOUSTACHE   MOUTHWASH   MOVIEGOER
MUDDINESS   MULTITUDE   MURDERESS   MUSKETEER   MYSTICISM   MYTHOLOGY


NAILBRUSH   NAKEDNESS   NAMEPLATE   NARRATION   NARRATIVE   NASTINESS
NAVIGATOR   NEBULISER   NEBULIZER   NECESSITY   NECTARINE   NEEDINESS
NEURALGIA   NEUROLOGY   NEWSAGENT   NEWSBREAK   NEWSFLASH   NEWSGROUP
NEWSHOUND   NEWSPAPER   NEWSPRINT   NEWSSTAND   NIGHTFALL   NIGHTGOWN
NIGHTLIFE   NIGHTMARE   NIGHTSPOT   NIGHTTIME   NINETIETH   NITPICKER
NONENTITY   NONSMOKER   NORMALITY   NOSEBLEED   NOSTALGIA   NOTEPAPER
NOTORIETY   NUMBSKULL   NUMERATOR   NUTRITION


OBEDIENCE   OBJECTION   OBJECTIVE   OBSCENITY   OBSCURITY   OBSESSION
OCCUPANCY   OESTROGEN   OFFSPRING   ONSLAUGHT   OPERAGOER   OPERATION
OPPRESSOR   OPTOMETRY   ORANGUTAN   ORCHESTRA   ORDINANCE   ORGANISER
ORGANIZER   ORPHANAGE   OSTEOPATH   OSTRACISM   OUTRIGGER   OVERDRAFT
OVERSIGHT   OVULATION   OWNERSHIP   OXIDATION


PACEMAKER   PACKHORSE   PAGEANTRY   PAINTBALL   PAINTWORK   PALMISTRY
PANELLIST   PAPARAZZI   PAPERBACK   PAPERWORK   PARAMEDIC   PARAMETER
PARCHMENT   PARENTAGE   PARQUETRY   PARRAKEET   PARSONAGE   PARTRIDGE
PARTYGOER   PASSENGER   PATCHWORK   PATERNITY   PATHOLOGY   PATRIARCH
PATROLLER   PATRONAGE   PAYMASTER   PEACETIME   PEASANTRY   PEDOMETER
PENINSULA   PENITENCE   PENSIONER   PEPPERONI   PERFORMER   PERFUMERY
PERIMETER   PERIPHERY   PERISCOPE   PESSIMISM   PESSIMIST   PESTICIDE
PETROLEUM   PETTICOAT   PETTINESS   PETULANCE   PHILATELY   PHONECARD
```

9. Nine-Letter Words

PHYSICIAN	PHYSICIST	PICANINNY	PILFERAGE	PINEAPPLE	PINSTRIPE
PIPSQUEAK	PISTACHIO	PITHINESS	PLACEMENT	PLAINNESS	PLAINTIFF
PLANELOAD	PLASTERER	PLATITUDE	PLAYGROUP	PLAYHOUSE	PLAYTHING
PLUMPNESS	PLUTONIUM	PNEUMONIA	POCKETFUL	POIGNANCY	POLITBURO
POLLUTANT	POLLUTION	POLYESTER	POLYGRAPH	POLYTHENE	POLYVINYL
POMPOSITY	POORHOUSE	POPPYCOCK	PORCELAIN	PORCUPINE	PORTFOLIO
PORTRAYAL	POSTERITY	POTASSIUM	POTPOURRI	POWERBOAT	POWERPLAY
PRANKSTER	PRECEDENT	PRECISION	PRECURSOR	PREGNANCY	PRESCHOOL
PRESENTER	PRESIDENT	PRESSROOM	PRETENDER	PRINCIPAL	PRINCIPLE
PRINTHEAD	PRIVATION	PROBATION	PROCEDURE	PROCESSOR	PROFANITY
PROFESSOR	PROFUSION	PROGNOSIS	PROJECTOR	PROMOTION	PROPELLOR
PROPRIETY	PROTECTOR	PROTESTOR	PROUDNESS	PROVISION	PROXIMITY
PSEUDONYM	PSYCHOSIS	PTARMIGAN	PUBLICIST	PUBLICITY	PUBLISHER
PULSATION	PUPPETEER	PURCHASER	PUREBLOOD	PURGATIVE	PURGATORY
PUSHINESS					

QUADRELLA	QUADRUPED	QUALIFIER	QUEERNESS	QUICKSAND	QUIETNESS
QUOTATION					

RACEHORSE	RACETRACK	RACKETEER	RACONTEUR	RADIATION	RADIOLOGY
RAINCHECK	RAINMAKER	RAINSTORM	RAINWATER	RASPBERRY	RATEPAYER
RATIONALE	READINESS	REARGUARD	REBELLION	RECEPTION	RECESSION
RECIPIENT	RECTANGLE	REDUCTION	REFLECTOR	REFRESHER	REGISTRAR
REGULATOR	REHEARSAL	REJECTION	REJOINDER	RELEVANCE	REMAINDER
REMISSION	RENDITION	REPAYMENT	RENOVATOR	REPELLENT	REPRIEVAL
RESIDENCE	RESIDENCY	RESONANCE	RESTRAINT	RETARDANT	RETENTION
RETICENCE	RETRIEVAL	RETRIEVER	REVERENCE	REVULSION	RIDGEBACK
RIDGELINE	RIGMAROLE	RIVERBANK	RIVERBOAT	RIVERSIDE	ROADHOUSE
ROOMINESS	ROSEWATER	ROUGHNECK	ROUGHNESS	ROUNDNESS	ROWDINESS
RUINATION	RUNAROUND				

SACCHARIN	SACRILEGE	SADDLEBAG	SAILCLOTH	SAINTHOOD	SALESGIRL
SALESLADY	SALESROOM	SALTINESS	SALTWATER	SALVATION	SAMARITAN
SANCTUARY	SANDSTONE	SANDSTORM	SAUCERFUL	SAXOPHONE	SCALLYWAG
SCARECROW	SCAVENGER	SCHNAPPER	SCHNITZEL	SCHOOLBAG	SCHOOLBOY
SCHOOLDAY	SCHOOLKID	SCIENTIST	SCORECARD	SCORELINE	SCOUNDREL
SCRABBLER	SCRAMBLER	SCRAPBOOK	SCRAPHEAP	SCRAPYARD	SCREWBALL
SCRIBBLER	SCRIMSHAW	SCRIPTURE	SCROUNGER	SCRUBLAND	SECLUSION
SECRETARY	SEMBLANCE	SEMICOLON	SEMIFINAL	SENIORITY	SENSATION
SENTIMENT	SEPARATOR	SERVIETTE	SERVILITY	SERVITUDE	SEVENTEEN
SEVERANCE	SEXUALITY	SHAKEDOWN	SHAREWARE	SHARPENER	SHARPNESS
SHEEPSKIN	SHELLFIRE	SHELLFISH	SHIRTTAIL	SHOEMAKER	SHOESHINE
SHOPFRONT	SHOREBIRD	SHORELINE	SHORTENER	SHORTFALL	SHORTHORN
SHORTNESS	SHORTSTOP	SHOVELFUL	SHOWINESS	SHOWPIECE	SHRINKAGE
SHRUBBERY	SIDEBOARD	SIGHTSEER	SIGNATORY	SIGNATURE	SILLINESS
SIMPLETON	SIMULATOR	SINCERITY	SINGALONG	SITUATION	SIXTEENTH
SKINFLINT	SKYWRITER	SLACKNESS	SLEAZEBAG	SLEEKNESS	SLEEPOVER
SLINGSHOT	SLOWCOACH	SMARTARSE	SMARTNESS	SMOKINESS	SNAKEBITE
SNAKESKIN	SNORKELER	SNOWDRIFT	SNOWFIELD	SNOWFLAKE	SNOWSTORM
SOAPINESS	SOAPSTONE	SOCIALISM	SOCIALIST	SOCIALITE	SOCIOLOGY

SOCIOPATH	SOFTCOVER	SOLICITOR	SOLILOQUY	SOLITAIRE	SOPHOMORE
SOUNDNESS	SOUPSPOON	SOURDOUGH	SOVEREIGN	SPACESHIP	SPACESUIT
SPADEWORK	SPAGHETTI	SPEAKEASY	SPEARMINT	SPECIALTY	SPECTACLE
SPECTATOR	SPEEDBOAT	SPEEDSTER	SPHINCTER	SPICINESS	SPIDERWEB
SPINNAKER	SPLENDOUR	SPRINGBOK	SPRINKLER	SQUABBLER	STABILITY
STABLEBOY	STAFFROOM	STAGEHAND	STAGNANCY	STAIRWELL	STALENESS
STARGAZER	STARLIGHT	STATEHOOD	STATEROOM	STATIONER	STATISTIC
STATUETTE	STEAMBOAT	STEAMSHIP	STEELYARD	STEEPNESS	STERILITY
STIFFNESS	STILLNESS	STIMULANT	STOCKROOM	STOCKYARD	STONECROP
STONEFISH	STONEWARE	STOPLIGHT	STOPWATCH	STOREROOM	STORYBOOK
STORYLINE	STOVEPIPE	STRAGGLER	STRANGLER	STRATEGEM	STREAMBED
STREETCAR	STRONGBOX	STRONTIUM	STRUGGLER	STUDHORSE	STUPIDITY
STUTTERER	STYROFOAM	SUAVENESS	SUBBRANCH	SUBEDITOR	SUBMITTAL
SUBSTANCE	SUBWOOFER	SUCCESSOR	SUGARCANE	SULKINESS	SULTANATE
SUNBATHER	SUNFLOWER	SUNSCREEN	SUNSTROKE	SUPERBRAT	SUPERHERO
SUPERNOVA	SUPERSTAR	SUPPORTER	SUPREMACY	SURROGACY	SUSPENDER
SWAMPLAND	SWEARWORD	SWEATBAND	SWEATSHOP	SWEETCORN	SWEETENER
SWEETNESS	SWEETSHOP	SWIFTNESS	SWORDFISH	SYMBOLISM	SYMPOSIUM
SYNAGOGUE					

TABLELAND	TABLEWARE	TACTICIAN	TAILENDER	TAILLIGHT	TANGERINE
TARANTULA	TARDINESS	TARPAULIN	TATTOOIST	TAXIDERMY	TECHNIQUE
TELEPATHY	TELEPHOTO	TEMPTRESS	TENSENESS	TERRITORY	TERRORISM
TERRORIST	TESTAMENT	THERAPIST	THESAURUS	THICKENER	THICKHEAD
THIRTIETH	THREESOME	THRESHOLD	THROWAWAY	THROWBACK	THUMBNAIL
TIDEWATER	TIGHTNESS	TIGHTROPE	TIGHTWIRE	TIMEFRAME	TIMEPIECE
TIMESCALE	TINDERBOX	TIREDNESS	TOADSTOOL	TOLERANCE	TOLLBOOTH
TOMBSTONE	TOOTHACHE	TOOTHPICK	TORMENTOR	TOUCHDOWN	TOUGHNESS
TOWNHOUSE	TRACKSUIT	TRADENAME	TRADITION	TRAINLOAD	TRATTORIA
TRAVELLER	TRAVERSAL	TREACHERY	TREADMILL	TREASURER	TREATMENT
TRIATHLON	TRIBALISM	TRIBUTARY	TRICKSTER	TRIMESTER	TROOPSHIP
TRUCKLOAD	TRUMPETER	TUCKERBOX	TUNNELLER	TURBIDITY	TURNABOUT
TURNSTILE	TURNTABLE	TURQUOISE	TWENTIETH	TYPESTYLE	

ULTIMATUM	UMPTEENTH	UNDERFELT	UNDERLING	UNDERPASS	UNDERSIDE
UNDERTONE	UNDERVEST	URINATION	UROLOGIST	USHERETTE	UTTERANCE

VAGUENESS	VALENTINE	VALUATION	VANDALISM	VAPORISER	VAPORIZER
VARIATION	VASECTOMY	VEGETABLE	VEHEMENCE	VELODROME	VENGEANCE
VENTRICLE	VERBOSITY	VERMILION	VIABILITY	VIBRATION	VICEREGAL
VIEWPOINT	VIGILANCE	VIGILANTE	VIOLATION	VIOLINIST	VIRGINITY
VISCOSITY	VISIONARY	VOYEURISM	VULGARITY		

WAGONLOAD	WAISTBAND	WAISTLINE	WALKABOUT	WALKATHON	WALLCHART
WARMONGER	WASHBASIN	WASHBOARD	WASHCLOTH	WASTELAND	WATCHBAND
WATERBIRD	WATERFALL	WATERFOWL	WATERLILY	WATERLINE	WATERSHED
WATERSIDE	WAVEFRONT	WEARINESS	WEEKENDER	WEEKNIGHT	WEIRDNESS
WELLBEING	WHEELBASE	WHIRLPOOL	WHISPERER	WHITEBAIT	WHITENESS
WHOLEMEAL	WILLPOWER	WINDBREAK	WINDCHILL	WINDSTORM	WINEGLASS
WITTICISM	WITTINESS	WOMANHOOD	WOMANISER	WOMANIZER	WOODCRAFT

WOODINESS	WORDINESS	WORDSMITH	WORKBENCH	WORKFORCE	WORKGROUP
WORKHORSE	WORKPLACE	WORKSHEET	WORSHIPER	WRISTBAND	WRONGDOER

XYLOPHONE

YARDSTICK	YESTERDAY	YOUNGSTER

ZILLIONTH	ZIRCONIUM	ZOOKEEPER	ZOOLOGIST

9.1.4 NOUNS MORE OFTEN USED IN OTHER PARTS OF SPEECH

ABDOMINAL	ABSORBANT	ABSORBENT	ACROBATIC	AEROBATIC	AESTHETIC
AFTERCARE	ALLOWABLE	ANTIVENIN	ARTHRITIC	ASCENDENT	ASTHMATIC
AUTOMATIC	AUXILIARY	AXIOMATIC			
BACTERIAL	BALLISTIC	BILINGUAL	BIMONTHLY	BOTANICAL	BREAKABLE
BREAKEVEN	BRILLIANT				
CAESAREAN	CAESARIAN	CAUSATIVE	CELESTIAL	CLASSICAL	CLOCKWORK
COASTWARD	CONFIDENT	CORPORATE	CORROSIVE	COURTSIDE	CRITERION
CROSSBRED	CROSSOVER	CUTTHROAT			
DEFEATIST	DEFECTIVE	DEFENSIVE	DEFICIENT	DEPENDANT	DESIRABLE
DIALECTIC	DIGESTIVE	DILUTABLE	DISSIDENT	DISPARATE	DRINKABLE
ECCENTRIC	EFFECTIVE	EFFICIENT	ELEMENTAL	ENERGETIC	EPHEMERAL
ERGONOMIC	ESSENTIAL	EXCLUSIVE	EXPECTANT	EXPEDIENT	EXQUISITE
FACTORIAL	FANTASTIC	FIRSTBORN	FIVEPENCE	FLEDGLING	FORMATIVE
FORTUNATE	FOURPENCE				
GEOMETRIC	GERIATRIC	GOODNIGHT	GROTESQUE	GYMNASTIC	
HAPHAZARD	HARDBOUND	HARDCOVER	HEREAFTER	HORSEBACK	HUMANKIND
HYDRAULIC					
IMMOVABLE	IMPERFECT	IMPROMPTU	INAUGURAL	INCAPABLE	INCOGNITO
INCUMBENT	INCURABLE	INNERMOST	INSOLUBLE	INSOLVENT	INSURGENT
INTENSIVE	INTESTATE	INTIMATER	INTRUSIVE	INVISIBLE	IRREGULAR
ITINERANT					
LEASEHOLD					
MAKESHIFT	MALIGNANT	MASCULINE	MEANWHILE	MEDIAEVAL	MEDICINAL
MERCURIAL	MIDSTREAM	MIDSUMMER	MIDWINTER	MISERABLE	MONGOLOID
MULTILANE	MUNICIPAL				
NECESSARY	NIGHTWEAR	NINEPENCE	NINESCORE	NOCTURNAL	NONPROFIT
NORTHEAST	NORTHERLY	NORTHWARD	NORTHWEST	NOSTALGIC	
OBSESSIVE	OBSERVANT	OBSTETRIC	OFFENSIVE	OFFSEASON	OPERATIVE
OUTERWEAR					
PARALEGAL	PARALYTIC	PARAMOUNT	PEDIATRIC	PERENNIAL	PERMANENT
PERPETUAL	PERSONNEL	PERTINENT	PHENOMENA	PICTORIAL	PITUITARY
PNEUMATIC	POSTERIOR	POSTHASTE	POTENTIAL	PRACTICAL	PRAGMATIC
PREDINNER	PREMATURE	PRESEASON	PREVALENT	PRIMITIVE	PSYCHOTIC
QUADRATIC	QUARTERLY				
READYMADE	RECESSIVE	RENEWABLE	REPELLANT	REPENTANT	REQUISITE
RESISTANT	RESULTANT	RHEUMATIC			
SCHEMATIC	SECONDARY	SECTIONAL	SENSITIVE	SHIPBOARD	SHOREWARD
SHORTHAND	SLAPSTICK	SOFTBOUND	SOMEPLACE	SOMETHING	SOMEWHERE

SOPORIFIC	SOUTHERLY	SOUTHWARD	SPIRITUAL	STAUNCHER	STILLBORN
STRATEGIC	STYLISTIC	SUBATOMIC	SUBNORMAL	SUCCULENT	SYNTHETIC
TECHNICAL	TEMPORARY	TENTATIVE	TOUCHWOOD	TOWNSFOLK	TRACKSIDE
TRANSIENT	TRICOLOUR	TRIWEEKLY			
UMBILICAL	UNDECIDED	UNDERGRAD	UNDERHAND	UNDERWEAR	UNINSURED
UNIVERSAL	UNMARRIED	UNSAYABLE	UTTERMOST		
VENERABLE					
WATCHABLE	WHEREFORE	WHIRLWIND	WIDEAWAKE	WOMANKIND	WOMENFOLK

9.1.5 NON-PLURALS IN COMMON USE

ABHORRENT	ABYSMALLY	ADAMANTLY	ADAPTABLE	ADDICTIVE	ADMIRABLE
ADMIRABLY	ADORINGLY	ADVERSELY	ADVISABLE	AGREEABLE	AGREEABLY
AIMLESSLY	AIRWORTHY	ALGEBRAIC	ALLEGEDLY	ALONGSIDE	AMAZINGLY
AMBIGUOUS	AMBITIOUS	AMOROUSLY	ANCESTRAL	ANCHORMAN	ANCHORMEN
ANCILLARY	ANECDOTAL	ANGELICAL	ANOMALOUS	ANONYMOUS	ANTARCTIC
ANTIAGING	ANTITHEFT	ANXIOUSLY	APATHETIC	ARBITRARY	ARDUOUSLY
ASSERTIVE	ASSUMABLE	ASSUREDLY	ATROCIOUS	ATTENTIVE	AUDACIOUS
AUTHENTIC	AVAILABLE	AVOIDABLE	AWARDABLE	AWESOMELY	AWESTRUCK
AWKWARDLY					
BARBAROUS	BAREFACED	BASICALLY	BEACHWEAR	BEARDLESS	BEAUTIFUL
BEDRIDDEN	BELATEDLY	BIGHEADED	BILATERAL	BIZARRELY	BLAMELESS
BLATANTLY	BLESSEDLY	BLOODSHOT	BOMBASTIC	BOOGEYMAN	BOOGEYMEN
BOOKSHELF	BOUNDLESS	BOUNTIFUL	BOWLEGGED	BRAINLESS	BREAKNECK
BRONCHIAL	BROTHERLY	BUCKTEETH	BUCKTOOTH	BUDGETARY	BUILDABLE
BUOYANTLY					
CALLOUSLY	CAMERAMAN	CAMERAMEN	CANDLELIT	CAREFULLY	CATCHABLE
CATEGORIC	CATTLEMAN	CATTLEMEN	CAVERNOUS	CELLARMAN	CELLARMEN
CENTRALLY	CERTAINLY	CHEERLESS	CHILDLESS	CHILDLIKE	CINEMATIC
CITIZENLY	CLAIMABLE	CLEANABLE	CLEARABLE	CLERGYMAN	CLERGYMEN
CLIMBABLE	CLOCKWISE	CLOUDLESS	COGNITIVE	COLORFAST	COLORLESS
COLOURFUL	COMPACTLY	COMPETENT	COMPLIANT	CONCISELY	CONDUCIVE
CONGENIAL	CONGRUENT	CONSCIOUS	CONTINUAL	COPIOUSLY	CORDIALLY
CORRECTLY	CORRUPTLY	COUNTABLE	COURTEOUS	COWRITTEN	CRAFTSMAN
CRAFTSMEN	CROOKEDLY	CROTCHETY	CRUCIALLY	CUNNINGLY	CURIOUSLY
CURRENTLY	CUSTODIAL	CYNICALLY			
DANGEROUS	DEBATABLE	DECEITFUL	DECIDEDLY	DECIDUOUS	DEFIANTLY
DEFINABLE	DELICIOUS	DELIRIOUS	DESIRABLY	DESKBOUND	DESPERATE
DEVIOUSLY	DEVOTEDLY	DIAGNOSES	DIAGNOSIS	DIAMETRIC	DIFFERENT
DIFFICULT	DIGITALLY	DISHONEST	DISPROVEN	DISTANTLY	DIVERGENT
DIVERSELY	DIVIDABLE	DIVIDEDLY	DIVISIBLE	DOUBTLESS	DOWNRIGHT
DOWNRIVER	DRAFTSMAN	DRAFTSMEN	DRIVEABLE	DRUNKENLY	DUBIOUSLY
DUSTPROOF	DUTIFULLY				
EARNESTLY	EASYGOING	EFFECTUAL	EGOTISTIC	EIGHTFOLD	ELECTORAL
ELEGANTLY	ELSEWHERE	ELUSIVELY	EMBRYONIC	EMINENTLY	EMOTIVELY

9. Nine-Letter Words

ENDLESSLY	ENIGMATIC	ENJOYABLE	ENVIOUSLY	EQUITABLE	EROGENOUS
ERRONEOUS	ERRORLESS	ESTUARINE	ETERNALLY	ETHICALLY	EVANGELIC
EVERYBODY	EVIDENTLY	EXCELLENT	EXCESSIVE	EXCITABLE	EXCITEDLY
EXCUSABLE	EXEMPLARY	EXPANSIVE	EXPENSIVE	EXPRESSLY	EXTENSIVE
EXTREMELY	EXUBERANT				

FANATICAL	FATEFULLY	FAULTLESS	FAVORABLE	FAVORABLY	FEDERALLY
FEETFIRST	FELLOWMAN	FELLOWMEN	FEROCIOUS	FERVENTLY	FICTIONAL
FIELDMICE	FIELDSMAN	FIELDSMEN	FINANCIAL	FIRSTHAND	FISHERMAN
FISHERMEN	FISHWIVES	FITTINGLY	FOOLHARDY	FOOLISHLY	FOOLPROOF
FOOTLOOSE	FORBIDDEN	FORGETFUL	FORGOTTEN	FORLORNLY	FORTHWITH
FORWARDLY	FOURSCORE	FRANTICLY	FRATERNAL	FRIGHTFUL	FRIVOLOUS
FRONTWAYS	FRUITLESS	FURIOUSLY	FURTIVELY		

GAINFULLY	GALLANTLY	GARRULOUS	GENERALLY	GENETICAL	GENITALIA
GENTLEMAN	GENTLEMEN	GENUINELY	GLAMOROUS	GLANDULAR	GLARINGLY
GLEEFULLY	GLOWINGLY	GRADUALLY	GRANDIOSE	GRAPHICAL	GROOMSMAN
GROOMSMEN	GUARDEDLY	GUARDSMAN	GUARDSMEN	GUESSABLE	

HABITABLE	HALTINGLY	HAMSTRUNG	HANDWOVEN	HANDWROTE	HARMFULLY
HAUGHTILY	HAZARDOUS	HEADFIRST	HEALTHILY	HEARTFELT	HEATPROOF
HELLISHLY	HEREUNDER	HEXAGONAL	HIDEOUSLY	HILARIOUS	HOMEBOUND
HOMEGROWN	HOMICIDAL	HONORABLE	HONORABLY	HOPEFULLY	HOTHEADED
HOUSEKEPT	HOUSELESS	HOUSEWIFE	HUMORLESS	HURRIEDLY	HUSBANDLY

IDENTICAL	IDEOLOGIC	ILLEGALLY	ILLEGIBLE	ILLEGIBLY	ILLICITLY
ILLOGICAL	IMAGINARY	IMBECILIC	IMMEDIATE	IMMENSELY	IMMORALLY
IMPARTIAL	IMPASSIVE	IMPATIENT	IMPETUOUS	IMPORTANT	IMPRECISE
IMPRUDENT	IMPULSIVE	INANIMATE	INAUDIBLE	INAUDIBLY	INCESSANT
INCLEMENT	INCLUSIVE	INCORRECT	INDELIBLE	INDELIBLY	INDIGNANT
INDULGENT	INELEGANT	INEQUABLE	INFANTILE	INFERTILE	INGENIOUS
INITIALLY	INJURIOUS	INNOCUOUS	INORGANIC	INSIDIOUS	INSINCERE
INSIPIDLY	INSISTENT	INSTANTLY	INSURABLE	INTENSELY	INTERBRED
INTERCITY	INTERCLUB	INTERLAID	INTERWOVE	INTRICATE	INTRINSIC
INTUITIVE	INVENTIVE	INVERSELY	INVISIBLY	IRRITABLE	ISOSCELES

JUDICIOUS

KNOWINGLY

LABORIOUS	LAGGARDLY	LANGUIDLY	LATERALLY	LAUGHABLE	LAUGHABLY
LAWLESSLY	LAZYBONES	LEAKPROOF	LEARNABLE	LEASTWAYS	LEASTWISE
LECHEROUS	LEGENDARY	LEISURELY	LENGTHILY	LENIENTLY	LETHARGIC
LIBELLOUS	LIBERALLY	LINGUALLY	LITERALLY	LOGICALLY	LONGINGLY
LUCRATIVE	LUDICROUS	LUSTFULLY	LUXURIANT	LUXURIOUS	

MAGICALLY	MALICIOUS	MALLEABLE	MANDATORY	MARITALLY	MARVELOUS
MASSIVELY	MASTERFUL	MEDICALLY	MEMORABLE	MEMORANDA	MENSTRUAL
MERCILESS	METABOLIC	MICROBIAL	MIDDLEMAN	MIDDLEMEN	MIDWEEKLY
MIGRATORY	MILLENNIA	MINIMALLY	MINISCULE	MISERABLY	MISSHAPEN

MOLECULAR	MOMENTARY	MOMENTOUS	MONEYLESS	MONOTONIC	MONSOONAL
MONSTROUS	MONTHLONG	MOUNTABLE	MUNDANELY	MURDEROUS	MUSICALLY

NATURALLY	NAUGHTILY	NAVIGABLE	NEGLIGENT	NERVELESS	NERVOUSLY
NEUTRALLY	NIGHTLONG	NOISELESS	NOMINALLY	NONCOMBAT	NONLETHAL
NONPAYING	NONSHRINK	NOTORIOUS	NUMERICAL		

OBLIVIOUS	OBNOXIOUS	OBSCENELY	OBSCURELY	OBSTINATE	OBVIOUSLY
OCTAGONAL	ODOURLESS	OFFHANDED	OFFICIOUS	OFFSCREEN	OMBUDSMAN
OMBUDSMEN	OMINOUSLY	ONEROUSLY	OPPORTUNE	OPTIMALLY	OTHERWISE
OURSELVES	OUTERMOST	OUTRIDDEN	OUTSPOKEN	OUTWARDLY	OVENPROOF
OVERBOARD	OVERDRANK	OVERDRAWN	OVERDRUNK	OVEREAGER	OVEREATEN
OVERFLOWN	OVERFUSSY	OVERGROWN	OVERHASTY	OVERHEARD	OVERLADEN
OVERLARGE	OVERPROOF	OVERSEXED	OVERSLEPT	OVERSPENT	OVERSWEET
OVERTAKEN	OVERTHREW	OVERWOUND	OVERWROTE	OWNERLESS	

PAINFULLY	PALATABLE	PANORAMIC	PANTIHOSE	PAPERLESS	PARALYSIS
PARASITIC	PAROCHIAL	PARTIALLY	PASSIVELY	PATCHABLE	PATIENTLY
PATRIOTIC	PATROLMAN	PATROLMEN	PECUNIARY	PENDULOUS	PENKNIVES
PENNILESS	PENSIVELY	PERCHANCE	PERFECTLY	PERMEABLE	PERVASIVE
PIGHEADED	PILOTLESS	PITIFULLY	PLAINSMAN	PLAINSMEN	PLAINTEXT
PLAINTIVE	PLANETARY	PLAUSIBLE	PLAUSIBLY	PLAYFULLY	PLENTIFUL
PLOUGHMAN	PLOUGHMEN	POINTEDLY	POINTLESS	POISONOUS	POLICEMAN
POLICEMEN	POLITICAL	POMPOUSLY	PONDEROUS	POPULARLY	POSTNATAL
POWERLESS	PREDATORY	PRECISELY	PREFROZEN	PRESENTLY	PRESHRANK
PRESHRUNK	PRICELESS	PRIMAEVAL	PRIMARILY	PRINTABLE	PRIVATELY
PROACTIVE	PROFANELY	PROFUSELY	PROGNOSES	PROMINENT	PROVEABLE
PRUDENTLY	PSYCHOSES				

QUARRYMAN	QUARRYMEN	QUIZZICAL

RACEGOING	RADICALLY	RAMPANTLY	RAPTUROUS	RAUCOUSLY	RAUNCHILY
REACHABLE	REALISTIC	RECEPTIVE	RECLUSIVE	RECURRENT	REDHANDED
REDHEADED	REDUCIBLE	REDUNDANT	REFERENDA	REFUTABLE	REGARDFUL
REGRETFUL	REGULARLY	RELIANTLY	RELIGIOUS	RELUCTANT	REMOVABLE
REPAIRMAN	REPAIRMEN	REPAYABLE	REPUGNANT	REPULSIVE	REPUTABLE
REPUTABLY	REPUTEDLY	RESENTFUL	RESILIENT	RESURGENT	RETHOUGHT
REWRITTEN	RIDERLESS	RIGHTEOUS	ROUGHSHOD	ROUNDSMAN	ROUNDSMEN
ROUTINELY					

SARCASTIC	SARTORIAL	SATIRICAL	SCHOLARLY	SCORELESS	SEAWORTHY
SECRETIVE	SEDENTARY	SEDUCTIVE	SEEMINGLY	SEGMENTAL	SELECTIVE
SELFISHLY	SEMIRURAL	SEMISWEET	SENSELESS	SENSUALLY	SEPARABLE
SERIOUSLY	SEVENTHLY	SHADELESS	SHALLOWLY	SHAMELESS	SHAPELESS
SHIPSHAPE	SHOCKABLE	SHOOTABLE	SIDEBURNS	SIGNALMAN	SIGNALMEN
SIMILARLY	SINCERELY	SKETCHILY	SKILFULLY	SKINTIGHT	SLAPHAPPY
SLEEPLESS	SLEEPWEAR	SLENDERLY	SMOKELESS	SNOWBOUND	SOLDIERLY
SORROWFUL	SOUNDLESS	SOUTHMOST	SPARINGLY	SPASMODIC	SPATIALLY
SPEAKABLE	SPECIALLY	SPHERICAL	SPIDERMAN	SPIDERMEN	SPINELESS
SPOKESMAN	SPOKESMEN	SPORTSMAN	SPORTSMEN	SPRIGHTLY	SQUEAKILY

9. Nine-Letter Words

SQUEAMISH	STACKABLE	STAINLESS	STATESIDE	STATESMAN	STATESMEN
STATEWIDE	STAUNCHLY	STEADFAST	STEPCHILD	STOPPABLE	STOREWIDE
STRANGELY	STRAPLESS	STRENUOUS	STRESSFUL	STRINGENT	STRONGISH
STYLISHLY	SUBLIMELY	SUBSTRATA	SULPHURIC	SUMMARILY	SUMPTUOUS
SUPERRICH	SUPREMELY	SWORDSMAN	SWORDSMEN	SYMMETRIC	SYMPHONIC
SYNTHESES	SYNTHESIS				

TACTFULLY	TALKATIVE	TEACHABLE	TEARFULLY	TEDIOUSLY	TELLINGLY
TENACIOUS	THANKLESS	THEOLOGIC	THEREFORE	THEREUPON	THIRSTILY
THIRTYISH	THREEFOLD	THRIFTILY	TILLERMAN	TILLERMEN	TOLERABLE
TOOTHLESS	TOPFLIGHT	TRACEABLE	TRACKABLE	TRACKLESS	TRADESMAN
TRADESMEN	TRAINABLE	TRAUMATIC	TREATABLE	TRUSTABLE	TURBULENT
TWELFTHLY	TWENTYISH	TWOSTROKE	TYPICALLY		

ULTRATHIN	UNABASHED	UNADORNED	UNALIGNED	UNALTERED	UNAMUSING
UNANIMOUS	UNASHAMED	UNASSURED	UNAUDITED	UNAVENGED	UNBEKNOWN
UNBLENDED	UNBRANDED	UNBRUSHED	UNCEASING	UNCERTAIN	UNCHANGED
UNCHARTED	UNCLAIMED	UNCLEARED	UNCLEARLY	UNCOLORED	UNCOUNTED
UNCROWDED	UNDAMAGED	UNDAUNTED	UNDEFINED	UNDERDONE	UNDERGONE
UNDERLAID	UNDERLAIN	UNDERPAID	UNDERSIZE	UNDERSOLD	UNDERTOOK
UNDERWENT	UNDILUTED	UNDIVIDED	UNDOUBTED	UNEATABLE	UNELECTED
UNEQUALLY	UNETHICAL	UNEXCITED	UNEXPIRED	UNEXPOSED	UNFAILING
UNFEELING	UNFERTILE	UNFOCUSED	UNFOUNDED	UNFRANKED	UNHAPPILY
UNHATCHED	UNHEALTHY	UNHELPFUL	UNHURRIED	UNIFORMLY	UNIMPEDED
UNINDEXED	UNINJURED	UNINVITED	UNKNOWING	UNLABELED	UNLIKABLE
UNLIMITED	UNLIVABLE	UNLOVABLE	UNLUCKILY	UNMANAGED	UNMATCHED
UNMERITED	UNMOVABLE	UNMUSICAL	UNNATURAL	UNNOTICED	UNOPPOSED
UNPLANNED	UNPOPULAR	UNPRESSED	UNPRINTED	UNREFINED	UNREFUTED
UNRELATED	UNRENEWED	UNRIDABLE	UNRIVALED	UNSALABLE	UNSAVOURY
UNSCARRED	UNSCATHED	UNSCENTED	UNSECURED	UNSELFISH	UNSIGHTLY
UNSKILLED	UNSMILING	UNSPARING	UNSPOILED	UNSTAMPED	UNSTERILE
UNTAINTED	UNTAMABLE	UNTEMPTED	UNTENABLE	UNTHANKED	UNTOUCHED
UNTRAINED	UNTREATED	UNTRODDEN	UNUSUALLY	UNVARYING	UNWATCHED
UNWEIGHED	UNWORLDLY	UNWORRIED	UNWRITTEN	UPPERMOST	

VALIANTLY	VARIOUSLY	VEHICULAR	VERITABLE	VERSATILE	VERTEBRAE
VEXATIOUS	VIBRANTLY	VICARIOUS	VICIOUSLY	VIOLENTLY	VIRTUALLY
VIVACIOUS	VOICELESS	VOLUNTARY	VORACIOUS		

WATERLESS	WEBFOOTED	WAYWARDLY	WEIGHTILY	WHEREUPON	WHICHEVER
WHIMSICAL	WHOLESOME	WHOSOEVER	WILLINGLY	WINDBLOWN	WINDBORNE
WINDSWEPT	WITHDRAWN	WITHSTOOD	WITTINGLY	WOEBEGONE	WOMANLESS
WONDERFUL	WORLDWIDE	WORRIEDLY	WORRISOME	WORTHLESS	

YACHTSMAN	YACHTSMEN	YELLOWISH

ZEALOUSLY

9.2 LESS FAMILIAR NINES WHICH ARE HOOK WORDS

9.2.1 FRONT HOOKS OF EIGHTS TO MAKE NINES

FRONT HOOKS WITH VOWELS

ABASEMENT	ABATEMENT	ABIOGENIC	ABODEMENT	ABUILDING	*ACEPHALIC*
ACELLULAR	*ACRITICAL*	AEOLIPILE	AESTHESIA	AESTIVATE	*AETHEREAL*
AETIOLOGY	AFOREHAND	AFORESAID	AFORETIME	AGELASTIC	AHISTORIC
AHUNGERED	*ALACKADAY*	ALIENABLE	ALIKENESS	ALITERACY	ALITERATE
ALIVENESS	ALONENESS	ALUMINOUS	AMENDABLE	AMORALIST	AMORALITY
AMORNINGS	AMOROSITY	AMUSINGLY	AMYOTONIA	ANUCLEATE	APERIODIC
APERTNESS	APETALOUS	*APLANETIC*	APRIORITY	ARHYTHMIC	ASEPALOUS
ASEXUALLY	ASKEWNESS	ASMOULDER	ASPLENIUM	*ASTOMATAL*	ASTRADDLE
ASTRINGER	*ASYLLABIC*	ASYMMETRY	ASYNDETIC	ASYNERGIA	*ASYSTOLIC*
ATEMPORAL	ATHEISTIC	ATHEMATIC	ATHEOLOGY	ATONALITY	ATONICITY
AVASCULAR	AVENGEFUL	AVENTAILE	AVIRULENT	AVOCATION	*ECARINATE*
ECOMMERCE	*EIRENICAL*	EIRENICON	ELATERITE	ELECTRESS	ELOCUTORY
EMENDABLE	EMOTIVITY	ENUCLEATE	EPICRITIC	EPISTOLET	*ERADICANT*
EROSTRATE	ESQUIRESS	ESTOPPAGE	ESTRANGER	ETHIONINE	EVAGINATE
EVALUABLE	EVALUATOR	EVENTLESS	EVINCIBLE	EVINCIBLY	EVOCATION
ICONICITY	*IODOMETRY*				
OECUMENIC	OESOPHAGI	*OPACIFIER*	OPINIONED	OUROSCOPY	OZONATION
UPLIGHTER					

OTHER FRONT HOOKS

BEASTINGS	BEERINESS	BLACKLAND	BLADDERED	BLANKNESS	BLATHERER
BLINDWORM	*BLOCKABLE*	BLUSTROUS	BOOZINESS	BRASHNESS	BRICKYARD
BRIGHTISH	*BRUSHLIKE*	BURSIFORM	CAMPHORIC	CANNULATE	CHALUTZIM
CHARMLESS	CHASTENER	*CHEATABLE*	CHEMOSTAT	CHIDLINGS	CHOROLOGY
CLAPBOARD	CLAVATION	CLEANNESS	COVERABLE	COVERSLIP	COVERTURE
CREMASTER	CRENATURE	CRESTLESS	CRETINOID	CROQUETTE	CRUSTLESS
CUPBEARER	DECAUDATE	DEDUCIBLE	DEDUCTIVE	DEMERSION	DEMISSION
DEMISSIVE	DEMULSIFY	DENERVATE	DEPILATOR	DEVALUATE	DEXTRORSE
DIREFULLY	DRIFTLESS	FACTUALLY	FLABELLUM	FLAUGHTER	FLUSHNESS
FLUSTRATE	*FLUXMETER*	FRATCHING	FROCKLESS	GANTELOPE	GLANDLESS
GLUGGABLE	GMELINITE	GRAPESEED	GRATIFIER	GREENGAGE	GRIMINESS
GUNFOUGHT	HAIRINESS	HARBOROUS	HARQUEBUS	HESSONITE	HODOGRAPH
HODOMETER	HODOMETRY	HOOLACHAN	JASPEROUS	JOCULARLY	KALEWIVES
LACTIVISM	*LACTIVIST*	*LEERINESS*	LIMITABLE	LOCELLATE	*MACRODONT*
MANGULATE	MAXILLARY	*METHANOIC*	METHOXIDE	METHYLATE	METHYLENE
MISOGAMIC	MUSEFULLY	NAVICULAR	NEOLITHIC	NEVERMORE	NOOSPHERE
PENTANGLE	PETIOLATE	PINKINESS	PINNATELY	PINSETTER	PLACELESS
PLATINIZE	*PLEASABLE*	PLIGHTFUL	PLUSHNESS	POENOLOGY	*PREABSORB*
PREACCUSE	*PREADJUST*	PREASSIGN	*PREASSURE*	*PREBIDDEN*	*PREBOUGHT*
PREBUTTAL	PRECEPTOR	*PRECHOOSE*	*PRECHOSEN*	*PRECHARGE*	PREDEFINE
PREDESIGN	PREDIGEST	*PREEXPOSE*	PREFERRER	PREFIGURE	PREFORMAT
PREFREEZE	*PREGROWTH*	*PREHANDLE*	*PREHARDEN*	PREHEATER	PREHIRING
PREIMPOSE	*PREINSERT*	*PREINVITE*	PRELATION	*PRELOCATE*	PREMARKET
PREMODIFY	PREMOTION	PRENUMBER	*PREOBTAIN*	PREORDAIN	PREREVIEW
PRESCREEN	PRESCRIPT	PRESERVER	*PRESETTLE*	PRESTRESS	PRESTRIKE

PRESURVEY	PREVIEWER	PREVISION	PROOFLESS	*PROSELIKE*	PROSINESS
PUNGENTLY	PUSTULATE	RANTIPOLE	REDUCTIVE	REJECTIVE	RELATEDLY
REMIGRATE	REMISSIVE	RERADIATE	REVALUATE	REVERSION	REVOCABLE
ROYSTERER	RUNCINATE	SCHILLING	SCOPULATE	SCRAGGILY	*SCRUNCHIE*
SEDUCIBLE	*SEXERCISE*	SFORZANDI	SFORZANDO	SGRAFFITI	SGRAFFITO
SHOVELLER	SLANGUAGE	SLAVISHLY	SLIGHTISH	SLIMINESS	SLUMBERER
SPARTICLE	SPINELIKE	SPORTABLE	SPORTANCE	SPUTTERER	*SQUITTERS*
STICKSEED	STONELESS	STRAPLINE	STRIPLING	SUNBEATEN	SUNBONNET
SUNBRIGHT	SUNSTRUCK	SUNTANNED	SWELLHEAD	SWINGBEAT	SWORDPLAY
TACTUALLY	TALLIABLE	*TANOREXIC*	TARTINESS	TAURIFORM	THEREAWAY
THEREFROM	THEREINTO	THERENESS	THEREUNTO	THEREWITH	THITHERTO
THORNBILL	THORNLESS	THORNLIKE	THUMBLING	TRACHITIS	TRAILHEAD
TRAILLESS	TRAINBAND	TRAINLESS	*TRANSOMED*	TROUSSEAU	TRUSTLESS
TRUTHLESS	TURGENTLY	TZADDIKIM	VIDEOGRAM	WASSAILER	WEDGEWISE
WHEELLESS	WHEREFROM	WHEREINTO	WHERENESS	WHEREUNTO	WHEREWITH
WIMPISHLY	WITCHWEED	WOOZINESS	YRAVISHED	ZOOGAMETE	ZOOGAMOUS
ZOOPHYTIC					

9.2.2 END HOOKS OF EIGHTS TO MAKE NINES

END HOOKS WITH '(A)E'

ABSCISSAE	AMYGDALAE	ANTEFIXAE	APOLOGIAE	ASPIRATAE	AURICULAE
AVIFAUNAE	BALLISTAE	BASILICAE	BLASTULAE	BRANCHIAE	BRUCELLAE
CATHEDRAE	CERCARIAE	CISTERNAE	CLAUSULAE	COMATULAE	CONFERVAE
CUTICULAE	ECCLESIAE	ENDAMEBAE	ENTAMEBAE	EPHEMERAE	EPIFAUNAE
EPITHECAE	FENESTRAE	FIBRILLAE	GASTRULAE	GLABELLAE	HEPATICAE
LODICULAE	*MYXAMEBAE*	NUBECULAE	PALESTRAE	PALPEBRAE	PENUMBRAE
PETECHIAE	PLACENTAE	POSTCAVAE	*PUERPERAE*	QUADRIGAE	RACHILLAE
RETINULAE	SEMUNCIAE	SENSILLAE	SHIGELLAE	SILICULAE	STROBILAE
SUBCOSTAE	TESSELLAE	TRICHINAE	TROCHLEAE	VAGINULAE	VESICULAE
VIBRISSAE	VULSELLAE	YERSINIAE	ZOOGLOEAE		

OTHER END HOOKS WITH 'E'

ACANTHINE	ACETAMIDE	AFFRONTEE	ALIZARINE	ANGUIPEDE	ANTISTATE
APPRAISEE	AVENTAILE	BACCHANTE	BACKSLIDE	BALLADINE	BANDEROLE
BASOPHILE	*BATTLEAXE*	BAUDRICKE	BENZIDINE	BERBERINE	BOUTONNEE
CACOMIXLE	CANEPHORE	CAPONIERE	*CAPSOMERE*	CARTOUCHE	CHLORDANE
CIRRIPEDE	COCHLEARE	CONFRONTE	*CORPORALE*	CROSSBITE	CURCUMINE
CURTALAXE	CUSPIDORE	CYANAMIDE	DANCETTEE	DARRAIGNE	*DEBONAIRE*
DEBUTANTE	DECLASSEE	DEDICATEE	DELEGATEE	*DEMIVOLTE*	DESPOTATE
DETRAQUEE	DIPLOMATE	DIRIGISME	*DISSEISEE*	*DISSEIZEE*	DISTRAITE
DISULFIDE	ECSTASISE	ENDOSMOSE	ENSHEATHE	ENSHRINEE	EPHEDRINE
ETRANGERE	EUCARYOTE	EUKARYOTE	EXIGEANTE	FIGURANTE	FISSIPEDE
FURFUROLE	GAILLARDE	GARAGISTE	GASTNESSE	GRANDSIRE	GUANIDINE
HARMALINE	HISTAMINE	HISTIDINE	HOSPITALE	INSHEATHE	INTERESSE
INTERVALE	INTIMISTE	ISOCHRONE	KHALIFATE	LAVALIERE	MAGDALENE
MANDOLINE	MESCALINE	MILLEPEDE	MISCEGENE	MULTIPEDE	MULTITONE
MUSCADINE	NIGROSINE	OENOPHILE	OSTRACODE	OVERBORNE	PALMIPEDE
PANTALONE	PARAFFINE	PAROCHINE	*PARVOLINE*	PASTORALE	*PATHOGENE*
PENTOSANE	PEREGRINE	*PERIODIDE*	PHENAZINE	*PHENETOLE*	PHOSPHIDE

PHOSPHINE	PHOSPHORE	PHOTOGENE	PINNIPEDE	PLEONASTE	POLYPHONE
PONTIFICE	PRETERITE	PRINCESSE	PROLAMINE	PROTAMINE	PROTOXIDE
PROVEDORE	QUARTETTE	QUINOLINE	QUINTETTE	REAEDIFYE	REFORMATE
RELOCATEE	REMEDIATE	REPLICASE	RESTRINGE	*RHEOPHILE*	RHODAMINE
RICERCARE	SAFRANINE	SARABANDE	SCELERATE	SCLEREIDE	SEMIMATTE
SERAPHINE	SHEEPCOTE	SIMPLISTE	SLUGHORNE	SQUADRONE	STRONGYLE
SYNOPSISE	SYPHILISE	TETROXIDE	THIOPHENE	THYROXINE	TOLUIDINE
TORCHIERE	TRACHEIDE	TRITICALE	TYRANNISE	UNDERBITE	VERATRINE
VISAGISTE	VITELLINE	XYLOIDINE			

END HOOKS WITH OTHER VOWELS

AQUATINTA	ARGUMENTA	BOUSOUKIA	BOUZOUKIA	CALYPTERA	CANEPHORA
CATAPHORA	DIDRACHMA	DIPLOMATA	DISHDASHA	ESOTERICA	EXANTHEMA
FANFARONA	HIERATICA	HYPODERMA	*HYPOTHECA*	JAMBOLANA	*MAIASAURA*
MATACHINA	NICOTIANA	PARAMENTA	PHANTASMA	*PHILOMELA*	PRINCIPIA
SLIVOVICA	SOUVLAKIA				

ASTRAGALI	*CANNELONI*	CHORIAMBI	DECEMVIRI	EUCALYPTI	*LEYLANDII*
MATACHINI	*MOSASAURI*	PASTORALI	*PHOSPHORI*	PORTOLANI	QUARTETTI
QUINTETTI	RICERCARI	STRELITZI	TRIUMVIRI	ZAMINDARI	ZEMINDARI

CABALLERO	*DESTRUCTO*	MAGNIFICO	PASTICCIO	PORTOLANO	PULVILLIO
QUARTETTO	QUINTETTO	SOLFEGGIO			

END HOOKS WITH '(E)D'

ACULEATED	ADUNCATED	ANNULATED	*APERTURED*	APPANAGED	AREOLATED
ARILLATED	*ARSEHOLED*	BACKBONED	BALDPATED	*BAREBONED*	BARNACLED
BILOBATED	*BLUENOSED*	BURNOOSED	*BURNOUSED*	*CAPITATED*	CARINATED
CASEMATED	CLODPATED	*CRISPATED*	*CRISTATED*	*CROSSTIED*	CRUSTATED
CULTRATED	DIGITATED	*DUNGAREED*	ECHINATED	FASCIATED	FASCICLED
GARGOYLED	HARDNOSED	*HOOKNOSED*	JALOUSIED	*LIGULATED*	LOBULATED
LOCULATED	LUNULATED	LYOPHILED	MEMBRANED	MOONFACED	MURICATED
MUSTACHED	NICOTINED	OBVOLUTED	OCELLATED	PEDIGREED	PEDUNCLED
PHYSIQUED	PINAFORED	*PINTSIZED*	*PORTIERED*	PUNCTATED	REMARQUED
ROSTRATED	SAPPHIRED	SEMIDOMED	SLIPCASED	STELLATED	SURPLICED
TARTRATED	TENTACLED	TORQUATED	TRABEATED	TRAMLINED	TRESSURED
TRIANGLED	TRIVALVED	TUBERCLED	TUNICATED	UNCINATED	*UNDERAGED*
UNIVALVED	VAGINATED	VAMBRACED	VARICOSED	VERJUICED	*WHEYFACED*
WORMHOLED					

END HOOKS WITH '(A)L'

AGNOMINAL	AMBROSIAL	*ANAPHORAL*	ANTEFIXAL	ASPHYXIAL	AVIFAUNAL
BASILICAL	BLASTEMAL	BRANCHIAL	CACUMINAL	CALCANEAL	*CALVARIAL*
CERCARIAL	CISTERNAL	CLAUSTRAL	COLLEGIAL	COLLUVIAL	*CONFERVAL*
CRITERIAL	DECENNIAL	DEMENTIAL	DIARRHEAL	DICHASIAL	DYSPNOEAL
DYSTOCIAL	ECCLESIAL	EFFLUVIAL	ENDOSTEAL	*EPENDYMAL*	EPICEDIAL
EPIFAUNAL	ERYTHEMAL	FENESTRAL	FORAMINAL	GYMNASIAL	HEPATICAL
HERBARIAL	HYPOGAEAL	*LISTERIAL*	*MAGNESIAL*	MANUBRIAL	*MESOGLEAL*
MILIARIAL	OCCIPITAL	*PALESTRAL*	PALPEBRAL	PAROEMIAL	PENUMBRAL
PETECHIAL	PLACENTAL	POSTCAVAL	PRESIDIAL	PROTOZOAL	PTERYGIAL

9. Nine-Letter Words

PYCNIDIAL	*PYORRHEAL*	RHIZOBIAL	*SACRARIAL*	SCIATICAL	SEMUNCIAL
SENSORIAL	SIGNORIAL	SPORIDIAL	*SPOROZOAL*	STOMODEAL	SUBCOSTAL
SUBMENTAL	SUDAMINAL	SYMPODIAL	SYMPOSIAL	SYNCYTIAL	SYNEDRIAL
TEGMENTAL	TENTORIAL	THERIACAL	TRAPEZIAL	TRICHINAL	TRIENNIAL
TRIFORIAL	TRIHEDRAL	UNDERSEAL	UREDINIAL	UROPYGIAL	VACCINIAL
VERTEBRAL	VESTIGIAL	*VIBRISSAL*	*ZOOGLOEAL*		

END HOOKS WITH 'N'

AMBROSIAN	BACTERIAN	BASILICAN	CALCANEAN	*CALVARIAN*	CARETAKEN
CASTELLAN	CERCARIAN	COLLEGIAN	*DEMERARAN*	DYSTOPIAN	EPICEDIAN
FELLATION	FOREKNOWN	FORESHEWN	FORESHOWN	FORSPOKEN	HERBARIAN
HYDROZOAN	HYPOGAEAN	MAGNESIAN	*MALVASIAN*	*MARSUPIAN*	MAUSOLEAN
MISCHOSEN	MISDRIVEN	MISSPOKEN	MISTHROWN	MOLLUSCAN	OUTBROKEN
OUTDRIVEN	OUTTHROWN	OVERBLOWN	OVERGIVEN	OVERRIPEN	PANDEMIAN
PLANARIAN	*PRECHOSEN*	PROTOZOAN	RESTRIVEN	ROUGHHEWN	SANNYASIN
SCHLIEREN	SCHNECKEN	SEPTARIAN	SIGHTSEEN	SPATLESEN	SPOROZOAN
STRONTIAN	SUBTOPIAN	WIREDRAWN			

END HOOKS WITH 'R' OF VERBS

ALKALISER	APHORISER	APHORIZER	APPETISER	APPETIZER	APPRAISER
ARCHAISER	ASTRINGER	BACKBITER	BARBECUER	*BEGRUDGER*	BELITTLER
BLOCKADER	*BOMBARDER*	*BOTANISER*	*BOTANIZER*	*CANONISER*	*CANONIZER*
CANOODLER	CARACOLER	CASTRATER	CATALYSER	CATALYZER	CHASTISER
CIVILISER	CIVILIZER	COINSURER	*COLONISER*	COLONIZER	*COLORISER*
COLORIZER	COMANAGER	CONCEIVER	CONCLUDER	CONSERVER	CONSPIRER
CONSTRUER	CONTINUER	CONTRIVER	CONVERSER	CONVINCER	*DECOUPLER*
DEGREASER	*DEIONISER*	DEIONIZER	DENOUNCER	DESCRIBER	DESOLATER
DETANGLER	DETHRONER	*DIALOGUER*	DISBURSER	*DISGORGER*	DISGRACER
DISGUISER	DISPERSER	*DISPLACER*	*DISPROVER*	DISSOLVER	DISSUADER
DISUNITER	*DOWNSIZER*	DYNAMITER	*ENFEEBLER*	*ENKINDLER*	ENTANGLER
ENVELOPER	ESCALADER	ESTRANGER	*ETHERISER*	ETHERIZER	*EULOGISER*
EULOGIZER	EXCHANGER	EXERCISER	EXORCIZER	EXPEDITER	*FARADISER*
FARADIZER	*FINALISER*	FINALIZER	*FLATLINER*	*FLUIDISER*	FLUIDIZER
FOREBODER	*FRACTURER*	FREEBASER	GARROTTER	GLISSADER	HARANGUER
HESITATER	*HUMANISER*	HUMANIZER	IDEALISER	IDEALIZER	ILLUMINER
IMMUNISER	*IMMUNIZER*	IMPRESSER	INCREASER	INFRINGER	INSCRIBER
INTRIGUER	INVEIGLER	*LEGALISER*	LEGALIZER	*LINOTYPER*	LOCALISER
LOCALIZER	*MACERATER*	MASSACRER	*MAXIMISER*	MAXIMIZER	MEDICINER
MELODISER	MELODIZER	*MEMORISER*	MEMORIZER	*MINIMISER*	MINIMIZER
MISGUIDER	*MISJUDGER*	MISPRIZER	*MISQUOTER*	MISSHAPER	MOBILISER
MOBILIZER	MORTGAGER	NICKNAMER	NOVELISER	NOVELIZER	*OPTIMISER*
OPTIMIZER	OUTPLACER	OVERCOMER	OVERRIDER	OVERRULER	OVERTIMER
PAGANISER	PAGANIZER	PARALYSER	PARALYZER	PERCEIVER	PERSUADER
PLEASURER	POLARISER	POLARIZER	POSTPONER	PRACTICER	PRACTISER
PREJUDGER	PRESERVER	PROLONGER	PUNCTURER	*PYROLYSER*	PYROLYZER
QUANTISER	QUANTIZER	REASSURER	RECHARGER	*REDOUBLER*	REHEARSER
REINSURER	RENOUNCER	*REPRIEVER*	RESEMBLER	RIDICULER	*SANITISER*
SANITIZER	SATIRISER	*SATIRIZER*	*SATURATER*	SCHEDULER	*SCHMOOZER*
SENTENCER	SEQUENCER	SERENADER	SHUNPIKER	SIDELINER	SNOWSHOER
SQUIGGLER	STAMPEDER	STRADDLER	SURPRISER	TAILGATER	TELEVISER

THEORISER	THEORIZER	THROTTLER	TOTALISER	TOTALIZER	TRAVERSER
TREPHINER	TRICYCLER	UNBUNDLER	UNCOUPLER	*UNDERLIER*	*UNIONISER*
UNIONIZER	UNRIDDLER	VIGNETTER	VITALISER	VITALIZER	VOCALISER
VOCALIZER	*VOLUMISER*	*VOLUMIZER*			

OTHER END HOOKS WITH ' R'

ANTILIFER	*ANTINUKER*	ARTIFICER	AURICULAR	BARRETTER	BASELINER
BLASTULAR	*BLUELINER*	CAPITULAR	CARABINER	CASTRATOR	CLAUSULAR
CLITELLAR	CRIBELLAR	CUTICULAR	*DOWNCOMER*	FIBRILLAR	FLAGELLAR
FLEXTIMER	FRONTAGER	GASTRULAR	GLABELLAR	*GLADIOLAR*	HARDLINER
HOROLOGER	LITERATOR	MINIBIKER	MULTIUSER	NAVICULAR	NEBBISHER
NONDANCER	*OBLIGATOR*	OPERCULAR	*OPUSCULAR*	PENDICLER	PERFECTOR
PHALANGER	PRESBYTER	RESPONSER	RETICULAR	RETINULAR	RINGSIDER
ROSTELLAR	SCUTELLAR	SPIRILLAR	*STROBILAR*	*SUBPHYLAR*	SUSPENSER
TESSELLAR	TROCHLEAR	*TWEENAGER*	VESICULAR	WARDROBER	

END HOOKS WITH 'T'

BACKDROPT	CABRIOLET	DAYDREAMT	DISCOVERT	DISTRAINT	FOREMEANT
HARTBEEST	LANDDROST	MASTODONT	MISLEARNT	MULTIPLET	*NEUROMAST*
OUTDREAMT	OUTLEARNT	OVERBURNT	OVERLEAPT	OVERPLANT	OVERSLIPT
POLYGLOTT	SEPTUPLET	SEXTUPLET	SPRINGLET	STEGODONT	TRANSFIXT
VIDEOTEXT					

END HOOKS WITH 'Y'

ADULATORY	ALLOPATHY	ALLOTTERY	AMPULLARY	*ANAGLYPHY*	ANTIPHONY
ASPERSORY	ASSERTORY	BACILLARY	BLEACHERY	*BOUTIQUEY*	BRANCHERY
BRIMFULLY	*BUSINESSY*	CALCULARY	CAPSULARY	CHANDLERY	*CHARCOALY*
CHICANERY	*CINNAMONY*	COLOPHONY	*CONNIVERY*	CONTRASTY	COSTUMERY
CREMATORY	CURSITORY	DANDRUFFY	*DAYDREAMY*	DEMOCRATY	DEVIATORY
DICTATORY	EDUCATORY	ELEVATORY	EMANATORY	EMBRACERY	ENGRAVERY
EPIGRAPHY	ETHNARCHY	EUDAEMONY	EVOCATORY	EXECUTORY	EXPIATORY
FLOURISHY	*FOOTWEARY*	FORMULARY	FREEBOOTY	GOSSAMERY	GRANULARY
HAWTHORNY	*HEADACHEY*	HEPTARCHY	HISTOGENY	HUCKSTERY	IMMODESTY
IMPLICITY	INCENSORY	LAUDATORY	LOGOMACHY	MAGISTERY	MALINGERY
MAMILLARY	MEDIATORY	MEDULLARY	MOUNTAINY	MYOGRAPHY	MYSTAGOGY
NARRATORY	*NONSTICKY*	NUMMULARY	OENOPHILY	OLIGARCHY	OPSIMATHY
ORTHODOXY	OSTEOGENY	OUTDOORSY	OVERWEARY	*PALPATORY*	PAPILLARY
PARAFFINY	PATHOGENY	PEDERASTY	PENTARCHY	PERIPTERY	PHOTOGENY
PHYLARCHY	PISCATORY	POLYARCHY	POLYPHONY	PRODITORY	PROVISORY
PULSATORY	PUPILLARY	RADIATORY	RAKEHELLY	SCAPULARY	SCHMALTZY
SCOUTHERY	SECRETORY	SEIGNEURY	SEIGNIORY	SERGEANTY	SERJEANTY
SINGSONGY	*SINGULARY*	SLAISTERY	*SOAPSUDSY*	SPLINTERY	SPLUTTERY
SQUEAKERY	SQUIRRELY	*STARGAZEY*	STIPULARY	STITCHERY	SUBAHDARY
SUBLUNARY	TAUTONYMY	TETRAPODY	TETRARCHY	THEOSOPHY	TRIPLOIDY
TRIUMVIRY	UNTHRIFTY	VEXILLARY	VIBRATORY	VILLAGERY	VISCOUNTY
WHIFFLERY	WHIPCORDY	ZAMINDARY	ZEMINDARY	ZOOMORPHY	

OTHER END HOOKS

ABOIDEAUX	ABOITEAUX	ALLELUIAH	*ANTIMONYL*	BROMELIAD	BULGINESS
CANTHARID	CENTINELL	CENTONELL	CHAROSETH	*CHOCKFULL*	DAHABIYAH
DJELLABAH	ENSORCELL	FASCISTIC	FINICKING	FLAMBEAUX	*GALABIYAH*

GALLABEAH	GALLABIAH	GESNERIAD	GOLLIWOGG	HAFTAROTH	HAFTOROTH
HAGGADOTH	*INTIFADAH*	KABELJOUW	KHANSAMAH	LITERATIM	MACARONIC
MADRASSAH	MAHARAJAH	MEPHITISM	MESHUGGAH	MESOPHYLL	MICROCARD
MISENROLL	MOSCHATEL	MRIDANGAM	MULTIPLEX	NERVINESS	OVERTHINK
PANNIKELL	PARANOIAC	PAROEMIAC	PICKADILL	POURTRAYD	PRELATESS
PRIEDIEUX	PROCURESS	PRODROMIC	REDISTILL	RITORNELL	SANDARACH
SHAMIANAH	SHILLALAH	SNEESHING	SPECKLESS	SPELDRING	SPRINGALD
SULPHURYL	SYMPOSIAC	TARANTASS	TARTINESS	TELESTICH	TREADLESS
TRICKLESS	TROCHILIC	TYRANNESS	VIRTUOSIC	YESHIVOTH	ZOOPHORIC

9.3 SELECTED COMPOSITE LESS FAMILIAR NON-HOOK NINES

TWO-LETTER WORD PLUS SEVEN-LETTER WORD

ABACTINAL	ABERRANCY	ABNEGATOR	*ABSOLVENT*	ABSURDITY	ADDRESSER
ADEMPTION	ADMEASURE	ADMISSIVE	ADMIXTURE	ADMONITOR	ADNASCENT
ADNOMINAL	ADSORBATE	ADSORBENT	ALBURNOUS	ALCHEMISE	ALCHEMIST
ALFILARIA	ALLOCATOR	ALLOTTERY	*AMBIPOLAR*	AMUSEABLE	ANABIOSES
ANABIOSIS	ANABIOTIC	*ANAEROBIA*	ANAEROBIC	ANALGESIA	*ANAMNIOTE*
ANAPHASIC	ANAPLASIA	ANASTATIC	ANATOMISE	ANATOMIST	ANATOMIZE
ANECDYSES	*ANECDYSIS*	ANELASTIC	ANESTROUS	ANEUPLOID	ANHEDONIC
ANHYDRASE	ANHYDRIDE	ANHYDROUS	ANISOGAMY	ANOESTRUM	*ANOSMATIC*
ARABILITY	ARBLASTER	ARENATION	ARRESTIVE	ASSAYABLE	ASSONANCE
ASSURGENT	ATTEMPTER	ATTUITION	AWFULLEST	AWFULNESS	

BALECTION	*BASALTINE*	BASILICON	*BAZILLION*	BEFORTUNE	BEGLOOMED
BEGOGGLED	BELEAGUER	BEMONSTER	BEPATCHED	BEPLASTER	BESCATTER
BESMEARER	BESPANGLE	BESPATTER	BESPECKLE	BETRODDEN	BIATHLETE
BIAXIALLY	BICAMERAL	BICOASTAL	BIDENTATE	BIFOLIATE	BIFURCATE
BIGEMINAL	BIGENERIC	*BILECTION*	BILOCULAR	BINERVATE	BINOMINAL
BINUCLEAR	BIPARTITE	BIPINNATE	BIPYRAMID	*BIRADICAL*	BISECTION
BISERIATE	BISERRATE	BISULCATE	BISULFATE	BISULFIDE	BIVALENCE
BIVALENCY	BIVARIANT	BIVARIATE	BOLECTION	*BYPRODUCT*	

CHAPTERAL	CHARTLESS	CHELATION	CHILLNESS	CHORALIST

DASHINGLY	DEACIDIFY	DEAERATOR	DEALATION	DECANTATE	DECERTIFY
DECESSION	*DECLUTTER*	DECOHERER	DECOLLATE	DECOMPLEX	DECONGEST
DECONTROL	*DECUBITAL*	DECUBITUS	DECUMBENT	DECURRENT	DECURSIVE
DEFALCATE	DEFEATURE	DEFLEXION	DEFLEXURE	DEFLUXION	DEGARNISH
DELEGATOR	DELIGHTER	DELIMITER	DENITRATE	DENITRIFY	DENOMINAL
DENOTABLE	DEOXIDATE	DEOXIDISE	DEOXIDIZE	DEPICTURE	*DEPIGMENT*
DEPREDATE	DEPREHEND	DEPROGRAM	DEREPRESS	DERISIBLE	*DESCANTER*
DESPOILER	DESULPHUR	DETERSION	DETORSION	DEVITRIFY	DIACTINAL
DIANOETIC	*DIAPHONIC*	DIASTATIC	DIATOMIST	*DIAZOTISE*	*DIBROMIDE*
DIESTROUS	*DIGENESES*	*DIGENESIS*	DIGENETIC	*DIGESTANT*	*DIGLOTTIC*
DIGRAPHIC	DIMORPHIC	DIRECTRIX	*DISCANTER*	*DISPELLER*	DISCUMBER
DISHALLOW	DISPONDEE	*DISULFATE*	*DITHIONIC*	DIVALENCE	DIVESTURE
DIVIDUOUS	DIVISIBLY	DIVULGATE	DIZYGOTIC	DODECAGON	

EASTERNER	EMBRANGLE	EMBREATHE	EMBRITTLE	*EMBROILER*	EMPLASTER
EMPLASTIC	EMUNCTION	*ENACTABLE*	ENCAPSULE	ENCHANTER	ENCHORIAL
ENCODABLE	ENCRIMSON	ENCRINITE	ENCURTAIN	ENDECAGON	ENDENIZEN
ENDUNGEON	ENDURABLE	ENDURABLY	ENGARLAND	*ENGLACIAL*	ENGRAINER
ENGROSSER	ENHEARTEN	ENHYDROUS	*ENJOINDER*	ENLIVENER	ENSHELTER
ENTRAINER	ENVERMEIL	ENWREATHE	*EROTOLOGY*	ESCAPABLE	EXANIMATE
EXCAUDATE	EXCLAIMER	EXCLOSURE	EXCURRENT	EXCURSIVE	EXORATION
EXOSMOTIC	EXPLAINER	EXPLICATE	EXPOSTURE	EXPOUNDER	EXSECTION
EXTEMPORE	EXTENSILE	EXTENSITY	EXTORSIVE	EXTORTIVE	

GIANTLIKE	GOSPELLER	GUSHINGLY	GUSTATION	GUSTATIVE

HALITOTIC	*HASTATELY*	HAVERSINE	HEDERATED	HESTERNAL

INAPTNESS	INBREATHE	*INBREEDER*	INBROUGHT	INCAPABLY	INCAUTION
INCERTAIN	*INCITABLE*	INCORRUPT	INCREMATE	INCURABLY	INCURIOUS
INCURRENT	INCURSIVE	INCURVATE	INCURVITY	INDECORUM	INDENTURE
INDICTION	INDIGNIFY	INDISPOSE	INDOCIBLE	INDRAUGHT	INDUBIOUS
INDUCTILE	INDWELLER	INEBRIETY	INELASTIC	INERRABLE	INERRANCY
INERUDITE	INEXACTLY	INFIGHTER	INFLEXURE	INFLUXION	INFORTUNE
INFUSIBLE	INHARMONY	INHERITOR	INHUMANLY	INNERVATE	INNOXIOUS
INODOROUS	INPATIENT	INPAYMENT	INQUIETLY	INQUINATE	INQUORATE
INSATIATE	INSATIETY	INSECTARY	INSECTILE	INSECTION	INSENSATE
INSHELTER	INSOLUBLY	INSTILLER	INSWINGER	INTENABLE	*INTERRACE*
INTORSION	INTUMESCE	INUNCTION	INUTILITY	INVALIDLY	INVARIANT
INVIOLATE	*INVOCABLE*	INWREATHE	INWROUGHT	ISALLOBAR	ISENERGIC
ISOSMOTIC					

JASPILITE	*JOSHINGLY*

KAZILLION

LAMINABLE	*LASHINGLY*	LAUNDRESS	LICENSURE	LIENTERIC	*LIPOLITIC*

MIDINETTE	*MOBLOGGER*	MONODICAL	MYOLOGIST

NEOLOGIST	NOBILIARY	NOMINABLE	NOVICIATE	NOVITIATE

OBCORDATE	OBOVATELY	OBSEQUENT	OBVERSION	ONRUSHING	*ONSHORING*
OOGENESES	OOGENESIS	OOGENETIC	*OOLOGICAL*	OPEROSELY	OROLOGIST
OSTENSIVE	*OUTREASON*	OUTROOPER			

PALUSTRAL	PETAURINE	*PICHOLINE*	PIVOTABLE	POSTILLER	POSTRIDER

REACTUATE	READVANCE	*REANALYSE*	REANALYZE	REANIMATE	REAROUSAL
REBAPTISE	REBAPTIZE	REBLOSSOM	REBOUNDER	REBUTMENT	RECAPTION
RECATALOG	*RECAUTION*	RECERTIFY	RECHANNEL	RECHARTER	*RECITABLE*
RECLAIMER	RECOINAGE	RECOMFORT	RECOMPILE	*RECONFINE*	*RECONSIGN*
RECONSOLE	*RECONSULT*	RECONTOUR	RECOUNTER	*RECREATOR*	RECUMBENT

RECURSIVE	*RECURVATE*	REDELIVER	REDESCEND	*REDICTATE*	*REDIGRESS*
REDISPOSE	*REDIVORCE*	REDRESSER	REEDITION	*REELEVATE*	*REEMBRACE*
REENACTOR	REENGRAVE	*REENLARGE*	*REENSLAVE*	REENTRANT	*REEXECUTE*
REEXHIBIT	*REEXPLAIN*	*REFINABLE*	*REGLORIFY*	REFITMENT	REFLEXION
REFLUENCE	REFOUNDER	REFRESHEN	REFULGENT	REGARDANT	REGUERDON
REIMAGINE	REIMPLANT	*REINFLAME*	REINSPIRE	REITERANT	*REJUSTIFY*
RELACQUER	*RELAUNDER*	RELIQUEFY	*RELIVABLE*	*RELOCATOR*	REMINDFUL
REMIXTURE	*REMODELER*	REMOISTEN	REMONTANT	REMOVABLY	RENASCENT
REOBSERVE	REOPERATE	*REOXIDISE*	REOXIDIZE	REPARABLE	REPASSAGE
REPASTURE	REPATTERN	REPERCUSS	REPERUSAL	*REPIGMENT*	REPLEADER
REPORTAGE	REPREHEND	*REPRESSER*	REPRESSOR	REPRINTER	REPULSION
REQUALIFY	REQUESTER	REQUICKEN	REREBRACE	RERELEASE	RESALABLE
RESECTION	*RESEIZURE*	RESERVICE	*RESHARPEN*	RESHINGLE	*RESITUATE*
RESOLUBLE	RESOLVENT	RESORBENT	*RESPECIFY*	RESPECTER	RESPONSOR
RESTARTER	*RESTATION*	*RESTRETCH*	*RESUBJECT*	*RESUSPEND*	RETESTIFY
RETEXTURE	RETHINKER	RETIREDLY	RETORSION	RETORTIVE	RETOUCHER
RETRACTOR	*RETRAINEE*	RETREATER	RETRIBUTE	RETRODDEN	REUSEABLE
REUTILISE	*REVARNISH*	*REVIBRATE*	REVICTUAL	*REVIOLATE*	REVOCABLY
REWILDING	*REWIRABLE*	REWROUGHT			
SHOREWEED	SHOUTLINE	SIDEBONES	SIDELIGHT	SIPHONATE	SOBRIQUET
STAIRHEAD	*STAIRLESS*	STAIRLIFT	*STAIRLIKE*	STAIRWISE	STINKHORN
STINKWOOD	STRAYLING				
TESTATION	TOPIARIST				
UNABATING	*UNABETTED*	*UNABIDING*	*UNABJURED*	*UNABORTED*	UNABRADED
UNABUSIVE	UNACTABLE	UNADAPTED	*UNADEPTLY*	UNADMIRED	UNADOPTED
UNADVISED	*UNALARMED*	*UNALERTED*	UNALLAYED	*UNALLEGED*	*UNALLOWED*
UNALLOYED	*UNAMASSED*	UNAMENDED	UNAMERCED	UNAMIABLE	*UNANNEXED*
UNANNOYED	UNANXIOUS	UNAPTNESS	UNARMORED	*UNAROUSED*	*UNARRAYED*
UNASSAYED	UNASSUMED	UNATTIRED	UNATTUNED	UNAVERAGE	*UNAVERTED*
UNAVOIDED	UNAWARDED	UNAWESOME	UNBALANCE	UNBANDAGE	UNBAPTISE
UNBAPTIZE	UNBASHFUL	UNBEARDED	UNBEGUILE	UNBELIEVE	UNBELOVED
UNBEMUSED	UNBESPEAK	UNBESPOKE	*UNBIGOTED*	UNBLOODED	UNBLOTTED
UNBLUNTED	*UNBLURRED*	*UNBOARDED*	UNBOUNDED	UNBRIDGED	UNBRIEFED
UNBROILED	*UNBROWNED*	UNBRUISED	UNBUDGING	UNBURTHEN	*UNCANDLED*
UNCANDOUR	UNCANNILY	UNCAPABLE	UNCAREFUL	*UNCATERED*	UNCHARITY
UNCHARNEL	*UNCHARRED*	UNCHEERED	*UNCHILLED*	UNCHRISOM	UNCIVILLY
UNCLARITY	UNCLASSED	UNCLEANED	UNCLEANLY	*UNCLIMBED*	UNCLOYING
UNCOATING	UNCOMBINE	UNCONFINE	UNCONFORM	UNCONFUSE	UNCONGEAL
UNCORDIAL	UNCORRUPT	UNCOURTLY	UNCRUDDED	UNCRUMPLE	*UNCRUSHED*
UNCURABLE	*UNCURABLY*	UNCURDLED	UNCURIOUS	UNCURRENT	UNCURTAIN
UNDATABLE	UNDAWNING	UNDEBASED	UNDECAYED	UNDECEIVE	UNDECIMAL
UNDEFACED	*UNDEBATED*	*UNDECAGON*	UNDEFILED	UNDELAYED	*UNDELETED*
UNDELIGHT	UNDELUDED	*UNDERIVED*	UNDESERVE	UNDIGNIFY	UNDRAINED
UNDREADED	UNDREAMED	UNDRILLED	UNDROWNED	UNDUTEOUS	UNDUTIFUL
UNDYNAMIC	*UNEAGERLY*	UNEARTHLY	UNEMPTIED	UNENDOWED	UNENGAGED
UNENJOYED	*UNENSURED*	UNENTERED	UNENVIOUS	UNENVYING	UNEQUABLE
UNEQUALED	UNESSAYED	UNESSENCE	UNEXALTED	UNEXCUSED	UNEXTINCT

UNEXTREME	UNFADABLE	*UNFANCIED*	*UNFAVORED*	UNFEARING	UNFEIGNED
UNFIGURED	UNFITNESS	UNFLEDGED	UNFLESHLY	UNFLOORED	UNFLYABLE
UNFORTUNE	UNFRAUGHT	UNFREEDOM	UNFREEMAN	UNFREEMEN	UNFRETTED
UNFUELLED	UNFURNISH	UNFUSSILY	UNGAINFUL	UNGALLANT	UNGARBLED
UNGENTEEL	UNGENUINE	UNGERMANE	UNGHOSTLY	UNGLOSSED	UNGODLILY
UNGRASSED	UNGRAVELY	*UNGREASED*	UNGROOMED	UNGROUPED	UNGRUDGED
UNGUESSED	UNHANDILY	UNHANDLED	UNHARBOUR	UNHARMFUL	UNHARMING
UNHARRIED	UNHASTING	UNHAUNTED	UNHEARTED	UNHEEDFUL	UNHEEDING
UNHIRABLE	UNHONORED	UNHOPEFUL	*UNHOSTILE*	*UNHUMANLY*	UNHUMBLED
UNHURTFUL	UNILLUMED	UNIMPOSED	UNINCITED	*UNINVOKED*	UNJEALOUS
UNKINDLED	UNKNELLED	*UNLABORED*	UNLIGHTED	UNLOCATED	UNLOGICAL
UNLYRICAL	UNMAKABLE	UNMANACLE	UNMANLIKE	*UNMANNISH*	UNMANURED
UNMATURED	UNMEANING	UNMINDFUL	UNMIXABLE	UNMIXEDLY	UNMONEYED
UNMORALLY	*UNMORTISE*	UNMOTIVED	UNMOURNED	UNMOVABLY	UNNAMABLE
UNNEEDFUL	*UNNUANCED*	UNOBVIOUS	UNORDERED	UNORDERLY	UNPAINFUL
UNPALSIED	UNPARTIAL	*UNPATCHED*	UNPAYABLE	UNPENNIED	UNPERFECT
UNPERVERT	UNPIERCED	UNPILOTED	UNPITIFUL	UNPITYING	UNPLAGUED
UNPLAINED	UNPLANKED	UNPLANTED	UNPLEASED	UNPLEATED	UNPLEDGED
UNPLIABLE	UNPLIABLY	UNPLUCKED	UNPOINTED	UNPOLICED	UNPOLITIC
UNPOTABLE	UNPRECISE	UNPREDICT	UNPROVIDE	UNPROVOKE	UNPURSUED
UNQUAKING	UNQUALIFY	UNQUEENLY	UNQUELLED	UNQUIETLY	*UNRAVAGED*
UNRAZORED	UNREACHED	UNREADILY	UNREALISE	UNREALISM	UNREALITY
UNREALIZE	UNREBATED	UNREBUKED	UNREDUCED	UNRELAXED	UNREMOVED
UNRESERVE	UNRESTFUL	UNREVISED	UNREVOKED	UNRIPENED	*UNROASTED*
UNROSINED	UNROYALLY	UNRUMPLED	UNSAINTLY	*UNSALABLY*	UNSALUTED
UNSAMPLED	UNSATIATE	UNSCANNED	UNSCOURED	UNSCYTHED	UNSECULAR
UNSEDUCED	UNSEEABLE	UNSERIOUS	UNSEVERED	UNSHAPELY	*UNSHIRTED*
UNSHOCKED	UNSHRIVED	UNSHRIVEN	UNSHUNNED	UNSHUTTER	UNSICKLED
UNSIGHING	*UNSIMILAR*	UNSISTING	UNSIZABLE	UNSKILFUL	UNSKINNED
UNSMITTEN	*UNSOBERLY*	UNSOLACED	UNSOLIDLY	*UNSOOTHED*	UNSOUNDED
UNSOUNDLY	UNSOURCED	UNSPILLED	UNSPOTTED	UNSPRAYED	UNSQUARED
UNSTAINED	*UNSTALKED*	*UNSTARRED*	UNSTIFLED	UNSTILLED	UNSTINTED
UNSTIRRED	UNSTOCKED	UNSTRIPED	UNSTUDIED	UNSTYLISH	UNSUBDUED
UNSUBJECT	UNSULLIED	UNSUSPECT	UNSWADDLE	*UNSWOLLEN*	UNTACTFUL
UNTENABLY	UNTENURED	UNTIMEOUS	UNTOILING	UNTRESSED	UNTRUSSER
UNTUMBLED	UNTUNABLE	UNTUNABLY	UNTUNEFUL	UNTUTORED	*UNTWILLED*
UNTYPABLE	UNTYPICAL	UNUSHERED	UNUTTERED	UNVISITED	UNWAKENED
UNWARLIKE	UNWASTING	UNWEARIED	UNWEETING	UNWINKING	UNWISHFUL
UNWITTILY	UNWOMANLY	UNWOUNDED	UNWREAKED	UNWREATHE	UNWRINKLE
UNWROUGHT	UNZEALOUS	UPBOUNDEN	UPBRAIDER	UPBROUGHT	*UPBUILDER*
UPBURNING	*UPCOUNTRY*	*UPDRAUGHT*	UPRIGHTLY	UPSITTING	UPSWOLLEN
UPTHUNDER	*UPTITLING*	UPTRILLED	UPWROUGHT	USABILITY	

WEBLOGGER	WESTERNER	WOFULNESS	WOMANLIKE

SEVEN-LETTER WORD PLUS TWO-LETTER WORD

COMMON TWO-LETTER WORD ENDINGS

AL

ADENOIDAL	AGNATICAL	*ALBITICAL*	ALIMENTAL	AMYLOIDAL	ARMIGERAL
ARSENICAL	ARTISANAL	AZIMUTHAL	BAPTISMAL	*BISMUTHAL*	BOTULINAL
CAROTIDAL	CATARRHAL	*CHAPTERAL*	CHELOIDAL	*CHILIADAL*	CHOROIDAL
COITIONAL	COLLOIDAL	CONFORMAL	*COTHURNAL*	CRINOIDAL	DECAGONAL
DECAPODAL	DEISTICAL	DEMONICAL	DIALECTAL	DICTIONAL	DISAVOWAL
DISCOIDAL	DISTICHAL	DRUIDICAL	DUUMVIRAL	DYNAMICAL	*EKISTICAL*
ELEGIACAL	EMBRYONAL	EMPIRICAL	EMPTIONAL	ENDEMICAL	EPIDERMAL
ERISTICAL	EROSIONAL	ERRATICAL	ETHERICAL	ETHMOIDAL	*EUGENICAL*
EVASIONAL	EXODERMAL	FACTIONAL	*FACTOIDAL*	*FANTASMAL*	FISSIONAL
FLEXIONAL	FLUXIONAL	*FRACTURAL*	FUNGOIDAL	GALENICAL	GENERICAL
GEORGICAL	GNOSTICAL	HERETICAL	*HEXAPODAL*	HORIZONAL	HYPNOIDAL
IDIOTICAL	*INTROITAL*	ISMATICAL	ISODONTAL	JURIDICAL	KINETICAL
LEVITICAL	LITHOIDAL	*LUNATICAL*	*MARTINGAL*	MASTOIDAL	MIRIFICAL
MISSIONAL	MONADICAL	MONARCHAL	NEGROIDAL	NONAGONAL	NYMPHICAL
OOLOGICAL	ORGANICAL	*OVATIONAL*	OVIDUCTAL	PACTIONAL	PARADOXAL
PARODICAL	PASSIONAL	PERCENTAL	PHACOIDAL	PIGMENTAL	PIRATICAL
POLEMICAL	POLYGONAL	PORIFERAL	*POSTFIXAL*	PREBENDAL	PREVERBAL
PROSAICAL	PYRAMIDAL	PYRITICAL	QUANTICAL	QUINOIDAL	RECOUNTAL
RECRUITAL	*REDRESSAL*	REMNANTAL	RHABDOMAL	RHIZOIDAL	*RHOMBICAL*
ROTIFERAL	SATANICAL	SATYRICAL	SEGMENTAL	SEISMICAL	SEXTANTAL
SIGMOIDAL	SORITICAL	STATIONAL	STEROIDAL	STOMACHAL	STYPTICAL
SUCTIONAL	SYNAGOGAL	SYNODICAL	SYRINGEAL	*TANGENTAL*	TENSIONAL
TETANICAL	THERMICAL	THYROIDAL	TOPONYMAL	TORSIONAL	TRIDENTAL
TRIONYMAL	TRIUMPHAL	TUITIONAL	TYPHOIDAL	VENATICAL	VENEFICAL
VERIDICAL	VERSIONAL	*VISCOIDAL*			

AN

ACALEPHAN	AMOEBAEAN	ANNELIDAN	*ARANEIDAN*	CAERULEAN	DECAPODAN
EPICUREAN	ISOKONTAN	MOLLUSKAN	*OCTOPODAN*	PORIFERAN	PROTISTAN
ROTIFERAN	SACRISTAN				

ED

AIRHEADED	BASTIONED	BEDROOMED	BENEMPTED	BICOLORED	*BIFOCALED*
BIOFUELED	CALIBERED	CEILINGED	CHAPLETED	CHEVRONED	*CHIGNONED*
CORONETED	CORSLETED	CREEPERED	CROSIERED	*EARRINGED*	EGGHEADED
FANTAILED	FATHEADED	FETLOCKED	*FIREARMED*	FLOREATED	GALLOONED
GLACIERED	*HILLOCKED*	IMPASTOED	INFARCTED	KINGDOMED	*LEGGINGED*
LEOTARDED	MANSARDED	*MINARETED*	MURRAINED	*ORPHREYED*	OVERALLED
PALFREYED	PANNIERED	*PARASOLED*	PARSLEYED	PIGTAILED	PINHEADED
PINTAILED	PORTICOED	PROWESSED	RAINBOWED	RAMPICKED	*RANCOURED*
RATTAILED	REDNECKED	RINGLETED	SAPHEADED	*SATCHELED*	SHICKERED
SLICKERED	SNEAKERED	STONKERED	SUNBEAMED	*TAPROOTED*	TENDRILED
THICKETED	*TOURISTED*	TOWHEADED	TREFOILED	TRIDENTED	TRIFORMED
TUSSOCKED	UNCLEANED	VERANDAED	WHISKERED		

EE

ABANDONEE	COHABITEE	CONFIRMEE	CONSULTEE	COUNSELEE	DEBAUCHEE
GARNISHEE	PRESENTEE	RECOVEREE	*RETRAINEE*	TROLLOPEE	WARRANTEE

EN

BENIGHTEN	DRYBEATEN	GESTALTEN	MISFALLEN	REFRESHEN	TENDENZEN
THOUGHTEN	UPBOUNDEN	WITHOUTEN			

ER *extensions of verbs*

ABANDONER	ABOLISHER	ABSCONDER	ADDRESSER	ARRAIGNER	ASPHALTER
ASSAULTER	ATTEMPTER	*ATTRACTER*	AUGMENTER	*BALLASTER*	BANQUETER
BARGAINER	BARKEEPER	*BATFOWLER*	BENEFITER	BENIGHTER	BESEECHER
BESMEARER	*BEWITCHER*	BLACKENER	*BLEMISHER*	BLETHERER	BLUNDERER
BLUSTERER	BOLSTERER	*BOULDERER*	*BROADENER*	BROIDERER	BURNISHER
BUTCHERER	CARAVANER	CARPOOLER	CASHIERER	CATALOGER	CAUTIONER
CHAMBERER	*CHAMFERER*	CHANNELER	CHARTERER	*CHIRRUPER*	CLAMBERER
CLAMOURER	CLATTERER	*COHABITER*	COMPANDER	COMPOSTER	CONDEMNER
CONFIRMER	*CONGEALER*	CONJOINER	*CONQUERER*	CONSENTER	CONSORTER
CONSULTER	CONTESTER	CURTAILER	DEBAUCHER	*DEBRIEFER*	DECLAIMER
DEFAULTER	DEFRAUDER	DEFROSTER	DEGAUSSER	DELIGHTER	DELIMITER
DELIVERER	*DESCANTER*	DESCENDER	DESPAIRER	DESPOILER	DEWATERER
DIGRESSER	*DISAVOWER*	*DISCANTER*	DISCARDER	DISCERNER	DISOBEYER
DISPLAYER	DISRUPTER	*DISTENDER*	DISTORTER	DISTURBER	DRAUGHTER
DUNGEONER	*EARBASHER*	*EMBROILER*	ENCHANTER	ENGRAINER	ENGROSSER
ENLIVENER	ENTRAINER	EXCERPTER	EXCLAIMER	EXHAUSTER	EXHIBITER
EXPLAINER	EXPLOITER	EXPOUNDER	EXPRESSER	FASHIONER	FERMENTER
FLATTENER	*FLAVOURER*	FLUTTERER	FRITTERER	FRUITERER	FURBISHER
GAINSAYER	GALUMPHER	GARNISHER	*GLADDENER*	GRAUNCHER	*GUERDONER*
HARBOURER	*HARNESSER*	HARPOONER	HEARKENER	*HEARTENER*	HUSBANDER
IMPEACHER	IMPLANTER	IMPLEADER	IMPOUNDER	IMPRINTER	*INBREEDER*
INDWELLER	INFIGHTER	INFLICTER	*INGRAINER*	INHABITER	INHIBITER
INITIALER	INSTALLER	INSTILLER	INVEIGHER	JEOPARDER	KITCHENER
LACQUERER	LAMPOONER	LAUNDERER	*LEAFLETER*	LIGHTENER	*LIPREADER*
LOBSTERER	LOGROLLER	MARSHALER	MAUNDERER	MEANDERER	MENTIONER
MISCALLER	*MISDEALER*	MISLEADER	MISSIONER	*MONOSKIER*	MURTHERER
NEGLECTER	NETWORKER	NOURISHER	OUTPOURER	OUTWORKER	OVEREATER
PALAVERER	PERSISTER	PERTURBER	PERVERTER	PLANISHER	*PLENISHER*
PODCASTER	PLUNDERER	PONTOONER	PORTIONER	PORTRAYER	POTBOILER
POULTERER	*PRECOOKER*	PREDICTER	*PREVAILER*	PREVENTER	PROCEEDER
PROCESSER	PROGRAMER	*PROTECTER*	PROTESTER	PURLOINER	QUARRELER
QUARTERER	QUICKENER	*QUIETENER*	RANSACKER	REBOUNDER	RECHARTER
RECLAIMER	RECOUNTER	RECOVERER	RECRUITER	*REDBAITER*	REDRESSER
REFLECTER	REFOUNDER	*REFRAINER*	*REMODELER*	REPLEADER	*REPRESSER*
REPRINTER	RESCINDER	RESPECTER	RESPONDER	RESTARTER	RETHINKER
RETOUCHER	RETREATER	ROISTERER	SAUNTERER	SCALLOPER	*SCAMPERER*
SCATTERER	SCHNORRER	SCISSORER	SHAMPOOER	*SHATTERER*	SHEBEENER
SHELTERER	SKYJACKER	*SKYSURFER*	*SLACKENER*	*SLICKENER*	SMATTERER
SMOTHERER	SNICKERER	SNIGGERER	SOJOURNER	SPELUNKER	SQUELCHER

STAGGERER	STENCILER	STOMACHER	*SUBSISTER*	SUBSOILER	SUBVERTER
SUGGESTER	SURFEITER	*SURPASSER*	*SUSPECTER*	SUSTAINER	SWAGGERER
TAMBOURER	TARNISHER	TENSIONER	THUNDERER	TIGHTENER	TORMENTER
TORPEDOER	TOUGHENER	TOURNEYER	TRINKETER	TRIUMPHER	TWITTERER
UNBOSOMER	UNDERDOER	*UNDERGOER*	UNTRUSSER	UPBRAIDER	*UPBUILDER*
VARNISHER	VICTUALER	*VODCASTER*	WADSETTER	WARRANTER	*WEATHERER*
WEBCASTER	WHIMPERER	WITNESSER			

ER *other*

ARBLASTER	BALLADEER	BERSERKER	CARBINEER	CHORISTER	*DAYWORKER*
EASTERNER	GAZETTEER	HERRINGER	HUNDREDER	ICEBOATER	*IMAGINEER*
LOWLANDER	*MANHUNTER*	*MIDLANDER*	MISSILEER	*NETBALLER*	NONFARMER
NONPLAYER	NONWORKER	NUNATAKER	OUTBACKER	OUTHAULER	OUTLANDER
OUTPORTER	*PALMISTER*	PARADOXER	PASQUILER	PILGRIMER	PISTOLEER
POTTINGER	PRIVATEER	PROVENDER	*REBIRTHER*	ROUTINEER	SIXTEENER
SOPHISTER	SUNDOWNER	THEOLOGER	TUTWORKER	VERSIONER	WESTERNER

ES

AGONISTES	ASCARIDES	AUSTRALES	BOLIVARES	ENTRALLES	ESPANOLES
HOATZINES	LEVATORES	MUDEJARES	OCEANIDES	OCTOPODES	PARADORES
PAROTIDES	PERICONES	PICADORES	PYRAMIDES	QUETZALES	ROTATORES
TELAMONES	TEMBLORES				

ET

BOTTOMSET	CLARIONET	CUSHIONET	DOLPHINET	*FLANNELET*	*KITCHENET*
LETTERSET	SPINNERET	SULPHURET	THERMOSET	TIERCELET	*TUMBLESET*

IS

AUSTRALIS	DIGITALIS	EXODERMIS	HETEROSIS	LITHIASIS	MELANOSIS
MORPHOSIS	TAENIASIS	VIBRIOSIS			

OR

ATTRACTOR	AUGMENTOR	COMBUSTOR	CONDEMNOR	CONFESSOR	CONFIRMOR
CONSIGNOR	CONSULTOR	CONTEMNOR	CONVERTOR	CORRUPTOR	COUNSELOR
DEFLECTOR	DEPRESSOR	DISRUPTOR	DISSECTOR	EMBRACEOR	ESCHEATOR
EXCERPTOR	EXPOSITOR	FERMENTOR	HUNDREDOR	*INFLECTOR*	INFLICTOR
INFRACTOR	INHERITOR	INHIBITOR	*NEGLECTOR*	NONFACTOR	PERCUSSOR
PLAYACTOR	PRECENTOR	PREDICTOR	PRELECTOR	PROSECTOR	*RECEIPTOR*
RECOVEROR	*REDRESSOR*	*REENACTOR*	REFRACTOR	REGRESSOR	REPOSITOR
REPRESSOR	REQUESTOR	RETRACTOR	SUBSECTOR	SUSPENSOR	TRISECTOR
WARRANTOR					

UM

ARBORETUM	ASPHALTUM	BOTULINUM	EXCERPTUM	POLYGONUM	SALICETUM

US

BOTULINUS	COMPLEXUS	COTHURNUS	INTROITUS	QUADRATUS	SINGULTUS
STROBILUS	TROCHILUS				

OTHER TWO-LETTER WORD ENDINGS

ABSCISSIN	ACALEPHAE	ADENOMATA	ALUMINATE	AMARANTIN	AMYGDALIN
ANGIOMATA	*ASCIDIATE*	AUTOMATON	BANQUETTE	BASILICON	BETHANKIT
BITTERNUT	BOLIVIANO	BRACHIATE	CEMBALIST	CENTAUREA	CEREBRATE
CHIASMATA	CHONDRIFY	CHONDRITE	CINGULATE	CLOISONNE	COLUMELLA
COROLLATE	CORYPHENE	COUPLEDOM	CRIMINATE	DACTYLIST	DECIDUATE
DIGITALIN	DOUBLETON	ECTHYMATA	ENCOMIAST	ENFREEDOM	EPITHETON
FAGOTTIST	FALCULATE	FIBROMATA	FIMBRIATE	*FISTULATE*	FLEURETTE
FOSSULATE	*FOVEOLATE*	GANGLIATE	GLOMERATE	GROUNDSEL	*HEGUMENOI*
HEGUMENOS	*HYDROMATA*	*HYGROMATA*	IDIOTICON	*ILLUVIATE*	INDUSIATE
KERYGMATA	KHEDIVATE	*LABELLATE*	LACINIATE	LAMELLATE	LAMINARIN
LANGUETTE	LAZARETTE	LAZARETTO	LEPORIDAE	LINGULATE	LIXIVIATE
LUCIFERIN	MARROWSKY	*MATELOTTE*	MEDULLATE	MESHUGAAS	*NARCOMATA*
NATHEMORE	NEUROMATA	NOODLEDOM	NYMPHALID	NYMPHETTE	OSTEOMATA
OUTLINEAR	PANDURATE	PASSERSBY	PATELLATE	PERCHERON	PERIOSTEA
PERSONATE	PIGNORATE	PINNULATE	*PLANULATE*	PLASTICKY	PLUMULATE
POTTINGAR	PRESTERNA	PRETERMIT	PRINCEDOM	PROCUREUR	*PROSOMATA*
PYRALIDID	PYRAMIDON	*QUIDDITCH*	RELIQUEFY	RHIZOMATA	RIPIENIST
ROTUNDATE	ROUNDELAY	SAGITTATE	SARCOMATA	SATINETTE	SAVAGEDOM
SCHOLIAST	SCOTOMATA	SERRANOID	SERRATION	SIGNORINA	SIGNORINE
SIGNORINO	*SINGLEDOM*	SINGLETON	SIXTEENMO	SMASHEROO	SOPRANINO
SOPRANIST	SOREDIATE	SPATULATE	SPICULATE	SPINULATE	SQUIREDOM
STAMINATE	*STINKEROO*	SUBCELLAR	SUBLINEAR	TAMBOURIN	TANGHININ
TEREBRATE	TERMINIST	TIMPANIST	TRACHEATE	TRAMPETTE	TRILITHON
TYMPANIST	*TYPHOIDIN*	VARIOLATE	*VEXILLATE*	VISCERATE	

THREE-LETTER WORD PLUS SIX-LETTER WORD

ABSCONDER	ACETABULA	ADOBELIKE	AIRHEADED	AIRMOBILE	AIRSTREAM
AIRSTRIKE	ALABASTER	ALEWASHED	ALLCOMERS	AMAUROSES	ANABIOTIC
ANABRANCH	*ANACLINAL*	ANAPHASIC	ANASTATIC	ANIMALIST	*ANTALKALI*
APOENZYME	APOSTATIC	ARBLASTER	*ARCMINUTE*	ARENATION	ASPHALTER
ASSURGENT	AWESTRIKE				

BALKINGLY	*BALLASTER*	BANDOLINE	*BANGALORE*	BARGAINER	BARGANDER
BARIATRIC	BARPERSON	BARRACOON	*BATFOWLER*	BEDROOMED	*BEDSITTER*
BEDSPRING	*BEDWARMER*	*BEDWETTER*	BEEFEATER	BENTONITE	*BETATOPIC*
BINOCULAR	*BINOVULAR*	BIOACTIVE	*BIODIESEL*	*BIOENERGY*	BIOETHICS
BIOFOULER	*BIOFUELED*	BIOHAZARD	*BIOMARKER*	BIOMETRIC	BIOMINING
BIOPARENT	*BIOPIRACY*	*BIOPIRATE*	*BIOREGION*	BIOSAFETY	BIOSENSOR
BIOSOCIAL	*BIOSTATIC*	*BIOTERROR*	*BIOWEAPON*	*BISPHENOL*	*BITSTREAM*
BOOGERMAN	BOOGERMEN	BORGHETTO	*BOWHUNTER*	BOWSTRING	BOWSTRUNG
BOXKEEPER	BOXWALLAH	BOYCOTTER	*BOYSHORTS*	BRAINCASE	BUMSUCKER
BUSHELLER					

CABINMATE   CADASTRAL   CANTINGLY   CARESSIVE   CATAMOUNT   CATRIGGED
CHAINFALL   CHAINWORK   CHAPARRAL   CHAVENDER   CHEVELURE   CHISELLER
CISALPINE   COGNATION   COGNOMINA   COLLIGATE   COLLINEAR   COLOSTOMY
CONDIDDLE   CONDOLENT   CONFLUENT   CONFORMAL   CONFORMER   CONJOINER
CONJUGATE   CONNATION   CONNOTATE   CONSIGNOR   CONSOLATE   CONSOLUTE
CONSORTER   CONTEMPER   CONTESTER   CONVOLUTE   COPRESENT   CORRODENT
CORRUGATE   COSMOLINE   COWFEEDER   CURSENARY   CURTAILER   CUTTINGLY

DAYCENTRE   DAYFLOWER   DAYSAILER   DAYSAILOR   DAYSPRING   DAYWORKER
DEFLECTOR   DEFLORATE   DEFROSTER   DEIPAROUS   DIESINKER   DIMORPHIC
DIMWITTED   DISANCHOR   DISANOINT   DISATTIRE   DISATTUNE   DISAVOUCH
DISAVOWAL   DISAVOWER   DISBODIED   DISBRANCH   DISBURDEN   DISBURSAL
DISCANDIE   DISCANTER   DISCARDER   DISCLIMAX   DISCOMFIT   DISCUMBER
DISEMBODY   DISENTAIL   DISENTOMB   DISESTEEM   DISFLUENT   DISFOREST
DISGODDED   DISHALLOW   DISHUMOUR   DISILLUDE   DISINFEST   DISINFORM
DISINHUME   DISINVENT   DISINVEST   DISINVITE   DISLUSTRE   DISOBLIGE
DISPLAYER   DISPRAISE   DISPRISON   DISPROFIT   DISPURVEY   DISRELISH
DISSEIZIN   DISSEIZOR   DISSEMBLE   DISSHIVER   DISSIMILE   DISSOCIAL
DISSONANT   DISSUNDER   DISTENDER   DISTHRONE   DOCTRINAL   DOGFOUGHT
DOGHANGED   DOGGERMAN   DOGGERMEN   DORBEETLE   DRYBEATEN   DRYSALTER
DRYWALLED   DUOBINARY   DUODENARY

EARBASHER   EARRINGED   ECOPHOBIA   ECOREGION   ECOSPHERE   EGOTHEISM
ENDAMEBIC   ENDAMOEBA   ENDLEAVES   ENDOBLAST   ENDOGAMIC   ENGAGEDLY
ENGENDURE   ENGROSSER   EXOENZYME   EXOPLANET   EXOPODITE   EXOSPHERE
EXOSPORAL   EXOTROPIC   EYEBRIGHT   EYEOPENER

FANTAILED   FATHEADED   FERMENTOR   FETLOCKED   FILLISTER   FLUVIATIC
FLYBRIDGE   FLYLEAVES   FLYPOSTER   FLYSCREEN   FLYSTRIKE   FORBEARER
FORBIDDER   FORGATHER   FORMALIST   FORMATTER   FORMICATE   FORWANDER
FROLICKER   FURBEARER   FURCATION

GALDRAGON   GALRAVAGE   GASHOLDER   GENITALIC   GEOBOTANY   GEOCORONA
GEODESIST   GEOMANTIC   GEOSPHERE   GEOSTATIC   GEOTROPIC   GERFALCON
GOOSANDER   GORBLIMEY   GUMSHIELD   GUMSUCKER   GUNCOTTON   GUTBUCKET

HAGBUTTER   HAGRIDDEN   HAMFATTER   HEMELYTRA   HERRINGER   HESTERNAL
HETEROSES   HETEROTIC   HINTINGLY   HISSINGLY   HOSTELLER   HOTDOGGER
HOWSOEVER   HUMBUCKER   HUMDINGER   HUMORALLY   HYPEREMIC   HYPOBLAST

ICEBOATER   IMPACTION   IMPACTIVE   IMPAVIDLY   IMPLEADER   INKHOLDER
INSENSATE   INSTALLER   INSTILLER   ISOBUTANE   ISOBUTENE   ISOCLINAL
ISOENZYME   ISOGAMETE   ISOHYDRIC   ISOHYETAL   ISOMETRIC   ISOOCTANE
ISOPOLITY   ISOSTATIC   ISOSTERIC   ISOTROPIC

JAMPACKED   JAYHAWKER   JEWELFISH   JOBHOLDER   JOBSEEKER   JOLTINGLY
JOYRIDDEN   JUNEATING   JUTTINGLY

KATABASES   KEYBUTTON   KEYLOGGER   KEYWORKER   KITCHENET

LAPSTRAKE LAPSTREAK LARGHETTO LASTINGLY LATRATION *LAWGIVING*
LAWMONGER LEAPOROUS LEAVENOUS *LEGWARMER* LEPROSERY LIBRATION
LINCRUSTA LINOLEATE *LIPREADER* LOGNORMAL LOWLANDER *LURKINGLY*
LYMPHATIC

MALADROIT MALENGINE MALLANDER MALTALENT MANDATARY *MANHUNTER*
MANLIKELY *MEGATONIC* MELANURIA MELANURIC MELTINGLY MESENTERA
MESOBLAST MESSALINE METABASES *METARCHON* METESTRUS MIDCOURSE
MIDDORSAL *MIDLANDER* MISADJUST *MISADVICE* MISADVISE MISALLEGE
MISAUNTER MISAVISED MISBELIEF MISBESTOW MISBUTTON *MISCALLER*
MISCHARGE *MISCHOOSE* MISCOLOUR MISCREANT MISCREDIT *MISDEALER*
MISDEFINE MISDESERT *MISDIVIDE* MISGOTTEN MISGOVERN MISGROWTH
MISGUGGLE MISINTEND MISLEADER MISLEARED MISLOCATE MISORIENT
MISPHRASE MISPRAISE MISRECKON MISREGARD MISRELATE MISRENDER
MISSINGLY MISSTRIKE *MOBLOGGER* MOCKINGLY MONAXONIC MONOCULAR
MONORCHID MONOVULAR MORPHOTIC MOSKONFYT

NEGLECTOR *NETBALLER* NETMINDER NEWFANGLE NEWMARKET NIDAMENTA
NIDDERING NILPOTENT NIPCHEESE NITRATINE NITRATION NITWITTED
NONACTIVE NONARTIST NONATOMIC NONAUTHOR NONBELIEF NONBINARY
NONBITING NONBONDED NONBUYING NONCAKING NONCAMPUS NONCAREER
NONCASUAL NONCAUSAL *NONCEREAL* *NONCODING* NONCOITAL NONCOKING
NONCOUNTY NONCREDIT NONCRISES NONCRISIS NONDEGREE *NONDEMAND*
NONDESERT NONDOCTOR NONDOLLAR NONDRIVER *NONDRYING* NONEDIBLE
NONENDING NONENERGY NONEROTIC NONETHNIC NONEXEMPT NONEXPERT
NONEXTANT NONFACTOR NONFADING NONFAMILY NONFARMER *NONFEUDAL*
NONFILIAL NONFINITE *NONFISCAL* NONFLYING NONFORMAL NONFOSSIL
NONFROZEN *NONFUNDED* NONGHETTO *NONGLAZED* *NONGLOSSY* NONGOLFER
NONGRADED NONGREASY NONGROWTH *NONHEROIC* NONHUNTER NONIMPACT
NONINJURY NONINSECT NONJOINER NONKOSHER NONLAWYER NONLEADED
NONLEAGUE NONLEGUME *NONLIABLE* NONLINEAL NONLINEAR NONLIQUID
NONLIVING *NONLOVING* NONMANUAL NONMARKET *NONMATURE* NONMENTAL
NONMETRIC NONMOBILE *NONMODERN* *NONMORTAL* NONMOVING NONMUTANT
NONMUTUAL NONNATIVE *NONNEURAL* NONNORMAL *NONORALLY* *NONPARITY*
NONPAROUS NONPERSON NONPLANAR *NONPLAYER* *NONPLIANT* NONPOETIC
NONPOLICE NONPOROUS *NONPOSTAL* *NONPROVEN* NONPUBLIC NONRACIAL
NONRANDOM NONREADER *NONRETURN* NONRHOTIC NONRIOTER NONRULING
NONSACRED NONSALINE NONSCHOOL *NONSECRET* NONSECURE NONSELVES
NONSERIAL NONSEXIST NONSEXUAL NONSIGNER NONSKATER NONSOCIAL
NONSPEECH *NONSTAPLE* *NONSTATIC* NONSTEADY NONSYSTEM *NONTALKER*
NONTARGET NONTHEIST *NONTRAGIC* NONTRIBAL NONUNIQUE NONURGENT
NONUSABLE *NONVACANT* NONVECTOR *NONVENOUS* NONVERBAL *NONVESTED*
NONVIABLE NONVIEWER NONVIRGIN *NONVIRILE* NONVISUAL NONVOTING
NONWINGED NONWORKER NONWRITER *NOOTROPIC* NORSELLER NUNNATION
NUTBUTTER NUTPECKER

OLECRANAL ONOMASTIC ORATRICES ORTHOAXES OUTBACKER OUTBIDDEN
OUTBIDDER *OUTBRAZEN* OUTCAUGHT OUTCHARGE OUTCRAFTY OUTDEBATE
OUTDESIGN OUTFIGURE OUTFITTER *OUTGALLOP* *OUTGAMBLE* OUTGROWTH

9. Nine-Letter Words

OUTHANDLE	OUTHAULER	OUTHUSTLE	OUTJOCKEY	*OUTJUGGLE*	OUTLANDER
OUTLAUNCE	OUTLAUNCH	OUTLINEAR	OUTLUSTRE	OUTMANTLE	*OUTMASTER*
OUTPORTER	OUTPOURER	OUTPREACH	*OUTPURSUE*	*OUTREASON*	*OUTRECKON*
OUTREDDEN	OUTRELIEF	OUTRUNNER	OUTSCHEME	*OUTSCREAM*	OUTSPRANG
OUTSPRING	OUTSPRUNG	OUTSTRAIN	OUTSTRIDE	OUTSTRIKE	*OUTSTRIVE*
OUTSTRODE	*OUTSTROKE*	*OUTSTROVE*	OUTSTRUCK	*OUTTHIEVE*	*OUTTHRUST*
OUTTONGUE	OUTTRAVEL	OUTWORKER			

PALEOCENE	*PALEOLITH*	*PALMISTER*	PANEGOISM	PANHANDLE	PANSEXUAL
PANTHEISM	PANTHEIST	PANTINGLY	PARABASES	PARADORES	PARAGOGIC
PARALALIA	PARALEXIA	*PARALEXIC*	PARALOGIA	PARATONIC	PARAVAUNT
PARBUCKLE	PARFLECHE	*PARGETTER*	*PAROTITIC*	PAROTITIS	PARROQUET
PARSIMONY	*PARURESES*	*PARURESIS*	PASSERINE	*PASSINGLY*	PATROLLER
PEASOUPER	PECTINEAL	PEDAGOGIC	*PEGLEGGED*	PENDRAGON	PENHOLDER
PENULTIMA	PERBORATE	PERCENTAL	PERFERVID	PERFERVOR	PERFUSION
PERICONES	PERIODATE	PERMUTATE	PERORALLY	*PERORATOR*	PEROXIDIC
PERRADIAL	PERRADIUS	PERSISTER	PERTUSSAL	*PERUSABLE*	PETAURIST
PEWHOLDER	PHILANDER	*PHOCOMELY*	PHONATION	PICADORES	PIGMENTAL
PIGTAILED	PINHEADED	PINHOOKER	*PINNATION*	PINTAILED	*PINWRENCH*
PODCASTER	PODIATRIC	*POLLUCITE*	POSTILLER	POTBOILER	*POTHOLDER*
POTHUNTER	*POTWALLER*	*POWFAGGED*	PREATOMIC	*PREATTUNE*	PREBATTLE
PREBIOTIC	*PREBUDGET*	*PRECAUDAL*	PRECENSOR	PRECOITAL	*PRECOOKER*
PRECREASE	PRECRISIS	PREDATIVE	*PREDEBATE*	*PREDEDUCT*	PREDEVOTE
PREEXCITE	PREEXILIC	PREFACIAL	PREFEUDAL	PREHALLUX	PREHEATER
PRELATISH	PRELECTOR	PREMERGER	PREMODERN	PREMONISH	PREMOSAIC
PRENOMINA	PRENOTION	PRENUBILE	PREOCULAR	*PRERECTAL*	*PREREFORM*
PRERETURN	PRESCIENT	PRESCUTUM	PRESELECT	*PRESENILE*	*PRESIGNAL*
PRESTERNA	PRETRAVEL	PREVENTER	PREVERBAL	PREVIABLE	*PROACTION*
PROCAMBIA	*PROCESSER*	PROCONSUL	PROCREANT	PROEMBRYO	PROENZYME
PROESTRUS	*PROFAMILY*	PROFLUENT	PROKARYON	PROLATELY	PROMACHOS
PROMETRIC	*PROMODERN*	PROMOTIVE	PRONATION	PRONUCLEI	PRONUNCIO
PRORATION	PRORECTOR	*PROREFORM*	PROSCRIBE	PROSECTOR	PROSIMIAN
PROSOMATA	PROSTATIC	*PROSTERNA*	PROTHALLI	PROTHESES	PROTHESIS
PROTHETIC	PROTHORAX	PROVENDER	PROZYMITE	PULSATIVE	PULVILLAR
PULVILLUS	PURSUABLE	PUTSCHIST			

QUAKINGLY	QUARENDER

RADIONICS	RAGPICKER	RAMPICKED	*RANCOURED*	RANSACKER	RANTINGLY
RASCAILLE	*RATTAILED*	REDACTION	*REDBAITER*	REDBREAST	REDNECKED
REDSTREAK	*REEKINGLY*	RENTALLER	REPARABLE	REPLEADER	RESCINDER
RESNATRON	RESPONDER	RESTARTER	REWROUGHT	RIGWIDDIE	RIGWOODIE
ROCKINGLY	RODFISHER	ROTOVATOR	ROTUNDATE	RUMRUNNER	

SAILORING	*SALURETIC*	SAPHEADED	SAWTIMBER	SEABOTTLE	SEAFARING
SEASTRAND	SECUNDINE	SEGMENTAL	SERRATION	SERREFILE	SERVILELY
SEXLINKED	SHEARLING	SIFTINGLY	SIXTEENER	SKIMOBILE	*SKYBRIDGE*
SKYSURFER	SODBUSTER	*SOLLICKER*	*SOSTENUTI*	SOSTENUTO	SPADESMAN
SPYMASTER	STYLOBATE	SUBACIDLY	SUBACTION	SUBAERIAL	SUBAGENCY
SUBALPINE	SUBALTERN	SUBAPICAL	SUBASTRAL	SUBCANTOR	SUBCAUDAL
SUBCAVITY	SUBCELLAR	SUBCENTER	SUBCHASER	SUBCLAUSE	SUBCLIMAX
SUBCOLONY	*SUBCONSUL*	SUBCORTEX	SUBCOUNTY	SUBDEACON	*SUBDEALER*

SUBDEPUTY	SUBDERMAL	SUBDORSAL	SUBENTIRE	SUBFAMILY	SUBGENERA
SUBINCISE	SUBJACENT	SUBJUGATE	SUBLETHAL	SUBLETTER	SUBLINEAR
SUBLUNATE	*SUBLUXATE*	SUBMARKET	SUBMATRIX	SUBMICRON	SUBMUCOSA
SUBNEURAL	*SUBNUCLEI*	SUBOCTAVE	SUBOCULAR	*SUBOSCINE*	SUBPERIOD
SUBPHYLUM	SUBPOTENT	SUBREGION	SUBSACRAL	SUBSAMPLE	SUBSCHEMA
SUBSCRIPT	SUBSECTOR	*SUBSISTER*	SUBSOCIAL	SUBTENANT	SUBTENURE
SUBTORRID	SUBTROPIC	SUBURSINE	SUBVERSAL	SUBVISUAL	SUBWARDEN
SUBWRITER	SUNBEAMED	SUNDOWNER	*SUNGAZING*	SUNRISING	SUNSEEKER
SURMASTER	SURMULLET	*SURPASSER*	SURREALLY	SURREINED	SURREJOIN
SYNCLINAL	SYNDROMIC				
TARANTARA	*TARBOUCHE*	TARNATION	TEACUPFUL	TEAKETTLE	TEASELLER
TEASINGLY	*TEATASTER*	THOLOBATE	TIPSTAVES	TITRATION	TOMBOYISH
TOPMAKING	TOPMINNOW	TORTRICES	TORULOSES	TORULOSIS	TOWHEADED
TUPTOWING	TUTWORKER				
UDOMETRIC	UNICOLOUR	*UNIJUGATE*	UNILINEAL	UNILINEAR	UNIPAROUS
UNIPLANAR	*UNIPOTENT*	*UNIRAMOSE*	UNIRAMOUS	UNISERIAL	UNISEXUAL
UNISONANT	UNSCANNED	UNSCOURED	UNSEDUCED	UNSEEMING	UNSMITTEN
UNSPILLED	UNSPOTTED	UNSPRAYED	*UNSTALKED*	UNSTILLED	UNSTINTED
UNSTIRRED	UNSWADDLE				
VARIOLITE	VIGNETTER	VISCERATE			
WADSETTER	WAGHALTER	WAITINGLY	WARBONNET	WARRANTER	*WASTINGLY*
WEBCASTER	*WEBLOGGER*	*WEBMASTER*	WEETINGLY	WINKINGLY	
ZOOBIOTIC	ZOOLATRIA	ZOOLITHIC	ZOOMANTIC	ZOOMETRIC	ZOOPHOBIA
ZOOSTEROL	ZOOTHEISM	ZOOTROPHY			

SIX-LETTER WORD PLUS THREE-LETTER WORD

COMMON THREE-LETTER WORD ENDINGS

AGE

ARREARAGE	BAILLIAGE	BARRELAGE	BEGUINAGE	BUTLERAGE	CAREENAGE
CARTONAGE	CELLARAGE	CLIENTAGE	CONSULAGE	COOPERAGE	COUSINAGE
DACOITAGE	ESCORTAGE	FACTORAGE	FLOWERAGE	FORESTAGE	FOSTERAGE
GABIONAGE	GALLONAGE	GROUNDAGE	HARBORAGE	HERMITAGE	KNIGHTAGE
MATRONAGE	PERSONAGE	PETROLAGE	PORTERAGE	RECOINAGE	REPASSAGE
REPORTAGE	SECRETAGE	SIPHONAGE	SQUIREAGE	STREETAGE	TAMPONAGE
TELFERAGE	VASSALAGE	VILLANAGE	WAITERAGE	*WEIGHTAGE*	

ANT

ALTERNANT	ARRESTANT	*ATTESTANT*	BENIGNANT	CAUTERANT	COLOURANT
DEMANDANT	*DIGESTANT*	EXCEPTANT	FABRICANT	FORMICANT	GERMINANT
HUMECTANT	*INFECTANT*	INFESTANT	INJECTANT	INSULTANT	INTENDANT
REGARDANT	REITERANT	REVERTANT	THRILLANT	TRENCHANT	TREPIDANT

9. Nine-Letter Words

ARY

CURSORARY	FORMICARY	INSECTARY	LAMPADARY	LEGIONARY	REGIONARY
SONNETARY					

ATE

ACETYLATE	ADSORBATE	ALUMINATE	*BICORNATE*	BIDENTATE	BROMINATE
BUSTICATE	CALIPHATE	CASEINATE	*CATKINATE*	COELOMATE	CRENELATE
CUSPIDATE	DECANTATE	DEGUSTATE	DEMENTATE	EPARCHATE	EXARCHATE
EXTIRPATE	FECUNDATE	FORMICATE	GRATINATE	HETMANATE	HUMECTATE
JUNIORATE	*KALIPHATE*	LECTORATE	MARGINATE	MASTERATE	MASTICATE
METHYLATE	METRICATE	OBSIGNATE	OXYGENATE	PASTORATE	PECTINATE
PERIODATE	PERSONATE	PHENOLATE	*POLLENATE*	PONDERATE	POTENTATE
PROTONATE	RECTORATE	RELUCTATE	RETARDATE	ROTUNDATE	RUBRICATE
RUSTICATE	SEGHOLATE	SHOGUNATE	SIPHONATE	*STOLONATE*	SULFURATE
TYCOONATE	VERMINATE	VIZIERATE			

DOM

BEADLEDOM	BEGGARDOM	BISHOPDOM	COUPLEDOM	ENFREEDOM	KAISERDOM
NIGGERDOM	NOODLEDOM	PRINCEDOM	RASCALDOM	SAVAGEDOM	*SINGLEDOM*
SQUIREDOM	THRALLDOM	UNFREEDOM			

ENE

FULLERENE	PENTYLENE	WOLVERENE

ESS

ANCHORESS	ARCHERESS	*BUGGINESS*	CHAPELESS	COHEIRESS	DEACONESS
DOCTORESS	DRAGONESS	FARMERESS	GAOLERESS	*GERMINESS*	GRAVELESS
GROVELESS	HERMITESS	JAILERESS	JAILORESS	JERKINESS	LARGENESS
LEGGINESS	MINGINESS	PANDERESS	PATRONESS	PERKINESS	*PIGGINESS*
PORTERESS	PUNKINESS	PYTHONESS	RECTORESS	SEXTONESS	SOLEMNESS
SULTANESS	TAILORESS	VARLETESS	VICTORESS	VISTALESS	WRITERESS

IDE

ACETYLIDE	*FULLERIDE*	GRAVESIDE	MATRICIDE	NIGHTSIDE	*PLANESIDE*
QUEENSIDE	SHORESIDE	*TOLUIDIDE*	TRAILSIDE		

HIP

AUGURSHIP	BEDELSHIP	*BLOCKSHIP*	CLERKSHIP	COUNTSHIP	DEVILSHIP
DONORSHIP	DRILLSHIP	ELDERSHIP	ENVOYSHIP	GIANTSHIP	GUARDSHIP
GUIDESHIP	GUILDSHIP	JUDGESHIP	KNAVESHIP	LAIRDSHIP	LIGHTSHIP
MAJORSHIP	MAYORSHIP	MINORSHIP	*MOTORSHIP*	QUEENSHIP	RIDERSHIP
RIVALSHIP	ROGUESHIP	RULERSHIP	SAINTSHIP	SCALDSHIP	SIZARSHIP
SKALDSHIP	STORESHIP	TUTORSHIP	UNCLESHIP	VICARSHIP	VIZIRSHIP

ION

ABJECTION	ABRUPTION	ADDUCTION	ADVECTION	ANTHEMION	ASPERSION
BISECTION	DEFLEXION	DEJECTION	DETERSION	DETORTION	EGRESSION
EXSECTION	EXSERTION	IMPACTION	IMPLEXION	INDENTION	INDICTION
INFLUXION	INGESTION	INSECTION	INTORTION	IRRUPTION	OLFACTION

POSTILION	PREFIXION	RECURSION	REDACTION	REFECTION	REFLEXION
RELICTION	RESECTION	RETORTION	*STRICTION*	SUBACTION	

ISH

BITTERISH	BROGUEISH	CLEVERISH	DRAGONISH	GENTILISH	*GRANNYISH*
GRAVELISH	JARGONISH	*JOCKEYISH*	KITTENISH	LICKERISH	LIQUORISH
LOAFERISH	MAIDENISH	MARROWISH	MONKEYISH	*MUCKERISH*	*NARROWISH*
NIGGERISH	PARSONISH	PRETTYISH	QUIVERISH	SALLOWISH	SPIDERISH
SPLEENISH	*SQUALLISH*	STRICTISH	TALLOWISH	TOMBOYISH	UPLANDISH
VANDALISH	VAPOURISH	VIRAGOISH	*WINTERISH*		

ISM

ABSURDISM	ALBINOISM	*ANALOGISM*	ATONALISM	*AUTEURISM*	AUTHORISM
BASHAWISM	BRUTALISM	*CAESARISM*	CAREERISM	CARNALISM	CARTELISM
CASUALISM	CAUTELISM	CRETINISM	CROTALISM	CURIALISM	DALTONISM
DESPOTISM	*DIALOGISM*	DIAPIRISM	DRAGONISM	EPIGONISM	ETHNICISM
EUNUCHISM	EUPHONISM	*EXOGENISM*	EXOTICISM	EXPERTISM	FETICHISM
FETISHISM	*FLUNKYISM*	FUSIONISM	GALLICISM	GANDERISM	GASCONISM
GENTILISM	*GOTHICISM*	HECTORISM	HERBALISM	HEROINISM	HOODOOISM
HOYDENISM	HYBRIDISM	IRENICISM	*ISOBARISM*	JESUITISM	JOCKEYISM
KAISERISM	KLEPHTISM	LABIALISM	LABOURISM	LICHENISM	NIGGERISM
ORPHANISM	PANDERISM	PEDANTISM	PENNALISM	PHYSICISM	PLURALISM
PLUTONISM	POETICISM	PRETTYISM	RACIALISM	RANTERISM	RASCALISM
RITUALISM	RUSTICISM	SCIENTISM	SERIALISM	SEXUALISM	SOVIETISM
SPIRALISM	SPIRITISM	SUTTEEISM	SWARAJISM	TRENDYISM	UNREALISM
VERBALISM	VIKINGISM	VOODOOISM	VULCANISM	VULGARISM	ZEALOTISM

LET

BRANCHLET	CRATERLET	LANDAULET	PRINCELET	SLEEVELET	STREAMLET
TIERCELET	TONGUELET				

MAN/MEN

ATTACKMAN	BOOGERMAN	*BOOGIEMAN*	*BRAKESMAN*	BRIDESMAN	BUSHELMAN
COLOURMAN	CORNERMAN	DEATHSMAN	DOGGERMAN	EIGHTSMAN	EXCISEMAN
FLUGELMAN	FRAUDSMAN	GARAGEMAN	GRANTSMAN	GROUNDMAN	GUILDSMAN
KENNELMAN	KLOOCHMAN	*LENGTHMAN*	LETTERMAN	LIVERYMAN	ONCOSTMAN
PANTRYMAN	PHRASEMAN	PLANTSMAN	PLEASEMAN	POINTSMAN	RADDLEMAN
RANZELMAN	REDDLEMAN	RUDDLEMAN	SAFETYMAN	SALARYMAN	SCHOOLMAN
SCYTHEMAN	SELECTMAN	SHANTYMAN	SHARESMAN	SHORESMAN	SICKLEMAN
SIGHTSMAN	SPADESMAN	SPOILSMAN	STABLEMAN	STEARSMAN	STEERSMAN
STRONGMAN	SWITCHMAN	SYNODSMAN	THIRDSMAN	*TINKERMAN*	VENIREMAN
VESTRYMAN	WASHERMAN	WHEELSMAN	WHERRYMAN		

OSE

ARABINOSE	CORYMBOSE	LICHENOSE	QUARTZOSE

OUS

ACANTHOUS	ANALOGOUS	*ARGENTOUS*	BIOGENOUS	BURDENOUS	CANKEROUS
CARBONOUS	CAUTELOUS	CELLAROUS	CERULEOUS	CHITINOUS	*CINDEROUS*
CLAMOROUS	COBALTOUS	*CORYMBOUS*	CRATEROUS	CRETINOUS	DEXTEROUS

9. Nine-Letter Words

EPIGONOUS EPONYMOUS EXOGENOUS FERVOROUS FIBRINOUS FLAVOROUS
FRACTIOUS FULGOROUS *GERMANOUS* GINGEROUS GLAIREOUS GLUTENOUS
HYBRIDOUS INGENUOUS ISOLOGOUS ISOMEROUS ISOPODOUS LEAPEROUS
LICHENOUS LUBRICOUS METEOROUS NECTAROUS NICKELOUS OXYGENOUS
PANDEROUS *PECTINOUS* PESTEROUS POMACEOUS PRISONOUS PULVEROUS
PUMICEOUS *QUARTZOUS* RANCOROUS ROSACEOUS RUBINEOUS SPIRITOUS
SPONGEOUS STUPOROUS SULFUROUS *TARTAROUS* TETTEROUS *THALLIOUS*
TREMOROUS TRIGONOUS TRIMEROUS UNISONOUS *UROPODOUS* VERMINOUS
VILLANOUS WONDEROUS

URE

ADMIXTURE CANNELURE COMFITURE CONFITURE DEFEATURE DEFLEXURE
DEPICTURE DIVESTURE IMPOSTURE INDENTURE REPASTURE STRICTURE

OTHER THREE-LETTER WORD ENDINGS

ACARIDEAN *AFTERSHOW* ALBINOTIC ALPHASORT ANILINGUS *ANTIARMOR*
ARCHILOWE BANNERALL BETRODDEN *BITTERNUT* BORDEREAU *BOTTOMSET*
BRAINSICK *BREASTFED* BREASTPIN BREEZEWAY BREGMATIC *BRIDLEWAY*
BURLEYCUE *CADDISFLY* CAMERATED CANDLENUT CANDLEPIN *CANTHITIS*
CARBONADO CARROTTOP *CELLARWAY* CHAINSHOT CHASSEPOT CHEESEVAT
CHEMOSORB CHINAROOT CHOKEDAMP CHROMAKEY CHROMATID CHROMATIN
CHROMOGEN CLOSEDOWN COLONITIS COLOURWAY *CONFERREE* CONSOLUTE
CORDONNET COTYLEDON *CROTONBUG* CRUISEWAY CRYPTOGAM CUPOLATED
CYSTIDEAN *DAEDALEAN* DAMASKEEN DAMSELFLY *DIGLOTTIC* *DIMWITTED*
DIPLONTIC DOBSONFLY DOCTORAND DOODLEBUG DOUBLETON *DOUCHEBAG*
DRECKSILL DYNAMOTOR EARTHSTAR ENAMORADO FARANDOLE FELLAHEEN
FIBRILLIN FILLIPEEN *FLOORSHOW* FLORIDEAN *FLOWERBED* FLUORSPAR
FORESTAIR FORGATHER FRANCOLIN FULLERENE GASPEREAU GLOSSATOR
GOGGLEBOX GOLDENEYE GOLDENROD GOLOSHOES GONOPHORE GOVERNALL
GRAPESHOT GREENSAND GREENSICK GROUNDNUT GROUNDOUT GROUNDSEL
HEARTSICK *HEARTSINK* HEARTSORE HELIOSTAT HETEROPOD HETEROSIS
HETEROTIC HODMANDOD HOLDERBAT HOLLOWARE HOUSELEEK HOUSEROOM
HUBRISTIC *HYBRISTIC* *HYDRASTIS* HYDROSERE *INDIGOTIC* INDIGOTIN
INSECTEAN INTERNODE *JUNGLEGYM* KINEMATIC *KNIFEREST* LAMINARIN
LEGGINGED LENTICULE *LETTERSET* LITHIASIS LITTERBAG LUMINAIRE
LUMINARIA MANGOSTAN MANTICORA MANTICORE MAQUISARD MARQUETRY
MARROWFAT MARROWSKY *MARTINGAL* MELANOSIS MELANOTIC MOCKERNUT
MONKEYPOD *MONKEYPOT* MORPHOGEN MORPHOSIS MORPHOTIC *MOUTONNEE*
MUSKETOON NECTAREAN *NIMBLEWIT* NITWITTED NYMPHALID ONIONSKIN
ORGIASTIC PASTEDOWN PENNONCEL PERMITTEE *PERSONNED* PHASEDOWN
PHENYLENE *PHOTOSCAN* *PHYLLOMIC* PINKERTON PLASMAGEL PLASMATIC
PLOUGHBOY POETICULE *POTATOBUG* PRAISEACH PRINCEKIN RATHEREST
RATTLEBAG *RATTLEBOX* *RECONSOLE* REFORMADO *REGGAETON* *REMIXTURE*
RIBAUDRED RILLETTES *RUSTICANA* SADDLEBOW SCAZONTIC SCHIZOPOD
SCRAPEGUT SCRUTOIRE SENHORITA SHADOWBOX SHIRRALEE *SILVEREYE*
SINGLETON *SKETCHPAD* SLUICEWAY SOOTHSAID SOUTHSAID SPONGEBAG
SPRITSAIL *SQUILLION* STREETBOY STROMATIC STROUPACH STRUMATIC
SUPERBOLD SUPERSALE SUPERSALT SUPERSELL SUPERSHOW SUPERSOFT
SUPERSOLD TABULATOR TAENIASIS TALLITHES TALLITHIM *THEIRSELF*

THREADFIN	THRENETIC	*TINKERTOY*	TITTLEBAT	TONSILLAR	TRENCHAND
TRENCHARD	*TRUCKSTOP*	TUCKERBAG	*TUMBLESET*	TURBANNED	ULTRASOFT
UNCATERED	URTICARIA	VIBRIOSIS	*VOLUMETRY*	VOMITORIA	WARRANTEE
WHITEDAMP	*WINTERFED*	*WONDERKID*	WOODENTOP	YESTEREVE	

FOUR-LETTER WORD PLUS FIVE-LETTER WORD

COMMON FIVE-LETTER WORD ENDINGS

FULLY

BALEFULLY	BANEFULLY	BASHFULLY	DOLEFULLY	DOOMFULLY	EASEFULLY
HATEFULLY	HEEDFULLY	HELPFULLY	HURTFULLY	MINDFULLY	MOANFULLY
NEEDFULLY	PUSHFULLY	RESTFULLY	RUTHFULLY	SONGFULLY	SOULFULLY
TOILFULLY	TUNEFULLY	WAILFULLY	WAKEFULLY	WISHFULLY	WISTFULLY
ZESTFULLY					

MAKER

| AUTOMAKER | CASEMAKER | DRUGMAKER | LOSSMAKER | ODDSMAKER | PLAYMAKER |
| SHOTMAKER | SNOWMAKER | STAYMAKER | TOOLMAKER | | |

METER

AEROMETER	*AUTOMETER*	BOLOMETER	*DOSEMETER*	DUROMETER	ERGOMETER
FADOMETER	FLOWMETER	FOCIMETER	OCTAMETER	PHONMETER	PYROMETER
RATEMETER	ROTAMETER	TAXAMETER	TAXIMETER	TELEMETER	TILTMETER
VOLTMETER	WATTMETER	WAVEMETER			

OLOGY

ARCHOLOGY	BATTOLOGY	BUMPOLOGY	CARPOLOGY	CARTOLOGY	*CONIOLOGY*
DISCOLOGY	DITTOLOGY	FESTOLOGY	GARBOLOGY	GISMOLOGY	*HERBOLOGY*
HISTOLOGY	ICONOLOGY	IRIDOLOGY	LIMNOLOGY	LITHOLOGY	*MEREOLOGY*
MUSEOLOGY	*PALEOLOGY*	PESTOLOGY	PHONOLOGY	SCATOLOGY	SEMIOLOGY
TAUTOLOGY	TELEOLOGY	TROPOLOGY			

STONE

ALUMSTONE	BAKESTONE	*BILESTONE*	BLUESTONE	BONDSTONE	BUHRSTONE
BURRSTONE	CALMSTONE	CAUMSTONE	COPESTONE	CORNSTONE	CURBSTONE
DOORSTONE	DRIPSTONE	DROPSTONE	FIRESTONE	FLAGSTONE	FLOWSTONE
FOOTSTONE	FREESTONE	GLADSTONE	GOLDSTONE	GREYSTONE	GRITSTONE
HOLYSTONE	HORNSTONE	*JACKSTONE*	KERBSTONE	LOADSTONE	LODESTONE
MARLSTONE	MERESTONE	PENISTONE	SILTSTONE	SLABSTONE	STARSTONE
TOADSTONE	TURNSTONE	VEINSTONE	WHETSTONE	WHINSTONE	WOODSTONE

WOMAN/WOMEN

ANTIWOMAN	BATSWOMAN	BONDWOMAN	BUSHWOMAN	BYREWOMAN	CHARWOMAN
CLUBWOMAN	*DOORWOMAN*	FIREWOMAN	FOREWOMAN	FREEWOMAN	*IRONWOMAN*
JURYWOMAN	KINSWOMAN	OARSWOMAN	POSTWOMAN	*SHOPWOMAN*	*TIREWOMAN*

OTHER FIVE-LETTER WORD ENDINGS

AEROBIONT	AEROGRAPH	*AEROLOGIC*	AEROMOTOR	AERONOMIC	*AEROPAUSE*
AEROPHONE	*AEROPULSE*	*AEROSCOPE*	AEROSHELL	AEROSPACE	*AEROSPIKE*
AEROTAXES	AEROTAXIS	AEROTRAIN	*AIRSTRIKE*	ALBESCENT	ALBESPINE
ALEWASHED	ALMSGIVER	ALMSHOUSE	AMASSABLE	AMYLOPSIN	ANANTHOUS
ANGASHORE	ANTECHOIR	ANTENATAL	*ANTIABUSE*	ANTIALIEN	*ANTIARMOR*
ANTIAUXIN	ANTIBLACK	ANTICLINE	ANTICLING	ANTICODON	ANTICRIME
ANTIDOTAL	ANTIDRAFT	ANTIELITE	ANTIFRAUD	ANTIGENIC	ANTIGLARE
ANTIGRAFT	ANTIHELIX	ANTIHUMAN	ANTILABOR	ANTIMACHO	*ANTIMUSIC*
ANTINODAL	ANTINOISE	ANTINOMIC	ANTINOVEL	ANTIPARTY	ANTIPODAL
ANTIPOLAR	ANTIQUARK	ANTIRADAR	*ANTIROYAL*	ANTISENSE	*ANTISHAKE*
ANTISHARK	ANTISHOCK	ANTISLEEP	ANTISMOKE	ANTISOLAR	ANTISTICK
ANTISTORY	*ANTISTYLE*	ANTITOXIC	ANTITOXIN	ANTITRADE	ANTITRAGI
ANTITRUST	ANTITUMOR	ANTITYPAL	ANTITYPIC	ANTIULCER	ANTIUNION
ANTIURBAN	*ANTIVENOM*	ANTIVIRAL	ANTIVIRUS	ANTIWHITE	*ANTIWORLD*
AQUABOARD	AQUADROME	*ARCHDRUID*	ARCHDUCAL	ARCHFIEND	ARCHIMAGE
ARCHONTIC	*ARCHRIVAL*	*ARCHSTONE*	*ARCOGRAPH*	AUTOCLAVE	*AUTOCRINE*
AUTOCRIME	AUTOCROSS	*AUTOCUTIE*	AUTOFLARE	AUTOGAMIC	AUTOGENIC
AUTOGRAFT	AUTOGUIDE	*AUTOLYSIN*	AUTOLYSIS	AUTOLYTIC	*AUTOMAGIC*
AUTONOMIC	AUTOPHONY	AUTOPOINT	*AUTOREPLY*	AUTOROUTE	*AUTOSPORE*
AUTOTELIC	AUTOTIMER	*AUTOTOXIC*	AUTOTOXIN	*AUTOTYPIC*	

BACKDRAFT	BACKFIELD	BACKHOUSE	*BACKPLATE*	*BACKSHORE*	BACKSIGHT
BACKSPEER	BACKSPEIR	*BACKSTAIR*	BACKSTALL	*BACKSTAMP*	*BACKSTORY*
BACKSWEPT	BACKSWORD	BAKEHOUSE	*BALDFACED*	BALDMONEY	BALKANISE
BALLASTER	BANDONION	*BANDSHELL*	BASEPLATE	*BEADHOUSE*	BEANFEAST
BEARGRASS	*BEDEHOUSE*	BEEFEATER	BEESTINGS	*BELLYLIKE*	BENEDIGHT
BENTGRASS	*BETATOPIC*	BIRDHOUSE	*BIRDWATCH*	*BITEPLATE*	*BLUECURLS*
BLUEJEANS	BLUEPOINT	BLUESHIFT	*BLURREDLY*	*BOARHOUND*	BOATSWAIN
BODYSHELL	*BOLOGRAPH*	*BONETIRED*	*BOOKLIGHT*	BOOKLOUSE	BOOKPLATE
BOOMSLANG	BOONDOCKS	BORESCOPE	*BRASSWARE*	BRATWURST	BRIMSTONY
BROWRIDGE	BRUTALIST	BUCKHOUND	BUCKTHORN	BUCKWHEAT	BULLFINCH
BULLSNAKE	*BULLWADDY*	BUTTSTOCK			

CALFDOZER	*CALLAIDES*	*CALLBOARD*	*CALMSTANE*	CAMERATED	CAMPANILE
CAMPSHIRT	*CAMPSTOOL*	CAMSTEARY	CANEBRAKE	CANEFRUIT	CAPITALLY
CARBAMATE	CARBAMIDE	CARBAMINO	CARBANION	CARBAZOLE	*CARBONIUM*
CARBURATE	CARDAMINE	CARDPHONE	CAREGIVER	CARNALIST	*CARNIVORY*
CARROUSEL	*CARTHORSE*	CASEBOUND	*CALMSTANE*	CENTURIAL	CEROGRAPH
CHAMFERER	CHARBROIL	CHARLOTTE	CHARMEUSE	*CHARTABLE*	CHATELAIN
CHINAWARE	CLAMSHELL	CLAPBREAD	*CLAYSTONE*	*CLIPSHEAR*	CLIPSHEET
COALHOUSE	COATSTAND	COHOUSING	COLDBLOOD	*COLEOPTER*	COLLAGIST
COLLODIUM	COMPTABLE	COMPTROLL	CONDOLENT	COOKSTOVE	COOLHOUSE
COONHOUND	*COPYFIGHT*	COPYTAKER	CORDGRASS	CORFHOUSE	CORKBORER
CORNBORER	*CORNBRAID*	CORNBRASH	CORNBREAD	CORNSTALK	CORYDALIS
CORYPHENE	*COTHURNAL*	COVETABLE	*CRABEATER*	CRABGRASS	CRAPSHOOT
CRAWDADDY	CROPBOUND	CROWBERRY	CULLENDER	*CYANURATE*	

DARKFIELD	DEADHOUSE	DEADLIGHT	DEADSTOCK	*DEAFBLIND*	DECKHOUSE
DEEPFROZE	DEEPWATER	DEERBERRY	*DEERGRASS*	DEERHOUND	DELEGABLE
DELEGATOR	*DELETABLE*	DELIMITER	DELIRIANT	*DEMOSCENE*	DEREPRESS
DIESINKER	DISANOINT	DISAVOUCH	*DISAVOWER*	DISCLIMAX	DISCOBOLI
DISCUMBER	DISHALLOW	DISHCLOUT	DISHTOWEL	DISSHIVER	DISSUNDER
DIVESTURE	*DOLLARISE*	DOOMSAYER	DOOMWATCH	*DOORFRAME*	DOORPLATE
DOPESHEET	DOWNBURST	DOWNCOURT	DOWNDRAFT	DOWNFIELD	DOWNFORCE
DOWNLIGHT	DOWNRANGE	DOWNSHIFT	DOWNSLIDE	DOWNSLOPE	DOWNSPOUT
DOWNSTAGE	DOWNSTAIR	DOWNSTATE	DOWNSWING	DRAGHOUND	*DRAGSTRIP*
DRAWKNIFE	DRAWPLATE	DRAWSHAVE	*DRAYHORSE*	*DROPCLOTH*	*DROPFORGE*
DROPLIGHT	*DROPSONDE*	DRYSALTER	DUCKBOARD	DUCKSHOVE	*DUMPTRUCK*
DUSTSHEET	*DUSTSTORM*				

EASTABOUT	EASTBOUND	ECHOVIRUS	*EDITRICES*	EPICLESES	*EPICRISES*
ERGOGENIC	ERGOGRAPH	ERGOMANIA	ERSTWHILE	*EUROCREEP*	EVERGLADE
EVERWHERE	EVILDOING	EXPOSABLE	EXPOSTURE		

FACEPLATE	*FACEPRINT*	*FACTSHEET*	FAIRYLIKE	*FALLBOARD*	FARMSTEAD
FARMWIVES	*FEEDGRAIN*	FEEDSTOCK	*FEEDWATER*	FERMENTER	*FERMIONIC*
FEUDALIST	*FILLAGREE*	*FILLESTER*	*FILMGOING*	FILOPLUME	FILOPODIA
FILOSELLE	*FILOVIRUS*	*FIREBOARD*	FIREBRAND	FIREBRICK	FIRECREST
FIREDRAKE	FIREHOUSE	FIREMANIC	FIRETHORN	*FIRETRUCK*	*FISCALIST*
FISHPLATE	FIVEPENNY	FLAGRANCE	FLAGSTICK	FLANNELLY	FLAPTRACK
FLATBREAD	*FLATSTICK*	*FLOGGABLE*	FLOPHOUSE	FLOPTICAL	FLUSHABLE
FOILBORNE	FOLKLORIC	FOOTBOARD	*FOOTBRAKE*	FOOTCLOTH	FOOTPLATE
FOOTSTALK	*FOOTSTALL*	*FOOTSTOCK*	FOREANENT	FOREBRAIN	FORECABIN
FORECADDY	FOREGLEAM	FOREJUDGE	FORENIGHT	FOREPOINT	FOREREACH
FORESHANK	FORESHEET	FORESHOCK	FORESKIRT	FORESLACK	*FORESPAKE*
FORESPEAK	FORESPEND	FORESPENT	FORESPOKE	FORESTAGE	FORESTAIR
FORESTEAL	FORESWEAR	FORESWORE	FORESWORN	FORETEACH	FORETEETH
FORETHINK	FORETOKEN	FORETOOTH	FOREWEIGH	FORMALIST	FOULBROOD
FOURPENNY	FREEBOARD	*FREEDIVER*	FREESHEET	FREEWHEEL	*FREEWRITE*
FREEWROTE	*FRETBOARD*	FROGMARCH	FROGMOUTH	*FROGSPAWN*	FRUGALIST
FULLBLOOD	FUNDAMENT	*FUNDRAISE*			

GAMARUCHE	GANGBOARD	*GAOLBREAK*	GASHOLDER	GAZEHOUND	GEARWHEEL
GERMANISE	GERMPROOF	GIGAHERTZ	GILLFLIRT	GLOBALIST	*GLOWSTICK*
GLUTAMATE	GLUTAMINE	GOLDBRICK	GOLDCREST	GOLDFINNY	GOLDSPINK
GOLDSTICK	GOODFACED	*GOODFELLA*	GOODWIVES	*GOREHOUND*	GOWDSPINK
GRANDAUNT	GRANTABLE	GRAYBEARD	*GRAYHOUND*	*GRAYSCALE*	GRAYWACKE
GRAYWATER	*GREYSCALE*	GRUBSTAKE	GUDEWIVES	*GYROPILOT*	GYROPLANE
GYROSCOPE	GYROVAGUE				

HACKBERRY	HALFLIVES	HALLSTAND	HALFPENCE	*HALFTRACK*	HALOBIONT
HALOCLINE	HANDBLOWN	HANDCLASP	HANDSPIKE	*HANDSTAMP*	HARDBOARD
HARDCOURT	*HARDGOODS*	HARDGRASS	HARDPARTS	HARDSTAND	HARMDOING
HARPYLIKE	HEADBOARD	*HEADCOUNT*	HEADFRAME	*HEADGUARD*	HEADLEASE
HEADPEACE	HEADPIECE	HEADSCARF	HEADSTALL	HEADSTICK	HEADSTOCK
HEAPSTEAD	HEELPIECE	*HEELPLATE*	*HELLDIVER*	HERBIVORY	HEREABOUT
HERETICAL	HETEROSES	HIDEBOUND	HILLCREST	*HILLSLOPE*	HINDBERRY

HINDBRAIN	HOARFROST	HOMEBUILT	HOMECRAFT	*HOMEPLACE*	HOMESTALL
HOMESTAND	HOMOGRAFT	*HOMOLOGIC*	HOMOLYSES	HOMOLYSIS	HOMOLYTIC
HOMOPHONE	HOMOPOLAR	HOMOTAXES	HOMOTAXIS	HOMOTONIC	HOMOTYPAL
HOMOTYPIC	*HOOFBOUND*	HOOPSKIRT	HOOTNANNY	HORNWRACK	*HOTELLING*
HOURPLATE	*HOWLROUND*	HYMNODIST	*HYPOBARIC*	HYPOBLAST	*HYPOGENIC*
HYPOMANIA	HYPOMANIC	HYPOTAXES	HYPOTAXIS	HYPOTONIC	

IMIDAZOLE	IRONBOUND	IRONSMITH

JACKFRUIT	JACKLIGHT	*JACKPLANE*	JACKSHAFT	JACKSMELT	JACKSMITH
JACKSNIPE	JACKSTRAW	JELLYLIKE	JERKWATER	JILLFLIRT	JOBSWORTH
JOINTRESS	*JOINTWEED*	JOKESMITH			

KAILYAIRD	KATABASES	KATABASIS	KENTLEDGE	*KERFLOOEY*	KETOGENIC
KILOCURIE	KILOGAUSS	KILOLITER	*KILOLITRE*	*KILOTONNE*	KINESCOPE
KINETICAL	KINGCRAFT	*KITEBOARD*	*KNEEPIECE*	*KNITTABLE*	KNOTGRASS

LAKEFRONT	LAKESHORE	LAMASERAI	LAMPBLACK	*LAMPBRUSH*	LAMPSHELL
LANDBOARD	LANDFORCE	LANDGRAVE	LANDLOPER	*LANDSHARK*	LANGRIDGE
LANGSPIEL	LATESCENT	LATICLAVE	LEADPLANT	LEADSCREW	LEAFSTALK
LEVATORES	LICKPENNY	*LIFEWORLD*	*LIMESCALE*	LIMEWATER	LINEAMENT
LINEARISE	*LINGBERRY*	LINTSTOCK	LINTWHITE	LITERATUS	*LOADSPACE*
LOANSHIFT	LOCATABLE	LOCKHOUSE	LOCOPLANT	LOGOGRAPH	LOGOTHETE
LONGBOARD	LONGCLOTH	LONGHOUSE	LONGSHORE	*LUCKPENNY*	*LUNATICAL*
LUTESCENT					

MAILPOUCH	MAINBRACE	MAINPRISE	MAINSHEET	MAKEREADY	MALLENDER
MANSLAYER	MANYPLIES	*MARSHALER*	MARSQUAKE	MASTHOUSE	*MATELOTTE*
MAULSTICK	*MEATSPACE*	MEGACURIE	MEGADEATH	MEGAFARAD	MEGAFAUNA
MEGAGAUSS	*MEGALITRE*	*MEGAPIXEL*	MEGASCOPE	MEGASPORE	*MEGATHERE*
MEGATONIC	MELTWATER	*MENOPOLIS*	MENTALIST	MERCURATE	MESSALINE
METABASES	METABASIS	METACARPI	*METAGENIC*	METAPHASE	METATARSI
METAVERSE	METESTICK	*MIDISKIRT*	*MILKTOAST*	MILLBOARD	*MILLHOUSE*
MILLWHEEL	*MINDSHARE*	MINELAYER	*MINESHAFT*	*MINIDRESS*	MINIRUGBY
MINISTATE	*MINITOWER*	*MINITRACK*	MISONEIST	MISSTRIKE	MOLDBOARD
MONOBASIC	MONOCEROS	MONOCHORD	MONOCLINE	MONOESTER	MONOGENIC
MONOGRAPH	MONOLATER	MONOLAYER	MONOLOGIC	MONOPHASE	MONOPHONY
MONOPODIA	MONOPULSE	MONORHINE	*MONOSKIER*	MONOSTELE	MONOSTICH
MONOSTYLE	MONOTYPIC	MOONBLIND	*MOONCHILD*	MOONPHASE	MOONQUAKE
MOONRAKER	MOONSHINY	MORTCLOTH	*MOSSGROWN*	MOSSPLANT	MUCKENDER
MUCKSWEAT					

NAILBITER	NEARSHORE	NECKVERSE	*NEWSMAKER*	NEWSTRADE	NICKPOINT
NONGLAZED	*NONGLOSSY*	NONGROWTH	NOSEGUARD	NOSEPIECE	NOSEWHEEL

OCTASTYLE	OLEOGRAPH	OLEORESIN	ONTOGENIC	ONTOLOGIC	*OUTSCREAM*
OUTSTRAIN	OUTSTRIDE	OUTSTRIKE	OUTSTRODE	*OUTSTROKE*	*OUTSTROVE*
OUTSTRUCK	*OVERACUTE*	OVERALERT	OVERBOUND	*OVERBRAKE*	*OVERBREED*
OVERBRIEF	OVERBUILD	OVERBUILT	OVERCARRY	*OVERCHEAP*	OVERCHILL
OVERCLAIM	*OVERCLASS*	OVERCLEAR	*OVERCLOSE*	OVERCLOUD	*OVERCOLOR*

OVERCOUNT	OVERDATED	OVERDIGHT	OVEREATER	OVEREMOTE	OVEREXERT
OVERFLOOD	OVERFLUSH	OVERFOCUS	*OVERFRANK*	OVERGLAZE	OVERGLOOM
OVERGORGE	OVERGRAIN	OVERGRASS	*OVERGRADE*	OVERGREAT	OVERGREEN
OVERHASTE	*OVERHONOR*	OVERINKED	OVERISSUE	OVERLABOR	OVERLEARN
OVERLIGHT	OVERLUSTY	OVERMATCH	OVERMERRY	OVERMOUNT	OVERPAINT
OVERPERCH	OVERPLAID	OVERPOISE	OVERPRESS	OVERPRIZE	OVERPROUD
OVERQUICK	OVERRIGID	OVERROAST	OVERSAUCE	OVERSCALE	OVERSHADE
OVERSHARP	OVERSHINE	OVERSHIRT	OVERSHONE	OVERSKIRT	OVERSMOKE
OVERSPICE	*OVERSPILT*	OVERSTAIN	OVERSTAND	OVERSTANK	OVERSTARE
OVERSTINK	OVERSTOOD	OVERSTORY	OVERSTREW	OVERSTUDY	OVERSTUNK
OVERSWEAR	OVERSWELL	OVERSWING	OVERSWORE	OVERSWORN	OVERSWUNG
OVERTEACH	*OVERTHICK*	*OVERTIGHT*	*OVERTIMID*	OVERTOWER	OVERTRADE
OVERTREAT	OVERTRICK	OVERTRUST	OVERWATCH	OVERWEIGH	OVERWREST

PACKBOARD	*PACKFRAME*	PACKSHEET	PAINTRESS	PALMHOUSE	PALSGRAVE
PALSYLIKE	PANDURATE	PANTDRESS	PANTHEIST	*PARABLAST*	PARABRAKE
PARACLINE	*PARAGLIDE*	PARALOGIA	PARAMESES	PARARHYME	*PARASOLED*
PARATAXES	PARATAXIS	PARATONIC	PARAVAUNT	*PASSALONG*	PASSAMENT
PASTALIKE	PASTORATE	PAYSAGIST	PELLAGRIN	PENETRANT	PENTOXIDE
PERIBLAST	PERIBOLOS	PERIBOLUS	PERICLINE	PERICONES	PERIDROME
PERIGONIA	PERINATAL	PERISTYLE	*PERITRACK*	PERMALLOY	PESTHOUSE
PLANTABLE	*PLAYACTOR*	*PLAYDOUGH*	PLAYFIELD	*PLAYGOING*	PLEASEMEN
PLEDGABLE	PLOWSHARE	*PLUGBOARD*	POETASTER	POKEBERRY	*POKELOGAN*
POLEMARCH	*POLLENATE*	*POLLTAKER*	POLYAMIDE	POLYAMINE	POLYAXIAL
POLYBASIC	*POLYDEMIC*	POLYGAMIC	POLYGENIC	*POLYIMIDE*	POLYTONAL
POLYWATER	POLYZONAL	POLYZOOID	PONTLEVIS	*POORMOUTH*	PORTHOUSE
PORTREEVE	POSTAXIAL	POSTCRASH	POSTFAULT	POSTHORSE	POSTHOUSE
POSTNASAL	POSTRIDER	POSTTRIAL	*POSTVIRAL*	PRODROMAL	PROSODIST
PROSTOMIA	PUBESCENT	PUTTYLIKE	PYRETHRUM	PYROCLAST	PYROGENIC
PYROLATER	PYROMANIA				

QUADRATUS	QUADRILLE	*QUIDDITCH*	QUITCLAIM

RAINBOWED	RAINSPOUT	RAINTIGHT	RAKESHAME	RANGELAND	*RANKSHIFT*
REARHORSE	REARMOUSE	REDDLEMAN	REDECRAFT	*REENACTOR*	*REENLARGE*
REENSLAVE	REENTRANT	*REINFLAME*	*RESHARPEN*	*RESTRETCH*	RICKSTAND
RINGSTAND	ROADCRAFT	ROADSTEAD	ROCKBOUND	*ROCKHOUND*	ROCKSHAFT
ROCKSLIDE	ROCKWATER	ROOFSCAPE	*ROOTBOUND*	*ROOTSTALK*	ROOTSTOCK
ROSEFINCH	ROSTRALLY	*ROTACHUTE*	ROTAPLANE	ROTATABLE	ROTATORES
ROTAVIRUS	ROTIFERAL	ROTOGRAPH	*ROTOSCOPE*	RUBESCENT	RUDDLEMAN
RUNECRAFT					

SAFELIGHT	SAGEBRUSH	*SAILMAKER*	SAILPLANE	SAILRATUS	SALTPETER
SALTPETRE	SANDBLAST	SANDGLASS	SANDSPOUT	SCARPETTI	SCARPETTO
SCARPINES	SEALPOINT	SEEDEATER	*SEEDSTOCK*	SELDSHOWN	*SELENOSES*
SEMIANGLE	SEMIBREVE	*SEMICURED*	SEMIDEIFY	SEMIDWARF	SEMIERECT
SEMIFLUID	SEMIGROUP	SEMILUNAR	*SEMIPIOUS*	*SEMIPOLAR*	SEMIRIGID
SEMIROUND	SEMISOLID	SEMITONAL	SEMITONIC	*SEMITRUCK*	*SEMIURBAN*
SEMIVOCAL	SEMIVOWEL	SEMIWORKS	SENESCENT	SENTENTIA	SERASKIER
SHADBERRY	*SHAGGABLE*	SHEWBREAD	*SHINGUARD*	SHIPBORNE	SHIPOWNER

SHITFACED	SHOEBLACK	SHOPBOARD	SHOTFIRER	SHOTMAKER	SHOTPROOF
SHOWBREAD	SHOWMANLY	SHOWPLACE	SICKLEMAN	SICKNURSE	SIDELIGHT
SIDESHOOT	*SIDEWHEEL*	SIGHTABLE	SIGNBOARD	SILKALINE	SINGSPIEL
SKIDPROOF	*SKIMBOARD*	*SLAMDANCE*	SLIPCOVER	*SLIPNOOSE*	*SLIPSHEET*
SLOETHORN	SLOGANISE	SNAPHANCE	SNOWBERRY	SNOWBLINK	SNOWBRUSH
SNOWCLONE	SNOWFLECK	SNOWFLICK	*SNOWGLOBE*	SNOWMAKER	SNOWSCAPE
SNOWSLIDE	SOAPBERRY	*SOFTGOODS*	SOFTSHELL	SOILBORNE	SOLEPLATE
SOLEPRINT	SOMASCOPE	SOMEWHILE	SONGCRAFT	SONGSMITH	SOOPSTAKE
SOOTFLAKE	SORITICAL	SPAEWIVES	SPINDRIFT	SPOTTABLE	STABLEMAN
STAGHOUND	*STAGNANCE*	*STARBURST*	STARDRIFT	STARSHINE	STEPBAIRN
STEPSTOOL	STIRABOUT	STUDENTRY	SUBAPICAL	SUBSAMPLE	SUBSTRACT
SURFPERCH	*SURFRIDER*	*SWATHABLE*			

TACKBOARD	TAILBOARD	TAILENDER	TAILPIECE	TAILPLANE	TAILSLIDE
TAILSTOCK	TAILWATER	TAILWHEEL	TALIGRADE	*TALLGRASS*	TARTARISE
TAXIPLANE	TEAKETTLE	TEARSHEET	TEARSTAIN	*TEARSTRIP*	TEATASTER
TEGULATED	TELEGENIC	TELEPHONY	TELEPOINT	TELEVISOR	TELLURATE
TELLURITE	TEMPTABLE	TENEBROSE	*TENTMAKER*	TEXTPHONE	THENABOUT
THIOFURAN	THROBLESS	*THRUPENNY*	*TILTROTOR*	*TIMESAVER*	*TIMESHARE*
TOADEATER	TOADGRASS	*TOGAVIRUS*	TOLLHOUSE	TOOLHOUSE	*TOPOGRAPH*
TORCHABLE	TORTRICES	TOWNSCAPE	*TREEHOUSE*	TRIMETHYL	TRUEPENNY
TUNESMITH	TUNGSTATE	*TURFGRASS*	TURNAGAIN	TURNROUND	TWALPENNY
TWAYBLADE	TWINBERRY	TWOSEATER	TYPEWRITE	TYPEWROTE	TYPOGRAPH
TYPOLOGIC	TYPOMANIA	*TYROPITTA*			

UNBEGUILE	UNBELIEVE	UNBELOVED	UNBEMUSED	UNBESEEMS	UNBESPEAK
UNBESPOKE	UNDEBASED	*UNDEBATED*	UNDEFACED	UNDEFILED	UNDELAYED
UNDELIGHT	*UNDERIVED*	UNDESERVE			

VAGINOSES	VAINGLORY	VANTBRACE	*VANTBRASS*	VENATICAL	VENTRALLY
VERBALIST	VIEWPHONE	VILLAGREE	VIRESCENT	VITASCOPE	

WAKEBOARD	WALDFLUTE	WALDGRAVE	WALLBOARD	WARMBLOOD	WASHSTAND
WAVEGUIDE	WAVESHAPE	*WEARPROOF*	WELLANEAR	WELLHOUSE	*WESTABOUT*
WESTBOUND	WHINBERRY	*WHIPSNAKE*	WHIPSTALL	WHIPSTOCK	*WICKTHING*
WILDGRAVE	WINDBLAST	WINDBOUND	WINDHOVER	WINDPROOF	WINDSHAKE
WINDTIGHT	WINEBERRY	*WINEMAKER*	WINEPRESS	*WINGCHAIR*	*WIREFRAME*
WIREGRASS	WIREPHOTO	WOLFBERRY	WOLFHOUND	WOODBLOCK	*WOODBORER*
WOODGRAIN	WOODHORSE	WOODHOUSE	WOODLOUSE	WOODMOUSE	*WOODPRINT*
WOODREEVE	WOODSPITE	WOODSTOVE	WORDBOUND	WORDBREAK	WORKHOUSE
WORKMANLY	WORKPIECE	*WORKPRINT*	*WORKSPACE*	WORKTABLE	WRAPROUND

FIVE-LETTER WORD PLUS FOUR-LETTER WORD

COMMON FOUR-LETTER WORD ENDINGS

ABLE

ADOPTABLE	*ALARMABLE*	ALTERABLE	AMASSABLE	*AMUSEABLE*	ANNEXABLE
ASSAYABLE	*ATONEABLE*	AUDITABLE	*BOARDABLE*	*BOUNDABLE*	*BROWSABLE*
CANOEABLE	*CHANTABLE*	CHARTABLE	CHASEABLE	*CHOKEABLE*	CLASSABLE

CLOSEABLE	COLORABLE	COMPTABLE	COVETABLE	CROSSABLE	DANCEABLE
DEFERABLE	*DELAYABLE*	DRAFTABLE	DRAINABLE	DRAPEABLE	DRILLABLE
EJECTABLE	ELECTABLE	*ENACTABLE*	ENTERABLE	ERECTABLE	EXACTABLE
EXPOSABLE	FIGHTABLE	*FLICKABLE*	FLOATABLE	*FLOODABLE*	FLUSHABLE
FOCUSABLE	*FORCEABLE*	FORGEABLE	FRAMEABLE	FRANKABLE	GAUGEABLE
GLEANABLE	*GORGEABLE*	GRANTABLE	GRASPABLE	GRAZEABLE	GROUPABLE
GUARDABLE	IMAGEABLE	*INDEXABLE*	INFERABLE	*JUDGEABLE*	KNEADABLE
LABELABLE	LACERABLE	LEACHABLE	LIMITABLE	*LODGEABLE*	*LOWERABLE*
MEDICABLE	MOTORABLE	MOULDABLE	MOUTHABLE	*MUNCHABLE*	ORDERABLE
PAINTABLE	*PAROLABLE*	PEACEABLE	PERCEABLE	PIVOTABLE	PLACEABLE
PLANTABLE	PLEADABLE	*POACHABLE*	POINTABLE	*PRICEABLE*	*PURGEABLE*
QUELLABLE	RAISEABLE	RAZORABLE	*RECITABLE*	REFERABLE	*RELAXABLE*
RIGHTABLE	RINSEABLE	*SCALEABLE*	SCOLDABLE	SCOOPABLE	SCRAPABLE
SCREWABLE	*SERVEABLE*	SEVERABLE	SHAKEABLE	SHAMEABLE	SHAREABLE
SHAVEABLE	SHIFTABLE	SIGHTABLE	*SLAKEABLE*	SLICEABLE	*SMASHABLE*
SMELLABLE	SMOKEABLE	SOUNDABLE	SPALLABLE	SPAREABLE	SPELLABLE
SPENDABLE	SPILLABLE	SPOILABLE	STAGEABLE	STAINABLE	STATEABLE
STEALABLE	*STICKABLE*	*STONEABLE*	SUPERABLE	*SWATHABLE*	*TASTEABLE*
TEMPTABLE	THINKABLE	*TORCHABLE*	TOUCHABLE	TRACTABLE	TRADEABLE
TRAILABLE	*TRUCKABLE*	TWISTABLE	UNCAPABLE	UNMIXABLE	UNPAYABLE
UTTERABLE	VAPORABLE	VENGEABLE	VISITABLE	WEIGHABLE	WIELDABLE
WOUNDABLE	*WRITEABLE*	YIELDABLE			

ABLY

ALLOWABLY	ALTERABLY	AVAILABLY	AVOIDABLY	COLORABLY	COUNTABLY
DRINKABLY	ENJOYABLY	*GAUGEABLY*	INCURABLY	*INFERABLY*	*MEDICABLY*
PEACEABLY	PROVEABLY	RENEWABLY	*RIGHTABLY*	*SCALEABLY*	*SHAMEABLY*
SUPERABLY	TEACHABLY	THINKABLY	TRACEABLY	VENGEABLY	

ALLY

ACTINALLY	ANTICALLY	BIPEDALLY	*COASTALLY*	*DOMICALLY*	EDICTALLY
ENTERALLY	EPOCHALLY	FLUIDALLY	FRONTALLY	GENICALLY	HUMORALLY
LUDICALLY	MANICALLY	*MESICALLY*	OHMICALLY	ONTICALLY	OPTICALLY
ORBITALLY	*OSMICALLY*	PANICALLY	PIVOTALLY	*QUANTALLY*	SEVERALLY
SONICALLY	STOICALLY	SUGARALLY	TELICALLY	THERMALLY	TONICALLY
TOPICALLY	TOXICALLY	*XERICALLY*			

ANCE

EXULTANCE   FAINEANCE   IMPEDANCE   PLEASANCE

FISH

ANGELFISH	BLACKFISH	BLINDFISH	*CLINGFISH*	*CRAMPFISH*	CROSSFISH
DEVILFISH	GLOBEFISH	GOOSEFISH	*HOUNDFISH*	JEWELFISH	LEMONFISH
PILOTFISH	*QUEENFISH*	*RAZORFISH*	SABLEFISH	SCALDFISH	*SNAILFISH*
SNAKEFISH	SNIPEFISH	SPADEFISH	SPIKEFISH	SQUAWFISH	STINGFISH
STOCKFISH	SWEETFISH	SWELLFISH	TRUNKFISH	UNDERFISH	*VIPERFISH*
WRECKFISH	*ZEBRAFISH*				

9. Nine-Letter Words

FORM

ACINIFORM	CIRRIFORM	CLAVIFORM	CORNIFORM	DISCIFORM	LENTIFORM
LIBRIFORM	PENNIFORM	*PROREFORM*	STYLIFORM	TERRAFORM	VILLIFORM

HEAD

BLUNTHEAD	BREADHEAD	*CLARTHEAD*	CLOSEHEAD	*CRISPHEAD*	CROSSHEAD
FLINTHEAD	FLOORHEAD	GREENHEAD	JOLLYHEAD	JUICEHEAD	*METALHEAD*
NEGROHEAD	*RIVERHEAD*	SCALDHEAD	SCAREHEAD	*SMACKHEAD*	*SNAKEHEAD*
STAIRHEAD	STEELHEAD	*WATERHEAD*			

HOOD

ANGELHOOD	BEASTHOOD	FAIRYHOOD	GIANTHOOD	*GIPSYHOOD*	MONKSHOOD
QUEENHOOD	SMOKEHOOD	SWINEHOOD			

LAND

BENCHLAND	BRUSHLAND	CLOUDLAND	*CROWNLAND*	*LINKSLAND*	LOTUSLAND
MARCHLAND	MOVIELAND	NORTHLAND	PENNYLAND	RANGELAND	SEDGELAND
SHRUBLAND	SOUTHLAND	VIDEOLAND	*WHEATLAND*		

LESS

ANGERLESS	ARMORLESS	*ARROWLESS*	*BADGELESS*	BEINGLESS	*BENCHLESS*
BERRYLESS	*BLADELESS*	BLINDLESS	BLOOMLESS	*BOUGHLESS*	BOWELLESS
BRACTLESS	BRAKELESS	*BRANDLESS*	BRAZELESS	*BREADLESS*	BRIEFLESS
BRINELESS	*BROODLESS*	CHAINLESS	CHAPELESS	CHARTLESS	*CHEEKLESS*
CHIEFLESS	COVERLESS	CRAFTLESS	CRIMELESS	CROWNLESS	DAUNTLESS
DEATHLESS	*DECAYLESS*	DEPTHLESS	*DITCHLESS*	DOWERLESS	DREADLESS
DREAMLESS	FAITHLESS	FAVORLESS	*FEASTLESS*	FENCELESS	*FEVERLESS*
FIBERLESS	FIBRELESS	FLAMELESS	FLECKLESS	*FLOCKLESS*	*FLOODLESS*
FLOORLESS	FLOURLESS	FORCELESS	*FRAMELESS*	FRONDLESS	FRONTLESS
FROTHLESS	*GLARELESS*	*GLEBELESS*	*GLOOMLESS*	GRACELESS	GRADELESS
GRAPELESS	*GRATELESS*	GRAVELESS	*GREEDLESS*	GRIEFLESS	*GROVELESS*
GUARDLESS	GUIDELESS	GUILELESS	GUILTLESS	*HAVENLESS*	*HINGELESS*
HONEYLESS	*HONORLESS*	IDEALLESS	IMAGELESS	INDEXLESS	JOINTLESS
JUDGELESS	JUICELESS	KNIFELESS	LIEGELESS	LIGHTLESS	LINERLESS
LIVERLESS	*LOGICLESS*	LOVERLESS	MATCHLESS	*MERITLESS*	MIRTHLESS
MOTORLESS	MOUTHLESS	*MUSICLESS*	NIGHTLESS	ORDERLESS	PEACELESS
PIECELESS	PLACKLESS	PLANTLESS	PLEATLESS	PLUMBLESS	PLUMELESS
PRIDELESS	PRINTLESS	PUNCHLESS	PUTTYLESS	QUALMLESS	QUEENLESS
RANCHLESS	REACHLESS	REALMLESS	RETCHLESS	RHYMELESS	RIGHTLESS
RIVALLESS	RIVERLESS	*TABLELESS*	TAINTLESS	TEACHLESS	*TEETHLESS*
TENORLESS	*THEFTLESS*	THEMELESS	THROBLESS	THUMBLESS	TITLELESS
TOUCHLESS	TOWERLESS	TRACELESS	TRADELESS	TRIBELESS	TROTHLESS
TROUTLESS	TRUCELESS	*TRUNKLESS*	UDDERLESS	*VAPORLESS*	*VENOMLESS*
VIZORLESS	VOWELLESS	*WAGONLESS*	WIELDLESS	WOUNDLESS	WRATHLESS
WREAKLESS	*YEASTLESS*	*YOUTHLESS*			

LIKE

ADOBELIKE	ADULTLIKE	*APRONLIKE*	*ARROWLIKE*	BAIRNLIKE	*BASINLIKE*
BEASTLIKE	*BELLYLIKE*	BERRYLIKE	BLADELIKE	*BLOODLIKE*	BOARDLIKE
BRUTELIKE	*CAMELLIKE*	*CHOIRLIKE*	*CIGARLIKE*	*CIVETLIKE*	*CLOTHLIKE*

CLOUDLIKE	*CLUMPLIKE*	COURTLIKE	*CRAPELIKE*	*CREAMLIKE*	DEATHLIKE
DIRGELIKE	DOUGHLIKE	DREAMLIKE	*DUNCELIKE*	DWARFLIKE	EARTHLIKE
FAIRYLIKE	*FENCELIKE*	*FIBERLIKE*	FIENDLIKE	*FLAMELIKE*	FLINTLIKE
FLUIDLIKE	FROSTLIKE	*FRUITLIKE*	FUGUELIKE	GABLELIKE	GAUZELIKE
GHOSTLIKE	GIANTLIKE	*GLADELIKE*	*GLANDLIKE*	GLASSLIKE	*GLOBELIKE*
GLUMELIKE	GNOMELIKE	*GOURDLIKE*	GRAPELIKE	GRASSLIKE	*GRAVELIKE*
GUARDLIKE	*HARPYLIKE*	*HINGELIKE*	HORSELIKE	HUMANLIKE	*IVORYLIKE*
JELLYLIKE	JEWELLIKE	*JUDGELIKE*	LEECHLIKE	*LEMONLIKE*	*LEMURLIKE*
MAPLELIKE	MARCHLIKE	*MARSHLIKE*	*METALLIKE*	*MOUSELIKE*	MOUTHLIKE
NIGHTLIKE	NURSELIKE	NYMPHLIKE	*PALSYLIKE*	*PASTALIKE*	PETALLIKE
PLANTLIKE	PLATELIKE	*PLUMELIKE*	PURSELIKE	PUTTYLIKE	*RANCHLIKE*
RAVENLIKE	*RESINLIKE*	*RIDGELIKE*	RIVERLIKE	*SABERLIKE*	SAINTLIKE
SATYRLIKE	SCALELIKE	SCREWLIKE	*SEWERLIKE*	*SHALELIKE*	SHEAFLIKE
SHEEPLIKE	SHEETLIKE	SHELFLIKE	SHREWLIKE	SHRUBLIKE	*SIEVELIKE*
SINUSLIKE	SLATELIKE	SLEEPLIKE	SNAILLIKE	*SNIPELIKE*	*SNOUTLIKE*
SPADELIKE	*SPEARLIKE*	STAGELIKE	*STAIRLIKE*	*STEEDLIKE*	*STONELIKE*
STORMLIKE	STRAWLIKE	*SUGARLIKE*	*SWINELIKE*	SWORDLIKE	SYLPHLIKE
SYRUPLIKE	*TANGOLIKE*	*THIEFLIKE*	THUMBLIKE	TIGERLIKE	TOOTHLIKE
TORCHLIKE	TOWERLIKE	TRUTHLIKE	*TULIPLIKE*	TUMORLIKE	UNGODLIKE
UNMANLIKE	*VAPORLIKE*	*VAULTLIKE*	*VIRUSLIKE*	*WALTZLIKE*	*WEDGELIKE*
WHALELIKE	WITCHLIKE	WOMANLIKE	YEASTLIKE		

LINE

ANTICLINE	*BROADLINE*	CABALLINE	CORALLINE	COUNTLINE	DRIVELINE
FIBROLINE	*FROSTLINE*	GIRTHLINE	*HOUSELINE*	INTERLINE	*LAUGHLINE*
METALLINE	PERSELINE	SHOUTLINE	SIBYLLINE	SIGHTLINE	TOUCHLINE
TRUCKLINE					

LING

BRANDLING	COURTLING	FIRSTLING	FLESHLING	FOUNDLING	GREENLING
HEARTLING	MONTHLING	PLANTLING	RIDGELING	SAINTLING	SHAVELING
STEERLING	STRAYLING	TROUTLING	VETCHLING	WORLDLING	YOUNGLING

MENT

ABASHMENT	ADDLEMENT	ALINEMENT	ALLAYMENT	ANNEXMENT	ARRAYMENT
AVISEMENT	BESETMENT	BEVELMENT	BLASTMENT	*COPAYMENT*	DEBARMENT
DETERMENT	DEVILMENT	*DIZENMENT*	EDUCEMENT	EJECTMENT	ELOINMENT
ELOPEMENT	*EMBOWMENT*	ENACTMENT	ENUREMENT	ERASEMENT	EXACTMENT
EXILEMENT	EXTOLMENT	FLESHMENT	HERRYMENT	*IMBUEMENT*	INTERMENT
INUREMENT	*INURNMENT*	*PARLEMENT*	PASSEMENT	RABATMENT	RAVELMENT
REBUTMENT	RECALMENT	REFITMENT	*REVELMENT*	REVETMENT	ROUSEMENT
SCAPEMENT	STREWMENT	VENGEMENT			

NESS

ACRIDNESS	ADULTNESS	*AGILENESS*	*ALGIDNESS*	ALIENNESS	AMPLENESS
APARTNESS	AWFULNESS	BEINGNESS	*BLONDNESS*	*BOUNDNESS*	*BRAVENESS*
BROADNESS	BROWNNESS	BRUTENESS	*BUSTINESS*	*BUTCHNESS*	BUXOMNESS
CAGEYNESS	CAMPINESS	CHILDNESS	CHILLNESS	*CIVILNESS*	CORNINESS
CRUELNESS	*DAILYNESS*	DATEDNESS	DAZEDNESS	*DOPEYNESS*	DOUCENESS
DROLLNESS	DWARFNESS	DYINGNESS	EQUALNESS	ERECTNESS	EXACTNESS

FADEDNESS	*FATALNESS*	FETIDNESS	*FIRSTNESS*	FIXEDNESS	FLEETNESS
FLUIDNESS	*GAMEYNESS*	GAUNTNESS	GELIDNESS	GIVENNESS	GLUEYNESS
GOOEYNESS	GRANDNESS	GRAVENESS	GREENNESS	HOKEYNESS	HOMEYNESS
HUMANNESS	*IDEALNESS*	INANENESS	INAPTNESS	*INNERNESS*	IRATENESS
JADEDNESS	JOINTNESS	LARGENESS	LEVELNESS	*LICITNESS*	LITHENESS
LIVIDNESS	LOATHNESS	*LOCALNESS*	*LOYALNESS*	LUCIDNESS	LURIDNESS
MATEYNESS	*MAZEDNESS*	MIXEDNESS	*MUCIDNESS*	NAIVENESS	NOBLENESS
NOTEDNESS	OFTENNESS	OTHERNESS	OUGHTNESS	OVERTNESS	*PEARTNESS*
PLANENESS	*PLUMBNESS*	PRIMENESS	PRONENESS	QUICKNESS	RABIDNESS
RAPIDNESS	*REGALNESS*	RIGHTNESS	RIGIDNESS	RURALNESS	TACITNESS
TANGINESS	TAPERNESS	TEPIDNESS	THINGNESS	THREENESS	TRITENESS
TUMIDNESS	UNAPTNESS	UNFITNESS	UTTERNESS	VALIDNESS	VAPIDNESS
VEXEDNESS	*VITALNESS*	VOCALNESS	WHOLENESS	WOFULNESS	*WOMANNESS*
WRONGNESS	YOUNGNESS				

SHIP

AUGURSHIP	BEDELSHIP	*BLOCKSHIP*	CLERKSHIP	COUNTSHIP	DEVILSHIP
DONORSHIP	DRILLSHIP	ELDERSHIP	ENVOYSHIP	GIANTSHIP	GUARDSHIP
GUIDESHIP	GUILDSHIP	JUDGESHIP	KNAVESHIP	LAIRDSHIP	LIGHTSHIP
MAJORSHIP	MAYORSHIP	MINORSHIP	*MOTORSHIP*	QUEENSHIP	RIDERSHIP
RIVALSHIP	ROGUESHIP	RULERSHIP	SAINTSHIP	SCALDSHIP	SIZARSHIP
SKALDSHIP	STORESHIP	TRANSSHIP	TUTORSHIP	UNCLESHIP	VICARSHIP
VIZIRSHIP					

SIDE

BEACHSIDE	GRAVESIDE	NIGHTSIDE	*PLANESIDE*	QUEENSIDE	SHORESIDE
TRAILSIDE					

SOME

CURVESOME	EIGHTSOME	*GREEDSOME*	*GREENSOME*	HEARTSOME	HYDROSOME
LAUGHSOME	LIGHTSOME	LITHESOME	PRANKSOME	QUIETSOME	TOOTHSOME
TRICKSOME	YOUTHSOME				

TONE

ALUMSTONE	BAKESTONE	*BILESTONE*	BLUESTONE	BONDSTONE	BUHRSTONE
BURRSTONE	CALMSTONE	CAUMSTONE	*CLAYSTONE*	COPESTONE	CORNSTONE
CURBSTONE	*DOLOSTONE*	DOORSTONE	DRIPSTONE	DROPSTONE	FIRESTONE
FLAGSTONE	FLOWSTONE	FOOTSTONE	FREESTONE	GLADSTONE	GOLDSTONE
GREYSTONE	GRITSTONE	HORNSTONE	*JACKSTONE*	KERBSTONE	LOADSTONE
LODESTONE	MARLSTONE	MERESTONE	MICROTONE	ORTHOTONE	PENISTONE
SILTSTONE	SLABSTONE	STARSTONE	TOADSTONE	TOUCHTONE	TURNSTONE
VEINSTONE	WHETSTONE	WHINSTONE	WOODSTONE		

WARD

AFTERWARD	DEATHWARD	EARTHWARD	FIELDWARD	FRONTWARD	*GRAVEWARD*
NIGHTWARD	RIGHTWARD	RIVERWARD	SPACEWARD	STERNWARD	

WARE

AGATEWARE	*BRASSWARE*	CHINAWARE	CREAMWARE	DELFTWARE	HOLLOWARE
METALWARE	TREENWARE	*TRIALWARE*	VAPORWARE		

WEED

BROOKWEED	BUGLEWEED	*CLEARWEED*	CRAZYWEED	*FEVERWEED*	GREENWEED
HORSEWEED	*JOINTWEED*	RIVERWEED	ROSINWEED	SHOREWEED	SLINKWEED
SMARTWEED	SNAKEWEED	STICKWEED	STINKWEED	*SUPERWEED*	

WISE

ALTARWISE	ANGLEWISE	BROADWISE	*CHORDWISE*	COASTWISE	FRONTWISE
GUESTWISE	*PENNYWISE*	PIECEWISE	SCARFWISE	SHOALWISE	SLANTWISE
SLOPEWISE	SNAKEWISE	SPIREWISE	SPOKEWISE	SPOONWISE	STAIRWISE
TABLEWISE	TAPERWISE				

WOOD

BEECHWOOD	BLACKWOOD	BLOODWOOD	*BRIARWOOD*	*BRIERWOOD*	BRUSHWOOD
CANOEWOOD	CEDARWOOD	COPSEWOOD	DEVILWOOD	EAGLEWOOD	EARLYWOOD
FRUITWOOD	GREENWOOD	HEARTWOOD	*IVORYWOOD*	LANCEWOOD	*LEMONWOOD*
LIGHTWOOD	MATCHWOOD	*MOOSEWOOD*	PRICKWOOD	ROUNDWOOD	SAPANWOOD
SATINWOOD	SNAKEWOOD	STINKWOOD	*TIGERWOOD*	TORCHWOOD	TULIPWOOD
UNDERWOOD	ZEBRAWOOD				

WORK

BLADEWORK	CHAINWORK	*CLASSWORK*	EARTHWORK	FALSEWORK	*FLUSHWORK*
FROSTWORK	GLASSWORK	GRILLWORK	GROUPWORK	INTERWORK	PIECEWORK
PLAINWORK	PRESSWORK	QUILLWORK	SCALEWORK	SHELLWORK	*SHIFTWORK*
STAIRWORK	STEELWORK	STONEWORK	*STUMPWORK*		

WORT

ADDERWORT	BIRTHWORT	*BLOODWORT*	CORALWORT	FEVERWORT	*GIPSYWORT*
GLASSWORT	LASERWORT	LIVERWORT	MARSHWORT	MITERWORT	MITREWORT
MONEYWORT	NAVELWORT	PEARLWORT	PENNYWORT	QUILLWORT	SPEARWORT
STONEWORT	STRAPWORT	TOOTHWORT			

OTHER FOUR-LETTER WORD ENDINGS

ACARIDEAN	*AEROSCOPE*	AEROSHELL	*AEROSPIKE*	*AFTERBODY*	AFTERCLAP
AFTERDAMP	AFTERDECK	AFTERGAME	AFTERHEAT	AFTERMOST	*AFTERPAIN*
AFTERPEAK	AFTERSHOW	AFTERTIME	AFTERWORD	AITCHBONE	ALLOTROPE
ALLOTROPY	ALPHASORT	*ALPHATEST*	AMBERJACK	*ANGASHORE*	ANGLESITE
ANGLEWORM	ANIMALIER	ANIMALIST	ANTICLING	ANTICRIME	*ANTISHAKE*
ANTISHARK	ANTISHOCK	ANTISLEEP	ANTISMOKE	ANTISPAST	ANTISTICK
ANTISTORY	ARGILLITE	ASPERGILL	*AUDIOBOOK*	AUDIOGRAM	AUDIOLOGY
AURISCOPE	AUTOSCOPY	*AUTOSPORE*	AVIZEFULL		

BACKSHORE	BACKSPEER	BACKSTALL	*BACKSTAMP*	*BACKSTORY*	BACKSWEPT
BACKSWORD	BANDALORE	*BANDSHELL*	BANGSRING	BARCAROLE	BARREFULL
BASALTINE	BASILICON	*BEECHMAST*	*BIRDSFOOT*	*BIRTHNAME*	BIRTHROOT
BISONTINE	*BITCHFEST*	BLACKDAMP	BLACKGAME	BLACKLEAD	BLACKPOLL
BLACKTAIL	BLACKWASH	*BLASTEMIC*	BLEAREYED	BLOODROOT	BLOODWORM
BOATSWAIN	BOOMSLANG	BORESCOPE	BRAILLIST	BRAINCASE	*BRAINDEAD*
BRAINFART	*BRAINFOOD*	*BRAINSTEM*	*BRAINWAVE*	BREADROOM	BREADROOT
BREAKTIME	*BREAKWALL*	*BRIARROOT*	BRICKWALL	BRIDEMAID	BRIDEWELL

319

9. Nine-Letter Words

BRIMSTONY	BRINGDOWN	BROADLEAF	BROADTAIL	BROMELAIN	BROOKLIME
BROOMCORN	BROOMRAPE	*BROWNTAIL*	*BRUSHMARK*	BUDGETEER	*BUILDDOWN*
BULLYCIDE	BURSARIAL	*BUSTICATE*	*BUTEONINE*	BUTTERINE	BUTTSTOCK

CABINMATE	CABLEGRAM	CAIRNGORM	*CALLAIDES*	*CALMSTANE*	CAMELHAIR
CAMPODEID	*CAMPSTOOL*	CANALBOAT	*CANDYGRAM*	CANDYTUFT	CANTORIAL
CARBONOUS	CARRYTALE	CARTELIST	CATERWAUL	CAULDRIFE	*CAUMSTANE*
CEASEFIRE	CEDARBIRD	*CHAINFALL*	CHAMPLEVE	*CHANTILLY*	CHASEPORT
CHEERLEAD	*CHEMOKINE*	CHEMOSORB	CHILIAGON	CHINAROOT	CHIROLOGY
CHOKEBORE	CHOKEDAMP	CHURNMILK	CLAMPDOWN	CLAMSHELL	*CLEANLILY*
CLEAREYED	CLEARSKIN	CLEARWING	*CLIMBDOWN*	CLINGFILM	*CLIPSHEAR*
CLOSEDOWN	*CLOWNFISH*	COLORBRED	COLTSFOOT	COMPOTIER	COMPTROLL
CONDOLENT	CORALLITE	CORALLOID	CORALROOT	CORNOPEAN	CORNSTALK
CORSETIER	COTANGENT	COURBARIL	*COVERSINE*	CRAMPBARK	CRAPSHOOT
CREAMLAID	CREAMWOVE	CREWELIST	*CRIMEWAVE*	CROSSBAND	CROSSFALL
CROSSTALK	CROSSTOWN	CROSSTREE	CROSSWALK	*CROWSFEET*	*CROWSFOOT*
CRYPTOGAM	CULPATORY	CURIALIST	CURSENARY	*CYBERPORN*	

DAIRYMAID	*DANCEHALL*	DANDYFUNK	DANDYPRAT	DAVENPORT	DEADSTOCK
DEATHBLOW	*DEATHTRAP*	DELPHINIA	DEVONPORT	*DICKYBIRD*	*DISCOLOGY*
DODDYPOLL	DODGEBALL	DOGMATORY	*DOLLYBIRD*	*DOORNBOOM*	DOUCEPERE
DOUGHBALL	DOUGHFACE	DOWNSLOPE	DOWNSPOUT	DOWNSTATE	DOWNSWING
DRAGSTRIP	DRAWSHAVE	DREAMHOLE	DRESSMADE	DRESSMAKE	*DRILLHOLE*
DROMEDARE	DUCKSHOVE				

EAGLEHAWK	EARTHBORN	EARTHFALL	EARTHFAST	EARTHFLAX	EARTHRISE
EARTHSTAR	EARTHWOLF	EAVESDRIP	EDEMATOSE	*EIGHTBALL*	EIGHTFOIL
ELDERCARE	ENTERTAKE	ENTERTOOK	EVENTRATE	EVERYWHEN	*EXTRABOLD*
EXTRAPOSE	EXTRAVERT				

FARCEMEAT	FARMSTEAD	*FAULTLINE*	FEEDSTOCK	*FEVERROOT*	FIBROLITE
FIELDVOLE	FIREDRAKE	FLAGSTICK	*FLAREBACK*	*FLASHCARD*	FLASHLAMP
FLASHOVER	FLASHTUBE	*FLATSTICK*	FLESHWORM	FLINTLOCK	FLOODTIDE
FLOODWALL	*FLOORSHOW*	FLUOROTIC	FLUORSPAR	FOLIOLOSE	FOOTSTALK
FOOTSTALL	*FOOTSTOCK*	FORCEMEAT	FORESHANK	FORESLACK	FORESPEAK
FORESPEND	FORESPENT	FORESPOKE	FORESTEAL	FORESTINE	FORESWEAR
FORESWORE	FORESWORN	FORTHCAME	FORTHCOME	FRIARBIRD	FRIEDCAKE
FROGSPAWN	*FRONTLIST*	FRONTPAGE	*FUNGISTAT*	FUSILLADE	

GARRETEER	GAVELKIND	GEODESIST	GISMOLOGY	GIZMOLOGY	GLADSTONE
GLANDERED	*GLASSWORM*	*GLIDEPATH*	*GLOBETROT*	*GLOWSTICK*	GOLDSPINK
GOLDSTICK	GONIATITE	GOOSEFOOT	GOOSEHERD	GOOSENECK	GOWDSPINK
GRANDAUNT	*GRAPELICE*	GRAPESHOT	GRAPETREE	GRAPHEMIC	*GRASSBIRD*
GRASSHOOK	*GRASSPLOT*	*GRASSQUIT*	*GRAVESITE*	GREATCOAT	*GREENBONE*
GREENHAND	GREENMAIL	GREENROOM	GREENSAND	GREENSICK	GREENWASH
GREENWING	GRILLROOM	GRISTMILL	GRONEFULL	GRUBSTAKE	GUANOSINE
GUESTBOOK	GUIDEWORD	GUILDHALL	GUNNYSACK	GYROSCOPE	

HAIRYBACK	HANDSPIKE	*HANDSTAMP*	HANDSTURN	*HARESTAIL*	HAVERSINE
HAWKSBILL	HEADSTALL	HEADSTICK	HEADSTOCK	HEAPSTEAD	*HEARTFREE*
HEARTSEED	HEARTSICK	*HEARTSINK*	HEARTSORE	HEDGEBILL	*HELIOGRAM*

HELIOLOGY	HELIOSTAT	HELIOTYPE	HELIOZOIC	*HILLSLOPE*	HOMESTALL
HOMOSPORY	*HONEYTRAP*	HONORARIA	*HORNYWINK*	HORSEBEAN	HORSEMINT
HORSEPOND	*HORSERACE*	HORSETAIL	HOUSECARL	HOUSECOAT	HOUSEKEEP
HOUSELEEK	HOUSEROOM	HOWSOEVER	*HUMIDICES*	*HYDRAZOIC*	*HYDROCAST*
HYDROLASE	HYDROSERE	HYDROSOMA	HYDROSTAT	HYDROVANE	HYDROZOON
HYPERACID	HYPERARID	HYPERBOLA	HYPERBOLE	HYPERCUBE	HYPEREMIC
HYPERFINE	HYPERMART	*HYPERNOVA*	*HYPERREAL*	HYPERTEXT	HYPOSTOME

IDIOTICON	*IMINOUREA*	IMPELLENT	INGLENEUK	INGLENOOK	INNERWEAR
INTERARCH	INTERBANK	INTERCELL	INTERCLAN	INTERCROP	INTERDASH
INTERDEAL	INTERDICT	INTERDINE	INTERFILE	INTERFIRM	INTERFLOW
INTERFOLD	INTERFUSE	INTERGANG	INTERGREW	INTERGROW	INTERJOIN
INTERKNIT	*INTERKNOT*	INTERLACE	INTERLARD	INTERLEAF	INTERLEND
INTERLENT	*INTERLOAN*	*INTERLOOP*	INTERMALE	INTERMESH	INTERMURE
INTERNODE	INTERPAGE	INTERPLED	INTERPONE	INTERPOSE	*INTERRACE*
INTERTERM	INTERTILL	INTERUNIT	INTERVEIN	INTERWIND	INTERZONE
INTRACITY	IVORYBILL				

JACKSHAFT	JACKSMELT	JAMBOLANA	*JARLSBERG*	JASPERISE	*JELLYROLL*
JESSERANT	JOINTWORM	JOLLYBOAT			

KNIFEREST

LABELLATE	*LABELLIST*	LABELLOID	*LABELMATE*	LACERTINE	LAKESHORE
LAMPSHELL	*LANDSHARK*	*LASERDISC*	*LASERDISK*	*LATERBORN*	LEADSCREW
LEAFSTALK	LIBELLANT	LIBERTINE	LIBRATORY	LIGHTFACE	LIGHTFAST
LIGHTWAVE	LINTSTOCK	LITHOCYST	LITHOLOGY	LITHOPONE	LITHOTOME
LIVERLEAF	*LOADSPACE*	LONGSHORE	LOWERMOST	*LUNCHMEAT*	LUTESCENT

MACROGLIA	MADREPORE	MAISTRING	MANGANITE	MANGETOUT	*MANOSCOPY*
MAQUISARD	MARCHPANE	MARESCHAL	MARIALITE	*MARSHBUCK*	MATCHBOOK
MATCHPLAY	MAULSTICK	*MEATSPACE*	*MEDALPLAY*	*MELONGENE*	MENTALIST
MENTORIAL	METALLIST	METALLOID	METESTICK	METROLOGY	*MICROBLOG*
MICROGLIA	MICROLITH	*MICROLOAN*	MICROLOGY	MICROPORE	*MICROSITE*
MICROVOLT	MICROWATT	MICROWIRE	MILLENARY	MILLEPORE	MILLERITE
MINDSHARE	*MINESHAFT*	MINISTATE	*MISCHOOSE*	*MOLLYHAWK*	MONADNOCK
MONOSKIER	MONOSTELE	MONOSTICH	*MOOSEBIRD*	MOOSEYARD	MORPHETIC
MORPHOTIC	MOULDWARP	*MOUNDBIRD*	*MOUSEOVER*	*MOUSETAIL*	MOUTHFEEL
MOUTHPART	MUSCARINE				

NARCOTINE	NEARSHORE	*NEVERMIND*	NIGHTBIRD	NIGHTFIRE	NIGHTGEAR
NIGHTGLOW	NIGHTMARY	*NIGHTTIDE*	*NONCEREAL*	NORTHMOST	*NYMPHETIC*

OAKENSHAW	OCEANARIA	OLIVENITE	ONIONSKIN	ORRISROOT	ORTHOAXES
ORTHOAXIS	ORTHOEPIC	OUTERCOAT	OUTRELIEF	OVERSHADE	*OVERSHARP*
OVERSHONE	OVERSMOKE	*OVERSPICE*	OVERSTANK	OVERSTINK	OVERSTORY
OVERSTREW	OVERSWEAR	OVERSWELL	OVERSWING	OVERSWORE	OVERSWORN
OVERTEACH	*OVERTHICK*	*OVERTIMID*	OVERTOWER	OVERTRADE	OVERTRUST

PADDYWACK	*PANTYHOSE*	PASTEDOWN	PASTELIST	PATERCOVE	*PEACHBLOW*
PERISTOME	PESTOLOGY	*PETALODIC*	PETERSHAM	PETITTOES	PHASEDOWN
PHONOGRAM	PHONOLITE	PHONOLOGY	*PHOTOCARD*	PHOTOCELL	PHOTOGRAM

PHOTOLYSE	PHOTOMASK	*PHOTOSCAN*	PHOTOTUBE	PIANOLIST	PINCHFIST
PITCHBEND	PLAINSONG	PLASTICKY	PLATEMARK	POLLYANNA	*POLYSEMIC*
PORTATILE	*POUNDCAKE*	*PRESSGANG*	PRESSMARK	*PRIMAVERA*	PROMODERN
PRONGBUCK	PRONGHORN	PROOFROOM	PROSELYTE	PSALMBOOK	PSALMODIC
PSEUDAXES	PSEUDAXIS	PUBESCENT	PULMONARY	PUNCHBALL	*PUNCHBOWL*
PUNCHLINE	PUTTYROOT				

QUARTZITE	*QUEENCAKE*	QUICKLIME	QUINTROON

RADIOGOLD	RADIOGRAM	RADIOTHON	RAINSPOUT	RAKESHAME	RATHERIPE
RAZORBACK	RAZORBILL	*RAZORCLAM*	RECONDITE	*RECONFINE*	*RECONSIGN*
RECONSOLE	RECTORIAL	*REENSLAVE*	REGARDANT	RETROCEDE	RETRODICT
RETROFIRE	RETROFLEX	RETROPACK	RETROVERT	RHINOLITH	RHINOLOGY
RIDGEPOLE	*RIDGETREE*	RIFLEBIRD	RIGHTMOST	ROADSTEAD	ROCKSHAFT
ROOFSCAPE	*ROOTSTALK*	ROOTSTOCK	*ROTOSCOPE*	*ROUGHBACK*	ROUGHCAST
ROUNDARCH	*ROUNDBALL*	ROUNDHAND	*ROUNDHEEL*	*ROUNDTRIP*	ROUNDWORM
ROYALMAST	RUBESCENT				

SABREWING	SAINTFOIN	*SAINTLILY*	SALLYPORT	SANDSPOUT	SATISFICE
SAUCEBOAT	*SCALETAIL*	SCARFSKIN	SCENARISE	SCOPELOID	SCREWBEAN
SCRIPTORY	SCRUMDOWN	*SEEDSTOCK*	SEMISOLID	SERREFILE	SEVENFOLD
SHAMEFAST	SHANKBONE	*SHAPEWEAR*	SHAVETAIL	SHEEPFOLD	*SHEETROCK*
SHELFROOM	SHELLBACK	SHELLBARK	*SHOOTDOWN*	*SHORTARSE*	SHORTCAKE
SHORTGOWN	SHREWMICE	*SIDEROTIC*	SIDESHOOT	SIGILLATE	SIGMATRON
SIMULACRE	SKIMOBILE	*SLEEPAWAY*	SLIMEBALL	SLINGBACK	SLUNGSHOT
SMACKDOWN	SMEARCASE	SNAKEBIRD	SNAKEROOT	SNEAKERED	SNOWSCAPE
SOFTSHELL	SOMASCOPE	SONNETEER	SOOPSTAKE	SOOTHFAST	SOOTHSAID
SOUNDBITE	SOUNDCARD	*SOUNDPOST*	SOUTHSAID	SOUTHWEST	SPACEBAND
SPARTEINE	SPEEDBALL	*SPEEDREAD*	SPEEDWELL	SPELDRING	SPELLBIND
SPELLDOWN	SPICEBUSH	SPIKENARD	SPILLOVER	SPLAYFEET	SPLAYFOOT
SPOILFIVE	SPOONBAIT	SPOONBILL	*SPOONHOOK*	*SPOONWORM*	*SPRIGTAIL*
SPRITSAIL	*SQUAWBUSH*	SQUAWROOT	STACKROOM	STACKYARD	STAIRFOOT
STAIRSTEP	STANDAWAY	*STANDDOWN*	*STANDFAST*	STANDGALE	*STANDOVER*
STATELILY	STEENBRAS	*STEENBUCK*	STEINBOCK	*STENOBATH*	STENOTYPE
STEPSTOOL	STERNFAST	STERNMOST	STERNPORT	STERNPOST	STILLROOM
STILTBIRD	STINGBULL	*STINKBIRD*	STINKHORN	STOKEHOLD	STOKEHOLE
STOMACHAL	STONEBOAT	STONECAST	STONECHAT	STONEHAND	STONESHOT
STONEWASH	STOOLBALL	STOOPBALL	STORMBIRD	STOWNLINS	STRAPHANG
STRAPHUNG	STYLOBATE	STYLOLITE	*STYLOPISE*	*STYLOPIZE*	SUGARBUSH
SUGARCOAT	SUGARLOAF	SUGARPLUM	*SUPERATOM*	SUPERBANK	*SUPERBIKE*
SUPERCEDE	SUPERCITY	SUPERCLUB	SUPERCOIL	SUPERCOLD	SUPERCOOL
SUPERCUTE	SUPERFARM	SUPERFAST	SUPERFINE	SUPERFIRM	SUPERFLUX
SUPERFOOD	SUPERFUND	SUPERFUSE	SUPERGENE	SUPERGOOD	SUPERHIVE
SUPERHYPE	SUPERJOCK	SUPERLAIN	*SUPERLOAD*	*SUPERLONG*	SUPERMALE
SUPERMART	SUPERMIND	SUPERMINI	SUPERRACE	SUPERREAL	SUPERROAD
SUPERSAFE	SUPERSALE	SUPERSALT	SUPERSELL	SUPERSHOW	SUPERSIZE
SUPERSOFT	*SUPERSOLD*	SUPERSTUD	SUPERTHIN	*SUPERTRAM*	SUPERWAVE
SUPERWIDE	SUPERWIFE	SWEATSUIT	SWEEPBACK	SWEETMEAL	SWEETMEAT
SWEETVELD	SWINEHERD	SWINGBOAT	*SWINGTAIL*	SWINGTREE	*SWORDBILL*
SWORDTAIL	SYLVANITE				

TABESCENT	TABLEMATE	TACHOGRAM	TAILSTOCK	TALLYSHOP	TARGETEER
TAXONOMER	TEARSTAIN	*TEARSTRIP*	TELESCOPY	TEMPORISE	*TENIACIDE*
TEPIDARIA	TERRAMARA	TERRAMARE	TETRADITE	TETRAGRAM	TETRALOGY
THEIRSELF	THERMOTIC	THORNBACK	*THICKLEAF*	*THORNBIRD*	THORNTREE
THREEPEAT	THYMIDINE	*TIGHTKNIT*	*TIMESAVER*	TOOTHCOMB	TOUCHLINE
TOUCHMARK	TOWNSCAPE	TOXICOSES	TRACKBALL	TRACKROAD	TRANSAXLE
TRANSCODE	TRANSDUCE	TRANSFARD	*TRANSGENE*	TRANSMOVE	TRANSMUTE
TRANSVEST	TRASHTRIE	TRIACTINE	TRIERARCH	TRIGONOUS	*TRUCKSTOP*
TUNGSTATE	*TUNGSTITE*	TYRANNOUS			

ULTRACOLD	ULTRACOOL	ULTRAFAST	ULTRAFINE	ULTRAHEAT	ULTRALEFT
ULTRAPOSH	ULTRAPURE	ULTRARARE	ULTRARICH	ULTRASAFE	ULTRASLOW
ULTRASOFT	*ULTRATINY*	ULTRAWIDE	UMBELLATE	UMBRATILE	UNCESSANT
UNDERBAKE	UNDERBORE	UNDERBOSS	UNDERBRED	UNDERBRIM	UNDERBUSH
UNDERCARD	UNDERCART	UNDERCAST	UNDERCLAD	UNDERCLAY	UNDERCLUB
UNDERCOOL	*UNDERDAKS*	UNDERDECK	UNDERDOER	*UNDERDOSE*	UNDERDRAW
UNDERDREW	UNDERFIRE	UNDERFLOW	UNDERGIRT	*UNDERGOER*	UNDERGOWN
UNDERHAIR	*UNDERHEAT*	UNDERHUNG	UNDERKEEP	UNDERKEPT	*UNDERKILL*
UNDERKING	*UNDERLEAF*	*UNDERLOAD*	UNDERMOST	UNDERNOTE	UNDERPART
UNDERPLOT	*UNDERRIPE*	UNDERSAID	UNDERSELF	UNDERSHOT	UNDERSIGN
UNDERSOIL	UNDERSONG	UNDERSPIN	UNDERTANE	UNDERTIME	UNDERTINT
UNDERVOTE	UNDERWING	*UNDERWIRE*	UNDERWORK	UNGODLILY	*UNMANNISH*
UNPENNIED	UNREDREST	UREDOSORI			

VEXILLATE	VIDEODISC	VIDEODISK	VILLAGREE	*VIREONINE*	VIRESCENT
VITASCOPE	*VOICEMAIL*	VOLKSLIED	VRAICKING		

WAISTBELT	*WALLYBALL*	WALLYDRAG	*WATCHLIST*	WATERBUCK	WATERLEAF
WAULKMILL	WHALEBOAT	WHALEBONE	WHEATMEAL	WHIPSTALL	WHIPSTOCK
WHITEBASS	WHITEBEAM	WHITECOAT	*WHITECOMB*	*WHITEDAMP*	WHITEFACE
WHITELIST	WHITETAIL	WHOLEFOOD	WINDSHAKE	WOLFSBANE	*WORKSPACE*
WORLDBEAT	WORRYGUTS				

ZINKENITE

9.4 SOME OTHER LESS FAMILIAR NON-HOOK NINES

ABOMINATE	ACIDULATE	ACIDULENT	ACONITINE	ACROTERIA	ADENOSINE
ADIPOCERE	AEPYORNIS	AERIALITY	AEROLITIC	AFTERINGS	*AGENTIVAL*
AGRESTIAL	ALBERTITE	ALEATORIC	*ALEURONIC*	*ALGOMETER*	ALIENATOR
ALMANDITE	AMETROPIA	AMOURETTE	ANABOLITE	ANALOGISE	ANALOGIST
ANDESITIC	ANDOUILLE	ANDRADITE	ANDROECIA	*ANGOSTURA*	ANHEDONIA
ANHYDRITE	*ANIDROSES*	ANNUALISE	ANORECTAL	ANORTHITE	ANTHELION
ANTIBUSER	*ANTIMERIC*	*APHRODITE*	APSIDIOLE	ARAGONITE	ARCUATION
ARECOLINE	AREOMETER	AREOSTYLE	ARGENTINE	ARGENTITE	*ARISTOTLE*
AROMATASE	ARSENIATE	ARSENIOUS	ARTEMISIA	ARTERIOLE	ARTERITIS
ARYTENOID	*ASSORTIVE*	ASTRODOME	ASTROLABE	ATONALIST	ATTAINDER
ATTOLASER	AUBRIETIA	AUDITORIA	AUDITRESS	AUSLANDER	AUSTENITE
AVENTURIN	AVOUTERER				

```
BACTEROID  BADINERIE  BAIGNOIRE  BANDELIER  BANDOLEER  BANDOLERO
BANDOLIER  BARITONAL  BASTINADE  BEARNAISE  BRASILEIN  BRIOLETTE
BUTADIENE

CADENTIAL  CAFETORIA  CALENTURE  CANTONISE  CARBONISE  CAREERIST
CARNALISE  CARNITINE  CARNOTITE  CARTELISE  CASEATION  CATARHINE
CAUTERISE  CENSORIAL  CENSORIAN  CENTRIOLE  CERATODUS  CIGUATERA
CINERATOR  CINEREOUS  CITIGRADE  COADUNATE  COBALTINE  COETERNAL
COINTREAU  CONSORTIA  CONTADINE  COPATAINE  CORNEITIS  CORNELIAN
CORNETIST  COVARIATE  CRENATION  CRENULATE  CRETINISE  CROTALINE
CROUSTADE  CURTILAGE  CUSTODIER

DALTONIAN  DARNATION  DAWSONITE  DEAMINASE  DEAMINATE  DEAMINISE
DECALITER  DECALITRE  DECIMATOR  DECLINATE  DECURSION  DEDICATOR
DEFOLIANT  DEINOSAUR  DELAPSION  DEMANTOID  DENTALIUM  DENTATION
DENTURIST  DERMATOID  DESOLATOR  DESTINATE  DETONABLE  DETRITION
DETRUSION  DIABLERIE  DIABOLISE  DIACONATE  DIAERETIC  DIALOGISE
DIALOGITE  DIAMAGNET  DIAMETRAL  DIATOMITE  DIETARIAN  DIETARILY
DILATATOR  DINOCERAS  DIOPTRATE  DIPLOTENE  DIPTEROUS  DISTINGUE
DIVINATOR  DOGMATISE  DOLABRATE  DOLERITIC  DORTINESS  DOSIMETER
DRAGONISE

EALDORMAN  EALDORMEN  ECRITOIRE  EDEMATOUS  EGLANTINE  EIGENTONE
ELAEOLITE  ELAIOSOME  ELASTOMER  ELATERIUM  ELEDOISIN  ELEUTHERI
ELUTRIATE  EMANATION  EMENDATOR  EMICATION  ENAMELIST  ENANTHEMA
ENDOCRINE  ENDOERGIC  ENDORSIVE  ENERVATOR  ENTERITIS  EPICENTRA
EPIDOSITE  EPIGAEOUS  EPILATION  EPINEURAL  EPINEURIA  EPISODIAL
EPISTERNA  EPISTOLER  EPULATION  EPURATION  ERGATANER  EROTICISE
ERUDITION  ERVALENTA  ESCRIBANO  ESOTROPIA  ESTAMINET  ESTIVATOR
ESTRADIOL  ESTUARIAL  ESTUARIAN  ETHANOATE  EUCLIDEAN  EUDEMONIA
EUDIALYTE  EUGLENOID  EUTHERIAN  EVAGATION  EVANITION  EVAPORITE
EVITATION  EVITERNAL  EXARATION  EXODONTIA  EXUDATION

FACTORISE  FEDERATOR  FERALISED  FESTINATE  FILIGRANE  FLORIATED
FLORICANE  FOEDERATI  FOETATION  FOGRAMITE  FOLIATURE  FORESTIAL
FORTALICE  FORTILAGE  FRONTENIS

GABERDINE  GABIONADE  GALANTINE  GAMINERIE  GANNISTER  GARNITURE
GASOMETER  GAULEITER  GENDERISE  GENERALIA  GENIALISE  GENICULAR
GENITIVAL  GENOCIDAL  GENTILISE  GEOMETRID  GERMANITE  GERUNDIAL
GILSONITE  GIRANDOLA  GIRANDOLE  GITTARONE  GOSLARITE  GRADATION
GRANDIOSO  GRANITISE  GRANITITE  GRANITOID  GRANIVORE  GRANOLITH
GRANULATE  GRANULITE  GRANULOSE  GRATICULE  GRENADINE  GRINDELIA

HARIOLATE  HERALDIST  HESITATOR  HETAERIST  HIERODULE  HODIERNAL

IATROGENY  IDEALOGUE  IGNORABLE  INAMORATO  INCRETION  INDAGATOR
INDUVIATE  INEBRIANT  INEBRIATE  INEBRIOUS  INGRATELY  INHALATOR
INOPINATE  INTEGRAND  INTEGRANT  INTENSATE  INUNDATOR  INUSITATE
INVERTASE  IONISABLE  IONOPAUSE  IPRINDOLE  IRISATION  IRREDENTA
IRRELATED  IRRIDENTA  ISOLATIVE  ISOPTERAN  ISOTHERAL  ITERATION
ITERATIVE  ITINERATE
```

KAOLINITE   KETONURIA

LACERTIAN   LANGOUSTE   LANTERLOO   *LAODICEAN*   LAPIDEOUS   LARCENIST
LARCENOUS   LARGITION   *LATIMERIA*   LAUDATION   *LEARINESS*   LEGENDIST
LEVANTINE   *LEVIGATOR*   *LEVITATOR*   LIBERATOR   *LICTORIAN*   LIDOCAINE
LINEARITY   LINEATION   LINEOLATE   LORGNETTE   LUTEINISE   LYONNAISE

MACEDOINE   MADELEINE   MADRILENE   MAGNESITE   MANNERIST   MARINIERE
MATRONISE   MEANDROUS   MEDIATISE   MELATONIN   MELIORATE   MELIORIST
MENADIONE   MENTATION   MEROPIDAN   MESTRANOL   METEORIST   METEOROID
MINUTIOSE   *MIRANDISE*   MONTADALE   MORGANITE   MORTALISE   MUGEARITE
MULTITOOL

NANOMETER   NANOMETRE   NANOTESLA   NARCOTISE   NATROLITE   NAUTILOID
NECROTISE   NECTAREAL   NECTARIAL   NECTARIED   NEFARIOUS   NEGOCIANT
NEGOTIANT   NEGRITUDE   NEMERTAIN   NEOLOGIAN   NEOLOGISE   NEOPILINA
NEOPLASIA   NEOTEINIA   NEOTERISE   NEOTERISM   NEOTERIST   NEOTERIZE
NERVATION   NEURATION   NEUROGLIA   NEUTRONIC   NIAISERIE   NIELLATED
NIGRITUDE   *NITRAMINE*   NODULATED   NONPAREIL   NORMATIVE   *NOUGATINE*
NUCLEATOR   NUMERAIRE

OBEISANCE   OCTENNIAL   OCTONARII   *OENOTHERA*   OMNIRANGE   *OPERATISE*
ORANGEADE   ORANGERIE   ORATORIAN   ORDINAIRE   *ORGANOTIN*   ORNITHINE
ORTANIQUE   OSMETERIA   OSTIOLATE   OSTRACEAN   OVERHAILE

PANELISED   PANETTONI   PARANOEIC   *PARDALOTE*   PARHELION   PEARLISED
PEDANTISE   PELORISED   *PELTATION*   *PENTOSIDE*   PERDITION   PERITONEA
PERNIONES   PERTUSION   PERVASION   PIGEONITE   PIGNERATE   *PINTADERA*
PISTAREEN   *PISTOLERO*   *PISTOLIER*   PLANETOID   POLIANITE   POLONAISE
PONDEROSA   POSIGRADE   POTENTISE   PREDATION   PRELATISE   PRELUSION
PRETORIAL   PRETORIAN   PROGESTIN   PROLATION   PROLATIVE   *PROSCENIA*
PROTOGINE   PSALTERIA   PTERIDINE

RACIATION   RADIALISE   RADIATELY   RADIATIVE   RANDOMISE   *RAVIGOTTE*
REBOATION   RECENSION   RECLINATE   RECLUSION   REDINGOTE   REFLATION
REISTAFEL   RELIGIOSE   RELIGIOSO   REMOULADE   REPLETION   *REPLICANT*
REPTATION   REPTILOID   RESENTIVE   RESONATOR   RETIARIUS   REVALENTA
REVELATOR   RHETORISE   *RHIGOLENE*   RHODANATE   RHODANISE   RHODOLITE
RHODONITE   RHOEADINE   RHOTACISE   RITUALISE   RODGERSIA   *ROOTINESS*
ROSANILIN   ROSEATELY   ROSMARINE   ROUTINISE   RUTILATED

SALIMETER   SALOMETER   SALTATION   SANATORIA   SANBENITO   SANITORIA
SANTOLINA   *SAPONATED*   SAPROLITE   SARDONIAN   SARTORIAN   SATIATION
SATURNIID   SATURNINE   SCIAENOID   SCIENTIAL   SCLEROTIA   SCLEROTIN
SCORODITE   SECTARIAL   SECTARIAN   SECTORIAL   SECURITAN   SEIGNORAL
SEMAINIER   SEMANTIDE   SEMANTRON   SEPIOLITE   SEPTATION   SEPTENNIA
SERIALITY   SERIATELY   SERIATION   SERINETTE   SEROTINAL   SEROTONIN
SERRULATE   SIGNEURIE   SILTATION   SINOLOGUE   SINUATELY   SINUATION
SLOGANEER   SOLFERINO   *SONICATOR*   SORTATION   SORTILEGE   SPARTERIE
SPIRATION   SPORULATE   STAMINEAL   STAMINODE   *STAVUDINE*   STENOPAIC
STERADIAN   STERCULIA   STERILANT   STINGAREE   STORIATED   STORNELLI

9. Nine-Letter Words

STRIATION	STRIATURE	STRIDENCE	STRIDLING	SUCTORIAN	SUDATORIA
SULFONATE	*SUPERNATE*	SUPINATOR			

TANAGRINE	TANALISED	TARRIANCE	TASIMETER	*TEARINESS*	TECTORIAL
TELEGONIC	TELEOSAUR	TELLURIAN	TELLURION	TENAILLON	TENDINOUS
TENEBROUS	*TENIAFUGE*	*TENSORIAL*	TENTORIUM	TENURABLE	TERATOGEN
TEREDINES	TERPENOID	TERPINEOL	TERRICOLE	TERVALENT	*TEUTONISE*
THEOMANIA	THERALITE	THREONINE	TIERCERON	TINGUAITE	TOERAGGER
TONSORIAL	TOPIARIAN	TORBANITE	TORMENTIL	TOURNEDOS	*TOURTIERE*
TRAGEDIAN	TRAGULINE	TREHALOSE	TREILLAGE	TREMATODE	TREMATOID
TREMOLANT	TREMOLITE	TREPONEMA	TRETINOIN	TRIALOGUE	TRIBUNATE
TRICERION	*TRICLOSAN*	TRICOTINE	TRIECIOUS	TRIHEDRON	TRILINEAR
TRILOBATE	TRILOBITE	TRINOMIAL	TRISAGION	*TRISERIAL*	*TRITANOPE*
TRIVALENT	*TROPAEOLA*	*TROPEOLIN*	TULAREMIA	TURBINATE	

UITLANDER	ULIGINOSE	UNTIRABLE	URALITISE	URANINITE	URCEOLATE
UREOTELIC	URINATIVE	UROKINASE	UROLAGNIA		

VARIEGATE	VARIOLOID	VECTORIAL	VELOUTINE	VENERATOR	VERITATES
VERNALISE	VERNATION	VETTURINI	VETTURINO	*VIOSTEROL*	VOISINAGE
VULNERATE					

WANTONISE	*WEAPONISE*	WEARISOME	WINTERISE